MATTHEW

MATTHEW

by
John M Riddle

40 Beansburn, Kilmarnock, Scotland

ISBN-13: 978 1 910513 93 4

Copyright © 2017 by John Ritchie Ltd.
40 Beansburn, Kilmarnock, Scotland

www.ritchiechristianmedia.co.uk

All rights reserved. No part of this publication may be reproduced, stored in a retrievable system, or transmitted in any form or by any other means – electronic, mechanical, photocopy, recording or otherwise – without prior permission of the copyright owner.

Typeset by John Ritchie Ltd., Kilmarnock
Printed by Bell & Bain Ltd., Glasgow

Contents

Preface	7
Chapter 1	9
Chapter 2	26
Chapter 3	37
Chapter 4	47
Chapter 5	64
Chapter 6	95
Chapter 7	113
Chapter 8	130
Chapter 9	157
Chapter 10	184
Chapter 11	209
Chapter 12	227
Chapter 13	253
Chapter 14	280
Chapter 15	298
Chapter 16	316
Chapter 17	342
Chapter 18	361
Chapter 19	379
Chapter 20	397
Chapter 21	415

Matthew

Chapter 22	433
Chapter 23	451
Chapter 24	470
Chapter 25	504
Chapter 26	531
Chapter 27	578
Chapter 28	614

Preface

This book represents the substance of Bible Class discussions on Friday evenings between April 2010 and August 2012 at Mill Lane Chapel, Cheshunt. As in the case of previous publications in this series, the original notes were written without any thought of their eventual appearance in the public domain, and, again, the current volume does not purport to be a commentary in the usual sense of the word.

Our brother, now in heaven, and of happy memory, Mr George Waugh, said of Matthew, that 'he once wrote books for Caesar, but latterly he was enabled to write a book for God'. Instead of relieving people of their money, he made immense wealth freely available by writing the Gospel of Matthew.

When "wise men" came from the east and eventually arrived at the place "where the young child was", they "fell down, and worshipped him", opening their treasure and presenting to Him "gifts; gold, and frankincense, and myrrh". Those "wise men" have their successors. Through Matthew, not to mention Mark, Luke and John, the Holy Spirit, has put us in a position to worship God's beloved Son, and to present the untold treasure of "the things concerning himself". J G Bellett reminds us that while we find great delight in reading the New Testament epistles, which declare 'the doctrine of the Lord', there can be no greater delight than occupation with 'the Lord of the doctrine' as we read the Gospel records.

As before, the Bible Class at Cheshunt remains indebted to John Ritchie Ltd., for their willingness to publish its notes, something first mooted by Mr John Grant, and to Mr Fraser Munro and the John Ritchie 'team' for their invaluable help in formatting and editing the material submitted to them. The Bible Class also continues to be grateful to Miss Lesley Prentice for having

Matthew checked and corrected the original manuscripts, something she continues to do, and to Mr Eric Browning for his considerable help in sending copies of current studies by Email to an ever-widening readership.

John Riddle
Cheshunt, Hertfordshire
November 2017

THE GOSPEL OF MATTHEW

"The book of the generation of Jesus Christ"

Read Chapter 1:1-17
It has been nicely said that the Old Testament commences with one man (Moses) writing about four men (Abraham, Isaac, Jacob, and Joseph), whereas the New Testament commences with four men (Matthew, Mark, Luke, and John) writing about one Man: "Jesus Christ, the Son of David, the son of Abraham" (Matt. 1:1).

The first mention in Scripture of the word "four" occurs in connection with one river dividing into four: "And a river went out of Eden to water the garden; and from thence it was parted, and became into four heads" (Gen. 2: 10), reminding us that one Man came from the paradise of God, and that His perfect life was characterised by four streams. The four Gospels each portray the Lord Jesus differently. Over Matthew's Gospel it could be written "Behold, thy *King*" (John 19: 14); over Mark "Behold my *servant*" (Isaiah 42: 1); over Luke "Behold the *man*" (John 19: 5); over John "Behold your *God*" (Isaiah 40: 9).

Matthew's Gospel presents the Lord Jesus as the awaited Messiah (or Christ) of Old Testament prophecy, and so we read a great deal about His relationship with the Jewish nation. He is "the King of the Jews" (2: 2). It has been pointed out that there are sixteen parables in Matthew and all but four begin: "The kingdom of heaven is like...", whereas there are twenty parables in Luke, and all but two begin with the words, "There was a certain man..." or their equivalent.

Matthew then is the Gospel of the King, and concerns the Man who spoke with the authority of the Sovereign. He said "I say unto you" some thirty times in Matthew's Gospel. Who better than Matthew, a civil servant, to write about this! The man who wrote books for Caesar, now writes a book for God! In passing, it is worth noting that some students divide the Gospel of Matthew

Matthew

with reference to the words, "When Jesus had ended (or 'finished') these sayings...made an end of commanding his twelve disciples...finished these parables " (7: 28; 11: 1; 13: 53; 19: 1; 26: 1).

Matthew wrote, under divine inspiration, to combat problems faced by New Testament Hebrew believers, and thus in Chapter 1, he proves the Lord Jesus to be *(i) the son of Joseph - legally* (vv.1-17) : "And Jacob begat Joseph the husband of Mary, of whom was born Jesus, who is called Christ" (v.16): hence Joseph is addressed as "thou son of David" (v.20); *(ii) the son of Mary - actually* (vv.18-25): "she was found with child of the Holy Ghost...that which is conceived in her is of the Holy Ghost...she...brought forth her firstborn son" (vv.18, 20, 25).

Matthew Chapter 1 comprises two major sections: *(1)* the ancestry of the King (vv.1-17); *(2)* the advent of the King (vv.18-25).

1) THE ANCESTRY OF THE KING, vv.1-17
Matthew relates here the ancestry of the Lord Jesus in order to prove that He has the right to reign. In the words of Wm. MacDonald (*Matthew: Behold your King*), the "truth is that the genealogy is indispensable. It lays the foundation for all that follows. Unless it can be shown that Jesus is a legal descendant of David through the royal line, it is hopeless to try to prove that He is the Messiah-King of Israel. Matthew begins where he must begin - with documentary evidence that Jesus inherited legal right to the throne of David through His stepfather, Joseph". These verses can be divided as follows: *(a)* the dominant names (v.1); *(b)* the detailed ancestry (vv.2-17).

a) The dominant names, v.1
"The book of the generation (from *genesis,* meaning 'an origin, a lineage, or birth') of Jesus Christ, the son of David, the son of Abraham" (v.1). The dominant names in the Lord's genealogy are David and Abraham. In this connection, we should notice the following:*(i)* the book; *(ii)* the subject; *(iii)* the ancestors.

i) The book. It is "The book of the generation of Jesus Christ". John Heading (*What the Bible Teaches - Matthew*) points out that "the word 'book' (*biblos*) cannot mean in context the whole Gospel by Matthew, but only this first genealogical paragraph". The expression, "The **book** of the generation of Jesus Christ", should be compared with "the **book** of the generations of Adam" (Gen. 5: 1). These expressions are unique in Scripture. Adam was

Chapter 1

God's king over creation: "thou hast made him a little lower than the angels, and hast crowned him with glory and honour. Thou madest him to have dominion over the works of thy hands; thou hast put all things under his feet" (Psalm 8: 5-6). Adam, God's king over creation, failed, but Christ, God's King over all, can never fail.In Genesis, "the book of the generations of Adam" details Adam's *successors* (the "book of the generations of Adam, Gen. 5: 1 - 6: 8, is followed by the "generations of Noah", Gen. 6: 9), whereas in Matthew's Gospel, "the book of the generation of Jesus Christ" details His *ancestors* according to the flesh.

Attention is drawn to a vital change in the wording of the "generation of Jesus Christ": in His genealogy, the Lord's ancestors were begotten *of men* ("Abraham *begat* Isaac; and Isaac *begat* Jacob; and Jacob *begat* Judas and his brethren"), whereas the Lord Jesus was born *of a woman*: "and Jacob *begat* Joseph the husband of Mary, *of whom was born* Jesus, who is called Christ" (v.16). It should be carefully noted that He is *not* the son of Joseph. In this connection it must be said that the word "whom" ("of whom was born Jesus") is in the feminine gender, indicating not Mary and Joseph, but Mary alone. The Lord Jesus was "the Son of man", but He was no man's son. The change of expression is preparatory for a change in circumstances.

ii) The subject. It is "The book of the generation of *Jesus Christ*". "*Jesus*" is the name given to Him in manhood. It is His personal name. "*Christ*" is the name given to Him prior to manhood. It is His official title, meaning 'the anointed one'. Matthew is therefore emphasising that the "Jesus" known to the Jews is none other than the "Christ". When the high priest said, "I adjure thee by the living God, that thou tell us whether thou be the Christ, the Son of God", the Lord's reply brought immediate condemnation: "They answered and said, He is guilty of death" (Matt. 26: 63-66). In their judgment, He was not "Jesus Christ". He was just "Jesus of Nazareth".The genealogy that follows proves that He has every right to be called "Jesus Christ" (v.18).

iii)The ancestors. The Lord Jesus is "the son of David, the son of Abraham". David was a man after God's own heart (1 Sam. 13: 14), and Abraham "was called the Friend of God" (James 2: 23). How much more the Lord Jesus!

Wm. Kelly (*Lectures on Matthew*) asks and answers the question, "Why are these two names thus selected; and why put together in this brief summary? Because all the hopes of Israel were bound up with what was revealed to these two persons. David was the great head of the kingdom, the one in whom the true line of Messiah's throne was founded ... Abraham, again, was the one in whom it was said all the nations of the earth should be blessed. Thus the opening words prepare us for the whole of the Gospel. Christ came with all the reality of the kingdom promised to David's son. But if He were refused as the Son of David, still, as the son of Abraham, there was blessing not merely for the Jew, but for the Gentile". See Galatians 3: 13-14.

It should be noted that Matthew refers to Him as "the son of David" before "the son of Abraham".David is mentioned first, because it is Matthew's purpose to emphasise **the kingship of Christ.** In fact, the New Testament commences with "Jesus Christ, the son of David" and ends with "I am the root and offspring of David" (Rev. 22: 16). It is noteworthy that in the following genealogy, only David is mentioned as having office: he is "David **the king**" (v.6).

The order of the names, "the son of David, the son of Abraham", is an appropriate introduction to the Gospel.The "son of David" was **Solomon**, and the glory and strength of his kingdom is proverbial. The expression, "Son of David", therefore points to a glorious reign. The Lord Jesus is "greater than Solomon", and so He will ultimately "sit upon the throne of his glory" (Matt. 25: 31). Matthew **Chapters 1-25** are occupied with the King and His kingdom. The "son of Abraham" was **Isaac**, and he was placed on the altar. The expression, "son of Abraham", therefore points to the Lord's death and resurrection. Matthew **Chapters 26-28** are occupied with these closing scenes of His life on earth. It should be noted that Matthew does not record the ascension. He emphasises His earthly kingdom.

At Calvary, it was written over Him, "This is Jesus the King of the Jews" (Matt. 27: 37).As "the son of David", He is "the **king** of the Jews": as "the son of Abraham", He is "the king of the **Jews**".

b) The detailed ancestry, vv.2-17
"So all the generations from Abraham to David are fourteen generations; and from David until the carrying away into Babylon are fourteen generations; and from the carrying away into Babylon unto Christ are fourteen generations" (v.17). It has been said that 'Matthew was balancing his books'. Fourteen plus fourteen plus fourteen, giving a total of forty-two generations. It has also been pointed out that forty-two is the product of six multiplied by seven: the number of man and the number of completeness. But whether that is a realistic way of looking at the subject is questionable!

Chapter 1

The three sections have been described as follows: *(i)* the origin of the Davidic line (vv.2-6a); *(ii)* the decline of the Davidic line (vv.6b-11); *(iii)* the eclipse of the Davidic line (vv.12-16). E.W.Bullinger points out that the first begins with the call of Abraham, and ends with the call of David; the second begins with the construction of the temple, and ends with the destruction of the temple; the third begins with the nation under Babylon, and ends with the nation under Rome.

Various suggestions have been made in connection with the "fourteen generations". John Heading points out that the number "fourteen", used to define the three groupings in the genealogy, "has given rise to many explanations by the expositors, because Matthew's intention is not explained. We are not therefore committed to any particular suggestion". John Heading continues: 'For example, the number acts as an artificial aid to memory' and, 'The number impresses David's name on each group, for in Hebrew the numerical values of the letters in his name add up to fourteen'. There are other suggestions!

i) The origin of the Davidic line, vv.2-6a

"From Abraham to David are fourteen generations" (vv.2-6): Abraham, Isaac, Jacob, Judas, Phares, Esrom, Aram, Aminadab, Naasson, Salmon, Booz, Obed, Jesse, David. The addition is correct (of course) - fourteen generations! There are no omissions. It is in strict accord with 1 Chron. 1: 34; 2: 1-15. Abraham heads the list and then there are thirteen occurrences of the word "begat".

This section of the genealogy, together with the opening line of the next section, is remarkable for its **inclusions**: "Judas beget Phares and Zara of **Thamar**...Salmon begat Booz of **Rachab**...Booz begat Obed of **Ruth**... David the king begat Solomon of **her that had been the wife of Urias**" (vv.3,5,6). Andrew Wilson (*Matthew's Messiah*) makes the pertinent observation that "No doubt there are some females who might feel aggrieved that more of Christ's female ancestors were not mentioned. After all, they played no small part in Christ's descent...why does he not mention women like Sarah and Rebecca - women of faith - instead of a woman like Tamar who disguised herself as a prostitute?"

William Kelly has a superb piece here: "There are four women, and only four, who appear in the line, and upon every one of them there was a blot... What are we not taught by this? If the Messiah deigns to link Himself with

Matthew

such a family - if God is pleased so to order things that out of that stock, as concerning the flesh, His own Son, the Holy One of Israel, was to be born - surely there could be none too bad to be received of Him. He came to 'save His people from their sins', not to find a people that had no sins". How remarkable, bearing in mind that "Judas begat Phares and Zara of Thamar" (v.3), that no reference is made to Judah's son, Shelah, by his wife, but only to those born out of immorality (Gen. 38: vv.5, 29-30).

Wm. Kelly continues: "But that is not all. 'Phares begat Ezrom...and Salmon begat Booz of Rachab' (vv.3-5). And who and what was she? A Gentile, and once a harlot!...'And Booz begat Obed of Ruth'...Ruth, loving as she was, yet to a Jew was from a source particularly odious...She was a Moabitess, and thus forbidden by the law to enter the congregation of the Lord to the tenth generation (Deut. 23: 3-4)...Thus was given a still deeper testimony that grace would go out and bless the very worst of the Gentiles. Whether the Jews like it or not, God had Rahab, the once immoral Gentile, and Ruth, the meek daughter of Moab, brought, not only into the nation, but into the direct line from which the Messiah was to arise". The "extremely dark and dirty background" (Andrew Wilson) against which, it should be said, Matthew sets the integrity of Mary and Joseph, is emphasised further by the inclusion of "her that had been the wife of Urias" (v.6). Bathsheba's name not given, and the description of her is quite deliberate. It is remarkable that she should be in the Lord's ancestry. We might have expected Abigail (1 Sam. 25: 39-42).

Bearing all this, and much more, in mind, it is striking to remember that the Lord Jesus said of John the Baptist, "For John came unto you in the way of righteousness, and ye believed him not: but the publicans and harlots believed him" (Matt. 21: 32). It is even more striking to remember that when the Messiah came, He was called "the friend of publicans and sinners" (Matt. 11: 19) and spoke so graciously to the woman "taken in adultery" (John 8: 3), and to the woman who had "had five husbands", saying "and he whom thou now hast is not thy husband" (John 4.18). The "woman in the city, which was a sinner", of whom Simon the Pharisees said, "This man, if he were a prophet, would have known who and what manner of woman this is that toucheth him: for she is a sinner", was wonderfully blessed: "thy faith hath saved thee; go in peace" (Luke 7: 36-50). Moreover, the Lord brought wonderful blessing into the life of the "woman of Canaan" (Matt. 15: 22), otherwise known as 'the Syrophenician woman' (Mark 7: 26). She was a Gentile ("the woman was a Greek").

Chapter 1

To sum it all up, when the Messiah came, He took a particular interest in people like Tamar, Rahab, Ruth and Bath-sheba! He still does!

ii) The decline of the Davidic line, vv.6b-11
"From David until the carrying away into Babylon are fourteen generations":Solomon, Roboam (Rehoboam), Abia (Abijah), Asa (unchanged), Josphat (Jehoshaphat), Joram (Jehoram), Ozias (Uzziah), Joatham (Jotham), Achaz (Ahaz), Ezekias (Hezekiah), Manasses (Manasseh), Amon (unchanged), Josias (Josiah), Jechonias (*not* Jehoahaz, Jehoiakim, or Zedekiah, *but* Jehoiachin).There are fourteen occurrences of "begat". Once again, the addition is correct - of course: fourteen generations! But this is going to change! We might have expected reference to the glory of Solomon, but this is not mentioned. On reflection, this is not surprising: this is the genealogy of "a greater than Solomon"! It has to be said that in this section of the genealogy we have a 'mix' of kings. Godliness certainly does not 'run in the blood'.

This section of the genealogy is remarkable for its *exclusions.* The complete genealogy is found in 1 Chron. 3: 1-16, from which it will be observed that Ahaziah, Joash and Amaziah are missing in Matthew's list. The answer seems to be that all three sprang from Athaliah. "Hence they are completely passed over. We find God thus marking His resentment at the introduction of that wicked and idolatrous stock from the house of Ahab. Athaliah's descendants are not mentioned even to the third generation. This appears to be the moral reason why we find three persons left out at this particular point" (Wm. Kelly). We do read that the Lord visits "the iniquity of the fathers upon the children unto the third and fourth generations of them that hate me" (Exodus 20: 5, 34: 7; Num. 14: 18; Deut. 9), and "it is not until the fourth generation that God allows another king to be listed in Matthew's genealogy" (Andrew Wilson). Ellicott's Commentary concurs, but in a different context: "Apparently the motive for the omission was simply the desire of bringing the names in each period into which the genealogy is divided to the arbitrary standard of fourteen. Possibly, however, as it was thus necessary to omit three names, the choice of these may have been determined by the fact that they belonged to the time of Athaliah's disastrous influence in the history of the monarchy of Judah". David said of the wicked, "Let his posterity be cut off; and in the generation following let their name be blotted out" (Psalm 109:13).It should also be noted that the fact that according to Matthew, "Joram (Jehoram) begat Ozias (Uzziah)", omitting three intervening generations, demonstrates that "the word 'begat' does not necessarily imply an adjacent family connection of father-son" (John Heading).

There is a further *exclusion*, although this is matched by an *inclusion*, so maintaining the "fourteen generations" in the genealogy (v.17). In the genealogy, Josias (Josiah) is succeeded by Jechonias (Jehoiachin), but in actual fact, Jehoiachin was Josiah's grandson: he was the son of Jehoiakim. It is said of him, "Thus saith the LORD, Write ye this man childless, a man that shall not prosper in his days: for no man of his seed shall prosper, sitting upon the throne of David, and ruling any more in Judah" (Jer. 22: 30). In fact Jehoiachin, who is described as "Jeconiah, the captive" (RV), had seven sons (cf. 1 Chron. 3: 17-18), but it has been pointed out that the "verse does not say that he is to be absolutely childless, but only that he is to be legally counted so, no son or descendant succeeding to him" (C. von Orelli). E.W.Bullinger concurs: not "no sons", but "no sons to sit on the throne of David". His grandson, Zerubbabel, became governor of Judah (Hag. 1: 1), but neither he nor any of his descendants ever ruled as king. Jehoiachin's uncle, Zedekiah, reigned after him, but died before him (Jer 52.10,11). Jehoiachin was therefore the last of the Judaean kings.

The question therefore arises, 'How can the Lord Jesus fulfil the promises made to David when, although legally the son of David through Joseph, the exclusion from the throne of any descendant of Jechonias (Jehoiachin or Coniah), according to Jeremiah 22: 30, made this impossible?' The answer lies in the fact that Mary was also of the line of David (Luke 3: 31). 'At His birth, the Lord Jesus was a true Son of David "after the flesh" (Rom. 1: 3), because Mary was a descendant of David. He is also a true Son of David by legal right, because His legal father (though not His actual father) was a son of David. But none other can claim the throne, since they are disqualified by the exclusion placed on Jeconias' (Martin Anstey, *The Romance of Bible Chronology*). But although he had no successor on the throne, the legal line continued, which brings us to:

iii) The eclipse of the Davidic line, vv.12-16
"From the carrying away into Babylon unto Christ are fourteen generations" (vv.12-17). It has been suggested that in 1 Chron. 3: 17, "Jeconiah; Assir" (AV) might read 'Jeconiah-Assir' meaning 'Jeconiah the prisoner' (JND margin), and that his son is Salathiel. So we begin: Salathiel (Shealtiel), Zorobabel (Zerubbabel: evidently the grandson of Shealtiel, 1 Chron.3: 18-19), Abiud, Eliakim, Azor, Sadoc, Achim, Eliud, Eleazar, Matthan, Jacob,

Joseph, Christ. Salathiel (Shealtiel) and Zorobabel (Zerubbabel) are certainly found in the Old Testament (Ezra 3: 2; Neh. 12: 1; Hag. 1: 1), but the remaining names, apart, of course, from Joseph and Christ, are outside the Scriptures.

There are twelve occurrences of "begat", plus the vital change of wording, "Joseph the husband of Mary, of whom was born Jesus, who is called Christ" (v.16). But this is only thirteen generations, and we are specifically told that "from the carrying away into Babylon unto Christ are fourteen generations" (v.17). It could be argued that Jechonias is included twice - at the end of the second section of the genealogy (v.11), and at the beginning of the third (v.12). Against this, however, it has to be said that Solomon's name occurs twice but that his name is only needed once to give fourteen generations in the first and second sections of the genealogy. The commentaries appear to give no explanation, and the question remains unresolved, unless Mary's name is to be included. At first glance, this seems improbable. After all, it hardly seems realistic to count Joseph and Mary as two "generations". On the other hand, Matthew is not likely to have miscalculated the number of generations!

One thing is very clear, "when we come to difficulties, we should conclude that the problem is in our lack of knowledge rather than in the Book's fallibility. Bible problems should challenge us to study and search for the answers: 'It is the glory of God to conceal things, but the honour of kings is to search out a matter' (Prov. 25: 2)" (Wm. Macdonald). This brings us to:

2) THE ADVENT OF THE KING, vv.18-25
"Now the birth of Jesus Christ was on this wise: When as his mother Mary was espoused to Joseph, before they came together, she was found with child of the Holy Ghost...Joseph, thou son of David, fear not to take unto thee Mary thy wife; for that which is conceived in her is of the Holy Ghost. And she shall bring forth a son, and thou shalt call his name JESUS: for he shall save his people from their sins" (vv.18, 20, 21).

"Now the birth of Jesus Christ was on this wise"

Read Chapter 1: 18-25
In our first study we suggested that Matthew Ch.1 may be divided as follows *(1)* the ancestry of the King (vv.1-17); *(2)* the advent of the King (vv.18-25).

Matthew

1) THE ANCESTRY OF THE KING, vv.1-17

In this connection we noticed that since Matthew presents the Lord Jesus as the Messiah-King of Israel, the genealogy is indispensable. Matthew demonstrates that He is the legal descendent of David. He commences with "The book of the generation of Jesus Christ, the son of David, the son of Abraham" (v.1). William Kelly asks the question, "Why are these two names thus selected; and why put together here in this brief summary?", and answers: "Because all the hopes of Israel were bound up with what was revealed to these two persons...David was the great head of the kingdom, the one in whom the true line of Messiah's throne was founded...Abraham was the one in whom it was said that all the nations of the earth should be blessed".

2) THE ADVENT OF THE KING, vv.18-25

Matthew introduces his account of the Lord's birth as follows, "Now the birth of Jesus Christ was on this wise" (v.18), and we should notice: *(a)* the conception of the King (vv.18-20);*(b)* the mission of the King (v.21);*(c)* the credentials of the King (vv.22-23); *(d)* the identity of the King (v.23); *(e)* the birth of the King (vv.24-25).

a) The conception of the King, vv.18-20

Consideration must be given to the following: *(i)* its accomplishment by the Holy Spirit (v.18); *(ii)* its explanation to Joseph (vv.19-20)

i) Its accomplishment by the Holy Spirit."Now the birth of Jesus Christ was on this wise: When as his mother Mary was espoused to Joseph, before they came together, she was found with child of the Holy Ghost" (v.18). The words "*Now* the birth of Jesus Christ was on this wise" emphasises that His birth was on totally different lines to His ancestors. The following should be carefully noted:

-The time of His conception. It was while "his mother Mary was espoused to Joseph, before they came together". The expression, "his mother Mary", should be carefully noted. We do not have, for obvious reasons, the expression, 'his father Joseph'. Mary was "espoused to Joseph". Wm.MacDonald writes as follows: "In Bible times betrothal was a form of engagement, but it was more binding than engagement is today; it could be broken only by divorce". He then quotes A.T.Robertson: "Betrothal with the Jews was a serious matter, not lightly entered into and not lightly broken. The man who betrothed a maiden was legally husband (Gen. 29: 21; Deut.

Chapter 1

22: 23) and 'an informal cancelling of betrothal was impossible' (McNeile). Though they did not live together as husband and wife till actual marriage, breach of faithfulness on the part of the betrothed was treated as adultery and punished with death". Hence we read, "Joseph her husband" (v.19); "fear not to take unto thee Mary thy wife" (v.20).

The Lord Jesus was conceived before Mary and Joseph "came together", thus fulfilling the ancient scripture, "Behold, a virgin shall be with child" (vv.22-23). Mary herself bore witness to the fact. Having been told, "thou shalt conceive in thy womb, and bring forth a son, and shalt call his name JESUS", she replied, "How shall this be, seeing I know not a man?" (Luke 1: 31-34).

- *The means of His conception.* "She was found with child of the Holy Ghost". Mary knew this too: having said "How shall this be, seeing I know not a man?", the angel Gabriel answered: "The Holy Ghost shall come upon thee, and the power of the Highest shall overshadow thee: therefore also that holy thing which shall be born of thee shall be called the Son of God" (Luke 1: 34-35).

A little thought will shew the necessity for the miraculous conception of the Lord Jesus in this way. If, as some suggest, He was begotten of human generation, that is, the son of Joseph as well as Mary, the whole concept of Incarnation would be destroyed, and, we could draw no distinction between Jesus of Nazareth and ourselves. The whole issue turns on His identity. As the Son of God, He is eternal. The very prophecy which anticipates His birthplace, also draws attention to the eternity of the Lord Jesus. "But thou Bethlehem Ephratah, though thou be little among the thousands of Judah, yet out of thee shall he come forth unto me that is to be ruler in Israel; whose goings forth have been from of old, from everlasting" (Micah 5: 2). The words, "from everlasting" are, literally, 'from the days of eternity'. The passage clearly states that Israel's Messiah, Who is eternally existent, was at some future date to be born as man at Bethlehem. He lived before He was born! Since normal parentage implies commencement of existence, it follows that the conception of the Lord Jesus through the mysterious power of the Holy Spirit was the only way in which the Son of God could become incarnate.

Further to the above, had the Lord Jesus been begotten of human generation, He would have derived sinful human nature. The New

Matthew

Testament emphasises the consequences of our connection with Adam: "Wherefore, as by one man sin entered into the world, and death by sin; and so death passed upon all men, for that all have sinned...Therefore as by the offence of one judgment came upon all men to condemnation, even so by the righteousness of one the free gift came upon all men unto justification of life. For as by one man's disobedience many were made sinners, so by the obedience of one shall many be made righteous" (Rom 5: 12, 18, 19). The very fact that we derive from Adam guarantees our sinful nature. David, tracing the cause of his lapse with Bath-sheba, concludes: "Behold, I was shapen in iniquity; and in sin did my mother conceive me" (Psalm 51: 5). David's transgression sprang from David's nature, and his conclusion applies without exception to us all. But, and here is a most important fact, the Lord Jesus was not descended from Adam, and therefore the entail of sin, in which we all participate, was broken by His conception in the power of the Holy Spirit. He is in fact "the last Adam...the second man". Through the conception of the Lord Jesus in the womb of the virgin, uncontaminated human nature was conveyed to Christ. Consequently we read, "therefore also that *Holy thing* that shall be born of thee, shall be called the Son of God". The incarnation then secured the entry into perfect manhood of the Son of God.

If, in view of the statement, "Behold *a virgin* shall be with child", the question is asked, 'Is it possible?', the answer is simply, "For with God nothing shall be impossible" (Luke 1: 37). If a second question is asked, 'Is it necessary?', the answer is: the *Sonship* of Christ (His eternal Sonship) demanded it; the *sinlessness* of Christ demanded it; our *salvation* demanded it.

ii) Its explanation to Joseph. "Then Joseph her husband, being a just man, and not willing to make her a publick example, was minded to put her away privily. But while he thought on these things, behold, the angel of the Lord appeared unto him in a dream, saying, Joseph, thou son of David, fear not to take unto thee Mary thy wife: for that which is conceived in her is of the Holy Ghost" (vv.19-20). The importance of the words,"that which is conceived in her is of the Holy Ghost", cannot be over-emphasised. For reasons already given, they are vital. We should notice in them reference to the Lord's *humanity:* "that which is conceived in her"; and we should notice in them reference to His *deity*: "is of the Holy Ghost".

It should be noted that while Luke emphasises the role of Mary, Matthew emphasises the role of Joseph. This is in keeping with the Kingly emphasis of the Gospel. Notice that Joseph is addressed as "Joseph, thou **son of David**".The divine intervention - "behold, the angel of the Lord appeared unto him" - was essential. Otherwise Joseph would not have believed Mary's explanation. See Luke 1: 26-38. Matthew looks at the situation from Joseph's point of view (see v.19): Luke looks at it from Mary's point of view: "Behold the handmaid of the Lord; be it unto me according to thy word" (Luke 1: 38). It is worth noticing "the angel of the Lord appeared unto him in a dream" on four occasions: "while he thought on these things (1: 20)…when they were departed (2: 13)…when Herod was dead (2: 19)…when the family returned to Israel (2: 22)".

We must take the opportunity to notice the commendable way in which Joseph in described. He was a man of righteousness, a man of principle. But equally a man of compassion: he loved Mary. We should notice the following:

i) He was a just man. "Then Joseph her husband, being a ***just man***, and not willing to make her a public example, was minded to put her away privily" (v.19).

ii) He was a kind man. "Then Joseph her husband, being a just man, and ***not willing to make her a public example***, was minded to put her away privily" (v.19). R.V.G.Tasker comments on both these aspects of Joseph's character as follows: "One of the slanders which the early Christians had to answer was that Jesus was born out of wedlock; for, it was asked, why did not Joseph report the matter at once to the authorities, when he discovered that Mary was pregnant during the period of their betrothal? Matthew records the answer. It is not denied that Mary became pregnant before Joseph had consummated the marriage; but it is urged that, although as a law-abiding man he was well aware that he ought to make the matter public, he nevertheless refrained from doing so from a desire to shield his betrothed from shameful exposure, and had begun to envisage the possibility of divorcing her secretly".

iii) He was a thoughtful man."But while he ***thought*** on these things, behold, the angel of the Lord appeared unto him in a dream" (v.20). Wm. MacDonald puts it nicely: "It was while this gentle and deliberate man was mapping his strategy to protect Mary that the angel of the Lord appeared to him in a dream…He should have no misgivings about marrying Mary. Any suspicions he might have concerning her moral purity were groundless. Her pregnancy was a miracle of the Holy Spirit" (Wm.MacDonald).

iv) He was an obedient man."Then Joseph being raised from sleep ***did*** as the angel of the Lord had bidden him, and took unto him his wife" (v.24).

b) The mission of the King, v.21
"And she shall bring forth a son, and thou shalt call his name JESUS: for he shall save his people from their sins".Careful notice must be taken of the following:

i)The birth of the King."And she shall bring forth a son". Luke tells us that "the days were accomplished that she should be delivered. And she brought forth her firstborn son, and laid him in a manger" (Luke 2: 6-7). While the conception of the Lord Jesus was divine, His birth was perfectly natural.

ii)The name of the King."Thou shalt call his name JESUS", meaning 'Jehovah is salvation' or 'Jehovah, the Saviour'. It is said that there is a play on Hebrew words here: "Thou shalt call his name JESUS (*ieshua*): for he shall save (*ioshua*) his people from their sins".

It is not without significance that ***Joseph*** is told: "Thou shalt call his name JESUS", whereas in Luke's Gospel, ***Mary*** is told "thou shalt conceive in thy womb, and bring forth a son, and shalt call his name JESUS" (Luke 1:31). It fell to Joseph, "son of David", to announce His birth in Matthew's Gospel, and to Mary, His mother, to announce His birth in Luke's Gospel, which stresses His true and perfect humanity.

iii)The work of the King."He shall save his people from their sins". It is said that the "he" is emphatic: "he" - and none other - "shall save his people from their sins". While it is true that "his people" today are both Jews and Gentiles, in the current context, the reference is to the believing Jews. He had come to save His people, not merely from their enemies, but "from their sins". This involved His death: "He was wounded for our transgressions, he was bruised for our iniquities: the chastisement of our peace was upon him; and with his stripes we are healed. All we like sheep have gone astray; we have turned every one to his own way; and the Lord hath laid on him the iniquity of us all...Therefore will I divide him a portion with the great, and he shall divide the spoil with the strong; because he hath poured out his soul unto death: and he was numbered with the transgressors; and he bare the sin of many, and made intercession for the transgressors" (Isaiah 53: 5, 6, 12).

Chapter 1

c) The credentials of the King, vv.22-23
"Now all this was done, that it might be fulfilled which was spoken of the Lord by the prophet, saying, Behold a virgin shall be with child, and shall bring forth a son, and they shall call his name Emmanuel, which being interpreted is, God with us". This is the first occurrence of Matthew's formula ("that it might be fulfilled which was spoken"), used by him to introduce passages from the Old Testament. See 2: 15, 17, 23; 4: 14; 8: 17; 12: 17; 13: 35; 21: 4; 27: 9.

Matthew refers here to Isaiah 7: 14: "Behold, a virgin shall conceive, and bear a son, and shall call his name Immanuel". The wording of the prophecy calls for close attention:

i) "Behold". The very use of this word indicates that something momentous is to follow. It is frequently used in this way in Scripture. "If Ahaz and others who were present were at all familiar with this formula, they would immediately realise that an announcement of supreme importance was about to be made. Isaiah is not going to declare the birth of any child, but of a significant Child" (E.J.Young).

ii) "A virgin shall conceive, and bear a son". A great deal has been written about this great statement, including attempts to lessen its force by making the word "virgin" mean something other than the obvious. In Hebrew, one word for virgin is *'bethulah'*, but that word could also be used of a betrothed virgin, or of a married woman, for example, "Lament like a virgin *('bethulah')* girded with sackcloth for the **husband** of her youth" (Joel 1: 8). E.J.Young observes that if Isaiah had used *'bethulah'*, "he would have left us in confusion. We could not have known precisely what he had in mind...In the light of these deliberations it appears that Isaiah's choice of *'almah'* was deliberate. It seems to be the only word in the language which unequivocally signifies an unmarried woman."

On the ground of common sense alone, the argument that the passage refers to a young married woman is nonsense. There would be nothing unusual in a young married woman conceiving and bearing a son! That would be no sign at all to Ahaz! The accuracy of the language must be noted; if a young woman, married or unmarried for that matter, conceived, she would no longer be a virgin. It remains that Mary was a virgin before the Lord Jesus Christ was conceived, and she was a virgin after He was born, and remained so until the commencement of normal marital relationships. This is clearly stated in Matt 1: 24-25.

iii) "Behold __the__ virgin". Whilst the AV reads, "Behold, a virgin", M.C.Unger and others point out that the Hebrew here and the Greek of Matt 1: 23 (see JND) have the definite article. It has been suggested that this implies someone well-known, and Isaiah's own wife has been included in the speculation. The presence of Shear-jashub is sufficient to disprove this suggestion! The inclusion of the definite article surely refers to the ancient promise: "And I will put enmity between thee (the serpent) and the woman, and between thy seed and *her* seed; it shall bruise thy head, and thou shalt bruise his heel" (Gen 3:15). The statement is unique. In Scripture, the progenitor is always male, with this one exception, and this implies something totally unparalleled. Hence, "God sent forth his Son, come of woman" (Gal 4: 4 JND). This leads to:

d) The identity of the King, v.23
"They shall call his name Emmanuel (or 'Immanuel', Isaiah's spelling) which being interpreted is, God with us". This explains the reason for the manner of His conception. E.J.Young cites John Calvin here: "Calvin rightly maintains that the name cannot be applied to anyone who is not God. No one else in the Old Testament bears this name. For these reasons, the prophecy must be interpreted only of that One to whom these conditions apply, namely, Jesus the Christ, the Son of the Virgin and the Mighty God." "Emmanuel", which conveys His absolute deity, together with His perfect humanity, is a description of His identity, rather than a name by which He was known on earth.

Matthew thus commences with "Emmanuel", meaning "God with us", and ends similarly: "Lo, I am with you always" (28: 20) where the order of the original words is "Lo, I *with you* am". We should not forget either that He is with His assembled people: "For where two or three are gathered together in my name, there am I in the midst of them" (Matt. 18: 20).

e) The birth of the King, vv.24-25
"Then Joseph being raised from sleep did as the angel of the Lord had bidden him, and took unto him his wife: and knew her not till she had brought forth her firstborn son: and he called his name JESUS". Mary was a virgin both before and after the birth of the Lord Jesus. Although married: Joseph "knew her not till she had brought forth her firstborn son".

In summary, it could be said that the Lord Jesus was: *(i)* conceived by the **Spirit of God** in order to become *(ii)* the Saviour of the **people of God,** in accordance with the predictions of *(iii)* the **word of God,** and thus His incarnation secured *(iv)* the **presence of God**.

THE GOSPEL OF MATTHEW

"Where is he that is born king of the Jews?"

Read Chapter 2: 1-23
If in Chapter 1, Matthew brings before us the Ancestry of the King, and the Advent of the King, then in this chapter he brings before us the Adoration of the King. The events described here are peculiar to Matthew and in keeping with the overall design and purpose of his Gospel. In the words of R.V.G.Tasker, 'the child…was acknowledged even in His infancy, and by representatives of the non-Jewish world, to be *par excellence*, the *King of the Jews'*.

Matthew 2 comprises three major sections: *(1)* the recognition of the King (vv.1-12); *(2)* the refuge in Egypt (vv.13-18); *(3)* the return to Israel (vv.19-23).

1) THE RECOGNITION OF THE KING, vv.1-12
We should notice here: *(A)* the arrival of the magi (vv.1-2); *(B)* the agitation in Jerusalem (v.3); *(C)* the answer of the priests and scribes (vv.4-6); *(D)* the assignment by Herod (vv.7-8); *(E)* the adoration of the Lord (vv.9-11); *(F)* the avoidance of Judaea (v.12).

A) THE ARRIVAL OF THE MAGI, vv.1-2
"Now when Jesus was born in Bethlehem of Judaea in the days of Herod the king" (or 'Now Jesus **having been born** in Bethlehem of Judaea in the days of Herod the king', JND), behold, there came wise men (*magos*) from the east (compare Gen. 4: 16; 11: 2 margin) to Jerusalem, saying, Where is he that is born King of the Jews? For we have seen his star in the east, and are come to worship him". Men came from the west in John 12: 20. Reference is made to "Herod the *king*", and to "he that is born *king* of the Jews". The contrast could not have been greater.

Chapter 2

- *"Herod the king"*. According to Wm.MacDonald, 'Herod the Great was a descendant of Esau and therefore a traditional enemy of the Jews. He himself had become a convert to Judaism, but his conversion was more nominal than real. After the death of Julius Caesar, he was promoted from governor to king of Judaea, 40BC'. It was towards the end of his reign that the wise men arrived in Jerusalem. It has been pointed out that Herod's 'strength and cruelty matched the Old Testament description of Rome: "a beast...dreadful and terrible...it devoured and break in pieces, and stamped the residue with the feet of it" (Dan. 7: 7)' (J.Heading).

- *"King of the Jews"*. Of the Lord Jesus it was prophesied, "Behold, thy King cometh unto thee, meek, and sitting upon an ass, and a colt the foal of an ass" (Matt. 21: 5). Herod was *made* a king: the Lord Jesus was "***born*** King of the Jews".

It is not without significance that Matthew's Gospel commences with the question, "Where is he that is born **King of the Jews?**" and ends with that same King on a cross: "And sitting down they watched him there; and set up over his head his accusation written, ***THIS IS JESUS THE KING OF THE JEWS***" (27: 36-37). See also 27: 27-30.

The visit of the "wise men" (or 'magi') is of absorbing interest, and attention is drawn to the following: *(a)* the source of their information; *(b)* the means of their guidance; *(c)* the time of their arrival; *(d)* the object of their visit.

a) The source of their information
Quite clearly, they were party to information not available to either the political or religious world. And they were Gentiles! As J. Heading rightly observes, 'God gave no revelation concerning the birth of Christ to the Roman authorities, to these wicked Herods, or to the religious leaders and teachers in Jerusalem and Judaea: it was hidden "from the wise and prudent" (Matt. 11: 25)'. With this in mind, it should be said that apparently only the wise men saw the star, or if this were not the case, then most definitely, only the wise men understood its significance. "The secret of the Lord is with them that fear him" (Psalm 25: 14).

It has been suggested that having seen the star, they associated its appearance with Balaam's prediction that a star would come out of Jacob (Num. 24: 17). Others suggest that the Magi connected this remarkable phenomenon with Daniel's seventy-weeks prophecy which foretold the time of Christ's first coming (Dan. 9: 24-25). But on balance, it does *not* seem likely that the magi were directly guided by the scriptures. They were obviously unaware that Micah had predicted the exact place of Messiah's birth. It therefore seems more probable that the knowledge was communicated to them supernaturally. After all, they are quite specific, "Where is he that is born **King of the Jews?** For we have seen **his** star (*autou ton astera*: as distinct from the myriads of other stars), in the east, and are come to worship **him**".

b) The means of their guidance
"We have seen his star in the east". As Wm.MacDonald observes, 'We do not know where they lived in the East, how many there were, or how long their journey lasted. (Only the designers of Christmas cards seem to know). It was the star in the East that somehow made them aware of the birth of a king'. R.V.G.Tasker states that the magi actually said, 'We saw his star at its rising' (*en te anatole*) as distinct from *en tais anatolais*, which rightly means "in the east". The sense therefore is not that the star actually moved in front of them as they travelled from the East, but that from the East they saw its rising. J.Heading concurs: 'They saw the "star in the east", namely, **when they were in the east** relative to Jerusalem; the star itself was in the west'. It is worth saying that the "wise men" were guided by a combination of divine revelation (they knew that it was "*his* star") and observable events. It must be said that these particular "wise men" were certainly not the successors of "the magicians...astrologers...sorcerers, and the Chaldeans" in Nebuchadnezzar's kingdom (Dan. 2: 2), who 'had their own methods of interpreting dreams and understanding the signs of the stars' (J.Heading). These wise men were different. Since Zacharias, Mary, Joseph, the shepherds, Simeon, and Anna, all received information in connection with the Lord's birth by divine revelation, it seems to be a safe assumption the "wise men" here must have done so as well.

Various scientific explanations have been offered to account for the star itself, including the suggestions that it was a conjunction of planets, or a supernova (a star that suddenly becomes brighter). But J.Heading points out that 'all these rotate with the sun, and would not fix a direction for the guidance of the wise men, particularly as the last few miles from Jerusalem to Bethlehem ended with the star exactly over the house where the young Child lay'. J.Heading speaks, surely, for us all, in saying, 'We believe that "his star" was something miraculous for a miraculous occasion, near enough to the earth for the wise men to have taken a vertical bearing from the star to the house exactly underneath when it became stationary (Matt. 2: 9). So it may have been the "cloud of glory" that rested over the tabernacle, and that gave guidance to the children of Israel in their wilderness march from Egypt'.

c) The time of their arrival
It is quite clear that 'the Lord's birth preceded the visit of the wise men by an unspecified period of time' (Wm.MacDonald). The magi arrived when the Lord was *"a young child".* In fact, this chapter could be called 'the chapter of the young child'. The expression is used nine times: vv.8, 9, 11, 13 (twice), 14, 20 (twice), 21. Notice too that the expression "*young child* and his mother" occurs five times: vv.11, 13, 14, 20, 21. The order is important.

d) The object of their visit
This is clearly stated: "We have seen his star in the east, and are come to *worship him".* It could be said that this is the crowning piece of information in connection with the arrival of the magi. In the Millennium, "the Gentiles shall come to thy light (Zion's light), and kings to the brightness of thy rising" (Isaiah 60: 3). This, surely, is prefigured here.

B) THE AGITATION IN JERUSALEM, v.3
"When Herod the king had heard these things, he was troubled, and all Jerusalem with him". H.A.Ironside calls this 'most distracting to the aged wretch who sat upon the throne at that time'. We should notice the hostility of Herod, reminding us that "the powers that be" have little, if any, time for the Lord Jesus. At least five things might be noted of Herod: the chapter refers to his disconcertedness (v.3); his duplicity (vv.7-8); his danger (vv.12-13); his depravity (v.16); his death (v.19). R.V.G.Tasker observes that 'It is not surprising that news of the enquiry made by these astrologers on their arrival should have speedily reached the ears of King Herod, and that he should have been greatly perturbed in consequence, for the last thing in the world that ill-tempered tyrant could contemplate with composure was the presence of a rival king in Jewry; and even if the inhabitants of Jerusalem did not share his fear of the new-born child, they would certainly be alarmed at the prospect of a fresh exhibition of Herod's anger' (R.V.G.Tasker). It has also been suggested that the news could well have been received with alarm by the religious leaders since it would mean the end of their finely-tuned religious practices. The claims of Christ always disturb men and women, even - at times - the Lord's people.

If His first advent, with all its comparative secrecy, caused disturbance, then

His second advent will cause universal disturbance, "every eye shall see him, and they also which pierced him: and all kindreds of the earth shall wail because of him" (Rev. 1: 7).

C) THE ANSWER OF THE PRIESTS AND SCRIBES, vv.4-6

"And when he had gathered all the chief priests and scribes of the people together, he demanded of them where Christ should be born. And they said unto him, In Bethlehem of Judaea: for thus it is written by the prophet; And thou Bethlehem, in the land of Juda, art not the least among the princes of Juda: for out of thee shall come a Governor, that shall rule my people Israel". The reference to Bethlehem, meaning the 'house of bread', reminds us that as "the true bread from heaven" (John 6: 32), the Lord Jesus came in the same way as the manna – quietly and without ostentation (Exodus 16: 14-15).

The magi saw "his star in the east" and went to the wrong place! The passage does not say that the star led them to the wrong place. Quite naturally, they went to Jerusalem. Where else would the King be born? But supposition gave way to the Scriptures, emphasising the vital importance of the word of God.

We should notice the attitude of the religious men. They knew the book, but had no desire to go five miles to Bethlehem! Their heads were filled with theology, but they had no heart for the Christ of God. As Paul later pointed out, the people of Jerusalem "knew him not, nor yet the voices of the prophets which are read every sabbath day" (Acts 13: 27). From John 7: 40-43 we learn that it is possible to know the Scriptures, but not to perceive the identity of Jesus of Nazareth.

The passage as it stands in Micah should be compared with its quotation by the priests and scribes. Micah wrote: "But thou, Beth-lehem Ephratah, though thou be little among the thousands of Judah, yet out of thee shall he come forth unto me that is to be ruler in Israel; whose goings forth have been from of old, from everlasting" (Mic. 5: 2). It has been pointed out that 'the priests and scribes omitted the words, "whose goings forth have been from of old, from everlasting", since this points to the divine character of the King just born, and this they would desire to avoid with its reminder of Isaiah 57: 15, "the high and lofty One that inhabiteth eternity"' (J.Heading).

D) THE ASSIGNMENT BY HEROD, vv.7-8

"Then Herod, when he had privily (he evidently did not wish to give the impression to all and sundry that he had a particular interest in the "young child") called the wise men, inquired of them diligently (*akriboo*, to learn by exact enquiry) what time the star appeared ('how long since the star appeared', JND margin). And he sent them to Bethlehem; and said, Go and search diligently (*akribos exetazo*, accurately to seek out) for the young child; and when ye have found him, bring me word again, that I may come and worship (*proskuneo*) him also". This is an opportue moment to stress that the Lord's people should always have pure motives, and that duplicity should be studiously avoided. See 2 Cor. 2: 17; 1 Thess. 2: 5-6.

E) THE ADORATION OF THE LORD, vv.9-11
"When they had heard the king, they departed: and, lo, the star, which they saw in the east, went before them, till it came and stood over where the young child was. When they saw the star, they rejoiced with exceeding great joy. And when they were come into the house, they saw the young child with Mary his mother, and fell down, and worshipped him: and when they had opened their treasures, they presented unto him gifts; gold, and frankincense, and myrrh". We should notice five things here: *(a)* where they went; *(b)* how they went; *(c)* when they stopped; *(d)* who they worshipped; *(e)* what they offered.

a) Where they went
Although it is not specifically stated, there seems little doubt that they went to Bethlehem. While this may seem obvious, it is of importance if we are to correctly understand the sequence of events. It seems clear that since Joseph was told to flee to Egypt after the departure of the wise men (v.13), the visit of the magi took place *after* the Lord Jesus had been brought into the temple at Jerusalem when he was approximately six weeks old. From Jerusalem, He was taken back to Bethlehem, thence to Egypt. However, this *appears* to conflict with the statement that after the Lord Jesus had been presented to the Lord at Jerusalem, Joseph and Mary returned to **Nazareth** (Luke 2: 39). The answer is that Luke evidently omits any reference to the intervening flight to Egypt in saying "and when they had performed all things according to the law of the Lord, they returned into Galilee, to their own city of Nazareth".

b) How they went
The star which the wise men had seen in the east reappeared at this point (v.9). It is simply called "the star, which they saw in the east" (again, 'the star, which they saw at its rising': *en te anatole*), not 'the star that they followed

from the east'. But what is meant by "the star...went before them, till it came and stood over where the young child was?" Does this mean that it actually moved a short way ahead of them as they made the five-mile journey to Bethlehem? This hardly seems necessary. It seems more likely that the star reappeared over the place "where the young child was", so obviating the necessity for the wise men to make house to house enquiries. The star "went before them", not in the sense of moving immediately ahead, but of going in advance.

c) When they stopped
As noted above, they stopped when they reached "the house" immediately underneath the star. Amongst other things, this indicates that there was nothing unusual about the place: "the house" did not glow with supernatural light! The magi needed the star to point out **the exact house**: "it came and stood over where the young child was". The humility that marked the King was matched by His humble surroundings!

The wise men certainly didn't park their camels outside a stable. We are not told, in any case, that the Saviour was born in a stable! They were led to a "house" (v.11). 'The Lord Jesus was laid in a manger, "because there was no room for them in the inn" (Luke 2: 7), all available space being occupied by an influx of people coming to Bethlehem for the enrolment. But we can rightly assume that they moved to a "house" (v.11) as soon as such accommodation became free' (J.Heading).

d) Who they worshipped
The magi "rejoiced" when they saw the **star** (v.10), but they "worshipped" when they saw **Him** (v.11)! The star led them to Christ (v.9), but they did not worship the means by which they found Him, and there is no need to say that they did not worship Mary! The subject of worship (that is, sincere worship) is mentioned some eight times in Matthew's gospel: 2: 2; 2: 11; 8: 2; 9: 18; 14: 33; 15: 25; 18: 26; 28: 9. The book begins and ends in this way. The "wise men...fell down, and worshipped him" (2: 11): the eleven disciples "worshipped him" (28: 17).

As Wm.Macdonald points out, 'These Gentiles diligently sought Christ, while Herod planned to kill Him, while the knowledgeable priests and scribes were as yet indifferent, and while the people of Jerusalem were troubled. All these attitudes were omens of the way in which the Messiah would be received'.

Chapter 2

e) What they offered
There was a variety in their worship: "they presented *unto him* gifts; gold, frankincense, myrrh". (Compare Luke 8: 3, where godly women "ministered *unto him* of their substance"). On a practical note, Joseph and Mary were poor people, soon to make the long journey to Egypt, so in the overruling wisdom of God "gold" was offered, not to mention the "frankincense" and the "myrrh" which would have been used in attending to the young child. It is worth noting that Matthew is the 'gospel of treasure' (*thesauros*): in worship (2:11); in wisdom (12: 35); in words (13: 52). It was written by Levi - a man who handled money!

'Gold is a type or figure of deity and glory; it speaks of the bright, shining perfection of His divine Person. Frankincense is an ointment, or perfume; it suggests the fragrance of the life of sinless perfection. Myrrh is a bitter herb, sometimes used in embalming; it presages the sufferings which He would endure in bearing away the sins of the world' (Wm.MacDonald). Gold was the currency of kings; frankincense was the currency of priests; myrrh was the currency of undertakers.

It is worth pointing out that in the Millennium, Gentiles will bring Israel's Messiah "gold and frankincense" (Isaiah 60: 6). But no reference is made to myrrh! Since Isaiah was speaking of Christ's second advent, myrrh would be inappropriate, because He will not suffer then. In Matthew, the myrrh is included because His first coming is in view with its attendant suffering, whereas Isaiah describes "the glories that shall follow". The "gold and frankincense" which will be brought in the Millennium reminds us that the Lord Jesus will be "priest upon his throne" (Zech. 6: 13).

The magi brought gold, frankincense and myrrh. Like the magi, we too must worship with full hands (Deut 16: 16-17). Do *we* open our treasures? Do we *have* any treasures to offer?

F) THE AVOIDANCE OF JUDAEA, v.12
"And being warned of God in a dream that they should not return to Herod, they departed into their own country another way". They went back 'a different way'. Worshipping the Lord Jesus makes a difference! It has been said that no one who meets Christ with a sincere heart ever returns the same way. True encounter with Him transforms all life.

John Heading points out that "another way" would have incurred difficulty. 'A

33

glance at a map showing main roads at that time proves that the main road went from Bethlehem to Jerusalem, from Jerusalem to Jericho eastwards, and then over the Jordan northwards from the top of the Dead Sea. To reach the top of the Dead Sea "another way" would mean crossing inhospitable mountainous country east of Bethlehem. Obedience to God's voice does not always bring a bed of ease'.

2) THE REFUGE IN EGYPT, vv.13-18

In these verses we should notice *(A)* the safety of the Lord Jesus (vv.13-15) and *(B)* the slaughter of the young children (vv.16-18).

a) The safety of the Lord Jesus, vv.13-15

'From early childhood the threat of death hung over our Lord. The storm clouds gathered with unprecedented speed and fury. It was apparent that He was born to die. But there was an appointed time, and He could not die until then' (Wm.MacDonald). We must remember that "Christ died for our sins according to **the scriptures**" (1 Cor. 15: 3). His death could **only** take place as foretold.

Events follow a familiar pattern. The beautiful picture described in the previous verses gives place to the ugly picture of Herod's anger, graphically reminding us that the enemy cannot rest when anything precious to God is taking place. But everything was under divine control: Joseph was warned of looming danger and guided accordingly. Following the angel's warning (v.13), the family sought refuge in Egypt. We are not told how long they stayed there, only that they were refugees until the death of Herod (v.15). As H.A.Ironside observes, Joseph 'furnishes us with a most precious example of implicit obedience to the will of God, even under most perplexing and difficult circumstances'.

At this point, a statement in the Old Testament became clothed with a new meaning (v.15). God had said through the prophet Hosea, "Out of Egypt have I called my son" (Hos. 11: 1). In its original setting, this refers to the deliverance of Israel from Egypt at the time of the exodus. But the statement is capable of a double meaning. The Messiah's history would closely parallel that of the nation of Israel; here the prophecy is fulfilled by His return to the land of Israel from Egypt.

b) The slaughter of the young children, vv.16-18

"Then Herod, when he saw that he was mocked (in sense of 'deluded' or

Chapter 2

'deceived') of the wise men, was exceeding wroth, and sent forth, and slew all the children (*pais*, male children) that were in Bethlehem, and in all the coasts thereof, from two years old and under, according to the time which he had diligently enquired of the wise men" (v.16). This tragic verse speaks for itself. It is not known how many children perished. Herod evidently set the age limit according to the time when the star first appeared to the wise men. This gives us some clue as to the approximate age of the Lord Jesus at the time.

The weeping that followed the slaughter of the young children fulfilled the prophecy, "Thus saith the Lord: A voice was heard in Ramah, lamentation and bitter weeping; Rahel (Jeremiah's spelling) weeping for her children refused to be comforted for her children because they were not" (Jer. 31: 15). In the prophecy, Rachel represents the nation of Israel. She weeps at the deportation of her children, but her weeping is restrained because the exiles would return (vv.16-17). But here, 'Matthew quotes only the verse of weeping, and not the verses of rejoicing, because so far as the mothers in Bethlehem were concerned, only tragedy had hit them' (supplied by J.Waldron). C.L.Feinberg points out that 'Matthew's method of quoting an Old Testament reference does not automatically imply a direct fulfillment' and continues, 'For proof see the immediate context in Matthew 2.15, where Hosea 11.1 in its original context unmistakably speaks of the nation of Israel, but by analogy and higher fulfilment refers to Christ'.

3) *THE RETURN TO ISRAEL, vv.19-23*
On his return to the land of Israel following instructions from the angel (vv.19-20), and having received further instruction by dream when hesitating to enter Judaea in view of the evident cruelty of the Archelaus, who had succeeded his father, Joseph travelled northward to Galilee and settled in Nazareth.

For the fourth time in this chapter (cf. vv.6, 15, 18, and now v.23), Matthew reminds us that prophecy was being fulfilled. He does not mention any prophet by name but simply says that the prophets in general had foretold that the Messiah would be called a Nazarene. There is no verse in the Old Testament that states this is so many words. Many scholars suggest that Matthew is quoting Isaiah 11: 1: "There shall come forth a rod (*netzer:* a shoot) from the stem (stump) of Jesse". The word *netzer* derives from the Hebrew *natzer*, meaning 'to shine or blossom', implying fruitfulness. The word Nazarene comes from this. However, Wm.Macdonald finds the connection somewhat remote and suggests that since Nazareth was a town which was regarded with contempt (see John 1: 46), the scorn which was heaped upon this 'unimportant' town naturally fell on its inhabitants as well, and that the words "He shall be called a Nazarene" (v.23) mean that He would be treated with contempt and mockery. He quotes Isaiah 53: 3 and Psalm 22: 6 in support, and concludes, 'So while the prophets might not have used the exact words, this was undeniably the spirit of several of their prophecies'.

THE GOSPEL OF MATTHEW

"This is my beloved Son"

Read Chapter 3: 1-17
This chapter comprises two main sections: *(1)* the ministry of John the Baptist (vv.1-12); *(2)* the baptism of the Lord Jesus (vv.13-17).

1) THE MINISTRY OF JOHN THE BAPTIST, vv.1-12
These verses may be divided as follows: *(a)* the preaching of John (vv.1-2); *(b)* the preacher himself (vv.3-4); *(c)* the people's response (vv.5-9); *(d)* the preacher's contrasts (vv.10-12).

a) The preaching of John, vv.1-2
"In those days (in the "days" that the Lord Jesus "dwelt...in Nazareth", 2: 23) came John the Baptist, preaching in the wilderness of Judaea, and saying, Repent ye: for the kingdom of heaven is at hand". We should notice:

i) Where he preached. He "came...preaching in the wilderness of Judaea" (v.1). He is described as "The voice of one crying in the wilderness" (v.3). Marks tells us that "John did baptize in the wilderness, and preach the baptism of repentance for the forgiveness of sins" (Mark 1: 4). Luke tells us that as a child, John "grew, and waxed strong in spirit, and was in the deserts till the day of his shewing unto Israel" (Luke 1: 80), and that "word of God came unto John the son of Zacharias in the wilderness" (Luke 3: 2). We should notice:

- *That he was prepared in the wilderness.* In this, he resembled Moses (Ex. 3: 1), and Paul (Gal. 1: 17). We, too, need to get away from the atmosphere of this world in order to be alone with God. See Mark 6: 31. But more than that, he **grew** in the desert! See Luke 1: 80 above. If we are going to "grow in grace, and in the knowledge of our Lord and Saviour Jesus Christ" (2 Pet. 3: 18), we will need spiritual solitude.

Matthew

- *That he preached in the wilderness*. The man with God's word was not found in places connected with institutionalised religion, but in the wilderness! Read Luke 7: 24-25, and note the words, "What went **ye out** into the wilderness for to see?". God's word was not found in the temple or in the synagogues. It was preached by a man outside Judaism. Divine blessing did not come through the religious practices of the day, or of any day.

ii) What he preached. He preached "Repent ye: for the kingdom of heaven ('the kingdom of the heavens', JND) is at hand" (v.2). The Lord Jesus preached the same message (see Matt 4: 17). It is very important to understand that repentance, attested here by baptism, was preparatory for salvation. With this in mind we should notice exactly what John said. He "preached the baptism of repentance *for* the remission of sins" (Luke 3: 3), meaning '*unto* the remission of sins'. ***Their sins were not forgiven at their baptism.*** Baptism had no saving power. Sins can only be forgiven through faith in Christ. John's baptism was therefore *preparatory.* See Acts 18: 25 and 19: 1-5, especially Acts 19: 4: "John verily baptized with the baptism of repentance, saying unto the people, that they should **believe on him which should come after him,** that is, on Christ Jesus". This is more than adequately confirmed by John himself: "Behold the Lamb of God, which taketh away the sin of the world" (John 1: 29). By being baptised, men and women expressed their new attitude to sin. This change of attitude was so fundamental that it was expressed in baptism as death to the old life. It was the realisation of the gravity of sin in this way that would result in men and women turning to Christ for forgiveness.

The baptism of John was in preparation for the Lord's coming and is therefore not applicable now. The Bible teaches that Christians should be baptised, but baptism today is for people who *have* turned to the Lord Jesus and trusted in Him as their Saviour.

The expression, "the kingdom of heaven" (this is the first of thirty-two occurrences) is found only in Matthew's Gospel. It is the sphere in which God's rule is acknowledged. John called 'the nation of Israel to turn its back on sin, and thus be in a proper moral and spiritual condition to receive the King' (Wm.Macdonald).

b) The preacher himself, vv.3-4
These verses should be read in conjunction with Luke 3: 4-6; John 1: 23. We must notice:

Chapter 3

i) The prophetic confirmation. "For this is he that was spoken of by the prophet Esaias, saying, The voice of one crying in the wilderness, Prepare ye the way of the Lord, make his paths straight". See also Mark 1: 3; Luke 3: 4-6; John 1: 23.

Matthew refers here to Isaiah 40: 3-5. According to David Gooding, 'the heart of that prophecy was a metaphor drawn from an ancient custom that when an emperor or some other eminent personage was about to visit a city, the citizens could be required to prepare a well-constructed approach road along which he could advance with due pomp and dignity on his way into the city'. In Isaiah 40, the way was to be prepared for none other than the Lord Himself: "Prepare ye the way of the Lord....say unto the cities of Judah, Behold your God!". (Isaiah 40: 3, 9-10). Matthew was therefore in no doubt about the identity of the Lord Jesus. The work of John was to announce the coming of "the Lord God" Himself, for the Lord Jesus was "God...manifest in the flesh" (1 Tim 3: 16).

But what kind of approach road were people required to build when the Lord Jesus (the Lord God") came? It was the approach road of repentance. John preached "the baptism of *repentance*" (Luke 3: 3) or as Matthew has it, "I indeed baptize you with water unto repentance" (v.11). Repentance has been defined as 'seeing sin as God sees it'. It involves a change of mind about sin, leading to 'turning *from* sin and turning *to* God' (W.E.Vine).

ii) The personal details. "And the same John had his raiment of camel's hair, and a leathern girdle about his loins; and his meat was locusts and wild honey". We should notice:

- *His dwelling.* We have already commented on this. He was raised in the wilderness, and preached in the wilderness.

- *His dress.* His clothing came from the wilderness: "his raiment of camel's hair (serviceable and unostentatious), and a leathern girdle about his loins (to 'gird the loins' meant readiness to serve: a man tucked his long voluminous garment into his belt to facilitate movement)". He certainly didn't follow the fashions! He was not "gorgeously apparelled" (Luke 7: 25). Like Elijah before him (2 Kings 1: 8), his dress reflected his calling: it was a severe ministry - "Repent". He was not "a man clothed in soft raiment...behold, they that wear soft raiment are in king's houses" (Matt. 11: 8). Without suggesting for a moment that Christians ought to wear some kind of uniform (official or

Matthew

unofficial!), *our* dress should reflect *our* calling. See, for example 1 Timothy 2: 9-10.

- *His diet.* He had a strange diet. His food came from the wilderness - "locusts and wild honey". It was an unusual combination. Locusts were pronounced fit for human consumption, as opposed to other "unclean" insects (Lev. 11: 21-22). So John's food was both clean and sweet, even though it was the diet of the poor. He did not "live delicately" (Luke 7: 25). The word of God is both clean (Psalm 119: 140) and sweet (Psalm 119: 103). It is certainly not available in the godless society around us: it is found in the quietness of God's presence. But we mustn't expect everybody to understand this: "John came neither eating or drinking, and they say, He hath a devil" (Matt. 11: 18). The world will think that we're strange too!

Looking at it from another point of view, God provided for John in the desert. He had the necessities of life. "Your heavenly Father knoweth that ye have need of all these things" (Matt. 6: 32). It's usual to look at a wilderness as a lonely, uninhabited, and unrewarding place. That's just the way unsaved people see the Christian life. But it certainly wasn't the case so far as John was concerned. It was the place where God taught him, provided for him, and prepared him. But now, after thirty preparatory years, his service had begun.

c) The people's response, vv.5-9
Parallel passages are found in Mark 1: 4-5 and Luke 3: 7-8. In this connection we should notice:

i) The response of the common people. "Then went out to him Jerusalem, and all Judaea, and all the region round about Jordan, and were baptized of him in Jordan, confessing their sins" (vv.5-6).

ii) The response of the religious leaders. "But when he saw many of the Pharisees and Sadducees (the first reference to them) come to his baptism, he said unto them, O generation of vipers, who hath warned you to flee from the wrath to come? Bring forth therefore fruits meet for repentance: and think not to say within yourselves, We have Abraham to our father: for I say unto you, that God is able of these stones to raise up children unto Abraham" (vv.7-9). They were:

- *People trying to hide their true nature*. "O generation of vipers! (referring to their true parentage: see Gen. 3: 1)" (v.7). (Luke does not distinguish between the ordinary people and the religious leaders here: see 3: 7). These people were not baptized: "But the Pharisees and lawyers rejected the counsel of God against themselves, being not baptized of him" (Luke 7: 30). David Gooding describes them as 'vipers in front of a bush fire: trying to escape the flames but without any intention of having their evil natures changed'. They are told to "Bring forth... fruits meet for repentance" (v.8).

- *People relying on their ancestry.* "And begin not to say within yourselves, We have Abraham to our father: for I say unto you, That God is able of these stones to raise up children unto Abraham" (v.9). They were reliant upon national descent for divine favour, rather than on repentance and confession of sin. But national descent would not exempt them from "the wrath to come". Sadly, they persisted in this 'religious conceit' (J.Heading): "They answered and said unto him, Abraham is our father. Jesus saith unto them, If ye were Abraham's children, ye would do the works of Abraham" (John 8: 39). John was evidently referring to literal stones (compare 4: 3), and therefore saying that the creation of "children unto Abraham" from "stones" (*lithos*) was less difficult than the conversion of these people! Believers are "living stones (*lithos*)" (1 Pet. 2: 5).

d) The preacher's contrasts, vv.10-12
Parallel passages are found in Mark 1: 7-8 and Luke 3: 9-19. In the verses above, John makes five contrasts:

i) He contrasts two types of tree. "And now also the axe is laid unto the root of the trees: therefore every tree which bringeth not forth good fruit is hewn down, and cast into the fire" (v.10). Compare Matthew 7: 16-20: note the words, "By their fruits ye shall know them". The axe lay ready to fell the tree. The "good fruit" required is clearly identified in v.8: "Bring forth therefore fruits meet for **repentance**". John baptized "with water unto **repentance**". Failure to "bring...forth good fruit" would bring divine judgment. As N.Crawford *(What the Bible Teaches - Luke)* points out, 'the axe at "the root of the trees" is a figurative way of saying that God's judgment has already been determined, and will be carried out in due time, when the sinner least expects it'. Compare 2 Peter 2: 3, "Whose judgment now of a long time lingereth not, and their damnation slumbereth not".

ii) He contrasts two preachers. "*I* indeed baptize you with water unto repentance: but *he* that cometh after me is **mightier than I**, whose shoes *I am not worthy to bear* (perhaps meaning, 'not worthy to carry the shoes of the King'): *he* shall baptize you with the Holy Ghost, and with fire" (v.11). Compare Luke 3: 15-16: "And as the people were in expectation, and all men mused in their hearts of John, whether he were the Christ or not; John answered, saying unto them all...one mightier than I cometh, the latchet of whose shoes I am not worthy to unloose". John was constantly aware of his own unworthiness and inferiority, and the worthiness and superiority of Christ. This led him to say, "He must increase, but I must decrease" (John 3: 30). The greatest of the prophets exclaimed, "I am not worthy" when preaching about Christ. (Others also said "I am not worthy": see Matt. 8: 8 and Luke 15: 21). The Lord Jesus is not only better than men. He is better than the best of men! The song of heaven is, "***Thou*** art worthy" (Rev. 4: 11).

iii) He contrasts two types of baptism. "I indeed baptize you **with water** unto repentance: but he that cometh after me...shall **baptize you with the Holy Ghost, and with fire"** (v.11). In describing the superiority of Christ, John refers to their respective baptisms. He baptised "with water" and, as David Gooding observes, 'John could put repentant people in water' but 'Only One who was God could put people in the Holy Spirit, or the Holy Spirit in people'.

iv) He contrasts two types of baptism by Christ. "He shall baptize you with (*en*, meaning 'in') the Holy Ghost, and with fire" (v.11). This is a very solemn statement. Quite possibly, this refers to the two classes of people mentioned earlier: "every tree...which bringeth not forth good fruit, is hewn down, and cast into the fire" (v.10). Those that ***did*** bring "forth good fruit" would be baptised "with (in) the Holy Ghost", and those that ***did not*** bring "forth good fruit" would be baptised "with fire". The 'baptism of the Spirit' took place once, and that was on the day of Pentecost. See Acts 1: 5, "And, being assembled together with them, (the Lord Jesus) commanded them that they should not depart from Jerusalem, but wait for the promise of the Father, which, saith he, ye have heard of me. For John truly baptized with (in) water; but ye shall be baptized with (in) the Holy Ghost not many days hence". See also Acts 11: 15-16. It was an act of great ***blessing.*** But to be baptised "with fire" will be an act of terrifying ***judgment.*** The Lord Jesus bestows the greatest possible blessings on those who bring "forth good fruit" which, today, is "repentance toward God, and faith toward our Lord Jesus Christ" (Acts 20: 21). He will execute judgment on all who refuse to repent and believe.

v) He contrasts two commodities on the threshing floor. "Whose fan is in his hand, and he will throughly purge his floor, and gather his wheat into the garner; but he will burn up the chaff with unquenchable fire" (v.12). Notice that it is "*his* wheat". John now uses a different metaphor and refers to winnowing. There is no such thing as universal salvation. All too many people find refuge in the idea that God is duty bound to bless everybody, and that He is too kind to cast men and women into hell. There *will* be a *separation* in eternity. Men and women will either be saved in "the garner" of heaven, or lost in the "unquenchable fire" of hell. We must urge people to "flee from the wrath to come".

2) THE BAPTISM OF THE LORD JESUS, vv.13-17
These verses can be divided as follows: *(a)* the testimony of John on earth (vv.13-15); *(b)* the testimony of God from heaven (vv.16-17).

a) The testimony of John on earth, vv.13-15
Matthew alone records the conversation between John the Baptist and the Lord Jesus at His baptism. We should notice two things here:

i) John's reticence to baptise the Lord. "Then cometh Jesus from Galilee to Jordan unto John, to be baptized of him. But John forbad him, saying, I have need to be baptized of thee, and comest thou to me?" (vv.13-14). The word "forbad" is in the imperfect tense, and could be rendered 'had it in mind to prevent him', or, 'was for hindering him'. Hence the RV, 'would have hindered him'. See *Vincent's Word Studies of the New Testament*. This was *before* John saw the Holy Spirit descending and remaining on the Lord Jesus, identifying Him as the Lamb of God and Son of God. Up to that moment, John knew him only as a relative, albeit a very wonderful relative. John was thoroughly aware of the moral excellence of the Lord Jesus. Hence his words, "I have need to be baptized *of thee,* and comest thou to me?" But John was not, even then, aware of His true identity. In his own words, "I knew him not".

This speaks eloquently about the life and character of the Lord Jesus during what are often called 'the silent years' in Nazareth. John knew that He was totally different from everybody else who requested baptism, and more than that, he was totally different from John himself! There was no need for repentance on the part of *this* candidate! *He* did not have to "bring forth...fruits worthy of repentance". He did not have to say, 'What shall I do then?' By saying, "I have need to be baptised of thee, and comest thou to me?", John bore testimony to the perfect manhood of the Lord Jesus. Very shortly afterwards, he would hear the testimony of God Himself: "This is my beloved Son, in whom I am well pleased". The perfect life of the Lord Jesus was recognised by John the Baptist on earth, and by God in heaven.

ii) The Lord's reason for being baptised. In view of His sinlessness, why was the Lord Jesus baptised? Even John could not understand the reason! We must listen carefully to the Saviour's explanation: "And Jesus answering said unto him, Suffer it to be so now: for thus it becometh us to fulfil all righteousness" (v.15). It is often suggested that although the Lord Jesus was totally sinless, He showed by His baptism that He was willing to stand in the place of those who were sinful, and therefore He anticipated His death on behalf of others at Calvary. This is a very attractive suggestion, but it does not quite fit the Lord's words, "thus it becometh **us** to fulfil all righteousness". These words point us to the correct meaning. "*It becometh us*", means, 'it is fitting, suitable, proper, right' *(Linguistic Key to the Greek New Testament)*. The Lord's answer to John, "suffer it to be so now", confirms that John was right in saying, "I have need to be baptized of thee", but that it was nevertheless fitting that He should be baptised, not because He needed to repent, but because He wished to identify Himself with what was right. 'By identifying Himself with those He came to redeem, Jesus inaugurated His public ministry as the Messiah. In regard to the Jewish religious observances, such as synagogue worship, attendance at feasts, and payment of the temple tax, Jesus always met the duties of a faithful Jew' (King James Study Bible).

It is beautiful to notice the way in which the Lord Jesus graciously acknowledges the part of John the Baptist in this: "thus it becometh **us** to fulfil all righteousness". It is nothing less than divine approval of his ministry. But there is more. As we have seen, the Lord Jesus had no need to be baptised, but He did not stand aloof from those who did, and was willing to identify Himself with them. This is a wonderful example to us all. In that sense, He has 'left us an example, that we should follow his steps' (1 Pet. 2: 21). We should always be glad to associate ourselves with those who desire to please God by turning from error, even if we haven't fallen into that same error ourselves. The Lord Jesus did not identify Himself with the nobility, but with "publicans" and "harlots" (Matt. 21: 32; Luke 7: 29). These were people who were deeply conscious of their shortcomings. What wonderful grace! We should also note that the Lord's baptism gave moral strength to His preaching. "The baptism of John, whence was it? from heaven, or of men?" (Matt. 21: 25). Had He not been baptised, the chief priests and elders might have found reason to deny His right to ask the question.

b) The testimony of God from heaven, vv.16-17

"And Jesus, when he was baptized, went up straightway out of the water: and, lo, the heavens were opened *unto him*, and he saw the Spirit of God descending like a dove, and lighting upon him: and lo a voice from heaven, saying, This is my beloved Son, in whom I am well pleased".

It is worth pointing out that Luke's record of the Lord's baptism, unlike that of Matthew and Mark, does not mention John the Baptist at all. Luke follows the ministry of John to its end (3: 19-20) and concentrates solely on the identity of the Lord. John had identified Him, and now God identifies Him. It is also worth noticing that only Luke refers to the fact that the Lord prayed at His baptism: "Now when all the people were baptized, it came to pass that Jesus also being baptized, and praying" (Luke 3: 21). The prayer life of the Lord Jesus is emphasised particularly in Luke's Gospel.

We should notice two important things here: *(i)* the Spirit from heaven (v.16); *(ii)* the voice from heaven (v.17).

i) The Spirit from heaven, v.16. "He saw the Spirit of God descending like a dove, and lighting upon him". This does not mean that He was not already indwelt by the Holy Spirit, but that He was anointed with the Holy Spirit for service. See Isaiah 61: 1, Acts 10: 38. The Holy Spirit came upon Him, not as "a mighty rushing wind" or as "fire", but "like a dove", indicating the gentleness and purity of His ministry. See Matt. 10: 16. Read Isaiah 42: 3. The Lord's service was undertaken in the power of the Holy Spirit. See, for example, Luke 4: 2, 14, 18. It is often pointed out that in the Old Testament, the dove "found no rest for the sole of her foot" (Gen 8: 9), but here the Holy Spirit found complete rest in Christ. It is said that the body of the dove does not produce bile, and this would emphasise the beauty and accuracy of the picture.

ii) The voice from heaven, v.17. "And lo a voice from heaven, saying, This is my beloved Son, in whom I am well pleased". It has been beautifully said that the Lord Jesus was 'The subject of His Father's love' - "Thou art my beloved Son", and 'the object of His Father's delight' - "in thee I am well pleased". The Lord Jesus was able to say, "I do always those things which please him (the Father)" (John 8: 29). At the end of the Old Testament, we have closed doors since there was nothing to bring God pleasure (Mal. 1:10). At the beginning of the New Testament, we have opened heavens because in Christ there was everything to bring God pleasure!

THE GOSPEL OF MATTHEW

"Tempted of the devil"

Read Chapter 4: 1-11
This chapter may be divided into four sections as follows: *(1)* the confrontation in the wilderness (vv.1-11); *(2)* the commencement of His preaching (vv.12-17); *(3)* the call of the disciples (vv.18-22); *(4)* the crowds that followed Him (vv.23-25). In the first case, we have the Lord *fasting* (v.2); in the second case, we have the Scriptures *fulfilled* (v.14); in the third and fourth cases, we have people *following* (vv.20, 22, 25).

1) THE CONFRONTATION IN THE WILDERNESS, vv.1-11
"Then was Jesus led up of the Spirit into the wilderness to be tempted of the devil" (v.1). Matthew (here) and Luke (4: 1-13) give us detailed accounts of the Lord's temptation, whereas Mark's record (1:12-13) is quite abbreviated, although he does tell us, uniquely, that the Lord was "with the wild beasts". John does not mention the Lord's temptations.

It should be said at the very outset that the temptations were not permitted to ascertain whether or not the Lord would pass or fail, but to tell us something about Him. They proved the reality of His own words, "the prince of this world cometh, and hath nothing in me" (John 14: 30). The temptation by the devil was not only something he was permitted to do, it was something he was constrained to do, in order to **demonstrate the moral fitness of the Lord Jesus for the work that lay before Him**. It must also be said that the temptation was real: the New Testament categorically states that He "suffered being tempted" (Heb. 2: 18), not because it was possible for Him to sin and therefore He was obliged to fight against yielding to temptation, but because, being utterly holy, the very suggestions of the devil were repulsive to Him. Unlike ourselves, of whom James says "every man is tempted when he is drawn away of his own lust, and enticed", the Lord Jesus, being God, "cannot be tempted with evil" (James 1: 13-14). We must now notice the following:

Matthew

a) The point at which the temptations occurred, v.1

"***Then*** was Jesus led up of the Spirit into the wilderness". It was after His baptism. It was in fact *immediately* after His baptism. Marks says exactly that: "And immediately the Spirit driveth him into the wilderness". At His baptism, God said from heaven, "This is my beloved Son, in whom I am well pleased" (Matt. 3: 17). Satan now attempts to change that statement. There is a very important lesson here. The Scriptures often demonstrate that the greatest temptations follow the greatest blessings. In the words of N.Crawford (*What the Bible Teaches - Luke*), Satan 'still makes a special target of any person or thing that brings glory to God'. He is near at our holiest and strongest moments: more so than at any other time. It was shortly after Peter had made his great confession, "Thou art the Christ, the Son of the living God", that the Lord said, "Get thee behind me, Satan" (Matt. 16: 16, 23).

b) The prevailing power when the temptations occurred, v.1

The Lord Jesus was "led up of ***the Spirit*** into the wilderness". Luke puts it slightly differently: "Jesus...was led by the Spirit into the wilderness" (4: 1) or "led by the Spirit *in* the wilderness" (JND, RV). That is, He was "led by the Spirit" during the whole course of the temptation. Mark employs a more forceful expression: "And ***immediately***, the Spirit ***driveth*** him into the wilderness." The words, "immediately" and "driveth", bring the Servant before us. It is the Servant ***enduring*** conditions in the wilderness. We should not, of course, understand this to mean that the Saviour needed to be driven like an unwilling slave. Rather that He was, as at all times, under the compulsion of the Holy Spirit. However, the fact that Mark uses the word "driveth" may well indicate the deep pain and revulsion with which the Saviour contemplated the prospect of confrontation with Satan. As we have already noted, He "***suffered*** being tempted" (Heb. 2: 18). We should carefully note that the Lord did not proceed recklessly into the wilderness: He did so in the power of the Holy Spirit.

c) The place in which the temptations occurred, v.1

"Then was Jesus led up of the Spirit into ***the wilderness***". Adam had every ***advantage.*** Just think of Eden, where there was no lack in anything. It was a place of beauty and plenty. The Lord Jesus faced every ***disadvantage***. Just think of the wilderness, where everything was lacking. It was a place of barrenness and emptiness. In Eden, God gave Adam, "every herb bearing seed...and every tree, in which is the fruit of a tree yielding seed" (Gen 1: 29), and said, "Of every tree in the garden thou mayest ***freely eat***" (Gen. 2:

16). But of the Lord Jesus, Matthew says, "And when he had fasted forty days and forty nights, He was afterward an *hungred*" (4: 2).

J.G.Bellett (writing on Mark) puts it magnificently: 'Everything that had surrounded Adam, the first man, might well have pleaded for God against the enemy. The sweetness of the whole scene, the beauty of that garden of delights, with its rivers which parted hither and thither, the fruits and the perfume, with the willing service of ten thousand tributary creatures, all had a voice for God against the accuser. The Lord Jesus was in the wilderness which yielded nothing, but left Him "an hungred", and the wild beasts (not in Eden!) were with Him, and all might have been pleaded by the accuser against God. All was *against* Jesus, as all had been *for* Adam; but He stood as Adam had fallen. The man of the dust *failed*, with all to favour him; the Man of God *stood*, with all against Him'.

We must add, of course, that Israel failed in the wilderness. It began with the golden calf at Sinai, and went on, and on, and on. But Christ, the true Israel, never failed in the wilderness. In fact, Israel's *disobedience* kept her in the wilderness (it should have been eleven days' journey from Horeb to Kadesh-Barnea, see Deuteronomy 1: 2): the Lord's *obedience* took Him into the wilderness and kept Him there for forty days and nights.

d) The person through whom the temptations occurred, v.1

Whilst Matthew and Luke say "tempted of the *devil*" (meaning 'the accuser' or 'the slanderer'), Marks says "he was there in the wilderness forty days, tempted of *Satan*" (meaning 'the adversary'). Satan sought constantly to both discredit and oppose the Lord Jesus in His service. He is given various other titles in Scripture. We should notice: *(i) his devotees*: he is called, "the god of this world" (2 Cor. 4: 4); *(ii) his dominion*: he is called, "the prince of this world" (John 16: 11 etc); *(iii) his domain:* he is called, "the prince of the power of *the air*" (Eph. 2: 2).

The very Creator, whose creation had been marred by Satan, not only stepped into His creation, but confronted Satan himself. He had come to deliver men and women from Satan's power, and proved His complete superiority over him. Had He been defeated in the wilderness, we would have been totally without hope. What we are now to see is vital to our salvation.

e) The period during which the temptations occurred, v.2

"And when he had fasted *forty days and forty nights*, he was afterward an hungred". Mark and Luke imply that the Lord Jesus was tempted throughout that period: "Being forty days tempted of the devil" (Luke 4: 2). Luke also makes clear, with Matthew, that the utmost pressure was exerted on the Lord at the end of the period: "and in those days he did eat nothing: and when they were ended, he afterward hungered. And the devil said unto him..." (Luke 4: 2-3 with Matthew 4: 2-3).

In Scripture, the figure "forty" is the number of probation. Israel was forty years in the wilderness, and failed time and time again. Moses was away on the mount for forty days and forty nights (Exodus 24: 18), and Israel lapsed into idolatry (Exodus 32). Elijah was given a meal sufficient to sustain him for forty days and forty nights (1 Kings 19: 8), and had to be replaced at the end of the time (1 Kings 19: 16). Unlike Israel in the wilderness, the Lord Jesus triumphed over Satan during the forty days and forty nights in the wilderness. Unlike Elijah, there was no need to replace Him after forty days and forty nights in the wilderness.

f) The principles on which the temptations occurred, vv.3-10
The temptations can be summarised as follows: *(i)* Satisfy Thyself: "command that these stones be made bread" (vv.3-4); *(ii)* Shew Thyself: "cast thyself down" (vv.5-7); *(iii)* Spare Thyself: "all these will I give thee, if thou wilt fall down and worship me" (vv.8-10).

It is most interesting to compare Matthew and Luke's record of the temptations. The principal difference is the order in which they are given. It is generally held that Matthew gives the chronological order, and this is supported by the 'time words' in his narrative: "when...afterwards...when... then...again...then...then" (Matt 4: 2-11). Luke, however uses the word "and" on numerous occasions in his account, omitting 'time words'. In keeping with his general design, Luke places last the particular point he wishes to emphasise. This is why he sometimes differs in his order of events, when compared with Matthew and Mark. It is fitting that Matthew, who emphasises the King and the kingdom, should end by drawing our attention to "all the kingdoms of the world" (v.8). Luke, on the other hand ends with reference to the way in which the Saviour refused to indulge in sensationalism. He made no attempt to impress men and women with the miraculous. There are other differences between the two records.

There is perhaps another reason for the order given by Matthew. E.W.Rogers has pointed out that Matthew records them as, in principle, they occurred to Israel when they were in the wilderness. 'He retraces Israel's wilderness history showing Christ as perfect in contrast with their sad imperfections. They murmured because they had no bread (Exodus 16). They tempted the Lord and limited the Most High because they had no water (Exodus 17: see particularly v.7), and in the absence of Moses they got Aaron to make a golden calf to which they bowed down and worshipped' (Exodus 32).

It can also be said that the three temptations as recorded by **Luke** (not by Matthew), follow the order in Genesis 3: 6 ("when the woman saw that the tree was **good for food**, and that it was **pleasant to the eyes,** and a tree to be desired **to make one wise**"), and the order in 1 John 2: 16 ("For all that is in the world, "the lust of **the flesh**, and the lust of **the eyes,** and the **pride of life**"). It has also been said "Just as the first temptation was to the body and the second to the soul, so the third was in the realm of the spirit; it had to do with worship, which is an exercise of the spirit' (Wm.Macdonald). Compare 1 Thessalonians 5: 23

i) Self-satisfaction, vv.3-4
In saying, "If thou be the Son of God, command that these stones be made bread", the tempter was not casting doubt on the Lord's identity, but saying in effect, '**Since** thou be the Son of God...' There was nothing sinful in hunger. Adam and Eve would have been hungry even if they hadn't sinned! But it would have been sin for the Lord Jesus to have distrusted God in the wilderness. Wm. Kelly puts it clearly: 'Didn't God know that there was no bread there? And was it not His Spirit who had led Him there? Had God told Him to leave the wilderness, or to make the stones into bread? He would not use His own power independently of God's word...Here, in the face of Satan, our Lord finds His strength; not in doing miracles, or in any provision that He might have made for Himself, but in the word of God...and He will not step out of the trial till it is over; He will not shift His circumstances or lift one little finger for Himself: He waits upon God'.

It was God's will for Him to be hungry in the wilderness to prove that in the most adverse circumstances, He was undeviating in His loyalty to the word of God, and therefore stronger than the great enemy who faced Him. For the Lord Jesus, the will of God was far more important than His own physical well-being. He would not take any step at all that would oppose the will of God. This is why He said, quoting from Deuteronomy 8: 3, "It is written, Man shall not live by bread alone, but by every word that proceedeth out of the mouth of God" (v.4). The context of the Deuteronomy quotation is helpful. In the early verses (vv.2-4) Moses reminded the people that they were utterly dependent on the Lord in the wilderness, and that they should not forget this when they arrived in Canaan (vv.7-20).

We should notice the exact wording of the quotation, "**Man** shall not live by bread alone...." This is most significant. In the garden of Eden, man was tempted by Satan, rejected God's will, and was defeated. Here in the wilderness is another Man tempted by Satan, but His loyalty to God's will cannot be altered, and He is victorious. The Lord Jesus overcame Satan, not by exercising His power as the Son of God, but by simply resting in God's will as Man. When the Lord Jesus came, He said, "**My meat is to do the will of him that sent me**" (John 4: 34). He lived, not by "bread alone, but by every word that proceedeth out of the mouth of God" (v.4). He would not step outside the word and will of God. To that end, He never performed a miracle for His own benefit. Satan might say "command that these stones be made bread", but the Lord Jesus lived by the word of God.

We might well ask the question: 'What is more important to us: our comfort and interests, in which case we will almost certainly do everything possible to please ourselves, or God's will, in which case we will wait for His guidance and obey His word. It must not be forgotten either that we must employ the word of God in resisting temptation. It has been pointed out that the words, "It is written", are in 'the Greek passive perfect tense, implying a past act with effects lasting to the present. The Lord therefore meant that the written word still had its same power, authority and value: see Heb. 4: 12; 1 Pet. 1: 24-25' (supplied by Justin Waldron).

ii) Self-advertisement, vv.5-7
"If thou be the Son of God, cast thyself down" (v.6). The "pinnacle of the temple" was probably the southern wing of the temple, and Josephus, who lived at the time, tells us that 'any one looking down would be giddy, whilst his sight could not reach such an immense depth'. The first temptation involved literal stones, and there can be little doubt that the second temptation involved the literal temple. Precisely how this took place is not revealed.

The Lord had said that man should "live...by every word that proceedeth out of the mouth of God" (v.4) so the devil now approaches the Lord Jesus with a Bible under his arm, saying in effect 'since that is the case, here is a word from God for you: "He shall give his angels charge concerning thee: and in their hands they shall bear thee up, lest at any time thou dash thy foot against a stone" (v.6). In view of this, according to the devil, the Lord could 'cast himself down'. He said in effect, 'Think of the tremendous impression it would make, and there is Biblical support for my suggestion'. But the tempter had misquoted and misapplied Psalm 91: 11-12 in several ways:

- **Firstly,** the tempter had quoted it out of context: the section reads "Because thou hast made the Lord, which is my refuge, even the most High, thy habitation, there shall no evil befall thee...For he shall give his angels charge over thee, to keep thee in all thy ways. They shall bear thee up in their hands, lest thou dash thy foot against a stone" (vv.9-12). Satan may have quoted the Bible, but he tried to make the verse mean something other than its true meaning. As Wm. Macdonald observes, 'It is true that God had promised to preserve Him, but that guarantee presupposed that the Messiah would be living in the will of God'. This meant absolute trust in God (v.9). Because He did this, it could be said that "he shall give his angels charge over thee, to keep thee in all thy ways" (v.11). Note too that the Scripture did **not** say, as the devil implied, 'Cast thyself down, because God has given his angels charge concerning thee, lest thou shouldest dash thy foot against a stone'.

- **Secondly**, the tempter did not, for obvious reasons, quote the verse following his (incomplete) quotation: "Thou shalt tread upon the lion and adder: the young lion and the dragon shalt thou trample under feet" (v.13).

- **Thirdly**, the tempter had endeavoured to make one part of Scripture contradict another, and without entering 'in to nice distinctions or analysing what Satan had said' (Wm.Kelly), the Lord simply said, "It is written again, Thou shalt not tempt the Lord thy God" (v.7), referring to Deuteronomy 6: 16. This is very important: it is all too easy to give a meaning to a verse in the Bible which is not supported by the rest of the Bible: any meaning like that must be wrong!

In this temptation, Satan attempted to attack the perfect trust of the Lord Jesus in the will of God, by asking Him to put God to the test. It is when we doubt a person that we make experiments to discover how far they are to be trusted. The Lord Jesus had no need to find out whether or not God could be trusted: He had no need to demonstrate His confidence; He trusted God completely and absolutely. Do remember too, that in saying "Thou (Satan) shalt not tempt the Lord thy God", the Lord Jesus was stating His deity.

Matthew

We might ask ourselves the question: 'What are we trying to do: impress people, or simply work within the purpose and will of God for us as revealed in His word?

iii) Self-preservation, vv.8-10
"All these ('the kingdoms of the world') will I give thee, if thou wilt fall down and worship me" (v.9). This was Satan's biggest offer: the wilderness - the temple - the world! How Satan was able to show the Lord Jesus all the kingdoms of the world and their glory, remains a mystery. It must, presumably, have been in some kind of a vision, since no mountain would have been sufficiently high for the purpose. One thing is quite certain: the Lord Jesus will have all those kingdoms one day. God will say to Him: "Ask of me, and I shall give thee the heathen for thine inheritance, and the uttermost parts of the earth of the earth for thy possession" (Psalm 2: 8). See also Revelation 11: 15. There is a sense in which the kingdoms of the world do belong to the devil at the present time (see Luke 4: 6): he is described as "the god of this world" (2 Cor. 4: 4) and John states that 'the whole world lieth in the wicked [one]" (1 John 5: 19, JND). But it has to be said that Satan's dominion was not delivered to him by God, but by man, to whom God originally gave dominion. During the course of the Eastbourne Bible Readings in 1973, E.W.Rogers pointed out that the word "delivered" can be translated 'betrayed', and it is perfectly true that the word *(paradidomi)* is often used in that way in the New Testament. Man has betrayed his trust.

Satan offered Christ the crown without the cross: he suggested a kind of short cut to glory. Just suppose, though totally impossible, that the Lord Jesus had accepted:

- **He would have not gone to Calvary.** There could, therefore, have been no salvation for us. We would have remained in Satan's power, and perished eternally. The death of the Lord Jesus meant defeat for Satan: no wonder he tried to prevent this happening.

- **He would have acknowledged Satan's superiority**. Notice the answer of the Lord Jesus, quoting Deuteronomy 6: 13: "It is written, Thou shalt worship the Lord thy God, and him only shalt thou serve" (v.10). To worship someone is to serve them. The Lord Jesus worshipped God, and served God alone. Can you think of anything more disastrous than for Christ to serve Satan? No wonder He commanded the tempter to go: "Get thee hence,

Satan" (v.10). "Then the devil leaveth him, and, behold, the angels came and ministered unto him" (v.11) Compare Mark 1: 13. They fulfilled the role assigned to them in Psalm 91: 11-12!

In conclusion, the Lord Jesus answered Satan by His knowledge and application of the Word of God: "It is written". This is exactly how we too can defeat the great enemy. Paul says, "Take...the sword of the Spirit, which is the Word of God" (Eph. 6: 17). 'In all three temptations Jesus quoted from the Pentateuch...like David He used only one of the five stones (Deuteronomy) to defeat the giant' (Wm. Macdonald). Before leaving this, we should ask the question: 'Do acquisitions absorb *us* - or do we accept what God gives us?

The sum of the matter is this: 'God's King must reign in righteousness...the King was tested and proved to be all that God the Father had declared at His baptism - the One in whom He had found all His delight' (H.A.Ironside).

g) The purpose for which the temptations took place
There are at least four ways in which we can regard the purpose for which the temptation took place:

i) To prove the impeccability of Christ. The temptations proved His purity and impeccability. That is why divine approval was given before, not after, the temptations. The temptations did not bring divine approval - they proved the correctness of it at His baptism.

ii) To prove the complete superiority of Christ over Satan. We should notice that He went to confront the enemy. It has been said that the devil challenged the first man, but the second Man challenged the devil. He did so in the power of the Spirit of God. In the wilderness, the Lord Jesus took the battle to Satan, and defeated him utterly, as we have seen. He triumphed where Adam was defeated. His commission was to "destroy the works of the devil" (1 John 3: 8). At the end of forty days and forty nights, at a time of extreme weakness, the Lord Jesus could say authoritatively, "Get thee hence, Satan". The Lord Jesus could not be broken.

iii) To provide an example for us. In His guidance by the Holy Spirit, in His dependence on God, and in His use of the word of God. Apply all this to yourself!

iv) To prepare the Lord for priesthood. In the wilderness, the Lord Jesus

Matthew

'sounded out the strength of the enemy, and measured the might of the foe'. We can come to Him, not because He has experience of sin, but because He knows the strength of the enemy. See Hebrews 4: 15-16. We must remember that whilst the Lord Jesus does not sympathise with our sins, He "suffered being tempted" (Heb.2: 18). Only One perfectly holy can be so deeply pained by the suggestion.

"Follow me"
Read Chapter 4: 12-25
In introducing this chapter, we suggested that the passage may be divided into four sections as follows: *(1)* the confrontation in the wilderness (vv.1-11); *(2)* the commencement of His preaching (vv.12-17); *(3)* the call of the disciples (vv.18-22); *(4)* the crowds that followed Him (vv.23-25).

1) THE CONFRONTATION IN THE WILDERNESS, vv.1-11
In these verses, we noticed the following in connection with the Lord's temptations: *(a)* the point at which they occurred (v.1): it was after the Father had said, "This is my beloved Son, in whom I am well pleased"; *(b)* the prevailing power when they occurred (v.1): He was "led up of the Spirit into the wilderness"; *(c)* the place in which they occurred (v.1): it was in "the wilderness"; *(d)* the person through whom they occurred (v.1): He was "tempted of the devil"; *(e)* the period during which they occurred (v.2): it was over a period of "forty days and forty nights" with particular reference to the end of that period; *(f)* the principles on which they occurred (vv.3-4); self-satisfaction (vv.3-10): self-advertisement (vv.5-7): self-preservation (vv.8-10); *(g)* the purpose for which they occurred: to prove His impeccability, to prove His complete superiority over Satan, to provide an example for us, and to prepare Him for priesthood.

2) THE COMMENCEMENT OF HIS PREACHING, vv.12-17
In these verses, we should notice: *(a)* the point in time (v.12); *(b)* the place (vv.12-13); *(c)* the prophecy (vv.14-16); *(d)* the preaching (v.17)

a) The point in time, v12
"Now when Jesus had heard that John was cast into prison, he departed into Galilee". According to Matthew, the first place He visited in Galilee was Nazareth (see v.13). Parallel passages are found in Mark 1: 14 and Luke 4: 14-15. The Lord remained in Nazareth until the townspeople there attempted to kill Him for daring to say that God was quite prepared to pass by His own unbelieving people in favour of Gentiles (Luke 4: 16-30). Having

Chapter 4

passed "through the midst of them" the Lord "went his way, and came down to Capernaum" (Luke 4: 30-31).

There is good reason for believing that the Lord's ministry began previously, and that Matthew makes no reference to events in the early chapters of John's Gospel, which includes details of His visit to "Cana of Galilee" (John 2: 1). His particular concern is to emphasise that the long-awaited Messiah had come in fufilment of Old Testament prophecy, and was now embarking on His *public* preaching with the message, "Repent: for the kingdom of heaven is at hand" (v.17).

However, we should notice that the Lord Jesus waited until the public ministry of John the Baptist had ended before commencing His own public ministry. The Lord made no attempt to eclipse John. He did nothing to put John 'in the shade' or to 'push him out of the way'. On the contrary, He later spoke of John in the highest terms. He paid the highest tribute to the man who had served Him so well. See Matthew 11: 7-15. There was continuity in the preaching. John had said, "Repent ye: for the kingdom of heaven is at hand" (Matt. 3: 2), and now the Lord Jesus preached in the same way. As Justin Waldron observes, 'When John the Baptist was imprisoned, Herod must have thought that he had silenced the voice of God. But no sooner had John been imprisoned than God spoke again through His Son. This illustrates for us the truth that "the word of God is not bound" (2 Tim. 2: 9)'. There can be no doubt that rejection of the King's forerunner intimated that the King Himself would be similarly treated. The Lord himself made this clear: "Elias is come already, and they knew him not, but have done unto him whatsoever they listed. Likewise shall the Son of man suffer of them. Then the disciples understood that he spake unto them of John the Baptist" (Matt. 17: 10-13).

b) The place, vv.12-13
"He departed into Gailee; and leaving Nazareth, he came and dwelt in Capernaum, which is upon the sea coast, in the borders of Zabulon and Nephthalim". John Heading notes that the Lord "departed into Galilee", and asks the question 'From where?' with the answer, 'Perhaps from the Jerusalem area'. Capernaum was about twenty miles northwest from Nazareth, towards the north of the Sea of Galilee. It was in this area that "most of his mighty works were done" (Matt. 11: 20). John Heading suggests that Matthew adds, "in the borders of Zabulon and Nephthalim", in order to make the relevance of his quotation from Isaiah 9: 1-2 more apparent.

Matthew

Naphtali was located along the western shore of Galilee, and Zebulon lay to the west of Naphtali.

c) The prophecy, vv.14-16

The Lord Jesus "came and dwelt in Capernaum, which is upon the sea coast, in the borders of Zabulon and Nephthalim: that it might be **fulfilled** which was spoken by Esaias the prophet, The land of Zabulon, and the land of Nephthalim, by the way of the sea, beyond Jordan, Galilee of the Gentiles: the people that sat in darkness saw great light; and to them that sat in the region and shadow of death light is sprung up". The words, "that it might be fulfilled" are quite specific, and quite unambiguous. It was revealed to Zacharias, the father of John the Baptist, that his son would be called "the prophet of the Highest" who would "give light to them that sit in darkness and in the shadow of death" (Luke 1: 76-79). The light could not have been greater (John 8: 12).

But why is Isaiah 9: 2 cited in the New Testament with reference to the Lord Jesus? Isaiah 9: 1 refers to two Assyrian invasions of Israel, the northern of the two kingdoms into which the nation was divided after the death of Solomon. Reference is made to these invasions in 2 Kings 15: 29; 17: 6. Zebulon and Naphtali were two of the ten tribes which made up Israel, and it now becomes clear why they alone are mentioned. They were located in the most despised part of the land, 'in Galilee of the nations, among the poorest of Israel, where Gentiles were mixed up with them - people who could not even speak their own tongue properly' (Wm. Kelly). The description "probably arose because of its position which made it 'the frontier' between the heart of the land and the external world' (F.Cundick). It was here that the Lord spent most of His time on earth. Not in sophisticated, religious Judaea and Jerusalem, but in despised "Galilee of the Gentiles". Their "dimness" (AV), or darkness' (JND), would be alleviated by "great light", and the prophecy was fulfilled with the coming of the Lord Jesus to that area. We should add that Isaiah 9: 2 also refers to the future as the subsequent verses show.

In endeavouring to tempt the Lord Jesus, the devil showed Him "all the kingdoms of the world, and the glory of them" (v.8), but now we have another perspective: "the people that sat in **darkness** saw great light; and to them that sat in **the region and shadow of death** light is sprung up". Ironic, isn't it! Things are not always what they seem to be!

d) The preaching, v.17
"From that time (compare vv. 16: 21) Jesus began to preach (*kerusso*, to herald), and to say, Repent: for the kingdom of heaven is at hand". "The kingdom of heaven" is a term used only in this Gospel. 'It speaks of heaven's rule over earth. This was now ready to be set up if there had been a readiness on the part of Israel to receive it. But it could be set up only on a foundation of national repentance; and for this the people were not prepared. They would not receive the King' (H.A.Ironside). Had He been received, and His credentials were unassailable, then Israel's blessings would have been as "the days of heaven upon the earth" (Deut. 11: 21). They will be ultimately! But only after national repentance. See Zechariah 12: 10-14.

3) THE CALL OF THE DISCIPLES, vv.18-22
In these verses we should notice at least three things about the four disciples, "Simon called Peter, and Andrew his brother...James the son of Zebedee, and John is brother" (vv.18, 21). They were *(a)* ordinary people; *(b)* occupied people; *(c)* obedient people.

a) They were ordinary people
All four were fishermen. Not high-ranking religious leaders, or great intellectuals, but ordinary fishermen. Paul puts it like this: "Not many wise men after the flesh, not many mighty, not many noble, are called" (1 Cor. 1: 26). As the Countess of Huntingdon observed, the Lord did not say, 'not *any* noble', but 'not *many* noble', and we can understand 'where she was coming from!' In any case, 'not any wise men after the flesh' would have excluded Paul himself!

This should encourage us. Some time later, after the Lord Jesus had returned to heaven, Peter and John were arrested, and appeared before the Jewish Sanhedrin. "Now when they saw the boldness of Peter and John, and perceived that they were unlearned and ignorant men, they marvelled" (Acts 4: 13). But we mustn't get the impression that the description "unlearned and ignorant" means that they were crude and illiterate. W.E. Vine writes: 'While *agrammatoi* ("unlearned") may refer to their being unacquainted with Rabbinical learning, *idiotai* ("ignorant") would signify 'laymen', in contrast with the religious officials'.

The fact remains that whatever our educational ability, business acumen, or cultural background, the Lord has important work for us all to do.

b) They were occupied people

Simon and Andrew were "casting a net into the sea" (v.18). James and John were "in a ship...mending their nets" (v.21). The Lord always calls busy men, and this can be amply illustrated from Old and New Testaments. For example, Moses was keeping "the flock of Jethro his father in law" (Exodus 3: 1), and Gideon was threshing "wheat by the winepress, to hide it from the Midianites" (Judges 6: 11). When it comes to the Lord's service, layabouts need not apply! Service for Christ is not a soft option. Zeal and faithfulness in secular work is one important qualification for spiritual work. These verses illustrate the fact that a variety of ability is needed in the Lord's service.

i) In the first case, two men were *"casting a net"*. In Matthew 13, the Lord Jesus refers to a drag net (*sagene*) which was used for deep-water fishing (v.47), but the nets here (*amphiblestron*, v.18; *diktuon*, vv.20-21) were used in inshore fishing. "And he said unto them, Follow me, and I will make you fishers of men" (v.19). Wm. Macdonald comments as follows: 'Their responsibility was to follow Christ. His responsibility was to make them fishers of men'.

ii) In the second case, two men were *"mending nets"*. The same Greek word (*katartizo*) is used, for example, in Galatians 6: 1 ("**restore** such an one") and in Ephesians 4: 12 ("for the **perfecting** of the saints"). When the Lord Jesus "ascended up on high, he led captivity captive, and gave gifts unto men...And he gave some...evangelists (people who 'cast nets'); and some, pastors and teachers (people who 'mend nets')" (Eph. 4: 8-11).

c) They were obedient people

"And they straightway left their nets, and followed him" (v.20); "And they immediately left the ship and their father, and followed him" (v.22). To quote Harold Paisley, 'The call and obedience of these two sons of Zebedee is another illustration of the sacrifices demanded by true discipleship. Christ and His claims were foremost, so they forsook home and business for His sake and the gospel'. How about us? Are we ready to serve Him - just where we are? Or does it have to be said of us, even as Christians:

> *Room for pleasure, room for business,*
> *But for Christ the crucified,*
> *Not a place where He can enter*
> *In the heart for which He died.*

Chapter 4

We should notice two further things: first of all, in both cases, the response was immediate: "and they *straightway* left their nets, and followed him" (v.20): "And they *immediately* (same word) left the ship and their father, and followed him (v.22). In a very real sense, Paul followed in their footsteps: "What things were gain to me, those I counted loss for Christ. Yea doubtless, and I count all things but loss for the excellency of the knowledge of Christ Jesus my Lord" (Phil. 3: 7-8). In the first case, he uses the past tense (v.7): in the second he uses the present tense (v.8). Something like thirty years lay between v.7 and v.8, and Paul hadn't changed his mind one iota!

Secondly, in the case of James and John, their father was not left to fend for himself. See Mark 1: 20. He did have the "hired servants". The Lord does not make unreasonable demands on others when He calls His disciples. Luke tells us that James and John were business partners with Simon (and Andrew too, presumably). See Luke 5: 10.

It is very interesting to notice the use of "straightway" in Mark's record (1: 16-20). Simon and Andrew were unhesitating in responding to the Lord's call (v.18), and the Lord was unhesitating in calling James and John (v.20). He never had to hesitate, did He? He could never make a mistake!

4) THE CROWDS THAT FOLLOWED HIM, vv.23-25
In these verses we should notice the following: *(a)* the Lord's priority (v.23); *(b)* the Lord's ability (v.24); *(c)* the Lord's popularity (v.25).

a) The Lord's priority, v.23
"And Jesus went about all Galilee, teaching in their synagogues, and preaching (*kerusso,* heralding) the *gospel* of the kingdom, and healing all manner of sickness and all manner of disease among the people". Compare Matthew 9: 35, which has been described as another "summary verse" (Justin Waldron).

Teaching and preaching were placed first. While the Saviour certainly "went about doing good, and healing all that were oppressed of the devil" (Acts 10: 38), this was not His priority. In His own words, "Let us go into the next towns, that I may preach there also: for therefore came I forth". This He did: "And he preached in their synagogues throughout all Galilee, and cast out devils (demons)" (Mark 1: 38-39). Galilee was a thickly-populated area: 'From north to south, Galilee was sixty-three miles long and thirty-three miles wide. According to Josephus, its population was about three million' (John Phillips).

This is the first reference in the New Testament to the Gospel: "the gospel of the kingdom". There can be no doubt that "the gospel of the kingdom" was "Repent: for the kingdom of heaven is at hand" (v.17). The Gospel message today proclaims the need for "repentance toward God, and faith toward our Lord Jesus Christ" (Acts 20: 21). It is "the gospel of the grace of God" (Acts 20: 24), and God's purpose is "to take out...a people for his name" (Acts 15: 14). It is noteworthy that Paul described his service as "preaching the kingdom of God" (Acts 20: 25). Whatever the dispensation, the expression "kingdom of God" emphasises divine rule in the lives of men and women, so that believers today have been "delivered from the power (*exousia*, meaning 'authority') of darkness, and...translated...into the kingdom of his dear Son" (Col. 1: 13).

At the end-time, "this gospel of the kingdom shall be preached in all the world for a witness unto all nations; and then shall the end come" (Matt. 24: 14). The preachers are described as "the servants of our God", and there will be "an hundred and forty and four thousand" of them "of all the tribes of the children of Israel" (Rev. 7: 3). As a result of their preaching, there will be "a great multitude, which no man could number, of all nations, and kindreds, and people, and tongues" who will stand "before the throne, and before the Lamb, clothed with white robes, and palms in their hands" (Rev. 7: 9). The apostle John was told, "These are they which came out of great tribulation, and have washed their robes, and made them white in the blood of the Lamb" (Rev. 7: 14). Whether it is "the gospel of the grace of God", or the "gospel of the kingdom" preached by John the Baptist, the Lord Jesus, and by God's servants at the end-time, the basis is the same: the message rests upon the death and resurrection of the Lord Jesus. The objective is the same: to bring men and women under divine authority. It is the result that is different: "the gospel of the grace of God" secures a heavenly people, while "the gospel of the kingdom" secures a people waiting expectantly and prepared for the coming of the King on earth.

b) The Lord's ability, v.24
"And his fame went throughout all Syria: and they brought unto him all sick people that were taken with divers diseases and torments, and those which were possessed with devils, and those which were lunatick, and those that had the palsy; and he healed them". If the Lord "went about all Galilee,

teaching in their synagogues" (v.23), over which we could write "to the Jew first", then over "his fame...throughout all Syria" we could write "and also to the Greek". The news of what He was doing throughout "all Galilee" (v.23) spread to "all Syria" (v.24). No case, whatever its nature - physical or mental - was to difficult for Him! As John Heading points out, 'The miracles of the Lord were characterised by three features that distinguished them from the works of men: they were instantaneous, they were complete, and they were lasting'.

c) The Lord's popularity, v.25
"And there followed him great multitudes of people from Galilee, and from Decapolis, and from Jerusalem, and from Judaea, and from beyond Jordan" (v.25). Decapolis was a territory with ten confederated cities in northeastern Palestine. The people were largely Gentiles. But following the Lord in this way did not constitute true discipleship. In another connection, the Lord said: "Not every one that saith unto me, Lord, Lord shall enter into the kingdom of heaven; but he that doeth the will of my Father which is in heaven" (Matt. 7: 21-23). This is the 'acid test' (John Heading). Having been attracted to Him on account of what He did, but having then listened to His teaching, "many of his disciples went back, and walked no more with him" (John 6: 66).

THE GOSPEL OF MATTHEW

"Blessed"

Read Chapter 5: 1-12

Matthew chs.1-9 can be divided as follows: *(i)* the presentation of the King (chs.1-4); *(ii)* the preaching of the King (chs.5-7); *(iii)* the power of the King (chs.8-9).

In chs.5-7, generally known as 'the Sermon on the Mount', the King describes the character and conduct of His subjects, and it should be said that His teaching is applicable at any given time. The fact that the Lord's teaching can be described as the laws of the "kingdom of heaven" does not confine them to the future revelation of that kingdom on earth. There is no scriptural justification for linking them to a specific age or dispensation, and to say that these chapters refer only to the future and have no voice for today, can only deprive us of a great deal of necessary instruction and encouragement. This approach is nothing less than a tacit denial of Paul's teaching that "all scripture is...profitable for doctrine, for reproof, for correction, for instruction in righteousness" (2 Tim. 3: 16). There is certainly an abundance of "doctrine", "reproof", "correction", and "instruction in righteousness" in 'the Sermon on the Mount!'

The term, "kingdom of heaven" (literally, 'the kingdom of the heavens'), with its allusion to Daniel 2: 44; 4: 26; 7: 13-14, is peculiar to Matthew's Gospel, whereas parallel passages in Mark and Luke use the term "the kingdom of God". The Jewish readers of Matthew's Gospel would have no difficulty in understanding the expression, "the kingdom of the heavens", whereas Gentile readers, with their idolatrous background, would tend to think of "the heavens" in terms of unseen spiritual powers. Hence, in order to correct that impression, Mark and Luke use the term, "the kingdom of God", but it is the same kingdom, with the same emphasis on divine **rule.** When the Lord Jesus came, "the kingdom of heaven was at hand" (Matt.

4: 17), and He displayed the power of the King (Matt. 12: 28). Believers today have been "delivered from the power of darkness, and ...translated... into the kingdom of His dear Son" (Col. 1: 13). That is, they are subject to His authority. He reigns in the hearts and lives of His people. When Christ returns to earth, He will establish His kingdom publicly for all to see, prior to which, both now and in the dark days that lie ahead, His people can rightly pray "thy kingdom come". The principles of the 'sermon' are timeless', and therefore for present application.

Introduction, vv.1-2

"And seeing the multitudes, he went up into a mountain: and when he was set, his disciples came unto him: and he opened his mouth, and taught them, saying..."

The movements of the Lord Jesus should be noted: He "went up...and when he was set (sat down)...opened his mouth". These movements emphasise His dignity of movement and bearing. It has been said that "the setting to the 'Sermon on the Mount' - *a mountain* - and the posture of the preacher - when he was *set* (sitting being the usual practice of the Rabbi when teaching) - suggest that Matthew is deliberately portraying the Lord Jesus as the second and greater Moses who, on a another 'mountain', imparts a new 'law', though to be sure a very different kind of law from that promulgated by Moses from Mount Sinai. The 'law' prescribed by the Lord Jesus is no external code of rules which can be followed to the letter, but a series of principles, ideals and motives for conduct, more akin to the 'law' which Jeremiah foretold the Lord would put in men's 'inward parts', and 'write it in their hearts' when he established a new covenant with them (Jer. 31: 33)" (R.V.G.Tasker).

It is therefore interesting to compare the law and 'the Sermon on the Mount'. Mountains were involved in both cases, but while Moses ascended the mount to *receive* the law, the Lord Jesus ascended the mount to *impart* the laws of His kingdom. The law was largely negative, outward, and in outline. The 'sermon' was largely positive, inward, and filled out the outline. It should also be said that the Lord delivered two 'sermons on the mount'. The second is found in Matthew chs.24-25, when the Lord "sat upon the mount of Olives". The verses currently before us should be compared with Luke 6: 20-23, which is part of what has been called 'the Sermon on the Plain'. It should be said, however, that some expositors believe that Matthew has placed together the Lord's teaching at various times and in various places to form one continuous 'sermon' or body of teaching.

In considering the 'beatitudes', we must notice the repeated contrasts: first, a **description of the disciple** ("Blessed are..."), then a **declaration of the blessing** ("for..."). The word "blessed" conveys more than 'happy'. It carries the ideas of spiritual prosperity, consciousness of divine favour, and spiritual happiness. The qualities described comprise the character of all who are subject to the reign of the King, and who therefore belong to His kingdom. In consequence "anyone who claims to be God's son, or to know Him, or to belong to His kingdom, or to be a member of His body, the Church, in whom these qualities are conspicuous by their absence, is 'a liar and knows not the truth'" (R.V.G. Tasker).

It should be noted that while the first seven 'beatitudes' (vv.3-9) emphasise the **character** of the disciples, the final two 'beatitudes' (vv.10-12) emphasise the **conditions** in which they find themselves.

The first beatitude, v.3

"Blessed are the poor in spirit: for theirs is the kingdom of heaven"

i) The description of the disciple: "Blessed are the poor in spirit". The Lord does not refer here to material poverty, but rather to a low estimate of ourselves - or **no** estimate of ourselves. It is the complete opposite of arrogance. Proverbs 13: 7 describes someone who is "poor in spirit". As R.V.G Tasker points out, "The best commentary on the first beatitude is the parable of the Pharisee and the publican (Luke 18:10-14), where the publican "would not lift up so much as his eyes unto heaven, but smote upon his breast, saying, God be merciful to me a sinner".

To be "poor in spirit" leaves **no room for pride or self-righteousness.** In this connection, the following should be noted: "God resisteth the proud, and giveth grace to **the humble**" (1 Peter 5: 5); "If any man among you seemeth to be wise in this world, let him become **a fool**, that he may be wise" (1 Cor. 3: 18); "Unto me, who am less than the **least of all saints...**" (Eph. 3: 8); "For I am **the least** of the apostles, that am not meet to be called an apostle, because I persecuted the church of God" (1 Cor. 15: 9); "For thus saith the high and lofty One that inhabiteth eternity, whose name is Holy; I dwell in the high and holy place, with him also that is of a **contrite and humble spirit**"

(Isaiah 57: 15). (Notice here that it is those of "a contrite and humble spirit" who enjoy God's presence, which is exactly the Lord's teaching in Matt. 5: 3). See also Isaiah 66: 2. Widening this, those that recognise that they are "poor" recognise "that they can do no good thing without divine assistance, and that they have no power in themselves to help them do what God requires them to do" (R.V.G.Tasker).

We should notice that this section of the 'beatitudes' ends with "peacemakers" (v.9): to be "poor in spirit" is the foundation for that noble work. In fact to be "poor in spirit" sets out the basis of conduct on which the other 'beatitudes' rest.

ii) The declaration of blessing: they are "blessed" because "theirs is the kingdom of heaven". They possess "all things" (2 Cor. 6: 10). In Hannah's words, "He raiseth the poor out of the dust, and lifteth up the beggar from the dunghill, to set them among princes, and to make them inherit the throne of glory" (1 Sam. 2: 8). But, looking at it another way, "the kingdom of heaven belongs to such, for from that kingdom the proudly self-sufficient are inevitably excluded" (R.V.G.Tasker).

To be "poor in spirit" is exemplified by the Lord Jesus. He "humbled himself", and God "hath highly exalted him" (Phil. 2: 8-9). Paul counted "all things but loss, for the excellency of the knowledge of Christ Jesus my Lord" (Phil. 3: 8).

The second beatitude, v.4

"Blessed are they that mourn: for they shall be comforted"

The words, "Blessed are they that mourn", seem contrary to nature. So do the words of Solomon: "It is better to go to the house of *mourning* than to go to the house of feasting" (Eccl. 7: 2), but read on - Solomon does explain himself.

i) The description of the disciple: "Blessed are they that mourn". This follows in proper sequence. The Lord does not refer here to mourning in the usual sense, although His words could certainly be applied in that way, but to mourning in the spiritual sense. The "poor in spirit" are sorrowful for their own sins and failings. Compare Psalm 34: 18. This is the result of self-examination. The mourning here is sorrow born out of conviction of sin. Paul mourned in this way when he cried "O wretched man that I am! who shall deliver me from the body of this death?" (Rom 7: 24). He mourned over the strength of the flesh. This ought to cause us all to mourn. Careless gaiety does not become the children of God. See 1 Corinthians 5: 2: "And ye are puffed up, and have not rather *mourned*". Days of mourning are days of meaning. We must not trivialise life.

It must also be said that those "that mourn" are also sorrowful for the evil that is rampant in the world, and the cause of so much suffering and misery. The tears of Jeremiah are a case in point (see Jer. 9: 1, 18; 13: 17; 14: 17). Wm.Macdonald rightly points out that "This is mourning for the Son of man's sake: in other words, it is that sorrow which a person endures in fellowship with the Lord Jesus. As someone has said, it is 'an active sharing and bearing of the world's hurt and sin like Jesus weeping over Jerusalem'"

ii) The declaration of blessing: they are "blessed" because "they shall be comforted". Those that mourn in this way receive spiritual comfort. See, for example, "godly sorrow worketh repentance to salvation not to be repented of...behold this selfsame thing, that ye sorrowed after a godly sort, what carefulness it wrought in you, yea, what clearing of yourselves...In all things ye have approved yourselves to be clear in this matter" (2 Cor. 7: 10-11). On the wider canvass, time will come when - with the establishment of the kingdom on earth - all wrongs will be put right and the King will inaugurate a reign of perfect righteousness.

Thinking of divine comfort in its widest sense, God is the "God of all **comfort;** who **comforteth** us in all our tribulation, that we may be able to **comfort** them which are in any trouble, by the **comfort** wherewith we ourselves are **comforted** of God" (2 Cor. 1: 3-4). See also Romans 15: 4, "For whatsoever things were written aforetime were written for our learning, that we through patience and **comfort** of the scriptures might have hope"; 1 Thessalonians 4: 18, "Wherefore **comfort** one another with these words". The Lord's coming is a tremendous source of comfort. Notice the Lord's words concerning Lazarus: "but now he is **comforted**" (Luke 16: 25).

The third beatitude, v.5

"Blessed are the meek: for they shall inherit the earth"

The word 'meek' (*praus* or *praos:* see W.E.Vine) is only used on three other occasions in the New Testament: see Matt. 11: 28-29; 21: 5-9; 1 Pet. 3: 4.

i) The description of the disciple: "Blessed are the meek". Meekness is not weakness. It has been described as 'power under control'. "Meekness" has the ideas of mildness, gentleness, ability to absorb spiritual injury. It is the Christian's spiritual 'shock-absorber'. As W.E.Vine points out, 'The common assumption is that when a man is meek it is because he cannot help himself; but the Lord was "meek" because He had the infinite resources of God at His command. Described negatively, meekness is the opposite to self-assertiveness and self interest. The Lord Jesus was "*meek* and lowly in heart" (Matt. 11: 29). He came "*meek*, and sitting upon an ass, and a colt the foal of an ass" (Matt. 21: 5). (Do notice that, significantly, this is not said in John 12: 15). Meekness is part of the "fruit of the Spirit" (Gal. 5: 22-23). Moses exhibited this quality in a remarkable degree: He was "very *meek*, above all the men which were upon the face of the earth" (Num. 12: 3). Paul besought the believers at Corinth "by the *meekness* and gentleness of Christ" (2 Cor. 10: 1).

ii) The declaration of blessing: they are "blessed" because "they shall inherit the earth". Psalm 37 is cited here, where, having said "For yet a little while, and the wicked shall not be", David continues, "But *the meek shall inherit the earth*, and shall delight themselves in the abundance of peace" (vv.10-11). The words, "inherit the earth" have the idea of administration. While there may well be a reference here to redeemed Israel in the millennial age, it must be remembered that "the saints shall judge (in the sense of 'administer') the world" (1 Cor. 6: 2-3). 'The meek do not inherit the world at the present time; rather they inherit abuse and dispossession. But they will literally inherit the earth when Christ, the king, reigns for a thousand years of peace and prosperity' (Wm.Macdonald).

The fourth beatitude, v.6

"Blessed are they which do hunger and thirst after righteousness: for they shall be filled"

i) The description of the disciple: "Blessed are they which do hunger and thirst after righteousness". We should welcome hunger and thirst like this! The *practice* of righteousness is before us here, rather than the righteous *standing* enjoyed by every believer. We should "hunger and thirst for righteousness" for *ourselves*, and for *the world*. Not only should we desire to do what is right and just ourselves, but we should long to see God's final triumph over evil, and His kingdom fully established.

ii) The declaration of blessing: they are "blessed" because "they shall be filled". In Paul's words, "And this I pray...that ye may be sincere and without offence till the day of Christ, being *filled* with the fruits of righteousness, which are by Jesus Christ, unto the glory and praise of God" (Phil. 1: 9-11). Isaiah puts it like this: "the work of righteousness shall be peace; and the effect of righteousness quietness and assurance for ever" (Isa. 32: 17). Righteousness is linked with "peace, and joy in the Holy Ghost" in Paul's description of "the kingdom of God" (Rom. 14: 17). The Millennium will see a *reign* of righteousness, but there is something even better: "We...look for new heavens and a new earth, wherein *dwelleth righteousness"* (2 Pet. 3: 13).

The fifth beatitude, v.7

"Blessed are the merciful: for they shall obtain mercy"

i) The description of the disciple: "Blessed are the merciful". They are totally unlike Joab and Abishai of whom David said, "these men the sons of Zeruiah be too hard for me" (2 Sam. 3: 39). It involves comforting the distressed - helping the poor - a supportive ministry - displaying kindness. We tend to be snobbish - very 'middle class' - ignoring the great need all around us. The Lord's people should have "bowels and mercies" (Phil. 2: 1). This 'beatitude' touches our relationship with others. To show mercy is to display grace and kindness towards those who have no claim whatsoever upon it. The person who shows mercy does not demand his rights, however much he might appear justified in doing so. If we stand upon 'our rights' we could well descend into vindictiveness rather than exhibiting mercy. It has been rightly said 'The question of attitude towards law breakers is not involved here. It is not a matter of the system of justice overlooking flagrant breaches of the law of the land' (E.L.H.Ogden).

ii) The declaration of blessing: they are "blessed" because they "shall obtain mercy". The 'repentant sinner first obtains mercy at the cross. To bestow it is God's prerogative. Showing it to others is the business of the child of God, who in doing so will continue to obtain it' (E.L.H.Ogden). The Lord Jesus taught His disciples to say: "And forgive us our sins; for we also forgive every one that is indebted to us" (Luke 11: 4). This should be compared with Eph. 4: 32, which sets out our position before God: "And be ye kind one to another, tenderhearted, forgiving one another, even as God for Christ's sake *hath* forgiven you". The Lord's teaching in Luke 11 is more forcibly expressed in Matt. 6: 14-15, "For if ye forgive men their trespasses, your heavenly Father will also forgive you: but if ye forgive not men their trespasses, neither will your Father forgive your trespasses". There is no contradiction. Our practice must correspond with our position. An unforgiving spirit on our part will disrupt our fellowship with God. How can we enjoy His forgiveness and blessing if we have an unforgiving spirit towards others? James points out that "he shall have judgment without mercy, that hath shewed no mercy" (James 2: 13). Herod showed no mercy to either James or to the keepers of the prison housing Peter, and he in turn was shown no mercy (Acts 12: 1-2, 19-24).

The sixth beatitude, v.8

"Blessed are the pure in heart, for they shall see God"

i) The description of the disciple: "Blessed are the pure (*katharos*, meaning pure as being cleansed) in heart". This refers, not to salvation, but to the character we must display as saved people. We have been purified: see Acts 15: 9 and 1 Peter 1: 22. But this must be worked out practically: "And every man that hath this hope in him purifieth himself, even as he is *pure*" (1 John 3: 3); "Whatsoever things are *pure*...if there be any virtue, and if there be any praise, think on these things" (Phil. 4: 8); "Follow peace with all men, and *holiness*, without which no man shall see the Lord" (Heb. 13: 14). Compare Ephesians 5: 5.

David describes the "pure in heart" in Psalm 24: 3-4: "Who shall ascend the hill of the Lord? And who shall stand in his holy place? He who has clean hands and a pure heart, who does not lift up his soul to what is false, and does not swear deceitfully". A pure heart is one whose motives are unmixed, whose thoughts are holy, whose conscience is clean: a heart 'undivided in its affections, uncompromising in its attitudes, and unsinning in its actions' (E.L.H.Ogden).

ii) The declaration of blessing: they are "blessed" because "they shall see God". Humanly speaking, this is a paradox. "No man hath seen God at any time" (John 1:18). Yet Moses endured, "seeing him who is invisible" (Heb. 11: 27). We see Him now by faith. There can be no perception of God without purity. A pure heart is the condition for seeing God. He will not hide Himself from, "the pure in heart".

Matthew

As to the future, the question is sometimes asked, 'will we see God?' The Lord's words help here: "He that hath seen me, hath seen the Father". It has been said that all we will ever see of God we shall see in Christ, for He is God. We have "the light of the knowledge of the glory of God in the face of Jesus Christ" (2 Cor. 4: 6). We will most certainly see Him literally (1 John 3: 2; Rev. 22: 4).

The seventh beatitude, v.9

"Blessed are the peacemakers: for they shall be called the children ('sons') of God"

i) The description of the disciple: "Blessed are the peacemakers". James connects the previous 'beatitude' with this as follows: "But the wisdom that is from above is first *pure*, then *peaceable*" (James 3: 17). See Hebrews 12: 14, "Follow *peace* with all men, and holiness, without which no man shall see the Lord"; 1 Thess. 5: 13, "Be at *peace* among yourselves".

The need always exits for 'building bridges', 'mending fences', 'repairing relationships', and bringing people together. The danger always exists of a 'short fuse', a short temper, which can only damage, perhaps irreparably, a situation. The Lord Jesus acted as a 'peacemaker'. When "the ten" heard about the request of James and John to sit on either side of the Lord in His glory, they "began to be much displeased" with them. But Jesus called them to him..." (Mark 10: 41-42).

ii) The declaration of blessing: they are "blessed" because "they shall be called the sons (JND) of God". That is, have the character of God Himself. After all, He has made possible the greatest peace of all!

As already noted, while the preceding 'beatitudes' emphasise the *character* of the Lord's people, the final two 'beatitudes' emphasise the *conditions* in which they are found. The conditions intimate clearly "that the instruction set forth here is intended, not, as many have insisted, for the millennial kingdom of Christ, for then there will be no persecution for the sake of righteousness, but for the disciples of Christ during the time of His rejection, when His followers are exposed to the hatred of a godless world' (H.A.Ironside).

Chapter 5

The eighth beatitude, v.10

"Blessed are they which are persecuted for righteousness' sake: for theirs is the kingdom of heaven"

i) The description of the disciple: "Blessed are they which are persecuted for righteousness' sake". Here, it is persecution for "*righteousness' sake*". That is, because of our testimony. Righteousness and truth arouse hatred and rejection. In v.11, it is for "my sake". 'These are believers who suffer for doing the thing that is right. Their unshakeable integrity condemns the ungodly world and brings out its venomous hostility. Men hate a righteous life because it exposes their own unrighteousness' (Wm.Macdonald).

ii) The declaration of blessing: they are "blessed" because "theirs is the kingdom of heaven". See 1 Peter 4: 14, "If ye be reproached for the name of Christ, happy are ye: for the Spirit of glory and of Christ resteth upon you". Persecuted believers can rejoice because they have "everlasting consolation and good hope through faith" (2 Thess. 2: 16), and have been called to God's "kingdom and glory" (1 Thess. 2: 12)

The ninth beatitude, vv.11-12

"Blessed are ye, when men shall revile you, and persecute you, and shall say all manner of evil against you falsely for my sake. Rejoice, and be exceeding glad: for great is your reward in heaven: for so persecuted they the prophets which were before you"

i) The description of the disciple: "Blessed are ye, when men shall revile you, and persecute you, and shall say all manner of evil against you falsely for my sake". These verses continue the theme of persecution, and emphasise that this can take place by speech as well as by deed. It should also be noted that the Lord now puts the subject on to a personal level. The change should be noticed: it is now "blessed are *ye*". It is now made personal to the disciples - they would suffer. As noted above, it is not now persecution for "*righteousness' sake*" but "persecution for *my sake*".

ii) The declaration of blessing: "Rejoice, and be exceeding glad: for great is your reward in heaven: for so persecuted they the prophets which were before you". The persecuted are 'to rejoice and be exceeding glad because: *(a)* it is proof that they belong to Christ, *(b)* proof of their faithfulness to Christ, and *(c)* proof of their identity with Christ' (E L.H. Ogden). 'To suffer for Christ's sake is a privilege that should cause joy and gladness. A great reward awaits those who thus become companions of the prophets in tribulation. These Old Testament spokesmen for God were embodied consciences who stood true to the Lord in spite of the most staggering suffering' (Wm.Macdonald).

E.L.H.Ogden points out that 'the true believer does not, however, look upon persecution as a means of gaining a reward. This was not the purport of the Lord's statement. He knows, nevertheless, that however dark the days of persecution may be, he will for his faithfulness receive a crown of life (Rev. 2; 10). Paul was able to speak of his experiences as "light affliction which...worketh for us a far more exceeding and eternal weight of glory" (2 Cor. 4:17)'.

'Here then in the Beatitudes we have a full-length portrait of the citizen of Christ's kingdom. Notice the emphasis on righteousness (v.6), peace (v.9), and joy (v.12), and compare with Romans 14: 17: "The kingdom of God does not mean food and drink but righteousness and peace and joy in the Holy Spirit"' (Wm.Macdonald).

Note: this study makes use of notes taken of an address by Mr. Ray Dawes at Cheshunt, 10.12.1994, and of an article by E.L.H.Ogden which appeared some years ago in 'Assembly Testimony'.

"Ye are the salt of the earth...Ye are the light of the world"

Read Chapter 5: 13-30
In his 'Synopsis of the Books of the Bible', J.N.Darby states that the 'Sermon on the Mount' describes the character of the Kingdom, and of the people in it, and supposes the rejection of the King. These three things should be kept constantly in mind when studying the passage.

After the introduction (vv.1-2), Matthew Chapter 5 may be divided as follows: *(1)* the description of His subjects (vv.3-12); *(2)* the distinctiveness of His subjects (vv.13-16); *(3)* the demands on His subjects (vv.17-48): "Ye have heard that it hath been said...but *I* say unto you". It should be noted that in vv.1-10 the pronouns used are "their's" and "they", but in vv.11-16, the pronouns are "ye", "you" and "your". So the principles in vv.1-10 are applied personally in vv.11-16.

Chapter 5

1) THE DESCRIPTION OF HIS SUBJECTS, vv.3-12

They are "poor in spirit" (v.3); they "mourn" (v.4); they are "meek": they do not insist on their rights (v.5); they "hunger and thirst after righteousness" (v.6); they are "merciful" (v.7); they are "pure in heart", and because of this God will reveal himself to them (v.8); they are "peacemakers" (v.9); they rejoice under persecution (vv.10-12). It could be said that the beatitudes cover *(i)* what they are *in themselves*: they are "poor in spirit... mourn... meek... hunger and thirst after righteousness" (vv.3-6), and "pure in heart" (v.8); *(ii)* what they are in relation to *others*: they are "merciful...peacemakers" (vv.7,9); *(iii)* what they are in relation to *adversaries*: they rejoice (v.12) when persecuted "for righteousness sake" (v.10) and for the Lord's sake (v.11). This brings us to:

2) THE DISTINCTIVENESS OF HIS SUBJECTS, vv.13-16

Having referred to "your reward in heaven", the Lord turns their attention back to earth. The distinctiveness of God's people is expressed in two ways: *(a)* "Ye are the salt of the earth" (v.13); *(b)* "ye are the light of the world" (v.14). In general terms, the following should be noted

i) In saying, "*Ye* are the salt of the earth" and "*Ye* are the light of the world", the "Ye" is emphatic here, meaning that 'you, and you alone' are the "salt of the earth" and "the light of the world". This emphasises the privilege and dignity belonging to the citizens of the kingdom of heaven.

ii) In saying, "Ye *are* the salt of the earth" and "Ye *are* the light of the world", the Lord emphasises what disciples are in themselves. He did not say 'ye have the salt of the earth' or 'ye have the light of the world', but that "ye *are* the salt of the earth" and "the light of the world". His disciples are both "salt" and "light". The teaching in vv.3-10 shows how this is achieved.

iii) In saying, "Ye are the *salt* of the earth" and "ye are the *light* of the world", the Lord indicates the nature of their testimony for God in the world. *"Salt"* supposes corruption: *"light"* supposes darkness. *"Salt"* implies prevention against corruption, and emphasises evil *moral* conditions. *"Light"* emphasises evil *spiritual* conditions.

iv) In saying, "Ye are the salt of the earth" and "ye are the light of the world", the Lord emphasises the distinctiveness of His disciples, but at the same time, indicates that their effectiveness lies, in the first case, by contact - mingling or mixing - with others, and in the second, by maintaining separation from others. Light does not mingle with darkness! R.V.G.Tasker points out that 'the most obvious *general* characteristic of salt is that it is essentially different from the medium into which it is put. It power lies precisely in this difference.

v) In both cases, the danger of failure is emphasised. In the first case, the salt could lose its savour (v.13). In the second, the light could be hidden (v.15). In both instances, therefore, personal responsibility is emphasised.

a) "Ye are the salt of the earth", v.13
As noted above, the Lord refers firstly to the description of His disciples and, secondly, to the danger of failure.

i) The description. "Ye are the salt of the *earth*". This refers to the 'purifying, perpetuating and antiseptic qualities' (W.E.Vine) which should be resident in every believer. The sphere, "earth", refers to general conditions in the world, to the atmosphere of life in the world. It tells us that the world, left to itself, will become progressively more corrupt. It was like that before the Flood: "The earth also was corrupt before God, and the earth was filled with violence. And God looked upon the earth, and, behold, it was corrupt; for all flesh had corrupted his way upon the earth" (Gen. 6: 11-12). The words, "Ye are the salt of the earth" therefore remind us that the very presence and testimony of God's people should be an *influence against the corruption of the age.* He expects them to be an influence for Him in a corrupt world. Salt does not remove corruption, but curtails its spread. Our presence should have a moderating effect on the conduct and conversation of people in our company. Our presence should make a difference.

ii) The danger. "But if the salt have lost his savour, wherewith shall it be salted?" See Mark 9: 50: "Salt is good: but if the salt hath lost his *saltness,* wherewith will ye season it?". The disciples, "called to be a moral disinfectant in a world where moral standards are low, constantly changing, or non-existent, can only discharge this function if they themselves retain their virtue - and this calls for much self-discipline - not least in speech, for, as Paul said, a Christian's speech must be 'alway with grace, and seasoned with salt' (Col. 4: 6)" (R.V.G.Tasker). The Lord's teaching here visualises a condition in which someone has lost their total credibility for God. They are of no further use to *men.* They have no further testimony. As believers they are completely rejected - "trodden under foot of *men*" or, according to Luke's record, "It is neither fit for the land, nor yet for the dunghill; but men cast it

Chapter 5

out" (Luke 14: 34-35). The total lack of moral guidance by the professing 'church' is a case in point.

b) "Ye are the light of the world", vv.14-16
Once again, as noted above, the Lord refers firstly to the description of His disciples and, secondly, to the danger of failure.

i) The description. "Ye are the light of the ***world"*** (v.14). The sphere, "the world", refers to mankind in alienation from God. It has to be asked, in what sense are believers "the light of the world?", or for that matter, in what sense is the Lord Jesus "the light of the world" (John 8: 12)? The answer, in relation to the Lord Jesus, is that men and women know nothing at all apart from Him about the things that matter. He is "the light of the world" in the sense that He brings illumination and knowledge about matters otherwise totally unknown. We have "the light of the knowledge of the glory of God in the face of Jesus Christ" (2 Cor. 4: 6). It therefore follows that the Lord's people are "the light of the world" not only in that they speak about matters completely outside the realm of the natural man, but that they exhibit the truth of those matters in their lives (v.16).

The Lord Jesus not only said, "I am the light of the world", but "*I* am come a light into the world" (John 12: 46), and "As long as I am in the world, *I* am the light of the world" (John 9: 5). But He was going to depart, and to His servants remaining He says, "*Ye* are the light of the world". We who "were sometimes darkness" are now "light in the Lord" and are to "walk as ***children of light***" (Eph. 5: 8). As "the light of the world", the children of God are here to illuminate the darkness of the world around them.

ii) The danger. This is emphasised as the Lord develops the subject of our responsibility as "the light of the world". He uses two metaphors: "a city" (v.14) and "a candlestick (lampstand)" (v.15). Both illustrations emphasise the same lesson: If the light is to shine, it must be in a conspicuous position, and unobscured by intervening objects. So:

- ***"A city that is set on a hill cannot be hid".*** It is a point of reference - a landmark - for direction and guidance. A "city set on a hill (*oros,* usually translated 'mountain')" is visible to those who live on lower levels. It can also be seen from afar. Put another way, it is a beacon to travellers, and unbelievers should be able to tell from our lives the direction in which they are going, either to heaven, or to hell. Bearing in mind the background -

darkness - if we are living as we should, our lives will stand out: our testimony "***cannot*** be hid". It ***must*** stand out against this world's darkness.

- A lampstand in a house. If "a city set on a hill ***cannot be hid***", then a lamp is not lit with a view to ***being hid***. "Neither do men light a candle, and put in under a bushel, but on a candlestick; and it giveth light (*lampo*) unto all that are in the house". It would be absurd to put a candle ("lamp") under a meal-tub (*modios*, translated "bushel") instead of placing it on a lampstand ("candlestick", AV), and then expect the occupants of the house to see it! (R.V.G.Tasker). Compare Philippians 2: 14-15, "Do all things without murmurings and disputings; that ye may be blameless and harmless, the sons of God, without rebuke, in the midst of a crooked and perverse nation, among whom ye shine (*phaino*) as lights (*phosteer*) in the world".

Should we protest that we have little ability or little opportunity, then we should notice that the Lord moves from "a ***city*** that is set on a hill" to "all that are in the ***house***". We may not be able to shine like a city on a hill, but we can shine like a lamp in a room! Wm.Macdonald points out that the bushel is "a unit of measure used in business" and "Christ's followers should not allow the claims of business to douse their witness for Him".

Privilege determines responsibility, and therefore the Lord says: "Let your light (*phos*) so shine (*lampo*) before men, that they may see your good works, and glorify your Father which is in heaven" (v.16). ***Where should it shine?*** Answer: "before men" (the disciples must not hide themselves). ***What constitutes the shining?*** Answer: "your good works". So the light should shine through our ***lives***. We must emulate Dorcas who was "full of good works" (Acts 9: 36). It should also shine through our ***lips*** (Phil.2: 15-16).

What is the object? Answer: "glorify your Father". (This is the first mention of "Father" in New Testament). H.A.Ironside points out that "mere profession is not enough. The life should speak for God. As we live Christ before men, we let our light shine. Thus they recognise our good works and see in them an evidence of sincerity". This brings us to:

3) THE DEMANDS ON HIS SUBJECTS, vv.17-48
What is involved in the "good works" of v.16? This section answers. Verses 17-20 form a general introduction, and vv.21-48 give specific examples.

Chapter 5

a) The general introduction: vv.17-20
In these verses, the Lord Jesus makes two important points: *(i)* that His ministry was in complete harmony with the law and the prophets (vv.17-19); *(ii)* that His ministry involved standards far above the teaching of the scribes and Pharisees (v.20).

The necessity for the Lord's teaching at this point is clear. He was unorthodox by the standards of the day. He was not a scribe or a Pharisee, but He was none the less a teacher. That was unorthodox for a start! Then, He condemned and exposed the traditions of the scribes and Pharisees. Then, He mixed with people that the religious leaders would have shunned. So, where did He stand in relation to the law and the prophets? In saying, "Think not that I am come to destroy the law, or the prophets" (v.17), the Lord was probably referring to accusations against Him. So, what will such unorthodox ministry produce? The answer is true righteousness: "except your righteousness shall exceed the righteousness of the scribes and Pharisees, ye shall in no case enter into the kingdom of heaven" (v.20). We must therefore consider:

i) The relationship between His teaching and the teaching of the law and the prophets, vv.17-19. "Think not that I am come to destroy the law, or the prophets: I am come not to destroy, but to *fulfil*" (v.17). We should notice two matters here: firstly, that He did this in His own life personally: He came to fulfil *(pleroo)* the law. Secondly, that He 'filled out' the law: He demonstrated its real meaning. The Greek word *pleroo* means to 'fill to the full'.

The law was inviolable. "For verily, I say unto you, Till heaven and earth pass, one jot or one tittle (so the word of God is inspired to the extent of the smallest letter in the Hebrew alphabet and the tiniest stroke distinguishing one Hebrew letter from another!: compare 1 Cor. 2: 13) shall in no wise pass from the law, till all be fulfilled" (v.18). Not only so, He enjoined the observance of the law: "Whosoever therefore shall break one of these least commandments, and shall teach men so, he shall be called the least in the kingdom of heaven: but whosoever shall **do** and **teach** them (the Lord Jesus was described as a prophet mighty in **deed** and **word**", Luke 24; 19: see also Acts 1: 1), the same shall be called great in the kingdom of heaven" (v.19). Standing in the kingdom depended on respect for the law, and compliance with it.

Matthew

ii) ***The relationship between His teaching and the teaching of the scribes and Pharisees, v.20.*** "For I say unto you, That except your righteousness shall exceed the righteousness of the scribes and Pharisees, ye shall in no case enter into the kingdom of heaven". What His teaching required far exceeded the practices and teaching of the scribes and Pharisees. We should notice that in v.19, the Lord discusses *position* in the kingdom - he refers to the "least" and the "great", but in v.20, He discusses actual *presence* in the kingdom.

Had we only v.19, we might have thought that the scribes and Pharisees had a very real advantage. After all, they copied the law, and taught the law: their whole life was the law of God. But v.20 adjusts that impression: "Except your righteousness shall exceed the righteousness of the scribes and Pharisees..." Their righteousness comprised external and formal practices. The kingdom of heaven demanded righteousness of the highest standard.

Notice that the word "except" is used three times in relation to the kingdom: *(i)* repentance was essential, see Matthew 18: 3, "***Except*** ye be converted"; *(ii)* regeneration was essential, see John 3: 5, "***Except*** a man be born of water and of the Spirit"; *(iii)* righteousness was essential; here, "***Except*** your righteousness shall exceed...." This is developed in vv.21-30, with reference to two commandments: in vv.21-26 with reference to the sanctity of life, the sixth commandment: "Thou shalt not kill", and with reference to the sanctity of marriage, the seventh commandment: "Thou shalt not commit adultery". The Lord Jesus develops the teaching of the law in these two matters.

While Paul states that "by the deeds of the law there shall no flesh be justified in his sight" (Rom. 3: 20), and that we have become "dead to the law" (Rom. 7: 4), this does not mean that we can forget the Lord's teaching here. Matthew 5 sets out the standards and demands of the law, and Romans 8: 3-4 states that "what the law could not do, in that it was weak through the flesh, God sending His own Son in the likeness of sinful flesh, and for sin, condemned sin in the flesh: that the ***righteousness of the law might be fulfilled in us***". Not fulfilled ***by*** us, but fulfilled ***in*** us: that is, through the power of the Holy Spirit. What the law demanded in Matthew 5, we should supply - but not by our own achievement: it is through the indwelling Holy Spirit. The law is not the means of sanctification, anymore than it is the means of justification.

Chapter 5

b) The specific examples, vv.21-30

These are "Thou shalt not kill" (vv.21-26); "Thou shalt not commit adultery" (vv.27-28). Both are introduced with the words, "Ye have heard that it was said by them of old time" (vv.21, 27) and both continue with the words, "But I say unto you" (vv.22, 28). This pattern continues for the remaining part of the chapter (vv.31-48) with the repeated words "It hath been said" (vv.31, 33, 38, 43) followed by the words, "But I say unto you" (vv.32, 34, 39, 44). It must be clearly stated here that the Lord Jesus is not, for one moment, "impinging in the least degree upon the permanent validity of the sixth and seventh commandments... What He is saying is that God's demands in these matters are far more comprehensive and exacting than current interpretations of them by the scribes might seem to suggest. Murder, He insists, has its birth in anger fostered by an uncontrolled spirit of revenge, and such anger is itself an infringement of the sixth commandment. Similarly, adultery is but the final expression of lustful thoughts harboured in the imagination...." (R.V.G.Tasker). Causeless anger is murder in embryo. Cain was angry, and slew Abel (Gen. 4: 5, 6, 8). Herod was "exceeding wroth", and slew children (Matt. 2: 16).

i) "Thou shalt not kill", vv.21-26.

"Ye have heard that it was said by them of old time, Thou shalt not kill: and whosoever shall kill shall be in danger of the judgment". The quotation in v.21 appears to combine Exodus 20: 13 with Numbers 35: 30-31. The way in which the scribes and Pharisees applied this blinded men to its spiritual implications: they emphasised only the letter of the law, i.e., physical murder, and totally ignored the spirit of the law. The Lord Jesus emphasised that the law dealt with *attitudes* as well as *actions*. The act of murder derived from the attitude of anger. These verses emphasise two things:

- *The danger of anger towards a brother, vv.21-22*. We should notice the three stages in the development of anger. 'The concepts behind "angry... Raca...fool" represent downward stages in the loss of self-control in one's description of the character of another man. In effect, the man's character is being murdered!' (J.Heading). *Firstly,* anger unexpressed, or harbouring thoughts of hatred: "whosoever is angry with his brother without a cause" (v.22); *secondly,* anger expressed in contempt: "whosoever shall say to his brother, Raca (vain, worthless fellow)" (v.22); *thirdly,* anger expressed in abuse: "whosoever shall say, Thou fool (godless, a moral reprobate: the word *moros* describes a wicked, graceless, abandoned wretch, a worthless scoundrel in heart, J.Heading)" (v.22). Note that the references to "the judgment...the council...hell fire" represent the increasing severity of judgment in view of the increasing measure of anger. The reference to Judaism ("the council", referring to the Sanhedrim, "the altar", etc.) remind us of the immediate circumstances of the disciples. This was not the era of the church, which commenced on the day of Pentecost. As Wm.Macdonald points out, "there is no mistaking the severity of the Saviour's words. He teaches that anger contains the seeds of murder. He states that abusive language contains the spirit of murder. And He warns that cursing language implies the very desire to murder". The last (with reference to "hell fire") can be understood by reference to 1 John 3: 14-15 etc., "He that loveth not his brother abideth in death. Whosoever hateth his brother is a murderer and ye know that no murderer hath eternal life abiding in him". Ephesians 4: 20-27 are now compulsory reading, particularly v.26: "Be ye angry, and sin not: let not the sun go down upon your wrath".

- The danger of the brother towards whom anger is harboured, vv.23-26.
"Therefore, if thou bring thy gift to the altar, and there rememberest that thy brother hath ought against thee, leave there thy gift before the altar, and go thy way; first be reconciled to thy brother, and then come and offer thy gift" (vv.23-24). Whilst we should take the initiative if we 'have ought against our brother', here we must take the initiative if 'our brother has ought against us'. Notice where the Lord Jesus placed the priority: not on offering the gift - it was to be left before the altar - but on reconciliation. This, surely, applies to the Lord's supper. "These words, of course, are written in a Jewish context; the whole idea of bringing a gift to the altar belongs to Judaism. But it is no less applicable in the Christian dispensation. It means, for instance, that we should not go to the Lord's Supper and partake of the bread and wine if we have sinned against a brother. God gets no worship from a believer who is not on speaking terms with another" (Wm.Macdonald).

Our attitude should not be: 'If someone has something against us, then that's their responsibility: they must sort it out'. We should carefully notice the Lord's teaching in vv.25-26: if the man accused (i.e. the man whose brother is accusing him) ***does nothing to clear the matter up, and therefore fails to achieve reconciliation,*** he also is in a dangerous position. He may find himself accused by his "adversary" (the brother who has something against him) in court, and - albeit falsely - end up in prison, from which he will not emerge until he has "paid the utmost farthing". The section emphasises the danger of doing nothing when brotherly relationships break down.

Chapter 5

ii) "Thou shalt not commit adultery", vv.27-28. Whatever society may say, adultery is wrong. See 1 Thessalonians 4: 3-8. The Lord Jesus referred not only to the outward act, but to the inward thought. A man may never be guilty of the act, but he may guilty of the thought and desire. It has been said:

> *Sow a thought and you reap an act.*
> *Sow an act and you reap a habit.*
> *Sow a habit and you reap a character.*
> *Sow a character and you reap a destiny.*

In vv.29-30, the Lord urged His disciples to strike at the very root of anything that would produce unholy actions. Thus, "If thy right *eye* offend thee" (v.28), with reference to the lustful look, and "If thy right *hand* offend thee" (v.29), perhaps referring to the outburst of anger with murderous intent. There was to be no quarter in dealing with the dangers. Believers are told: "Make not provision for the flesh, to fulfil the lusts thereof" (Rom. 13: 14); "Mortify therefore your members which are upon the earth; fornication…" (Col. 3: 5); "Neither yield ye your members as instruments of unrighteousness unto sin" (Rom. 6: 13); "Glorify God in your body" (1 Cor. 6: 20). The solemn words, "and not that thy whole body should be cast into hell" are not easily explained. Most commentators conveniently pass over them! It is difficult to make this refer to believers. R.V.G.Tasker gives what appears to be the best explanation in saying that the Lord Jesus is "expressing in metaphorical language that a limited but morally healthy life is better than a wider life which is morally depraved". The latter will take a man or a woman "into hell" (*geena*, the "eternal fire").

Note: This study includes material taken from an address by Mr.Richard Catchpole at Cheshunt, 14th.January, 1995.

"Be ye therefore perfect"

Read Chapter 5: 31-48
As we have already noted, after the introduction (vv.1-2), this chapter may be divided as follows: *(1)* the description of His subjects (vv.3-12); *(2)* the distinctiveness of His subjects (vv.13-16); *(3)* the demands on His subjects (vv.17-48): "Ye have heard that it hath been said…but I say unto you".

Matthew

1) THE DESCRIPTION OF HIS SUBJECTS, vv.3-12
This may be divided as follows: *(i)* what they are *in themselves*: they are "poor in spirit... mourn... meek... hunger and thirst after righteousness" (vv.3-6), and "pure in heart" (v.8); *(ii)* what they are in relation to *others*: they are "merciful...peacemakers" (vv.7,9); *(iii)* what they are in relation to *adversaries*: they rejoice (v.12) when persecuted "for righteousness sake" (v.10) and for the Lord's sake (v.11).

2) THE DISTINCTIVENESS OF HIS SUBJECTS, vv.13-16
The distinctiveness of God's people is expressed in two ways: *(i)* "Ye are the salt of the earth" (v.13); *(ii)* "ye are the light of the world" (vv.14-16). In the first case, His disciples were to be distinctive in their association with the world, and in the second they were to be distinctive in their disassociation with the world.

3) THE DEMANDS ON HIS SUBJECTS, vv.17-48
These verses commence with the Lord's statement that He had not come to "destroy the law, or the prophets...but to fulfil" (v.17). The verb "to fulfil" (*pleroo*) signifies 'to make full...to fill to the full" (W.E.Vine), or 'to fill up'. He had not come to do as the scribes and Pharisees, and insist on the letter of the law alone, but rather to emphasise the spirit of the law. Hence His reference to the commandments, "Thou shalt not kill" (vv.21-26), and "Thou shalt not commit adultery" (vv.27-30), are introduced with the words, "Ye have heard that it was said by them of old time" (vv.21, 27), and continue with the words, "But I say unto you" (vv.22, 28). This pattern continues for the remaining part of the chapter (vv.31-48) with the repeated words "It hath been said" (vv.31, 33, 38, 43) followed by the words, "But I say unto you" (vv.32, 34, 39, 44). In all, the Lord Jesus deals with six matters:

A) Murder vv.21-26
We have already considered the Lord's teaching on this subject. To summarise, "murder... has its birth in anger fostered by an uncontrolled spirit of revenge, and such anger is itself an infringement of the sixth commandment" (R.V.G.Tasker).

B) Adultery, vv.27-30
We have already considered the Lord's teaching on this subject as well. To summarise: "adultery is but the final expression of lustful thoughts harboured in the imagination" (R.V.G.Tasker). We must 'beware of the second look' – or 'second thought'. In the words of the proverb: 'You can't

stop a bird flying over your head, but you can stop it making a nest in your hair'. This brings us to:

C) *Divorce, vv.31-32*
"It hath been said, Whosoever shall put away his wife, let him give her a writing of divorcement: But I say unto you, That whosoever shall put away his wife, saving for the cause of fornication, causeth her to commit adultery: and whosoever shall marry her that is divorced committeth adultery". The following should be borne in mind:

i) The Lord Jesus is not setting aside the provision made in the law of Moses, but condemning the practice of Pharisees who quoted Deuteronomy 24: 1 ("When a man hath taken a wife, and married her, and it come to pass that she find no favour in his eyes, because he hath found some uncleanness in her: then let him write her a bill of divorcement...") in justifying a much laxer attitude to divorce than was here permitted. In the Old Testament, divorce, though not envisaged in the divine ideal for marriage, was allowed in order to save an unfortunate woman from a loveless marriage. It is important to remember that the passage refers to the very earliest point in a marriage. This is the explanation given by the Lord Jesus: "For the hardness of your heart he wrote you this precept" (Mark 10: 3-5). But even this had been evidently abused, and men were divorcing their wives at the slightest whim. Hence the question, "Is it lawful for a man to put away his wife **for every cause?**" (Matt. 19: 3). The school of Shammai (those who followed Rabbi Shammah) allowed divorce only on the ground of adultery. The school of Hillel (those who followed Rabbi Hillel, with his more liberal views) allowed divorce for the most amazing reasons. J.C.Ryle cites Lightfoot's *Horae Hebraicae* on Matthew 5: 31. 'The school of Hillel saith, If a wife cooks her husband's food ill by over-salting it, or over-roasting it, she is to be put away'. Edersheim notes that the same liberal school allowed divorce on the grounds that a man had found another woman more attractive than his wife. Others allowed a man to divorce his wife for spinning in the streets, or if she spoke disrespectfully about his parents in his presence. The mind boggles!

ii) The Lord Jesus specified "fornication" as the one ground for divorce. It is quite clear, these verses allow divorce on one ground only: immorality. Not mental cruelty, incompatibility, desertion, irretrievable breakdown, irrecoverable brain damage, or any other reason. **The only ground is immorality**. If otherwise than immorality (to be precise, "fornication"), then the husband who puts away his wife and remarries becomes guilty of adultery (Matt.19: 9); the woman who has been wrongly put away and then remarries, commits adultery (Matt. 5: 32); and the person who marries the wife wrongly put away also commits adultery (Matt. 5: 32 and 19: 9).

But 'immorality' must be qualified. The precise word is "fornication". This is the word used by the Lord Jesus in Matthew, and it is here that able men divide. There are two major camps:

- *That "fornication" includes immorality of all kinds.* That is, pre-marital and post-marital immorality, including, therefore, adultery. However, if the Lord Jesus meant adultery as the one ground of divorce, as it is often alleged, then it is surprising that He did not say so. In any case, if we accept that fornication *(porneia)* and adultery *(mochos)* are synonymous, then both Matthew 5 & 19 involve an absurd situation. The woman is put away for the cause of adultery, and is caused to commit adultery!

- *That "fornication" must be distinguished from "adultery".* That is, that "fornication" refers to pre-marital unchastity alone. The fact that *only Matthew,* writing *for Jews*, includes the 'exception clause', gives support for the view that a man could only divorce his wife if there had been evidence of pre-marital unchastity. Under the Jewish betrothal laws, a betrothed maiden was regarded as a wife, although - technically - this was not actually the case. This is clear from Deuteronomy 22: 23-34 ("betrothed to an husband...his neighbour's wife"), and illustrated in Matthew 1: 18-20, where Joseph is called "her husband", and Mary, "thy wife...his wife", even "before they came together". There is, therefore, a particularly Jewish context to Matthew 5 and Matthew 19, which is inapplicable in Mark and Luke, where there is no 'exception clause'. In further support for this view, it is often stated that *(i)* where the word "fornication" is used *alone,* it signifies immorality generally, but *(ii)* where it is used with adultery, as in the current passage, it refers specifically to pre-marital unchastity as opposed to post-marital infidelity.

Believers should remember God's purpose in marriage. It is stated in Gen. 2: 24, and cited by the Lord Jesus in Matthew 19: 4-8. They should also remember Paul's clear statement in Romans 7: 1-3. The subject continues to be debated on all points, and strong pleas are entered for careful consideration of all its aspects, and for grace and kindness towards believers who find themselves in a desperate position through, so far as we can judge, no fault of their own.

D) Swearing, vv.33-37

It should be said that this does not refer to 'a judicial oath, that is, to an oath administered by a magistrate... if the declaration be simply God's authority, introduced by the magistrate to declare the truth, the whole truth, and nothing but the truth, I do not see that the Lord in any wise absolves the Christian's obligation to this' (Wm.Kelly).

We must notice: *(a)* the clarity of the original command (v.33); *(b)* the duplicity of the religious leaders (vv.34-36); *(c)* the simplicity of the Lord's command (v.37).

a) The clarity of the original command

"Again ye have heard that it hath been said by them of old time, Thou shalt not forswear thyself, but shall perform unto the Lord thine oaths" (v.33), meaning 'Thou shalt not swear falsely', that is, undo one's swearing - become a perjurer. The Lord Jesus here refers to:

- ***Numbers 30: 2***: "If a man vow a vow unto the Lord, or swear an oath to bind his soul with a bond: he shall not break his word, he shall do according to all that proceedeth out of his mouth".

- ***Deuteronomy 23: 21-23***: "When thou shalt vow a vow unto the Lord thy God, thou shalt not be slack to pay it".

b) The duplicity of the religious leaders

The Lord Jesus continues: "***But I say*** unto you, Swear not at all; neither by heaven; for it is God's throne..." James urged this upon his readers (of Jewish ancestry): "But above all things, my brethren, swear not, neither by heaven, neither by the earth, neither by any other oath: but let your yea be yea; and your nay, nay; lest ye fall into condemnation" (James 5: 12).

It is important to understand that the Pharisees taught that if a vow or an oath did not actually name God, then it was not actually binding. In other words, as the passage shows, they left a loophole through which to slide by differentiating between God and what belonged to Him. The Lord Jesus condemned this duplicity. We must say what we mean and mean what we say. It is significant that Matthew alone records this part of the Saviour's teaching. It has a particularly Jewish application.

He instances four ways in which the Jews were accustomed to swearing:

Matthew

by heaven, by the earth, by Jerusalem, and by the head. 'This teaching was represented, however, by the scribes as implying that if only swearing was not to a false proposition and did not profane the actual name of God, there was no need to regard oaths as binding' (R.V.G.Tasker). In each case, the Saviour shews that it was impossible to say that there was no reference to God.

- *"Neither by heaven*; for it is God's throne". The reference is to Isaiah 66: 1, cited by Stephen in Acts 7: 48-50: "Howbeit the Most High dwelleth not in temples made with hands: as saith the prophet, Heaven is my throne..." (Note that Isaiah 66: 2 continues by saying, "But to this man will I look, even to him that is poor and of a contrite spirit, and that trembleth at my word", v.2). Matthew 5: 34 must be read in conjunction with Matt. 23: 22, "he that sweareth by heaven, sweareth by the throne of God, and by him that sitteth thereon".

- *"Nor by the earth*; for it is his footstool". Reference is made again to Isaiah 66: 1, "Thus saith the Lord, The heaven is my throne, and the earth is my footstool". In passing, this is so reassuring. He is in complete control of this world and its affairs. Earth does not direct heaven: "the heavens do rule" (Dan. 4: 21).

- *"Neither by Jerusalem*: for it is the city of the great King." Reference is made here to Psalm 48: 2. "Beautiful for situation, the joy of the whole earth is mount Zion, on the sides of the north, the city of the great King".

- *"Neither shalt thou swear by thy head*, because thou canst not make one hair white or black." The part of the head that the Jews swore by was the hair. The sense is that while 'the head might be thought to be a man's absolute possession, God alone can make a man look old, or preserve the dark hair of his youth' (McNeile).

In summary, to swear by any of these, in order to avoid pronouncing the Divine Name, and so to have grounds for failing to enact a vow, was totally false. The first three implied His presence, and the last implies the absolute power of God to which all are subject. Examples of their double talk are cited by the Lord Jesus later in Matthew's Gospel, viz:

- *Chapter 15: 5-6*. "For God commanded saying, Honour thy father and mother: and, He that curseth father or mother let him die the death. But ye say, Whosoever shall say to his father or his mother, It is a gift (i.e. that thing/money) by whatsoever thou mightest (otherwise) be profited by me; and honour not his father and his mother, he shall be free". Traditional teaching gave a man freedom to exclude his parents from the support/help required by the fifth commandment, simply by saying, in the form of a vow, "Corban". In effect, 'that by which you might have received advantage from me is hereby dedicated as an offering'. Its actual dedication was not really contemplated: it was dedicated (and therefore unavailable) only as regards the parent who hoped to receive it.

- *Chapter 23: 16-22*. "Woe unto you, ye blind guides, which say, Whosoever shall swear by the temple, it is nothing: but whosoever shall swear by the gold of the temple, he is a debtor! Ye fools and blind: for whether is greater, the gold, or the temple that sanctifieth the gold?...whoso shall swear by the temple, sweareth by it, and by him that dwelleth therein".

These passages will help us to see the force of the Lord's words, "But let your communication be, Yea, yea; Nay, nay: for whatsoever is more than these cometh of evil". This brings us to:

c) The simplicity of the Lord's command
In view of the questionable practices of the day, the Saviour, far from abrogating the law, urges a higher standard than the law. His people were not to be bound by rules to their word: there should be a *reality* about their word which did not require policing by the law. A possible translation is 'But let your Yea be (i.e. really mean) yea and your Nay (mean) nay'. The words, "For whatsoever is more than these cometh of evil", can be understood to mean 'cometh of the evil one'.

Paul made this the standard of his word. "When I therefore was thus minded, did I use lightness? And the things that I purpose, do I purpose according to the flesh, that with me there should be yea, yea, *and* nay nay. But as God is true, our word toward you was not yea *and* nay. For the Son of God, Jesus Christ, who was preached among you by us, even by me and Silvanus and Timotheus, was not yea *and* nay, but in him was yea. For all the promises of God in him are Yea, and in him Amen, unto the glory of God by us" (2 Cor. 1: 17-20). In addressing the Corinthians, the apostle was obliged to remind them of their word. "And herein I give my advice: for this is expedient for you, who have begun before, not only to do but also to be forward a year ago. Now therefore perform the doing of it: that as there was a readiness to will, so there may be a performance also out of that which ye have" (2 Cor. 8: 10-11).

The Lord's people should be marked by integrity in their speech. Half truths are as bad as downright lies. Our intentions should be genuine: "Be not rash with thy mouth, and let not thine heart be hasty to utter anything before God...When thou vowest a vow unto God, defer not to pay for it; for he hath no pleasure in fools: pay that which thou hast vowed. Better is it that thou shouldest not vow, than that thou shouldest vow and not pay" (Eccl. 5: 1-6).

E) *Legal Recompense, vv.38-42*
"Ye have heard that it hath been said, An eye for an eye, and a tooth for a tooth". We must notice *(a)* the original command (v.38); *(b)* the new command (vv.39-42).

a) The original command
In dealing with this subject, the Lord Jesus refers to three relevant Old Testament passages:

- *Exodus 21: 22-24*. In relation to an expectant mother: "If a man strive, and hurt a woman with child, so that her fruit depart from her, and yet no mischief follow: he shall surely be punished...And if any mischief follow, then thou shalt give life for life. Eye for eye, tooth for tooth, hand for hand, foot for foot".

- *Leviticus 24: 19-20*. In relation to a neighbour: "And if a man cause a blemish in his neighbour; as he hath done, so shall it be done to him; breach for breach, eye for eye, tooth for tooth: as he hath caused a blemish in a man, so shall it be done to him again"

- *Deuteronomy 19: 16- 21*. In relation to a false witness: "If a false witness rise up against any man...the judges shall make inquisition: and, behold, if the witness be a false witness, and hath testified falsely against his brother; then shall ye do unto him, as he had thought to do unto his brother....And thine eye shall not pity; but life shall go for life, eye for eye, tooth for tooth, hand for hand, foot for foot".

In each case, the injured party, including the man who would have been injured if the false witness had succeeded, had legal right to exact justice. As Wm.Macdonald points out: 'This was both a command to punish...and it was a limitation on punishment: the penalty must not exceed the crime'. He also points out 'that the authority to take revenge was vested in the *government*...not in the private victim'.

b) The new command, vv.39-42
In dealing with this subject, the Lord Jesus clearly teaches that while it is not wrong for a man to be punished according to the injury he has inflicted upon another ("An eye for an eye, and a tooth for a tooth" is perfectly righteous), believers ought to be *more* than righteous: they ought to be *gracious*. Grace gives more than is asked for by law. This is exemplified in Ephesians 4: 28. The law said "Thou shalt not steal", but grace says, "Let him that stole steal no more: but rather let him labour, working with his hands the thing which is good, that he may have *to give* to him that needeth".

We may regard this new command in three ways: *(i)* the commandment imparted; *(ii)* the commandment exemplified; *(iii)* the commandment applied.

i) The commandment imparted
There was to be no insistence on legal restitution by the Lord's people. "But I say unto you, That ye resist not evil (or 'one that is evil'): but whosoever shall smite thee on thy right cheek, turn to him the other also. And if any man will sue thee at the law, and take away thy coat, let him have thy cloke also. And whosoever shall compel thee to go a mile, go with him twain, Give to him that asketh thee, and from him that would borrow of thee turn not thou away". The Lord Jesus is teaching that 'a disciple should be ready to suffer loss rather than to resort to personal vindictiveness' (R.V.G.Tasker). It ought to be said at this juncture that these verses do *not* refer to the responsibilities of "the powers that be" (Rom 13: 1). They *are* required to "execute wrath upon him that doeth evil" (Rom. 13: 4), and will answer to God for their evident failure to do so. But the Lord's people are required to act on the principle that "where sin abounded, grace did much more abound". This is enjoined in the Epistles.

- "See that none render evil for evil unto any man; but ever follow that which is good, both among yourselves and to all men" (I Thess. 5: 15).

- "Not rendering evil for evil, and railing for railing: but contrariwise blessing" (1 Pet. 3: 9).

- "Dearly beloved, avenge not yourselves but rather give place unto wrath; for it is written, Vengeance is mine; I will repay, saith the Lord. Therefore if thine enemy hunger, feed him. If he thirst, give him drink. For in so doing thou shalt heap coals of fire upon his head. Be not overcome of evil, but overcome evil with good" (Rom. 12: 19-21).

It is important to see that the Saviour is teaching that His disciples should not insist upon their rights with a view to revenge. The fact that Paul appealed to Caesar did not infringe the Lord's teaching here. His reasons for appealing to Caesar were quite different.

ii) The commandment exemplified
Notice that the Saviour exemplified His own teaching. This was always the case: see Acts 1: 1: "The former treatise have I made, O Theophilus, of all that Jesus began both to *do* and teach".

- "Christ also suffered for us, leaving us an example...who, when he was reviled, reviled not again: when he suffered, he threatened not; but committed himself (His cause) to him that judgeth righteously" (I Pet. 2: 21-23). There was no spirit of revenge in the Lord Jesus: "Father forgive them, for they know not what they do". There was no spirit of revenge in Stephen either: "Lord, lay not this sin to their charge" (Acts 7: 60).

- On the cross, the "soldiers...took His garments (plural of 'cloak' i.e. outer garments)... and also his coat" (the same word in Matthew 5: 40)" (John 19: 23). But the One who could have been encircled by "more than twelve legions of angels" allowed His enemies to strip Him.

- The idea behind "compel thee to go a mile" is enforced service. "Compel" is a word of Persian origin meaning the mounted messenger of the Persian king. The Lord Jesus was the perfect Servant: He "came not to be ministered unto, but to minister, and to give his life a ransom for many" (Mark 10: 45).

- "Give to him that asketh thee, and from him that would borrow of thee turn not away". This is rather different from what has gone before, but continues the same principle: the child of God should not stand upon his rights when confronted by the claims of others. The Lord Jesus was constantly thronged by people seeking His help and blessing - so much so that His kinsfolk said, when they learned that "they could not so much as eat bread", "He is beside himself" (Mark 3: 21). The Saviour certainly withheld nothing from men and women.

Before passing to the final section of Matthew Ch.5, we must pause and carefully note that if vv.39-43 are applicable to the attitude we must adopt in relation to a hostile world, then they are also applicable to the child of God and his brethren in the Lord. So:

iii) The commandment applied
The passage reminds us how to act when a brother injures us: "I say unto you, That ye resist not evil: but whosoever shall smite thee on thy right cheek, turn to him the other also" (v.39). That is, indicate our willingness to endure, to put up with what has been done, albeit unrighteously. It reminds us how to act when a brother infringes our rights: "And if any man will sue thee at the law, and take away thy coat, let him have thy cloak also" (v.40). See 1 Corinthans 6: 7. It reminds us how to act when a brother burdens us: "And whosoever shall compel thee to go a mile, go with him twain" (v.41). It reminds us how to act when a brother needs us; "Give to him that asketh thee, and from him that would borrow of thee turn not thou away" (v.42).

F) Enemies, vv.43-48
Once again, we may divide these verses into *(a)* the original command (v.43); *(b)* the new command (v.44); *(c)* the reason for the new command (vv.45-48).

a) The original command, v.43
"Ye have heard that it hath been said, Thou shalt love thy neighbour, and hate thine enemy". The reference in the first part of the verse is to Leviticus 19: 18. The words "and hate thine enemy" are generally taken to be a reference to Deuteronomy 23: 4-6, where, speaking of the Ammonites and the Moabites, God says "Thou shalt not seek their peace nor their prosperity all the days of thy life". The Saviour continues: "But I say unto you..." So:

b) The new command, v.44
"But I say unto you, Love your enemies, bless them that curse you, do good to them that hate you, and pray for them that despitefully use you". The Saviour is therefore sweeping away all distinctions. Again, He exemplified His own teaching at Calvary: "Father, forgive them; for they know not what they do" (Luke v23: 34).

But how can we possibly love our enemies? The answer must lie in the words, "the love of Christ constraineth us" (2 Cor. 5: 14), and "the love of God is shed abroad in our hearts by the Holy Ghost which is given unto us" (Rom. 5: 5). The Scriptures never place impossible obligations upon us. The 'Good Samaritan' certainly loved his enemy!

c) The reason for the new command, vv.45-48

To do so is to shew a family characteristic: "That ye may be the children (*huios*, meaning 'sons') of your Father which is in heaven: for he maketh his sun to rise on the evil and the good, and sendeth rain on the just and the unjust" (v.45). God bestows blessings alike on "the evil and on the good… on the just and on the unjust". The Lord's people are to show kindness to all men in the same way that the Father makes no distinction.

Not to do so is to fail to shew the distinctiveness of the children of God who are to live by a higher standard than the despised tax-collectors. (Matthew, the writer, was once a tax-collecter!) There is nothing distinctive about loving and greeting members of our fraternity only: "For if ye love them which love you, what reward have ye? do not even the publicans the same? And if ye salute your brethren only, what do ye more than others? do not even the publicans so?" (vv.46-47). 'If our standards are no higher than the heathen's, it is certain that we will never make an impact on the world' (Wm.Macdonald).

"Be ye therefore perfect (i.e. 'complete') even as your Father which is in heaven is perfect" (v.48). That is, following v.45 with vv.46-47, we are to be complete in our love. There is to be no differentiation in our love, even as God is complete in His love: that is, it is extended to all. As Wm.Macdonald rightly points out, the Lord Jesus did 'not mean that this is the way by which we *become* sons of God….Rather He meant that this is how we *manifest ourselves* as sons of God. We demonstrate that we are His sons by behaving like Him'.

THE GOSPEL OF MATTHEW

"Take heed"

Read Chapter 6: 1-18
It has been said that 'if the principles of the 'Sermon on the Mount' will be practised in the coming Kingdom, it would be rather strange if those who will participate in that kingdom *then* do not practise those principles *now*!' The Lord's teaching, rightly understood and practised, will enable us to have an 'abundant entrance' into "the everlasting kingdom of our Lord and Saviour Jesus Christ" (2 Pet. 1: 11).

Matthew Chapter 6 may be divided into two major sections: *(1)* the Lord's comparison between rewards on earth and rewards in heaven (vv.1-18): the word "reward" occurs in vv.1, 2, 4, 5, 6, 16, 18; *(2)* the Lord's comparison between treasure on earth and treasure in heaven (vv.19-34): the words "treasures" and "treasure" occur in vv,19, 20, 21, and in the final analysis we "lay up" treasure in heaven by seeking first "the kingdom of God and his righteousness" (v.33).

1) REWARDS ON EARTH AND REWARDS IN HEAVEN, vv.1-18
It might be helpful to notice repeated words and phrases in these verses. It has been rightly said that this is a good guide to the overall lessons and meaning of a passage. In this connection, the following should be noted:

i) "Father". This occurs ten times in these verses. It should be said that the words "our Father which art in heaven" imply consciousness of dwelling on earth and an earthly kingdom. Believers today are "partakers of the heavenly calling" (Heb. 3: 1) and are "blessed...with all spiritual blessings in heavenly places in Christ". Once "dead in trespasses and sins", God "hath quickened us together with Christ...and hath raised us up together, and made us sit together in heavenly places in Christ Jesus" (Eph. 1: 1, 4-6). Without being pedantic, the expression 'heavenly Father' is a more appropriate form of address today, but we certainly come as children to a Father. J.Waldron points out that the repetition of "Father" is the key to understanding these verses. Almsgiving, prayer and fasting should all be undertaken for His approval, not for other people.

ii) *"Reward".* As already noted, this word occurs seven times in the current passage. While the words "shall reward thee openly" could refer to our time on earth, it is more likely that they refer to the future. While the disciples at the time would not have been aware of "the judgment seat of Christ" (2 Cor. 5: 10), we now know that when the Lord returns, He will "bring to light the hidden things of darkness, and will make manifest the counsels of the hearts: and then shall every man have praise of God" (1 Cor. 4: 5).

iii) *"Secret".* This occurs six times in the passage (twice in vv.4, 6, 18). It has been nicely said that 'the secret of the Christian life is the life of a Christian in secret'. This recalls the oft-quoted words of the Psalmist: "He that dwelleth in the secret place of the most High shall abide under the shadow of the Almighty" (Psalm 91: 1).

iv) *"Hypocrites".* This occurs three times in the passage (vv.2, 5, 16). The word hypocrisy 'primarily denotes a reply, an answer...then play-acting, as the actors spoke in dialogue' (W.E.Vine). We must make sure that we don't 'put on an act' to impress other people. Paul and his colleagues certainly avoided this (1 Thess. 2: 3-6). "All things are naked and opened unto the eyes of him with whom we have to do" (Heb. 4: 13).

v) *"Verily, I say unto you".* This expression occurs three times in the passage (vv.2, 5, 16). These words, or similar ("I say unto you"), occur some fourteen times in the 'Sermon on the Mount', beginning with 5: 18. See also 5: 20, 22, 26, 28, 32, 34, 39, 44; 6: 2, 5, 16, 25, 29. It has been said that these words are like a spine to the whole section. They emphasise the Lord's authority. The Old Testament words, "Thus saith the Lord", give place to "I say unto you" in the New Testament. The Lord has come!

In these verses (vv.1-18), the Lord delivers three warnings: *(A)* in relation to almsgiving (vv.1-4); *(B)* in relation to prayer (vv.5-15); *(C)* in relation to fasting (vv.16-18). Almsgiving is *manward*; prayer is *Godward*; fasting is *selfward.* (Compare Titus 2: 12). The passage commences with the words, "Take heed" (v.1), translated "beware" in Matthew 7: 15; 10: 17; 16: 6.

Chapter 6

A) Almsgiving, vv.1-4
Commentators often say that since in some manuscripts the word "alms" (v.1) is replaced by 'righteousness' (hence, 'Take heed that ye do not your righteousness before men', JND margin), the opening verse is a general introduction to the Lord's teaching on almsgiving, prayer and fasting. (The word "alms" in vv.2-4 is not subject to the same amendment). However, leaving things as they are, we must notice, first of all, that there is no conflict between the Lord's words, "Let your light so shine **before men**" (5: 16), and His words here, "do not your alms **before men**" (v.1). It has been nicely said 'Show what you are tempted to hide, and hide what you are tempted to show'. This sets out the difference between the two verses very clearly indeed!

Almsgiving means the shewing of mercy. 'Alms' or 'almsgiving' (*eleemosume*) is connected with *eleemon* meaning 'merciful' (W.E.Vine). See Romans 12: 8, "he that showeth mercy (*eleeo*), with cheerfulness". See also Hebrews 13: 16. Mark 12: 41-42 must be read in connection with giving alms "in secret". The Lord insists on pure motives. We should note some instances of almsgiving from the book of Acts:

i) **Acts 3: 3.** The lame man "asked an alms", and was told by Peter: "Silver and gold have I none". The man's greater need was addressed. (Compare Matthew 9: 2-8; "Son, be of good cheer, thy **sins** be forgiven thee").

ii) **Acts 9: 36.** "Dorcas" was "full of good works (note this: "**full** of good works") and almsdeeds which she did". It was her testimony in this way that gave added publicity to the miracle performed through Peter: "And it was known throughout Joppa; and many believed in the Lord" v.42). Are our "good works" enhancing our testimony?

iii) **Acts 10: 31.** "Cornelius, thy prayer is heard, and thine alms are had in **remembrance** in the sight of God".

iv) **Acts 24: 17.** Paul before Felix: "Now after many years, I came to bring alms to my nation, and offerings". It has been pointed out that Paul, a Benjamite, meaning 'son of my right hand', brought alms in the spirit "let not thy left hand know what thy **right hand** doeth". Rather subtle! However, without being subtle, the man who "obtained mercy" (1 Tim.1: 13) now shews mercy.

B) Prayer, vv.5-15

We should notice: *(a)* the place of prayer (vv.5-6); *(b)* the practice of prayer (vv.7-8); *(c)* the pattern for prayer (vv.9-13); *(d)* the proviso in prayer (vv.14-15).

a) The place of prayer, vv.5-6

"And when thou (it is personal prayer) prayest, thou shalt not be as the hypocrites are: for they love to pray standing in the synagogues and in the corners of the streets, that they may be seen of men. Verily I say unto you, They have their reward. But thou, when thou prayest, enter into thy closet, and when thou hast shut thy door, pray to thy Father which is in secret; and thy Father which seeth in secret shall reward thee openly". This speaks for itself.

The word "closet" (*tameion*) or 'chamber', denotes 'firstly, a store-chamber, then, any private room, secret chamber' (W.E.Vine). Put another way, the word originally meant storehouse or larder. So having entered to pray, we emerge with far more than when we went in! It is worth noticing that there is a reward for praying: "thy Father which seeth in secret shall reward thee openly". Perhaps this means that prayer will be answered for all to see. Elijah took the widow of Zarephath's dead son up to his room in the loft, prayed, and "brought him down out of the chamber into the house, and delivered him unto his mother" (1 Kings 17: 19-23). Elisha actually "shut the door" of the room where the Shunammite's son lay dead, prayed, and the Lord raised the boy (2 Kings 4: 32-37).

b) The practice of prayer, vv.7-8

"But when ye pray, use not vain repetitions, as the heathen do for they think that they shall be heard for their much speaking. Be not ye therefore like unto them: for your Father knoweth what things ye have need of, before ye ask him". The prophets of Baal "called on the name of Baal from morning even until noon" and "when midday was past...they prophesied until the time of the offering of the evening sacrifice", but it didn't get them very far! (1 Kings 18: 26-29). At Ephesus, the mob shouted "Great is Diana of the Ephesians" for two hours, but that didn't get them very far either! (Acts 19: 34).

There is a very big difference between repetition and 'vain repetition'. Paul "besought the Lord ***thrice***" (2 Cor.12: 8). The Lord Jesus "went away again, and prayed the third time, saying the ***same words***" (Matt. 26: 44). The words, "for they (the heathen) think that they shall be heard for their much speaking", remind us that multiplied words are no substitute for earnestness of heart. Other things to be avoided (avoided like the plague) in prayer are, preaching in prayer and making announcements in prayer! The words, "your Father knoweth what things ye have *need* of (not 'what you would like'), before ye ask him", remind us that prayer is not giving information to God, but a right attitude towards Him. John 6: 5-6 are recommended reading on the subject.

c) The pattern for prayer, vv.9-13
It has been said that this prayer is particularly designed for saints in tribulation days: see particularly vv.10-13. There can be no doubt that it *will* be most appropriate at the end-time, but we cannot limit the prayer to any given period.

It is generally called 'the Lord's prayer'. But, without trying to be too pedantic, it could be better called 'the disciples' prayer'. Later teaching by the Lord Jesus on the subject of prayer, let alone in the Epistles, makes it clear that this prayer was particularly suited to the period of His presence with the disciples on earth. Notice, for example, that no mention is made here of His name. But when the time came for the Lord Jesus "to depart out of this world" (John 13: 1), He gave His disciples new guidelines for prayer: "And in that day ye shall ask me nothing. Verily, verily, I say unto you, Whatsoever ye shall ask the Father *in my name*, he will give it you. Hitherto ye have asked nothing in my name: ask, and ye shall receive, that your joy may be full...At that day ye shall ask *in my name*: and I say not unto you, that I will pray the Father for you: for the Father himself loveth you, because ye have loved me, and have believed that I came out from God" (John 16: 23-27). Notice, too, that there is no reference to the basis on which we now pray: we can "come boldly to the throne of grace" because "we have a great high priest that is passed through the heavens, Jesus the Son of God" (Heb. 4: 14-16), and we can have "boldness to enter into the holiest by the blood of Jesus" (Heb. 10: 19).

Amongst other things, as we have already noticed, the prayer anticipates the 'end-time' when 'the request for daily bread and an imminent expectation of the kingdom would be a real issue for Jewish Tribulation saints (Rev. 13: 7-8, 16-17)' (David Newell). But this does not mean, for one moment, that we should dismiss the prayer as irrelevant to ourselves. For a start, 'The emphasis is not on a method, or on a subject, or on a form of words to be used, but on the very act of praying' (Norman Crawford). With this in mind we should notice that the prayer is in two distinct but complementary parts:

Matthew

God's interests are placed first (vv.9-10), and our interests follow (vv.11-13). The lesson for us is clear: do **we** put His interests first in our lives? Notice that the Lord did not say, '*if* ye pray', but "*when* ye pray". See also vv.5, 6, 7, 16, 17 in connection with almsgiving and fasting.

i) God's interests. "Our Father which art in heaven, Hallowed be *thy* name. *Thy* kingdom come. *Thy* will be done in earth, as it is in heaven" (vv.9-10).

- His name. "Hallowed be thy name" (v.9). Whilst we are told that the address, "Our Father which art in heaven", is not appropriate language for a heavenly people (which is certainly true, as we have seen, in the light of later New Testament teaching), it remains that He *is* "our Father" and that He *is* "in heaven". There can be no doubting the relevance of the prayer during the Great Tribulation at the end-time, but surely coming as children to a Father is a privilege that *we* also enjoy. We are certainly on firm New Testament ground. In the Old Testament, the word "father" is rarely used of God, and then only with reference to Israel collectively (Isaiah 1: 2; 63: 16; 64: 8). The Old Testament believers knew Him as Jehovah, Elohim and El Shaddai, and 'only with the coming of the Son has God been revealed as Father (John 1: 18; 4: 23; 17: 5-6)' (David Newell). In the words of Thomas Watson (*The Lord's Prayer,* 1692), 'The name Jehovah carries majesty in it; the name Father carries mercy in it'.

But the intimacy that believers now enjoy must not diminish our reverence for Him one iota. The word "hallowed" means, literally, 'to make holy', and here it expresses the desire of every believer that God's name may be revered and honoured. "For who in the heaven can be compared unto the Lord? who among the sons of the mighty can be likened unto the Lord? God is greatly to be feared in the assembly of the saints, and to be had in reverence of all them that are about him" (Psalm 89: 6-7). See also Psalm 111: 9.

At the moment, men do anything but 'hallow' God's name. His name is blasphemed, and ultimately "the man of sin" who "opposeth and exalteth himself above all that is called God" will sit "in the temple of God, shewing himself that he is God" (2 Thess. 2: 3-4). But the prayer of God's people *will* be answered. It will be said, "Blessed be the Lord God, the God of Israel, who only doeth wondrous things. And blessed be his glorious name for ever" (Psalm 72: 18-19).

- *His kingdom*. "Thy kingdom come" (v.10). While it is perfectly true that "the kingdom of God cometh not with observation (margin, 'outward show')…for, behold, the kingdom of God is within you ('in the midst of you', JND)" (Luke 17: 20-21), and "the kingdom of God is not meat and drink; but righteousness, and peace, and joy in the Holy Ghost" (Rom. 14: 17), the kingdom *will* be established *publicly* on earth. See, for example Dan. 2: 44, "And in the days of these kings shall the God of heaven set up a kingdom, which shall never be destroyed: and the kingdom shall not be left to other people. But it shall break in pieces and consume all these kingdoms, and it shall stand for ever". Once again, the prayer of God's people will be answered.

- *His will*. "Thy will be done in earth, as it is in heaven" (v.10). All do God's bidding in heaven. All *will* do His bidding on earth. Since believers, though on earth, are citizens of heaven (Phil. 3: 20-21), it follows that we should do His will now: "as the servants of Christ, doing the will of God from the heart" (Eph. 6: 6).

While we are certainly waiting for the Lord to "descend from heaven with a shout" (1 Thess. 4: 16), when He will take us to His "Father's house" (John 14: 2), it should nevertheless be our constant desire for the establishment of His kingdom on earth, when "every knee" shall "bow, of things in heaven, and things in earth, and things under the earth; and that every tongue" shall "confess that Jesus Christ is Lord to the glory of God the Father" (Phil. 2: 10-11).

ii) Our interests: "Give *us* this day our daily bread. And forgive *us* our debts, as we forgive our debtors. And lead *us* not into temptation; but deliver *us* from evil" (vv.11-13). It is our interests as they are now, without for one moment denying that the Lord had in mind end-time conditions as well.

- *Provision for us.* "Give us this day our daily bread" (v.11). Living as we do in the Western world, with comparative affluence and security, we seldom, if ever, pray, like this. But there are countless numbers of God's people in the world today, let alone past generations of believers, who face drought, famine and starvation. There are also countless numbers of believers whose faith in Christ has brought persecution and deprivation that we have never experienced. Leaving aside the sufferings of godly men and women at the end-time, when "no man might buy or sell, save he that had the mark…of the beast" (Rev. 13: 17), believers in Muslim countries today, many of them expelled from their employment and evicted from home and family, have to ask God to meet their daily needs.

We must never forget that "Every good gift and every perfect gift is from above, and cometh down from the Father of lights" (James 1: 17). We are all dependent on Him, and none of us knows whether sea-changes will take place in our circumstances.

- **Forgiveness for us.** "And forgive *us* our debts, as we forgive our debtors" (v.12). This should be compared with Eph. 4: 32, which sets out our position before God: "And be ye kind one to another, tenderhearted, forgiving one another, even as God for Christ's sake ***hath*** forgiven you". There is no contradiction. Our practice must correspond with our position. An unforgiving spirit on our part will disrupt our fellowship with God. How can we enjoy His forgiveness and blessing if we have an unforgiving spirit towards others?

- **Deliverance for us**. "And lead *us* not into temptation; but deliver *us* from evil" (v.13). But does God ever "lead us...into temptation?" We are assured that this is never the case: "Let no man say when he is tempted, I am tempted of God: for God cannot be tempted with evil, neither tempteth he any man" (James 1: 13). The "temptation" here must therefore refer to trial, which is the other meaning of *peirasmos.* The word is used by James in both senses: he uses it in connection with testing under trial (1: 2) and with solicitation to do evil (1: 14). The words, "lead us not into temptation" are therefore a prayer for deliverance from trials and pressures which might cause us to fail. It is an admission of our weakness and frailty. In the words of John Phillips, 'We are living in a perilous world, and we are made of highly flammable material'. How thankful we are that the Lord "knoweth our frame: he remembereth that we are dust" (Psalm 103: 14).

The deliverance "from evil" refers to the evil that men would endeavour to inflict on us. Compare 2 Tim. 4: 18, "And the Lord shall deliver me from every evil work, and will preserve me unto his heavenly kingdom". This refers, not to deliverance from injury and death, but from the spiritual damage that Satan endeavours to inflict upon God's people through physical suffering.

The final doxology at the close of v.13 ("For thine is the kingdom, and the power, and the glory, for ever. Amen") 'is not found in the oldest witnesses to the Greek text, and is almost certainly a later liturgical addition' (R.V.G.Tasker). See RV/JND with their margin notes.

d) The proviso in prayer, vv.14-15

The Lord's teaching in Luke 11: 4 ("forgive us our sins; for we also forgive every one that is indebted to us") is more forcibly expressed here: "For if ye forgive men their trespasses, your heavenly Father will also forgive you: but if ye forgive not men their trespasses, neither will your Father forgive your trespasses". We should distinguish here between *judicial* forgiveness, and *parental* forgiveness. The former concerns our standing before God (see, again, Eph. 4: 32), the latter with our communion with God. But even with regard to judicial forgiveness, there can be no forgiveness for us unless there is true repentance of sin, which must include an unforgiving spirit towards others. See also Colossians 3: 13.

C) Fasting, vv.16-18

"Moreover when ye fast, be not, as the hypocrites, of a sad countenance: for they disfigure their faces, that they may appear unto men to fast. Verily I say unto you, They have their reward. But thou, when thou fastest, anoint thine head, and wash thy face; that thou appear not unto men to fast, but unto thy Father which is in secret: and thy Father which seeth in secret, shall reward thee openly". In the New Testament, fasting is associated with:

i) Mourning. "Can the children of the bridechamber mourn, as long as the bridegroom is with them? but the days will come, when the bridegroom shall be taken from them, and then shall they fast" (Matt. 9: 15). This is not appropriate for us - we have the Bridegroom with us!

ii) Prayer. "As they ministered to the Lord, and fasted, the Holy Ghost said..." (Acts 13: 2); "And when they had ordained them elders in every church, and had prayed with fasting" (Acts 14: 23); "Defraud ye not one the other, except it be with consent for a time, that ye may give yourselves to fasting and prayer" (1 Cor. 7: 5).

Wm.MacDonald rightly observes that "in these passages, it appears that fasting accompanied prayer as an acknowledgement of deep earnestness in discerning the will of God and of a solemn awareness of the responsibility of obeying His guidance". He continues: "while fasting is not clearly commanded in the New Testament, it is encouraged by the promise of reward". Now read Neh. 1: 4, Luke 2: 37 and, of course, Matt. 4: 2.

Matthew

C.H.Mackintosh puts it with his customary clarity: 'The exercise of fasting stands in immediate connection with prayer, and we think the connection is most instructive. Fasting implies abstention from things natural and earthly; prayer implies occupation with things spiritual and heavenly. The former closes the channel of communications between nature and the scene around; the latter opens the channel between the spiritual man and the scene above'.

Finally, do note the Lord's teaching here in v.17. It does not become us to have miserable faces! A cheerful countenance is not incompatible with inward mourning. Our demeanour and appearance should reflect the fact that we represent the risen Christ.

"Seek ye first"

Read Chapter 6: 19-34
We have already noted that the Lord's teaching in this chapter may be divided as follows: *(1)* He compares rewards on earth with rewards in heaven (vv.1-18): the word "reward" occurs in vv.1, 2, 4, 5, 6, 16, 18; *(2)* He compares treasure on earth with treasure in heaven (vv.19-34): the words "treasures" and "treasure" occur in vv.19, 20, 21, and in the final analysis we "lay up" treasure in heaven by seeking first "the kingdom of God and his righteousness" (v.33).

1) REWARDS ON EARTH AND REWARDS IN HEAVEN, vv.1-18
This section of the chapter comprises three warnings against ostentation: *(a)* in almsgiving (vv.1-4); *(b)* in prayer (vv.5-15); *(c)* in fasting (vv.16-18).

2) TREASURE ON EARTH AND TREASURE IN HEAVEN, vv.19-34
These verses are relevant to the Lord's commission in Matthew 10 when the disciples were sent out in faith: "Provide neither gold, nor silver, nor brass in your purses; nor scrip for your journey, neither two coats" (Matt. 10: 9-10). There can be little doubt that they will also be relevant in the coming Tribulation period at the end-time, when the Gospel of the Kingdom will be presented afresh. But the Lord's teaching here is equally applicable to *us*. It is repeated in the New Testament epistles: "Charge them that are rich in this world, that they be not highminded, nor trust in uncertain riches, but in the living God, who giveth us richly all things to enjoy" (1 Tim. 6: 17); "Let your conversation be without covetousness (literally, 'love of silver')" (Heb. 13: 5). See also Philippians 3: 18-19, "For many walk... who mind earthly things".

Chapter 6

In comparing treasure on earth with treasure in heaven, the Lord Jesus warns His disciples against *(a)* covetousness (vv.19-24), and *(b)* cares (vv.25-34). In the first case, the Lord deals with the **accumulation of wealth** and speaks particularly to the **rich**, warning them against **ambition**. In the second, He deals with the **attitude to the necessities** of life and speaks particularly to the **poor**, warning them against **anxiety**. Both are mentioned in Matthew 13: 22, where the seed could be choked by "the **care** of this world" and by the "deceitfulness of **riches**".

a) His warning against covetousness, vv.19-24
The Lord deals with the subject of covetousness in three ways: He refers *(i)* to storing (vv.19-21): "Lay not up for yourselves treasures upon earth...but lay up for yourselves treasures in heaven"; *(ii)* to seeing (vv.22-23): "The light of the body is the eye: if therefore thine eye be single...But if thine eye be evil"; *(iii)* to serving (v.24): "Ye cannot serve God and mammon".

i) Storing, vv.19-21
In this connection, we should notice that it is possible to accumulate wealth in two places: "Lay not up for yourselves treasures upon **earth**...but lay up for yourselves treasures in **heaven**". The Lord uses the plural in vv.19-20 ("yourselves"), but the singular in v.21 ('thy treasure', RV). The words, "Lay not up (*thesaurizo*) for yourselves" are, literally, 'treasure not up for yourselves'. Compare Luke 12: 33-34. See also James 5: 3, "Ye have heaped treasure together for the last days". The expression is used in a better sense in 1 Corinthians 16: 2, "Upon the first day of the week, let every one of you lay by him in store". See also 2 Corinthians 12: 14.

The Lord does not refer here to wealth *per se*, but to passion for possessions: the hoarding and amassing of possessions. The church at Laodicea illustrates v.19: "I am rich, and **increased** with goods, and have need of nothing: and knowest not that thou art wretched, and miserable, and poor" (Rev. 3: 17). The church at Smyrna illustrates v.20: "I know thy works, and tribulation, and poverty, (but thou art rich)". (Rev. 2: 9). The 'rich young ruler' chose "treasures upon earth" as opposed to "treasures in heaven" (Matt. 19: 21). In this connection, the Lord makes two important points:

- **The treasures of earth can be insecure.** They are subject to moth, rust and thieves. Listen to Solomon: "For riches certainly make themselves wings; they fly away, as an eagle toward heaven" (Prov. 23: 5). Paul warns against "trust in **uncertain** riches" (1 Tim. 6: 17). The "moth" (*ses*) is the clothes moth. So the Saviour is referring to clothing. "Rust" (*brosis*) is literally 'an eating', so the Saviour is referring to metal objects. The word "corrupt" here (*aphanizo*) means 'to consume'. It should be said that some commentators prefer 'devour by vermin' to 'rust', on the ground that the 'stores' in question would be more likely to consist of grain, etc. The expression "break through" (*diorusso*) is, literally, 'dig through'.

Note: our inheritance is not subject to such risks! It is "an inheritance incorruptible, and undefiled, and that fadeth not away, reserved in heaven for you" (1 Pet. 1: 4).

- *The treasures of earth can completely absorb us.* "For where your treasure is, there will your heart be also". What we value claims our love and affection, Hence: "Love not the world, neither the things that are in the world" (1 John 2: 15). It is infinitely more worthwhile to "lay up for yourselves treasures in heaven". Remember, "We brought nothing into this world, and it is certain we can carry nothing out" (1 Tim. 6: 7). ('How much did so-and-so leave?' – answer 'Everything!'). Paul "suffered the loss of all things" (Phi. 3: 8), but he anticipated a "crown of righteousness" (2 Tim. 4: 8). If the Lord were to come, nothing else would matter except "treasures in heaven!" Where is *our* affection? Paul writes, "Set your affection (mind) on things above, not on things on the earth" (Col. 3: 1-2)

It is not so much what we possess, but our attitude to it that is important. A man may have immense wealth, and not treasure it. A man may have little, and treasure it immensely. Note 1 Timothy 6: 9-10: "they that **desire to be rich** fall into temptation and a snare…For the **love of money** is a root of all kinds of evil: which some reaching after have been led astray from the faith, and have pierced themselves through with many sorrows" (RV).

The question must be asked, 'What is treasure in heaven?' The Lord does not define "treasure in heaven" here, but the New Testament leaves us in no doubt about the answer. The following should be of immense value to us: "Well done, thou good and faithful servant" (Matt. 25: 21); "then shall every man have praise of God" (1 Cor. 4: 5); "thou hast a little strength, and hast kept my word, and hast not denied my name" (Rev. 3: 8). This is "treasure" indeed, and we 'lay it up' by our faithfulness and labour. A man by his labour and zeal acquires treasure on earth, and a child of God does so in respect of treasure in heaven. Paul calls this "fruit that may abound to your account" (Phil. 4: 17). Read 1 Timothy 6: 18-19. Moses sets us a good example here: see Hebrews 11: 26. What about the "cup of cold water"? (Matt. 10: 42). The idea of reward and treasure are present in the following: "I have fought a good fight...a *crown* of righteousness" (2 Tim. 4: 7-8); "Feed the flock of God...a *crown* of glory" (1 Pet. 5: 2- 4); "be thou faithful unto death...a (margin, 'the') *crown* of life" (Rev. 2: 10).

ii) Seeing, vv.22-23
In this connection, we should notice two conditions: "if therefore thine eye be single...if thine eye be evil". The underlying teaching is that how and what we look at controls our entire life. The idea of "light" is really 'lamp' (a portable lamp): thus the eye gives direction and plots the pathway for living. See Eph. 1: 18, "The eyes of your understanding (JND 'heart') being enlightened".

Since the section lies between vv. 19-21 and v.24, where it is evident that the Lord is speaking of our attitude to money, it is therefore clear that He is also referring to money here. Hence the words, "if therefore thine eye be single... if thine eye be evil", refer to a proper and improper attitude to money. So:

- *The single eye.* The believer with clear vision. He is well focussed. He looks at things from a spiritual standpoint. The word "single" (*haplous*) means singleness of purpose, that is, as opposed to two treasures (vv.19-21) and two masters (v.24). In this case, "thy whole body shall be full of light". The expression, "thy whole body" is a metaphor for the whole life. "Light" refers to what is of God: "God is light" (1 John 1: 5).

Abraham had a 'single eye'. "He *looked* for a city which hath foundations, whose builder and maker is God" (Heb. 11: 10). It is rather significant that it was after Lot (his name means 'a veil') had left Abraham that God said to the patriarch, "Lift up now thine *eyes*" (Gen. 13: 14). The veil had gone! With the other Patriarchs, Abraham saw the promises "afar off", with the result that they "confessed that they were strangers and pilgrims on the earth" (Heb. 11: 13). Moses had a 'single eye': he "endured, as *seeing* him who is invisible", and this enabled him to esteem "the reproach of Christ greater riches than the treasures in Egypt" (Heb. 11: 27, 26). At his death (age 120), "his *eye* was not dim, nor his natural force abated" (Deut. 34: 7).

- *The evil eye.* This does not refer to a lustful look. It is "evil" (*poneros*) in the sense of labour, pain, sorrow. We are told that it could be translated 'out of order', that is, malfunctioning, as in the case of Laodicea: "And knowest not that thou art wretched, and miserable, and poor, and *blind*, and naked" (Rev. 3: 17). See also 2 Peter 1: 9, "But he that lacketh these things is *blind*, and cannot see afar off".

However, the fact that the 'evil eye' is contrasted with the 'single eye', may well suggest, in the words of Wm.Macdonald that 'The man with the diseased eye has double vision. He is trying to live for two worlds. He doesn't want to let go of his earthly treasures, yet he wants treasures in heaven too. The teachings of Jesus seem impractical and impossible to him. He cannot see the wisdom of them. He lacks clear guidance: the whole subject is darkness to him'. In this case, "Thy whole body shall be full of darkness". 'In other words, if you know that Christ forbids trusting earthly treasures for security, yet you go ahead and do it anyway, the teaching you have failed to obey ("the light that is in thee") becomes darkness - a very intense form of spiritual blindness. You cannot see riches in their true perspective' (Wm.Macdonald).

iii) Serving, v.24
In this connection, we should notice two masters: "No man can serve (meaning bond-service, as a slave) two masters (*kurios*, meaning "lord")... ye cannot serve God and mammon". (We have an example of attempting to serve two masters in 2 Kings 17: 33). Notice the order: storing (vv.19-21), seeing (vv.22-23), service (v.24). The last can only be undertaken in view of the first and second!

The Lord did *not* say 'No man *should* serve two masters', but "no man *can* serve two masters". The law demanded unreserved devotion to God: "Thou shalt love the Lord thy God with *all* thy heart, and with *all* thy soul, and with *all* thy mind" (Matt. 22: 37). We cannot serve God with divided affections. Joshua made this clear: "Now therefore fear the Lord, and serve him in sincerity and in truth...And if it seem evil unto you to serve the Lord, choose you this day whom ye will serve...but as for me and my house, we will serve the Lord" (Joshua 24: 14-15).

The word "hate" ("hate the one, and love the other"), while used in the usually understood sense elsewhere, has here the meaning of disregarding a rival claim. See also Luke 14: 26, "If any man come to me, and hate not his father...he cannot be my disciple". The word "mammon" is an Aramaic expression meaning 'riches'. The Lord Jesus contrasts what He calls "the "mammon of unrighteousness" or "the "unrighteous mammon" with "the true riches" (Luke 16: 9-11). His concluding words to the covetous Pharisees

Chapter 6

were, "that which is highly esteemed among men is abomination in the sight of God" (Luke 16: 15). Justin Waldron asks, 'Are we like the people of Haggai's day (Hag 1: 3-6), or the people of Macedonia (2 Cor. 8: 1-5). This brings us to:

b) His warning against cares, vv.25-34
If His disciples were to give their attention to spiritual storing, seeing and serving, what about their daily needs? They might well be anxious about this, and thus the Saviour continues: "take no thought" (vv.25, 31, 34), meaning 'be not anxious' (RV): or 'be not careful' (JND), that is full of care. The word "thought" (*merimnao*) means 'drawn in both directions'. See also Matthew 10: 19 (with parallel passages in Mark 13: 11; Luke 12: 11) where the RV reads, 'be not anxious' (AV has "take no thought"). We are to be "careful (*merimnao*) for nothing", but prayerful about everything (Phil. 4: 6). There is a contrast between "take no thought" (v.25) and "seek ye first" (v.33).

We learn therefore that it is possible to be distracted by *affluence* (vv.19-24), and it is possible to be distracted by *anxiety* (vv.20-34). We are not to be careless, but we *are* to be care-free. Martha was "careful (same word) and troubled about many things" (Luke 10: 41). Compare Philippians 4: 6, "Be careful for nothing". See also 1 Peter 5: 7, "Casting all your care (*merimnao*, 'anxiety', RV) upon him, for he careth (*melei*) for you". A parallel passage is found in Luke 12: 22-31.

Having spoken about the way in which His disciples should regard wealth, the Lord now speaks about the things money can buy: "Therefore I say unto you, Take no thought for your life, what ye shall eat, or what ye shall drink; nor yet for your body, what ye shall put on. Is not the life more than meat, and the body than raiment?" (v.25). This introductory statement ("Is not the life more than meat, and the body than raiment?") emphasises God has given us life, and He can sustain it, and that God has given us a body, and He can clothe it. He has given the *greater* ("life...body"), and He can therefore give the *lesser* ("meat...raiment"). Note Luke 12: 15, "a man's life consisteth not in the abundance of the things which he possesseth". See also 1 Timothy 6: 6-8: "But godliness with contentment is great gain. For we brought nothing into this world, and it is certain we can carry nothing out. And having *food* and *raiment* let us be therewith content".

The verses that follow (vv.26-34) are easily divided: *(i)* the lesson from fowls

109

(vv.26-27); *(ii)* the lesson from flowers (vv28-30); *(iii)* the lessons applied (vv.31-34). We must not forget that the Saviour is speaking here about the necessities of life, not about the luxuries of life!

i) The lesson from fowls, vv.26-27

The lesson is clear: God feeds the fowls: how much more His children. "Behold the fowls of the air; for they sow not, neither do thy reap, nor gather into barns; yet your heavenly Father feedeth them. Are ye not much better than they?" (v.26).

The disciples are told to "**Behold** the fowls of the air", that is, 'to look earnestly and attentively', reminding us that nature is rich in lessons for us. See, for example, 1 Cor. 11: 14. The 'rich fool' said "I will pull down my barns, and build greater" (Luke 12: 15-21), but the birds do not "gather into barns". The rich man certainly made plans to 'lay up treasure', and we should notice that the Lord continued by citing the teaching of Matthew 6: 25-34. See Luke 12: 22-31. The question, "Are ye not *much better* than they?" (v.26) is one of those questions of which it can be said, 'To ask the question is to answer it'. However, if amplification is required, then Genesis 1: 26 will be more than ample! Man has been given a unique dimension: and God "breathed into his nostrils the breath of life; and man became a living soul". The emphasis on God's love should be noted: "Your heavenly **Father**". We can rely upon the love of God who saved us, and who will preserve us "unto his heavenly kingdom" (2 Tim. 4: 18), to undertake for our bodily needs. David said, "I have been young, and now am old; yet have I not seen the righteous forsaken, nor his seed begging bread" (Psalm 37: 25). We can pray with confidence, "Give us this day our daily bread" (Matt. 6: 11). Notice too the wording in the passage: "your heavenly **Father** feedeth them" (v.26); "Wherefore, if **God** so clothe the grass of the field" (v.30); "your heavenly **Father** knoweth" (v.32). What His *love* promises ("Father"); His *power* fulfils ("God").

Notice that in any case we cannot alter our circumstances. "Which of you by taking thought (anxious thought) can add ('put to' or 'increase') one cubit unto his stature?" (v.27). The word "stature" (*helikia*) could refer either to height or to life-span (it means, primarily, 'an age, as a certain length of life'). So anxious thought will never make you any taller, or make you live any longer! However, "cubit" seems to indicate that "stature" is used in its normal sense. The thought is that we cannot add to ourselves - only God does that. Hence v.28, "how they ("the lilies") grow".

Said the robin to the sparrow, *"I should dearly like to know
Why these anxious human beings rush around and worry so".
Said the sparrow to the robin, "Friend, I think that it must be
That they have no heavenly Father such as cares for you and me"*

ii) The lesson from the flowers, vv.28-30
Again, the lesson is clear: God clothes the lilies: how much more His children. "And why take ye thought for raiment? Consider (literally, 'learn thoroughly' or 'consider carefully, so as to learn') the lilies of the field, (thought to include gladiolus and iris species) how they grow; they toil not, neither do they spin: and yet I say unto you, That even Solomon in all his glory was not arrayed like one of these"(vv.28-29). The field (*agros*) is a cultivated field. The picture, then, is of flowers which give splashes of rich colour to the cornfields. The words, "they toil not, neither do thy spin", may refer to men in the first instance, and women in the second. Glory was **given** to Solomon, but glory **belongs** to the lilies!

So, to a disciple anxious about clothing, the Lord says, 'See what God can do with the lilies!' Man's clothing, under microscopic examination, will be seen to be blemished and imperfect. But God's provision for the lilies, and all else, will be seen under microscopic examination, to be wonderful and perfect! Even Marks & Spencer cannot claim that! The lesson follows: "Wherefore, if God so clothe the grass of the field, which today is, and tomorrow is cast into the oven, shall he not much more clothe you, O ye of little faith?" (v.30). The words, "grass of the field", probably refer to the same plant(s) in vv.28-29, whose reedy stems are fuel for the oven. It is said that "the oven" was three feet deep in the ground and plastered. It was heated with grass etc until sufficiently hot to bake.

The words, "O ye of little faith", occur four times in Matthew: 6: 30 (rebuking care); 8: 26 (rebuking fear: "Lord save us: we perish"); 14: 31 (rebuking doubt: "Lord save me"); 16: 8 (rebuking reasoning: "they reasoned among themselves, saying, it is because we have taken no bread").

iii) The lessons applied, vv.31-34
"Therefore take no (anxious) thought, saying, What shall we eat? or, What shall we drink? or, Wherewithal shall we be clothed? (For after all these things do the Gentiles seek): for your heavenly Father knoweth that ye have need (remember, the Lord is referring here to the necessities of life) of all these things" (vv.31-32). This is the second "Therefore" (see v.25), and the

statement summarises and applies vv.25-30. The Lord Jesus refers to two quests: the quest of the Gentiles (v.32); the quest of the disciples (v33).

- **The quest of the Gentiles, v.32.** People with no relationship with God: "For all these things do the Gentiles **seek**" (*epizeteo* meaning 'to seek earnestly' or 'crave'). Compare 1 Thessalonians. 4: 5: "even as the Gentiles, which know not God". The child of God should not be governed by the materialistic outlook of the unregenerate.

- **The quest of the disciples, v.33.** Our priority in life is to "seek (*zeteo*, 'to strive after')…first the kingdom of God (only five times in Matthew), and his righteousness". Paul expresses it differently, but it is the same priority: "For to me to live is Christ" (Phil. 1: 21). In the context of the Lord's teaching here, seeking "first the kingdom of God (that is, submission to His rule in our lives) and his righteousness", involves **storing** in the right place, **seeing** in the right way, and **serving** the right master. The injunction, "seek ye first the kingdom of God" is accompanied by a promise: "And all these things (see v.33) **shall** (not 'might') be added unto you". We cannot "add" one cubit to our stature, but God can 'add' (same word) to us! The Lord taught elsewhere "There is no man that hath left house, or brethren…for my sake, and the gospel's, but he shall receive an hundredfold now in this time…and in the world to come eternal life" (Mark 10: 28-30).

Taken together, vv.32-33 give us God's role in providing for us: "your heavenly Father knoweth that ye have need of all these things" (v.32), and our part: "But seek *ye* first the kingdom of God, and his righteousness" (v.33). Compare Psalm 34: 9-10.

The Saviour concludes: "Take therefore no thought (be not therefore anxious) for the morrow: for the morrow shall take thought for the things of itself. Sufficient unto the day is the evil thereof" (v.34) or 'Sufficient for each day is its own trouble'. That is, don't anticipate trouble: don't worry about what might happen or what could happen. We are to live 'a day at a time'. The "evil" here refers to adversity. As Wm.Kelly observes, 'When the next day comes, the evil might not be there, and if it is, *God* will still be there!'

> Precious thought my Father knoweth! In His love I rest:
> For whate'er my Father doeth must be always best.
> Well I know the heart that planneth nought but good for me,
> Joy and sorrow interwoven, Love in all I see.

THE GOSPEL OF MATTHEW

"Judge not that ye be not judged"

Read Chapter 7: 1-14
Matthew Chapter 7 can be broadly divided into three sections: *(1)* instruction regarding relationships (vv.1-14); *(2)* identifying dangers (vv.15-23); *(3)* implementing His word (vv.24-29).

1) INSTRUCTION REGARDING RELATIONSHIPS, vv.1-14
The Lord deals with this subject in five ways: *(a)* judging our brethren (vv.1-5); *(b)* speaking to the unregenerate (v.6); *(c)* praying to God (vv.7-11); *(d)* acting towards others (v.12); *(e)* forsaking the world (vv.13-14).

a) Our relationship with our brethren, vv.1-5
The words, "And why beholdest thou the mote that is in thy brother's eye, but considerest not the beam that is in thine own eye?" (v.3), make it clear that the Lord's opening injunction, "Judge not that ye be not judged" (v.1), has particular reference to the way in which His disciples should treat each other. Perhaps it is opportune to say that the context in which a passage or verse occurs is most important. It has been called 'the golden rule' of Biblical interpretation. It has been said that 'a text taken out of its context becomes a pretext' for just about anything!

Very clearly the Lord's teaching here cannot be applicable to every situation in the Christian life. Sadly, there are occasions when sin and wrong-doing have to be addressed, and two examples occurred at Corinth:

- "For what have I to do to judge them also that are without? do not ye *judge* them that are within?" (1 Cor. 5: 12). In this case, immorality was tolerated in the assembly at Corinth, and the believers there were "puffed up", possibly proud of their liberality and tolerance or, more likely, proud that it wasn't happening to them personally. In this connection Paul states his position clearly: "For I verily, as absent in body, but present in spirit, have *judged* already, as though I was present, concerning him that hath so done this deed" (1 Cor. 5: 3). It was necessary to take disciplinary action. We must distinguish between weakness and wickedness. We can bear and forebear with the former, but we must never bear and forebear with the latter.

- "If then ye have judgments of things pertaining to this life, set them to *judge* who are least esteemed in the church. I speak to your shame. Is it so, that there is not a wise man among you? no, not one that shall be able to *judge* between his brethren?" (1 Cor. 6: 4-5). In this case, believers were 'washing their dirty linen in public' or, in Paul's words, "brother goeth to law with brother, and that before unbelievers" (v.6). The matter should have been dealt with in the assembly.

The words, "Judge not that ye be not judged. For with what judgment ye judge, ye shall be judged: and with what measure ye mete, it shall be measured to you again" (vv.1-2), could not possibly apply to the above situations, but they can most certainly apply in personal relationships, especially when it comes to what Paul calls "evil surmisings" (1 Tim 6: 4), and an attempt is made to deal with the faults of fellow-believers. In this connection, the Lord issues two warnings:

i) He warns against superiority. This can only lead to a censorious spirit and to harsh judgment of others, which is far removed from the "spirit of meekness" (Gal. 6: 1) required in anybody who seeks to help a fellow-believer. In His teaching here, the Lord refers to recompence in kind ("For with what judgment ye judge, ye shall be judged) and in measure ("with what measure ye mete, it shall be measured unto you again"). The recompence in this way may await the judgment seat of Christ (see 2 Cor. 5: 10), but it seems more likely that the Lord is referring to recompence in the present time. It has been said that 'We can expect to be judged and condemned by others in the same way and to the same extent that we judge and condemn them' (John Phillips). Either way, it is the principle that "whatsoever a man soweth, that shall he also reap" (Gal. 6: 7). It must be said that the Lord is not referring to an elder's responsibility in the assembly, which may well involve addressing the suitability of a brother or sister for a particular task or ongoing responsibility. The Lord is speaking here about general relationships amongst His people.

It is worth noting that the words, "with what measure ye mete, it shall be measured to you again", occur again in Mark 4: 24 with reference to our interest in the word of God: "Take heed what ye hear: with what measure ye mete, it shall be measured to you: and unto you that hear shall more be given", and in Luke 6: 38 with reference to practical liberality: "Give, and it shall be given unto you; good measure, pressed down, and shaken together, and running over, shall men give into your bosom. For with the same measure that ye mete withal it shall be measured to you again". It is also important to remember that all who trust in the Lord Jesus will never be judged for their sins: "He that heareth my word, and believeth (on) him that sent me, hath everlasting life, and shall not come into condemnation (judgment); but is passed from death unto life" (John 5: 24).

ii) He warns against hypocrisy. "And why beholdest thou the mote that is in thy brother's eye, but considerest not the beam that is in thine own eye? Or how wilt thou say to thy brother, Let me pull out the mote out of thine eye; and, behold, a beam is in thine own eye? Thou hypocrite, first cast out the beam out of thine own eye; and then shalt thou see clearly to cast out the mote out of thy brother's eye" (vv.3-5).

The Lord Jesus refers here to someone who can see (or thinks he can see) what's wrong with the other man, without any consideration of the wrong in himself. We must remember that the Lord is addressing His disciples when He says, "Thou **hypocrite**". The "mote" (*karphos*) refers to a small dry stalk or a tiny piece of straw, and the "beam" (*dokos*) to a roof support. A parallel passage is found in Luke 6: 41-42. People who specialise in this sort of thing are found in Mathew 23: 23-25, and it may well be that the Lord had in mind the hypocrisy of the religious leaders when warning His disciples in this way. This is illustrated in Mark 7: 1-13. The Pharisees and scribes took exception to the way in which the Lord's disciples ate "bread with unwashen hands" (v.5), but they were guilty of something infinitely more serious - they neatly side-stepped the command, "Honour thy father and mother" by using the word "Corban" (v.11), which implied that the financial help that they should have given to parents was allegedly devoted to the Lord. The religious leaders saw a "mote" in the eyes of the Lord's disciples, and completely ignored the "beam" in their own eyes. In fact they were very good at identifying small things, and even better at overlooking important things: "Woe unto you, scribes and Pharisees, hypocrites! For ye pay tithe of mint and anise and cumin, and have omitted the weightier matters of the law, judgment, mercy, and faith" (Matt. 23: 23).

We must remember that the Lord is not saying that the "mote" does not exist, and that any perceived problem must be ignored. It is not a case of 'Don't be concerned', but 'Put yourself right first'. While the situation described in Galatians 6: 1 is obviously something quite serious ("if a man be overtaken in a fault"), the principle is clear: "ye which are spiritual restore such an one in the spirit of meekness; **considering thyself**, lest thou also be tempted". The words, "ye which are spiritual", refers to men in communion with God, and who can 'see clearly': men who do not have distorted vision: men without a "beam" in their eye. Both Old and New Testaments stress the need for personal integrity: "Only take heed *to thyself*...Take ye therefore good heed *unto yourselves*...Take heed *unto yourselves*" (Deut 4: 9, 15, 23); "Take heed therefore *unto yourselves*" (Acts 20: 28); "Take heed *unto thyself*" (1 Tim. 4: 16). Self-examination is necessary. Only then will we be able to "see clearly to cast out the mote out of thy brother's eye" (v.5). M.R.Vincent (*Word Studies in the New Testament*) makes the interesting observation: 'Pull out the beam; then thou shalt see clearly, not only the fault itself, but how to help thy brother get rid of it'. It has been said that clear sight is necessary if anyone is to attempt such a delicate operation as removing a little splinter from his brother's eye!

In another connection, this time with reference to the Lord's supper, we must remember the injunction: "Let a man examine himself, and so let him eat of that bread, and drink of that cup" (1 Cor. 11: 28).

The Lord Jesus had no "beam" in His eye. He alone had the moral right to wash the disciples' feet (John 13: 1-17). In the law of the "red heifer" (Numbers 19) only a clean person could sprinkle the unclean Israelite: "And a clean person shall take hyssop...and the clean person shall sprinkle on the unclean on the third day" (Num. 19: 18-19). The Lord Jesus acted as a "clean person" in washing the feet of His disciples. In all things, the Lord is "the *righteous* judge" (2 Tim. 4: 8).

b) Speaking to the unregenerate, v.6
"Give not that which is holy (pure) unto the dogs, neither cast ye your pearls (something beautiful, costly and the product of suffering) before swine, lest they trample *them* under their feet, and turn again and rend *you*". According to R.V.G.Tasker, the grammar leads to the meaning: 'Never think of giving that which is holy unto the dogs'. This confirms that not every kind of judgment comes under the ban in vv.1-2. While we must not engage in the hard censorious judgment of others, we must have what has been called 'a

sense of judgment' in our contacts with our fellow-men. How glad we are that it is all very different when it comes to our relationship with fellow-believers: "we speak wisdom among them that are perfect" (1 Cor. 2: 6).

Bearing in mind the Lord's words to the Syrophenician woman, "Let the children first be filled: for it is not meet to take the children's bread, and to cast it unto the dogs" (Mark 7: 27), it had been suggested that by "dogs" the Lord could be referring to the Gentiles, and that for a Jew to "invite a pagan to share his religious feasts…would be like throwing meat consecrated for sacrifice to an unclean pariah-dog" (R.V.G.Tasker). He continues: "Nor would he risk the jibes of his Gentile neighbours by placing before them spiritual 'food' which they could not assimilate; for that would be like trying to feed unclean pigs with pearls, the only result being that the pigs, finding the pearls inedible, trample them under foot and turn savagely upon the donors".

We may not wholly agree with R.V.G.Tasker's suggestion that the Lord is referring to Jew and Gentile here, but there is a great deal of mileage in his explanation. In fact, he continues by saying, "Similarly, the truths that Christ taught, His pearls of great price, must not be broadcast *indiscriminately* to those who would ridicule and despise them, and become increasingly antagonistic". Perhaps we can expand his suggestion and say that the vast range of subject matter in the word of God should not be taught indiscriminately. There is, of course, no prohibition on Gospel testimony to unbelievers. The Syrophenician woman said, "Yes, Lord: yet the dogs under the table eat of the children's crumbs" (Mark 7: 28). But many of those things which are 'part and parcel' of Christian truth, are not for unbelievers. "Pearls" are precious. Just imagine communicating the Song of Solomon to the unsaved. That would indeed be a case of giving "that which is holy unto the dogs" and casting "pearls before swine". The Lord did not cast His "pearls before swine" in 'the upper room'. He waited until Judas had left (John 13: 30-31) before delivering His 'upper room ministry' (John 14-16). We must remember that "the natural man receiveth not the things of the Spirit of God: for they are foolishness unto him: neither can he know them, because they are spiritually discerned" (1 Cor. 2: 14).

We should add that Peter alludes to both dogs and pigs when referring to false teachers: "But it is happened unto them, according to the true proverb, The dog is turned to his own vomit again, and the sow that was washed to her wallowing in the mire" (2 Pet. 2. 22). The "dogs" here are not our western pets, but scavengers - unclean animals. Paul told the Philippian believers to "beware of dogs" (Phil. 3: 2) when referring to the activities of the Judaisers. In view of these passages, it certainly seems possible that the Lord may have been alluding to false teachers in referring to "dogs" and "swine".

As a postscript, we really ought to add, even though it really has nothing to do with our subject here, that we should never discuss assembly matters with unbelievers, particularly when difficulty and dissension occur.

c) Praying to God, vv.7-11
Two matters should be noted here: *(i)* the exhortation (vv.7-8); *(ii)* the illustration (vv.9-11). Put differently, the Lord first emhasises our part (vv.7-8), and then God's part (vv.9-11).

i) The exhortation, vv.7-8
"Ask, and it shall be given you; seek, and ye shall find; knock, and it shall be opened unto you" (v.7). (The word "ask" means to ask as in the sense of addressing a superior. The Lord Jesus used a different word in His requests to the Father, meaning to ask as an equal). The three words, "ask...seek...knock", could be understood as different degrees of intensity. The words, "Seek, **and ye shall find**", recall Matthew 6: 33, "Seek ye first the kingdom of God, and his righteousness; and all these things shall be added unto you". The words, "Knock, **and it shall be opened unto you**", recall Revelation 3: 7-8, "I have set before thee an open door, and no man can shut it"; 1 Corinthians 16: 9, "A great door and effectual is opened unto me". The Lord opened that door!

The "present continuous imperatives mean 'keep on asking, seeking, knocking', while the verbs ('ask, seek, knock') suggest increasing intensity and earnestness" (David Newell on the parallel passage in Luke 11: 9-10). We have an example in Epaphras: "always labouring fervently for you in prayers" (Col. 4: 12). Are we prepared to "pray without ceasing?" (1 Thess. 5: 17).

The Lord's words, "For every one that asketh receiveth; and he that seeketh findeth; and to him that knocketh it shall be opened" (v.8), should not be taken as an unconditional promise. The New Testament has a great deal to say about the subject. For example: we are to pray in the Lord's name, that is, with reference to His glory and interests with God's glory in view: "And whatsoever ye shall ask in my name, that will I do, that the Father may be glorified in the Son" (John 14: 13); we are to ask in faith: "If any of you lack wisdom, let him ask of God...But let him ask in faith, nothing wavering" (James 1: 5-6); we are to pray in the Holy Spirit: "praying in the Holy Ghost" (Jude v.20); our prayers are to be backed by a godly life: "And whatsoever we ask, we receive of him, because we keep his commandments, and do those things whch are pleasing in his sight" (see 1 John 3: 22); we are to pray according to the will of God: "And this is the confidence that we have in him, that, if we ask any thing according to his will, he heareth us" (1 John 5: 14). It has to be said that although the Lord will hear the prayers of His godly people (Psalm 66: 18-19), the answer may sometimes be 'No'. Moses desired to see the land of Canaan, but was told, "speak no more unto me of this matter" (Deut. 3: 26). Paul "besought the Lord thrice" for deliverance from the "thorn in the flesh", but was told, "My grace is sufficient for thee" (2 Cor. 12: 9). The Lord Jesus requested three times, "If it be possible, let this cup pass from me" (Matt. 26: 39-44).

Prayer may not be answered because we "ask amiss" (James 4: 3). Sadly, it is possible to pray from wrong motives and with self-centredness. Sometimes the answer is 'Yes', but it is accompanied by delay. It has often been said that 'God's delays are not denials'. His timing is always perfect. There might be other reasons, totally unknown to us. Read Daniel 10: 12-14.

But the fact that we are urged to persist in prayer, does not mean that there is some unwillingness on the part of the Father to respond to His children's requests. This follows:

ii) The illustration, vv.9-11
The illustration given: "Or what man is there of you, whom if his son ask bread, will he give him a stone? (he will not give him something unusable or inedible). Or if he ask a fish, will he give him a serpent? (he will not give him something harmful)" (vv.9-10). He will not mock his son. He has his best interests in view. Two things call for attention.

- The Lord refers here to genuine needs, "bread...fish", not to self-gratification (James 4: 3). It would be a poor father (or mother) who indulges every whim and fancy of their children. (Frustrated children who scream in supermarkets need a short sharp lesson). Solomon certainly did not pray from selfish motives (1 Kings 3: 5-15).

- 'No normal human father, being asked by his child for bread, would refuse it or deceive the child by offering it something superficially similar

Matthew

but worthless and dangerous' (David Gooding on the parallel passage in Luke 11: 11-12). The 'superficial similarity' will be clear in the case of a loaf of bread and a stone (the loaves were quite small), and in the case of a fish and a serpent, but it is worth noting that Luke also mentions the case of an egg and a scorpion. In this case it should be remembered that a curled-up scorpion looks rather like an egg - until it stings you!

The illustration applied. "If ye then, being evil, know how to give good gifts unto your children, how much more shall your Father (emphasising His love) which is in heaven give good things (see James 1: 17) to them that ask him?" (v.11). This ("ye...being evil") is addressed to the disciples! We need to remember that although we are saved, we still have a fallen evil nature. But "how much more shall your Father which is in heaven give good things to them that ask him". Note "Give ***good*** things". He is wiser than us, and knows what is good for us, and what is not good for us. Remember too that while He knows exactly what we need, He does love to hear our voice! Notice that Hebrews 12: 9 uses the illustration of an earthly father when dealing with the way in which God disciplines His children (J.Waldron).

d) Acting towards others, v.12
"Therefore all things whatsoever ye ***would*** that men should do to you, do ye even so to them: for this is the law and the prophets". The Lord did ***not*** say, 'all things whatsoever men ***do to you***, do ye even so to them'. As Wm.MacDonald points out, 'Christianity is not simply a matter of abstinence from sin; it is positive goodness'. The Lord Jesus summarised "the law and the prophets" as follows: "Thou shalt love the Lord thy God with all thy heart, and with all thy soul, and with all thy might. This is the first and great commandment. And the second is like unto it, Thou shalt love thy neighbour as thyself. On these two commandments hang all the law and the prophets" (Matt. 22: 35-40). The Old Covenant demanded that people should not be self-interested: "Thou shalt love thy neighbour as thyself". But the New Covenant sets a ***higher*** standard, "That ye love one another, ***as I have loved you***" (John 15: 12). The Lord Jesus looked not "on his own things", but "on the things of others" (Phil. 2: 4). Such an attitude will prevent us from saying, "Suffer ***me first***" (Matt. 8: 21).

e) Forsaking the world, vv.13-14
"Enter ye in at the strait gate: for wide is the gate, and broad is the way that leadeth to destruction, and many there be that go in thereat; because strait

is the gate, and narrow is the way, which leadeth unto life, and few there be that find it" (vv.13-14).

It is very difficult to think of these verses in any other way than two gates, each leading to two ways which end in two destinations. The well-known and much used picture of the 'Two Ways' flashes immediately before or eyes! It may therefore be a little surprising to know that some commentators place the gates at the *end* of the two ways, saying that once either of these gates has been entered there is no possibility of return. In other words, there will be no possibility of transferring from the 'broad way' to the 'narrow way'. It will then be too late. Most of us will probably find this difficult to take on board, and R.V.G.Tasker, who inclines in this direction does admit that the traditional view is 'possible grammatically!'

It has been pointed out that while these verses are often used in a Gospel context, they are addressed to disciples! Wm.MacDonald puts it like this: the Lord Jesus "is saying, in effect, 'To follow Me will require discipline, perseverance, self-abnegation, faith and endurance. But it is the only life worth living. If you choose the easy way through life, you will have plenty of company, but you will miss God's best for you'". For the purpose of this study we suggest that as believers, we can either:

i) Determine to keep the company and share the pleasures of men and women who will ultimately suffer "destruction" (*apoleia*), meaning, not loss of being, but loss of well-being. It has to be said that many believers, or professing believers, opt for the 'wide gate' or 'broad way' approach to life. This is not to say that, like the people whose company they seek, they will be lost themselves. Or we can:

ii) Determine to keep the company and share with a relative few what might seem to be the privations and restrictions involved in following Christ, knowing that this will enable us to "lay hold on eternal life" now (1 Tim. 6: 12, 19) with its full enjoyment in eternity. Paul followed this road: "But what things were gain to me, those I counted loss for Christ. Yea doubtless, and I count all things but loss for the excellency of the knowledge of Christ Jesus my Lord: for whom I have suffered the loss of all things and do count them but dung, that I may win Christ" (Phil. 3: 7-8).

But be warned, people on the 'broad way' will "think it strange that ye run not with them to the same excess of riot, speaking evil of you" (1 Pet. 4: 4).

"A wise man...built his house upon a rock"

Read Chapter 7: 15-29
In our previous study, we noticed that this chapter may be broadly divided into three sections: *(1)* instruction regarding relationships (vv.1-14); *(2)* identifying dangers (vv.15-23); *(3)* implementing His word (vv.24-29).

1) INSTRUCTION REGARDING RELATIONSHIPS, vv.1-14
We have already seen that the Lord deals with our relationships in five ways: *(a)* with our brethren (vv.1-5); *(b)* with the unregenerate (v.6); *(c)* with God (vv.7-11); *(d)* with others (v.12); *(e)* with the world (vv.13-14). This brings us to:

2) IDENTIFYING DANGERS, vv.15-23
In these verses we should note how *(a)* false prophets (vv.15-20) and *(b)* false profession (vv.21-23) can be identified. In the first case, the Lord says, "by their fruits ye shall know them" (v.20); in the second, He says, "Not every one that saith...but he that doeth the will of my Father which is in heaven" (v.21): it is not what people say, but what they do.

It has been suggested that one reason for the fact that "few" find the 'strait gate' and follow the 'narrow way' lies in the activities of false prophets and the danger of false, or easy, profession

a) Identifying false prophets, vv.15-20
We should notice *(i)* the impression they give (v.15); *(ii)* the identification (v.16); *(iii)* the illustrations (vv.16-19); *(iv)* the identification repeated (v.20). It has been said that if in vv.1-5 we are not to be critical, then in these verses we are not to be naïve! The Old Testament has a lot to say about false prophets. See, for example, Deuteronomy ch.13. They were men who "speak a vision of their own heart, and not out of the mouth of the Lord... they are prophets of the deceit of their own heart" (Jer. 23: 16, 26). The New Testament has this to say: "Beloved, believe not every spirit, but try the spirits whether they are of God: because many false prophets are gone out into the world" (1 John 4: 1).

i) The impression they create. "Beware of false prophets, which come to you in sheep's clothing, but inwardly they are ravening wolves" (v.15). It should be remembered that it isn't what a man looks like - genial, engaging, self-effacing and quite harmless - but what he believes that is all-important. The most dangerous aspect of false teaching is, at first sight, its resemblance to the truth. As R.V.G.Tasker observes, "It may well be some time before its pernicious elements are detected, and the teachers themselves shown up in their true colours". Paul highlights the same danger in speaking of "false apostles, deceitful workers, transforming themselves into the apostles of Christ...whose end shall be according to their works" (2 Cor. 11: 13-15).

Paul warned the elders from Ephesus of this very danger: "I know this, that after my departing shall grievous *wolves* enter in among you, not sparing the flock. Also of your own selves (that is, from among the ranks of the elders) shall men arise, speaking perverse things (twisted or distorted things), to draw away disciples *after them*" (Acts 20: 29-30). In the first case, the enemy seeks to destroy what exists: in the second he seeks to establish something new. The elders would face dangers from both outside and inside the church. Centuries before, Nehemiah faced dangers from within and without. See Nehemiah chs. 4-5. Paul prefaces his prediction by saying, "Take heed therefore unto yourselves, and to all the flock...to feed (tend) the church of God" (v.28), and concludes by saying, "Therefore watch, and remember, that by the space of three years I ceased not to warn every one night and day with tears" (v.31). Our great bulwark against false teaching is vigilant shepherd care, which includes sound teaching.

It should also be said that false teachers act surreptitiously. Jude emphasises this by saying, "For there are certain men crept in unawares" (Jude v.4). The words "crept in unawares" translate one word *(pareisduno)* meaning 'to enter in by the side *(para,* beside, *eis,* in), to insinuate oneself into, by stealth, to creep in stealthily' (W.E.Vine). Compare Galatians 2: 4, "False brethren unawares brought in" *(pareisaktos:* 'brought in secretly'), and 2 Peter 2: 1, "false teachers...who privily (as in Galatians 2: 4) shall bring in damnable heresies". False teaching always begins surreptitiously. Truth can always be proclaimed openly. The false teacher, like the thief and the robber, "climbeth up some other way" (John 10: 1). In 1 John 2: 18-19, the false teachers "went out from us". In Jude, they creep in! 'Admission has been secretly gained' (RSV).

Remember too that one feature of false teaching is the way in which it oversteps the word of God. "Whosoever transgresseth, and abideth not in the doctrine of Christ, hath not God" (2 John 9). The word "transgresseth" *(parabaino,* or in some manuscripts, *proago)* really means 'goes forward', and emphasises the fact that the false teachers are unwilling to remain with the truth, that is, to 'abide in the doctrine of Christ'. They think they know better. They can explain things far more clearly than these 'fundamentalist Christians'. False teachers have always got something new and additional to say. Remember as well that a false teacher is known, not only by what he says, but by what he does *not* say: "If there come any unto you, and bring not this doctrine, receive him not into your house, neither bid him God speed" (2 John 10). Notice John's expressions: "who confess not...abideth not...bring not" (2 John 7, 9, 10).

ii) The identification. "Ye shall know them by their fruits" (v.16). The "fruits" are described at length in 2 Peter 2. The chapter commences as follows: "But there were false prophets also among the people, even as there shall be false teachers among you, who privily shall bring in damnable heresies, even denying the Lord that bought them" (2 Pet. 2: 1). "Damnable" means 'destructive'. It does not mean loss of being, but loss of well-being. So false teaching causes disturbance and uncertainty; it invades the security and peace which truth provides. That's the first way in which false teaching can be recognised. The word "heresies" means, primarily, a choice and, so, an opinion leading to a division. This is the second way in which false teaching can be recognized: it divides God's people.

Peter continues by drawing attention to a further "fruit" of false teaching: "even denying the Lord that bought them". As you can see, the false teachers are not actually denying the death of Christ: they are denying the authority to which He is entitled in the lives of those for whom He died. Whilst Peter does not use the usual word for "Lord" (*kurios*), he does use a word (*despotes*) which conveys absolute authority. Compare 2 Timothy 2: 21, "meet for the *master's* use"; Jude v.4, "denying our only *master* and Lord, Jesus Christ" (RV).

Amongst other things, false teaching has moral implications, and these are stressed as well in 2 Peter 2. False teachers are described as "spots they are and blemishes, sporting themselves with their own deceivings while they feast with you; having eyes full of adultery, and that cannot cease from sin; beguiling unstable souls: an heart they have exercised with covetous practices; cursed children" (vv.13-14). There is much more. Read the entire chapter.

iii) The illustrations, vv.16-19. These are quite self-explanatory: "Do men gather grapes of thorns, or figs of thistles? Even so every good tree bringeth forth good fruit; but a corrupt tree bringeth forth evil fruit. A good tree cannot bring forth evil fruit, neither can a corrupt tree bring forth good fruit. Every tree that bringeth not forth good fruit is hewn down, and cast into the fire". Attention is drawn to the following:

- Good fruit cannot be *expected* from a corrupt source (vv.16-17). Just as good natural fruit cannot be expected from "thorns" and "thistles", so good spiritual fruit cannot be expected from fallen men, however religious. It is not without significance that the Lord should refer to "thorns" and thistles" here. They are evidence of the curse (Gen. 3: 18).

- Further to this, it is *impossible* for good fruit to be produced from a corrupt source: "A good tree *cannot* bring forth evil fruit, neither can a corrupt tree bring forth good fruit" (v.18). As true believers, we should "be filled with the fruits of righteousness which are by Jesus Christ, unto the glory and praise of God" (Phil 1: 11). We should display the "fruit of the Spirit" (Gal 5: 22-23).

- It is inevitable that false teachers will suffer divine judgment: "Every tree that bringeth not forth good fruit is hewn down, and cast into the fire" (v.19). John the Baptist preached the same message, though with a wider application. He uses identical language in Matt. 3: 10. Peter makes the same point in saying of false teachers that they "bring upon themselves swift destruction" (2 Pet. 2: 1). This is evidently the meaning of Paul's words, "If any man love not the Lord Jesus Christ, let him be Anathema Maran-atha" (1 Cor. 16: 22). The coming of the Lord Jesus ("Maran-atha") is the occasion of a solemn warning. Paul's use of "Anathema" here hardly refers to the disinterested world at large. Its use in Galatians 1: 8-9 supports the suggestion that Paul has false teachers particularly in view here: "But though we, or an angel from heaven, preach any other gospel unto you than that which we have preached unto you, let him be *accursed* (*anathema*). As we said before, so say I now again, If any man preach any other gospel unto you than that ye have received, let him be *accursed*".

iv) The identification repeated. "Wherefore by their fruits ye shall know them" (v.20). The Lord's repetition here emphasises that this is the true test of false teachers.

One of the "fruits" of false teaching is the type of people it produces, and this follows. We have only to think of the countless multitudes who rest on their 'church' membership and their religious activities for salvation. All this is the product of false teaching.

a) Identifying empty profession, vv.21-23.
In these verses we should notice the following: *(i)* profession is not enough (v.21); *(ii)* profession must be accompanied by practice (v.21); *(iii)* profession will be popular (v.22); *(iv)* profession will be exposed (v.23).

i) **Profession is not enough, v.21.** "Not every one that *saith* unto me, Lord, Lord, shall enter into the kingdom of heaven". R.V.G.Tasker points out that it is "not only false teachers who make the narrow way difficult to find and still harder to tread. A man may also be grievously self-deceived, and fondly imagine that he is walking along the right road when he is not. He may use the believer's vocabulary, repeat the believer's formulas, recite the believer's creed, and take part in the believer's activities, without being a real believer himself".

ii) **Profession must be accompanied by practice, v.21.** "Not every one that saith unto me, Lord, Lord, shall enter into the kingdom of heaven; but he that *doeth* the will of my Father which is in heaven". The Lord Jesus later censured the religious hierarchy for the glaring discrepancy between what they said and what they did: "they say and do not" (Matt. 23: 3). There was no such inconsistency in Him: in the words of Luke, "The former treatise have I made, O Theophilus, of all that Jesus began to do and teach" (Acts 1: 1). Do notice the order here: "do" first, then "teach". Paul urged Timothy: "Take heed unto thyself, and unto the doctrine ('teaching")" (1 Tim. 4: 16). The first part of the statement recalls 1 Tim. 4: 12, "Be thou an example of the believers.", and the second part recalls "give attendance to reading, to exhortation, to doctrine" (1 Tim. 4: 13). There was to be no discrepancy between Timothy's personal life, and Timothy's public ministry. Note the same combination in Acts 20: 24. What we say may be right, but are we right? It has been well said that we have been saved by faith alone, but that the faith that saves is not alone. See Ephesians 2: 8-10.

James puts it very clearly indeed. Here it is, without comment: "But be ye doers of the word, and not hearers only, deceiving your own selves. For if any be a hearer of the word, and not a doer, he is like unto a man beholding his natural face in a glass: for he beholdest himself, and goeth his way, and straightway forgetteth what manner of man he was. But whoso looketh into the perfect law of liberty, and continueth therein, he being not a forgetful hearer, but a doer of the work, this man shall be blessed in his deed" (James 1: 22-25).

iii) Profession will be popular, v.22. "*Many* will say to me in that day, Lord, Lord, have we not prophesied in thy name? and in thy name have cast out devils (demons)? and in thy name done many wonderful works?" It is noteworthy that the modern 'charismatic phenomenon', with all its excesses, claims to have prophets and the ability to perform miracles.

iv) Profession will be exposed, v.23. "And then will I profess unto them, I never knew you; depart from me, ye that work iniquity". They said that they knew Him (v.22), but He did not know them. Since they had spoken and acted in His name (v.22), He had every right to judge them. The "many wonderful works" (v.22) are nothing less than the work of people "that work iniquity". Wm.MacDonald makes the valid observation that 'we should learn from this verse that not all miracles are of divine origin, and that not all miracle workers are divinely accredited. A miracle simply means that a supernatural power is at work. That power may be divine, or it may be satanic'. To dispense with simple obedience to the Word of God in favour of such sensational phenomena is perilous. The Lord will 'remind them that He never knew them with favour or acknowledged them as His own' (Wm. Macdonald). True believers are the people of whom the Lord said, "I am the good shepherd, and know my sheep, and am known of mine" (John 10: 14), and of whom Paul said, "The Lord knoweth them that are his" (2 Tim 2: 19).

3) IMPLEMENTING HIS WORD, vv.24-29
The word "sayings" occurs twice in these well-known verses, and we should notice that in the first case, His "sayings" (v.24) must be acted upon (vv.24-27), while in the second (v.28) they caused astonishment (vv.28-29).

a) His sayings must be acted upon, vv.24-27
Very clearly, these verses extend the Lord's teaching in vv.21-23. Profession will be tested by the storms of life. Mere acquaintance with the Lord's teaching will avail nothing when trouble comes. But obedience to His word is evidence of spiritual reality which will stand the tests of life. At the same time, these verses form a fitting conclusion to the entire 'Sermon'. We should notice *(i)* the wisdom of obedience (vv.24-25) and *(ii)* the

foolishness of disobedience (vv.26-27). The Lord uses the word "house" as a symbol of our lives.

i) The wisdom of obedience. "Therefore whosoever heareth these sayings of mine, and doeth them, I will liken him unto a wise man, which built his house upon a rock: and the rain descended, and the floods came, and the winds blew, and beat upon that house; and it fell not: for it was founded upon a rock" (vv.24-25). We have already quoted James: "But be ye doers of the word, and not hearers only, deceiving your own selves" (James 1: 22). Joshua was to be a 'doer of the word': "This book of the law shall not depart out of thy mouth; but thou shalt meditate therein day and night, that thou mayest observe to *do* according to all that is written therein" (Jos. 1: 8). As J. Waldron points out, 'We need to be like Ezra who "prepared his heart to *seek* the law of the Lord, and to *do* it, and to *teach* in Israel statutes and judgments" (Ezra 7: 10). The Lord Jesus said, "If ye know these things, happy are ye if ye *do* them" (John 13: 17).

As Wm.MacDonald observes, 'We are not left to guess the identity of the wise man. It is *the disciple* who not only hears these teachings (chs.5-7) but does them (v.24). His life has a solid foundation. When the inevitable testings come from above ("the rain descended"), from the side ("the winds blew"), and from beneath ("the floods came"), he is able to endure because his life is firmly grounded'. As J.Heading observes, "Some expositors suggest that the rock foundation here is Christ, but we feel that the Lord had not developed His teaching sufficiently at that point in His ministry to reach these heights. Rather we believe that it is His moral and spiritual teaching that constitutes the rock".

ii) The foolishness of disobedience. "And every one that heareth these sayings of mine, and doeth them not, shall be likened unto a foolish man, which built his house upon the sand: and the rain descended, and the floods came, and the winds blew, and beat upon that house; and it fell: and great was the fall of it" (vv.26-27). Once again, Wm.MacDonald suggests that "the foolish man" is a disciple. This is both thought-provoking and challenging. "The foolish man is the disciple who hears Christ's teachings but instead of practising them, lives like the rest of the people around him. This man will not be able to stand against the storms of adversity. He buckles under the severe stresses of life. Though he may be saved as far as his soul is concerned, his life is wasted, his testimony is nil, and he suffers loss at the Judgment Seat of Christ".

G.H.Lang puts it as follows: 'The eternal salvation of the builder is not the issue. The lesson is this: that every man...is spending his life - his time, strength, means - in building a life structure, a character, an exhibition of himself; and this product of his energy will be severely tested, as a building, by a tempest. If it stands the test, the builder will have permanent advantage from his life-work; if it collapses, he will find that he has lived and toiled in vain'.

b) His sayings caused astonishment, vv.28-29
"And it came to pass, when Jesus had ended these sayings, the people were astonished at his doctrine: for he taught them as one having authority, and not as the scribes". He said, "Ye have heard...but *I* say unto you" (Matt 5: 21-22 etc). In the words of J.Waldron, 'We might also add that His words had authority because He himself lived out what He taught (Acts 1: 1)'. He taught them with authority here. He taught them with grace in Luke 4: 22.

The 'Sermon' commences, "And when he was set, his *disciples* came unto him: and he opened his mouth, and taught them" (5:1-2). The 'Sermon' concludes, "And it came to pass, when Jesus had ended these sayings, the *people* (crowds', JND) were astonished at his doctrine". Evidently the "people" also gathered round, but the 'Sermon' is none the less addressed principally to the Lord's disciples. It is pertinent to *us.*

THE GOSPEL OF MATTHEW

"Himself took our infirmities, and bare our sicknesses"

Read Chapter 8: 1-18
Having delivered what is commonly called 'The Sermon on the Mount', in which the Lord Jesus describes the character of His kingdom and of its subjects, He now presents what H.A.Ironside calls 'His royal credentials', and gives, in the words of Wm.MacDonald, who refers to Isaiah 35: 5-6, 'conclusive evidence to the nation of Israel that He is indeed the Messiah of whom the prophets had written'.

In Chapters 8-9, Matthew records ten miracles performed by the Lord Jesus. They fall into three groups: *(i)* the cleansing of the leper, the healing of the centurion's servant, and the healing of Peter's mother-in-law (8: 1-17); *(ii)* the stilling of the storm, the deliverance of the demoniac, and the raising of the paralytic (8: 23 - 9: 8); *(iii)* the healing of the woman with the issue of blood, the raising of the ruler of the synagogue's daughter, the healing of two blind men, and the healing of a demon-possessed dumb man (9: 18-34).

The first group of miracles is separated from the second by an account of two would-be followers of the Lord Jesus (8: 18-22). The two aspirants speak to the Lord after He had given orders to cross the sea (v.18) but before the actual embarkation (v.23), thus forming a bridge between the first and second groups of miracles. The second group of miracles is separated from the third by the call of Matthew and subsequent events (9: 9-17).

We must now consider the first of these three groups, in which the Lord demonstrates: *(1)* His power over leprosy (vv.1-4); *(2)* His power over paralysis (vv.5-13); *(3)* His power over fever (vv.14-18). All three are pictures of sin. The practical lessons should be noted: in the **first** case, cleansed people are to obey the Word of God; in the **second**, concerned people

Chapter 8

are to have faith in the Word of God; in the *third*, healed people are to be engaged in the service of God.

1) HIS POWER OVER LEPROSY, vv.1-4

The chapter commences with a contrast between the "great multitudes" that followed the Lord, and a single leper at His feet (Mark 1: 40). He was evidently one of the comparative few in Israel who recognised the Saviour's true identity. This recognition did not come by "flesh and blood", but by divine revelation. See Matthew 16: 17. Matthew Henry observes that 'This is fitly recorded with the first of Christ's miracles...because that the leprosy was looked upon, among the Jews, as a particular mark of God's displeasure; and therefore Christ, to show that He came to turn away the wrath of God, by taking away sin, began with the cure of a leper'.

The cleansing of the leper illustrates the way of salvation. The leper had to cry, "Unclean, unclean", and "without the camp shall his habitation be" (Lev.13:45-46). Leprosy severed him from the place where God dwelt amongst His people. Sin distances people from God, and if unforgiven, it will distance them from God eternally. Luke emphasises, with his doctor's eye, the dire condition of the man: "behold a man *full* of leprosy" (Luke 5: 12). The parallel passages are found in Mark 1: 40-45; Luke 5: 12-16. We ought to say at this juncture that as a general rule, time and space will not permit extensive quotations from the parallel passages or lengthy comments on them. But it is a good practice to read them, and notice how they differ in emphasis. Matthew emphasises the following:

a) How the leper came to Christ, v.2

"And, behold, there came a leper and worshipped him, saying, Lord, if thou wilt, thou canst make make clean". Neither the medical world nor the religious world could help him, reminding us that "Neither is there salvation in any other: for there is none other name under heaven given amongst men, whereby we must be saved" (Acts 4: 12). Only the Lord could cleanse from leprosy, and He alone can cleanse from sin. We should notice:

i) His atttitude in approaching Christ. Only Matthew, characteristically, tells us that the leper "worshipped him". See also 2: 11; 9: 18; 14: 33; 15: 25; 18: 26; 20: 20; 28: 9, 17. The word 'worship' here (*proskuneo*) comes from two words: *pros* meaning 'towards' and *kuneo*, meaning 'to kiss'. Matthew's use of the word evidently reflects his presentation of the Lord Jesus as "the King of the Jews". Let's just say that Mark and Luke emphasise that the leper knelt or fell down before the Saviour, reminding us that there is no room for pride or self-sufficiency in the presence of Christ. This is the first occasion in the New Testament on which He is addressed as "Lord". J.Waldron points out that the Gentile centurion did so as well (v.6), so that we have a Jew and a Gentile calling Him "Lord", reminding us that "there is no difference between the Jew and the Greek (standing for Gentiles): for the same Lord over all is rich unto all that call upon him" (Rom. 10: 12).

ii) **His confidence in the ability of Christ.** "Lord, if thou wilt, thou canst make me clean". The man came to the Lord Jesus in faith. The Saviour immediately shows, not only His ability, but His willingness to help the man:

b) **How the leper was cleansed by Christ, v.3**
"And Jesus put forth his hand and touched him, saying, I will; be thou clean. And immediately his leprosy was cleansed". We should notice:

i) **The touch of Christ.** He "put forth his hand, and touched him". Blessing came through personal contact. It still does. Others would have avoided the leper because he was unclean.

ii) **The voice of Christ.** We can hardly begin to imagine the leper's joy when he heard the Lord say, "I will; be thou clean". At the same time, we can hardly imagine the Saviour's joy that the man had every confidence in Him. He loves to respond to faith. It was to be so different later. He was obliged to say of Jerusalem, "How often would I have gathered thy children together...and ye would not!" (Matt. 23: 37).

iii) **The power of Christ.** He accomplished the cleansing. "And immediately his leprosy was cleansed". Salvation is just like that: "Believe on the Lord Jesus Christ, and thou shalt be saved" (Acts 16: 31).

c) **How the leper was commanded by Christ, v.4**
This brings us to the practical lesson of the section, which is that *cleansed people are to obey the Word of God:* "And Jesus saith unto him, See thou tell no man; but go thy way, shew thyself to the priest, and offer the gift that Moses commanded, for a testimony unto them".

The ceremony connected with the cleansing of the leper is described in Leviticus 14. Here is part of it: "And the priest shall go forth out of the camp; and the priest shall look, and, behold, if the plague of leprosy be healed in the leper; then shall the priest command to take for him that is to be cleansed two birds alive and clean, and cedar wood, and scarlet, and hyssop: and the priest shall command that one of the birds be killed in an earthen vessel over running water: as for the living bird, he shall take it, and the cedar wood, and the scarlet, and the hyssop, and shall dip them and the living bird in the blood of the bird that was killed over running water: and he shall sprinkle upon him that is to be cleansed seven times, and shall pronounce him clean, and shall let the living bird loose in the open field" (Lev. 14: 1-7).

God never gives meaningless instructions or meaningless details in His word. We must remember too that all the Old Testament sacrifices are, in some way, pictures of the death of the Lord Jesus. So the two birds must in some way tell us about Him. Without going into detail, the first bird reminds us of the incarnation and death of the Lord Jesus. The bird was "killed in an earthen vessel". The "running water", a picture of the Holy Spirit, reminds us that the Lord Jesus "through the eternal Spirit offered himself without spot to God (Heb. 9: 14). The second bird reminds us of the resurrection and ascension of Christ. Hebrews 9: 12 tells us that "by his own blood he entered in once into the holy place, having obtained eternal redemption for us".

When studying the detail of Leviticus 14, don't forget the absolutely vital lesson: "go thy way, shew thyself to the priest, and offer the gift that *Moses commanded, for a testimony unto them"*. In other words, *obey* the Word of God. But there is more: the words "for a testimony unto them" strongly suggest that the Lord Jesus was presenting His credentials to the priest. The cleansing of lepers was one sign that the kingdom of God had come (Matt. 11: 5). But there is no record of any response. While we are not told whether the leper went to the priest, we are certainly told that he disobeyed the first command, "See thou tell no man". As a result of this, "Jesus could no more openly enter into the city, but was without in desert places; and they came to Him from every quarter" (Mark 1: 45). Disobedience always hinders the Saviour's work.

2) HIS POWER OVER PARALYSIS, vv.5-13
If leprosy is a picture of sin, so is paralysis: see Romans 5: 6. 'The faith of a Gentile centurion is now introduced in striking contrast to the unreceptiveness of the Jews. If Israel will not welcome her King, the despised pagans will acknowledge Him' (Wm.MacDonald).

Matthew Henry puts it quaintly but nicely in saying: 'Now good old Simeon's word began to be fulfilled, that He (the Lord Jesus), should be "a light to lighten the Gentiles", as well as "the glory of thy people Israel"'. A parallel passage is found in Luke 7: 1-10.

Although Capernaum (v.5) was wonderfully privileged, the Lord was obliged to say, "And thou, Capernaum, which art exalted unto heaven, shalt be brought down to hell: for if the mighty works, which have been done in thee, had been done in Sodom, it would have remained unto this day" (Matt. 11: 23). Privilege incurs responsibility, and this principle applies to us all.

The miracle emphasises that distance did not limit the Lord's power to heal. Elijah and Elisha were both used by the Lord to perform miracles, but in each case they were in immediate contact with the beneficiaries. See, for example 1 Kings 17: 21; 2 Kings 4: 32-35. But this is not the case here. See also Mark 7: 29-30. The Lord Jesus is infinitely greater than all who preceded Him - and infinitely greater than all who followed Him!

a) The concern of the centurion, vv.5-6

"There came unto him a centurion, beseeching him (*parakaleo:* stronger than 'asking him')". The differences between Matthew and Luke's record (look them up) are usually explained by saying that the centurion, a Gentile (v.10), dealt with the Lord via intermediaries. It is worth pointing out that "every centurion mentioned in the New Testament showed integrity in his attitude and actions (Matt 27: 54; Acts 10: 22; 22: 26; 23: 17; 27: 43)" (N. Crawford). It has been said that this centurion must have belonged to the army of Herod Antipas since there were no Roman armies in Galilee before AD 44.

The man's concern for his servant is most commendable. He earnestly said ("beseeching"), "Lord, my servant lieth at home sick of the palsy (one word *paralutikos*), grievously tormented" (v.6). Luke has: "And a certain centurion's servant, who was dear unto him, was sick, and ready to die" (Luke 7: 2). This is all the more praiseworthy when we remember that the word "servant" means a bondservant or slave. How much do **we** value people? Nobody should be 'beneath us'. "Sick (*kakos*), and ready to die" reminds us of the perilous position of men and women without salvation. The Lord Jesus used the word "sick" (*kakos*) to describe the spiritual condition of men and women. See Luke 5: 31-32. He issued a solemn warning in saying, "if ye believe not that I am he, ye shall die in your sins" (John 8: 24). This can only lead to "the second death" (Rev 21: 8).

Chapter 8

While Matthew, unlike Luke, does not mention the centurion's good standing in the community, and his love for God's people which was expressed in building them a synagogue (see Luke 7:4-5), it is worth asking ourselves the questions, 'What kind of testimony do **we** have in the community? and 'How much do **we** love the people of God?'

b) The response of the Saviour, v.7
"And Jesus saith unto him, I will come and heal him". As we shall see, the centurion's faith did not require the personal presence of the Saviour, but the Lord's willingness to come must be noted. For the Lord to visit the centurion's home would breach the accepted practice of the day: Jews were not permitted to visit Gentile homes lest they should be defiled in some way.

c) The faith of the centurion, vv.8-9
"The centurion answered and said, Lord, I am not worthy that thou shouldest come under my roof: but speak the word only, and my servant shall be healed". While this can be understood as a matter of courtesy - the centurion did not wish to offend Jewish sensibilities over visiting Gentile homes – it has to be said that the Lord Jesus saw only the man's faith. We must notice three very important things here:

i) He acknowledged his own unworthiness. "Lord, I am not worthy that thou shouldest come under my roof". According to Luke, the Jews said that "he was **worthy** (*axios:* referring to weight) for whom he should do this" (Luke 7: 4), but the man himself said, "I am **not worthy** (*hikanos,* referring to sufficiency)" (v.8). Now there's an important difference! It applies when it comes to salvation, and it applies to everything else as well. We do not **deserve** God's blessing in any way! There are some interesting differences in the words used by Matthew and Luke and whilst this is all very interesting, we mustn't let the technicalities divert us from the simple point that the centurion was a humble man. John the Baptist said "I am not worthy (*hikanos*)", and the prodigal son said "I...am no more worthy (*axios*)" (Luke 3:16; 15: 21).

ii) He acknowledged the power of the Lord's word. "But speak the word (*logos*) only, and my servant shall be healed" (v.8). Since the centurion was stationed near Capernaum, he evidently knew that the Lord Jesus could speak with power. Some time before, the local people "were all amazed, and spake among themselves, saying, What a word *(logos)* is this! For with authority and power he commandeth the unclean spirits, and they come out. And the fame of him went out into every place of the country round about" (Luke 4: 36-37). Whilst we cannot be absolutely sure of the chronology, we do know that the Lord had healed a nobleman's son lying desperately ill at Capernaum, which was some distance from Cana where the Saviour was at the time. See John 4: 46-54. On the assumption that this had taken place before events in Matthew ch.8 and Luke ch.7, the centurion could have had no doubt about the Lord's ability to save his servant from death, and **we** should have no doubts about His ability to save men and women either.

This brings us to the practical lesson of these verses: We now learn that if in the case of the leper, **cleansed people are to obey the Word of God,** then in this case, **concerned people are to have faith in the Word of God.**

This is why we must never allow anything to either replace or rival the word of God. The word of God remains the agency by which men and women are "born again": "Seeing ye have purified your souls in obeying the truth… being born again, not of corruptible seed, but of incorruptible, by the word of God, which liveth and abideth for ever" (1 Pet. 1: 23). It is called "the word of reconciliation" and the "word of truth" (2 Cor. 5: 19; 6: 7). Do **we** have every confidence in the Word of God? The centurion did not ask for "a sign from heaven" (Luke 11:16): He simply believed that the Lord Jesus could heal his servant.

iii) He acknowledged the Lord's authority. "For I am a man under authority, having soldiers under me: and I say to this man, Go, and he goeth; and to another, Come, and he cometh; and to my servant, Do this, and he doeth it" (v.9). J.C.Ryle (writing on Luke) puts it beautifully: 'He regards our Lord as one possessing authority over diseases, as complete as his own authority over his soldiers, or a Roman emperor's authority over himself. He believes that a word of command from Jesus is sufficient to send sickness away'.

d) The response of the Saviour, vv.10-13
i) He "marvelled". "When Jesus heard it, he marvelled" (v.10). The demeanour of the centurion made a deep impression on the Lord Jesus. If you think that this is a most inaccurate observation, do remember that the fact that the Saviour "marvelled" emphasises the reality of His human

nature. He was "in all things...made like unto his brethren" (Heb 2: 17), apart from sin (Heb 4: 15), without for one moment ceasing to be God. No wonder Paul exclaims, "And without controversy great is the mystery of godliness: God was manifest in the flesh" (1 Tim. 3: 16). 'We must believe and admire, without attempting to define or explain' (J.C.Ryle). The Lord Jesus "marvelled" on two occasions. In Mark 6: 6, He "marvelled because of their unbelief", and here He "marvelled" at the centurion's faith. The reason follows:

ii) **He commented.** He "said to them that followed, Verily I say unto you, I have not found so great faith, no, not in Israel" (v.10). He added (this is peculiar to Matthew): "And I say unto you, That many shall come from the east and west, and shall sit down with Abraham, and Isaac, and Jacob, in the kingdom of heaven. But the children (*huios*, meanng 'sons') of the kingdom shall be cast out into outer darkness: there shall be weeping and gnashing of teeth (indicating extreme suffering)" (vv.11-12). In the words of Wm.MacDonald, 'Gentiles would flock from all over the world to enjoy fellowship with the Jewish patriarchs, while the sons of the kingdom would be thrown into the outer darkness where they would weep and gnash their teeth. "Sons of the kingdom" are those who were Jews by birth, who professed to acknowledge God as King, but who were never truly converted'. "Outer darkness" refers to exclusion from the presence of God.

What follows is also peculiar to Matthew: "And Jesus said unto the centurion, Go thy way; as thou hast believed, so be it done unto thee (v.13). We must remember that "without faith it is impossible to please him" (Heb. 11: 6). The nation of Israel had every reason to believe on Him, but failed to do so: "He came unto his own, and his own received him not" (John 1: 11). There was no lack of evidence for His claim to be the Son of God. When John the Baptist sent two of his disciples to the Lord Jesus with the question, "Art thou he that should come? Or do we look we for another?", they were sent back to the castle of Machaerus (according to Josephus 'the black fortress on the east side of Jordan, on the shores of the Salt Sea') with the message, "Go and shew John again those things which ye do hear and see" (Matt. 11: 4). Sadly we read, "But though he had done so many miracles before them, yet they believed not on him" (John 12: 37).

But here is a believing Gentile. A man with "so great faith" (v.10). The Lord Jesus only spoke of 'great faith' on one other occasion, and once again it was a Gentile. Not now a man, but a Syrophenician woman: "O woman, great is thy faith: be it unto thee even as thou wilt" (Matt. 15: 28). Both cases remind us that as a result of Israel's unbelief, "salvation is come to the Gentiles", although the Lord will ultimately be recognised and acknowledged by His own people (Rom. 11: 11-12).

iii) He acted. "And his servant was healed in the selfsame hour" (v.13). The Lord's word is always completely reliable. We can trust Him completely. Compare the healing of the Syrophenician woman's daughter (Matt. 15: 28) and the healing of the nobleman's son (John 4: 46-54). N.Crawford nicely comments that 'the servant never saw the One who healed him. Peter has this in mind in writing, "Whom having not seen, ye love; in whom though now ye see him not, yet believing, ye rejoice with joy unspeakable and full of glory" (1 Pet 1: 8)'.

Luke proceeds to show that the Lord Jesus was not only able to save from death: He was also able to save the dead! See Luke 7: 11-17. But Matthew turns to another instance of the Lord's ability to heal:

3) HIS POWER OVER FEVER, vv.14-18
We should notice **(a)** the miracle performed privately (vv.14-15); **(b)** the miracles performed publicly (vv.16-17); **(c)** the move across the lake (v.18).

a) The miracle performed privately, vv.14-15
"And when Jesus was come into Peter's house, he saw his wife's mother laid (so the first so-called 'Pope' had a wife! see 1 Cor. 9: 5), and sick of a fever. And he touched her hand (compare v.3), and the fever left her: and she arose, and ministered unto him" (vv.14-15). Parallel verses are found in Mark 1: 29-34 and Luke 4: 38-41. Luke, the doctor, notes that it was "a *great* fever", and describes the miracle itself in a little more detail: "And he *stood over* her, and rebuked the fever; and it left her: and immediately she arose (to the amazement, surely, of the doctor at such a rapid recovery of complete health), and ministered unto them (Luke 4: 38-39).

This brings us to the practical lesson of these verses. If in the case of the leper we learn that *cleansed people are to obey the Word of God*, and in the case of the centurion's servant that *concerned people are to have faith in the Word of God*, then in this case we learn that *healed people are to be engaged in the service of God*. 'As soon as He touched her, the fever vanished. Ordinarily, fever leaves a person greatly weakened, but this cure was so instantaneous and complete that she was able to get out of bed and serve Him. This was a fitting expression of gratitude for what the Saviour had done for her. We should imitate her, whenever we are healed, by serving Him with renewed dedication and vigour' (Wm. MacDonald).

b) The miracles performed publicly, vv.16-17
"When the even was come, they brought unto him many that were possessed with devils: and he cast out the spirits with his word, and healed all that were sick: that it might be fulfilled which was spoken by Esaias the prophet, saying, Himself took our infirmities, and bare our sicknesses" (vv.16-17). Once again, Luke tells us, with his doctor's mind, that "he laid his hands on *every one* of them, and healed them".

In the first case, Peter's mother-in-law was cured because, "they *tell him* of her" (Mark 1: 30). In the second case, many were healed because "they *brought unto him* all that were diseased" (Matt. 8: 16; Mark 1: 32). The lesson is clear. We, too, must tell the Lord Jesus about people, and we must bring people to Him.

We should notice that only Matthew quotes from the Old Testament (Isaiah 53: 4) at this juncture. R.V.G.Tasker points out that "the Greek words in Matthew's version, *elaben* and *ebastasen*, translated *took* and *bare*, could mean either 'carried' in the sense of 'bore the burden of', or 'carried away', i.e. 'removed the burden'". He continues, "The latter gives the better sense in the present context, for though Jesus bore the burden of men's sins, there is no evidence that He endured physical maladies on their behalf'. This is correct, but the Lord certainly 'bore the burden' of human infirmities in His deep grief and sympathy at the misery around Him. We read that "he was moved with compassion" (Matt. 9: 36 etc); "he sighed" (Mark 7: 34); "Jesus wept" (John 11: 35). In the cases mentioned, He then removed the cause of such infirmities. We must remember that He is still "touched with the feeling of our infirmities" (Heb. 4: 15)

c) The move across the lake, v.18
Matthew then tells us that "when Jesus saw the great multitude about him, he gave commandment to depart unto the other side" (v.18). Unlike the Pharisees (Matt. 6: 1, 5, 16), the Lord Jesus never sought plaudits of men.

We should notice that "*he* gave commandment to depart unto the other side". Although the Lord knew exactly what would happen on Galilee (vv.23-28), He still gave the disciples instructions to set sail - right into a "great tempest!".

The terrified disciples learnt a great deal that night, and the tempests of life bring us valuable lessons too. The Saviour knew exactly what He was doing in issuing instructions for the crossing. The tempest was a case of "the stormy wind fulfilling his word" (Psalm 148: 8).

"What manner of man is this"

Read Chapter 8: 19-27
As we have already noted, Matthew chs. 8-9 lay before us the 'royal credentials' of the King (H.A.Ironside). We have already considered His power *(i)* over leprosy (8: 1-4); *(ii)* over paralysis (8: 5-13); *(iii)* over fever (8: 14-18). We must now notice His authority *(1)* over the lives of His disciples (vv.19-22); *(2)* over the power of nature (vv.23-27); *(3)* over the bondage of Satan (vv.28-34).

1) OVER THE LIVES OF HIS DISCIPLES, vv.19-22
Perhaps having seen "great multitudes about him" (8: 18), and thinking that this was an opportunity to become part of a popular movement, "a certain scribe came, and said unto him, Master (Luke has "Lord"), I will follow thee whithersoever thou goest" (v.19). He was followed by "another of his disciples" who said, "Lord, suffer me first to go and bury my father" (v.21).

Mark does not include these verses. He is describing the perfect Servant! It should be said that Luke instances the desire of three people to follow him. See Luke 9: 57-62, where we learn that the Lord expects His followers to be ***pilgrims*** (vv.57-58), ***preachers*** (vv.59-60) and ***ploughmen*** (vv.61-62). The word "follow" occurs in connection with each category: "Lord, I will follow thee...Follow me...Lord, I will follow thee" (Luke 9: 57, 59, 61). John had rebuked a man for "casting out devils (demons)" because "he followeth not with us" (Luke 9: 49), and the Lord spells out the implications of following Him in some detail. In each case the cost of discipleship is made very clear. It is worth pointing out at this juncture that 'Luke does not tell us that these three incidents took place at the same time, but in putting them together, he is giving us a composite picture of true discipleship. Matthew puts the first two together, but omits the third one completely (Matt. 8: 18-22)' (N.Crawford). We must now concentrate on Matthew's two references: *(a)* the desire of the scribe (vv.19-20); *(b)* the desire of the disciple (vv.21-22). The man in the first case was too hasty: the man in the second case was too tardy.

Chapter 8

a) The desire of the scribe, vv.19-20
"And a certain scribe came, and said unto him, Master (*didaskalos*, meaning 'teacher'), I will follow thee whithersoever thou goest". As J.C.Ryle says (writing on Luke), 'It was a step in advance of many. Thousands of people heard our Lord's sermons who never thought of saying what this man said. Yet he who made this offer was evidently speaking without thought'. Hence, "And Jesus saith unto him, The foxes have holes, and the birds of the air have nests (roosting places); but the Son of man hath not where to lay his head". It is rather striking to notice that Peter said virtually the same thing as the scribe. See Luke 22: 33. The man here was quite unlike Ittai the Gittite, who weighed it all up in saying "In what place my lord the king shall be, whether in death or in life, even there also will thy servant be" (2 Sam. 15: 18-22).

This is the first reference in the New Testament to the Lord Jesus as "the Son of man" (the title occurs thirty-two times in Matthew), and it should be noted that the first and last references to the Lord in this way refer to His head: "The Son of man hath not where to lay his *head*" (Matt. 8: 20); "And I looked, and behold a white cloud, and upon the cloud one sat like unto the Son of man, having on his *head* a golden crown" (Rev. 14: 14). Need we say more?

We learn, therefore, that following Him involves *the surrender of comfort*. It means "enduring hardness" (2 Tim. 2: 3). Peter was well-aware of this: "Lo, we have left all, and have followed thee" (Luke 18: 28). This involved sharing His poverty. Peter followed the footsteps of the Saviour, who "became poor" (2 Cor. 8: 9), in saying "silver and gold have I none" (Acts 3: 6). The work of the Saviour meant that He had no home of His own. How much *are* we prepared to give up for Him? Caleb "wholly followed the Lord" (Joshua 14: 8, 9, 14). Peter "followed him afar off" (Matt. 26: 58). Are we tenaciously following Him? Ruth counted the cost: "Intreat me not to leave thee, or to return from following after thee: for whither thou goest I will go", and when Naomi "saw that she was stedfastly minded to go with her, then she left speaking unto her" (Ruth 1: 16-18). How resolute is *our* discipleship? Hebrews 11 gives us examples of those who were willing to endure privation and hardship because they were "strangers and pilgrims on the earth" (Heb. 11: 13).

b) The desire of the disciple, vv.21-22
"And another of his disciples said unto him, Lord, suffer me first to go and

bury my father. But Jesus said unto him, follow me; and let the dead bury their dead". Luke has "And he said unto another (*heteros,* meaning a different kind of person), Follow me. But he said, Lord, suffer me first to go and bury my father. Jesus said unto him, Let the dead bury their dead: but go thou and preach the kingdom of God" (Luke 9: 59-60). We now learn that following Him involves **the surrender of family.**

It is usually pointed out that it is highly unlikely that the Lord Jesus was banning a man from attending his father's funeral! We know that He insisted that the care of elderly parents is a God-given duty which must not be avoided under any religious pretext whatsoever. See Matt. 15: 3-9. The usual view is therefore that the man's father was elderly and that his son was asking for permission to delay following the Lord Jesus until his father was dead. In other words, his father had a greater claim on his life than the Lord Jesus. This agrees with the Lord's words, "If any man come to me, and hate not ('give second place to, and if need be, to let go', D.Gooding) his father, and mother, and wife, and children, and brethren, and sisters, yea, and his own life also, he cannot be my disciple" (Luke 14: 26). The prior claim on our lives are the interests of the Lord Jesus. But the man said, **"Lord,** suffer **me first".** There is a certain emphasis on "**my** father". "Lord" and "me first" are a contradiction in terms! Rather like "Not so, Lord" (Acts 10: 14). Paul expressed the reverse: "Not I, but Christ" (Gal 2: 20).

The situation is illustrated in the life of Abraham. God had said to Abraham, "Get thee out of thy country, and from thy kindred, and from thy father's house, unto a land that I will shew thee" (Gen 12: 1). But "Terah took Abram his son (the complete reverse of God's command)…and they came unto Haran and dwelt there. And the days of Terah were two hundred and five years: and Terah died in Haran" (Gen. 11: 31-32). Abraham (or Abram as he was called then) waited till his father was dead before he fulfilled God's command! There was certainly no discussion when the Lord called James and John: "and straightway he called them: and they **left their father** Zebedee in the ship with the hired servants, and followed him" (Mark 1:19-20).

The explanation 'Let the (spiritually) dead, bury the (physically) dead' does not seem awfully satisfying, although the word "dead" is used in both senses in John 5: 21-25. It seems more probable that the Saviour meant 'Let those in close and immediate contact with the dead person make arrangements for their burial'. Norman Crawford puts it like this: 'Many a servant of Christ has been compelled to give "the things of the Lord" (1 Cor. 7: 32-33) priority over legitimate and earthly ties, such as those who go far from home and loved ones to carry the gospel to the ends of the earth. At times, they have said goodbye to a beloved father and mother, never expecting to see them again in this life'. We should also remember that many of God's children have given the Lord's interests first place in the teeth of gale force adversity from their own family circle. The Lord Jesus knew all about this, for there was a time when "neither did his brethren believe in him?" (John 7: 5). How real are His claims in *our* lives?

For the sake of *completeness on the subject*, attention is drawn to Luke 9: 61-62: "And another *(heteros)* also said, Lord, I will follow thee; but let me first go bid them farewell, which are at home at my house. And Jesus said unto him, No man, having put his hand to the plough, and looking back, is fit for the kingdom of God". (Compare 1 Kings 19: 20). We now learn that following Him involves **the surrender of friends.** It is impossible to serve Christ with a divided heart. Whilst Paul is referring to a soldier on active service in saying "No man that warreth entangleth himself with the affairs of this life" (2 Tim 2: 4), the same principle is applicable here. A ploughman who takes his eye off the fixed object at the far end of the field, inevitably loses direction and his work is impaired. The disciple who becomes distracted from his service by past friendships and family ties will soon be ineffective in the Lord's service. If we keep looking back, it will not be long before we go back. Paul said, "this one thing I do" (Phil. 3: 13). This man, like his predecessor, said "Lord...me first". Once again there is a certain emphasis on "*my* house". We must leave it there! Except to say that the Lord Jesus was the supreme example of His own ministry. He was thoroughly acquainted with the hardships His disciples would experience (Luke 9: 58): He left home and family in order to "preach the kingdom of God" (Luke 9: 60): He was not distracted or diverted in His service (Luke 9: 62). He has left us "an example" that we "should follow his steps" in every way (1 Pet. 2: 21).

2) OVER THE POWER OF NATURE, vv.23-27
We should notice at least four things here *(a)* the destination (v.23); *(b)* the danger (v.24); *(c)* the despair (v.25); *(d)* the deliverance (vv.26-27). Do notice that the narrative begins with the words, "his disciples followed him": there's the link with the previous verses. As we shall see, it led them straight into a storm! How often that happens!

Matthew

a) The destination, v.23

"And when he was entered into a ship, his disciples followed him". Luke has, "Now it came to pass on a certain day, that he went into a ship with his disciples: and he said unto them, Let us go over unto **the other side** of the lake. And they launched forth" (Luke 8: 22). The "other side" is identified as "the country of the Gadarenes, which is over against Galilee" (Luke 8: 26). Having completed His work there, "Jesus...returned" (Luke 8: 40) to the western side of Galilee. Quite obviously then, His purpose in visiting Gadara, was to help the demon-possessed man there. The Lord Jesus took the initiative: "he said unto them, Let us go over". He took the initiative in our case too!

Peter describes the work of the Lord Jesus as follows: "Who went about doing good, and healing all that were oppressed of the devil: for God was with Him" (Acts 10: 38). He came to "destroy the works of the devil" (1 John 3: 8). We mustn't think that all this belongs to the past. People are still in captivity to Satan. See, for example Eph 2: 2 and 1 John 5: 19 margin. The Lord Jesus made a journey across Galilee to help a poor man who was completely enslaved by Satan. But the journey was really much longer than that. He came from heaven to save the man, and **us,** from Satan's power.

How far are we prepared to travel in the interests of men and women? The furthest most of us are called to go, is to our own town. But are we prepared to go even as far as that? Did you say that you were too tired after a busy day, or after a busy week? Just read on.

Mark gives us a little piece of extra information: "And there were also with him other little ships" (Mark 4: 36), but the subsequent narrative centres, as in Matthew and Luke, on just one ship. The other ships are not mentioned again. Commentators assume that they, too, were engulfed by the storm, but were they? Or was the storm directed against one ship only? And if so, why? Perhaps we shouldn't read too much into the detail, but it *is* tempting! This brings us to:

b) The danger, v.24

"And behold, there arose a great tempest in the sea, insomuch that the ship was covered with the waves: but he was asleep". The Sea of Galilee is subject to sudden storms. It is some seven hundred feet below sea level, and the surrounding heights are 'furrowed with ravines like funnels down which winds rush with great velocity' (A.Plummer). This storm was unusually fierce. That much is perfectly clear. Matthew uses a most unusual word to describe the storm: "And behold, there arose a great **tempest** in the sea". The word "tempest" translates the Greek word *'seismos'*, from which come our 'seismic' and 'seismology', relating to earthquakes. In fact *'seismos'* is rendered "earthquake" everywhere else in the New Testament! The storm on the lake now appears to be very unusual indeed. It was evidently caused by fierce winds from above, and an earthquake or earth tremor from beneath. Satan was certainly behind the "great wind from the wilderness" which destroyed Job's family (Job 1: 19), and it is not without significance that he is called the "prince of the power of the air" (Eph. 2: 2). Whilst it is not specifically stated, there does *seem* to be grounds for concluding that the storm on the lake was another Satanic attempt to destroy the Lord Jesus.

The reason is not difficult to establish. Satan's dominion was under attack: the house of the "strong man" was being spoiled (Matt. 12: 28-29). At that very moment, the Saviour was *en route* to Gadara where He would free two men from Satan's power. We should not therefore be surprised when we encounter difficulties in spreading the gospel of Christ. See, for example 1 Thess. 2: 18, "Wherefore we would have come unto you, even I Paul, once and again; but **Satan hindered us**". There was a happy outcome to this: instead of going to Thessalonica, Paul wrote two letters that tell us about the return of Christ. There was a happy outcome to the tempest on Galilee. The Lord allowed it to take place, first to test the faith of the disciples, and then to prove that His power was greater than any storm. All this should remind us, when the hindrances and difficulties come, that "**greater** is he that is in you, than he that is in the world" (1 John 4: 4).

c) The despair, v.25
The storm-tossed ship presents an amazing contrast: "He was asleep...And his disciples came to him, and awoke him, saying, Lord (Luke has "Master, master"), save us: we perish". Mark has, "Master, carest thou not that we perish?" (Mark 4: 38). Jonah also slept in a boat during a storm (Jonah 1: 5), but "behold, a greater than Jonas is here"! (Matt 12: 41). (This contrast is 'ripe for development!'). Mark tells us that the Lord "was in the hinder part of the ship, asleep on a pillow" (Mark 4: 38).

i) The Saviour was asleep. "He was asleep". Only Luke says "he **fell** asleep": Luke always emphasises the perfect humanity of the Lord Jesus. We know from Psalm 121, that "He that keepeth Israel neither slumbers nor sleeps" (Psalm 121: 4). God is above His creation: He does not sleep. But the Lord Jesus is "God...manifest in the flesh" (1 Tim. 3: 16). In incarnation, without resigning for one moment, or in the slightest degree, His eternal deity, He deliberately took perfect humanity. He is "the man Christ Jesus" (1 Tim. 2: 5), and displayed this in His weariness, hunger and thirst. Quite clearly, none of these things are the result of sin.

The Lord Jesus could say more than any other, "I will both lay me down in peace, and sleep, for thou, Lord, only makest me to dwell in safety" (Psalm 4: 8). The words, "He giveth his beloved sleep" (Psalm 127: 2), are so appropriate when used of the Lord Jesus. He was able to sleep in perfect assurance of His Father's safekeeping.

ii) **The disciples were agitated.** "And his disciples came to him, and awoke him, saying, Lord, save us: we perish". It wasn't that they accused the Lord Jesus of sitting idly by and doing nothing to save them from drowning. It seemed to them that **everybody** on board was about to go down with the boat, but He appeared completely unconscious and unconcerned by imminent death. It was quite clear that the disciples had no idea that their Master was quite capable of dealing with the situation, although, it has to be said, they did say "Lord, Save us".

On a technical note, and we do need to pay attention to them, comparison will show that Matthew, Mark, and Luke, differ in their records at this point. Matthew says, "Lord, (*kurie*) save us: we perish." Mark says, "Master, (*didaskale*, meaning 'teacher') carest thou not that we perish?". Luke says, "Master, Master (*epistata*), we perish?" N.Crawford explains: 'It was "they", the disciples who came to Him, and all three forms of address were used, each one addressing the Lord according to their own appreciation of Him and their need'.

Life is full of storms, and the older you grow, the fiercer they become. Sometimes, circumstances seem just too much for us handle. This was just how the disciples felt: little did they know that their boat was unsinkable, even though it was filled with water. It was unsinkable because the Lord Jesus was on board. He was apparently doing nothing to help the situation, not even sitting shoulder to shoulder with them in the storm, but the fact that He was there made deliverance certain. Centuries before, God had said, "Fear not: for I have redeemed thee, I have called thee by thy name; thou art mine. **When thou passest through the waters**, I will be with thee; and through the rivers, they shall not overflow thee" (Isaiah 43: 1-2). The Lord Jesus says, "I will never leave thee, nor forsake thee" (Heb. 13: 5). Sometimes, He *appears* to be doing nothing - apparently asleep in our lives - letting things happen that we can't understand. But His very presence with us guarantees that even the greatest difficulties cannot destroy us, and at the right moment, He will prove that He is in complete control. We need to do only one thing - trust Him. The disciples were gently rebuked, because they didn't: "Why are ye so fearful, O ye of little faith?" (v.26). Years later, Peter wrote: "Casting all your care upon him, for he careth for you" (1 Pet. 5: 7). Perhaps he was thinking of that anguished cry on Galilee, "Carest Thou not that we perish?" (Mark 4: 38). If so, he had learnt that the Saviour *did* care.

It has been beautifully said that 'the violence of the storm did not awaken Him, but the cries of His disciples aroused Him immediately. A mother may sleep through a thunderstorm, but the faintest whimper of her baby instantly awakens her from rest' (H.S.Paisley).

d) The deliverance, vv.26-27
i) **He rebuked the disciples**. "And he saith unto them, Why are ye so fearful, O ye of little faith?" (v.26). Faith and fear are mutually exclusive. Matthew puts this first: Mark and Luke put this *after* he had rebuked the wind and sea. In Luke's record, "And he said unto them, Where is your faith?" (Luke 8: 25). The disciples had so much evidence that He was the Son of God, and in view of this how could *He* ever be drowned? Their faith had given way under pressure. Faith had given place to 'fearfulness' or, as the word (*deilos*) means, 'cowardice and timidity' (W.E.Vine). But it would be quite wrong for us to sit in judgment on the disciples. Perhaps the Saviour says *to us*, "Why are ye so fearful, O ye of little faith?" He may not still the storms in our lives, but He can control their effect on us. In the midst of the storms of life (caused by business, health, family, and so many other things) He still says: "Peace I leave with you, my peace I give unto you...Let not your heart be troubled, neither let it be afraid" (John 14: 27).

ii) He rebuked the storm. "Then he arose, and rebuked the wind and the sea ("the raging of the water", Luke 8: 24); and there was a great calm" (v.26). There is a distinct sense of calm dignity and authority in the words, "Then he arose". He actually stood in the storm-tossed waterlogged boat! The use of the word "rebuke" (*epitimao*) may suggest that the Lord 'treated the violent forces of nature as demonic' (R.H.Mounce). The "great tempest" (v.24) was followed by "a great calm". All that the Lord ever did was complete! The blind man saw... clearly" (Mark 8: 25); the dumb man "spake plain" (Mark 7: 35). Luke says, simply, "there was a calm" (Luke 8: 24). Mark has the well loved words, "Peace, be still" (Mark 4: 39), which are rather stronger than the English translation suggests! "Peace" is really 'Silence': "be still" is really, 'be muzzled'. The latter is used in Matt 22: 34 and 1 Pet 2: 15, but rendered "silence" in the AV. The Lord Jesus fulfilled Psalm 89: 9: "Thou rulest the raging of the sea: when the waves thereof arise, thou stillest them". Then there's Psalm 93: 4: "The Lord on high is mightier than the noise of many waters, yea, than the mighty waves of the sea". See also Psalm 107: 23-30 which describes the experiences of men "that go down to the sea in ships, that do business in great waters". These mariners proved that after crying "unto the Lord in their trouble...he bringeth them out of their distresses. He maketh the storm a calm, so that the waves thereof are still". But they never saw anything like this! It has been frequently pointed out that the sea does not automatically become calm when the wind drops. It takes some time for the swell to cease. In this case, the wind dropped, and the sea became calm immediately. It was the touch of the Creator Himself. The very God who said, "Let the waters under the heaven be gathered together in one place...and the gathering together of the waters called he Seas" (Gen. 1: 9-10), was present on the Sea of Galilee. He 'spoke' creation into existence: He spoke again, and creation immediately obeyed. It had no alternative.

We have seen the Lord Jesus "asleep", and we have seen Him silencing the storm. In the first case, we have watched a perfect Man, who displayed all the usual human characteristics - sin apart - in His life. Here, He slept. In the second case, we have watched the Creator-God. He displayed the attributes of deity. But He was not a dual personality. He was as much **God** when "he was asleep", as He was **Man** when He "rebuked the winds and the sea". The Lord Jesus is God and man in one unique Person. He is "Emmanuel...God with us" (Matt. 1: 23).

iii) **The effect on the disciples.** "But the men marvelled, saying, What manner of man is this, that even the winds and the sea obey him?" (v.27). (Compare "what manner of love", 1 John 3: 1; "what manner of persons ought ye to be", 2 Pet. 3: 11). Luke tells us that one kind of fear gave place to another: "And they, being afraid ("they feared exceedingly", Mark 4: 41), wondered, saying one to another, What manner of man is this! For he commandeth even the winds and water, and they obey him" (Luke 8: 25). The trembling of the disciples here is attributable to the calm, and not to the storm. "And they being afraid wondered" as they asked the question,

"What manner of man is this!" Fear, in the usual sense of the word, gave place to reverential awe.

3) OVER THE BONDAGE OF SATAN, vv.28-34
We will consider these verses in our next study, God willing.

"There met him two possessed with devils"

Read Chapter 8: 28-34
As we have already noted in at least two previous studies, Matthew chs. 8-9 lay before us the 'royal credentials' of the King (H.A.Ironside). We have already considered His power *(i)* over leprosy (8: 1-4); *(ii)* over paralysis (8: 5-13); *(iii)* over fever (8: 14-18), together with the fact that His authority is emphasised again in vv.19-34 as follows: *(1)* over the lives of His disciples (vv.19-22); *(2)* over the power of nature (vv.23-27); *(3)* over the bondage of Satan (vv.28-34).

1) OVER THE LIVES OF HIS DISCIPLES, vv.19-22
When the "scribe" said, "Master I will follow thee whithersoever thou goest", the Lord replied, "The foxes have holes, and birds of the air have nests; but the Son of man hath not where to lay his head" (vv.19-20). When "another of his disciples" said, "Lord, suffer me first to go and bury my father, the Lord replied, "Follow me; and let the dead bury their dead" (vv.21-22). We considered this in our last study.

2) OVER THE POWER OF NATURE, vv.23-27
We also considered this in our last study. The chorus in the old Sankey hymn, "Master the tempest is raging" (number 61), puts it beautifully:

> *The winds and waves shall obey My will!*
> *Peace!...be still!...*
> *Whether the wrath of the storm-tost sea,*
> *Or demons, or men, or whatever it be,*
> *No waters can swallow the ship where lies*
> *The Master of ocean, and earth, and skies:*
> *They all shall sweetly obey My will;*
> *Peace! be still! Peace! Be still!*
> *They all shall sweetly obey My will;*
> *Peace! peace! be still!*

3) OVER THE POWER OF SATAN, vv.28-34

The violent storm on Galilee was followed by the violent men in Gadara. The Bible describes a Christian in many ways. Here is one of them: "If any man be in Christ, he is a new creature (creation): old things are passed away; behold, all things are become new" (2 Cor 5: 17). This was certainly true of the Gadarene demoniacs. Their captivity to Satan's power gave place to liberty through Christ. We should notice *(a)* captivity to Satan (v.28); *(b)* liberty through Christ (vv.29-32); *(c)* testimony to others (vv.33-34).

a) Captivity to Satan, v.28

Justin Waldron suggests that we can look at this incident in three different ways: firstly, it shows us what society does: it restrains, isolates and threatens. Secondly, it shows us what Satan does: he robs men of self-control, friends and family, and condemns them to judgment. Thirdly, it shows us what Christ can do: He braved the storm to reach the men, and then He saved them by His word!

"And when he was come to the other side, into the country of the Gergesenes (or Gadarenes, RV: see JND margin), there met him two possessed with devils, coming out of the tombs, exceeding fierce, so that no man might pass that way." It is not without significance that Mark has, "And when he was come out of the ship, *immediately* there met him out of the tombs a man with an unclean spirit" (Mark 5: 2). The words "immediately...straightway... forthwith...anon" (*eutheos*) punctuate Mark's gospel, emphasising the promptitude coupled with calm dignity with which the Saviour went about His service. But we now learn that Satan can also be quick! See Mark 4: 15. His servants can be quick too! See Mark 6: 25,27.

It should be noted that Matthew tells us that there were two men, whereas Mark (5: 1-20) and Luke (8: 26-40) mention only one. It is usually said that Mark and Luke evidently refer only to the most prominent of the two, but a better explanation (Gareth Armstrong) suggests just as only one leper out of the ten returned to glorify God and give thanks to the Lord Jesus (Luke 17: 12-19), this may be the case here. Although two men were healed by the Lord, Mark and Luke concentrate on the man who desired to follow Him. We should notice that Matthew does not mention the way in which the Lord was worshipped, and for this information we are indebted to Mark and Luke: "When he saw Jesus afar off, he ran and worshipped him" (Mark 5: 6, cf. Luke 8: 28), leading Matthew Henry to say, 'He usually *ran upon* others with *rage,* but he *ran to* Christ with *reverence!*' We should notice the following:

Chapter 8

i) They were "possessed with devils". Mark, mentioning, as noted, only one man, describes him as "a man with an unclean spirit". (Mark 5: 2). He wasn't simply a mental case. This may have been a result, but as John Heading *(What the Bible Teaches - Matthew)* observes, 'We must always distinguish demon possession from mental disorder, which results from minute physical disorders of the brain'. Matthew makes it clear that Satan completely controlled both lives, and the state of the poor men provides us with an illustration of his power. Paul reminded the believers at Ephesus that they once "walked...according to the prince of the power of the air, the spirit that now worketh in the children of disobedience" (Eph. 2: 2). John tells us that 'the whole world lies in the wicked [one]" (1 John 5: 19, JND). Worse lies ahead. Read Revelation 12: 7-12; 13: 1-18.

Luke, referring to only one man, adds that he "had devils *a long time*" and "wear no clothes" (Luke 8: 27). This reminds us that Satan deprives men and women of their decency. The Lord Jesus refers to "the shame of thy nakedness" (Rev 3: 18). Men and women shamelessly indulge in sin.

ii) They came "out of the tombs". Both Mark and Luke make it clear that they lived "among the tombs" (Mark 5: 3; Luke 8: 27). 'These graves consisted of caves or holes hewn out of solid rock, and so lent themselves excellently as dwellings' (supplied by J.Waldron). A cemetery only reminds us of one thing. We now have a further illustration of the sorry state of sinful men. They are "dead in trespasses and sins" (Eph. 2: 1). Death is never annihilation: it is always *separation;* "being alienated from the life of God" (Eph. 4: 18). The demoniacs lived in the atmosphere of death, and that is precisely the position of unregenerate humanity today. But how few recognise the stark reality of their position! We should also add:

iii) They were uncontrollable. "They were exceeding fierce, so that no man might pass that way". But the Lord Jesus deliberately passed "that way!" (Timothy Miller). Satanic power could not stop Him and in any case, He had come to "destroy (undo) the works of the devil" (1 John 3: 8). Mark, referring to the one man only, tells us that "no man could bind him, no, not with chains: because he had been often bound with fetters and chains, and the chains had been plucked asunder by him, and the fetters broken in pieces: neither could any man tame him" (Mark 5: 3-4). Luke reads similarly: "he was kept bound with chains and in fetters; and he brake the bands", adding, "and was driven of the devil into the wilderness" (Luke 8: 29). In other words, he was beyond human control: not even brute force could pacify

Matthew

him. There was no human solution to the problem. Satan's power was just too great. The sons of Sceva proved this. When they attempted to exorcise an evil spirit, the man concerned "leaped on them, and overcame them, and prevailed against them, so that they fled out of that house naked and wounded" (Acts 19: 13-16). Satan's power is too strong for men to handle. No wonder the Lord Jesus called him "a strong man" (Luke 11: 21). The demon-possessed man was "driven of the devil into the wilderness", but the Lord Jesus was driven by the Holy Spirit "into the wilderness" (Mark 1: 12). It would be profitable to develop the contrast!

Matthew emphasises the danger that the two men posed *to others*: "They were exceeding fierce, so that **no man might pass that way**". Mark emphasises that the man on whom he concentrates was a danger *to himself*: he was "always…crying and cutting himself with stones" (Mark 5: 5). The inner torment of the man resulted in physical damage. Satan's power is damaging and harmful. He causes incalculable moral and spiritual injury, and if this is allowed to continue, it will result in eternal pain.

b) Liberty through Christ, vv.29-32
"And, behold, they cried out, saying, What have we to do with thee, Jesus, thou Son of God? Art thou come hither to torment us before the time?", reminding us that "the devils (demons) also believe, and tremble (*phrisso*, meaning 'shudder')", (James 2: 19). "And there was a good way off from them, an herd of many swine, feeding. So the devils besought him, saying, If thou cast us out, suffer us to go away into the herd of swine. And he said unto them, Go. And when they were come out, they went into the herd of swine: and, behold, the whole herd of swine ran violently down a steep place into the sea, and perished (not the usual *apollumi*, 'to perish', but *apothnesko*, 'to die') in the waters". But the Lord's sheep will never perish! See John 10: 28. One outstanding difference between Matthew's record and those of Mark and Luke, is the fact that the men scarcely get a mention at this stage in his narrative! That must be significant! Matthew stresses the presence of the King! The entire emphasis is on the effect of the Lord's word to the demons. No mention of the vast change in the two men, something emphasised by Mark (5: 15) and Luke (Luke 8: 35).

Whilst the men's voices were heard ("behold, they cried out"), it does seem that it was the demons who were speaking. Compare Luke 8: 28-30: "He cried out…and with a loud voice, said, What have *I* to do with thee, Jesus, thou Son of God most high? *I* beseech thee, torment me not (For he had commanded the unclean spirit to come out of the man…). And Jesus asked him, saying, What is *thy* name? And he said, Legion: because *many* devils were entered into him. And *they* besought him that he would not command *them* to go out into the deep". It therefore appears that Legion was the principal demon. Compare Mark 5: 6-9. (Compare Luke 8: 2 and 11: 26 which give two other cases of multiple demon-possession).

Once again, the details are absorbing. *Firstly,* the demons are actual beings: they are not mere influences. *Secondly*, the identity of the men is practically submerged in the identity of the demons. *Thirdly*, demon-possession and Christ are mutually exclusive: "What have we to do with thee, Jesus, thou Son of God?" This should be sufficient warning against any involvement with spiritism. *Fourthly*, the demon acknowledged the identity of the Lord Jesus. It is sobering to note again (compare Luke 4: 33-34) that demons recognised Him, but men did not. *Fifthly,* note the full title, "Jesus, thou Son of God". Luke has "Jesus Son of the Most High God" (Luke 8: 28, JND). This is explained in Gen 14: 19. The full weight of this title will become evident when He reigns on earth. *Sixthly,* the demons anticipated divine judgment: "art thou come hither to torment us before the time": compare Luke 8: 31 "they besought him that he would not command them to go out into the deep" ('the bottomless pit', JND). So they knew what would ultimately happen to them, and when it would happen. Demons are aware of their ultimate destiny. "Everlasting fire" is "prepared for the devil *and his angels*" (Matt. 25: 41). This is why the demons spoke of coming "torment". They were aware that a time of reckoning was coming.

Matthew Henry makes four observations in connection with the name, "Legion" as it occurs in Mark's Gospel. 'Now this intimates that the devils are *military powers*. The devils war against God and His glory, Christ and His gospel, men and their holiness and happiness. *They are numerous:* he owns, or rather he boasts, "we are many", as if he hoped to be too many for Christ Himself to deal with. *They are unanimous*: they are many devils, and yet but one legion engaged in the same wicked cause. *They are very powerful*: who can stand before a legion?'

At first glance, it seems rather strange that the Lord Jesus should give the demons permission to possess the "herd of many swine" (numbering about two thousand, Mark 5: 13). The animal rights movement would launch an immediate protest! John Heading observes that as a result of demon-possession, 'the behaviour of the swine was worse than the two men; the demons tormented and destroyed the swine'. It could be argued that the death of the pigs was nothing less than divine judgment on the owners for contravening Leviticus 11: 7; Deuteronomy 14: 8, but this assumes that the owners of the swine were Jews. We are told that there were a considerable number of non-Jewish people living in the area. The sight of the demon-possessed swine rushing madly into the lake, would certainly assure the healed man that his deliverance was complete. We might add that demons evidently desire to be embodied, a fact which *might* shed some light on Genesis 6: 1-4.

Once again, the details are absorbing. Notice that the demons did not turn to their dark master, the devil, for orders: they made their request to Christ. "So the devils besought him...." (v.31). The demons knew where ultimate authority lay. Bearing in mind that pigs were unclean animals, it was most appropriate that unclean spirits should possess unclean animals! We can only conjecture what happened to the demons, but see Luke 11: 24-26.

c) Testimony to others, vv.33-34
"And they that kept them fled, and went their ways into the city, and told everything, and what was befallen to the possessed of the devils. And, behold, the whole city came out to meet Jesus: and when they saw him, they besought him that he would depart out of their coasts". The loss of the pigs seems to have been paramount in the minds of the swineherds who, presumably, belonged to the non-Jewish population of the district. The man himself was just an afterthought! Pigs were evidently more important than people. Not only so, the Gadarenes were more concerned about their pigs than they were about their souls. See the **addendum.** In the Old Testament, king Ahab was far more interested in his animals than he was in his subjects. See 1 Kings 18: 5.

Notice, again, that Matthew makes no reference to the fact that they "came to Jesus, and found the man, out of whom the devils were departed, sitting at the feet of Jesus, clothed, and in his right mind: and they were afraid" (Luke 8: 35). Luke's threefold description of the man at this point makes a profitable little study in itself.

Luke tells us that "They also which saw it told them by what means he that was possessed of the devils was healed" (Luke 8: 36). Years later, Paul wrote to the Thessalonians in connection with their testimony in Macedonia and Achaia, and beyond: "For they themselves shew of us what manner of entering in we had unto you, and how ye turned to God from idols, to serve the living and true God" (1 Thess 1: 8-10). In both cases, onlookers bore witness to the power of Christ: they should be able to do the same in *our* case too. But this doesn't mean that a mass revival will follow. Christ was a threat to their self-centred and self-indulgent lives. There is a terrible anticlimax at the end of the narrative: "And, behold, the whole city came out to meet Jesus (that looks promising): and when they saw him, they besought him that he would depart out of their coasts (the apparent promise was unfulfilled)". Quite obviously the Lord Jesus did not match their expectations, fulfilling the prophecy: "he hath no form nor comeliness; and when we shall see him, there is no beauty that we should desire him" (Isaiah 53: 2). Sad and solemn, isn't it?

Unlike Matthew, Mark and Luke refer to the Lord's instructions to the ex-demoniac who now wished to follow Him: "Now the man out of whom the devils were departed, besought him that he might be with him: but Jesus sent him away, saying, Return to thine own house (Mark has 'thine own people', JND), and shew how great things God hath done unto thee. And he went his way, and published (*kerasso*, 'to be a herald, to proclaim, preach', W.E.Vine) throughout the whole city how great things Jesus had done unto him" (Luke 8: 38-39). He certainly covered a wide area: "He...began to publish in Decapolis how great things Jesus had done for him: and all men did marvel" (Mark 5: 20). Gadara lay in the district of Decapolis, meaning the 'ten cities', of which Damascus was the most famous. Later, the Lord Jesus "came unto the sea of Galilee, through the midst of the coasts of Decapolis" (Mark 7: 31). From Matthew's parallel record, we learn that "great multitudes came unto him" (Matt 15: 30). It seems as if he did a thorough job, doesn't it? What about *us?*

Addendum

"They besought him that he would depart out of their coasts"
(Matthew 8: 34)

Rabbi, begone!
Thy powers bring loss to us and ours
Our ways are not as Thine
Thou lovest men - we, swine!

Matthew

O get Thee gone, Omnipotence
And take this fool of Thine!
His soul? what care we for his soul?
Since we have lost our swine!

The Christ went sadly,
He had wrought for them a sign
Of love and tenderness divine –
They wanted swine!

Christ stands without your door and gently knocks,
But if your gold or swine the entrance blocks
He forces no man's hold, He will depart
And leave you to the treasures of your heart.

John Oxenham.

Quoted in *'The Collected Writings of Harold St. John'*
(Volume 1: Page 371)

THE GOSPEL OF MATTHEW

"Be of good cheer; thy sins be forgiven thee"

Read Chapter 9: 1-17
In this chapter, the Lord continues to lay before us His 'royal credentials'. The current passage may be divided as follows: **(1)** the cure of the paralytic (vv.1-8); **(2)** the call of Matthew (v.9); **(3)** the contention of the Pharisees (vv.10-13); **(4)** the concern of John's disciples (vv.14-17).

1) THE CURE OF THE PARALYTIC, vv.1-8
Joseph, the Lord's guardian was told that Mary would "bring forth a son, and thou shalt call his name JESUS: for he shall save his people from their sins" (Matt. 1: 21). This is now illustrated: "Son, be of good cheer; thy sins be forgiven thee" (v.2). David's words could be written over these verses: "Who forgiveth all thine iniquities: who healeth all thy diseases" (Psalm 103: 3). The Lord did both in the case of this man! These verses are of great interest to us for at least three reasons: they illustrate the Gospel message; they describe our role in bringing others to Christ; they emphasise the deity of the Lord Jesus. We know from Mark 2: 1-12 that this incident took place in Capernaum, which Matthew describes as "his own city" (v.1).

Parallel passages are found in Mark (Mark 2: 1-12) and Luke (Luke 5: 17-26), and they should be read! Luke introduces the subject at some length (Luke 5: 17). Matthew is not so copious in detail as his colleagues, but in the interests of brevity we must largely confine ourselves to his record of the miracle. The following should be noted:

a) The perseverance of his friends, v.2
"And, behold, **they** brought to him a man sick of the palsy, lying on a bed". The paralysed man certainly had some very good friends, and this illustrates Paul's exhortation, "With **one mind, striving together** for the faith of the Gospel" (Phil. 1: 27). This should be true of every assembly in its local evangelism. How well are **we** co-operating? Just imagine what

would have happened to the man if one friend lost his grip, or decided that he had something better to do! Or just imagine what would have happened if there had been disagreement or strife between them. Is it any different in the spiritual realm? We should all be "workers together" (2 Cor 6: 1). See also Philippians 1: 5. The New Testament does not say anything about 'loners!'

Leaving aside the details given by Mark and Luke (entry via the roof), we must notice that "they **brought to him** a man sick of the palsy, lying on a bed". N.Crawford *(What the Bible Teaches - Luke)* puts it like this: 'We can learn an excellent lesson from this story of a helpless man who received such timely help from the four who were able to carry him. Most people who are saved in our day, who are not related to believers, are brought to hear the Gospel through the influence of saved people who have concern for them'. Door to door visitation, tract distribution, personal work, are arduous and time-consuming. The obstacles of indifference and apathy are very real. People have such a **polite** way of rejecting the gospel. The four friends were not deterred, and we should not be deterred either. We must go 'the extra mile' if necessary (Matt 5: 41). Notice that they brought the man as he was - they had no other option anyway! We need to bring people as they are - warts and all.

They evidently had every confidence that the Lord Jesus could deal with the case. We must never lose the confidence expressed by Paul: "I am not ashamed of the gospel of Christ: for it is the power of God unto salvation" (Rom 1: 16). The friends believed that Christ could heal the man, and we must continue to believe that He can still save sinners.

b) The paralysis of the man, v.2
"And, behold, they brought to him a man **sick of the palsy**, lying on a bed", reminding us that "when we were **without strength**, in due time, Christ died for the ungodly" (Rom. 5: 6). Undoubtedly, the man was only too well aware of his helplessness. Tragically, so many people have no awareness whatsoever of their helpless spiritual condition.

c) The priority of the Lord Jesus, v.2
"Jesus seeing their faith, said unto the sick of the palsy, Son, be of good cheer; thy sins be forgiven thee". Only Matthew has "be of good cheer". The precise meaning of "**their faith**" is often debated. Was it the faith of four men, or five men? 'To limit this to the four who carried the man, makes

the man not only a paralytic, but a person without voice or will. Surely his faith was at least as strong as the four friends!' (N.Crawford). This must be right: salvation is always by faith. The man must have exercised faith to get up and walk!

Humanly speaking, we might have expected the Saviour to say, "Arise, and take up thy bed, and walk". But the Lord Jesus dealt with the most important problem first. He was certainly a very sick man indeed, but life with unforgiven sin is worse. The most important thing in life is to have our sins forgiven. The death of Christ is the only basis on which this can take place. Sins have only ever been forgiven on this basis, whether they were committed *before* or *after* His death at Calvary. See Rom 3: 25-26.

Whilst we are certainly to "do good unto all men" (Gal 6: 10) and to remember that the Lord Jesus "went about doing good" (Acts 10: 38), we must never forget that men and women need, above all else, to be saved from their sins. It was to that end that the Saviour came: "But now once in the end of the world hath he appeared *to put away sin by the sacrifice of himself* (Heb. 9: 26).

But there is more here: the man actually *heard* the Saviour say, "thy sins be forgiven thee". He was assured that his sins were forgiven by the Lord Jesus. The man could rest on the word of Christ Himself. If we ever have doubts about our salvation, we must do the same: "Verily, verily, I say unto you, he that heareth my word, and believeth (on) him that sent me, *hath everlasting life*, and shall not come into condemnation, but *is passed* from death unto life" (John 5: 24).

d) The problem of the scribes and Pharisees, vv.3-6

"And, behold, certain of the scribes (Luke mentions the Pharisees as well) said within themselves, This man blasphemeth" (v.3). Luke (and Mark) expand: "the scribes and the Pharisees began to reason, saying, Who is this that speaketh blasphemies? Who can forgive sins, but God alone?" (Luke 5: 21). They rightly thought that only God could forgive sins (see, for example, Isaiah 43: 25; 44: 22) but, as David Gooding points out, 'this was something startlingly new: He personally released a man from the guilt of his sins... The Old Testament gave no one, not priest, nor prophet, nor theologian any such authority. They could pronounce in God's name that God had forgiven, or would forgive, such and such a sin; but none had authority to pronounce forgiveness in his own name, as Christ had just done'. In answer to their

Matthew

unspoken protest, the Lord Jesus then 'provided the most stunning proof of His deity' (D.Newell). We should notice:

i) His perception proved His deity. The scribes and Pharisees uttered no words: they "said within themselves" (v.3), or as Mark and Luke put it, they 'reasoned in their hearts' (Mark 2: 6; Luke 5: 22). What is more, the Saviour didn't question them. He knew exactly what they were thinking: "And Jesus knowing their thoughts" (v.4) or "When Jesus perceived in his spirit that they so reasoned within themselves" (Mark 2: 8). That in itself, was evidence of His deity. One attribute of deity is omniscience. Notice that according to Mark, they "reasoned" (Mark 2: 8), and came to the wrong conclusion.

ii) His power proved His deity. The Lord Jesus now proves to them, on the basis of their own teaching, that He is God. The man's paralysis gave the Lord Jesus the opportunity to display His power as "the Son of man" (this was a divine title: see Dan 7: 13). The Rabbis taught that physical sickness was the result of some sin against God. See, for example, John 9: 1-3. We know that this was incorrect, but the Lord Jesus answered them on their own ground. If they believed that sickness was the result of sin, then they ought also to believe that healing was the result of the forgiveness of sin.

As already noted, they had said, "This man blasphemeth" (v.3), or "Who is this that speaketh blasphemies? Who can forgive sins, but God alone?" (Luke 5: 21). Very well, in raising the paralytic, the Saviour proved that the man's sins were forgiven, and that He therefore must be God, who alone can forgive sins. This is the force of His words: "Whether is easier, to say, Thy sins be forgiven thee; or to say, Arise and walk? (that is, both proved Him to be God). But that ye may know that the Son of man hath power (*exousia,* authority) **upon earth** (note: He can only forgive people's sins whilst they are on earth) to forgive sins, (then saith he to the sick of the palsy), Arise, and take up thy bed, and go unto thine house" (vv.5-6). They had already seen the authority (*exousia*) in His teaching (7: 29) and they were about to see it again in the raising of the paralytic (v.8), where the same word (*exousia*) is used.

e) The proof of forgiveness, vv.7-8
"And arose, and departed to his house (Luke adds, "glorifying God"). But when the multitude saw it, they marvelled, and glorified God, which had given such power (*exousia,* authority) unto men". (that's as far their understanding could go: "unto **men**") or, as Luke puts it, "And they were all amazed, and

they glorified God, and were filled with fear, saying, We have seen strange things today" (Luke 5: 26). The man arrived with his back on his bed, and left with his bed on his back! New life was firm evidence of forgiveness, and it was there immediately!

'Any one, pastor, priest or evangelist, can pronounce a formula of forgiveness, but such words are worthless unless supported by the evidence of life and character: no human authority, nor even texts of Scripture, will avail in any given case. The only acceptable proof of pardon lies in a man's ability to walk before God and his fellows in the ungrieved power of the Holy Ghost' (Harold St.John). He continues, 'There is no virtue in invisible faith'. Do people see evidence of forgiveness in *our* lives? It is highly unlikely that they will glorify God, but they ought to see the reality of new life in Christ. However, we are not left to make the best of it ourselves. The very command, "Arise, take up thy bed, and go unto thine house" (v.6), was accompanied by the power to do so. As Luke puts it elsewhere, "Immediately his feet and ankle bones received strength" (Acts 3: 7). The Lord Jesus both commands and *enables* His people.

2) THE CALL OF MATTHEW, v.9

"And as Jesus passed forth from thence, he saw a man, named Matthew, sitting at the receipt of custom: and he saith unto him, Follow me. And he arose, and followed him". At the time Matthew, or to give him his other name, Levi, was writing books for Caesar. Later, he wrote a book for God! We are reading it now! Luke calls Matthew a "publican" (Luke 5: 27) meaning a tax collector. He was not therefore a particularly popular person. A Jew employed in this way by the occupying Roman authorities was regarded as a traitor. It has been stated that the Romans had a customs post in Capernaum, where the Galilean fishermen had to pay tax on their catches in the lake. Others say that the main route from Syria to Egypt ran past Capernaum, and that all goods entering the territory of Herod Antipas were subject to duty at the toll post in Capernaum (supplied by J.Waldron).

Perhaps Matthew worked there. If, however, the customs post related to the fishing trade, then Peter, Andrew, James and John found themselves in fellowship with the man who relieved them of their money! This reminds us that the Gospel unites men and women. Old barriers, and old animosity, are done away in Christ. See Col 3: 11.

When the Lord Jesus said, "Follow me", Levi didn't argue. "Where the word of a king is, there is power" (Eccl. 8: 4). The Lord's command was weighted with divine authority. Matthew simply says, "And he arose, and followed him". Luke is a little more explicit: "And he left all, rose up, and followed him" (Luke 5: 28). The Lord said, "My sheep hear my voice, and I know them, and they follow me" (John 10: 27). Whilst the Lord Jesus only asserts His right in some cases to take men and women from their employment in order to serve Him, the fact remains that He says to *every one of us,* "Follow me". It is not an option: it is mandatory. In most cases, it is "Follow me" where we live and work. But it is "Follow me" none the less. He has every right to direct *our* lives: "He died for all, that they which live should not henceforth live unto themselves, but *unto him* which died for them and rose again" (2 Cor. 5: 15).

3) THE CONTENTION OF THE PHARISEES, vv.10-13
In these verses we should notice *(a)* the company that He kept (v.10); *(b)* the criticism that He received (vv.11-13).

a) The company that He kept, v.10
"And it came to pass, as Jesus sat at meat in the house, behold, many publicans and sinners came and sat down with him and his disciples". Significantly enough, Matthew does not mention himself, but we learn from Mark and Luke's record (Mark 2: 15; Luke 5: 29) that the meal took place in his house: "And Levi *made him* a great feast in his own house (Matthew does not tell us about the size of the banquet he provided!): and there was a great company of publicans and of others that sat down with them" (Luke 5: 29). Matthew placed himself, and his possessions, at the disposal of the Lord Jesus. Harold St.John (writing on Mark) puts it like this: 'The publican recognised at once that, for the future, his main business in life was to please his new Master; he therefore made a great feast, first to express the joy he felt, and next to win his old associates to the same alliance. He invited tax-gatherers, the most hated class of society, and sinners, probably non-practising Jews, and all manner of irreligious persons'. As H.S.Paisley (*What the Bible Teaches - Mark*) observes, 'Matthew showed his love for the Person of Christ and his love for the perishing world. These are still the marks of reality in a follower of Christ'. The four friends of the paralysed man and Levi had at least one thing in common: they brought others to the Lord. Do *we*?

We ought to notice that the Lord Jesus made it clear that He did not regard the feast in Matthew's house as a social occasion. It was an opportunity for

Chapter 9

Him to "call...sinners to repentance" (vv.12-13) It is important to observe the distinction between separation, and isolation. The Lord Jesus never compromised with men and women in any way, but at the same time, He did not distance Himself from them. In fact, He was called "a friend of publicans and sinners" (Matt. 11: 19). Where would any of us have been today if it had been otherwise? But some thought differently, and we come now to:

b) The criticism that He received, vv.11-13
"And when the Pharisees saw it, they said unto his disciples, Why eateth your master with publicans and sinners?" (v.11). Luke emphasises the animosity of the scribes and Pharisees towards the disciples: "Why do ye eat and drink with publicans and sinners?" (Luke 5: 30). Mark reads similarly (Mark 2: 16).

The Lord's oft-quoted reply follows: "They that be whole need not a physician, but they that are sick. But go ye and learn what that meaneth, I will have mercy, and not sacrifice: for I am not come to call the righteous, but sinners to repentance" (vv.12-13). Both Mark (2: 17) and Luke (5: 31-32) omit the words "But go ye and learn what that meaneth, I will have mercy, and not sacrifice". They are peculiar to Matthew who, writing particularly for Jewish believers, cites Hosea 6: 6 here: "For I desired mercy, and not sacrifice; and the knowledge of God more than burnt offerings". It is worth pointing out that when He was criticised, the Lord pointed to the Scriptures. Now that's a good example to us all! Sadly, while these people had the Scriptures, they didn't practise them, and they knew nothing of the spirit in which they were to be practised.

R.V.G.Tasker puts it nicely: 'Accordingly, Jesus bids these doctrinaires, in a passage found only in his Gospel, to read their Bible again, and to discover from Hosea 6: 6 how completely in accordance with the will of a merciful God it was that He should make contact with these 'sinners' instead of avoiding them in the interests of ritual correctness'.

The Lord's reply does not imply for one moment that the scribes and Pharisees were righteous, but that they *thought* they were righteous. 'Those, who assume themselves righteous, as these Pharisees, place themselves beyond the skill of the Great Physician' (H.S.Paisley). The Lord Jesus had no time for people who thought themselves better than others. He frequently condemned the scribes and Pharisees for their hypocrisy. The spiritual sickness of men and women is graphically described in Isaiah 1: 5-6: "The whole head is sick, and the whole heart faint".

Matthew

We rightly use this passage in Gospel preaching. It is a salutary warning to those who, like the proud Pharisees, "trusted in themselves that they were righteous" (Luke 18: 9). However, we *all* need to be warned against spiritual pride. It is not unknown for Christians to speak disparagingly of fellow-believers. None of us must think that we have 'arrived' spiritually. We all need His on-going help. To think otherwise is a recipe for disaster.

4) THE CONCERN OF JOHN'S DISCIPLES, vv.14-17

"Then came to him the disciples of John, saying, Why do we and the Pharisees fast oft (see Luke 18: 12), but thy disciples fast not" (v.14). Luke, but not Mark, includes praying in their question: "Why do the disciples of John fast often, and make prayers, and likewise the disciples of the Pharisees; but thine eat and drink?" (Luke 5: 33). Had John himself been present, he would have said, "He that hath the bride is the bridegroom: but the friend of the bridegroom, which standeth and heareth him, rejoiceth greatly because of the bridegroom's voice: this my joy therefore is fulfilled" (John 3: 29). John the Baptist was the "friend of the bridegroom", and Christ was the "bridegroom" Himself. The Lord Jesus uses the same illustration: "Can the children of the bridechamber mourn (Mark and Luke have "fast"), as long as the bridegroom is with them?" (v.15). Mark adds "As long as they have the bridegroom with them, they cannot fast" (Mark 2: 19). Luke puts it slightly differently: "Can ye make the children of the bridechamber fast, while the bridegroom is with them?" (Luke 5: 34). It has been pointed out that in the Old Testament, national salvation is likened to the joy of bride and bridegroom (Is. 54: 5-8; Jer. 2: 2; Hos. 2: 18-20), and that the Lord is therefore pointing out that His disciples had every reason to rejoice: the Saviour of Israel was now present!

However, the Lord continues: "but the days will come, when the bridegroom shall be taken from them, and then shall they fast" (v.15). Mark and Luke read similarly: "But the days will come, when the bridegroom shall be taken away from them, and then shall they fast in those days" (Mark 2: 20; Luke 5: 35). The words, "taken away", mean 'removed with violence', and were fulfilled when the Saviour was arrested, condemned and crucified. The best commentary on the words, "then shall they fast in those days", is given by the Lord himself: "Verily, verily, I say unto you, That ye shall **weep and lament,** but the world shall rejoice; and ye shall be **sorrowful**, but your sorrow shall be turned into joy" (John 16: 20).

Notice that at that time, there was no bride. The disciples are simply called,

Chapter 9

"the children of the bridechamber" (v.15). But the day of Pentecost marked the commencement of the church, of which Paul writes: "Christ also loved the church, and gave himself for it" (Eph. 5: 25). The church is destined to share eternity with Christ as His heavenly bride.

Having pointed out that the position of His disciples was essentially different to the position of the disciples of John and the Pharisees, the Lord goes further by demonstrating that His non-compliance with the religious traditions of the time emphasised the fact that Christianity and Judaism (the Jewish religion) did not mix. He had not come to 'patch up' the old religion (a new piece of cloth in an old garment), or give it a new lease of life (new wine in old wineskins), but to bring something entirely new.

In His own words: "No man putteth ('seweth', Mark 2: 21) a piece of new cloth unto an old garment; for that which is put in to fill it up taketh from the garment ('the piece that was taken out of the new agreeth not with the old', Luke 5: 36), and the rent is made worse. Neither do men put new wine into old bottles, else the bottles break, and the wine runneth out, and the bottles perish: but they put new wine into new bottles, and both are preserved" (vv.16-17), or, in Mark's words, "the new wine doth burst the bottles, and the wine is spilled, and the bottles will be marred: but new wine must be put into new bottles" (Mark 2: 22). The "old garment" and the "old bottles" are highly significant. The first picture gives the result of trying to keep the law. You're left with tattered garments. In fact, "all our righteousnesses are as filthy rags" (Isaiah 64: 6). They are already "rent", and the attempt to remedy the situation with "the new piece" only makes it worse. The second picture is a perfect description of Judaism: old, hard, and inflexible.

Our salvation does not lie in an attempt to improve our position under the law, but by receiving "the righteousness of God" through faith in Christ. In other words, a totally new garment. The 'freshness and power of the joy of the Spirit of Pentecost' (Harold St.John) could never be contained in the "old bottles" of worn-out Judaism. "If any man be in Christ, he is a new creature (creation): old things are passed away; behold, all things are become new" (2 Cor. 5: 17). Even so, many people still find it difficult to make the change from their old religion to the "newness of life" (Rom 6: 4) and "newness of spirit" (Rom 7: 6) that Christ brings. As N.Crawford observes, 'Their good works and external religion suit them well, and they desire nothing else'.

"Thy faith hath made thee whole"

Read Chapter 9: 18-26
Matthew 9: 18-38 may be divided into five parts, of which the first two represent corresponding sides of an integrated narrative: *(i)* healing for a sick woman (vv.20-22); *(ii)* life for a dead child (vv.18-19; 23-26); *(iii)* sight for blind men (vv.27-31); *(iv)* speech for a dumb man (vv.32-34); *(v)* compassion for scattered sheep (vv.35-38). In order to obviate spiritual indigestion (!), we will address the healing of the woman and the raising of the child (vv.18-26) in our current study, and devote our next study to the remaining verses (vv.27-38). Matthew 11: 2-5 is a good commentary on the whole section which provides further evidence that the Lord Jesus is "he that should come" (Matt. 11: 3).

Were we studying Luke's Gospel at this point, we would have noticed that chapter 8 describes the blessing of a man, a woman, and a child. In each case, human resources were extinguished. The demoniac (demonized man) "was kept bound with chains and in fetters; and he break the bands" (v.29). The woman with the "issue of blood" had "spent all her living upon physicians, neither could be healed of any" (v.43). The child was dead (v.49). The first case depicts deliverance from the *power* of sin: the second depicts deliverance from the *plague* of sin: the third depicts deliverance from the *penalty* of sin. Put another way, Luke ch. 8 demonstrates that the Lord Jesus is greater than the power of *demons*, greater than the power of *disease*, and greater than the power of *death.* He had come to "destroy ('undo', JND) the works of the devil" (1 John 3: 8).

There are at least four major points for consideration, the first of which is applicable to the entire narrative: *(1)* the intertwined events; *(2)* the interceding father (vv.18-19); *(3)* the interrupted journey (vv.20-22); *(4)* the imparting of life (vv.23-26). Parallel passages are found in Mark 5: 22-43 and Luke 8: 41-56.

1) THE INTERTWINED EVENTS
It is not without significance that Matthew specifically says, "While he spake these things unto them, behold, there came a certain ruler, and worshipped him" (v.18). What follows illustrates that divine blessing had nothing to do with the "old garment" and the "old bottles" (vv.16-17) of Judaism. Taken together, the three records (Matthew, Mark, Luke) yield some interesting comparisons. *(a)* In the *first case*, twelve years of suffering ended. In the

second, twelve years of joy ended. Norman Crawford (writing on Luke) observes that 'the sickness of the woman and the death of the maiden give a vivid picture of the spiritual condition of Israel's twelve tribes' and that, 'As in this case the coming of the Lord brought healing and life, so it will be when Israel recognises her true Messiah in the day when He comes as her Deliverer'. *(b)* The **first case** concerned an unnamed and unimportant woman (that is, humanly speaking) who was evidently approaching the end of life. The **second case** concerned a named girl, belonging to an important family, at the beginning of life. *(c)* In the **first case**, Jairus came quite openly. In the **second case**; the woman came quietly and unobstrusively. But both fell at His feet (Luke 8: 41, 47). *(d)* In the **first case**, we have a woman defiled by an issue of blood, and therefore 'outside'. In the **second case**, we have the daughter of a synagogue ruler, and therefore very much 'inside'. Both needed the blessing of Christ. It is worth remembering that the healing of the woman must have been a severe rebuke to Jairus. Her illness meant exclusion from the synagogue, and whilst Jairus may not have been personally involved, he represented a system which did nothing to help people in her condition. The kindness and mercy of Christ condemned the stern and unbending attitude of the synagogue. As we have noted, the Lord Jesus did not put new wine into old bottles. *(e)* In the **first case**, the Lord Jesus proved superior to human wisdom: in the **second case**, He proved superior to human religion. *(f)* In the **first case**, the woman touched the Saviour: in the **second**, the Saviour touched the child.

The last of these should be carefully noted, and Norman Crawford (*What the Bible Teaches - Luke*) is worth quoting in full here: 'It is important to note that this is the only occasion in the life of Christ when two miracles are intertwined. There is a reason for this. In the woman healed, we see salvation illustrated from the *human* standpoint in that all the efforts were her own. In the girl raised up, we see salvation from the *Lord's* standpoint, for in her case, all depended on Him. The woman's hand stretched out and laid hold on His garment. In the house, His hand stretched out and laid hold of the girl'.

With this in mind, we can now give orderly consideration to the narrative, which brings us to:

2) THE INTERCEDING FATHER, vv.18-19
We know him as Jairus from Mark and Luke's records (Mark 5: 22; Luke 8: 41), but his name is not given here. Jairus is the New Testament equivalent

of the Old Testament 'Jair' (Judges 10: 3), meaning 'Jehovah enlightens'. It is encouraging to learn that at least one synagogue ruler was enlightened enough to seek the Lord's help. They were usually hostile towards Him: see Luke 13: 14, John 9: 22, John 12: 42. While Jairus is described as "one of the rulers of the synagogue" (Mark 5: 22) or "a ruler of the synagogue" (Luke 8: 41), Matthew simply calls him "a certain ruler" (v.18). The status of Jairus certainly emphasises the impotence of human religion, and the fact that "he worshipped" the Lord Jesus (v.18), or "fell down at Jesus' feet" (Luke 8: 41), must have been an astonishing sight to the onlookers, particularly to any Pharisees present (it does seem that Jairus may well have come to Matthew's house (v.10), proving that he recognised Christ's authority to be infinitely higher than the authority of Judaism.

The desperate father cried, "My daughter is even now dead" or 'My daughter has by this died' (JND), and continued, "But come and lay thy hand upon her, and she shall live" (v.18). The text indicates the extremity of the situation. According to Luke, "He fell down at Jesus' feet, and besought him that he would come into his house: for he had one daughter, about twelve years of age, and she lay a dying" (Luke 8: 41-42). According to Mark he said, "My little daughter lieth at **the point of death**: I pray thee, come and lay thy hands on her, that she may be healed; and she shall live" (Mark 5: 23). Our private prayers, and our assembly prayers, would be quite different if we prayed with the earnestness of this man. We should notice the following:

i) **His attitude to the Lord Jesus.** As noted: "he worshipped" the Lord Jesus (v.18), or "fell down at Jesus' feet" (Luke 8: 41: Mark 5: 22 is similar). Before making his request, Jairus honoured the Lord Jesus. Putting the three records together, he cast himself on the Lord's mercy, and acknowledged that he was totally dependent on Him. Any pride or self-esteem as a "ruler of the synagogue" was completely abandoned.

ii) **His reality in the Lord's presence**. "But come and lay thy hand upon her, and she shall live" (v.18). Mark is similar, but Luke is more emphatic: he "besought him" (Luke 8: 41). The word 'beseech' here (*parakaleo*) is a great deal stronger than 'ask'. This was no mechanical request: it came from the depths of his heart. Do we pray like that? The reality of his plea was born of urgency. His daughter "lay a dying". We are surrounded by people in danger of "the second death". For completeness, we should also notice:

iii) **His affection for his daughter.** She was his "only daughter, about twelve years of age" (Luke 8: 42). Mark has, "my *little daughter*" (Mark 5: 23). This was no cold, dispassionate request. How often we pray "for all men" (1 Tim. 2: 1), but with very little actual interest in them. We've said the right thing, but that's about all.

iv) **His faith in the Lord.** "Come and lay thy hand upon her, and she *shall* live" (v.18). Mark (5: 23) is comparable, but Luke simply says that Jairus "besought him that he would come to his house".

There's not a great deal of mileage in condemning Jairus because his faith did not evidently rise to the level of the centurion's faith: "Lord, I am not worthy that thou shouldest come under my roof: but speak the word only, and my servant shall be healed" (Matt. 8: 8). The Lord Jesus accommodated the lesser faith of Jairus and "arose, and followed him" (v.19). It would be disastrous for us if the Saviour only acknowledged sublime faith!

It is noteworthy that Matthew says, "And Jesus arose, and followed him, and so did his disciples" (v.19). This is unique! The Lord followed Jairus! Had it been otherwise, the woman (v.20) would not have dared to have darted in front of the "ruler", especially in view of the stigma attaching to her condition. The Saviour deliberately made it as easy as possible for the woman. We should notice that Matthew does not mention the news of the child's death (see Luke 8: 49): he is concerned particularly with the power of the King and concentrates attention upon Him. This brings us to:

3) THE INTERRUPTED JOURNEY, vv.20-22
Generally speaking, interruptions are usually unexpected so far as we are concerned, but not in the Lord's case! It could be argued that the case of the twelve year old girl was far more important than the case of the woman. After all, a few more days wouldn't make much difference to her. She could always be healed on the return journey. But the Lord Jesus never thought like that: He cared deeply about every case, and nothing was too trivial or of lesser importance so far as He was concerned. This is a lesson we *all* need to learn.

i) Her condition, v.20
The "issue of blood" is called a "plague" in Mark 5: 29, 34. It would not be incorrect to describe her as a dying woman. Her life was slowly ebbing away. Leviticus 15 describes this particular condition as "uncleanness": it involved separation from the tabernacle. See Lev. 15: 19-31. 'According to the cruel

social custom of that time, her disease demanded that she must leave her house, be divorced by her husband, and that the gates of the synagogue and temple must be closed to her' (H.St.John). Moreover, according to Mark, it was a worsening condition: she had "suffered many things of many physicians, and had spent all that she had, and was nothing bettered, but rather grew worse" (Mark 5: 26). See also Luke 8: 43. The health of the woman aptly depicts the spiritual condition of men and women, and society generally. Men and women have an ongoing disease, and "many physicians" (Mark 5: 26) have not brought improvement: sinners are "nothing bettered" but 'rather grow worse'.

ii) Her confidence, vv.20-21

She "came behind him, and touched the hem of his garment: for she said within herself, If I may but touch his garment, I *shall* be whole". She touched the Lord Jesus in faith. Mark tells us that she "heard...came...touched...for she said, If I may touch but his clothes, I *shall* be whole" (Mark 5: 27-28). Later, the Saviour said, "thy *faith* hath made thee whole" (v.22). (Not faith in the 'magical properties' of his clothes, as some suggest, but faith in Him). We should notice that she touched "the hem of his garment". Like every pious Jew, the Lord Jesus wore a ribband of blue on the hem of his garment. This was a constant reminder to the *wearer* of the need for obedience and holiness. See Numbers 15: 38-41. The Pharisees enlarged the borders of their garments for the benefit of the *onlookers.* See Matthew 23: 5. But the woman didn't touch *them!* The Lord Jesus was known for His purity, and for his ability to help and save. The passage should be compared with Acts 19: 11-12 where Paul's ministry was accompanied by "the signs of an apostle" (2 Cor.12: 12).

iii) Her cure, v.22

She was healed immediately: "But Jesus turned him about; and when he saw her, he said, Daughter, be of good comfort (remember that she was "trembling", Luke 8: 47); thy faith hath made thee whole. And the woman was made whole from that hour". The woman was an outcast, but the Lord calls her "Daughter!" He called the paralytic, "Son" (v.2). Once again, Matthew is particularly concerned with the power of the King, and therefore omits the details given by Mark and Luke: "And *straightway* the fountain of her blood was dried up: and she felt in her body that she was healed of that plague" (Mark 5: 29); "and *immediately* her issue of blood stanched" (Luke 8: 44). The word "stanched" *(histemi)* means 'to stand still' (W.E.Vine). The Lord Jesus dealt with the source and symptoms of her problem. Medical cures take time: we have to be patient. But this was entirely different, and so were all the cases of healing performed by the Saviour. He deals with sin in exactly the same way: "Believe on the Lord Jesus Christ, **and thou shalt be saved**" (Acts 16: 31). There were no doctor's fees now. His blessings are "without money, and without price" (Isaiah 55: 1). "The **gift** of God is eternal life through Jesus Christ our Lord" (Rom. 6: 23). There was a cost to Him: He knew that "virtue (*dunamis*) had gone out of him" (Mark 5: 30). See also Luke 6: 19; 8: 46.

It is noteworthy that Matthew omits the detail supplied by Mark and Luke in connection with the woman's confession. Yet again, Matthew concentrates attention on the King. Nevertheless, it might be helpful to notice the details given by Mark and Luke.

According to Luke, the Saviour's question, "Who touched me?", brought the response: "Master (*epistates,* meaning, according to W.E.Vine, 'a chief, a commander, overseer, master': only used by Luke: see also 5: 5; 8: 24; 9: 33, 49; 17: 13) the multitude throng and press thee, and sayest thou, Who touched me?" (Luke 8: 45). Compare Mark 5: 30-31. The lesson is very clear. Curious crowds got nothing. The Saviour did not respond to curiosity, but He did respond to faith. The woman came with a deep sense of need, and with deep reality of faith, and was wonderfully blessed. But, as Harold St.John puts it in his unique way, the Lord did not permit her 'to filch a blessing from Him, and then depart unknown and unseen. This would never have satisfied the Lord nor contented the woman'.

We might be disposed to think that once the woman was healed, she could live happily ever after. No doubt she did, but that happiness was heightened by her confession and its results. With this in view, Mark tells us, the Saviour "looked round", not to find out who had touched Him, but to "**see her** that had done this thing" (Mark 5: 32). Luke gives us the result: "And when the woman saw that she was not hid, she came trembling" (Luke 8: 47). The Saviour was omniscient. He had at least two objectives: first, to encourage confession and, second, to confirm faith. Notice:

- **What the woman said to the Lord.** His first objective was achieved. "She came trembling, and falling down before him, she declared unto him, **before all the people**, for what cause she had touched him, and how she was healed immediately" (Luke 8: 47). Notice that whilst there was no fear in touching Him (v.44), there was fear in confessing Him (v.47). That is probably true of most of us. We must remember, however, that the Saviour is not looking for secret disciples. Do notice as well that "she declared *unto him*, before all the people". Her confession was both a witness to the bystanders and an expression of gratitude to the Lord Jesus. We must confess the Lord Jesus before *others*, but we must not forget to tell *Him* how much we appreciate all that He has done for us.

- *What the Lord said to the woman.* His second objective was achieved. "Daughter (the only occasion where this was said directly), be of good comfort: thy faith hath made thee whole: go in peace" (Luke 8: 48). *Firstly*, there was assurance for the woman. She had *His* word. She 'received His certificate of salvation' (H.St.John). Compare Romans 10: 9-10, "If thou shalt confess with thy mouth the Lord Jesus ('Jesus as Lord', JND), and shalt believe in thine heart that God hath raised him from the dead, thou shalt be saved. For with the heart man believeth unto righteousness, and with the mouth confession is made unto salvation". *Secondly*, the woman, having made public confession, was publicly vindicated. The crowd heard the Saviour bear public witness to the completeness of her cure. Else 'she would have still been the target of that same suspicion and prejudice from which she had suffered so long' (H.St.John). Mark says, "Go in peace, and *be* whole of thy plague" (Mark 5: 34). That is, 'continue whole and well'. There was no question of a recurrence of the illness. Our peace rests on the fact that God has said, "Their sins and iniquities will I remember no more" (Heb. 8: 12). Having confessed with her mouth and believed in her heart, the woman proved that "Whosoever believeth on him shall not be ashamed" (Rom. 10: 11).

To sum up: the woman knew she was cured (Luke 8: 44); the woman confessed she was cured (Luke 8: 47); the woman was assured she was cured (Luke 8: 48). Now for 'cured' substitute the word 'saved', and you have a good Gospel message! But the incident can also be used to illustrate the restoration of a backslider. After all, the woman once enjoyed healthy life, but something had gone seriously wrong, and all her attempts to recover enjoyment and peace had failed. In desperation she turns to Christ, and finds restoration and blessing. Perhaps we have all known 'better days'. David speaks for us all in saying, "He restoreth my soul" (Psalm 23: 3).

4) *THE IMPARTING OF LIFE, vv.23-26*
Whereas at this point in Mark's record of events, the tempo changes, and the Saviour speeds on His way, Matthew simply says, "and when Jesus

Chapter 9

came into the ruler's house" (v.23). Mark tells us that the Lord "suffered no man to follow him, save Peter, and James, and John the brother of James, and he cometh to the house of the ruler of the synagogue" (Mark 5: 37-38). The crowds are dismissed: the Saviour will allow no further interruption: speed was required, not to raise the girl, but to **alleviate sorrow**. He is still touched by human grief, and all our tears are in His bottle. See Psalm 56: 8.

On arrival, He saw "the minstrels ('flute-players', JND) and the people making a noise" and "said unto them, Give place ('Withdraw', JND); for the maid is not dead, but sleepeth (*katheudo*). And they laughed him to scorn" (vv.23-24). Their mourning, for what it was worth, turned to mockery! Mark is more explicit: "And he cometh to the house of the ruler of the synagogue, and seeth the tumult, and them that wept and wailed greatly. And when he was come in, he saith unto them, Why make ye this ado, and weep? The damsel is not dead, but sleepeth" (Mark 5: 38-40). Luke reads similarly. People still scoff at the words, "she is not dead, but sleepeth". We know, of course, that the girl was raised, but eventually died again. Compare 1 Thess. 4: 13-18, where Paul deals with "them also which sleep in Jesus". There is no question of further death when the Lord comes! The professional mourners who "laughed him to scorn" have their successors: "There shall come in the last days scoffers...saying, Where is the promise of his coming?" (2 Pet 3: 3-4). Don't expect people to listen with awe when you tell them that Christ is returning: you too are likely to be "laughed...to scorn". In this case, unbelief meant exclusion: "he...put them (the professional mourners) all out" (Luke 8: 54). When He returns, "all kindreds of the earth shall wail because of him" (Rev. 1: 7). There will be no mockery then.

Matthew, unlike Mark and Luke, makes no mention of Peter, James and John here, or of the girl's parents. He concentrates attention entirely on the power of the King. These three disciples were particularly privileged. It was to be just like that again: see Luke 9: 28-29 and Mark 14: 33. Harold Paisley, writing on Mark, puts it nicely: 'They witnessed His **grace** as the Saviour, His **glory** as the Sovereign, and His **grief** as the Sufferer'. But why only **those** three? There is, of course, a general answer, which covers all divine appointments: see 1 Cor 12: 18: "As it hath pleased him". But perhaps the Lord was fitting them for future responsibility and leadership. Perhaps He was strengthening them for future suffering. All three paid dearly for their loyalty to Christ.

In keeping with his overall purpose, Matthew simply says, "But when the people were put forth, he went in, and took her by the hand, and the maid arose" (v.25). Luke tells us that in raising the girl, the Lord Jesus used just two words, "Maid, arise" (Luke 8: 54). Mark tells us that he actually spoke in Aramaic: 'Talitha cumi' (Mark 5: 41) which means, literally, 'Little lamb, I say unto thee arise'. Aramaic was the language of the *people*: He did not employ classical Hebrew, Greek or Latin, but used words which conveyed tenderness and gentleness. There was no need for convalescence: "And her spirit came again, and she arose *straightway* (immediately)" (Luke 8: 55). Mark tells us that "straightway the damsel *arose and walked*; for she was of the age of twelve years. And they were astonished with a great astonishment" (Mark 5: 42). The Lord Jesus fulfilled Hosea 13: 14, "O death, I will be thy plagues: O grave, I will be thy destruction".

The fact that the Lord said, "The damsel is not dead, but sleepeth", has led some to question her actual death. Compare John 11: 11-14, where the Saviour uses the word "sleepeth" (*koimaomai*) to describe the death of Lazerus. But Luke is perfectly clear: "her spirit came again". That's quite conclusive language! In the words of J.C.Ryle, these words also emphasise the 'separate existence of spirits (referring to the human spirit), and their independence of the body'. The human spirit is 'something that subsists by itself, which after death, is somewhere else than where the body is. Where the soul of the child was in the interval we are not told. It was in the hand of the Father of spirits, to whom all souls at death return' (Matthew Henry).

Luke emphasises that new life needs feeding! "He commanded to give her meat" (Luke 8: 55). See also Mark 5: 43. The ability and desire to eat was, of course, proof positive, that the girl was alive again. Compare Luke 24: 41-43. New spiritual life needs feeding too: "As newborn babes, desire the sincere milk of the word, that ye may grow thereby" (1 Pet. 2: 2). The ability to desire and enjoy spiritual food is evidence of eternal life.

Instead of advertising a healing meeting, the Saviour "charged them that they should tell no man what was done" (Luke 8: 56). Compare Mark 9: 9, 30. The Lord Jesus never sought publicity. He was intent on carrying out the Father's will, and confidently left the issues of His service to Him. He was "obedient unto death, even the death of the cross. Wherefore *God also hath highly exalted him,* and given him a name which is above every name" (Phil. 2: 8-11). J.C.Ryle has a telling piece here: 'To do great works, and say nothing about them - to work powerfully, and yet noiselessly and quietly - is to walk in Christ's steps. The shallowest streams and the emptiest vessels make most noise'. Even so, Matthew tells us that "the fame hereof went abroad into all that land" (v.26).

"Thou son of David, have mercy on us"

Read Chapter 9: 27-38
In our last study, we suggested that Matthew 9: 18-38 may be divided into five parts, of which the first two represent the corresponding sides of an integrated narrative: *(i)* healing for a sick woman (vv.20-22); *(ii)* life for a dead child (vv.18-19; 23-26); *(iii)* sight for blind men (vv.27-31); *(iv)* speech for a dumb man (vv.32-34); *(v)* compassion for scattered sheep (vv.35-38).

1) HEALING FOR A SICK WOMAN, vv.20-22
Amongst the lessons connected with the healing of the "woman...diseased with an issue of blood twelve years" is the fact that she "came behind him, and touched the hem of his garment". *The woman touched the Lord*. It was an act of faith on her part, and illustrates salvation from the human standpoint. Men and women must trust in Christ for salvation.

He turned with, "Daughter, be of good comfort;
Thy faith hath made thee whole!"
And peace that passeth all understanding
With gladness filled her soul.

But there is far more to salvation than 'the decision we made', and the raising of the ruler's daughter, which follows, illustrates salvation from the Lord's standpoint: so

2) LIFE FOR A DEAD CHILD, vv.18-19; 23-26
In this case, *the Lord touched the girl*: "he went in, and took her by the hand, and the maid arose". There was nothing she could do: she was dead. It all depended on the Lord! It is just like that so far as we were concerned: "And you hath he quickened who were dead in trespasses and sins" (Eph. 2: 1).

The 'intertwined' events described in these verses (vv.20-26) therefore illustrate salvation from the human and divine standpoints. This brings us to:

3) SIGHT TO THE BLIND MEN, vv.27-31
"And when Jesus departed thence, two blind men followed him, crying, and

Matthew

saying, Thou son of David, have mercy on us, And when he was come unto the house, the blind men came to him: and Jesus said unto them, Believe ye that I am able to do this? They said unto him, Yea, Lord. Then touched he their eyes, saying, According to your faith be it unto you. And their eyes were opened" (vv.27-30). This miracle is unique to Matthew. The Lord Jesus gave sight to these two blind men near the beginning of His ministry, and He did exactly the same to two other blind men near its end (Matt. 20: 29-34). There was therefore no diminishing of His power. In this connection it is worth remembering that he cleansed the temple near the beginning of His ministry (John 2: 13-17) and again near its end (Matt. 21: 12-13). In this case, there was no diminishing of His convictions. Regrettably, we can lose or relax our convictions, but it was not so in His case!

We should notice the following: *(a)* the faith of the blind men (vv.27-29); *(b)* the command to the blind men (v.30); *(c)* the disobedience of the blind men (v.31).

a) The faith of the blind men, vv.27-29

J.C.Ryle points out that "strong faith in Christ may be sometimes found where it might least have been expected" and continues, "Who would have thought that two blind men would have called our Lord the 'Son of David'? They could not, of course, have seen the miracles that He did: they could only know Him by common report. But the eyes of their understanding were enlightened, if their bodily eyes were dark: they saw the truth which scribes and Pharisees could not see; they saw that Jesus of Nazareth was the Messiah". "Son of David" is the royal title of the Messiah. See Matt. 1: 1; 21: 9, 15. It is surely not too imaginative to say that the blind men would have known that when the Messiah came, His credentials would include giving sight to the blind (Luke 4: 18). As W.MacDonald observes, "Men say, 'Seeing is believing'. God says, 'Believing is seeing'. The Lord said to Martha, 'Did I not say to you that if you would believe you would see the glory of God?' (John 11: 40). The writer to the Hebrews noted, 'Through faith we understand' (Heb. 11: 3). The apostle John wrote, 'I have written to you who believe...that ye may know that ye have eternal life' (1 John 5: 13). God is not pleased with the kind of faith that demands a prior miracle. He wants us to believe Him simply because He is God".

It has been pointed out that before acceding to their request, the Lord tested the sincerity of the blind men. He did not heal them on the spot, but waited until they confirmed the genuineness of their faith. Hence His question,

Chapter 9

in the house, "Believe ye that I am able to do this?" (v.28). After all, some people make a lot of noise, but that is all! It was not so in this case, and the Saviour said, "According to your faith be it unto you. And their eyes were opened" (vv.29-30).

b) The command to the blind men, v.30
"And Jesus straitly charged them (*embrimaomai*: 'charged them sharply', JND), saying, See that no man know it". Wm.MacDonald suggests that the Lord sternly warned the two men in this way because "He did not want to foment a premature movement to enthrone Him as King. The people were not as yet repentant; He could not reign over them until they were born again. Also, a revolutionary uprising in favour of Jesus would bring terrible reprisals from the Roman government on the Jews. Besides all this, the Lord Jesus had to go to the cross before He could reign as King; anything that blocked His pathway to Calvary was at variance with the pre-determined plan of God". Compare John 6: 15. It would have been in Satan's interests for the Lord Jesus to become King without going to the cross. See Matthew 4: 8-9.

c) The disobedience of the blind men, v.31
"But they, when they were departed, spread abroad his fame in all that country". While we can well understand, and even admire, their exuberant testimony, it remains that the two men disobeyed the very Saviour whom they had confessed to be the "Son of David". We therefore learn 'that humble obedience is better than impulsive spontaneity' (supplied by J. Waldron). We may not always understand divine instructions, but we can rest in the knowledge that they are always given for good reasons. In this case, the reasons have been suggested above. It has been said that "Not even gratitude is a valid excuse for disobedience".

4) SPEECH TO THE DUMB MAN, vv.32-34
"As they went out, behold, they brought to him a dumb man possessed with a devil. And when the devil was cast out, the dumb spake: and the multitudes marvelled, saying, It was never so seen in Israel. But the Pharisees said, He casteth out devils through the prince of the devils". The word "dumb" (*kophos*) denotes 'blunted or dulled' (W.E.Vine) and is also used of deafness (Matt. 11: 5; Mark 7: 32, 37; 9: 25; Luke 7: 22). It has been suggested that the man might have been deaf and dumb, but this is not apparent from the text. But do notice that someone brought him to the Lord Jesus.

Once again, this miracle is unique to Matthew. Bearing in mind that Matthew writes particularly for Jewish believers, William Kelly is undoubtedly right in saying "I believe that all this is brought together for the same purpose. The Lord was giving type after type, pledge upon pledge, that Israel would not be forgotten, that Israel would be raised out of death: let them be ever so blind, they would see; ever so dumb, they would speak".

At the same time, there does appear to be a spiritual sequence in the miracles described in this chapter. Firstly, the Lord gave life to the dead (v.25); secondly, sight to the blind (v.29) and now, thirdly, speech to the dumb (v.33). We can put it like this: life (the child was raised) was followed by understanding (the blind could see), and understanding was followed by testimony (the dumb man spoke). How closely does this apply to us?

We should notice *(a)* the testimony of the man (v.33); *(b)* the testimony of the multitudes (v.33); *(c)* the testimony of the Pharisees (v.34).

a) The testimony of the man, v.33
"And when the devil was cast out, the dumb spake". It does seem evident that the man's dumbness was more than a physical disability. It was the result of demon-possession, and we can certainly add that Satan continues to rob men and women of the ability to praise God, causing Paul to say, "when they knew God, they glorified him not as God, neither were thankful" (Rom. 1: 21). We are not told what the man said, but Wm.MacDonald is probably right in saying that "we may assume that he used his restored power of speech in worship and witness for the One who had so graciously healed him". Is this true of us?

b) The testimony of the multitudes, v.33
"The multitudes marvelled, saying, It was never so seen in Israel". This recalls that having healed the man that was "deaf, and had an impediment in his speech", the onlookers "were beyond measure astonished, saying, He hath done all things well: he maketh both the deaf to hear, and the dumb to speak" (Mark 7: 32-37). What kind of testimony do we have? Our fellow men and women may not "marvel" at us, but they ought to see evidence of the power of Christ in our lives!

c) The testimony of the Pharisees, v.34
Whereas "the multitudes marvelled" or, in Mark's words, "the common people heard him gladly" (Mark 12: 37), the religious fraternity were of a different mind, and it is not without significance that the greatest opposition to the

Gospel still comes from institutionalised religion. "But the Pharisees said, He casteth out devils through the prince of the devils". On this occasion, the Lord made no recorded reply, but He certainly did so later when the Pharisees said, "This fellow doth not cast out devils, but by Beelzebub the prince of the devils" (Matt. 12: 24). The Lord called this 'the unpardonable sin' (Matt. 12: 31-32). It was blasphemously attributing the miracles which He performed by the Holy Spirit to the power of Satan. The Lord gave new life to the girl (v.25), sight to the blind (v.29), and now speech to the dumb, but the Pharisees remained spiritually dead, spiritually blind, and spiritually dumb. The Lord had been accused of blasphemy by the scribes (v.3), but now the religious leaders engage in blasphemy themselves. It has been pointed out that the opposition to the Lord Jesus in this way could well have been engendered by the jealousy of the religious leaders. "the multitudes... glorified God, which had given such power unto men" (v.8); "the fame hereof (the raising of the ruler's daughter) went abroad into all that land" (v.26); the blind men "spread abroad his fame in all that country" (v.31) and now "the multitudes marvelled, saying, It was never so seen in Israel" (v.33).

5) COMPASSION FOR SCATTERED SHEEP, vv.35-38

These verses have been described as the beginning of what is known as the 'Third Galilean Circuit'. This needs a little investigation. The Lord left Nazareth and took up residence in Capernaum, from where He "went about all Galilee" (Matt. 4: 12-25). This would be the 'First Galilean Circuit'. Having delivered the 'Sermon on the Mount', the Lord returned to Capernaum (Matt. 8: 5) from where he crossed the lake to "the country of the Gergesenes (Matt. 8: 28), returning to "His own city" (Matt. 9: 1). This would be the 'Second Galilean Circuit'. Now (v.35) He commences the 'Third Galilean Circuit'. The case rests!

We should notice two major points here: *(a)* His comprehensive ministry (v.35); *(b)* His compassionate heart (vv.36-38).

a) His comprehensive ministry, v.35
i) It was comprehensive in its scope. The Lord "went about all the cities and villages teaching (*didasko*)...and preaching (*kerusso*)". We could say that the area was thoroughly evangelised. What a challenge to *us*! The word "teaching" means exactly what it says – to give instruction, while the word "preaching" means to herald or proclaim. The two words do not evidently refer to two different things, but to different aspects of the Lord's work. He taught the people, and did so by addressing them publicly. While, at this

stage in His ministry the Lord's teaching was supported by authenticating miracles, the emphasis is none the less on teaching the Word of God. See also, for example, Mark 1: 38-39: "And he said unto them, Let us go into the next towns, that I may preach there also: for therefore came I forth. And he preached (*kerusso*) in their synagogues throughout all Galilee, and cast out devils (demons)".

ii) It was comprehensive in its content. The Lord preached "the gospel of the kingdom". That is, the rule of God in the hearts and lives of men and women. Their subjection to divine authority. For that rule to commence, repentance was necessary. See Matthew 4: 17, "From that time, Jesus began to preach, and to say, Repent: for the kingdom of heaven is at hand". Profession was in itself unavailing: "Not every one that saith unto me, Lord, Lord, shall enter into the kingdom of heaven; but he that doeth the will of my Father which is in heaven" (Matt. 7: 21).

iii) It was comprehensive in its effect. No problem was beyond His ability: "healing every sickness and every disease among the people". J.C.Ryle has a delightful piece here: "He was an eye-witness of all the ills that flesh is heir to; He saw ailments of every kind, sort, and description; He was brought into contact with every form of bodily suffering. None were too loathsome for Him to attend to: none were too frightful for Him to cure. He was the healer of "every sickness and every disease". There is much comfort to be drawn from this fact. We are each dwelling in a poor frail body: we never know how much suffering we may have to watch, as we sit by the bedsides of beloved relatives and friends; we never know what racking complaint we ourselves may have to submit to, before we lay down and die. But let us arm ourselves with the precious thought that Jesus is specially fitted to be the sick man's friend. The great High Priest to whom we must apply for pardon and peace with God, is eminently qualified to sympathise with an aching body, as well as to heal an ailing conscience. The eyes of Him who is the King of kings used often to look with pity on the diseased".

b) His compassionate heart, vv.36-38
The Lord did not teach and preach dispassionately. We should carefully note the following:

i) The Lord was affected deeply by what He saw: The Lord "was moved with compassion (*splanchnizomai*) on them, because they fainted, and were scattered abroad, as sheep having no shepherd" (v.36). Compare 1 Kings

22: 17; Numbers 27: 17. The word "compassion" means, literally, 'to be moved as to one's inwards' (W.E.Vine). In English we have the expression, 'My heart went out to him'. The word also occurs in Matthew 14: 14; 15: 32; 18: 27; 20: 34; Mark 1: 41, etc). How much are we touched by the desperate condition of men and women around us?

According to M.R.Vincent (*Word Studies of the New Testament*) the word "fainted" originally meant to 'flay, rend, or mangle', and Rienecker/Rogers (*Linguistic Key to the Greek New Testament*) state that the original form of the word is used in the papyri with the meaning 'to distress, to harass, to worry, to trouble'. M.V.Vincent also states that the words "scattered abroad" originally had the meaning of 'thrown' or 'cast', therefore meaning 'thrown down' or 'prostrated'. In a piece supplied by J.Waldron, 'This flock is so weary because of the heavy burdens laid on their shoulders by the religious leaders (Matt. 11: 28; 23: 4)'. The Lord's words, "they fainted, and were scattered abroad, as sheep having no shepherd", recall Ezekiel 34: 5-6, "And they (the sheep of Israel) were scattered, because there is no shepherd...My sheep wandered through all the mountains, and upon every high hill: yea, my flock was scattered upon all the face of the earth, and none did search or seek after them". The shepherds at that time, and when the Lord was here, had lamentably failed. The shepherd care of the Lord Jesus proclaimed Him to be the promised Shepherd (Ezek. 34: 23; 37: 24; Micah 5: 4).

We could summarise the condition of the "sheep" in the following way: they were without strength ("they fainted"); they were without direction ("they...were scattered abroad"); they were without care ("sheep having no shepherd").

ii) The Lord was aware of the need for workers. "Then saith he unto his disciples, The harvest truly is plenteous, but the labourers are few" (v.37). In Wm.MacDonald's words, 'the problem has persisted to this day: the need is always greater than the work-force'. See also Luke 10: 2; John 4: 35-38. We must remember that despite appearances, there is still a harvest to be reaped. The Lord has not yet come: we are therefore to be busy in the harvest field.

iii) The Lord asked His disciples to pray. "Pray ye therefore the Lord of the harvest, that he will send forth labourers into his harvest" (v.38). The need could only be met by servants sent by "the Lord of the harvest". It has often been said that 'a need does not constitute a call'. Workers should not go until they are sent. See Romans 10: 15. We should note that it is the Lord's harvest. It is probably best to understand the words, "the Lord of the harvest", with reference to God. He supplied the seed (His word); He supplied the men to sow the seed (John 4: 38). But, as ever, God's purposes are implemented by His Son. Hence, shortly after this, the Lord Jesus Jesus "sent forth" the twelve to the "lost sheep of the house of Israel" (Matt. 10: 5-6).

We must not leave the chapter without noticing the importance of prayer. The disciples were not to appeal to Missionary Societies for help, or make appeals at missionary report meetings (Acts 14: 27), but to pray that "the Lord of the harvest" will "send forth labourers into his harvest". In this connection we must listen again to J.C.Ryle (writing in 1856): "Personal working for souls is good; giving money is good; but praying is best of all. By prayer we reach Him, without whom work and money are alike in vain". By this "we obtain the aid of the Holy Ghost... Never, never may we forget that if we would do good to the world, our first duty is to pray!"

Addendum

The Lord's healings

by Jack Strahan

(A former Surgeon in the Erne Hospital, Enniskillen)

No discrimination.	-	"He healed them all".
No specialisation	-	He never referred to another specialist.
No procrastination	-	No future appointments: no waiting lists.
No interrogation	-	He never needed to take a case history to find out about the patients' illness. He knew!
No investigation	-	No blood tests. No X-rays. No scans. No biopsies, etc.

Chapter 9

No contamination	-	No masks, gloves etc. No protective measures. He was undefilable.
No incantations	-	Compare today's 'faith healers'.
No medication	-	His word. Sometimes His touch. Only rarely an application, e.g. John 9: 6.
No rehabilitation	-	No need for convalescence. His healings were immediate and complete.
No repetitions	-	No two cases the same, nor healed in the same way.
No re-evaluations	-	He never needed to review. There were no relapses.
No remuneration	-	He never accepted anything in return, but He did appreciate "Thanks".

Kindly sent by Jack Strahan, 31st May, 2010.

THE GOSPEL OF MATTHEW

"These twelve Jesus sent forth"

Read Chapter 10: 1-15
Having clearly presented His credentials, the King dispatches His messengers to the nation with the message, "The kingdom of heaven is at hand" (v.7). They did not undertake their assignment without adequate preparation, and we are indebted to Mark and Luke for helpful information in this connection.

Mark tells us that the Lord Jesus went up "into a mountain, and calleth unto him whom he would: and they came unto him. And he ordained twelve, that they should be with him, and that he might send them forth to preach, and to have power to heal sicknesses, and to cast out devils (demons)" (Mark 3: 13-15). The "twelve" are then named (vv.16-19). Mark carefully points out that they did not embark on their preaching until they had been adequately prepared. Their preparation is summed up in two words: "with him". The lesson is clear. Preachers need to be "with him" before they preach! But even that isn't enough. They need to be directed by Him. They must be sure that He has sent them! Luke, who emphasises the Lord's prayer life, tells us that "he went out into a mountain to pray, and continued all night in prayer to God. And when it was day, he called unto him his disciples: and of them he chose twelve, whom also he named apostles" (Luke 6: 12-13). The Lord Jesus prayed before choosing the apostles. Need we say more?

After "the twelve" had been "with him" (Mark 3: 14), accompanying Him, listening to Him and watching Him, He "began to send them forth two by two" (Mark 6: 7), sending them "to preach the kingdom of God, and to heal the sick" (Luke 9: 2). In Matthew's words, "These twelve Jesus sent forth, and commanded them, saying, Go not into the way of the Gentiles, and into any city of the Samaritans enter ye not: but go rather to the lost sheep of the house of Israel. And as ye go, preach, saying, The kingdom of heaven is at hand" (Matt. 10: 5-7).

Chapter 10

We must bear in mind that Matthew presents the Lord Jesus as Israel's promised King, and that "the twelve" were dispatched as the King's messengers with instructions to confine their preaching to "the lost sheep of the house of Israel". The Lord Jesus had "come unto his own ('things', or 'home')", but as events were to show, "his own ('people') received him not" (John 1: 11). Their commission differs considerably from the commission given at the end of Matthew's Gospel. By then, the King had been rejected and was about to return to the Father. The commission in Matthew 10 relates to Israel only, but the commission in Matthew 28 relates to all nations: "Go ye therefore, and teach all nations, baptizing them in the name of the Father, and of the Son, and of the Holy Ghost" (28: 19). As H.A.Ironside points out, it was appropriate "that the offer of the kingdom should first be extended to Israel, for they were, by natural birth, the children of the kingdom. It was to them that the promises had been given; and they looked forward for centuries to the coming of the King and the manifestation of His dominion over the earth, with Israel as the chosen nation, through whom blessing would come to all the rest of the world (Isa. 60: 1-16). When they refused to bow to the message as given by the Lord and His apostles, the kingdom was taken from them and given to another people (Matt. 21: 43)".

The chapter may be divided as follows: *(1)* the current commission (vv.1-15): these verses refer to the immediate preaching tour; *(2)* the coming conditions (vv.16-23): quite evidently, the persecution predicted by the Lord in these verses did not happen during the imminent preaching tour: the conditions described belong to a later period; *(3)* the care for the disciples (vv.24-42): these verses contain teaching to guide and encourage disciples in their work for Him.

1) THE CURRENT COMMISSION, vv.1-15
These verses bring before us *(A)* the King's men (vv.1-4) and *(B)* the King's mandate (vv.5-15).

A) The King's men, vv.1-4
The Lord had previously told His disciples to "Pray...the Lord of the harvest, that he will send forth labourers into his harvest" (9: 38), and now "the Lord of the harvest" sends *them!* The people who were sent were the people who prayed! The connection between "Pray" (9: 38) and "Go" (10: 5) is very clear! We know that this does not apply in every case, but we ought to remember that we might be the answer to our own prayers, especially in evangelism. If you are praying (of course you are!) that the Gospel will make

good headway in your district, then be prepared to pull your full weight in local assembly work. Now let's notice the following;

a) The description of the King's men
They are called "his twelve disciples" (v.1), and "the twelve apostles" (v.2). The word 'disciple' means, literally, 'a learner' (*mathetes,* from *manthano,* to learn), and W.E.Vine points out that 'A disciple was not only a pupil, but an adherent; hence they are often spoken of as imitators of their teacher; cp. John 8: 31; 15: 8'. The word 'apostle' means, literally, a 'sent one' (*apostolos,* from *apo* meaning from, and *stello,* meaning to send). This is the only occurrence of the word 'apostle' in Matthew's Gospel. While it is used in a wider sense elsewhere (see, for example, Acts 14: 4, 14), it is used here in a technical sense. See Acts 1: 21-26. Paul qualified for apostleship: "have I not seen Jesus Christ our Lord?" (1 Cor. 9: 1).

The lesson for us is so clear: we cannot expect the Lord to employ us in His service unless we have listened and adhered to His instructions. Obvious, isn't it?

b) The resources of the King's men
"He gave them power (*exousia,* meaning 'authority') against unclean spirits, to cast them out, and to heal all manner of sickness and all manner of disease" (v.1). In the Lord's service, no one is sent "at his own charges", meaning that he doesn't have to buy his own provisions, (1 Cor. 9: 7). When the Lord commissions His servants, He equips them for the task. The call of Gideon (Judges 6: 12-16) and the call of Ezekiel (Ezek. 2: 1-2) illustrate this perfectly. It is worth pointing out here the uniqueness of the Lord. He **conferred** power! Elisha, for example, performed miracles, but he did not, and could not, confer that ability on others.

c) The identity of the King's men
Looking now at the apostles themselves, it has to be said that naturally speaking, they look like unpretentious material! But that it is 'naturally speaking'. Listen to this: "And he (Andrew) brought him (Simon) to Jesus. And when Jesus beheld him, he said, Thou art Simon the son of Jona: thou shalt be called Cephas, which is by interpretation, A stone" (John 1: 42). The Lord saw the possibilities in Peter! "Thou art (what he was)…thou shalt be (what he would become)".

It is interesting to compare the list of apostles given by Matthew with those

Chapter 10

of Mark (3: 16-19) and Luke (6: 12-16 and Acts 1: 13). Matthew and Luke name them in pairs. Luke also names them in groups in Acts 1. Mark names them one by one. H.St.John has some insightful observations here: 'In Matthew, the gospel of fellowship, they are arranged in six pairs: we have to learn that "two are better than one....for if they fall, one will lift up his fellow" (Eccl. 4: 9-10). In Mark, each one of the twelve stands alone (note the "and" repeated eleven times) for while not forgetting the yoke of fellowship, each servant must wait directly upon his Master for guidance and support. The Gospel of Luke follows the same order, but the list given in Acts 1: 13 arranges the eleven in groups (four, three and two pairs), suggesting that the team spirit also has its value'.

The list should be an encouragement to us. These were men of little account so far as this world is concerned. If they had been asked, all of them could have said with Amos, "I was no prophet, neither was I a prophet's son...but *the Lord took me*" (Amos 7: 14-15). In New Testament language, "For ye see your calling, brethren, how that not many wise men after the flesh, not many mighty, not many noble, are called: But God hath chosen the foolish things of the world to confound the wise" (1 Cor. 1: 26-31). Here are a few observations on Matthew's list:

- "The first, Simon, who is called Peter and Andrew his brother" (v.2). Andrew is known as 'Simon Peter's brother', although he was the man who introduced Peter to the Lord. Peter is never called, 'Andrew's brother!' Andrew was quite content to 'play the second fiddle!'

- "James the son of Zebedee, and John his brother" (v.2). Mark alone records the fact that the Lord Jesus surnamed James and John, "Boanerges, which is, The sons of thunder". This could refer to their great zeal as seen, for example, in Luke 9: 54. James was the first martyr of "the twelve" (Acts 12: 1-2). John was self-effacing. He was "the disciple whom Jesus loved". In using this phrase, John was not claiming that the Lord loved him more than the other disciples, but simply that he so much appreciated the love of the Lord for him. He was the disciple "leaning on Jesus' bosom" in the 'upper room' (John 13: 23) and was therefore in a position to obtain the answer to Peter's question (John 13: 1-26), to understand the meaning of the empty grave-clothes (John 20: 8), and to recognise the risen Lord (John 21: 7). How important it is to keep close to Him!

- "Philip, and Bartholomew" (v.3). It is generally agreed that Bartholomew

Matthew

is also known as Nathanael (John 1: 45). He came from "Cana in Galilee" (John 21: 2). It is most helpful to notice that when Nathanael said, "Can there any good thing come out of Nazareth?", Philip didn't argue: he simply said "Come and see" (John 1: 46-47). That's worth remembering!

- "Thomas, and Matthew the publican" (v.3). Thomas is notable for his devotion to the Lord": it was Thomas who said, "Let us also go, that we may die with him" (John 11: 16) and, in blank despair, "Lord, we know not whither thou goest; and how can we know the way?" (John 14: 5). Did Thomas actually "reach hither" his finger and his hand? It seems likely that he cried immediately "My Lord and my God" (John 20: 27-28). Matthew is only here called "the publican". In other words, he **describes himself** in this way. As R.H.Mounce observes, "It reflects the author's amazement that Jesus would call into his service one who had served in such a disreputable occupation". After all, not many people in those days would want a tax-collector for a friend!

- "James the son of Alphaeus, and Lebbaeus, whose surname was Thaddaeus" (v.3). "It is suggested that James son of Alphaeus is so named in order to distinguish him from James the brother of John. Thaddaeus, (some manuscripts have Lebbaeus) is called Judas son of James" in both Luke 6: 16 and Acts 1:13. It is conjectured that Judas was his original name but, after stigma was attached to the name by Judas Iscariot, he changed it to Thaddaeus (meaning 'warmhearted')" (R.H.Mounce). Support for the suggestion may be found in John 14: 22, "Judas saith unto him, not Iscariot..."

- "Simon the Canaanite, and Judas Iscariot, who also betrayed him" (v.4). So far as Simon is concerned, "the Canaanite" is, literally, 'the Cananaean', deriving from a Hebrew root meaning 'zealous', and it is often suggested that he once belonged to the Zealot party, which wanted freedom for Israel. But he had gained freedom from sin! Norman Crawford notes that Simon the Zealot and Matthew "were at the two extremes of Jewish life. One belonged to a radical group among the Jews who were fanatically opposed to Rome and had taken a blood oath never to bow to her authority, and never to countenance those who did, and the other was an employee of Rome (he was a 'quisling') before the Lord called him. Round the Lord Jesus these two extremes met. We never read of a clash between them".

Matthew, Mark and Luke all end with reference to the Lord's betrayal by

Judas Iscariot. He 'is a solemn instance of how far a person may be under the influence and power of Christianity, and yet become an apostate' (Morrish's Bible Dictionary). Iscariot is said to be a Hebrew word "with the meaning, 'a man of Kerioth': Kerioth was a little place in Judah (Joshua 15: 25). Judas was thus the only Judean" (supplied by J. Waldron).

What a picture! The Lord brought together a 'mixed bunch'. With the exception of Judas Iscariot, they were welded together by a love for Him. Compare the mixed bunch that surrounded David in the cave of Adullam. See 1 Samuel 22: 2.

B) The King's mandate, vv.5-15
We can divide the 'King's mandate' as follows: *(a)* where they were to go (vv.5-6); *(b)* what they were to do (vv.7-8); *(c)* how they were to proceed (vv.9-15).

a) Where they were to go, vv.5-6
"**Go not** into the way of the Gentiles, and into any city of the Samaritans enter ye not: but **go rather** to the lost sheep of the house of Israel". The words, "any city of the Samaritans" refers to the area between Judaea and Galilee where a mixed population lived as a result of colonization (2 Kings 17: 24-28). The apostles were to go to "the lost sheep of the house of Israel". These had "no shepherd" (Matt. 9: 36), and were led by "blind guides" (Matt. 23: 16, 24). It has been said that these instructions are "consistent with the New Testament emphasis that God has directed His redemptive efforts to the Jew first and then to the Gentiles (cf. Rom. 1: 16; 2: 9-10)" (R.H.Mounce).

We should notice, however, that when the "seventy" were dispatched, they were told to go "before his face into every city and place, whither he himself would come" (Luke 10: 1). He had just sent messengers "before his face… into a village of the Samaritans, to make ready for him" (Luke 9: 52). The mandate was enlarged still further when the disciples were commanded to "Go…and teach all nations" (Matt. 28: 20). That mandate is still in force!

b) What they were to do, vv.7-8
"And as ye go, preach, saying, The kingdom of heaven is at hand. Heal the sick, cleanse the leper, raise the dead, cast out devils (demons): freely ye have received, freely give". John the Baptist (Matt. 3: 2) and the Lord Jesus (Matt. 4: 17) preached that "the kingdom of heaven is at hand", emphasising the need for repentance. The King had come to establish His kingdom, but

He could not reign over rebellious subjects. The King's messengers were to display their credentials and so authenticate their preaching. Had not the Scriptures stated that "your God will come with vengeance, even God with a recompence; he will come and save you. **Then** the eyes of the blind shall be opened, and the ears of the deaf shall be unstopped. Then shall the lame man leap as an hart, and the tongue of the dumb sing" (Is. 35: 4-6)? Compare Matthew 11: 2-6. As Wm. MacDonald observes, "The Jews demanded signs (1 Cor. 1: 22), so God graciously condescended to give them signs". Alas, in the face of all the available evidence, the King was still rejected.

The blessings of the King were to be made available "without money and without price" (Is. 55: 1). "As to remuneration, the Lord's representatives were to make no charge for their services. They had received their blessings without cost, and were to dispense them on the same basis" (Wm. MacDonald). In the Lord's own words: "freely ye have received, freely give".

It should be said that the message of "so great salvation; which at the first began to be spoken by the Lord, and was confirmed...by them that heard him", was also similarly authenticated: "God also bearing them witness, both with signs and wonders, and with divers miracles, and gifts of the Holy Ghost" (Heb. 2: 3-4).

c) How they were to proceed, vv.9-15
We should notice three things here: *(i)* their provision (vv.9-10); *(ii)* their accommodation (vv.11-13); *(iii)* their rejection (vv.14-15).

i) Their provision. "Provide neither gold, nor silver, nor brass in your purses, nor scrip for your journey, neither two coats, neither shoes, nor yet staves: for the workman is worthy of his meat" (vv. 9-10). The word "scrip" (*pera*) refers to 'a traveller's leathern bag or pouch for holding provisions' (W.E.Vine). It has been said that they must show by their attitude to material things that they were men of God.

Commentators suggest that the disciples were prohibited from providing themselves with financial means before commencing the journey, and that they were allowed to take only the most necessary items with them, so as not to rely on their own provision, but on God, who would care for them.

It is possible, however, to take an alternative view of these verses. They were to accept support ("the workman is worthy of his meat"), but bearing in mind that the word "provide" (*ktaomai*) means 'to procure for oneself, get, gain, acquire' (W.E.Vine), they were not to **make a trade** of their work. Their main concern was their **work** for God, not what they might get out of it. Paul was able to say, "we are not as many, which corrupt the word of God (make a trade of the word of God): but as of God, in the sight of God speak we in Christ" (2 Cor. 2: 17). The words, "the workman is worthy of his meat", are explained in 1 Corinthians 9: 11-14. However, it should be remembered that the Lord's teaching here does not authorise His servants today to expect support from unsaved people. The early preachers of the gospel "for his name's sake...went forth, taking nothing of the Gentiles" (3 John 7). In our present passage, however, the apostles were "Israelites preaching to Israelites, and it was a recognised principle among the Jews that the labourer deserves his food" (Wm. MacDonald).

ii) Their accommodation. "And into whatsoever city or town ye shall enter, enquire who in it is worthy; and there abide till ye go hence. And when ye come into an house, salute it. And if the house be worthy, let your peace come upon it: but if it be not worthy, let your peace return to you" (vv.11-13). While the instruction to stay in a "worthy" house could mean that it was not to be a disreputable place, it more likely refers to 'a household willing to receive the message; perhaps those who were disciples already would be living there' (J.Heading). They were to avoid giving offence to their hosts by leaving for better accommodation: "there abide till ye go hence". The words, "be content with such things as ye have" (Heb 13: 5) apply here! The servants of God must be courteous: "when ye come into an house, salute it". The word "salute" (*aspazomai*) means 'to greet' and in context here could be rendered 'pay respects'. But the Lord's servants were "not obligated to pray for God's peace on it, that is...pronounce a blessing on the family", if any household refused to accommodate them (Wm. MacDonald).

iii) Their rejection. "And whosoever shall not receive you, nor hear your words, when ye shall depart out of that house or city, shake off the dust of your feet. Verily I say unto you, It shall be more tolerable for the land of Sodom and Gomorrha in the day of judgment, than for that city", (vv.14-15). It has been said that time was precious, and time was not to be wasted when there was no prospect of fruitfulness. There was visual condemnation (v.14), and verbal condemnation (v.15). In this way, the Lord prepared His disciples to meet unbelief and impenitence in those to whom they preached. We have an example of this in Acts 13: 50-51, "But the Jews stirred up the devout and honourable women, and the chief men of the city (Antioch), and raised persecution against Paul and Barnabas, and expelled them out of their coasts. But they shook off the dust of their feet against them, and came to Iconium". The act of shaking off the dust of their feet signifies that those who reject the message will be rejected themselves and 'that the messengers would have nothing in common with rejectors of their Lord. They would take nothing from them, not even the dust of their city' (Norman Crawford, *What the Bible Teaches - Luke*). The law of privilege determining responsibility is clearly operative here: "It shall be more tolerable for the land of Sodom and Gomorrha in the day of judgment, than for that city". The Jewish cities had the privilege of listening to the King's messengers, but what an immense responsibility this placed upon them!

In our next study, God willing, we will address the second major division in the Lord's teaching (vv.16-23). As we will see, He describes the conditions which His servants will face after He had returned to heaven.

Note: A considerable amount of material in this study has been compiled from notes taken of an address by Mr. Bernard Osborne at Corsham, Wiltshire, on 5th May, 2008.

"Ye shall be brought before governors and kings for my sake"

Read Chapter 10: 16-23
In introducing this chapter, we suggested the following divisions: *(1)* the current commission (vv.1-15): these verses refer to the immediate preaching tour; *(2)* the coming conditions (vv.16-23): quite evidently, these were not experienced by the disciples at that particular time: they belong to a later period; *(3)* the counsel (a changed word here!) for the disciples (vv.24-42): the instructions and assurances in these verses were given to strengthen and encourage disciples at all times in their work for Him.

1) THE CURRENT COMMISSION, vv.1-15
As we have already noted, this related to Israel only: "Go not into the way of the Gentiles, and into any city of the Samaritans enter ye not: but go rather to the lost sheep of the house of Israel" (vv.5-6). This is consistent with Paul's statement that the "gospel...is the power of God unto salvation to every one that believeth; *to the Jew first*, and also to the Greek" (Rom. 1: 16). The commission in Matthew 28 relates to *all nations*: "Go ye therefore, and teach all nations, baptizing them in the name of the Father, and of the Son, and of the Holy Ghost" (28: 19).

These verses draw our attention *(a)* to the King's men (vv.1-4) and *(b)* to the King's mandate (vv.5-15). In connection with the former, we noted *(i)* their description ("disciples...apostles"); *(ii)* their resources ("He gave them power"); *(iii)* their identity (the names of "the twelve" are given). In connection with the latter, we noted *(i)* where they were to go (vv.5-6); *(ii)* what they were to do (vv.7-8); *(iii)* how they were to proceed (vv.9-15). This brings us to:

2) THE COMING CONDITIONS, vv.16-23

Quite clearly, these verses paint a far wider picture than vv.1-15. We must notice at least two differences:

- *In the first place,* the antagonism is far greater. The Lord had already warned His disciples that they would not find a ready ear everywhere they went: "whosoever shall not receive you, nor hear your words, when ye depart out of that house or city, shake off the dust of your feet" (v.14). Now He describes ferocious opposition: "they will deliver you up to the councils, and they will scourge you in their synagogues" (v17). When the apostles returned from their immediate preaching tour, they said nothing about persecution and scourging (Mark 6: 30; Luke 9: 10).

- *In the second place,* the sphere is far greater. The Lord had limited the ministry of "the twelve" to the "lost sheep of the house of **Israel**" (v.6), but now they are told that they would be "brought before **governors and kings** for my sake, for a testimony against them ('to them', RV) and the **Gentiles**" (v.18). However, at the same time, since the passage refers to preaching in "the cities of Israel" right up to the coming of "the Son of man" (v.23), it does appear that Lord Jesus makes particular reference here to the Jewish nation, not only as it existed when He was on earth and after His return to heaven, but as it will exist at the end-time. Before the Lord's public return, there will be a resumption of preaching in Israel. That is, after the Lord has returned for His believing people of the current dispensation (1 Thess. 4: 13-18). Once again, the nation will be told that "The kingdom of heaven is at hand". Further details are given by the Lord Jesus in His 'Olivet Discourse' (Matt. 24: 3-14).

When the Lord Jesus said, "Behold, I send you" (v.16), He made it very clear that their work for Him would involve grave danger. He did not send out His servants without warning them of the consequences. He repeated these warnings in His "upper room" ministry: "If the world hate you, ye know that it hated me before it hated you...These things have I spoken unto you, that ye should not be offended. They shall put you out of the synagogues: yea, the time cometh, that whosoever killeth you will think that he doeth God service (Saul of Tarsus thought like this: see Acts 26: 9)...But these things have I told you, that when the time shall come, ye may remember that I told you of them" (John 15: 18-21; 16: 1-4). Paul evidently had the Lord's teaching here in mind when he warned the believers at Thessalonica that dangers lay ahead, telling them that "no man should be moved by these afflictions: for yourselves know that **we are appointed thereunto**. For verily, when we were with you, we told you before that we should suffer tribulation; even as it came to pass, and ye know" (1 Thess. 3: 3-4). The apostles and early believers were left under no illusions: it would be 'rough going' for them in the extreme. We should be under no illusions either. The words, "For unto you it is given in the behalf of Christ, not only to believe on him, but also to suffer for his sake" (Phil. 1: 29), apply to **us** as well.

In considering the Lord's warnings to His disciples, we must notice the following: *(a)* the authority they carried: "I send you" (v.16); *(b)* the attributes they must exhibit: "be...wise as serpents, and harmless as doves" (v.16); *(c)* the animosity they would experience (vv.17-21): this would come from three sources, from religion (v.17), from the State (vv.18-20), and from family (v.21); *(d)* the endurance they must show (vv.22-23).

a) Their authority they carried, v.16

"Behold, I send you". The 'great commission' at the end of Matthew's Gospel carries the same authority: "All power (authority) is given unto me in heaven and in earth. Go ye therefore, and teach all nations (make disciples of all nations), baptizing them in the name of the Father, and of the Son, and of the Holy Ghost: teaching them to observe all things whatsoever I have commanded you" (Matt. 28: 18-20). This was their only authority. In the words of John the Baptist, "he that sent me...the same said unto me" (John 1: 33).

Here are some further examples: *(i)* Jeremiah was told, "Before I formed thee in the belly I knew thee; and before thou camest forth out of the womb *I* sanctified thee, and *I* ordained thee a prophet unto the nations" (Jer. 1: 5); *(ii)* Amos said: "I was no prophet, neither was I a prophet's son; but I was an herdman, and a gatherer of sycamore fruit: and the **Lord** took me as I followed the flock, and the **Lord** said unto me, Go, prophesy unto my people Israel" (Amos 7: 14-15); *(iii)* Paul said: "Paul, an apostle, (**not** of men, **neither** by man, **but** by Jesus Christ, and God the Father, who raised him from the dead") (Gal. 1: 1).

We have already noticed the Lord's words, "Pray ye therefore the Lord of the harvest, that *he* will send forth labourers into his harvest" (Matt. 9: 38). While it does not fall within our current study, it should be said that "thus saith the Lord" should be our *only* court of appeal in *all* matters of doctrine and practice. How deep are our convictions? Half-hearted convictions, or worse, will soon disappear entirely when the 'screw turns' and the pressure mounts.

b) The attributes they must exhibit, v.16

"Behold, I send you forth as sheep in the midst of wolves: be ye therefore wise as serpents, and harmless as doves". The Lord describes His servants in three ways:

i) As sheep. It all seems quite illogical, doesn't it? Sheep and wolves are at opposite ends of the spectrum. Paul warned the Ephesian elders that they could expect "grievous wolves...not sparing the flock" (Acts 20: 29). These were doctrinal 'wolves', whereas the Lord Jesus refers here rather to wolves who would savage them by brute force. The warning here is expanded in vv.17-18. It should be said that while the Jewish people are described as "sheep having no shepherd" (9: 36), the Lord's disciples, although "as sheep in the midst of wolves", were not sheep without a shepherd. The Lord Jesus was not "an hireling" who, "seeth the wolf coming, and leaveth the sheep, and fleeth" (John 10: 12). It wasn't illogical after all! Bearing in mind the ferocious attacks of their enemies, the Lord's servants needed to be... wise as serpents, and harmless as doves". So:

ii) As serpents. Scholars point out that the word "wise" (*phronimos*) means 'prudent, sensible, practically wise' (W.E.Vine). In this case, the Lord refers to the serpent's caution in avoiding danger. The Lord's people should not 'ask for trouble'. The word denotes 'wariness', not 'wiliness'. Serving Him is often fraught with difficulty and danger, without deliberately stirring it up, and the Lord's servants should avoid giving needless offence. On the other hand, while there is certainly 'such a thing as a righteous and holy zeal which is "not according to knowledge" (Rom. 10: 2)', we must not allow 'our so-called prudence...to degenerate into a compromising line of conduct, or downright unfaithfulness' (J.C.Ryle). To be "wise as serpents" means that we must "walk circumspectly (meaning diligently or carefully), not as fools but as wise" (Eph. 5: 15).

iii) As doves. The word "harmless" (*akeraios*) means 'unmixed, with absence of foreign mixture...pure...used metaphorically in the New

Testament of what is guileless, sincere' (W.E.Vine). The Lord's people are to be "blameless and harmless (*akeraios*), the sons of God, without rebuke, in the midst of a crooked and perverse nation" (Phil. 2: 15). It has been defined as 'purity of intention' (R.H.Mounce).

c) The animosity they would experience, vv.17-21

As we have already noted, opposition would come from three sources: *(i)* from religion (v.17); *(ii)* from the State (vv.18-20); *(iii)* from family (v.21), reminding us that "all that will live godly in Christ Jesus shall suffer persecution" (2 Tim. 3: 12).

i) From religion. "But beware ('be on your guard') of men (reminding us of the necessity to be "wise as serpents"); for they will deliver you up to the councils, and they will scourge you in their synagogues" (v.17). They were to be on their guard against unbelieving Jews who would haul them before their courts and flog them in their synagogues. According to a piece supplied by Justin Waldron, 'Apart from the great Sanhedrin in Jerusalem, which had seventy-one members, there were little courts (twenty-three members) in every town with more than one hundred and twenty inhabitants. These were closely connected to the synagogues'. Leaving aside the details for a moment, it is not without significance that the opposition here comes from men who considered themselves to be God's people. This is not the ill-will of **heathen** authorities.

Peter and John appeared before the 'great council' in Jerusalem (Acts 4: 5-22; 5: 27-41) where they were threatened and beaten (Acts 5: 40). Paul also appeared before the same council (Acts 23: 1-9), and writes, "Of the Jews five times received I forty stripes save one" (2 Cor. 11: 24). We have already noted the Lord's words, "They shall put you out of the synagogues: yea, the time cometh, that whosoever killeth you will think that he doeth God service" (John 16: 2). Having decided that "if any man did confess that he (the Lord Jesus) was the Christ, he should be put out of the synagogue", the man born bind was duly excommunicated (John 9: 22, 34). The "Good Shepherd" was on hand to help him (John 9: 35). He found His sheep. The church at Smyrna experienced "the blasphemy of them which say they are Jews, and are not, but are the synagogue of Satan" (Rev. 2: 9). There can be little doubt that the Lord refers here to a literal synagogue.

All this reminds us that the greatest enemy of the Gospel is institutionalised religion. The progress of the Ecumenical Movement with its so-called 'local councils of Christian churches' should sound the same warning in our ears "Beware of men".

ii) From the State. "And ye shall be brought before governors and kings (don't forget 1 Tim 2: 1-2) for my sake, for a testimony against them and the Gentiles" (v.18). Not now Jewish authorities, but Gentile authorities, although it should be said that in the book of Acts, it was often the Jews who were responsible for bringing the early preachers before Gentile authorities. As Wm. Kelly observes, "While hating the Gentile yoke, they would be quite willing to invoke Gentile authority where it became a question of Christ's followers". R.V.G. Tasker is at pains to point out that "by *governors* is meant Roman provincial governors, and by *kings* the Herodian princes who were sometimes given the courtesy-title 'kings'". While it could be said that the immediate reference is to these rulers, it can hardly be limited to them. The word "governors" (*hegemon*) is the general word for rulers, and the word "kings" is, again, a general word which need not be limited to 'Herodian princes'. The Lord's words here must apply not only to the duration of the Roman empire, but to the succeeding centuries, including our own day and beyond. Returning to New Testament times, John Heading points out that Paul, for one, "appeared before Sergius Paulus, Gallio, Felix, Festus and Agrippa, while at the end of his life he appeared before Nero, the cruel and abominable emperor in Rome". Ananias was told by the Lord that Paul was "a chosen vessel unto me, to bear my name before the Gentiles, and kings, and the children of Israel" (Acts 9: 15). Finally, we must not forget that the Lord Himself went where His disciples were to go. He appeared before a governor and a king (Luke 23:1-12: 1 Tim. 6: 13).

All this reminds us that in addition to opposition from religious sources, there is increasing opposition from the State. Recent legislation in the U.K. alone illustrates the point. Adherence to "all the counsel of God" is becoming fraught with increasing difficulty. To openly declare that "Neither is there salvation in any other: for there is none other name under heaven given among men, whereby we must be saved" (Acts 4: 12), is not politically correct, and it may not be too far in the future before further legislation is introduced to curb the message of the Gospel. Add equal-opportunity legislation, the legalisation (and promotion) of sodomy, the vilest of all human relationships, and the increasing rules and regulations in connection with Gospel work amongst children (surely a further satanically-engineered device to hinder God's work), and it may not be long before many of us appear before State courts to answer for our fidelity to the Word of God.

Does all this mean that we are left speechless, defenceless, and on 'a hiding to nothing'? Never! We must listen again to the Saviour:

- **The Lord's name will be honoured.** "And ye shall be brought before governors and kings for **my sake**, for a testimony against them (or **'to them'**, RV) and the Gentiles (v.18). The words 'a testimony to them' (RV) may refer to the Jews, in which case the statement embraces both Jew and Gentile. In the Epistle to the Philippians, Paul refers to the testimony of his imprisonment at Rome. It was public knowledge there that Paul was not in prison because he was a criminal. His words, "so that my bonds in Christ are manifest in all the palace" (Phil. 1: 13) are better rendered, 'so that my bonds have become manifest **as being in Christ** in all the praetorium and to all others'. In the words of M.R.Vincent *(Word Studies of the New Testament),* "The force of this statement lies in the fact that his imprisonment had become a matter of notoriety for Christ...All who came in contact with this prisoner would soon discover that he was in chains, not as a criminal, but as a Christian".

- **The Lord's help will be experienced.** "But when they deliver you up (not 'if they deliver you up'), take no thought (*merimnao*: to be anxious) how or what ye shall speak: for it shall be given you in that same hour what ye shall speak. For it is not you that speak, but the Spirit of your Father which speaketh in you" (vv.19-20). Peter experienced this: "And when they (the Jewish authorities) had set them (Peter and John) in the midst, they asked, By what power, or by what name, have ye done this? Then Peter, filled with the Holy Spirit, said unto them..." (Acts 4: 7-8). Paul experienced this: "At my first answer no man stood with me...Notwithstanding the Lord stood with me, and strengthened me; that by me the preaching might be fully known" (2 Tm. 4: 16-17). After all, since His servants would be "brought before governors and kings for **my sake"**, it is not surprising, in view of His marvellous grace, that He will undertake for them in every way. He is no man's debtor! (Needless to say, this does *not* refer to lazy preachers! In that case it is true to say that 'if a man stands up not knowing what he is going to say, no one will know what he has said when he sits down!').

It is worth noting that the Lord Jesus said, "For it is not you that speak, but the Spirit of *your* Father which speaketh in you" (v.20). He did not say, 'the Spirit of *our* Father', anymore than 'I ascend unto our Father and to our God' (John 20: 17). In saying "my Father" (for example, John 8: 49; 14: 7) the Lord emphasises His eternal Sonship. In saying "your Father" He emphasises what the Father had become to them (and us) in time.

iii) From family. "And the brother shall deliver up the brother to death, and the father the child: and the children shall rise up against their parents, and cause them to be put to death" (v.21). See also vv.34-36. While, as John Heading observes, "no such events are recorded in the Acts", believing Jews and converted Muslims have often been subjected to heartless treatment from relatives, and this continues to the present day. John Heading continues: "Turning to Christ and being baptised because of faith may lead to family persecution even unto death...In our country, lesser persecution may take place within the family circle when a young convert has parents who ridicule the truth of salvation through the blood of Christ". Following Christ often comes at a heavy cost.

d) The endurance they must show, vv.22-23
These verses merge past and future events, and look forward to the final mission to Israel.

There can be little doubt that these verses refer particularly to the unprecedented pressures of the coming 'great tribulation' (Matt. 24: 21) when "because iniquity shall abound, the love of many shall wax cold. But he that shall endure to the end, the same shall be saved" (Matt. 24: 12-13). It must be said here that salvation is *not* by endurance, but the *evidence* of salvation is seen by endurance. Compare Hebrews 3: 14. The Lord's words (v.22) do not imply that salvation is obtained "by faithfulness or devotedness. All is of grace. But where there is a genuine work of God in the soul there will be final perseverance, whether in the days of the great tribulation yet to come, or in this present evil age" (H.A.Ironside). Endurance in this way is evidence of love for Christ. It is "for *my name's sake*". That is, that His beloved name might be furthered and advantaged. Compare Acts 5: 41; 9: 16; 15: 26; 21: 13; 3 John v.7.

The words, "But when they persecute you in this city, flee ye to another" (v.23) make it clear that "the disciple of Christ is not to court persecution or needlessly expose himself in a fool-hardy way to danger" (H.A.Ironside). They were to be "wise as serpents" (v.16). Paul certainly acted in this way: see, for example, Acts 13: 51; 14: 6; 17: 10-15. The Lord's statement, "Ye shall not have gone over the cities of Israel, till the Son of man be come" (v.23), evidently mean that not all in Israel will hear the message, perhaps because of the raging opposition and persecution at the end-time. The public return of the Lord Jesus as "Son of man" (His title in relation to earth) will signal the end of the dark days of the tribulation, and the testimony of

Matthew

His witnesses will give place to the fulfillment of their preaching, and "then shall all the tribes of the earth mourn, and they shall see the Son of man coming in the clouds of heaven with power and great glory" (Matt. 24: 30). His coming will complete their unfinished work.

"The very hairs of your head are all numbered"

Read Chapter 10: 24-42

In our two previous studies, we suggested that the chapter may be divided as follows: *(1)* the current commission (vv.1-15): these verses refer to the immediate preaching tour; *(2)* the coming conditions (vv.16-23): quite evidently, these were not experienced by the disciples at that particular time: they belong to a later period, beginning in the book of Acts and extending to the end-time; *(3)* the counsel for the disciples (vv.24-42): the instructions and assurances in these verses were given to strengthen and encourage disciples at all times in their work for Him.

1) THE CURRENT COMMISSION, vv.1-15

As we have already noted, this related to Israel only: "Go not into the way of the Gentiles, and into any city of the Samaritans enter ye not: but go rather to the lost sheep of the house of Israel" (vv.5-6). These verses describe the men (vv.1-4) and their mission (vv.5-15).

2) THE COMING CONDITIONS, vv.16-23

Having noted that these verses envisage a wider sphere of service and a greater degree of opposition than anything described in vv.1-15, we noticed the following: *(a)* the authority they carried: "I send you" (v.16); *(b)* the attributes they must exhibit: "be...wise as serpents, and harmless as doves" (v.16); *(c)* the animosity they would experience (vv.17-21): this would come from three sources, from religion (v.17), from the State (vv.18-20), and from family (v.21); *(d)* the endurance they must show (vv.22-23).

But the Lord did not leave the matter there. He equipped them for the task that lay ahead, with all its problems and difficulties, by describing various aspects of their service for Him. This brings us to:

3) THE COUNSEL FOR THE DISCIPLES, vv.24-42

The Lord's teaching here may be summarised as follows: their service for Him involved *(a) conformity* (vv.24-25): "It is enough for the disciple that he be as his master" (v.25); *(b) confession* (vv.26-33): we must fearlessly (note the repetition of "fear not") confess Him (vv.26-31) in which case He will confess us (vv.32-33); *(c) conflict* (vv.34-39) involving the sacrifice of relationships (vv.34-37) and the sacrifice of ourselves (vv.38-39); *(d) compensation* (vv.40-42): the word "reward" occurs three times in these verses.

It will not escape notice that this is by no means a 'mixed bag' (we would not expect this anyway!). There is an evident continuity in the Lord's teaching. To be **conformed** to Him in bearing His reproach (vv.24-25) will involve **confessing** Him "before men" (vv.26-33), and this will inevitably bring **conflict** into our lives (vv.34-39) but the Lord is no man's debtor and there will be abundant **compensation** (vv.40-42).

a) Conformity, vv.24-25

Having said that "ye shall be hated of all men for my name's sake" (v.22) and that they would experience persecution (v.23), the Lord reminded His disciples, lest they should wonder why they should have to suffer such ill-treatment, that the servant must not expect to be treated better than his master: "The disciple is not above his master, nor the servant above his lord. It is enough for the disciple that he be as his master, and the servant as his lord". This is a general principle. Its application follows: "If they have called the master of the house Beelzebub, how much more shall they call them of his household?" While discipleship involves sharing the Master's rejection, "it is enough" for the disciple to "be as his master, and the servant as his lord". That in itself should be sufficient for us. It was certainly the case for Paul: "That I might know him, and the power of his resurrection, and the fellowship of his sufferings, being made conformable unto his death" (Phil. 3: 10). It has been pointed out (T. Miller) that Gehazi was not content to be "as his master", and in consequence, he forfeited his well-being: "he went out from his presence (Elisha's presence) a leper as white as snow" (2 Kings 5: 20,27)

The name "Beelzebub" or 'Beelzebul' (margin) is of uncertain origin, although it is generally thought to be connected with Baal-zebub, the god of Ekron (2 Kings 1: 2, 6). The Pharisees called Beelzebub "the prince of the devils (demons)" (Matt. 9: 34; 12: 24). The name may mean 'the lord of the high place' or 'lord of the house' (in which case, the Lord's expression, 'the master of the house', becomes even more significant), but it was commonly accepted amongst the Jews, following the Aramaic *Beelzeboul,* to mean 'the lord of the flies' or 'the lord of the dunghill'. It was both derisory and defamatory.

It was derisory: in using this name, they poured scorn and derision on the Saviour. It was defamatory: they said that he was empowered by "the prince of the devils" (Matt. 12: 24). The Lord's servants can therefore expect derision and defamation.

The repetition of the word "master" calls for comment. In the first two cases (vv.24,25) the word (*didaskalos*) means 'teacher', but in the third case, the word (*oikodespotes*) is translated exactly - "the master of the house" (v.25). It is elsewhere translated "the goodman of the house" (Matt. 20: 11; 24: 43; Mark 14: 14; Luke 12: 39). We must not overlook the twofold relationship: "disciple...master"; "servant...lord", or the fact that while He is "the master of the house", we are members of "his household (*oikiakos*)". The expression, "it is enough for the disciple to be as his master" also occurs in John 13: 16, in relation to menial tasks, and in John 15: 20, in relation, again, to persecution.

b) Confession, vv.26-33
The structure of these verses is beyond doubt: we are to confess Him (vv.26-31) and if this is the case, He will confess us (vv.32-33).

i) We must confess Him, vv.26-31. We must do so, fearlessly, in three ways:

- We are to have no fear in speaking for Him, vv.26-27. "Fear them not therefore (with all their derision and defamation): for there is nothing covered, that shall not be revealed; and hid, that shall not be known. What I tell you in darkness, that speak ye in light: and what ye hear in the ear, that preach ye upon the housetops". It is tempting to suggest that the Lord's words, "Fear them not therefore: for there is nothing covered, that shall not be revealed; and hid, that shall not be known" (v.26), refer to the future when "God shall judge the secrets of men by Jesus Christ" (Rom. 2: 16). However, it does seem that the words "covered" and "hid" refer to those who oppose and deride the Lord's servants, in which case He assures His disciples that they need have no fear in proclaiming His word, even though "the natural man receiveth not the things of the Spirit of God: for they are foolishness unto him" (1 Cor. 2: 14). In due time, what was "covered" and "hid" to the hearers would become abundantly clear. Peter gives us an example: "there shall come in the last days scoffers...saying, Where is the promise of his coming? For since the fathers fell asleep, all things continue as they were from the beginning of the creation...But the day of the Lord will come..." (2 Pet. 3: 1-10). What is "covered" and "hid" so far as the "scoffers" were concerned, will be "revealed" and "known". The teaching therefore given privately to the disciples ("what I tell you in darkness…what ye hear in the ear") can therefore be proclaimed publicly without fear and hesitation ("that speak ye in light…that preach ye upon the housetops"). The Lord Jesus exemplified this perfectly: "The Lord God hath given me the tongue of the learned, that I should know how to speak a word in season to him that is weary: he wakeneth morning by morning, he wakeneth mine ear to hear as the learned" (Isaiah 50: 4). He proclaimed what He had heard in His Father's presence "morning by morning".

Armed with the Word of God, we are to be fearless in our service, always bearing in mind that "The fear of man bringeth a snare: but whoso putteth his trust in the Lord shall be safe" (Prov. 29: 25). Jeremiah was told: "speak unto them all that I command thee: be not dismayed at their faces, lest I confound thee before them" (Jer. 1: 17). It is most important to listen at all times to the Lord's voice in His Word: it is equally important to convey what He tells us to other people.

- *We are to have no fear in suffering for Him, v.28*. "And fear them not which kill the body, but are not able to kill the soul: but rather fear him which is able to destroy both soul and body in hell". The martyrdom of Stephen illustrates the fact that men may "kill the body", but that is all. Stephen looked beyond death. As the Jews stoned him, he "kneeled down, and cried with a loud voice, Lord, lay not this sin to their charge". A short while before he had seen "the glory of God, and Jesus standing on the right hand of God" (Acts 7: 54-60). For the Lord's people, death, whatever its cause, is to be "absent from the body, and to be present with the Lord" (2 Cor. 5: 8); it is "to depart, and to be with Christ" (Phil. 1: 23). In fact, "death" is included in the list of benefits belonging to the believer! See 1 Corinthians 3: 21-23.

It is God alone who is "able to destroy both soul and body in hell". It is most important to notice that the Lord did ***not*** say that His disciples were to fear ***hell***, but to "fear ***him***, which is able to destroy both soul and body in hell" The Saviour made it perfectly clear that "he that heareth my word, and believeth (on) him that sent me, hath everlasting life, and shall not come into condemnation; but is passed from death unto life" (John 5: 24). The disciples were not to fear God because ***they*** were in danger of hell, but because His punishment of sinful men is a solemn reminder of His righteousness. To put it in Bible language, "The day of the Lord will come…seeing then that all these things shall be dissolved, what ***manner of persons ought ye to be*** in all holy conversation and godliness" (2 Pet. 3: 10-11). The epitaph of

John Knox reads: "Here lies one who feared God so much that he never feared the face of any man".

It is worth pointing out that the words, "able to destroy both soul and body in hell" do not refer to annihilation. The word "destroy" (*apollumi*) means 'ruin, loss, not of being, but of well-being' (W.E.Vine). The word "hell" (*geena*), which occurs twelve times in the New Testament, refers to the eternal fire.

- **We are to have no fear over His sufficiency for us, vv.29-31**. "Are not two **sparrows** sold for a farthing? and one of them shall not fall to the ground without your Father...Fear not therefore, ye are of more value than many sparrows". According to Morrish's Bible Dictionary, "In Palestine sparrows are plentiful" and "There are several species of sparrow in Palestine", although the entry states that "It is supposed that various kinds of small birds are alluded to by these names (*tsippor* and *strouthion*) being so called because of their 'chirping', which would include the sparrow". Sparrows, the cheapest thing on sale in the market, were bought and eaten by poor people. According to W.E.Vine a farthing (*assarion*) was 'one-tenth of a drachma, or one sixteenth of a Roman *denarius*'. Just think about it: the God who created the heavenly bodies and "calleth them all **by names** by the greatness of his might" (Isaiah 40: 25-26) is equally aware of every sparrow! According to Matthew, you could buy two sparrows for a farthing, whereas Luke tells us that you could by five sparrows for two farthings. It has often been said that this means that one was thrown in for nothing when you spent two farthings. But not one of them (not even the free one) is forgotten by God! If God took notice of the commonest and cheapest of birds, then we cannot doubt His interest and concern for His people! Perhaps the Lord was also saying that although His people would be treated by their enemies as valueless and expendable, they were of immense value to God! But this is not all. Sparrows are small birds, but the hairs of our head are even smaller! "But the very **hairs of your head** are all numbered. As Leon Morris (writing on Luke) observes, 'the importance of this does not lie in the actual count, but in the fact that God cares enough about His people to know the minutest detail about them. He knows things that they do not know themselves'. The numbering of the hairs on the head is proverbial (1 Sam 14: 45; 2 Sam 14: 11; 1 Kings 1: 52)

No wonder the Saviour concluded, "Fear not therefore..." When faced with pain and death for their loyalty to Christ, His people can rest in the fact that they are precious to God, and that every detail about them is known to Him.

ii) He will confess us, vv.32-33. "Whosoever therefore shall confess me before men, him will I confess also before my Father which is in heaven. But whosoever shall deny me before men, him will I also deny before my Father which is in heaven". We have to decide whether the Lord refers here to faithfulness or unfaithfulness on the part of true believers, or to believers ("whosoever…shall confess me") as opposed to unbelievers ("whosoever shall deny me").

It has to be said that in the context, the first suggestion appears to carry most weight, and support for this is found in 2 Tim. 2: 12, "If we suffer, we shall also reign with him: if we deny him, he also will deny us". He will not, of course, withdraw our salvation. That rests upon His death and resurrection. But He will not award us a position of honour in the kingdom. The Lord Jesus taught that "whosoever shall be ashamed of me, and of my words, in this adulterous and sinful generation, of him also shall the Son of man be ashamed, when He cometh in the glory of his kingdom, with the holy angels" (Mark 8: 38). We mustn't think that every Christian is going to wear a crown whatever happens! It must be said that Peter denied the Lord "before men", but this, surely, does not mean that he will be denied in heaven! John Heading must be right in saying that the denial "does not refer to a believer who in a moment of weakness fails to witness for his Lord before men". Having said this, there is considerable support amongst commentators for the view that the Lord refers to "that kind of denial that is habitual and final" (Wm. MacDonald), and that the people concerned will hear Him say, "I never knew you: depart from me, ye that work iniquity" (Matt. 7: 23).

c) Conflict, vv34-39
Faithfulness in our confession will inevitably bring conflict, and these verses highlight three areas where this will occur:

i) Conflict in family life, vv.34-36. The Lord Jesus prepared His disciples for conflict in the most difficult area of all - in family life: "Think not that I am come to send peace on earth: I came not to send peace, but a sword. For I am come to set a man at variance against his father, and the daughter against her mother, and the daughter in law against her mother in law. And a man's foes shall be they of his own household". The Saviour refers here to Micah 7: 6. In an earlier part of His teaching, the Saviour indicated the lengths to which such antagonism would go (v.21).

As H.A.Ironside points out, "This seems to be a strange statement in view of the angels' message at His birth: 'Glory to God in the highest, and on earth peace, good will toward men' (Luke 2: 14)". Quite clearly the Lord Jesus is not teaching here that He had come to deliberately foment antagonism within the family circle, but rather that this would be one result of His coming. The word "variance" (*dichazo*) means 'to cut apart, divide in two' (W.E.Vine). In some cases, unsaved family members tolerate and even smile benignly on believers in their midst, but this is not always the case by far, particularly where believers come from strong religious or cultural backgrounds. In passing, it should be said that **believers** should never show antagonism. Here it is the unsaved members of the family against the saved, not the saved against the unsaved!

ii) Conflict in our priorities, v.37. "He that loveth father or mother more than me is not worthy of me: and he that loveth son or daughter more than me is not worthy of me". While this could mean that the Lord's interests are put to one side in order to avoid family hostility, it has to be said that the idea of hostility and antagonism is not present here. In all circumstances, whether decidedly unfavourable (vv.35-36) or favourable (v.37), the Lord must be given first place. He is "worthy" of our complete devotion and unswerving loyalty. It is certainly not unknown for believers to put family and other interests before the Lord, forgetting that what He said about food, drink and clothing is equally applicable in every sphere of life: "But seek ye first the kingdom of God, and his righteousness; and all these things shall be added unto you (Matt. 6: 33). But the subject is narrowed still further: to be "worthy" of Him (v.37 twice) involves

iii) Conflict in personal life, vv.38-39. "And he that taketh not his cross, and followeth after me, is not worthy of me. He that findeth his life shall lose it: and he that loseth his life for my sake shall find it". A man carrying his cross was potentially dead. That man did not come back. He was severing his connection with this world. The truth is expounded in Gal 2: 20; 5: 24; 6: 14.

"For whosoever shall save his life shall lose it", meaning that we can put our own interests first, and in the **short term** appear to do extremely well out of it, but in **the long term** we will do extremely badly, for:

> *Only one life, 'twill soon be past:*
> *Only what's done for Christ will last.*

The Lord gave at least two illustrations of men who 'saved their lives' and lost them. See Luke 12: 16-21; 16: 19. "But "he that loseth his life for my sake shall find it", that is, we can put Christ's interests first, and in the **short term** appear to do extremely badly out of it, but in the **long term**, there could be no better way to use our lives. There doesn't seem to be much future in heeding His words, "let him deny himself, and take up His cross daily, and follow me" (Luke 9: 23), but in the light of eternity there can be no better approach to life. See Philippians 1: 21, 3: 4-8. This will be made abundantly clear when Christ returns, see 2 Timothy 4: 6-8.

d) Compensation, vv.40-42
In the privations and difficulties of true discipleship, there will be compensations in fellowship and hospitality. The order in which this is described is most interesting. It is tempting to say that the three examples are given in descending order, but each of them is obviously of great importance.

i) To receive a servant of Christ has the highest possible significance. "He that receiveth you **receiveth me**, and he that receiveth me receiveth him that sent me" (v.40). As Wm.MacDonald points out, "The reason for this is that the one who is sent represents the sender. An ambassador stands in the place of the government that commissions him. To receive the ambassador is to enjoy diplomatic relations with his country". R.H.Mounce points out that 'In the context of persecution (v.23), hospitality could involve harbouring at considerable risk those who are wanted by the authorities'.

ii) To receive a servant of Christ as a prophet or a righteous man, is to identify oneself with him and therefore both guest and host, since they both contribute to the same end, will receive the same reward. "He that receiveth **a prophet** in the name of a prophet shall receive a prophet's reward; and he that receiveth **a righteous man** (see Matt. 5: 10) in the name of a righteous man shall receive a righteous man's reward" (v.41).

The Lord therefore commenced with fine concepts: receiving the servant of Christ was to receive Him, and receiving a prophet or a righteous man would make the host eligible for the reward that prophets and righteous men receive. What follows looks, by comparison rather nondescript and unimportant, but this is far from the case:

iii) "And whosoever shall give to drink unto one of these little ones a cup of cold water only in the name of a disciple, verily I say unto you, he shall in no wise lose his reward" (v.42). While the word "receive" is not used here, the sense is certainly implied. The Lord is particularly forceful here, indicating that this was no lesser matter. Notice that it is not a matter of acting charitably in a general sense, but recognising that "these little ones" are disciples: the cup of cold water is given "in the name of a disciple". Perhaps there is a deliberate emphasis on 'small people' ("one of these little ones") and a 'small provision' ("a cup of cold water") in order also to emphasise that there was nothing 'small' about it! R.V.G.Tasker puts it nicely: "The smallest act of service to the most insignificant of Christ's disciples ("these little ones") will be rewarded as though it had been rendered to Christ Himself". The word rendered "little" (*micros*) is the opposite of *megas*, meaning "great".

Although found in the following chapter, the words, "And it came to pass, when Jesus had made an end of commanding his twelve disciples, **he** departed thence to teach and to preach in their cities" (11: 1), make a suitable conclusion to our present passage. But what an unexpected statement! We might have expected Matthew to say, 'And it came to pass, when Jesus had made an end of commanding his twelve disciples, he **sent them** thence to teach and to preach in their cities". But it doesn't say that at all! Having dispatched the twelve disciples to "preach, saying the kingdom of heaven is at hand" (v.7), He went himself "to teach and to preach in their cities". The "Lord of the harvest" (Matt 9: 38) was busy in the harvest-field.

When the disciples saw this, they might well have exclaimed: "It is enough for the disciple that he be as his master, and the servant as his lord" (v.25). He set them a perfect example. He was totally different from the scribes and Pharisees who "say, and do not". He asks us to do nothing that He has not done Himself, and it would be so gratifying if we could all say that in every way, "as he is, so are we in this world" (1 John 4: 17).

THE GOSPEL OF MATTHEW

"There hath not risen a greater than John the Baptist"

Read Chapter 11: 1-15
We commenced our three studies in the preceding chapter by saying that 'having clearly presented His credentials, the King dispatched His messengers to the nation with the message, "The kingdom of heaven is at hand" (10: 7)'. The immediate mission to "the lost sheep of the house of Israel" (10: 6) was the prelude to service that would continue until the time when "the Son of man be come" (10.23), and the Lord made it clear that in their preaching His servants would encounter fierce opposition.

It is therefore striking to notice that having warned His disciples of coming adversity (Ch.10), the Lord proceeded to "preach in their cities" (11:1), where he encountered those very trials Himself (Chs.11-12). For example:

- He warned His disciples that some cities would not receive **them** (10: 11-15): we now read that some cities did not receive **Him** (11: 20-24).

- He warned His disciples that **they** would encounter opposition from religious circles (10: 17): we now read that this happened to **Him** (12: 1-14).

- He warned His disciples that **they** would be accused of serving Beelzebub (10.25): we now read that **He** was faced with the same accusation (12: 22-24).

- He warned His disciples that one result of **His** coming would be family discord (10: 34-37): we now read that **He** experienced this Himself (12: 46-50).

In fact, the correspondence between Chapter 10 and Chapters 11-12 can be observed at the beginning of both passages. In Chapter10, the Lord Jesus gave His disciples "power against unclean spirits...and to heal all manner of sickness and all manner of disease" (10: 1), and in Chapter 11 He drew attention to His power in healing (11: 4-5). The similarity between these passages reminds us that "we have not an high priest which cannot be touched with the feeling of our infirmities; but was in all points tempted like as we are, yet without sin" (Heb. 4: 15). He has experienced what He tells us to expect.

Matthew Chapter 11 comprises two major sections which may be entitled as follows: **(1)** the response to the Lord (vv.1-24); **(2)** the response by the Lord (vv.25-30).

1) THE RESPONSE TO THE LORD, vv.1-24

These verses cover the following: **(A)** the uncertain prophet (vv.1-15): "Art thou he that should come, or do we look for another?" (v.3); **(B)** the unresponsive children (vv.16-19): "We have piped unto you, and ye have not danced; we have mourned unto you, and ye have not lamented" (v.17); **(C)** the unrepentant cities (vv.20-24): "if the mighty works, which were done in you, had been done in Tyre and Sidon, they would have repented long ago in sackcloth and ashes" (v.21).

A) The uncertain prophet, vv.1-15

The Lord's commendation of John the Baptist is recorded here and in Luke 7: 18-29. John spoke well of the Lord Jesus. People said, "John did no miracle: but all things that John spake of this man were true" (John 10: 41). We must now notice that the Lord Jesus spoke well of John. He did so on more than this occasion. See John 5: 33-35, "Ye sent unto John, and he bare witness unto the truth", and the Lord continued by describing him as "a burning and a shining light". This illustrates His teaching that "Whosoever therefore shall confess *me* before men, him will *I* confess also before my Father which is in heaven" (Matt. 10: 32).

We should now notice: *(a)* John's concern (vv.2-3); *(b)* the Lord's confirmation (vv.4-6); *(c)* the Lord's commendation (vv.7-15).

a) John's concern, vv.2-3

"Now when John had heard in the prison the works (*ergon*) of Christ, he sent two of his disciples, and said unto him, Art thou he that should come, or do we look for another?" John's faithfulness had landed him in deep trouble: "And many other things in his exhortation preached he unto the people. But Herod the tetrarch, being reproved of him for Herodias his brother Philip's wife, and for all the evils that Herod had done, added yet this above all, that he shut up John in prison" (Luke 3: 18-20). (Josephus tells us that Herod confined John in the fortress of Machaerus on the east side of the Dead Sea). This reminds us that "all that will live godly in Christ Jesus shall suffer persecution" (2 Timothy 3: 12). John's imprisonment evidently took place during the early months of the Lord's public ministry. See Matt 4: 12-17, Mark 1: 14-15, and John 3: 22-24.

Whilst other suggestions have been made, it is difficult to escape the conclusion that John was perplexed by his imprisonment. Perhaps he thought, "I have laboured in vain, I have sent my strength for nought" (Is. 49: 4). Although he was in prison, he was certainly not insulated from the outside world. He knew that Judaea and the surrounding country were ablaze with excitement: "And there came a fear on all (following the raising of the widow's son at Nain): and they glorified God, saying, That a great prophet is risen up among us; and, That God hath visited his people. And this rumour of him went forth throughout all Judaea, and throughout all the region round about. And the disciples of John shewed him of all these things" (Luke 7: 16-18).

This, in itself, was no problem to John. We know that he was only too delighted to give Christ pre-eminence. He had said, "He must increase, but I must decrease" (John 3: 30). His preaching was Christ-centred. See, for example, John 1: 30: "This is he of whom I said, after me cometh a man which is preferred before me: for he was before me". But after all this, he was *in prison* without any prospect of release! Here was John's problem. He had faithfully prepared "the way of the Lord", only to be apparently abandoned when the task was finished. We can understand why he said, "Art thou he that should come, or do we look for another?" If Jesus really was "the Lord", where was the "kingdom of heaven?" (Matt 3: 2). Whilst we would draw back from saying that John now had serious doubts about the Lord Jesus, he certainly needed reassurance and confirmation that the Lord was indeed the long-awaited Messiah. J.G.Bellett *(The Evangelists)* puts it like this: 'John had...testified to the Person of the Son of God. As to that he had no doubt. But it seems that he was not prepared for all the results of being the Lord's witness...He became impatient, not being prepared for all the cost of being the Lord's *prisoner* as well as *minister*". As Wm.Kelly observes, 'Even a prophet is not beyond Satan's assault'.

There are at least two lessons for us here: *(i)* John expressed his concern; *(ii)* John evidently forgot past evidence.

*i) **John expressed his concern.*** John took his doubts to Christ. He was unable to do this directly, but that didn't stop him. We all have doubts at times. None of us have sublime faith that soars above every problem and difficulty. Sometimes, our cherished expectations just don't materialise, and we begin to wonder if our convictions were right after all. Even John the Baptist was unsure for a moment. But he didn't sit in prison, and stew about it *ad infinitum!* He asked the Lord to explain the situation. Paul did the same, and received an answer, even if it did not mean deliverance from the problem. See 2 Corinthians 12: 7-9. Do remember the old hymn, and "Take it to the Lord in prayer".

Whilst John was obliged to communicate with the Lord Jesus via his two disciples, this does remind us that we do need the prayerful fellowship of God's people. John shared his concern with others. Aaron and Hur "stayed up" the hands of Moses, "the one on the one side, and the other on the other side" (Exodus 17: 12).

*ii) **John evidently forgot past evidence.*** In times of doubt, it is always helpful to rest upon what we **do** know. There was no doubt at all that Jesus **was** the promised Messiah. John had not been mistaken: "And John bare record, saying, I saw the Spirit descending from heaven like a dove, and it abode upon him...And I saw and bare record that this is the Son of God" (John 1: 32-34). Let's face it, there are many things in life **generally** that we do not understand, and things happen to us **personally** that we do not understand. We can only face these problems when we stand on the firm ground of God's word. What we **do** understand will help us when faced with things that we **do not** understand.

b) The Lord's confirmation, vv.4-6
There are at least two important things to note here: *(i)* the privacy; *(ii)* the proof.

*i) **The privacy.*** We should notice that the Lord Jesus did not publicly correct John. "Jesus answered and said unto **them** (the two disciples), Go and shew John again those things which ye do hear and see" (v.4). After they had gone, He publicly commended him (vv.7-15): He "began to say unto the multitudes concerning John..." (v.7). It is important to notice here that a private question was answered privately. Public disorders have to be addressed publicly. See Galatians 2:11-14.

The privacy of the enquiry and answer is particularly important in view of the **gentle** rebuke which follows: "And blessed is he, whosoever shall not be offended in me". Notice that the Lord does not even address John directly. The word "offended" (from the verb *scandalizo*) means, 'to put a snare or stumblingblock in the way'. As we have seen, John's imprisonment made him question his former convictions, and his momentary unbelief was a stumblingblock to him. But the Saviour's rebuke was not placarded 'all over town': it was gently administered in private, reminding us that "as a father pitieth his children, so the Lord pitieth them that fear him. For he knoweth our frame: he remembereth that we are dust" (Psalm 103: 13-14). This is a helpful lesson that we all need to learn. It is quite wrong to publicise other people's weaknesses.

Perhaps we should apply the Saviour's words here to ourselves. We are called to follow the Saviour when, humanly speaking, we seem to be 'on a hiding to nothing'. Is all the inconvenience of following Him really worthwhile? Christians often seem to get a 'pretty poor deal' in life. Listen to the Saviour's words: "Blessed are ye, when men shall revile you, and persecute you, and shall say all manner of evil against you falsely, for my sake. Rejoice, and be exceeding glad: for great is your reward in heaven" (Matt. 5: 11-12).

*ii) **The proof.*** The Lord answered John by citing His ministry and miracles. He did not make a formal statement about His Messiahship. He simply pointed to His deeds and His words: "The blind receive their sight, and the lame walk, the lepers are cleansed, and the deaf hear, the dead are raised up, and the poor *have the gospel preached unto them* (one word based on *euangelizo*)" (v.5). We should notice that nothing is said in the Old Testament in connection with Messiah raising the dead: this was even "greater than the miracles that were predicted" (Wm.MacDonald). Luke makes it clear that the two disciples actually saw all this happening: "And **in that same hour** he cured many of their infirmities and plagues, and of evil spirits; and unto many that were blind he gave sight. Then Jesus answering said unto them, Go your way, and tell John what things ye have seen and heard" (Luke 7: 21-22). While Wm. Kelly makes the telling comment, 'We have not, I believe, one case of curing the blind before Christ came', this would be equally true in connection with the deaf and the lame. The miracles performed by the Lord Jesus proved that He was "he that should come". He did "among them the works which none other man did" (John 15: 24). We must remember that the Lord Jesus did not perform special miracles just to impress John. He was already famed for His miracles, as John knew. See Luke 7: 16-18.

Matthew

It is important to remember that the Lord Jesus was appealing to the Word of God here. The witness of John's two disciples was corroborated by the prophetic Scriptures, in this case, Isaiah 35: 5-6 and Isaiah 61: 1. The first passage describes the effect of His future coming *to reign:* "Behold, your God will come with vengeance, even God with a recompence: he will come and save you. Then the eyes of the blind shall be opened, and the ears of the deaf shall be unstopped. Then shall the lame man leap as an hart, and the tongue of the dumb sing". The Lord Jesus displayed *at that time* the very power that He *will* display when He comes to establish His kingdom. The second passage describes the effect of His first coming *in grace and mercy:* "The Spirit of the Lord God is upon me, because the Lord hath anointed me to preach good tidings unto the meek; he hath sent me to bind up the broken-hearted, to proclaim liberty to the captives, and the opening of the prison to them that are bound". The Lord Jesus fulfilled the prophetic Scriptures, and made them 'more sure'. See 2 Peter 1: 19 margin.

We cannot leave this without emphasising the importance of reference to the Word of God when establishing an argument, or proving a point. Our first consideration should always be, "What saith the scripture?" (Rom 4: 3). The way to test any argument is set out in Isaiah 8: 20, "To the law and to the testimony: if they speak not according to this word, it is because there is no light in them".

c) The Lord's commendation, vv.7-15
The Lord Jesus now describes the greatness of John the Baptist to the multitudes. This paragraph is not without its difficulties. We can divide the verses as follows: *(i)* the character of John (vv.7-8); *(ii)* the prophets and John (vv.9-10); *(iii)* the kingdom and John (vv.11-13); *(iv)* Elijah and John (vv.14-15) The public commendation of John by the Lord Jesus is most important. It vindicated John, and settled any doubts in people's minds about him. J.C.Ryle (writing on Luke) puts it like this: 'His expressions are so peculiarly strong, that we might suppose they were specially intended to prevent any slur being thrown on John's character on account of his message'.

i) The character of John, vv.7-8.
He was neither "a reed shaken with the wind" (v.7), nor "a man clothed in soft (*malakos*, meaning 'effeminate' in its widest sense) raiment" (v.8). It is delightful to notice that although John was no longer in the public eye, His past ministry was not forgotten by the Lord Jesus. We have the sad proverb, 'out of sight, out of mind', but the Saviour does not forget any of His servants. He does not forget them now,

and He will not forget them in eternity. Notice as well that the Lord Jesus spoke highly of John 'behind his back'. It has been pointed out (T.Miller) that although John was not "reed shaken with the wind", he had become "a bruised reed", but of the gentle Saviour it is said, "A bruised reed shall he not break" (Is. 42: 3). We must notice:

- His steadfastness. John was the very opposite of "a reed shaken with the wind". (Compare 1 Kings 14: 15). He did not bow under pressure from anybody! He certainly didn't vary his preaching to suit his audience. He gave straight, challenging and searching answers to "the people", the "publicans" and "the soldiers" (Luke 3: 10-14). He was not intimidated by the religious fraternity. He called them "a generation of vipers!" (Luke 3: 7). People in high office didn't deter him either. Herod was "reproved by him for Herodias his brother Philip's wife" (Luke 3: 19). John was not "tossed to and fro, and carried about with every wind of doctrine" (Eph 4: 14). This reminds us that, like Timothy, we must "continue...in the things which thou hast learned and hast been assured of" (2 Tim 3: 14).

- His separation. John was the very opposite of "a man clothed in soft raiment". The Lord said, "Behold, they that wear soft raiment are in kings' houses". There was no ostentation about John. He was not the product of a materialistic society. He was a man whose ministry involved sacrifice and self-renunciation. He was 'roughly clothed, ill-housed and poorly fed' (J.Heading). For "soft raiment", read "camel's hair, and a leathern girdle about his loins" (Matt 3: 4). John 'loved not the world, neither the things that are in the world' (1 John 2: 15).

ii) The prophets and John, vv.9-10. "But what went ye out for to see? A prophet? yea, I say unto you, and much more than a prophet" (v.9). The people were "persuaded that John was a prophet". See Matthew 21: 23-27; Luke 20: 1-8. Compare Matthew 14: 5. But he was "more than a prophet". He was the forerunner of the Lord Jesus. He was "the prophet of the Highest" who would "go before the face of the Lord to prepare his ways" (Luke 1: 76). The Old Testament prophets spoke accurately and eloquently *about* the Lord Jesus, but John the Baptist *introduced* Him. John, "a prophet" but "more than a prophet", was himself the subject of prophecy! "For this is he, of whom it is written, Behold, I send my messenger before thy face, which shall prepare thy way before thee" (v.10). See Malachi 3: 1. John was the greatest of all the prophets: "Verily I say unto you, Among them that are born of women there hath not risen a greater than

John the Baptist" (v.11). But this is followed by an unexpected statement, bringing us to:

iii) ***The kingdom and John, vv.11-13.*** "Notwithstanding he that is least in the kingdom of God is greater than he" (v.11). Any explanation of these words must differentiate between John ***personally***, and John's ***position.***

- ***John personally.*** Quite obviously, the Lord Jesus did not mean that everyone in the kingdom of heaven, even the least, is greater in worth than John the Baptist. Would any of ***us*** dare to say that we are greater than John the Baptist? Just think about his steadfastness and moral courage again. We must remember that John was "faithful unto death". None of us are in the same league! We must look elsewhere for the answer.

- ***John's position.*** John announced the advent of the kingdom: "Repent ye: for the kingdom of heaven is at hand" (Matt. 3: 2). But John was not actually in that kingdom, which bestows blessings and privileges unknown to him. His own words, "I indeed baptize you with water unto repentance... but...he shall baptize you with the Holy Ghost" (Matt. 3: 11), emphasise the immeasurable privileges and blessings of all who trust in Christ. We have only to remember, for example, the unique character of the church, and the fact that it is the supreme example of "the manifold wisdom of God" (Eph 3: 10). Believers are "greater" than John in privilege and blessing (see John 3: 29), rather than "greater" than John in strength of character and devoted service.

Having contrasted the position of John and the position of those in membership of the kingdom, the Lord Jesus spoke to the multitude about entering the kingdom. He used startling language: "And from the days of John the Baptist until now the kingdom of heaven suffereth violence, and the violent take it by force" (v.12). This is not the easiest verse to understand! Some suggest that this refers to the violence of the enemies of the kingdom, in which case, they appear to be successful and the kingdom is taken "by force". But can we really imagine that the "kingdom of heaven" (elsewhere called "the kingdom of God") can be overcome and defeated? Violence, in the shape of pressure and persecution, serves to strengthen God's work! The verse must therefore refer to the way in which the kingdom is entered. The word "violent" *(biazo,* to force) refers to the attitude of those seeking to enter the kingdom. Luke puts it as follows: "The law and the prophets were until John: since that time the kingdom of God is preached, and every man presseth (*biazo*) into it" (Luke 16: 16). W.E.Vine observes that 'the verb suggests forceful endeavour'. But why was such 'forceful endeavour' necessary? It was certainly not necessary because of any reluctance on God's part! The 'forceful endeavour' was necessary in view of the obstacles placed in the way by the religious leaders: "But woe unto you, scribes and Pharisees, hypocrites! for ye shut up the kingdom of heaven against men: for ye neither go in yourselves, neither suffer ye them that are entering to go in" (Matt. 23: 13). Nothing has changed. Institutionalised religion is still one of the greatest barriers to faith in Christ. It is not always easy to overcome.

The words, "For all the prophets and the law prophesied until John" (v.13), evidently summarise what has been said. They remind us that the advent of John the Baptist marked the end of Old Testament anticipation, and the beginning of New Testament appropriation. Notice the two expressions, "***until*** John" (v.13) and "***until*** now" (v.12).

iv) Elijah and John, vv.14-15. "And if ye will receive it, This is Elias, which was for to come, He that hath ears to hear, let him hear". The coming of "Elijah the prophet" (Mal. 4: 5) raises some interesting questions. For example, was Malachi's prophecy actually fulfilled through the preaching of John the Baptist, or does it still await fulfilment? If the prophecy has been partially fulfilled in John, but awaits complete fulfilment, are we to expect the coming of Elijah himself, and does the Bible tell us anything more about his coming? These questions were addressed in our Malachi studies, and these notes follow the tentative conclusion reached then: namely, that Malachi's prophecy was fulfilled by John the Baptist. We should note the following in this connection.

- John was certainly not Elijah (see John 1: 19-21). But there was a correspondence between the two men. The angel made this clear to Zacharias: "And many of the children of Israel shall he turn to the Lord their God. And he shall go before him in the ***spirit and power of Elias***" (Luke 1: 16-17). We know that, like Elijah, John called the people back to God.

- John, however, is certainly described as the Elijah of prophecy. Our present passage (v.14) evidently states that there is more than 'a correspondence between John and Elijah': "and if ye will receive it, ***this is Elias, which was for to come***". The Lord Jesus later referred again to John in this way: "And his disciples asked him, saying, Why say the scribes that ***Elias must first come***? And Jesus answered and said unto them, ***Elias truly shall first come, and restore all things***. But I say unto you, That ***Elias is come*** *already*, and they knew him not, but have done unto him whatsoever they listed...Then the disciples understood that he spake unto them of John the Baptist" (Matt. 17: 10-13).

- John fulfilled Malachi's prophecy (Mal 4: 6). Through his ministry, men and women were convicted of sin, brought to repentance, and prepared for Messiah's coming. John certainly made "ready a people prepared for the Lord". See Acts 19: 4, "Then said Paul, John verily baptized with the baptism of repentance, saying unto the people, that they **should believe on him which should come after him, that is, on Christ Jesus**".

"I thank thee, O Father, Lord of heaven and earth"

Read Chapter 11: 16-30
In our previous study, we suggested that this chapter may be divided into two major sections: **(1)** the response to the Lord (vv.1-24); **(2)** the response by the Lord (vv.25-30).

1) THE RESPONSE TO THE LORD, vv.1-24
We noted that this section of the chapter covers the following: **(A)** the uncertain prophet (vv.1-15): "Art thou he that should come, or do we look for another?" (v.3); **(B)** the unresponsive children (vv.16-19): "We have piped unto you, and ye have not danced; we have mourned unto you, and ye have not lamented" (v.17); **(C)** the unrepentant cities (vv.20-24): "if the mighty works, which were done in you, had been done in Tyre and Sidon, they would have repented long ago in sackcloth and ashes" (v.21).

A) The uncertain prophet, vv.1-15
Following his condemnation of Herod's immoral behaviour, John the Baptist was imprisoned (Luke 3: 19-20), and it was from the castle of Machaerus (according to Josephus) that he despatched two of his disciples to the Lord Jesus with the question: "Art thou he that should come, or do we look for another?" (v.3). The Lord answered the question by telling them to "shew John again those things which ye do hear and see", and having sent them back to John, then speaks about him in most commendable terms - to the extent of saying that "among them that are born of women there hath not risen a greater than John the Baptist" (v.11).

The Lord then refers again, in another connection, to John the Baptist, which brings us to:

B) The unresponsive children, vv.16-19

He likens "this generation" (*genea,* meaning, in this case, people living at the same period)", referring particularly to the ruling fraternity (see Luke 7: 29-31), to "children (*paidarion,* meaning 'little chidren') sitting in the markets (market-places), and calling to their fellows" (v.16) M.R.Vincent *(Word Studies in the New Testament)* quotes Donald Francis *(Metaphors in the Gospels)* here, and the passage is worth reproducing in full. "He pictured a group of little children playing at make-believe marriages and funerals. First they acted a marriage procession; some of them piping as on instruments of music, while the rest were expected to leap and dance. In a perverse mood, however, these last did not respond, but stood still and looked discontented. So the little pipers changed their game and proposed a funeral. They began to imitate the loud wailing of eastern mourners. But again they were thwarted, for their companions refused to chime in with the mournful cry and to beat their breasts...So the disappointed children complained: 'We piped unto you and ye did not dance; we wailed, and ye did not mourn. Nothing pleases you. If you don't want to dance, why don't you mourn?...It is plain that you are in bad humour, and determined not to be pleased'".

The Lord then applies His illustration. Like the children who didn't want to solemnly play at funerals, these people didn't want anything to do with the solemn preaching of John the Baptist who "came neither eating and drinking", meaning that he refrained from normal food, leading to the charge that he was demon-possessed (v.18). And like the children who didn't want to joyfully play at weddings, they didn't want anything to do with the Lord Jesus who "came eating and drinking". They described him as "a man gluttonous, and a winebibber (a reference to Deuteronomy 21: 20), a friend of publicans and sinners" (v.19). So, to sum up, They neither accepted John's message of pending judgment and need for repentance, nor the message of forgiveness and joy from the Lord Jesus. Had they accepted the first, they would have accepted the second. But they rejected both, proving that "the god of this world hath blinded the minds of them which believe not" (2 Cor 4: 4). It has been rightly pointed out that the Lord was indeed "a friend of publicans and sinners", but not in the way that they meant: 'He befriended sinners in order to save them from their sins, but He never shared or approved their sins' (Wm.MacDonald).

J.C.Ryle (*Expository Thoughts on the Gospels - Matthew*) puts it in a nutshell: "they were as perverse and hard to please as wayward children". What he says next is superb: "Thousands of professing Christians are just as unreasonable as these Jews...whatever we teach and preach, they find fault; whatever be manner of our life, they are dissatisfied. Do we tell them of salvation by grace, and justification by faith? At once they cry out against our doctrine as licentious and Antinomian (meaning, 'against the law'). Do we tell them of the holiness which the Gospel requires? At once they exclaim that we are too strict, and precise, and righteous overmuch. Are we cheerful? They accuse us of levity. Are we grave? They call us gloomy and sour. Do we keep aloof from balls, and races, and plays? They denounce us as puritanical, exclusive, and narrow-minded. Do we feast, and drink, and dress like other people, and attend to our worldly callings, and go into society? They sneeringly insinuate that they see no difference between us and those who make no religious profession at all; and that we are no better than other men. What is all this but the conduct of the Jews over again?... He who spake these words knew the hearts of men!"

The final comment by the Lord Jesus, "But wisdom is justified of her children" (v.19), is usually explained by saying that unlike those that rejected both John the Baptist and the Lord Jesus, the "children" here are the people who showed their wisdom by recognising and accepting the divine message or, alternatively, recognised the divine wisdom of the message. This explanation, however, is far from satisfactory and it does seem, rather, that the Lord Jesus is speaking with heavy irony. These people were 'wise in their own conceits' (Rom. 11: 25; 12: 16), and could therefore easily justify their rejection of John and his message, and the Lord Jesus and His message. After all, when **we** don't want to accept something, however right, we can trot out good reasons quite quickly! Neither suited them, and therefore, in their great wisdom (!), they refused to accept both messages. Very clever, but utterly disastrous.

C) *The unrepentant cities, vv.20-24*
"Then began he to upbraid the cities wherein most of his mighty works were done, because they repented not" (v.20).

We have to decide whether the Lord's words here were uttered as a fearful denunciation alone, or as 'a woe of sadness', for 'at that point Christ seems to be overwhelmed at the thought of cities like Chorazin, Bethsaida (meaning 'house of fishing': a blind man was healed there: see Mark 8: 22-26) and Capernaum, which had witnessed His mighty works, and were still unrepentant and unsaved' (David Gooding, writing on Luke 10: 13-15). Compare the Lord's deep feelings about Jerusalem: Luke 13: 34. We must now listen to His solemn words: "Woe unto thee, Chorazin! (only mentioned here and in Luke 10: 13: said to have been at the northern tip of Galilee) woe unto thee, Bethsaida! for if the mighty works, which were done in you, had been done in Tyre and Sidon, they would have repented long ago in sackcloth and ashes. But I say unto you, It shall be more tolerable for Tyre and Sidon at the day of judgment, than for you. And thou, Capernaum (said to be the city of Nahum), which art exalted to heaven, shalt be brought down to hell (an allusion to Isaiah 14: 13-15): for if the mighty works, which have been done in thee (see, for example Mark 2: 1-12; Luke 4: 31-41), had been done in Sodom, it would have remained until this day. But I say unto you, That it shall be more tolerable for the land of Sodom in the day of judgment than for thee". Note that the men of Sodom and the "cities of the plain" (Gen. 19: 29) still face future judgment.

The great lesson in these verses is that privilege determines responsibility. Tyre and Sidon were the two great commercial ports of the Phoenician empire. They were famous for their riches and luxury. See Isaiah 23 and Ezekiel 27. Although they are condemned for their total disregard for the Lord, they never had the great privileges which belonged to the Galilean cities, which were therefore infinitely more culpable for their attitude to Him. Capernaum is also mentioned. This was the place where the Lord Jesus lived at one time. See Matt 4: 13; 9: 1. The words "exalted to heaven" evidently refer to the marvellous privilege of His presence in the city. But it would be "brought down to hell (*hades*)". To reject Christ incurs the most terrible consequences. In the words of Derek Kidner (see his introduction to Psalms 1-72, *Tyndale Old Testament Commentaries*): "the small towns of Galilee, having had their taste of heaven, now face a deeper hell than Sodom's". Wm.MacDonald makes the thought-provoking observation that the Lord 'had drawn near to the city of Sodom in one of His pre-incarnate appearances as the Angel of Jehovah (Gen. 18: 1-2, 22). But Capernaum's privilege was greater: the Lord had actually lived there and presented the most irrefutable evidences of His Messiahship. Sodom's sin was great: it was the pit of immorality. But Capernaum's sin was greater: it had rejected the holy Son of God. No sin is greater than that'.

We must not forget that *our* great privileges make *us* very responsible people as well. How do *we* respond to our unparalleled blessings? We must also notice that the Lord clearly teaches that there will be degrees of punishment on judgment day, and that 'these degrees will be according to light and privilege' (N.Crawford). Hence the words, "It shall be more tolerable for Tyre and Sidon at the day of judgment, than for you. The principle of privilege determining responsibility is clearly taught in Luke 12: 47-48: "And that servant, which knew his lord's will, and prepared not himself, neither did according to his will, shall be beaten with many stripes. But he that knew not, and did commit things worthy of stripes, shall be beaten with few stripes. For unto whomsoever much is given, of him shall much be required: and to whom men have committed much, of him they will ask the more".

But how did these three things affect the Lord? Did they engender resentment and bitterness on His part? This brings us to the second of the two major divisions of the chapter:

2) THE RESPONSE BY THE LORD, vv.25-30
Once again we see the touch of the Master Jeweller. We have been occupied with the dark background, but now our attention is drawn to some precious gems. "At **that** time (the dark background) Jesus answered and said, I thank thee, O Father, Lord of heaven and earth...All things are delivered unto me of my Father...Come unto me, all ye that labour and are heavy laden, and I will give you rest (the precious gems)". We must now notice **(A)** what the Lord said to His Father (vv.25-26), and **(B)** what the Lord said to His hearers (vv.27-30).

A) What He said to His Father, vv.25-26
"At that time Jesus answered and said, I thank thee, O Father, Lord of heaven and earth, because thou hast hid these things from the wise and prudent, and hast revealed them unto babes. Even so, Father; for so it seemed good in thy sight". Luke complements this in saying: "In that hour Jesus rejoiced in spirit" (Luke 10: 21) which, in passing, is the only occasion on which we read that "Jesus rejoiced".

The Lord Jesus exemplifies the injunction, "In every thing give thanks" (1 Thess. 5: 18). Paul followed His footsteps in saying, "I have learned, in whatsoever state I am, (therewith) to be content. I know both how to be abased, and I know how to abound: every where and in all things I am instructed both to be full and to be hungry, both to abound and to suffer need. I can do all things through Christ which strengtheneth me" (Phil. 4: 11-13). In his adversity, Jacob exclaimed "all these things are against me" (Gen.. 42: 36). But the Lord Jesus found cause for thanksgiving! The word "answered" simply refers to the way He answered His circumstances.

We must not overlook the fact that the Lord Jesus refers to the Father five times in vv.25-27: "O Father...Father...my Father...the Father...the Father". In the first two instances, the Lord is addressing His Father, and the very language ("O Father...Father") is permeated with profound love and devotion. We are privileged to listen with 'unshod feet'. We hear him say. "Hereafter I will not talk much with you: for the prince of this world cometh, and hath nothing in me. But that the world may know that I love the Father; and as the Father gave me commandment, even so I do" (John 14: 30-31). As A.W.Pink observes, 'This is the only time that Christ ever spoke of His love to the Father; it was now that He was to give supreme proof of it', that is, in going 'forth to meet Satan because He had received "commandment" from the Father to do so'. In His prayer, the Lord Jesus refers to:

i) *The supremacy of the Father*. "I thank thee, O Father, Lord of heaven and earth..." It is remarkable that although "the Son of man hath not where to lay his head" (Luke 9: 58), His Father was "Lord of heaven and earth" and owned 'every square inch of earth and heaven into the bargain' (David Gooding). Nebuchadnezzar was obliged to recognise that "he (the most High) doeth according to his will in the army of heaven, and among the inhabitants of earth: and none can stay his hand, or say unto him, What doest thou?" (Dan. 4: 35), but the Lord Jesus did not have to be brought to the conclusion that His Father was "Lord of heaven and earth". He spoke as a devoted Son. If the Lord Jesus spoke to the Father in this way, we too should address Him with adoring submission.

ii) *The sovereignty of the Father*. "I thank thee...that thou hast hid these things from the wise and prudent (referring, in context, to the proud Jewish leaders), and hast revealed them unto babes (referring, in context, to His unlettered and unpretentious disciples): even so, Father; for so it seemed good in thy sight". The best commentary on these words is found in 1 Cor 1: 18-31. Notice the words, "For it is written, I will destroy the wisdom of the wise, and will bring to nothing the understanding of the prudent. Where is the wise? where is the scribe? where is the disputer of this world? hath not God made foolish the wisdom of this world? For after that in the wisdom of God the world by wisdom knew not God, it pleased God by the foolishness of preaching to save them that believe...But we preach Christ crucified, unto the Jews a stumblingblock, and unto the Greeks foolishness; but unto them which are called, both Jews and Greeks, Christ the power of God, and the wisdom of God" (vv.19-24). Salvation is not through human wisdom, but by divine revelation. Had it been otherwise, then the vast mass of mankind would have been beyond hope. The "wise and prudent" said "we are Moses' disciples...dost thou teach us?" (John 9: 29, 34). The man born blind, a 'babe', said "I believe. And he worshipped him" (John 9: 38).

B) What He said to His hearers, vv.27-30
These verses may be summarised in two words: revelation and invitation. In the first case, He reveals the Father to men (v.27): in the second, He bestows blessings upon men (vv.28-30).

a) He reveals the Father to men, v.27
"All things are delivered unto me of my Father: and no man knoweth the Son, but the Father; neither knoweth any man the Father, save the Son, and he to whomsoever the Son will reveal him". We must notice:

i) He is the executor of the Father's will. "All things are delivered unto me of my Father". Having said, "I thank thee, O Father, Lord of heaven and earth", The Lord Jesus now reveals that the Father, who is supreme in every sphere, has committed everything to Him, reminding us that every purpose of God, Whose "fulness" dwells perfectly in Christ, will be completed by Him: "it pleased the Father that in him should all fullness dwell; and having made peace through the blood of his cross, by him to reconcile all things unto himself; by him, I say, whether they be things in earth, or things in heaven" (Col. 1: 19-20). It is important to remember that whilst there is absolute equality in the Godhead, the Scriptures assign initiative, plan and purpose to the Father, and the execution of those plans and purposes to the Son, which He carries out in the power of the Holy Spirit. In committing "all things" to the Son, the Father has displayed His love for Him: "The Father loveth the Son, and hath given all things into his hand" (John 3: 35). Nothing delights the Father more than to see His Son, Whom He loves infinitely and eternally, pre-eminent in "all things" (Col. 1: 17). Here are three further examples of the Lord's teaching in this connection: "all power is **given unto me** in heaven and in earth" (Matt 28: 18); "the Father...hath **given him** authority to execute judgment also because he is the Son of man" (John 5: 26-27); "thou hast **given him** power over all flesh" (John 17: 2).

It should be said, however, that in the context of our current passage, the words, "All things are delivered unto me of my Father", may have a particular meaning. In the words of Wm.Kelly, 'The throne of Israel may be refused Him; the Jews may reject, the leaders despise Him: all this may be, but what is the result? Not merely what was promised to David or Solomon but "All things are delivered unto me of my Father"'.

ii) **He reveals the Father.** "No man knoweth the Son, but the Father; neither knoweth any man the Father save the Son, and he to whomsoever the Son will reveal him". Compare John 10: 14-15. It is important to remember that the word "knoweth" (*epignosis*) denotes fulness of knowledge. We must remember that 'no one can disclose God save one who is God' (D. Newell), and that there are eternal and inscrutable mysteries about Christ and God which human wisdom and logic can never penetrate. "Canst thou by searching find out God? Canst thou find out the Almighty unto perfection?" (Job 11: 7). The Son is distinct from the Father, yet entirely one with Him. While the Lord did *not* say here, 'No man knoweth the Son, but the Father, and he to whomsoever the Father will reveal him', we should remember that after Peter had said, "Thou art the Christ, the Son of the living God" (Matt. 16: 16), the Lord Jesus replied, "Blessed art thou, Simon Bar-jona: for flesh and blood hath not revealed it unto thee, but *my Father* which is in heaven" (v.17).

We could know nothing at all about God had He not revealed Himself to us through His Son. "No man hath seen God at any time; the only begotten Son, which is in the bosom of the Father, he hath declared (revealed) him" (John 1: 18). But with all that we *do* know about the Father and the Son, we must still sing:

> But the high mysteries of Thy Name
> An angel's grasp transcend;
> The FATHER only (glorious claim!)
> The SON can comprehend.

It is equally true to say that with all that we know and enjoy of our Saviour, "No man knoweth ('fully knoweth') the Son, but the Father". In the instructions for the meal offering, *all* the frankincense was burnt on the altar (Lev. 2: 2). Only God could fully appreciate the beauty and sweetness of Christ.

Having said, "neither knoweth any man the Father save the Son, and he to whomsoever the Son will reveal him", emphasising His sovereignty, the Lord issues an invitation, emphasising human responsibility:

b) He bestows blessings upon men, vv.28-30
These well-known verses comprise *(i)* a call to salvation (v.28), and *(ii)* a call to service (vv.29-30).

Matthew

i) A call to salvation, v.28: "Come unto me, all ye that labour and are heavy laden, and I will give you rest". Compare Isaiah 14: 3. Very clearly, only God could use such language as this. The Lord Jesus is God manifest in the flesh. It has been pointed out that 'The people were weary and heavy laden (cf. 9: 36) because they were burdened with strict religious and other prescriptions laid on them by their religious leaders (cf. 23: 4). This call involves a plea: "Come unto me", and a pledge, "and I will give you rest"' (supplied by Justin Waldron). The Gospel preacher will rightly say that to "come" to Christ means to believe on Him (Acts 16: 31) and to receive Him (John 1: 12). The Gospel preacher will continue by stressing that in saying "Come unto *me*", it is clear that 'the object of faith is not a church, or a creed, or a clergyman, but the living Christ' (Wm.MacDonald). He will stress that "In order to truly come to Jesus, a person must be willing to admit that he is burdened with the weight of sin", and that the "rest" offered by the Lord Jesus "is a gift: it is unearned and unmerited" (Wm.MacDonald).

ii) A call to service, vv.29-30: "Take my yoke upon you, and learn of me; for I am meek and lowly in heart: and ye shall find rest unto your souls. For my yoke is easy, and my burden is light". In saying "Take *my* yoke upon you", the Lord Jesus refers to His own glad submission to His Father's will (cf. v.26), and therefore those who come to Him must take the same yoke and also gladly submit to the Father's will as they work alongside Him. To be 'yoked' with the Lord Jesus 'is to have a very gentle (AV "meek") and humble-minded Teacher, who is never impatient with those who are slow to learn, and never intolerant with those who stumble' (R.V.G.Tasker). Paul certainly learnt the ways of Christ. See 1 Corintians 10: 1. Wm.Kelly points out that 'the terms on which the Lord gives rest to the *sinner* are, "Come unto me (just as you are)... and I will *give* you rest". The terms on which the *believer* finds rest are, "Take my yoke upon you, and learn of me; for I am meek and lowly in heart: and ye shall *find* rest unto your souls"'. The Lord's closing words, "For my yoke is easy, and my burden is light", do not promise a comfortable life, but that like Jacob, for whom seven years service for Rachel "seemed unto him but a few days, for the love that he had to her" (Gen. 29: 20), our relationship with the Lord will mean that "his commandments are not grievous (meaning 'burdensome')" (1 John 5: 3).

It would be lovely if the Lord Jesus could say to us, as Paul said to an unnamed colleague (probably Epaphroditus), "I intreat thee also, true yokefellow..." (Phil. 4: 3).

THE GOSPEL OF MATTHEW

"Behold my servant, whom I have chosen"

Read Chapter 12: 1-21
This chapter brings us to a critical point in the life and ministry of the Lord Jesus. As Wm.MacDonald observes, "The malice and animosity of the Pharisees have been rising. Now they are ready to spill over". By the time we reach the end of this chapter, the Pharisees have "held a council against him, how they might destroy him (v.14), and even worse, accused him of acting in the power of Satan: "This fellow doth not cast out devils (demons), but by Beelzebub the prince of the devils (demons)" (v.24). In short, they totally rejected Him, and deliberately closed their eyes to the evidence that "the kingdom of God is come unto you" (v.28).

As we will see, while the rejection of the Lord Jesus in this chapter meant that "the kingdom of God" was not then publicly established, this did not mean that the Lord's ministry ended in failure, and that unbelief had triumphed. It meant rather that "the kingdom of God" came to be established in a totally different way, and this will become clear in Chapter 13, which commences with the words, "The *same day* went Jesus out of *the house* and sat by *the sea side*" (v.1). The Lord's movements in this way were deeply symbolic. The "house" is a picture of Israel. The Lord later said, "Behold, your *house* is left unto you desolate" (Matt. 23: 38). The "sea side" is a picture of the Gentile nations, which "make a noise like the noise of the seas; and to the rushing of nations, that make a rushing like the rushing of many waters!" (Isaiah 17: 12); "The waters which thou sawest...are peoples, and multitudes, and nations, and tongues" (Rev. 17: 15). It is therefore most significant that in this chapter, which emphasises the Lord's rejection by the Jews, we read, "I will put my spirit upon him, and he shall shew judgment to the *Gentiles*... And in his name shall the *Gentiles* trust" (vv.18, 21).

Matthew 12 may be divided as follows: *(1)* the Lord and the Sabbath (vv.1-14); *(2)* the character of the Servant (vv.15-21); *(3)* the blasphemy against the Spirit (vv.22-37); *(4)* the request for a sign (vv.38-45); *(5)* the disciples and their status (vv.46-50).

1) THE LORD AND THE SABBATH, vv.1-14

"The issue that opens the floodgates is the sabbath question" (Wm. MacDonald). The "madness" of the Pharisees (Luke 6: 11) over the way in which the Lord utterly routed them on this issue led, as we have already noted, to "a council against him, how they might destroy him" (v.14). The Pharisees criticised the Lord Jesus in connection with the conduct of His disciples in the cornfields (vv.1-8), and over the healing of the incapacitated man in the synagogue (vv.9-13), both on the sabbath day. No wonder the Lord Jesus likened Judaism to an old worn out garment, and old hard inflexible bottles! (Matt. 9: 16-17).

a) Eating on the sabbath day, vv.1-8

"And at that time Jesus went on the sabbath day through the corn: and his disciples were an hungred, and began to pluck the ears of corn, and to eat" (v.1). Parallel passages are found in Mark 2: 23-28 and Luke 6: 1-5. The disciples were not stealing. The law sanctioned their behaviour: "When thou comest into the standing corn of thy neighbour, then thou mayest pluck the ears with thine hand; but thou shalt not move a sickle unto thy neighbour's standing corn" (Deut 23: 25).

"But when the Pharisees saw it, they said unto him, Behold, thy disciples do that which is not lawful to do upon the sabbath day" (v.2), and it has to be quickly said that it was only 'unlawful' in the eyes of the Pharisees! Ploughing and reaping were forbidden on the sabbath (Exodus 34: 21), but not eating! After all, in the words of H.St.John, 'it is no harder to pick an ear of wheat than it is to lift one's food from the table on the sabbath day!' The preparation of food was perfectly lawful. See Exodus 12: 16. God's word is never unreasonable! But what God had intended as a blessing (Exodus 20: 8-11) had become a burden. While we are not told why the Pharisees condemned the disciples in this way, it is usually suggested that in their eyes picking the grain was 'harvesting', rubbing it in their hands was 'threshing', and separating the grain from the chaff was 'winnowing'. In other words, according to their rules and regulations, it was nothing less than 'work'.

The Lord Jesus later censured the Pharisees for "teaching for doctrines the commandments of men" (Matt 15: 9). The lawyers did not escape either:

"Woe unto you also, ye lawyers! For ye lade men with burdens grievous to be borne" (Luke 11: 46). We too should carefully avoid adding to the Word of God. It is also worth remembering that there is a big difference between preference and principle. Sometimes our preferences have the force of law! Remember too that, 'these very men, who pretended such strictness on one little point, were more than lax and indifferent about other points of infinitely greater importance...(Matt 23: 23-24)' (J.C.Ryle). We too must beware!

The Lord Jesus answered the criticism by the Pharisees. He did not leave His disciples to fight the battle alone. There is no difficulty in harmonising Matthew and Mark ("they said unto *him*") with Luke ("they said unto *them*"). The Lord still gives "grace to help in time of need" (Heb. 4: 16). In reply, the Lord Jesus cited two cases in the Old Testament, and it is worth noting David Newell's excellent point that the Lord Jesus **appealed** to the Scriptures as the ultimate authority (v.3), **accepted** the Scriptures as historically accurate (v.3), and **applied** the Scriptures to the current circumstances (vv.4-5).

i) **"*Have ye not read***" what David did, when he was an hungred, and they which were with him; how he entered into the house of God, and did eat the showbread, which was not lawful for him to eat...but only for the priests?" (vv.3-4). See 1 Samuel 21: 1-6, where although David technically transgressed the law (Lev. 24: 5-9), he did not incur condemnation. But the Lord's disciples had done nothing comparable: they had only broken an unreasonable law of the Pharisees, so how could they possibly be condemned?

By answering the Pharisees in this way, the Lord Jesus did far more than appeal to an Old Testament precedent. He exposed the emptiness of their religion. Very clearly, the ceremonial law, as distinct from moral law, was never intended to be exercised at the expense of compassion and mercy. We must remember, of course, that when David violated the *moral law*, he was severely condemned. See 2 Samuel 11-12. There is a striking correspondence between David (the Lord's Anointed) and his servants in the Old Testament, and the Lord Jesus (also the Lord's anointed) and His disciples in the New Testament. Both were subject to persecution: David by Saul, and the Lord Jesus by the religious leaders. Bearing in mind that Israel's Messiah was denied by His own people (John 1: 11) any concern with man-made external regulations was completely irrelevant.

ii) "Have ye not read in the law, how that on the sabbath days the priests in the temple profane the sabbath, and are blameless?" (v.5). As Wm.MacDonald clearly explains, 'the priests profaned the sabbath by killing and sacrificing animals, and by performing many other servile duties (Num. 28: 9-10). Yet they were guiltless because they were engaged in the service of God'. The Lord's comment on this is striking: "But I say unto you (indicating that what He was about to say was even more important than the ministry of the priests in the temple), That in this place is one greater than the temple" (v.6). Compare vv.41-42. If the priests were guiltless on the sabbath as they served in the house of God, then the disciples must be guiltless in the presence of the God of the house! In saying, "in this place is one greater than the temple", the Lord Jesus was asserting His absolute deity. The Saviour then refers for the third time to the Old Testament:

iii) "But if ye had known what this meaneth, I will have mercy, and not sacrifice, ye would not have condemned the guiltless, For the Son of man is Lord even of the Sabbath day" (vv.7-8). The Lord now refers to Hosea 6: 6: "For I desired mercy, and not sacrifice; and the knowledge of God more than burnt offerings". God put 'compassion before ritual...but they valued outward punctiliousness above human welfare' (Wm.MacDonald). In saying, "For the Son of man is Lord even of the sabbath day", the Lord Jesus was claiming equality with God. See Genesis 2: 1-3. He uses the title, "Son of man", which denotes His universal supremacy over the whole human race, and therefore over everything connected with the human race. It was He who had instituted the law in the first place, and therefore He was the One most qualified to interpret its true meaning' (Wm.MacDonald). He also had the right to free it from Pharisaical regulations.

It is worth noticing that Mark gives us a little more information, and in particular the Saviour's words, "The sabbath was made for man, and not man for the sabbath" (Mark 2: 27). The sabbath was introduced for man's **benefit:** "The sabbath was made for man", that is, for man's good. Man was not created to make burdensome rules for the sabbath, and thus destroy its true purpose.

b) Healing on the sabbath day, vv.9-14
These verses illustrate further the hypocrisy of the scribes and Pharisees. The connection with vv.1-8 is clear. The Pharisees, no doubt seething after their defeat over sabbath-keeping, now look for fresh grounds on which to indict the Lord Jesus on the same subject. But the Saviour was not

discouraged. He persevered in His service. Opposition did not deter Him. See Isaiah 42: 4. The same perseverance was seen in Paul. Read 1 Thess 2: 2. The Lord Jesus now takes the battle into "***their*** synagogue" (v.9), a very significant expression! Parallel passages are found in Mark 3: 1-6; Luke 6: 6-11. Notice:

i) The man's ailment, v.10. "And when he was departed thence, he went into their synagogue: and, behold, there was a man which had his hand withered" (v.10). Luke not only tells us that the Lord Jesus "entered into the synagogue and taught", but being "the beloved physician" (Col. 4: 14), with his precise medical mind, notes that it was his "right hand" (Luke 6: 6). Since the man's hand was "***restored*** whole, like as the other" (v.13), we *could* infer that it was not originally withered. There is a spiritual lesson here for us. In Scripture, the hand is a symbol for work. For example, "No man, having put his **hand** to the plough" (Luke 9: 62). The right hand is also a symbol of strength. See, for example, Exodus 15: 6 and Psalm 20: 6. Sometimes believers get 'withered hands'. They lose their spiritual strength and ability to work for God. Perhaps we have a "withered hand" when it comes to fellowship (Galatians 2: 9), or prayer (1 Timothy 2: 8).

ii) The Pharisees' attack, v.10. "And they asked him, saying, Is it lawful to heal on the sabbath days? that they might accuse him". They were still 'condemning the guiltless' (v.7). Luke tells us that "the scribes and Pharisees watched him" (Luke 6: 1). Compare Luke 14: 1. Can you think of anything more despicable? They had no interest in the disabled man, but were totally absorbed with accusing the Saviour. Once again, there is a spiritual lesson for us. It is sadly possible to have the same critical spirit. Of course, we must test everything by the Word of God, and sometimes people merit censure. But it is just awful when people either come to meetings purely for the purpose of 'picking holes' in others, or start to do this as meetings proceed. We do need to pray that God will give us grace to see what is good and commendable in one another, rather than concentrate on one another's deficiencies.

iii) The Lord's answer, vv.11-12. Luke tells us that the Lord "knew their thoughts" (Luke 6: 8) before they uttered a word. He was omniscient. "And he said unto them, What man shall there be among you, that shall have one sheep, and if it fall into a pit on the sabbath day, will he not lay hold on it, and lift it out? How much then is a man better than a sheep? Wherefore it is lawful to do well on the sabbath days". See also Luke 14: 5-6. In effect, the Lord Jesus made the Pharisees answer their own question! They were consumed with what they thought was "lawful" on the sabbath day (vv.2,10): now the Lord shows them what really *was* lawful! Compare Luke 13: 10-17.

Here is an extract from an address by Professor Blaiklock, entitled 'The Pharisees and the Sabbath'. 'Only when life was in danger did the Pharisees permit healing on the sabbath. They watched. The Lord brought the man forward. "Is it lawful to do good on the sabbath?", He asked: "to save life or to kill?" (Mark 3: 4). It was a skilful question, for the rabbis decreed that if a beast had fallen into a pit on the sabbath, the owner was to ascertain whether it was hurt. If not, he was to feed and bed it, but not extricate it until the next day. If it was hurt, he was to get it out and kill it. This was difficult and wasteful, so they had an escape regulation. The owner could get the beast out of the pit with the announced intention of killing it, and then not do so. In other words, they could twist their own laws for an animal, but not for a man'. Proverbs 12: 10 makes interesting reading here!

We can now understand why, according to Luke, the Lord Jesus said to the man, "Rise up, and stand forth in the midst" (Luke 6: 8). He was going to administer a public rebuke to the hypocritical Pharisees. He never shrank from confronting hypocrisy. See Matthew 23: 13-15.

iv) The Lord's action, v.13. "Then said he to the man, Stretch forth thine hand. And he stretched it forth: and it was restored whole, like as the other". Mark tells us that He "looked round about on them with anger, being grieved for the hardness of their hearts" (Mark 3: 5). He still grieves over hard hearts. How much are we grieved over the refusal of men and women to bow to the claims of Christ? How much are we grieved over our own hardness of heart when men and women around us are plunging towards eternal doom? Once again, the Lord Jesus demonstrated His divine power. The man's hand was not restored after a series of delicate operations followed by extensive therapy, but immediately. Salvation is just like that: "Believe on the Lord Jesus Christ, and thou shalt be saved" (Acts 16: 31).

v) The Pharisees' animosity, v.14. "Then the Pharisees went out, and held a council against him, how they might destroy him". Mark tells us that "the Pharisees went forth, and straightway took counsel with the Herodians against him, how they might destroy him" (Mark 3: 6). Luke tells us that "they were filled with madness; and communed one with another what they might do to Jesus" (Luke 6: 11). Rather than rejoicing in the blessing of a fellow-countryman, they were infuriated by the exposure of their own hypocrisy. They thought only of their party-position. Nothing causes people so much rage than to be shown the folly of their religion. It should also be noted that the power of unbelief is greater than the power of evidence. 'Miracles do not save or generate faith in those who observe them' (David Newell).

2) THE CHARACTER OF THE SERVANT, vv.15-21

"But when Jesus knew it, he withdrew himself from thence: and great multitudes followed him, and he healed them all" (v.15). The Lord would not allow His death to be hastened: compare John 7: 1. We should notice that the Lord Jesus was rejected by the religious world (v.14), but accepted by the common people. In fact, Mark tells us that "the common people heard him gladly" (Mark 12: 37). We must remember, however, that the Lord never sought publicity: "And he charged them that they should not make him known" (v.16). This leads Matthew, writing for people who knew the Old Testament, to observe that the Lord's reticence to court publicity had been foretold centuries before: "that it might be fulfilled which was spoken by Esaias the prophet, saying, Behold my servant...He shall not strive, nor cry; neither shall any man hear his voice in the streets" (vv.17-19). Matthew refers here to Isaiah 42: 1-4, which lies at the beginning of the first 'Servant Song' in the prophecy. While a detailed study of these verses is beyond the scope of this study, we cannot leave the passage without noting the following: *(a)* the identity of the Servant (v.18); *(b)* the activity of the Servant (vv.19-21).

a) The identity of the Servant, v.18

Having said, "Behold your God" (Isaiah 40: 9), the prophecy continues by saying, "Behold, my servant" (Isaiah 42: 1). God had other servants in the Old Testament. Here are three of them: *(i)* "Hast thou considered **my servant Job**" (Job 1: 8); *(ii)* "If there be a prophet among you, I the Lord will make myself known unto him in a vision. **My servant Moses** is not so" (Num. 12: 6-7); *(iii)* "For I will defend this city to save it for mine own sake, and for **my servant David's** sake" (Isaiah 37: 35). But this Servant is unique. He is the perfect Servant. More than that, this Servant is none other than God manifest in flesh! Although "being in the form of God", He "took upon him the form of a servant" (Phil.2: 6-7). The word translated "servant" in v.18 (*pais*) can mean both 'child' and 'servant' or 'attendant'. We must notice the following:

i) **He is acknowledged by God.** The words, "Behold my servant", are permeated with divine pleasure. This is abundantly clear from what follows, "my beloved, in whom my soul is well pleased". He is God's Servant in deed and in truth. We must listen to Him as He describes His service: "Wist ye not that I must be about *my Father's* business" (Luke 1: 49); "The works which *the Father* hath given me to finish, the same works that I do, bear witness of me" (John 5: 36).

ii) He is appointed by God. It is interesting to compare the original passage with Matthew's rendering: "Behold my servant, whom I uphold; mine elect, in whom my soul delighteth" (Is. 42: 1); "Behold my servant, whom I have chosen; my beloved, in whom my soul is well pleased" (v.18). W.E.Vine points out that the words "my beloved" give the other meaning of the Hebrew word rendered "mine elect". The words here, "whom I have chosen", refer to His eternal calling. As the "living stone" He is "chosen of God, and precious": as the "chief corner stone" He is "elect, precious" (1 Pet. 2: 4, 6). As the "Lamb of God", He was "foreordained before the foundation of the world" (1 Pet. 1: 20). These statements take us beyond human comprehension. No created intelligence could be entrusted with the great mission of man's salvation.

iii) He is approved by God. He is "my beloved, in whom my soul is well pleased". The Beloved Son (Matt. 3: 17) is the Beloved Servant (Matt. 12: 18). Compare Matthew 17: Moses and Elijah were present when God said of the Lord Jesus, "This is my beloved Son, in whom I am well pleased" (Matt. 17: 5), but this was *not* said of either of them! The Lord Jesus said, "I do always those things which please him" (John 8: 29).

iv) He is anointed by God. The words, "I will put my Spirit upon him" refer to His service: "The Spirit of the Lord God is upon me, because the Lord hath anointed me to preach good tidings unto the meek..." (Isaiah 61: 1). Similarly in connection with His future service: see Isaiah 11: 1-2: "The Spirit of the Lord shall rest upon him, the spirit of wisdom and understanding, the spirit of counsel and might, the spirit of knowledge, and of the fear of the Lord" (Isaiah 11: 1-2).

As already noted, it is of great significance to notice that the passage emphasises His service for God amongst Gentiles: "he shall shew judgment to the Gentiles". This is already true: "through their fall (Israel's fall through unbelief) salvation is come unto the Gentiles" (Rom. 11: 11). It will be true again when "all kings shall fall down before him: all nations shall serve him" (Psalm 72: 11).

b) The activity of the Servant, vv.19-21
We must notice *(a)* His meekness (v.19); *(b)* His gentleness (v.20); *(c)* His faithfulness (v.21).

Chapter 12

a) His meekness, v.19
"He shall not strive, nor cry; neither shall any man hear his voice in the streets". He was not a political rabble-rouser. He never led a demo. The original passage (Isaiah 42: 2) contains the words "nor lift up", meaning that He would not advance Himself. He never performed a miracle for His own benefit. He never sought prominence. After His transfiguration, He said to His disciples, "Tell the vision to no man, until the Son of man be risen again from the dead" (Matt. 17: 9). He waited the Father's time.

The setting of these verses also emphasises that He did not retaliate in the face of hostility: When "the Pharisees went out, and held a council against him, how they might destroy him", the Lord "withdrew himself from thence: and great multitudes followed him, and he healed them all; and charged them that they should not make him known" (vv.14-16). He could have consumed his enemies.

b) His gentleness, v.20
"A bruised reed shall he not break, and smoking flax shall he not quench". He was gentle, but *not* weak! Isaiah emphasises His gentleness: "He shall feed his flock like a shepherd: He shall gather the lambs with his arm, and carry them in his bosom" (Isaiah 40: 11). Paul wrote: "I...beseech you by the meekness and gentleness of Christ" (2 Cor. 10: 1)

The Lord Jesus did not 'break the bruised reed', whether the reed was John the Baptist, or Simon Peter. Neither did He quench the two dimly-burning flaxes *en route* to Emmaus. In fact, he rekindled their flagging spirits: "Did not our heart burn within us, while he talked with us by the way, and while he opened to us the scriptures?" (Luke 24: 32). The Lord Jesus is deeply interested in the *sound* (a bruised reed: a tune can be played on a reed), and *light* (a smoking flax) of His people.

c) His faithfulness, vv.20-21
His rule will be marked by firmness and strength. The words "till he send forth judgment unto victory. And in his name shall the Gentiles trust ('hope', JND)" represent the original Hebrew text: "He shall bring forth judgment to the Gentiles" (Isaiah 42: 1). He shall not fail nor be discouraged till he have set judgment in the earth: and the isles shall wait for his law" (Isaiah 42: 4). He will be steadfast in accomplishing the task before Him. "He shall not fail nor be discouraged *till* he have set judgment in the earth". Isaiah emphasises His strength: "Behold, the Lord God will come with a strong hand, and his arm shall rule for him" (Isaiah 40: 10).

Matthew

"This fellow doth not cast out devils, but by Beelzebub"

Read Chapter 12: 22-37
We have already noticed that this chapter may be divided as follows: *(1)* the Lord and the sabbath (vv.1-14); *(2)* the character of the Servant (vv.15-21); *(3)* the blasphemy against the Spirit (vv.22-37); *(4)* the request for a sign (vv.38-45); *(5)* the disciples and their status (vv.46-50).

1) THE LORD AND THE SABBATH, vv.1-14
Having been shown by the Lord Jesus that plucking and eating ears of corn on the sabbath day did not contravene the Scriptures (vv.1-8), and that healing on the sabbath day was in complete accord with their own practices in society (vv.9-13), the furious Pharisees "went out, and held a council against him, how they might destroy him" (v.14).

2) THE CHARACTER OF THE SERVANT, vv.15-21
The picture changes, and the madness of the Pharisees gives place to the meekness of the Saviour. Matthew refers to Isaiah 42: 1-4 in emphasising *(a)* the identity of the Servant: "Behold my servant, whom I have chosen; my beloved, in whom my soul is well pleased" (v.18); *(b)* the activity of the Servant: "he shall shew judgment to the Gentiles. He shall not strive, nor cry; neither shall any man hear his voice in the streets. A bruised reed shall he not break, and smoking flax shall he not quench, till he send forth judgment unto victory. And in his name shall the Gentiles trust" (vv.18-21). The passage emphasises His meekness (v.19); His gentleness (v.20); His faithfulness (vv.20-21).

A further demonstration of the healing power of the Lord Jesus, and the way in which the people responded, provoked further hostility on the part of the Pharisees. This brings us to:

3) THE BLASPHEMY AGAINST THE SPIRIT, vv.22-37
These solemn verses may be summarised as follows: *(a)* the amazement of the people (vv.22-23); *(b)* the accusation by the Pharisees (v.24); *(c)* the answer by the Lord (vv.25-32); *(d)* the abundance of the heart (vv.33-37).

a) The amazement of the people, vv.22-23
This arose from the healing of the demon-possessed blind and dumb man. "Then was brought unto him (not to the Pharisees) one possessed with a devil (demon), blind and dumb" (v.22). Luke also refers to this miracle (Luke

11: 14). According to R.V.G.Tasker the introductory word "Then" (v.22) does "not indicate 'at that moment' or 'directly after that', but is a literary device of the evangelists for linking together stories which are fundamentally similar". We should notice:

i) **The condition of the man, v.22.** He was "possessed with a devil (demon), blind and dumb". The Gospel preacher will point out that the man's condition is a vivid picture of unregenerate men and women, who "walk according to the prince of the power of the air, the spirit that now worketh in the children of disobedience" (Eph. 2: 2), who in consequence are blind, for "the god of this world hath blinded the minds of them which believe not" (2 Cor. 4: 4), and dumb for they cannot sing the "new song...even praise unto our God" (Ps. 40: 3). But there is more: the man was "the apt figure of the nation's condition, the Messiah unseen and His praise unuttered in their midst" (Wm.Kelly).

ii) **The cure of the man, v.22.** "And he healed him, insomuch that the blind and dumb both spake and saw". Believers can say with David, "My mouth shall praise thee with joyful lips" (Ps. 63: 5), and they can "offer the sacrifice of praise to God continually, that is, the fruit of our lips giving thanks to his name" (Heb. 13: 15). Believers have a faculty of sight which transcends natural vision: like Moses, they can endure "as seeing him who is invisible" (Heb. 11: 27).

iii) **The conclusion of the onlookers, v.23.** "And all the people were amazed, and said, Is not this the son of David?" "Son of David" is the royal title of the Messiah. See Matt. 1: 1; 21: 9, 15. In view of what they had seen they could only conclude that this was the Messiah through whom "the eyes of the blind shall be opened, and the ears of the deaf shall be unstopped.... and the tongue of the dumb sing" (Is. 35: 5-6). According to the competent authorities, "the form of the interrogative requires this to be rendered, 'Is this the son of David?', with the meaning 'Can it possibly be?', indicating their secret impression that this *must* be the case". In this way, the people avoided "the wrath of the ecclesiastics" which a direct statement would have brought upon them. (Supplied by Justin Waldron). But even so, the "wrath of the ecclesiastics" was not far away:

b) The accusation by the Pharisees, v.24
"But when the Pharisees heard it, they said, This fellow doth not cast out devils (demons), but by Beelzebub the prince of the devils (demons)".

Matthew

According to Mark, who refers particularly to the scribes, they "came down from Jerusalem" (Mark 3: 22). The Lord was evidently still in Galilee, probably in Capernaum. The fact that the people had even dared to ask the question, "Is not this the son of David?", enraged the religious leaders, and they came all the way from Jerusalem to collect evidence against him.

Since we have already encountered the name Beelzebub (Matt. 10: 25), all we need do here is to repeat our comments at that point. After all, a little revision never goes amiss! This is what we said: The name "Beelzebub" or 'Beelzebul' (margin) is of uncertain origin, although it is generally thought to be connected with Baal-zebub, the god of Ekron (2 Kings 1: 2, 6). The Pharisees called Beelzebub "the prince of the devils (demons)" (Matt. 9: 34; 12: 24). The name may mean 'the lord of the high place' or 'lord of the house'...but it was commonly accepted amongst the Jews, following the Aramaic *Beelzeboul* (the Greek manuscripts have 'Beelzebul'), to mean 'the lord of the flies' or 'the lord of the dunghill'. It was both derisory and defamatory. It was derisory: in using this name, they poured scorn and derision on the Saviour. It was defamatory: they said that he was empowered by "the prince of the devils" (Matt. 12: 24).

We ought to add, firstly, 'that the bitterest enemies of our Lord were unable to deny the reality of His miracles' and, secondly, that 'they had no way of holding out against His claims other than by the desperate shift of ascribing His miracles to Satan' (supplied by Justin Waldron). The fact that they called "the prince of the devils" by the derisory name 'Beelzebul', illustrates Peter's observation that false teachers "are not afraid to speak evil of dignities. Whereas angels, which are greater in power and might, bring not railing accusation against them before the Lord" (2 Pet. 2: 10-11).

c) The answer by the Lord, vv.25-32
We should notice that the Lord Jesus 'ignored the coarse insult and substituted the name, Satan' (H.St.John). The Lord answers this blasphemous accusation in two ways: he emphasises (i) the stupidity of the accusation (vv.25-29 and (ii) the gravity of the accusation (vv.30-32).

i) The stupidity of the accusation, vv.25-29. This is emphasised by the Lord's three questions (vv.26, 27, 29). We can summarise his reply like this:

- *Their statement was illogical, vv.25-26.* "And Jesus knew their thoughts (an affirmation of the Lord's omniscience), and said unto them, Every kingdom divided against itself is brought to desolation; and every city or house divided against itself shall not stand: and if Satan cast out Satan, he is divided against himself; *how then shall his kingdom stand?"* The fact that He had, allegedly, cast out demons by the power of the "prince of demons", implied self-destruction. In the words of Harold St.John (writing on Mark 3: 24-26), 'It implied that a political (a "kingdom...divided against itself"), domestic (a "house...divided against itself") and personal ("Satan...against himself") civil war has already broken out in the kingdom of evil'.

- ***Their statement was inconsistent, v.27.*** "And if I by Beelzebub cast out devils, *by whom do your children cast them out?* Therefore they shall be your judges". It has been suggested that the expression, "your children" ('your sons', JND), refers to the disciples or pupils of the Pharisees, and that their description in this way is in the same vein as "the sons of the prophets" (see, for example, 1 Kings 20: 35; 2 Kings 2: 3). On the other hand, some conservative commentators (including H.A.Ironside and J.Heading) suggest that the Lord refers here to His own disciples, being sons of Israel ("your children"), whom He empowered to cast out demons (Matt. 10: 1, 8; Luke 10: 17), but this explanation hardly seems tenable. The context does seem to suggest that the Lord is referring to the disciples of the Pharisees. According to Wm.MacDonald, 'Some of their Jewish associates, known as exorcists, claimed to have the power to cast out demons. Jesus neither admitted nor denied their claim. He simply used the claim to point out that if He cast out demons by Beelzebul, then the Pharisees' sons...also cast out demons by Beelzebul'. It is worth mentioning that there were evidently other groups who cast out demons. See Luke 9: 49-50.

- ***Their statement was ill-conceived, vv.28-29.*** They just hadn't understood what they were witnessing. "But if I cast out devils by the Spirit of God, then the kingdom of God (one of only four references to the "kingdom of God" in Matthew) is come unto you. Or else *how can one enter a strong man's house, and spoil his goods, except he first bind the strong man? And then he will spoil his house"*. Having completely confounded their argument that He cast out demons by Beelzebub, "the prince of the devils (demons)", the Lord then points out that the onlookers were correct. They had said, "Is not this the son of David?" (v.23). They said, in effect, that the Messiah had come to establish His kingdom, and the Lord now confirms their conclusion: "But if I cast out devils by the Spirit of God, then the kingdom of God is come unto you".

Matthew

In casting out demons by the Spirit of God, the Lord Jesus fulfilled the ancient prophecy, "The **Spirit of the Lord God** is upon me; because the Lord hath anointed me to preach good tidings unto the meek…to proclaim liberty to the captives, and the opening of the prison to them that are bound" (Is. 61: 1). Compare Isaiah 42: 1. Most certainly then, the King had come, and was in the process of establishing His kingdom. Peter describes His work in the power of the Holy Spirit: "God anointed Jesus of Nazareth with the **Holy Ghost** and with power; Who went about doing good, and **healing all that were oppressed of the devil**; for God was with Him" (Acts 10: 38). Luke gives us a splendid example: "And ought not this woman, being a daughter of Abraham, whom **Satan** hath bound, lo, these eighteen years, be loosed from her infirmity on the sabbath day? And when he said these things…all the people rejoiced for all the glorious things that were done by him" (Luke 13: 16-17).

In order to deliver men and women from bondage to the powers of darkness, the Lord Jesus had come to deal with the very "prince of the devils". This is evidently the meaning of the Lord's words, "Or else how can one enter a strong man's house, and spoil his goods, except he first bind the strong man?" They had accused Him of casting out demons by the "prince of the devils", but in actual fact He had come to annul his power! In order to deal with Satan's forces, he must first deal with the "prince" himself, whom He likens to a strong man guarding his house. In the words of John, "For this purpose the Son of God was manifested, that he might destroy ('undo', margin) the works of the devil" (1 John 3: 8). As noted above, He did this during His earthly ministry, but the basis of deliverance from Satan's power was established by the Lord's work on the cross: "Forasmuch then as the children are partakers of flesh and blood, he also himself likewise took part of the same; that **through death** he might **destroy him that had the power of death**, that is, the devil; and **deliver them** who through fear of death were all their lifetime subject to bondage" (Heb. 2: 14-15). How glad we are that the Lord Jesus continues to "spoil" (meaning 'to plunder') Satan's goods! Once **we** were subject to "the prince of the power of the air", but now we belong to Christ!

ii) **The gravity of the accusation, vv.30-32.** The solemnity of the Pharisees' attitude can be summarised as follows:

- **They opposed God's will, v.30.** "He that is not with me is against me; and he that gathereth not with me scattereth abroad". As R.V.G. Tasker points out, "the campaign between God and Satan had begun in earnest, and in that campaign neutrality is impossible." He continues: "Not to be allied with Jesus and the kingdom of God is to be allied with Satan and the kingdom of evil; and to try to prevent men and women from accepting Jesus as their King, as the Pharisees were trying to do (vv.23-24), is to disintegrate and scatter those who otherwise be 'the sons of the kingdom', enjoying its reign in their hearts, and that is the devil's main objective (v.30). It's worth pointing out that Mark 9: 40 does not contradict the Lord's teaching here: the subject there is *service*.

- **They blasphemed the Holy Spirit, vv.31-32**. "Wherefore I say unto you, All manner of sin and blasphemy shall be forgiven unto men: but the blasphemy against the Holy Ghost shall not be forgiven unto men. And whosoever speaketh a word against the Son of man, it shall be forgiven him: but whosoever speaketh against the Holy Ghost, it shall not be forgiven him, neither in this world, neither in the world to come". Mark uses equally strong language, "But he that shall blaspheme against the Holy Ghost hath never forgiveness, but is in danger of eternal damnation" and adds, "because they said, He hath an unclean spirit" (Mark 3: 29-30).

In the first place, there is **assurance of forgiveness**. The apostle Paul found forgiveness for blasphemy: "Who was before a **blasphemer,** and a persecutor, and injurious: but I obtained mercy" (1 Tim.1: 13). In the second place, there is **assurance of no forgiveness** for blasphemy "against the Holy Ghost." The reason is clear: it was in the power of the Holy Spirit that the Lord Jesus performed His miracles, and delivered men and women from Satan's power and control. In claiming that the Lord Jesus cast out demons by Satan's power, the Jewish leaders completely and utterly rejected both the Saviour Himself, and the divinely-provided evidence that He was the Christ, the Son of God. They were denominating the Holy Spirit as "Satan". Stephen's charge was immensely serious, "Ye do always resist **the Holy Ghost**: as your fathers did, so do ye" (Acts 7: 51), but this was even greater. It should be borne in mind that from the very beginning, the purposes and designs of God have been accomplished in the power of the Holy Spirit (cf. Gen. 1: 2), Himself God. The implications of assigning His power to Satan are solemn beyond words.

In the Old Testament, condemnation was pronounced on those who "call evil good, and good evil; that put darkness for light, and light for darkness; that put bitter for sweet, and sweet for bitter!" (Is. 5: 20). This was exactly what the scribes and Pharisees were doing, and not for the first time either. See Matthew 9: 34. Compare John 7: 20, 8: 48, 8: 52, 10: 20). The question arises: 'Can this sin be committed today?' Harold St.John (*An Analysis of the Gospel of Mark*) deals with the question as follows: 'The nature of that one unpardonable guilt and that unforgivable sinner, is defined in v.30 (that is, Mark 3: 30). If a man watched God in Christ revealing the grace of heaven, rescuing the victims of sin and disease and then, judging by what he had seen, imputed the deeds of the Redeemer to a Satanic source, he had uttered the one blasphemy which lay outside the circle of God's forgiveness'. He continues by saying that 'it is debatable whether such a sin could ever be committed today: when our Lord spoke, the Holy Spirit was present in a power which streamed forth from One Who was truly Man, but was also very God. Could such conditions ever recur?' However, recent statements by some so-called church leaders must bring them perilously near, if not under, the solemn judgment of this passage. It must also be said that other commentators take a similar but not identical view in saying that the solemn pronouncement of the Lord Jesus here has particular reference to those who, having seen the truth, *persist* in their opposition and rejection.

d) The abundance of the heart, vv.33-37

The connection with the preceding verses is clear: the Pharisees had accused the Lord Jesus of acting in the power of Satan (the very mention of this is horrifying), but the fact of the matter was that **they** were the people acting in Satan's power. Hence the Lord calls them "O generation of vipers" (v.34). As H.A.Ironside observes, 'They were the brood of the serpent, and they manifested the nature of that old serpent, which is the devil, in their attitude toward the Christ of God. Out of the abundance of their hearts their mouth spoke'. We should notice three contrasts:

i) A contrast between fruit, v.33.

"Either make the tree good, and his *fruit* good; or else make the tree corrupt, and his *fruit* corrupt: for the tree is known by his *fruit*". The Pharisees had accused him of casting out demons by the power of Satan. Was this a good work or a corrupt work? As Wm.MacDonald so rightly says, 'The fruit of His ministry had been good. He had healed the sick, given sight to the blind, caused the deaf to hear, made the dumb to talk, cast out demons, and raised the dead. Could a corrupt tree have brought forth such good fruit? Utterly impossible!' Yet they accused Him of acting in the power of Satan.

ii) A contrast between hearts, vv.34-35.
This takes the matter still further.

He speaks directly to them. They had accused Him: now He accuses them. "O generation of vipers (see also Matt. 3: 7), how can ye, being evil speak good things? For out of the abundance of the *heart* the mouth speaketh. A good man out of the good treasure of his *heart* bringeth forth good things: and an evil man out of the evil treasure bringeth forth evil things". Solomon warns against accepting the hospitality of someone with an evil eye, and adds, "as he thinketh in his heart, so is he" (Prov. 23: 7). How important to emulate the Psalmist, and say, "Thy word have I hid in my heart, that I might not sin against thee" (Ps. 119: 11), and talking about treasure, the Lord Jesus referred to a "householder, which bringeth forth out of his treasure things new and old" (Matt. 13: 52), which is rather different, to put it mildly, to the "evil man" with his "evil treasure" here.

iii) A contrast between words, vv.36-37. There can be litttle doubt that the Saviour is still referring to the Pharisees' accusation here: "But I say unto you, That every idle word that men shall speak, they shall give account thereof in the day of judgment. For by thy words thou shalt be justified, and by thy words thou shalt be condemned". The word "idle" (*argos*) has the sense here of 'ineffective, worthless' (W.E.Vine). Words are 'an accurate gauge' of a person's life, 'and form a suitable basis for condemnation or acquittal' (Wm.MacDonald).

Having said this, we must remember that David said, "I will take heed to my ways, that I sin not with my tongue" (Ps. 39: 1), and pray "Set a watch, O Lord before my mouth; keep the door of my lips" (Psalm 141: 3). We must not forget, either, that "If any man offend not in word, the same is a perfect man" (James 3: 2).

"Three days and three nights in the heart of the earth"

Read Chapter 12: 38-50
In previous studies we have noticed that this chapter may be divided as follows: *(1)* the Lord and the sabbath (vv.1-14); *(2)* the character of the Servant (vv.15-21); *(3)* the blasphemy against the Spirit (vv.22-37); *(4)* the request for a sign (vv.38-45); *(5)* the disciples and their status (vv.46-50).

1) THE LORD AND THE SABBATH, vv.1-14
Having been shown by the Lord Jesus that plucking and eating ears of corn on the sabbath day did not contravene the Scriptures (vv.1-8), and that healing on the sabbath day was in complete accord with their own

practices in society (vv.9-13), the furious Pharisees "went out, and held a council against him, how they might destroy him" (v.14).

2) THE CHARACTER OF THE SERVANT, vv.15-21
The picture changes, and the madness of the Pharisees gives place to the meekness of the Saviour. Matthew refers to Isaiah 42: 1-4 in emphasising *(a)* the identity of the Servant: "Behold my servant, whom I have chosen; my beloved, in whom my soul is well pleased" (v.18); *(b)* the activity of the Servant: "he shall shew judgment to the Gentiles. He shall not strive, nor cry; neither shall any man hear his voice in the streets. A bruised reed shall he not break, and smoking flax shall he not quench, till he send forth judgment unto victory" (vv.18-21). These verses emphasise His meekness (v.19); His gentleness (v.20); His faithfulness (vv.20-21).

3) THE BLASPHEMY AGAINST THE SPIRIT, vv.22-37
A further demonstration of the healing power of the Lord Jesus, and the way in which the people responded, provoked more hostility on the part of the Pharisees. The people said, "Is not this the son of David?", but the Pharisees would have none of this: "when the Pharisees heard it, they said, This fellow doth not cast out devils, but by Beelzebub the prince of the devils (demons)" (vv.23-24). Having demonstrated that this accusation was illogical (vv.25-26), inconsistent (v.27) and ill-conceived (v.28-29), the Lord warns the Pharisees that they had made themselves liable to eternal judgment: "Wherefore I say unto you, All manner of sin and blasphemy shall be forgiven unto men; but the blasphemy against the Holy Ghost shall not be forgiven unto men...it shall not be forgiven him, neither in this world, neither in the world to come" (vv.31-32). In attributing the power of the Holy Spirit to Satan, the Pharisees had made it clear that they, not the Lord, were the people empowered by Satan: "O generation of vipers, how can ye, being evil, speak good things" (v.34).

4) THE REQUEST FOR A SIGN, vv.38-45
"Then certain of the scribes and of the Pharisees answered him, saying, Master, we would see a sign from thee" (v.38). Together with the Sadducees, the Pharisees asked the same later: see Matthew 16: 1-4. Matthew places this event just before the parables of the kingdom, which are introduced with the words, "The **same day** went Jesus out of **the house** and sat by **the sea side**" (Matt. 13: 1), whereas Luke places it well after the transfiguration. The reference to a Gentile city (v.41) and to a Gentile queen (v.42) may well account for Matthew's inclusion of this incident at this point. It is in keeping

with the emphasis in the chapter on the Lord's rejection by the Jews, and the blessing of the Gentiles: "I will put my spirit upon him, and he shall shew judgment to the **Gentiles**...And in his name shall the **Gentiles** trust" (vv.18, 21).

We have already noted R.V.G.Tasker's observation (in connection with v.22) that the word "Then" (*tote*) does "not indicate 'at that moment' or 'directly after that', but is a literary device of the evangelist for linking together stories which are fundamentally similar". He also points out that the word "answered" (see 11: 25), 'does not indicate an answer to a specific question, but draws attention to the speaker's reaction to a particular situation'. The word "answered" (*apokrinomai*) occurs twice in vv.38-39: firstly with the meaning suggested above (v.38), and secondly with the usual meaning (v.39).

The word "generation" (*genea*) which occurs four times in these verses (vv.39, 41, 42, 45), evidently means 'the race, kind, family, stock, breed' (C.I. Scofield). The Lord refers to *(a)* the evil of the generation (vv38-39); *(b)* the sign to the generation (vv.39-40); *(c)* the judgment on the generation (vv.41-42); *(d)* the state of the generation (vv.43-45).

a) The evil of the generation, vv.38-39
According to Luke, it almost seems that the crowds were gathering in anticipation: "And when the people were gathered thick together, he began to say, This is an evil generation: they seek a sign" (Luke 11: 29). Compare John 6: 30: "What sign showest thou then, that we may see, and believe thee?" Wm.MacDonald sums up the situation: "In spite of all the miracles which Jesus had performed, the scribes and Pharisees had the temerity to ask Him for a sign. They implied, of course, that they would believe if He could prove Himself to be the Messiah. But their hypocrisy was transparent! If they had not believed as a result of so many wonders, why would they be convinced by one more?" However, it does seem that the "sign" demanded by the scribes and Pharisees was something quite different from the miracles performed by the Lord Jesus. Compare Matt. 27: 42. On other comparable occasions, they asked for "a sign from heaven" (Matt. 16: 1, Mark 8: 11).

We can be certain that the scribes and Pharisees did not genuinely want a sign to clear all doubt about the Lord's true identity, and to confirm that He was the Messiah. 'The desire for signs demonstrated the people's unbelief' (J.Heading). A "sign from heaven" is poles apart from faith in God. Thomas demanded evidence of the Lord's resurrection before he would believe, only to be told, "blessed are they that have not seen, and yet have believed" (John 20: 29). Peter certainly never forget the lesson: "Whom having not seen, ye love; in whom, though now ye see him not, yet believing, ye rejoice with joy unspeakable and full of glory" (1 Pet. 1: 8).

In replying to their request, the Lord describes them as "An evil and adulterous generation" (v.39). According to W.E.Vine, the word "evil" (*poneros*) 'denotes what is evil in influence and effect, malignant...what is destructive, injurious, evil'. While it is possible to understand the word "adulterous" here quite literally, it is more likely that it 'is used adjectivally to describe the Jewish people in transferring their affections from God' (W.E.Vine). R.V.G.Tasker rightly points out that it is used here "in the peculiarly biblical sense of 'unfaithful'". It has this meaning in James 4: 4. For an example of R.V.G.Tasker's "peculiarly biblical sense of 'unfaithful'", see Jeremiah 3: 9, "and it came to pass through the lightness of her whoredom, that she defiled the land, and committed adultery with stones and with stocks". In the words of Wm.MacDonald, 'they were adulterous because they were spiritually unfaithful to their God. They sought a sign when He, their Creator-God, stood in their midst'.

b) *The sign to the generation, vv.39-40*
"There shall no sign be given to it, but the sign of the prophet Jonas. For as Jonas was three days and three nights in the whale's belly (compare 1 Sam. 30: 2-13; Esther 4: 16) so ***shall*** (nothing could prevent this happening) the Son of man be three days and three nights in the heart of the earth". This should be compared with the Lord's answer to the question, "What sign shewest thou unto us, seeing that thou doest these things?", to which He replied, "Destroy this temple, and in three days I ***will*** (nothing could prevent this happening) raise it up...But he spake of the temple of his body" (John 2: 18-21). We know that even this "sign" failed to bring the Jews to repentance and faith. They did not believe "the sign of Jonas the prophet". See Matt. 28: 11-15; Luke 16: 31. The Lord Jesus was "declared to be the Son of God...by the resurrection from the dead" (Rom 1: 4). Jonah had been a sign to his generation (Luke 11: 30) and the Lord Jesus would be a sign to "this generation". As David Gooding points out, 'For the Ninevites the sign was the reappearance of a man, who had apparently been dead for three days...Jesus makes it clear that when He gives a sign it will be one of His own choosing, not one given at the demand of an unbelieving generation'. Two matters arise:

Chapter 12

- ***"three days and three nights"***. There is some debate in connection with the precise meaning of the Lord's words, "so shall the Son of man be three *days* and three *nights* in the heart of the earth". If the Lord Jesus was crucified on 'Good Friday', and left Joseph's tomb on 'Easter Sunday', how could He have been "three days and three nights in the heart of the earth?" This is what the lawyers call 'a nice question'. The usual answer is that in Jewish reckoning any part of a day and night counts as a complete period, and this would certainly be the answer if it were a question of "three days", but the Lord did say "three days and three nights!" It has been argued that the words "that sabbath day was an *high day*" (John 19: 31) indicate 'something special and distinct from a ordinary sabbath', arising from the fact that the feast of unleavened bread commenced on the fifteenth day of the first month and was regarded as a Sabbath, irrespective of the day of the week on which it fell (Lev. 23: 7). If it fell on the sixth day of the week, 'then two Sabbaths would follow one another' (J.Heading). On this basis, the Lord would have been crucified, not on 'Good Friday', but on Thursday. Make your own calculation, bearing in mind that the Lord rose before Mary Magdalene arrived at the tomb and it was "yet dark" (John 20: 1). Without doubt, the debate will continue!

- ***"in the heart of the earth"***. R.V.G.Tasker asserts that this does not mean 'in the grave', for the body of Jesus was not given earth burial but laid in a tomb hewn out of the rock. The expression (he suggests) indicates 'the nether-regions' or 'the abode of the dead'. It must be said, however, that on the cross, the Lord Jesus said, "Father, into thy hands I commend my *spirit:* and having said thus, he gave up the ghost" (Luke 23: 46). His spirit therefore went to the Father in heaven. Previously He had said to the repentant thief, "To day shalt thou be with me in paradise" (Luke 23: 43), and 'this assures us that the Lord Jesus was in paradise that very day. Paul, in 2 Corinthians 12: 2, 4 shows us that paradise and the third heaven are one and the same place. Thus on His death, the spirit and soul of the Lord Jesus went to the Father in heaven' (D.E.West, *Believer's Magazine, January 2011).* The expression "the heart of the earth" evidently *does* refer to burial: it is 'the most emphatic expression of real and total entombment' (supplied by J.Waldron).

c) The judgment on the generation, vv.41-42

These verses need little comment. "The men of Ninevah shall rise (*anestemi*) in the judgment with this generation, and shall condemn it: because they repented at the preaching of Jonah; and, behold, a greater than Jonas is here. The queen of the south shall rise up (*egeiro*) in the judgment with this generation, and shall condemn it: for she came from the uttermost parts of the earth to hear the wisdom of Solomon; and, behold, a greater than Solomon is here".

The Lord Jesus had greater wisdom than Solomon, and a better message than Jonah. The queen of Sheba made a long journey (Sheba was evidently in southern Arabia: probably modern Yemen) to hear the wisdom of Solomon and was transported with wonder at what she saw and heard, but the men of the Lord's generation 'had no journey to make, for Jesus was in their very midst' (David Gooding), and they despised, rejected, slighted and slandered Him. They would stand condemned "in the judgment" by her example. We should note, again, that both the queen of Sheba and the inhabitants of Nineveh were Gentiles. If non-Jews responded in this way to the wisdom and word of God, there can be no excuse for His own people in rejecting the wisdom and preaching of His own Son. Privilege determines responsibility. The greater the privilege, the greater the responsibility. Compare James 3: 1. The question has to be asked, 'At what point in the future will this particular resurrection take place?' If the Lord refers here to the judgment at the "great white throne" (Rev. 20: 11), at which it is generally said that only the wicked dead will be present, then what about the "men of Nineveh" and the "queen of the south?". Or will the "men of Nineveh" and the "queen of the south" be present as witnesses? Or is it a question of people who at least responded in measure to their privileges without actually exercising faith in God, as opposed to those who did not respond at all? Once again, this is a 'nice question!' However, we must take the opportunity to note some of the ways in which the Lord Jesus is "greater than Jonas", and "greater than Solomon".

i) "Greater than Jonas"
The following is taken from our Jonah studies in 1990. The four chapters of the book each emphasise at least one way in which the Lord Jesus is "greater than Jonas".

- **Chapter 1: The Lord is greater than Jonah in His obedience.** For example "Jonah rose up to flee unto Tarshish from the presence of the Lord" (v.2), but the Lord Jesus said, "I was not rebellious, neither turned away back" (Is. 50: 5); "Lo, I come: in the volume of the book it is written of me, I delight to do thy will, O my God" (Psalm 40: 6-8, quoted in Hebrews 10: 7.). He "became obedient unto death, even the death of the cross" (Phil. 2:

8). We could go much further. For example, Jonah had no power over the storm which threatened his life and the life of the mariners. The Lord Jesus "arose, and rebuked the wind, and said unto the sea, Peace be still. And the wind ceased, and there was a great calm" (Mark 4: 39). The presence of Jonah brought fear to the mariners, but the presence of the Lord Jesus brought peace to the disciples. He said, "It is I, be not afraid" (John 6: 20). There is much more.

- **Chapter 2: The Lord is greater than Jonah in His experience.** We must not underestimate Jonah's experience. It was quite horrible. He was under no misapprehension about the reason. When the mariners "took up Jonah, and cast him forth into the sea" (1: 15), they were actually acting on God's behalf: "For *thou* hadst cast me into the deep, in the midst of the seas" (2: 3). Compare Acts 2: 23, "Him, being delivered by the determinate counsel and foreknowledge of God, ye have taken, and by wicked hands have crucified and slain". The Lord Jesus suffered under divine judgment. On the third day Jonah reappeared "upon the dry land", and on the third day Christ rose in triumph from the grave.

- **Chapter 3: The Lord is greater than Jonah in His ministry.** It was never said of the Lord Jesus, "and the word of the Lord came unto him *the second time*," (v.1). Jonah had an eight-word sermon: "Yet forty days, and Nineveh shall be overthrown" (v.4). All we need to say at this juncture is that, by contrast, "God sent not his Son into the world to condemn the world; but that the world through him might be saved" John 3: 17). The Lord made it clear to James and John that "the Son of man is not come to *destroy* men's lives, but to *save* them" (Luke 9: 51-56).

- **Chapter 4: The Lord is greater than Jonah in His mercy.** Jonah evidently delighted in judgment. He failed to appreciate that it was God's "strange (meaning 'alien') work...his strange act" (Is. 28: 21). He failed to appreciate that God is "longsuffering to us-ward, not willing that any should perish, but that all should come to repentance" (2 Peter 3: 9). The publican cried, "God be merciful to me a sinner ('the sinner' JND)" (Luke 18: 13), and blind Bartimaeus cried, "Jesus, Thou son of David, have mercy on me" (Mark 10: 48). There was no reluctance on the part of the Saviour. It would have been a different story if they had cried to Jonah!

ii) "Greater than Solomon"
We will make no attempt to go into detail here, but simply confine ourselves

Matthew

to the wisdom, work, and wealth of Solomon. Just the briefest of suggestions for further study!

- **The Lord is greater than Solomon in His wisdom.** God gave Solomon "**wisdom** and understanding exceeding much, and largeness of heart, even as the sand that is on the sea shore" (1 Kings 4: 29). It was not long before Solomon displayed his God-given wisdom, not in handling the massive burden of state affairs, but in resolving a delicate problem posed by two mothers with one baby. See 1 Kings 3: 16-28. (They didn't have blood tests in those days!). The Scriptures refer to the "wisdom of words...the wisdom of the wise...the wisdom of this world...the wisdom of men" (1 Cor. 1: 17, 19; 2: 5; 3: 20. But God's wisdom is totally different: "Christ crucified" is a "stumblingblock" to the Jews, and "foolishness" to the Greeks, but to every child of God, He is "Christ the power of God, and the wisdom of God" (1 Cor.1: 23-24).

- **The Lord is greater than Solomon in His work.** Solomon was a builder. He built "the house of the Lord", "his own house", "the house of the forest of Lebanon", "the wall of Jerusalem", together with various other cities. He was also in the ship-building industry (1 Kings 9: 26). The "greater than Solomon" is not only the true "wisdom that is from above" (James 3: 17), He is a builder too. He said, "I will build my church, and the gates of hell shall not prevail against it" (Matt.16: 18).

- **The Lord is greater than Solomon in His wealth.** Solomon's material wealth was **abundant:** "Now the weight of the gold that came to Solomon in one year was six hundred threescore and six talents of gold, beside that he had of the merchantmen, and of the traffick of the spice merchants, and of the kings of Arabia, and of the governors of the country" (1 Kings 10: 4-15). There was gold everywhere (1 Kings 10: 16-21). We must remember the abundance of **our** spiritual wealth. Paul calls it "the exceeding riches of his grace in his kindness toward us through Christ Jesus" (Eph. 2: 7). Solomon's wealth was **superior.** Not just "gold", but "**best** gold"" (v.18) and "**pure** gold" (1 Kings 10: 18, 21). God does not bestow sub-standard blessings. Like his beloved Son, they are "unspeakable" (2 Cor. 9: 15). Solomon's wealth was **varied.** When the joint navies of Solomon and Hiram docked, the vessels discharged "gold, and silver, ivory, and apes, and peacocks" (1 Kings 10: 22). And so we could go on! Our wealth is no less varied. Just read Ephesians Chapter 1. The "greater than Solomon" has enriched us beyond measure, but at infinite cost. See 2 Cor. 8: 9.

d) The state of the generation, vv.43-45

These verses are usually explained with reference to Israel's idolatrous history. The "unclean spirit" is said to be the spirit of idolatry and that whilst at the time the nation was not given to idolatry, the rejection of their Messiah will ultimately render them vulnerable to the most fearful idolatry ever seen. They will worship the image of the beast (Matt. 24: 15; 2 Thess. 2: 4; Rev.13: 15).

However, it does seem that the Lord still has in mind the healing of the demoniac and the subsequent teaching: "how can one enter into a strong man's *house*, and spoil his goods, except he first bind the strong man?" (v.29). As already noted, in the words of John, "For this purpose the Son of God was manifested, that he might destroy ('undo', margin) the works of the devil" (1 John 3: 8). He did this during His earthly ministry, but the basis of deliverance from Satan's power was established by the Lord's work on the cross (Heb. 2: 14-15). Having died at Calvary and risen from the dead, so fulfilling His statement that the only sign that would be given was "the sign of the prophet Jonas" (v.39), all that was necessary for the blessing of Israel had been done: the *house* was "empty, swept and garnished ('put in order', W.E.Vine)" (v.44). Satan's power had been annulled. But there had been no national change of heart. The book of Acts makes it clear that the Lord remained unwanted and rejected, so that in the illustration the demon still calls it "*my* house". As in the illustration, so in reality: the nation which gave no welcome to the Saviour who died for them, became subject to increased Satanic power. The spiritual state of the nation worsened: having rejected the Saviour when He was with them, they continued to reject Him, and violently persecuted the men who urged them to accept Him. In the Lord's words, they were possessed with "seven other wicked spirits (suggests the totality of Satanic power) more wicked than himself". It is therefore most significant that the Lord "went...out of the *house*" and "sat by the sea side" (13: 1) or, in Paul's words, "seeing ye put it (the word of God) from you, and judge yourselves unworthy of everlasting life, Lo, we turn to the Gentiles" (Acts 13: 46). See also Acts 28: 25-28'

There is another lesson here: J.C.Ryle calls it 'a solemn warning to us never to be satisfied with religious reformation without heart conversion'. Peter puts it like this: "For if after they have escaped the pollutions of the world through the knowledge of the Lord and Saviour Jesus Christ, they are again entangled therein, and overcome, **the latter end is worse with them than the beginning**...But it is happened unto them according to the true proverb,

The dog (still a dog) is turned to his own vomit again; and the sow that was washed (but still a pig) to her wallowing in the mire" (2 Pet. 2: 19-22).

5) THE DISCIPLES AND THEIR STATUS, vv.46-50

Having been told that His mother and His brethren "stood without, desiring to speak with him", the Lord replied, "Who is my mother? And who are my brethren? And he stretched forth his hand toward his disciples, and said, Behold my mother and my brethren! For whosoever shall do the will of my Father which is in heaven, the same is my brother, and sister, and mother". We must not think that the Lord Jesus was disparaging His family in any way. He made careful provision for His mother at Calvary (John 19: 26-27), and His mother and His brothers were in the upper room after the Lord had ascended and before the day of Pentecost (Acts 1: 14). (Do notice that no reference is made here to Joseph. He was evidently dead). Mark 3: 20-21 gives us the reason for their visit.

In these verses, the Lord Jesus was not only teaching that it was more important to be a member of God's family than to be a member of a human family, but more than that, He intimated that "His ties with Israel would no longer be the controlling factor in His outreach...Obedience to God would bring men and women into vital relationship with Him...whether they were Jews or Gentiles" (Wm. MacDonald). God's family should be marked by obedience to His word. It is a question of family likeness. The Lord Jesus had come to "do the will of God" (Mark 3: 35). See, for example, John 4: 34, Luke 22: 42, Hebrews 10: 7. All who acted similarly were therefore related to Him. Are *we* displaying the family likeness? James certainly noted the importance of the Lord's teaching. See James 1: 22.

THE GOSPEL OF MATTHEW

"A sower went forth to sow"

Read Chapter 13: 1-23
The 'kingdom parables', which cover the entire period of the King's absence, including the present time, make it abundantly clear that although the King has been rejected, this does not mean that His interests have been thwarted, or even that His kingdom is in abeyance. This will become quite evident as we proceed. At least three things should be born in mind when studying these parables: *(A)* their setting; *(B)* their significance; *(C)* their sequence. It is worth noting, before we commence, that while the popular definition of a parable is 'an earthly story with a heavenly meaning', it is more correct to say that a parable is 'a form of teaching in which one thing is thrown beside another' (M.R.Vincent). The word parable (*parabole*) comes from *para* meaning 'beside' and *ballo* meaning 'to throw'. A parable is therefore a comparison or an illustration.

A) THE SETTING OF THE PARABLES
In this connection, we must notice *(a)* when they were given, and *(b)* where they were given.

a) When they were given
It is very important indeed to understand why the Lord Jesus introduced these parables at this stage in His ministry. In Chapter 12, two most significant things had happened:

i) **The Jewish leaders had completely rejected His ministry.** The Pharisees had "held a council against him, how they might destroy him (12: 14). That was bad enough. But worse followed. They accused him of acting in the power of Satan: "This fellow doth not cast out devils (demons), but by Beelzebub the prince of the devils (demons)" (v.24). They totally rejected His message, "Repent: for the kingdom of heaven is at hand" (4: 17), together with the evidence that "the kingdom of God is come unto you" (12: 28), and did so in the most fearful terms.

Matthew

ii) The Lord Jesus had announced new relationships. Spiritual relationships took precedence over earthly relationships: "Whosoever shall do the will of my Father which is in heaven, the same is my brother, and sister, and mother" (12: 50). He said, "My mother and my brethren are these that hear the word of God, and do it" (Luke 8: 21).

b) Where they were given
"The same day went Jesus out of the house and sat by the sea side" (v.1). The "house" is a picture of Israel. See, for example, Matthew 23: 38, "Behold, your house is left unto you desolate". The "sea side" is a picture of the Gentile nations which "make a noise like the noise of the seas; and to the rushing of nations, that make a rushing like the rushing of mighty waters!" (Isaiah 17: 12). See also Revelation 17: 15, "The waters which thou sawest...are peoples, and multitudes, and nations, and tongues".

B) THE SIGNIFICANCE OF THE PARABLES
This raises a most important question. The Lord Jesus was Israel's Messiah. If He had been summarily rejected by His own people, and had effectively severed natural ties, what about "the kingdom of God?" The Scriptures must be fulfilled, and Daniel had said, "In the days of these kings shall the God of heaven set up a kingdom which shall never be destroyed: and the kingdom shall not be left to other people, but it shall break in pieces and consume all these kingdoms, and it shall stand for ever" (Dan. 2: 44). But what of the intervening period? What of today? Is there no kingdom? Have the interests of God's kingdom lapsed, albeit temporarily?

The answer to these questions lies in the parables of Matthew 13. The parable of the sower, and its six attendant parables tell us that the kingdom of God has *not* gone away. As noted in introduction, these parables cover the period between the rejection of the kingdom of God as announced by Christ, and the establishment of that kingdom on earth by Christ at His second advent. With this in mind, we must note the following:

i) We are sometimes told that the kingdom is *'in abeyance'*, but it would be more correct to say that the ***public manifestation*** of the kingdom is 'in abeyance'. The kingdom itself is *not* in abeyance!

ii) We are told that the kingdom exists today *'in mystery'*, but is this really what the Lord Jesus meant in referring to "the ***mystery*** of the kingdom of God?" A "mystery" is something previously unrevealed, but now revealed.

The Old Testament did not visualise a kingdom without earthly territory, or without an earthly capital, or without an earthly king, but that is precisely what the Lord Jesus taught in the parables of the kingdom. See also Luke 17: 20: "The kingdom of God cometh not with observation (outward show)".

In these parables, the King is absent, whereas in later parables (Matthew 25) the King has returned, and it must be said again that the parables in Matthew 13 'cover the whole period of the King's absence between the first and second advents of Christ - the course of this present age' (Philip Harding). We learn, amongst other things, that the kingdom of God is now established not by public divine intervention (as it will), and definitely not by force of arms, or by political agreement, but by sowing "the word".

C) THE SEQUENCE OF THE PARABLES

The fact that there are seven parables (although some suggest, with good reason, that there are eight by including the 'parable of the householder', v.52) strongly suggests a complete series of events. The number "seven" has this significance in Scripture. It has been rightly said, that if the first four parables each convey different aspects of the enemy's work, and alert us to "his devices" (2 Cor. 2: 11), then the last three emphasise the work of the Lord. In the words of Archie Payne (*When the King Comes*), 'What a relief to turn from the dreadful work of the woman spreading corruption everywhere (v.33) to the outstanding figure of these (the fifth and sixth) parables". We should also notice that the first four parables were delivered publicly (by the sea), and the last three were delivered privately (in the house). The parable of the tares was *delivered* publicly, but explained privately.

The sequence commences with the parable of the sower, of which the Lord Jesus said, "Know ye not this parable? And how then will ye know all parables?" (Mark 4: 13). The seven 'parables of the kingdom' may be divided in the following way:

- **The propagation of the kingdom.** The parables of the sower (vv.3-9; 18-23) and of the tares (vv.24-30; 36-43). Notice that the Lord does not use the words, "The kingdom of heaven is like unto...", in introducing the first parable. This is evidently because he refers here to the 'planting' of the kingdom, rather than to the kingdom itself.

- **The pollution of the kingdom.** The parables of the mustard seed (vv.31-32) and of the leaven (v.33).

- ***The preciousness of the kingdom.*** The parables of the hid treasure (v.44) and of the pearl of great price (vv.45-46).

- ***The purifying of the kingdom.*** The parable of the drag-net (vv.47-50). This brings us to "the end of the world ('the consummation of the age', RV margin)" (v.49).

We must now consider the first parable. It is commonly called 'the parable of the sower', but could also be called, perhaps more accurately, 'the parable of the soils'.

1) THE PARABLE OF THE SOWER, vv.3-23
These verses may be divided as follows: *(a)* the details of the parable (vv.3-9); *(b)* the reason for parables (vv.10-17); *(c)* the explanation of the parable (vv.18-23).

a) The details of the parable, vv.3-9
Since the details in these verses are repeated and amplified later, comment can be deferred until we reach the Lord's explanation in vv.18-23. There is, however, one little detail that we ought to notice: in v.4, the seed "fell ***by*** the way side"; in v.5, it "fell ***upon*** stony places"; in v.7, it "fell ***among*** thorns; in v.8, it "fell ***into*** good ground. The prepositions are vital to a correct understanding of this parable. It has been said that in the first case the seed went on but not in; in the second it went in but not down; in the third it went down but not up; and in the fourth it went on, and in, and down, and up!

b) The reason for parables, vv.10-17
The disciples' question, "Why speakest thou unto them in parables?" (v.10) was answered with reference to the eyes and ears of the people (vv.13-15), and to the eyes and ears of the disciples (vv.16-17). (Notice Matthew's comments in vv.34-35). With this division in mind, the following should noted:

i) **Divine enlightenment**. "It is ***given*** (*didomi*) unto you to know the mysteries of the kingdom of heaven, but unto them it is not given" (v.11). Notice "you" and "them". David said, "The secret of the Lord is with them that fear him; and he will shew them his covenant" (Psalm 25: 14). The expression, "It is given", suggests divine sovereignty.

ii) **Divine enlargement**. "For whosoever hath, to him shall be given, and he shall have more abundance: but whosoever hath not, from him shall be taken away even that he hath" (v.12). Notice "hath", referring to the disciples, and "hath not", referring to the people. Paul said, "He that spared not his own Son, but delivered him up for us all, how shall he not with him also freely give us all things?" (Rom. 8: 32).

iii) Divine enjoyment. "Blessed are your eyes, for they see: and your ears, for they hear" (v.16). In these verses (vv.13-17), the Lord Jesus contrasts the eyes and ears of the people with the eyes and ears of the disciples:

- *The eyes and ears of the people, vv.13-15.* "Therefore speak I to them in parables: because they seeing see not; and hearing they hear not, neither do they understand" (v.13). The Lord continues by referring to Isaiah 6: 9-10 which emphasises that the nation's blindness and deafness was judicially imposed upon them: the natural faculties of seeing and hearing were unimpaired, but that was all: they were unable to grasp the significance of what they saw and heard, with this result: "Lest at any time they should be converted, and their sins should be forgiven them" (Mark 4: 12). To the Jews, the parables were just stories without much point. We must take a moment to digest this. The Jewish nation ("this people", not 'my people', Isaiah 6: 9) would not be allowed to understand, which is not an unsupportable and unreasonable statement when we remember that they had refused to recognise and accept their Messiah, even though He had proved His identity beyond all doubt. Their opportunity to do so would therefore be withdrawn. In other words, the people's inability to see and hear was judicial. They did not want to see and hear, and they would not, therefore, be able to do so. This is precisely the position in Acts 28 where Paul quotes the same passage in Isaiah 6 (it is quoted five times in the New Testament), and adds, "Be it known therefore unto you, that the salvation of God is sent unto the Gentiles, and that *they will hear it*" (Acts 28: 25-28).

- *The eyes and the ears of the disciples (vv.16-17).* "But blessed are your eyes, for they see: and your ears, for they hear. For verily I say unto you, That many prophets and righteous men have desired to see those things which ye see, and have not seen them; and to hear those things which ye hear, and have not heard them". This is quite self-explanatory. Compare 1 Peter 1: 10-12.

c) The explanation of the parable, vv.18-23
This brings us to the details in the parable where we should notice *(i)* the sower; *(ii)* the seed; *(iii)* the soil.

i) The sower

The Lord Jesus does not say that He is the sower. Compare the parable of the wheat and the tares (vv.24-30; 36-43). The Lord Jesus specifically states there that He *is* the sower (v.37), but not in connection with the parable of the sower. The reason is clear: the Lord Jesus was, of course, the sower *par excellence*, but we are also sowers. See Hebrews 2: "How shall we escape, if we neglect so great salvation; which at the first **began** to be spoken by the Lord..." (v.3). The "so great salvation" continues to be preached! In this parable, the seed is "the word" (Mark 4: 14), whereas in the parable of the tares, the good seed are the "children of the kingdom". We can sow the word, but only the Lord Jesus can sow the "children of the kingdom". We sow the seed, but salvation is His work alone, and we must not try to do it for Him by putting pressure on people to make decisions.

ii) The seed

As we have noticed, "the sower soweth the word". This is emphasised time and time again in the explanation. The expression, "the word", occurs six times in vv.19-23. Need we say more? We have no mandate to preach anything else but the Word of God. Natural seed is wonderfully viable: much more the Word of God. See Isaiah 55: 10-11 etc.

iii) The soil

The soil is the human heart. See v.19: "then cometh the wicked one, and catcheth away that which was sown in his **heart**". When the Bible talks about the heart, it means the centre of our lives - thoughts, emotions, and will. Our inner life. The human heart needs the Word of God: it is "deceitful above all things, and desperately wicked" (Jer.17: 9). Men and women must first hear the Word of God, although that in itself is not the guarantee that they will become members of the kingdom. Notice the expressions: "When any one heareth the word of the kingdom" (v.19); "he that heareth the word" (vv.20, 22, 23). But the Lord Jesus taught, "Take heed therefore **how** ye hear" (Luke 8: 18). The parable of the sower shows us that it is possible to hear in four different ways:

- **"By the way side"**. "When anyone heareth the word of the kingdom (essentially, repentance and faith), and understandeth it not, then cometh the wicked one, and catcheth away that which was sown in his heart" (v.19), or "Some fell by the wayside; and it was trodden down, and the fowls of the air devoured it...those by the wayside are they that hear; then cometh the devil, and taketh away the word out of their hearts, lest they should

Chapter 13

believe and be saved" (Luke 8: 5, 13). The wayside is hard ground, and describes hearts that have been hardened 'by the traffic of this world' (A Leckie). Satan waits to snatch away the good seed. People are impervious to its message. Their hard hearts rob them of interest and understanding. The message is lost on them. We have an example of this in Luke 8: 37. The last thing that Satan wants is for men and women to "believe and be saved" (Luke 8: 12).

Perhaps it might not be out of place to add that if Satan can rob God's people too in this way, he will be only too pleased. Even believers can hear the Word of God in some disinterested kind of way, and then forget and lose it. Satan cannot deprive us of our salvation, but he can certainly rob us of the good of God's Word.

As noted above, in each of the first four 'kingdom parables' in Matthew 13, the Lord Jesus refers to Satan's attempts to hinder the kingdom. It's a worthwhile study. In each case, the strategy is different. Check it out! The last three 'kingdom parables' make it clear that God's purposes cannot be overthrown by Satan. Check that out too!

- *"Upon stony places"*. "But he that received the seed into stony places, the same is he that heareth the word, and anon with joy receiveth it; yet hath he no root in himself, but dureth for a while: for when tribulation or persecution ariseth because of the word, by and by he is offended ('stumbleth'. RV)" (vv.20-21). The expression "stony ground" is really 'rocky ground' *(petrodes)*: the word 'is used of rock underlying shallow soil.' (W.E.Vine). In Mark's record, we should notice the double use of "immediately": "*immediately* receive it with gladness…*immediately* they are offended (stumbled)" (Mark 4: 16-17). So many people are like that: a sudden burst of enthusiasm, followed by a sudden decline. Notice the Lord's exact words here: "Immediately receive it with *gladness*" (Mark 4: 16). No repentance, no confession of sin, no sorrow for sin. In this connection, Acts 2: 41 must be read properly: "Then they that…received his word". Omit "gladly". God looks for tears of repentance: not 'all singing, all dancing' converts.

There seems to be every evidence of life. The seed "sprang up." But it was illusory: "no root" (Mark 4: 5-6). Growth before men, but no growth before God. The hard rock was underneath all the time. Truth will out when the test comes. Notice the emphasis: "when tribulation or persecution ariseth *because of the word"*.

Is it wholly inappropriate to ask about our own growth? Never mind about giving the right impression to other people: what does **God** see? Are our roots developing healthily? See, for example, Colossians 2: 7. We **will** encounter "affliction, or persecution...for **the word's sake**". The Christian life brings difficulties and problems: having trusted in the Lord Jesus for salvation, we must be prepared for them.

- **"Among thorns".** "He also that received seed among the thorns is he that heareth the word; and the care of this world, and the deceitfulness of riches, choke the word, and he becometh unfruitful" (v.22). Mark has: "And these are they which are sown among thorns; such as hear the word, and the cares of this world, and the deceitfulness of riches, and the lusts of other things entering in, choke the word, and it becometh unfruitful" (Mark 4: 18-19). Luke puts it like this: "When they have heard, go forth, and are choked with cares and riches and pleasures of this life, and bring no fruit to perfection" (Luke 8: 14). For many people, the burdens of life on one hand ('the distracting anxieties of the present age', H.S.Paisley), and prosperity in life on the other, take precedence over the claims of God's Word. It is a case of

> Room for pleasure, room for business,
> But for Christ the crucified,
> Not a place where He can enter
> In the heart for which He died.

What about **our** priorities? For those who are young, the "cares of this world" can take the form of constant worry and anxiety over school, and professional studies and examinations. They are important, but must not be allowed to monopolise time and encroach on the enjoyment of God's word. It is so important to give proper time to prayer and Bible reading. Later in life, business can buy us body, mind and soul, if we let it. So can other things. The Lord Jesus calls them "lusts", not in a moral sense, but in the sense of strong desires. The Lord Jesus had this to say to the church at Laodicea: "Thou sayest, I am rich, and increased with goods, and have need of nothing". But where was Christ in all this? He was not there at all: He was outside. See Revelation 3: 14-22. The "thorns" had been very effective at Laodicea. They seriously damaged Demas (2 Tim 4: 10). A relevant warning is given in 2 Tim 2: 4.

The three great spiritual enemies are all active in the parable: the devil is there (v.19); the flesh (or, minus the last letter and spelt backwards - self) is there (v.21); the world is there (v.22).

- *"Into good ground"*. "But he that received seed into the good ground is he that heareth the word, and understandeth it; which also beareth fruit, and bringeth forth, some an hundredfold, some sixty, some thirty" (v.23). Luke writes: "But that on good ground are they, which, in an honest and good heart, having heard the word, keep it, and bring forth fruit with patience" (Luke 8: 15). There was "good ground" in the heart of the dying thief (Luke 23: 39-43).

For the sower, there had been disappointments. But now we have hearts that have 'been prepared by grace; hardness was softened, shallowness was deepened, damaging roots were cleared away.' (J.Heading). The sower is encouraged. There are results from the labour. What are *our* hearts really like? Are they ready to receive the Word of God, believe it, and let it produce lasting fruit? But even good soil varies. Some soils have the capacity to produce better yields than others.

Finally, the question may be asked, 'Where is the church in all this? Or what about the relationship between the kingdom and the church?' The answer to the question is simple. The church is "the mystery...which in other ages was not made known unto the sons of men, as it is now revealed unto his holy apostles and prophets by the Spirit; that the Gentiles should be fellowheirs, and of the same body, and partakers of his promise in Christ by the gospel" (Eph. 3: 3-6). The Lord Jesus said to His disciples, "I have yet many things to say unto you, but ye cannot bear them now, Howbeit when he, the Spirit of truth, is come, he will guide you into all truth" (John 16: 12-13). Amongst other things, the church is the bride of Christ: He "loved the church, and gave himself for it". Believers of the present age will reign with Him. In the present age, our business is therefore to promote His interests by sowing "the word".

"The tares are the children of the wicked one"

Read Chapter 13: 24-43
The first four parables each convey different aspects of the enemy's work, and alert us to "his devices" (2 Cor. 2: 11): *(i)* in the parable of the sower, it is immediate opposition (v.19), but notice other influences - from within (v.21) and from the world (v.22); *(ii)* in the parable of the tares, it is imitation;

(iii) in the parable of the mustard tree, it is ostentation; *(iv)* in the parable of the leaven, it is corruption.

1) THE PARABLE OF THE SOWER, vv.3-9; 18-23
We have already considered this, noticing that in v.4, the seed "fell **by** the way side"; in v.5, it "fell **upon** stony places"; in v.7, it "fell **among** thorns; in v.8, it "fell **into** good ground. The prepositions are vital to a correct understanding of this parable. As we have also noted, it has been said that in the first case the seed went on but not in; in the second it went in but not down; in the third it went down but not up; and in the fourth it went on, and in, and down, and up! Having delivered the parable itself (vv.3-9), and answered the disciples' question, "Why speakest thou unto them in parables (vv.10-17), the Lord then explains the parable (vv.18-23). We come now to:

2) THE PARABLE OF THE TARES, vv.24-30; 36-43
As in the case of the parable of the sower, the details and explanation of this parable are separated, in this case, by two further parables (vv.31-33) and further teaching about parables in general (vv.34-35). For the purposes of our study we will note the details of the parable (vv.24-30) and then listen to the Lord's explanation in vv.36-43, before turning our attention to the intervening verses (vv.31-35).

a) The details of the parable, vv.24-30
All we need do at this juncture is to carefully read the parable: comment can be deferred until we reach the Lord's explanation in vv.36-43. However, it is worthwhile saying now that according to M.F.Unger, the most common tare found in grain fields in the Holy Land is bearded darnel, "a poisonous grass, almost indistinguishable from wheat while the two are growing into blade. But when they come into ear, they can be separated without difficulty". The reaction of the servants in the parable should be noted: "the servants of the house-holder came and said unto him, Sir, didst not thou sow good seed in thy field? From whence then hath it tares?" (v.27). Here is an illuminating little piece supplied by Justin Waldron: the servants were "shocked...they would not have been shocked if there were just a few of these darnels because they were common to the area – it's a grassy kind of weed. And it grows wherever it wants to grow. And they would not have been shocked if there were a few of them, because they always had weeds in the crop that they had to deal with. But they were shocked because the whole thing was full of them".

b) The explanation of the parable, vv.36-43

The Lord's explanation is a masterpiece of clarity and brevity. (Let preachers take note!). It is easily divided: *(i)* the sower (v.37); *(ii)* the field (v.38); *(iii)* the good seed (v.38); *(iv)* the tares (v.38); *(v)* the enemy (v.39); *(vi)* the harvest (vv.39-43).

i) The sower, v.37

"He that soweth the good seed is the Son of man". While, as we have said, the Lord Jesus does not say that *He* is the sower in the first parable, this is not the case in connection with the parable of the wheat and the tares (*zizanion*: a kind of darnel). The Lord Jesus specifically states here that He *is* the sower. The reason is clear: the Lord Jesus was, of course, the sower *par excelence*, but we are sowers as well: "How shall we escape, if we neglect so great salvation; which at the first **began** to be spoken by the Lord...." (Heb 2: 3). The "so great salvation" continues to be preached! In the parable of the tares, the Lord does not say "The seed is the word of God" (Luke 8: 11), but that "the good seed are the children of the kingdom". We can sow the word, but only the Lord Jesus can sow the "children of the kingdom". We sow the seed, but salvation is solely His work.

In the parable itself the Lord Jesus refers to "the servants of the householder" (v.27) and, as G.H.Lang (*Pictures and Parables*) points out, "Since this owner had servants it is a fair presumption that actually they sowed the field for him. Certainly God uses His servants in this work...But even so it is realistic and healthful for these servants to recognise the Lord as the proper Sower: "Sir, didst not thou sow good seed in thy field", not, 'Didst not thou give us good seed to sow'.

ii) The field, v.38

"The field is the world (*kosmos*)". In the former parable, the soil was the heart of the individual hearer, but in this parable "the field is the world". Notice, and this is most important, not the church, but "the world". In the parable itself, the Lord refers to the man sowing "good seed in **his** field". Whatever men and women may say, it remains that "all things were created by him, and for him" (Col. 1: 16). The world is "**his** field".

iii) The good seed, v.38

"The good seed are the children (sons) of the kingdom". In the words of Wm.MacDonald, 'it might seem bizarre and incongruous to think of living human beings being planted in the ground. But the point is that these sons of the kingdom were sown in the world. During His three years of public ministry, the Lord Jesus sowed the world with disciples who were loyal subjects of the kingdom'. This continued. See, for example, Acts 11: 19, "Now they which were scattered abroad upon the persecution (*thlipsis,* meaning 'a pressing' or 'pressure'; the RV has 'tribulation') that arose about Stephen (see Acts 8: 1) travelled as far as Phenice (the coastal plain of Syria including Tyre and Sidon), and Cyprus, and Antioch, preaching the word to none but unto the Jews only" (Acts 11: 19). We must note that these preachers are described as "scattered abroad" through persecution. But persecution wasn't an obstacle so far as God was concerned. It simply made the Gospel spread further. The word "scattered" (*diaspeiro*) was used in the Greek language for sowing seed. Satan attacked God's people, but God 'sowed' them! A packet of seeds produces a lot of plants, and God obtained some wonderful results from His "scattered" servants! Or shall we say, 'His sown servants!'

iv) The tares v.38
"The tares are the children ('sons', JND) of the wicked one". As already noted, the commonest of the four species of darnel was "the bearded, growing in the grain fields, as tall as wheat and barley, and resembling wheat in appearance" (W.E.Vine). It has been rightly said that "Satan has a counterfeit for every divine reality. He sows the world with those who look like disciples, talk like disciples, and., to some extent, walk like disciples. But they are not genuine followers of the King" (W.MacDonald). People who have 'the background' and 'know the language' are certainly amongst 'the tares'. Paul gives us a clear example: "For such are false apostles, deceitful workers, transforming themselves into the apostles of Christ. And no marvel; for Satan himself is transformed into an angel of light. Therefore it is no great thing if his ministers also be transformed as the ministers of righteousness" (2 Cor. 11: 13-15). The Lord Jesus warned His disciples against "false prophets, which come to you in sheep's clothing, but inwardly they are ravening wolves" (Matt. 7: 15). These 'sons of the wicked one' (JND) had their equivalent in the Old Testament "sons of Belial" (1 Sam 2: 12; 10: 27). While the word "Belial" was not the name of some pagan deity (it simply means "worthless"), it is used in the New Testament as a synonym for Satan: "What concord hath Christ with Belial?" (2 Cor. 6: 15).

v) The enemy, v.39
"The enemy that sowed them is the devil". We should notice that in the parable itself, the Lord said "while men slept, his enemy (the enemy of the owner of the field) came and sowed tares among the wheat, and went his

way" (v.25), but it should be noted that this was "not in itself a matter of reproach, nor did the householder blame his servants", rather that the Lord was emphasising that Satan acts invisibly and stealthily" (G.H.Lang). At the same time, it is a salutary warning against lack of vigilance. The field is the world and not, as already noted, the church. But this is a good opportunity to say the Lord's people must be alert. See Galatians 2: 4; 2 Peter 2: 1; Jude v.4. Remember Solomon's comments on the subject of sleeping: read Proverbs 24: 30-34.

vi) The harvest, vv.39-43
"The harvest is the end of the world; and the reapers are the angels" (v.39). This summarises and explains the parable itself: "The servants said unto him, Wilt thou then that we go and gather them (the tares) up? But he said, Nay; lest while ye gather up the tares, ye root up also the wheat with them. Let both grow together until the harvest: and in the time of harvest I will say to the reapers, Gather ye together first the tares, and bind them in bundles to burn them: but gather the wheat into my barn" (vv.28-30).

It must be said that "This parable does not justify, as some mistakenly suppose, the toleration of ungodly people in a local Christian church. Remember that the field is the world, not the church. Local churches are explicitly commanded to put out of their fellowship all who are guilty of certain forms of wickedness (1 Cor. 5: 9-13). The parable simply teaches that…the kingdom of heaven (which in this context evidently describes the sphere of profession) will include the real and the imitation, the genuine and the counterfeit, and that this condition will continue till the end of the age" (Wm.MacDonald). The people described here as "imitation…counterfeit" are certainly unmasked in Matthew 15: 1-20. The Pharisees were a case in point. Despite all their pedantic religious practices they remained "hypocrites" (v.7). They looked genuine, but proved otherwise. They were nothing more than "tares", and the Lord said of them, "Every plant, which my heavenly Father hath not planted, shall be rooted up" (v.13). Very clearly, He was referring to 'the parable of the tares' (see v.41).

The words "the end of this world ('the completion of the age', JND)" (v.40) are important. The parable anticipates the end-time when "the Son of man shall send forth his angels, and they shall gather out of his kingdom all things that offend, and them which do iniquity…Then shall the righteous shine forth as the sun in the kingdom of their Father" (vv.41-43). This should be compared with the preaching of John the Baptist (Matt. 3: 12). G.H.Lang points out that the "service of holy angels will assure that no mistake is made in distinguishing between wheat and darnel, and it will guarantee that no resistance by the wicked shall thwart justice. It was angels who destroyed Sodom, first putting righteous Lot into safety and then burning up the wicked (Gen. 19). It was a band of 'angels of woes' (JND) who plagued the Egyptians but spared the Israelites (Psalm 78: 49-55)...They are the executioners of the holy wrath of God as well as the protectors of His people, which dual work they will perform at the coming consummation of the age". The work of the angels in this way is also mentioned in 2 Thessalonians 1: 7-9, and Daniel 12: 3 should be read in connection with the words, "Then shall the righteous shine forth as the sun in the kingdom of their Father" (v.43).

Quite clearly, this parable does not envisage the church, with its peculiar hope. In fact, apart from an evident allusion in the parable of "the pearl of great price" (vv.45-46), there is no mention of the *ecclesia* in Matthew 13. Once again we must bear in mind that the church is "the mystery...which in other ages was not made known unto the sons of men, as it is now revealed unto his holy apostles and prophets by the Spirit; that the Gentiles should be fellowheirs, and of the same body, and partakers of his promise in Christ by the gospel" (Eph. 3: 3-6), and also that the Lord Jesus said to His disciples, "I have yet many things to say unto you, but ye cannot bear them now, Howbeit when he, the Spirit of truth, is come, he will guide you into all truth" (John 16: 12-13). While the parables of the kingdom most certainly include the present dispensation (the 'church age'), they cover the entire period commencing with the Lord's rejection and concluding with His return to establish His kingdom.

3) THE PARABLE OF THE MUSTARD SEED, vv.31-32
Commentators are certainly divided in their interpretation of the parables of the mustard tree and of the leaven. The suggestions that the parable of the mustard seed refers to the security of all who belong to the kingdom, and that the parable of the leaven refers to the quiet and unseen influence of God's work in human hearts, have some weighty proponents. Their conclusion is based on the fact that since the Lord refers here to "the kingdom of heaven" (vv. 31, 33; or "the kingdom of God", Luke 13: 18, 20), both parables must describe divine activity. Here, for example, is R.V.G.Tasker: "The inevitability of growth from what appears to be a very small beginning to a result seemingly out of all proportion to it is the truth set forth in the parable of the mustard seed (vv.31-32). Moreover the presence of the kingly reign of God is bound to penetrate the evil environment in which it is

exercised as effectively as yeast penetrates and transforms the flour into which it is put (v.33)".

Against this, it is quite clear from these parables that while the expression "kingdom of heaven" (called "the kingdom of God" in parallel passages) refers essentially to God's rule, it is subject nevertheless to constant attack by, amongst other things, imitation, corruption and infiltration. The 'parable of the sower' refers solely to "the word of the kingdom" (v.19) whereas the 'parable of the tares' mingles wheat and tares (v.26), and concludes, "The Son of man shall send forth his angels, and they shall **gather out** of his kingdom all things that offend, and them that do iniquity" (v.41). The final parable mingles good and bad fish (vv.47-50) and concludes, "So shall it be at the end of the world: the angels shall come forth, and **sever the wicked from the just"**. Both parables are prefaced, like the others, with the words "the kingdom of heaven is like unto..."

The figures employed by the Lord Jesus, in the parables of the mustard seed and leaven, strongly suggest that God's interests have been invaded by evil. If we are to be consistent with other references in the Scriptures, "the fowls of the air" (see, for example, vv.4,19) and "leaven" (see, for example, Matt. 16: 6-12) can only point in this direction. As W.Graham Scroggie *(A Guide to the Gospels)* rightly observes, "it may be laid down as a principle of interpretation that figures of speech are used consistently in discourse".

This brings us to the parable of the mustard seed: "The kingdom of heaven ("the kingdom of God", Luke 13: 18) is like to a grain of mustard seed, which a **man** took (a woman is specified in v.21), and sowed in his field ("cast into his garden", Luke 13: 19). Mark places the parable of the mustard seed after the parable of the patient but expectant farmer (Mark 4: 26-34), emphasising the difference between the progress of the kingdom from God's point of view, and its progress from man's point of view. With this in mind we must notice.

i) **Minute beginnings**. The "grain of mustard seed" is indeed...the least of all seeds" ("less than all the seeds that be in the earth", Mark 4: 31). We have only to think of the beginning of the "kingdom of God" in its present phase. Humble fishermen, described as "unlearned and ignorant men" (Acts 4: 13). In Paul's words, "God hath chosen the foolish things of the world, to confound the wise...and things which are despised, hath God chosen, yea, and things which are not, to bring to nought things that are" (1 Cor. 1: 27-28).

Matthew

*ii) **Massive developments.*** "But when it is grown, it is the greatest among herbs, and becometh a tree, so that the birds of the air come and lodge in the branches thereof". The Lord Jesus is alluding here to Ezek. 17: 22-23. Compare Dan. 4: 10-12, 20-22. In good ground, mustard seed will produce a tree of some ten to twelve feet high with sizeable branches. In Mark 4: 26-34, the first parable ended with ripe corn ready to be gathered, but the second, as here, with birds roosting in the branches. The Lord Jesus has already explained the significance of the "fowls of the air" (vv. 4, 19). The growth of a mustard seed is amazing, and from such small beginnings. Professing Christianity has also made spectacular growth. Witness its cathedrals and abbeys, its incense and its vestments, its popes and its bishops. But just look at all the birds in the branches! Christianity, so called, but having little or no correspondence to the Word of God, admits all shades of doctrine and practice, and all kinds of people, including emissaries of Satan.

Even J.C.Ryle (writing on Mark's Gospel), whilst interpreting the parable in a good sense, has to admit: 'I confess that I think the meaning of "the fowls of the air" is a point which admits some question...some think that it signifies the number of worldly and false professors who joined the church for mere carnal motives when it began to be grand and prosperous, as in the days of Constantine. When we remember that the "fowls of the air" in the parable of the sower, are declared by the Lord Himself to mean "Satan", we must admit that there is considerable force in this interpretation'. J.C.Ryle would be even more emphatic had he lived today! It is not without significance that the angel cries: "Babylon the great is fallen, is fallen, and is become the habitation of devils, and the hold of every foul spirit, and the cage of ***every unclean and hateful bird"*** (Rev.18: 2).

4) THE PARABLE OF THE LEAVEN, v.33
"The kingdom of heaven is like unto leaven, which a woman took, and hid in three measures of meal, till the whole was leavened". ***Not,*** it should be noted, "The kingdom of heaven is like unto leaven" (full stop!): the "kingdom of heaven is likened to the whole picture! "Leaven" (yeast) is always used in the Bible as a picture of pervasive evil. Its ability to convert sugar and allied substances, as starch, into alcohol and carbon dioxide, makes it an apt symbol of sin which, if unchecked, will completely change a person's life and character. It is not therefore difficult to understand why it was strictly forbidden in every sacrifice which speaks of the Lord Jesus. See Exodus 23: 18: Lev. 2: 11.

Paul uses the leaven as a picture of moral evil (1 Cor. 5: 6-8) and of doctrinal evil (Gal. 5: 9). The Lord Jesus mentioned three types of leaven: "the leaven of the **Pharisees"**, which was religious hypocrisy (Luke 12: 1); "the leaven of...the **Sadducees"** (Matt. 16: 6), which was doctrinal error (Matt. 22: 23, Acts 23: 8); "the leaven of **Herod**" (Mark 8: 15) which probably refers to the evil practices accompanying the Greek and Roman games introduced by the Herod family.

Having established the meaning of "leaven" in Scripture, we must now consider the Lord's words here. The church at Thyatira was censured by the Lord Jesus for allowing "that woman Jezebel, which calleth herself a prophetess, to teach and to seduce my servants to commit fornication, and to eat things sacrificed to idols" (Rev. 2: 20). The church at Thyatira was corrupted by leaven. In another connection, Zechariah refers to a woman sitting in the midst of an ephah (Zech. 5: 5-11). Without going into detail, the "woman" is Satan's counterfeit of the church, "Mystery, Babylon the Great, the mother of harlots and abominations of the earth", a great religious movement, here seeking to dominate trade. The "ephah" was a symbol of commerce (Lev 19: 35-36).

Evil doctrine is bed-fellow to evil practices which might suggest that leaven in "three measures of meal" stands for corruption of spirit, soul and body. Paul prayed that the Thessalonians might be preserved in all three spheres: see 1 Thess. 5: 23. The reference to "three measures of meal" should be compared with Genesis 18: 6, where Sarah was told, "make ready quickly three measures of fine meal, knead it, and make cakes upon the hearth". The Lord's reference therefore refers to corruption of the food supply. If the introduction of doctrinal and moral error is the beginning of the process ("hid in three measures of meal") then "the great whore that sitteth upon many waters" (Rev. 17: 1-6) represents the end of the process. She symbolises the final form of human religion of which it can be said, "the whole was leavened".

Having delivered the four parables "by the sea side" (v.1), Matthew comments: "All these things spake Jesus unto the multitude in parables; and without a parable spake he not unto them; that it might be fulfilled which was spoken by the prophet, saying, I will open my mouth in parables; I will utter things which have been kept secret from the beginning of the world" (vv.34-35). Matthew's reference here to the words of Asaph is not easily explained: "Give ear, O my people, to my law: incline your ears to the words of my mouth. I will open my mouth in a parable: I will utter dark sayings of old: which we have heard and known, and our fathers have told us" (Psalm 78: 1-3). Psalm 78 "was in no sense predictive, but simply a historical survey of God's dealings with Israel from the days of the Exodus to those of David" (Ellicott's Commentary). Matthew therefore appears to be pointing out that just as the fathers in Israel were to acquaint their children with Israel's history, which Asaph describes as "a parable" and "dark sayings" (the word means 'riddles') because the facts of their history conveyed important spiritual lessons, so the Lord Jesus had used parables to convey "things which have been kept secret from the beginning of the world". In this sense, the Lord had carried out the intentions of Asaph or, in Matthew's own words, He had "fulfilled (that) which was spoken by the prophet".

The four parables delivered "by the sea side" (v.1) are followed by three parables delivered in "the house" (v.36). We should remember, of course, that the parable of the tares (vv.24-30) was delivered by the sea, but explained in the house (vv.36-43). The remaining three parables are the parable of the treasure (vv.44), the parable of the pearl (vv.45-46), and the parable of the drag-net (vv.47-50). We will consider these in our next study.

"So shall it be at the end of the world"

Read Chapter 13: 44-58
For the purposes of our final study in this chapter we will divide the remaining verses into two major sections as follows: *(1)* the remaining parables (vv.44-52); *(2)* the rejection at Nazareth (vv.53-58).

1) THE REMAINING PARABLES, vv.44-52
If, as we have said, the first four parables each convey different aspects of the enemy's work, and alert us to "his devices" (2 Cor. 2: 11), then the last three emphasise the work of the Lord. In the words of Archie Payne (*When the King Comes*), already quoted, 'What a relief to turn from the dreadful work of the woman spreading corruption everywhere (in the parable of the leaven) to the outstanding figure of these (the fifth and sixth) parables, "The Man Christ Jesus"'. Despite the work of Satan during this age, God will fulfil His purpose in the restoration and blessing of Israel, in the formation of the church, and in the salvation of a great multitude of Gentiles at the end of the age. Referring to the fact that the Lord "went into the house" in declaring these parables, W.Kelly observes: "The multitude could not enter into them. They were the secrets of the family, and, therefore, the Lord calls the disciples within, and unfolds all to them". We should notice:

i) In the first two of these three parables, the treasure and the pearl are not **superficially visible.** In the case of the treasure, men just don't know that it exists! It is certainly not lying on the surface of the field! This reminds us that "the natural man receiveth not the things of the Spirit of God" (1 Cor. 2: 14).

ii) In the first two parables, the **common feature** is evidently that in order to gain the treasure and the pearl, both the "man" and the "merchant man" had to experience loss in acquiring the object of such value, pointing to the fact that the Lord gave His life before men and women could enjoy the blessings of divine possession and divine rule.

iii) In view of this, attention must be given to the **details** in both cases. Amongst other things, it should be noted that the treasure is found "in a field", that is, **on land,** whereas pearls are found in **the sea**. This could well point to God's earthly people **Israel** in the first place, and the **church** in the second, bearing in mind, as Wm.MacDonald points out, that 'the sea in Scripture is linked with the Gentiles, just as the land is linked with Israel. As the pearl comes out of the sea, so the church comes largely, though not exclusively, from the Gentile nations. It is sometimes called (inaccurately) the Gentile bride of Christ. This does not overlook the fact that there are converted Israelites in it, but it merely states that the dominant feature of the church is that it is a people called out from the nations for His name'.

iv) There is another significant difference between the first two parables. In the first case, "the kingdom of heaven is like unto a **treasure** hid in a field": the emphasis is on the "treasure". In the second case, "the kingdom of heaven is like", not a "pearl of great price", but "unto a **merchant man** seeking goodly pearls". The emphasis is on the "merchant man" which, it is strongly suggested, is the Lord himself.

v) Notice should be taken of the order of the two parables: the treasure is first, and the pearl second. If we are correct in suggesting that the treasure represents Israel and the pearl the church, then we might have expected the order to be reversed since the hope of the church will be realised before the hope of Israel. But the fact remains that while the purpose of God for Israel was made clear in the Old Testament, the church is called "the mystery...which in other ages was not made known unto the sons of men, as it is now revealed unto his holy apostles and prophets by the Spirit" (Eph. 3: 3-5).

Matthew

We come now to the three parables in question: *(A)* the parable of the treasure (v.44); *(B)* the parable of the pearl (vv.45-46); *(C)* the parable of the drag-net (vv.47-50). To these we will add *(D)* the parable of the householder (vv.51-52).

A) The parable of the treasure, v.44

"Again, the kingdom of heaven is like unto treasure hid in a field; the which when a man hath found, he hideth, and for joy thereof goeth and selleth all that he hath, and buyeth that field". Contrary to the explanation offered by some commentators, the parable does not depict 'the sinner seeking Christ, but the blessed Lord himself who came from heaven to earth to find that which to Him was of inestimable value: namely, His own people Israel' (H.A.Ironside). Support for this is found in the following: "Now therefore, if ye will obey my voice indeed, and keep my covenant, then ye shall be peculiar treasure unto me above all people: for all the earth is mine" (Exodus 19: 5); "For the Lord hath chosen Jacob unto himself, and Israel for his peculiar treasure" (Psalm 135: 4).

We have to enquire whether or not the detail is significant: the man finds the treasure, then hides the treasure, sells all he possesses, and buys the field in which the treasure lies. Does this mean that when the Saviour came, He found 'treasure' in a godly remnant in Israel, but rather than creating a great kingdom out of them, He paid the price to make them His own, and will at a future date display them for all to see? We know that in these parables, "the field is the world" (v.38). We also know that the Lord Jesus "gave himself a ransom for all" (1 Tim. 2: 6). He has 'bought the field'. At the moment, "the treasure" is hidden. That is, in the present dispensation, God is not dealing directly with Israel. The matter is not in public domain: the "treasure" is buried. He is currently continuing the work which began in the house of Cornelius when "God at the first did visit the Gentiles to take out of them a people for his name" (Acts 15: 14). Unlike the acquisition of the "pearl of great price" where the "merchant man" actually makes it his own, God has not yet taken up His earthly people Israel. The nation itself is prominent: it often dominates the news. But they "are not all Israel, which are of Israel: neither, because they are of the seed of Abraham, are they all children" (Rom. 9: 6-7), and although the nation largely exists today in unbelief, every believing Jew is precious to Him, and the day will come when Malachi 3: 17 will be fulfilled: "And they shall be unto me a peculiar treasure, saith the Jehovah of hosts, in the day that I prepare" (Mal. 3: 17, JND). With this in view, He will then gather "his elect from the four winds, from the uttermost part of the earth to the uttermost part of heaven" (Mark 13: 27). Until that day, a godly remnant will exist: "at this present time also there is a remnant according to the election of grace" (Rom. 11: 5), and this will still be the case once the church has been removed. It should be remembered that just as the Lord had hidden treasure in the days of Elijah, "seven thousand in Israel…which have not bowed unto Baal" (1 Kings 19: 18), so He will have a godly remnant in the end-time. That godly remnant will be persecuted by "the great dragon", and will flee "into the wilderness, where she hath a place prepared of God…where she is nourished for a time and times, and half a time" (Rev. 12: 6, 14).

B) The parable of the pearl, vv.45-46
"Again, the kingdom of heaven is like unto a merchant man, seeking goodly pearls: who when he hath found one pearl of great price, went and sold all that he had, and bought it". Whether or not we should press the fact that the "merchant man" was seeking "goodly pearls (plural)" is a moot question. Perhaps it is simply an allusion to what pearl-traders normally do – they look for pearls! Perhaps, too, we are intended to assume that he was also filled with joy (cf. v.44).

More to the point is the fact that whereas "treasure" comprises a number of items, perhaps many items, in this parable it is a "pearl of great price": one pearl. It has often been pointed out that the pearl is the outcome of irritation inside an oyster and that this, in turn, causes a secretion from which the pearl is formed, speaking to us of the suffering endured by the Saviour in order that He might procure the bride He loved. The Lord Jesus "loved the church, and gave himself for it; that he might sanctify and cleanse it with the washing of water by the word, that he might present it to himself a glorious church, not having spot or wrinkle, or any such thing; but that it should be holy and without blemish" (Eph. 5: 25-27). In the words of the parable, "he… found one pearl of great price" (v.46), reminding us of the singular uniqueness of the church in all its divine unity and beauty. Above all, a pearl displays a beauty untouched by human hands. It can be said that it is "one pearl of great price", not only in distinguishing it from all else, but in its own unique **oneness.** It has been nicely said that this "one pearl" is "of great price", not so much because of its own intrinsic value but because of the price paid for its possession.

C) The parable of the drag-net, vv.47-50
"Again, the kingdom of heaven is like unto a net, that was cast into the sea,

and gathered of every kind: which, when it was full, they drew to shore, and sat down, and gathered the good into vessels, but cast the bad away. So shall it be at the end of the world: the angels shall come forth, and sever the wicked from among the just. And shall cast them into the furnace of fire: there shall be wailing and gnashing of teeth".

We come now to 'the completion of the age' (v.49, JND). As already noted, it has been suggested that the parable of the drag-net refers to the salvation of a great multitude of Gentiles at the end of the age, and it must be said that the "sea" can most certainly be taken as depicting the Gentile nations. It has been suggested that the fish "of every kind" are Jews scattered throughout the nations, but the language strongly suggests activity amongst the Gentiles. It is therefore suggested that the parable of the drag-net represents:

- *either* the events described in Revelation ch.7, namely, the 144,000 true 'Jehovah's Witnesses' (vv.1-8), and the results of their labour in "a great multitude, which no man could number, of all nations, and kindreds, and people, and tongues" of whom it is said, "These are they which came out of great tribulation, and have washed their robes, and made them white in the blood of the Lamb" (vv.9-17). In this case the 'good fish' are those who receive and believe the message preached by the latter-day evangelists, and who had not "worshipped the beast, neither his image, neither had received his mark upon their foreheads" (Rev. 20: 4), whereas the 'bad fish' are those who took "the mark, or the name of the beast, or the number of his name" (Rev. 13: 17).

- *or*, possibly, to the division of the nations when "the Son of man shall come in his glory, and all the holy angels with him...and before him shall be gathered all nations: and he shall separate them one from another, as a shepherd divideth his sheep from the goats. To the goats He will say, "Depart from me, ye cursed, into everlasting fire, prepared for the devil and his angels" (Matt. 25: 31-33; 41).

Of the two suggestions, bearing in mind the imagery used by the Saviour, the former seems to be the best explanation. The 'fishing' is in the hands of men, but the separation is in the hands of the angels. It should be carefully noticed that as throughout the Scriptures, there are only two categories- the saved and the lost.

"Then shall the righteous shine forth as the sun in the kingdom of their Father.

Who hath ears to hear, let him hear" (v.43). The faithful will be vindicated. The age-old battle between right and wrong will be over. No longer will 'truth be on the scaffold'.

D) The parable of the householder, vv.51-52
"Jesus saith unto them, Have ye understood all these things? They said unto him, Yea, Lord. Then said he unto them, Therefore every scribe (much better than the Jewish scribes!) which is instructed unto the kingdom of heaven is like unto a man that is an householder, which bringeth forth out of his treasure things new and old". Some say that this means Old and New Testaments. Don't reject the idea out of hand! We must take note of Wm.Macdonald's comment here: 'Because they understood, they were obligated to share with others. Disciples are meant to be channels, not terminals, of blessing". The business of the Bible teacher is to draw attention to "what saith the scripture" (Gal. 4: 30). This obviously involves frequent travel along "old paths" (Jer. 6: 16). But many Bible highways are "unoccupied" (Judges 5: 6), and the Bible teacher will draw attention at times to passages and subject matter which will be new to his hearers. Not, of course, new to the word of God! Whether his subject matter is well known or lesser known, old or new, it must always be thoroughly biblical! To this end he will find "delight...in the law of the LORD; and in his law doth he meditate day and night" (Psalm 1: 2).

2) THE REJECTION AT NAZARETH, vv.53-58
"And it came to pass, that when Jesus had finished these parables he departed thence. And when he was come into his own country, he taught them in their synagogue" (vv.53-54). While it is often said that these verses refer to the second of two visits made by the Lord Jesus to Nazareth, the first being recorded in Luke 4: 1-30, it seems more likely that they are one and the same, and that Matthew "has deliberately left the story of Christ's rejection in Nazareth until here, immediately after the parables, to focus attention upon Christ's rejection in His own house - Israel." (A.Wilson, *Matthew's Messiah*). The passage says two things about the people at Nazareth ("his own country"): *(A)* "they were astonished" (vv.54-56); *(B)* "they were offended" (vv.57-58).

A) "They were astonished", vv.54-56
The word "astonished" (*ekplesso*) means 'amazed'. We must ask *(a)* what was it that amazed them? and *(b)* why were they amazed?

Matthew

a) What amazed them?
"Whence hath this man this wisdom and these mighty works?" (v.54); "Whence then hath this man all these things?" (v.56). They were amazed at His *"wisdom"* and His *"mighty works"*. Both were extraordinary. So it was the nature of His teaching (His wisdom) and the nature of His power (His works) that amazed them.

i) His wisdom. This had been evident as early as twelve years of age: "And all that heard him were astonished (*existemi*) at his understanding...And when they (Joseph and Mary) saw him they were amazed (*ekplesso*)" (Luke 2: 47-48). It was evident in His preaching at the outset of His public ministry: at Capernaum, "they were astonished (*ekplesso*) at his doctrine for he taught them as one having authority, and not as the scribes" (Mark 1: 22). It was evident in the way in which He was the Master of every situation, including the 'catch questions' from Pharisees/Herodians and the Sadducees (Matt. 22: 15-33; Mark 12: 13-27; Luke 20: 20-38). He said, "I speak that which I have seen with my Father" (John 8: 38), and therefore displayed what James calls "the wisdom that is from above" which is "first pure, then peaceable, gentle, and easy to be intreated, full of mercy and good fruits, without partiality, and without hypocrisy" (James 3: 17). How necessary to listen to His teaching! How thankful the Lord's people can be that they can enjoy His wisdom in everyday life!

ii)   His works. He had "done among them the works which none other man did" (John 15: 24). They said, being "beyond measure astonished (*ekplesso*)", that "He hath done all things well: he maketh both the deaf to hear, and the dumb to speak" (Mark 7: 37). He still does! He still completely changes lives: see 2 Corinthians 5: 17).

b) Why did this amaze them?
It amazed them because they didn't know who He was! He was unrecognised. "He was in the world, and the world was made by him, and the world knew him not" (John 1: 10). The religious leaders were bitterly opposed to Him: "We know that God spake unto Moses: as for this fellow, we know not from whence he is" (John 9: 29). These verses make it clear that whilst they thought they knew Him, they really didn't know Him at all!

i)   They thought that they knew Him. "Is not this the carpenter's son? Is not his mother called Mary? And his brethren, James, and Joses, and Simon, and Judas? And his sisters, are they not all with us?" (vv.55-56). Their comments are worth a closer look.

"Is not this the carpenter's son?" According to Mark, they said, "Is not this the carpenter (*tekton*)?" (Mark 6: 3). Both statements are factual. He was both the "carpenter's son" and "the carpenter" (different people said different things: taken together, this does seem to imply that Joseph was dead). As the "carpenter's son" He did not have a university education: he had not been trained in the religious schools of the day. They said, "How knoweth this man letters (*gramma*, meaning 'learning') having never learned". Quite clearly, the Lord Jesus didn't go about, like Simon the sorcerer, "giving out that himself was some great one" (Acts 8: 9), and He certainly didn't go around with a halo around His head. He was marked by humility. In any case, they were quite wrong to call Him "the carpenter's son". Joseph was His guardian. The Lord Jesus was 'the Son of man, but He was no man's son!'

"Is not his mother called Mary?" Very clearly, this indicates that they regarded Mary as quite an ordinary person. We know that she said, "My spirit hath rejoiced in God my Saviour" (Luke 1: 47). We must remember that her last recorded words were: "Whatsoever *he* saith unto you, do it" (John 2: 5).

"And his brethren...and his sisters, are they not all with us?". Once again, they were just ordinary people: there was nothing special about them. So the Lord Jesus was well aware of the problems and difficulties, the joys and sorrows, of family life. He had four "brothers" and at least two "sisters". This serves to remind us that people who trust in Him have a Saviour to whom they can bring not only the great problems of life but the ordinary problems of life as well. He is "touched with the feeling of our infirmities" (Heb. 4: 15). Christians can sing:

> *Jesus knows all about our troubles:*
> *He will guide till the day is done.*
> *There's not a friend like the lowly Jesus;*
> *No not one, no not one.*

It is worth remembering as well that there was a time in which "neither did his brethren believe on him" (John 7: 5), so the Lord Jesus knew what it was to be the 'odd man out' in the family. But they were there in the upper room after the Lord's ascension (Acts 1: 14)

But having said all this, the fact remains that while the people in Nazareth knew a lot about the Lord Jesus -

Matthew

ii) They still did not know Him. The section begins with "Whence hath this man this wisdom, and these mighty works" (v.54), and ends with "Whence then hath this man all these things" (v.56).

B) "They were offended", vv.57-58
The word translated "offended" means, literally, 'stumbled', but "offended" conveys its meaning very well. They said in effect, 'Who does He think He is - He has had no education - He's just the carpenter's son...What right has he got to say and do this'. Their failure to recognise His identity led to this! People today say in effect, 'What right has He got to be Lord of my life?

The Lord is still unrecognised and rejected, and people who follow Him may well discover that they are treated similarly. He was not popular in Nazareth, His home town, and His disciples today are not likely to be popular in their home environment, or anywhere else for that matter. It is worth pointing out as well that men and women are "offended" or stumbled because He proclaimed that it was necessary for Him to die and rise again in order that men and women might possess eternal life (John 10: 11,15,18). That is simply not acceptable to human reasoning. It proclaims that men and women are incapable of helping themselves when it comes to acceptance with God.

The Lord Jesus "did not many mighty works there (in Nazareth) because of their unbelief" (v.58), and the Gospel preacher is obliged to point out He will not perform 'a mighty work' in the lives of men and women if they persist in unbelief. People in Nazareth never saw the power of the Lord Jesus, and men and women will never experience His saving and delivering power if they fail to trust in Him. We should remember:

> He did not do "mighty works" to satisfy curiosity.
> He did not do "mighty works" to prove a point.
> He did "mighty works" to meet conscious need.
> He did "mighty works" in response to faith.

It is a question of "Believe on the Lord Jesus Christ, and thou shalt be saved". Paul and Silas did not say, 'Believe *about* the Lord Jesus Christ', but "Believe *on* the Lord Jesus Christ", meaning that for salvation there must be trust, reliance and dependence upon Him. The meaning of believing is clearly defined by John: "But as many as received him, to them gave he power to become the sons (children) of God, even to them that believe on his name" (John 1: 12). It is nothing short of tragic, as it was in Nazareth, when unbelief robs men and women of the saving power of Christ in their lives.

While Matthew does not say that He could not do "many mighty works there", but simply that "he did not many mighty works there", we ought to remember that according to Mark's record, "he could there do no mighty work, save that he laid his hand upon a few sick folk, and healed them. And he marvelled because of their unbelief" (Mark 6: 5-6).

THE GOSPEL OF MATTHEW

"Give ye them to eat"

Read Chapter 14: 1-21
This chapter may be divided in the following way: *(1)* the Lord's perception by Herod (vv.1-12): "This is John the Baptist; he is risen from the dead" (v.2); *(2)* the Lord's provision in the desert (vv.13-21): "this is a desert place...send the multitude away, that they may go into the villages and buy themselves victuals" (v.15); *(3)* the Lord's power in the storm (vv.22-33): "Jesus went unto them, walking on the sea" (v.25) ; *(4)* the Lord's perfection in healing (vv.34-36): "as many as touched him were made perfectly whole" (v.36).

1) HIS PERCEPTION BY HEROD, vv.1-12
Herod thought that the Lord was John the Baptist risen from the dead! In these verses we should notice *(A)* Herod's consternation (vv.1-2); *(B)* Herod's crime (vv.3-12)

A) Herod's consternation, vv.1-2
"At that time Herod the tetrarch (son of Herod the Great, Matt. 2: 1; Luke 1: 5) heard of the fame of Jesus, and said unto his servants, This is John the Baptist; he is risen from the dead; and therefore mighty works do shew forth themselves in him". Mark calls him by the courtesy title "king Herod" (Mark 6: 14), but he was in fact only a "tetrarch" (v.1) See also Luke 9: 7. W.E.Vine explains: it 'denotes one of four rulers, properly, the governor of the fourth part of a region; hence, a dependant princeling, or any petty ruler subordinate to kings or ethnarchs'.

Herod and his contemporaries had one thing in common: they all got it wrong. Herod's conscience told him that it was John the Baptist, and the theologians concluded (with reference to Malachi 4: 5) that "it is Elias", or "a prophet, or as one of the prophets" (Mark 6: 14-16). Compare Matthew 16: 14. J.Heading sums it all up: 'Superstition and rationalism can never fathom the Person of Christ'. That's why the Lord Jesus said to Peter, after he had confessed Him to be the Son of the living God, "Blessed art thou, Simon Bar-jona: for flesh and blood hath not revealed it unto thee, but *my Father which is in heaven*" (Matt. 16: 17). Compare 1 Corinthians 2: 14.

The following verses (vv.3-12) are largely self-explanatory (Wm.MacDonald calls them 'a literary flashback), and give us the circumstances of John's death which had taken place perhaps a year previously (Mark 1: 14; Luke 3: 20). This brings us to:

B) Herod's crime, vv.3-12
While Mark is more detailed than Matthew on this point (see Mark 6: 17-29), Matthew certainly gives us the salient facts: *(a)* John imprisoned (vv.3-5); *(b)* John executed (vv.6-11); *(c)* John buried (vv.12)

a) John imprisoned, vv.3-5.
"Herod had laid hold on John, and bound him, and put him in prison for Herodias' sake, his brother Philip's wife. For John said unto him, It is not lawful for thee to have her. And when he would have put him to death, he feared the multitude, because they counted him as a prophet". According to H.St.John: 'Josephus gives details of the place of John's imprisonment; it was a castle known as Machereus, the black fortress on the east side of Jordon, on the shores of the Salt Sea...It is, of course, possible that both the merry-making and the murder took place at the state capital, Tiberias'.

John was not afraid to reprove evil, and we learn the salutary lesson that telling the truth is not always popular. Many of the Old Testament prophets suffered for their fidelity to the Word of God (Heb. 11: 32-38). Stephen did so too, and so did the Lord Jesus: "But now ye seek to kill me, a man that hath told you the truth" (John 8: 40). It even happens amongst believers: Paul had to say to the Galatians, "Am I therefore become your enemy, because I tell you the truth?" (Gal. 4: 16).

The truth often provokes anger and malice, and it sometimes seems that our stand for righteousness will never be vindicated. John paid with his life for fearlessly condemning Herod. The Lord Jesus commended him in the highest terms in Matthew 11, but he awaits final vindication. We too have to wait for the day when "the Lord come, who will bring to light the hidden things of darkness, and will make manifest the counsels of the hearts: and *then* shall every man have praise of God" (1 Cor. 4: 5).

Matthew

It's worth noticing that according to Mark, John's reproof is cast in the imperfect tense: 'John kept on saying to Herod' (Mark 6: 18). He never accepted the situation, and never gave up trying to put it right. By the same token, Herodias never gave up her malice. That, too, is cast in the imperfect tense (Mark 6: 19). We must not overlook, either, the particular sin for which John reproved Herod; "It is not lawful for thee to have her" (v.4). Herodias had divorced her first husband, Philip, and married Herod. At the end of the Old Testament, God made a statement which has never been rescinded: "For the Lord, the God of Israel, saith that he hateth putting away (that is, divorce)" (Mal. 2: 16).

Before we leave this, we should notice that John's precepts were backed by practice. The man who said, "It is not lawful for thee to have thy brother's wife", was himself a "just man and an holy" (Mark 6: 20). He had the moral right to reprove Herod. Compare Matthew 23: 1-3 with Acts 1: 1.

b) John executed, vv.6-11
This section is full of practical lessons. To begin with, it all started off quite innocently: a birthday celebration. But it ended up with murder! These verses remind us that sin never stays still (T.Miller). One thing led to another. In this case immorality led to John's execution. A most appropriate commentary is found in James 1: 15. Here are some warnings:

i) Be careful how you celebrate, v.6. "But when Herod's birthday was kept". In Mark's words, "And when a convenient day was come, that Herod on his birthday made a supper to his lords, high captains, and chief estates of Galilee" (Mark 6: 21). In spite of the translation, 'And a holiday being come' (JND), which Darby doesn't seem too sure about himself (see his margin!), it does seem that it was a 'convenient day' for Herodias to get her revenge. The birthday celebrations gave good opportunity to settle an old score. The birthday party got progressively out of control, and Herod was mastered by events. We have to be very careful how, and where, we celebrate. Just take time to weigh up the possible consequences of your social engagements. See, for example, 1 Cor. 10: 27-33.

Be careful, too, about the social company you keep. Moses chose "rather to suffer affliction with the people of God, than to enjoy the pleasures of sin for a season" (Heb. 11: 25) Herod kept good company by social standards (see Mark 6: 21), but it didn't do him much good in the long run. He had to maintain the *status quo* in the presence of his friends (Mark 6: 26). On a technical note, the "lords" were the chief men or nobles, the "high captains" (literally, a commander of 1,000 soldiers) were military commanders, and the "chief estates" were the chief men of Galilee. Herod was surrounded by his own 'circle'. We must avoid partiality in our fellowship. See James 2: 1-9.

ii) Be careful what you watch, v.6. "The daughter of Herodias danced before them, and pleased Herod". We need no further details: the effect on Herod is sufficient commentary. The man lost his reason. We have said, 'be careful what you watch', and we'll add, 'be careful what you read'. Inevitably, sadly, but inevitably, we are confronted at times by things we would rather not have seen, and by writing we would rather not have read, and by comments and jokes that we would rather not have heard. All of which, if we let it, will invade the picture gallery of our minds. Here is the antidote: "Wherewithal shall a young man cleanse his way? by taking heed thereto according to thy word...Thy word have I hid in mine heart, that I might not sin against thee" (Psalm 119: 9, 11).

iii) Be careful what you promise, v.7. "Whereupon he promised with an oath to give her whatsoever she would ask". According to Mark, "the king said unto the damsel, Ask of me whatsoever thou wilt, and I will give it thee...unto the half of my kingdom" (Mark 6: 22-23). Beware of making rash promises: think about what you're saying. Better to say nothing at all, than to commit yourself to something that you will have cause to regret later. Remember Jephthah's vow (Judges 11: 30-31). The promises of God are never rash: see 2 Corinthians 1: 20. Abraham believed them completely: see Romans 4: 21.

iv) Be careful who influences you, v.8. "And she, being before instructed of her **mother,** said, Give me here John Baptist's head in a charger". It has been pointed out that Herod and Herodias are the New Testament counterparts of Ahab and Jezebel. Both Ahab and Herod wanted something to which they had no right. Both men were influenced by their wives, and two men lost their lives: Naboth in the Old Testament, and John in the New Testament. This may be an opportune moment to say that if you are courting and contemplating marriage, it is most important to think about the influence you are going to have on each other. Remember that emotional ties are very strong, and can cloud your judgment, whether you're a man or a woman.

v) Be careful about saving face, vv.9-11. "And the king was sorry: nevertheless for his oath's sake, and them which sat with him, he commanded it to be given her. And he sent, and beheaded John in the prison, And his head was brought in a charger, and given to the damsel: and she brought it to her mother". Herod would rather be known as 'a man of his word' - and a murderer - than a man who 'climbed down' - and saved the life of John the Baptist. It's always difficult admitting a mistake, and always embarrassing to 'go back on your word' - but rather do that than commit sin.

In completely different circumstances, Paul was obliged to change his plans in order to achieve the spiritual good of the assembly at Corinth. He was criticised for altering his announced route from Ephesus to Corinth, but did not hesitate to do so in view of developments in the assembly. Read 2 Corinthians 1: 15-23.

c) John buried, v.12
"And his disciples came, and took up the body, and buried it, and went and told Jesus". Cremation was, and is, a pagan practice. In the Old Testament, the patriarchs buried their dead: see, for example, Genesis 23: 1-20; 35: 19, 29. In the New Testament, "devout men carried Stephen to his burial" (Acts 8: 2). For the Christian, burial is deeply symbolic: it is likened to sowing a seed with expectation of new life. See 1 Corinthians 15: 35-44. Seed isn't burnt, it is sown!

In their sorrow, John's disciples "told Jesus". That does not mean that He didn't know about the death of John. Compare John 11: 14. He is omniscient: but we can still come and tell Him about our sadness and sorrows, and in so doing, "obtain mercy, and find grace to help in time of need" (Heb. 4: 16).

2) HIS PROVISION IN THE DESERT, vv.13-21
It might be helpful to notice that two feasts are placed very closely together. "Herod... made a supper to his lords" (Mark 6: 21), and the Lord Jesus fed the multitude in the wilderness. The first ended disastrously: but not the second!

The 'feeding of the five thousand' has the distinction of being recorded in all four Gospels (Matthew 14: 13-21; Mark 6: 30-44; Luke 9: 10-17; John 6: 1-14). Of the four accounts, Matthew's is the shortest. We can divide these verses as follows: *(A)* privacy in a desert place (v.13); *(B)* provision in a desert place (vv.14-21).

A) PRIVACY IN A DESERT PLACE, v.13
"When Jesus heard of it, he departed thence by ship into a desert place

apart". William Kelly points out that the death of John was 'the harbinger of a storm still more violent and a deed of blood darker far - the awful sin of His own rejection', and continues, 'He would not hurry the moment, but retires'. Support for this can be found in Luke 13: 32. On the other hand, it seems more likely that the Lord felt the death of John deeply, and wished to grieve over the death of the man who had heralded His coming (M.Baker). The Lord Jesus is not insensitive to human suffering (Heb. 4: 15).

Mark's emphasis is rather different: "And the apostles (the only place in Mark's Gospel where this expression occurs) gathered themselves together unto Jesus, and told him all things, both what they had done and what they had taught. And he said unto them, Come ye yourselves apart into a desert place, and rest a while: for there were many coming and going, and they had no leisure so much as to eat. And they departed into a desert place by ship privately" (Mark 6: 30-32). In this connection we should notice *(i)* their report to Him (v.30), and *(ii)* His response to them (vv.31-32). The lessons are clear *(i)* it is important to be alone with Christ; *(ii)* it is important to be active for Christ: the Lord Jesus said, "Come ye yourselves apart into a desert place, and rest *a while*". It wasn't permanent. The apostles were not to forget their responsibility. Time spent **with** Christ prepared them **for** service for Christ.

B) PROVISION IN A DESERT PLACE, vv.13-21
Very clearly, the crowds carefully noted the course of the boat, and by the time it arrived at its destination, they were there too! "And Jesus went forth, and saw a great multitude" (v.14). There was to be no privacy for Him. Notice three things.

a) The way He drew the crowds, v.13
"They followed him on foot out of the cities". Mark credits them with even greater enthusiasm: They 'ran together there on foot' (Mark 6: 33, JND). Whilst we may question their motives (see John 6: 1-2), we must also question our enthusiasm. How keen are we to hear His voice? There is something seriously wrong when interest in His word diminishes. We are often told that 'meetings are not everything'. That is true, but attendance at assembly meetings is a pretty accurate gauge of spiritual reality. These people certainly wanted to get to their meeting!

b) The way He cared for the crowds, v.14
While He had "departed thence by ship into a desert place **apart**", He was

not insensitive to the needs of the crowd. He set aside His own interests in the interests of the multitude: He "saw a great multitude, and was moved with compassion toward them, and he healed their sick" (v.14). In Paul's language, "He looked not on his own things, but....on the things of others" (Phil. 2: 4). The depth of His care for the multitudes is expressed in the words, "moved with compassion toward them". The word means, literally, 'to be moved as to one's inwards' (W.E.Vine), and is perhaps best understood by the expression we use when someone is in deep distress, 'my heart went out to him'. It has also been defined as 'love with grief'. The ministry of the Saviour flowed from deep compassion. He did not take a cold, clinical interest in the multitude. He yearned over them with compassion.

Both Mark and Luke mention the Lord's teaching ministry here: "he...was moved with compassion toward them, because they were as sheep not having a shepherd: and he began to teach them many things" (Mark 6: 34); "And the people, when they knew it, followed him: and he received them, and spake unto them of the kingdom of God, and healed them that had need of healing" (Luke 9: 11). Matthew omits reference to the Lord's teaching, mentioning only His power to heal, and thus largely confining himself to the feeding of the multitude, emphasising that "Where the word of a king is, there is power" (Eccl. 8: 4).

c) The way He provided for the crowds, vv.15-21
As already noted, the miracle which follows is the only one recorded in all four Gospels. It is one of two similar miracles. Both are mentioned by the Lord Jesus in Matthew 16: 9-10. The passage is brimful of important lessons for us: here are some of them:

i) They were fed despite human inadequacy, vv.15-16. Notice the way in which the disciples summed up the situation. **Firstly,** "This is a desert place": there was no possibility of sustaining life there. **Secondly,** "the time is now passed": time was running out: the situation was urgent. **Thirdly,** "send the multitude away, that **they** may go...and **buy themselves** victuals": they must make their own arrangements, and do the best they can to help themselves. This is good human reasoning. It illustrates salvation by works. But the Saviour looked at the situation differently: He did not agree with their solution: "But Jesus said unto them, They need not depart; give ye them to eat".

- In the first place, this made the disciples feel their total inadequacy. The task was impossible for them. At this point, the Lord was addressing Philip: "Whence shall we buy bread, that these may eat? And this he said to prove him: *for he himself knew what he would do*" (John 6: 6). It would have been delightful if Philip had expressed absolute faith in Christ, but - like us so often - he didn't: "Shall we go and buy two hundred pennyworth of bread, and give them to eat?" Even then, it would not be enough, not even for a snack (John 6: 7). Remember that a penny was the rate of pay for a day's work at that time! See Matthew 20: 2. The disciples looked at the problem through human eyes, and were totally overwhelmed. It is important to remember that, humanly speaking, we cannot meet the spiritual needs of men and women.

- In the second place, it is important to remember that when the Lord Jesus asks us to do something, He gives us the resources. His commands carry the ability to obey. "Not that we are sufficient of ourselves to think anything as of ourselves; but our sufficiency is of God: who also hath made us able ministers of the new testament" (2 Cor. 3: 5-6).

ii) They were fed from existing resources, vv.17-18. "And they say unto him, We have here but five loaves, and two fishes. He said, Bring them hither to me". We know that Andrew acted as spokesman, "There is a lad here, which hath five barley loaves, and two small fishes: but what are they among so many?" (John 6: 9). We too may not seem to have much to offer. Perhaps we feel devoid of ability and usefulness. But in His hands, our limited resources can be greatly used. God says to us all, "What is that in thine hand?" (Exodus 4: 2). The loaves and fishes were probably the lad's meal for the day, but he gave them to the Saviour, and we can be sure that he had a far better meal than he expected! Now compare 2 Kings 4: 42-44.

iii) They were fed in an orderly way, v.19. Everything was done in an orderly manner: "he commanded the multitude to sit down on the grass". According to Mark, "they sat down in ranks, by hundreds, and by fifties" (Mark 6: 40). Now read 1 Corinthians 14: 33, 40. The words used by Mark are most interesting: "companies" (v.39) means, literally, 'a drinking party' (W.E.Vine): however, the word is descriptive more of posture at the party rather than the purpose of the party!; "ranks" (v.40) means, literally, 'a garden-bed or plot (probably from *prason*, referring to a leek)'. W.E.Vine goes on to explain: 'used metaphorically in Mark 6: 40 of ranks of persons arranged in orderly groups'.

iv) They were fed with the disciple's help, v.19. "And looking up to heaven, he blessed (*eulogeo,* to speak well of), and brake, and gave the loaves to his disciples, and the disciples to the multitude". We must notice that the Lord Jesus gave thanks for the meal. He looked to the Source of "every good gift and every perfect gift" (James 1: 17). One feature of unsaved people is their ingratitude to God. See Romans 1: 21. One feature of saved people is their thankfulness: "In everything give thanks" (1 Thess. 5: 18).

In the words of J.C.Ryle, 'None but He Who at the first created all things, and sent down manna in the desert, could thus have "spread a table in the wilderness"'. The food was miraculously supplied by Christ, but responsibility for its distribution was given to the disciples. He uses us in exactly the same way. The good news of salvation does not originate with us, but it is conveyed through us. Hence the need to be "vessels unto honour, sanctified, and meet for the master's use, and prepared unto every good work" (2 Tim. 2: 21). Mark has rather a nice touch here: the apostles had returned, and "told him all things, both what **they** had done and, what **they** had taught" (Mark 6: 30), but in almost the next breath we are told that they are distributing food to the multitude! (Mark 6: 41). From the spectacular to the mundane, or was it? There is a lesson here!

We must not fail to notice that the Lord was at the very centre of operations (T.Miller). While He never sought publicity, always awaiting His Father's time (Matt. 17:9; Phil. 2: 9), He nevertheless had "in all things...the preeminence" (Col. 1: 18).

v) They were fed to complete satisfaction, vv.20-21. "And they did all eat, and were *filled*". Every miracle that the Lord Jesus accomplished was perfect - not one of them was incomplete or inadequate. This is equally true today: He completely meets the need of all who trust Him. He gives "a good measure, pressed down...and running over" (Luke 6: 38). Whilst there was no 'over-supply', there was evidently more than sufficient. Hence, "they took up of the fragments that remained twelve baskets full". These were small baskets (*kophinos*): larger ones (*spuris*) were used later (Matt 15: 37). We still "eat", and we are still "filled", but there is always plenty remaining. His provision is inexhaustible. There was much more left at the end than there was at the beginning!

Chapter 14

"Lord, save me"

Read Chapter 14: 22-36
We have already noticed that this chapter may be divided as follows: *(1)* the Lord's perception by Herod (vv.1-12): "This is John the Baptist; he is risen from the dead" (v.2); *(2)* the Lord's provision in the desert (vv.13-21): "this is a desert place...send the multitude away, that they may go into the villages and buy themselves victuals" (v.15); *(3)* the Lord's power in the storm (vv.22-33): "Jesus went unto them, walking on the sea" (v.25) ; *(4)* the Lord's perfection in healing (vv.34-36): "as many as touched him were made perfectly whole" (v.36).

1) HIS PERCEPTION BY HEROD, vv.1-12
Having "heard of the fame of Jesus" (v.1), Herod's guilty conscience led him to say, "This is John the Baptist; he is risen from the dead; and therefore mighty works do shew forth themselves in him" (v.2). According to Herod, the man of whom it was said, "John did no miracle" (John 10: 41), was now performing miracles! Matthew then relates the sordid events ending with John's death at the hands of Herod's executioner (vv.3-12).

2) HIS PROVISION IN THE DESERT, vv.13-21
While the Lord Jesus "departed thence by ship into a desert place apart", the people evidently realised where He was going, and hurried there "on foot" so that when "Jesus went forth" (disembarked) at Bethsaida (Bethsaida Julias, Luke 9:10), they were there to meet Him (vv.13-14). For "a desert place apart" (v.13) read "a great multitude" (v.14). The disappearance of any prospect of peace and quiet would have caused the best of men some irritation, but the Lord "was moved with compassion toward them, and he healed their sick" (v.14). Moreover, He displayed His deity in fully answering the question, "Can God furnish a table in the wilderness?" (Psalm 78: 19). This brings us to:

3) HIS POWER IN THE STORM, vv.22-33
These verses refer to: *(A)* His prayer at the commencement of the voyage (vv.22-23); *(B)* His power during the course of the voyage (vv.24-31); *(C)* His presence during the remainder of the voyage (vv.32-33).

A) His prayer at the commencement of the voyage, vv.22-23
We should notice at least three things here: *(a)* His concern for the disciples (v.22); *(b)* His containment of popularity (vv.22-23); *(c)* His continuance in prayer (v.23).

Matthew

a) His concern for the disciples, v.22
"And straightway Jesus constrained his disciples to get into a ship, and to go before him unto the other side, while he sent the multitudes away". Mark tells us that the disciples were bound for Bethsaida (Mark 6: 45), and it is worth saying that there were two places of the same name! (We have already referred to Bethsaida Julias). The parallel passage in John 6: 1-15 sheds additional light here: "Then those men, when they had seen the miracle that Jesus did, said, This is of a truth that prophet which should come into the world. When Jesus therefore perceived that they would come and take him by force, **to make him a king,** he departed again into a mountain himself alone" (vv.14-15).

Quite evidently, the Lord Jesus had no wish for His disciples to be embroiled in the political aspirations of the crowd: "And straightway (immediately) he constrained His disciples to get into the ship". Later, the Lord Jesus was to say, "My kingdom is not of this world: if my kingdom were of this world, then would my servants fight, that I should not be delivered to the Jews: but now is my kingdom not from hence" (John 18: 36).

b) His containment of popularity, vv.22-23
The Lord Jesus had come "to minister (serve), and to give his life a ransom for many" (Matt. 20: 28). The time had not yet come to reign, but when it does, it will be preceded, not by euphoria, but by repentance. See Zechariah 12: 10-14. The Lord Jesus was never influenced by the heady wine of popularity. It endangered the purpose for which He had come. He therefore sent the crowds away to contain the situation: otherwise they would have followed Him, and the danger could have spread. The words, "And when he had sent the multitudes away (note His authority), he went up into a mountain apart to pray (note His dependence on the Father)" (v.23), now assume additional significance. There is a lesson here for us all: popularity can be dangerous for us all: we must meet it with humble prayer. Compare Luke 5: 12-16.

c) His continuance in prayer, v23
We must never forget that the Lord Jesus was never too busy to pray. It has been rightly said that 'if we are too busy to pray, then we are too busy'. Mark stresses the busy life of the Lord Jesus. Prior to crossing the lake *en route* for the "desert place", "there were many coming and going, and they had no leisure so much as to eat" (Mark 6: 31). What started as a trip across the lake to peace and quiet, ended as another busy day with the Lord at work until "evening", with the disciples saying "the time is now past; send the

multitude away" (v15). The crowds gave the Lord and His disciples no rest, and this is one reason why He found it so important to spend time in prayer.

Mark tells us that He prayed at the **beginning** of the day: "And in the **morning**, rising up a great while before day, he went out, and departed into a solitary place, and there ***prayed***" (Mark 1: 35). He now prays at the **end** of the day: "And when he had sent the multitudes away, he went up into a mountain apart to ***pray***: and when the **evening** was come, he was there alone" (v.23). He didn't go to the mountain for rest and recuperation! Here is another reason why both the disciples and the crowds were sent away - so that He could be **alone** with God. After such a busy day, we might have expected Him to "rest a while" (Mark 6: 31), but He prayed. Do notice that the Lord achieved His object in crossing the lake: He "went by ship into a desert place **apart** (v.13) and now He "went up into a mountain **apart** to pray". Nothing can thwart His purposes! We should notice that Matthew adds, "and when the evening was come, he was there **alone**". It is worth mentioning that the Lord always prayed alone, whether or not He was with His disciples. That isn't the paradox it seems!

Humanly speaking, it might have seemed more important for Him to be with His 12 disciples, or to continue His work among the people who were so anxious to hear Him. But if an army is going to be successful in battle, it must have adequate supplies, and be in constant touch with headquarters. This is what prayer is all about. The Lord Jesus found it necessary to be in touch with His Father. We must never forget the lesson. We need to be in constant contact with God. "Pray without ceasing" (1 Thess. 5: 17).

B) *His power during the course of the voyage, vv.24-31*
The Lord sent His disciples straight into trouble! But, as we shall see, it was all part of their spiritual education. The disciples began the voyage across the lake to Bethsaida (Mark 6: 45), and found it hard going: "But the ship was now in the midst of the sea, tossed with waves: for the wind was contrary" (v.24). According to Mark, they were "toiling in rowing; for the wind was contrary unto them" (Mark 6: 48). These words are a pretty accurate description of life generally. Eliphaz summed it up like this: "Man is born unto trouble, as the sparks fly upward" (Job 5: 7). We must never think, either, that God's people are exempt from the problems, pressures and difficulties which confront men and women generally. But there is a difference. God's people have a Saviour who says, "I will never leave thee, nor forsake thee" (Heb. 13: 5). It wasn't long before this became evident.

The fact that the "ship was now in the midst of the sea" reminds us of the significance of the sea: "But the wicked are like the troubled sea, when it cannot rest, whose waters cast up mire and dirt. There is no peace, saith my God, to the wicked" (Isaiah 57: 21). When Israel was "in the midst of the sea" in this sense, God said: "I have surely **seen** the affliction of my people which are in Egypt, and have **heard** their cry…for I **know** their sorrows; and am **come down** to deliver them out of the hand of the Egyptians" (Exodus 3: 7-8). The great "I Am" of Exodus 3: 14 and John 8: 58, knows exactly what kinds of problems and difficulties face us. He knows exactly when it's tough going in life ("toiling in rowing"), and we don't seem to be getting anywhere. But does He care?

Matthew answers the question by using two small but significant expressions in his narrative: *(a)* "Jesus went unto them" (v.25); *(b)* "Jesus spake unto them" (v.27). Mark uses four small expressions: "he **saw** them…he **cometh** unto them…he **talked** with them…he **went up** unto them" (Mark 6: 48, 50, 51).

a) He "went unto them", v.25

This is certainly thought-provoking. We know that by the time the Saviour reached them, the boat was "about five and twenty or thirty furlongs" from the shore (John 6: 19). Say, between three and four miles. Matthew and Mark both note the adverse weather conditions, and so does John: "And it was now dark, and Jesus was not come to them. And the sea arose by reason of a great wind that blew" (John 6: 18-19). Not only so, but the Saviour was praying, and almost certainly facing the opposite direction. Yet, "He saw them toiling in rowing" (Mark 6: 48). Quite obviously, this was not natural vision. This was divine omniscience. Natural barriers, such as distance, do not limit the Son of God, and the Gospels abound with examples of His perfect knowledge. Incidents that were happening miles away (see, for example, John 11: 14), or that had happened in the lives of people He had never met before (see, for example John 1: 48 and 4: 18-19 etc), were all known to Him. "**All things** are naked and open unto the eyes of him with whom we have to do" (Heb. 4: 13); "The eyes of the Lord run to and fro throughout the whole earth" (2 Chron. 16: 9).

In His care for the disciples, the Lord was prepared to cross the lake to reach them. "And in the fourth watch of the night (between 3 a.m. and 6 a.m. Roman time) Jesus went unto them, walking on the sea" (v.25). Two thousand years ago, He came from heaven to earth, with all its darkness and distress, and this is even more wonderful than the events during that stormy night on Galilee. The disciples could hardly be blamed for the circumstances that made it so difficult for them on the lake. But the Bible says, **"while we were yet sinners,** Christ died for us" (Rom. 5: 8). We were guilty before God, and that made the willingness of the Lord Jesus to come from heaven to save us even more amazing.

The presence of the Saviour, who came "walking on the sea", can be equally real to **us** in the darkness and storms of life. "When thou passest through the waters, I will be with thee; and through the rivers, they shall not overflow thee" (Isaiah 43: 2). He knew exactly where to find them, and He knows exactly where we are too. J.C.Ryle comments: 'There are thoughts of comfort here for all true believers... We are never beyond the reach of His care. Our way is never hid from Him. He knows the path that we take, and is still able to help. He may not come to our aid at the time we like best, but He will never allow us utterly to fail. He that walked upon the water never changes. He will always come at the right time to uphold His people. Though He tarry, let us wait patiently'.

Notice that He came "**walking** on the sea". Not staggering in the face of the adverse wind and turbulent sea, or running, but "walking!" He came to them with perfect calm and control: He was unhurried and unhindered. Now let's shift the emphasis: "He went unto them, walking **on the sea**". The Man 'who could walk on the tossing waters of the sea, was Master over all circumstances' (H.St.John). We ought also to notice that He came to them in the most unexpected way. How often we too experience His help from the most unexpected direction! There is no need to comment on the fact that 'natural laws' were suspended when this happened. After all, He had created the natural laws that govern the universe, and is therefore greater than those laws. The Creator must be greater than His work.

Mark adds: "He cometh unto them, walking upon the sea, **and would have passed by them**" (Mark 6: 48). Various suggestions have been made. Perhaps He was teaching His disciples the lesson that whilst we cannot do without Him, He can do without us. He could cross the lake without the necessity to board their boat. Whilst it is certainly true that we are not indispensable, this explanation does seem rather harsh. On the Emmaus road, "He made as though he would have gone further. **But they constrained him saying, Abide with us**" (Luke 24: 28-29). The Saviour had no intention of forcing Himself upon either those two disciples, or upon the twelve disciples in the boat. He awaited their invitation on both occasions. He awaits our request for His help and presence in the storms of life. It is always gladly accepted.

b) He "spake unto them", vv.26-31
In these verses, the Lord speaks first to the twelve disciples together (vv.26-27), and then to Peter (vv.28-31).

i) He spoke to the disciples, vv.26-27. "And when the disciples saw him walking on the sea, they were troubled, saying, It is a spirit; and they cried out for fear" (v.26). Mark carefully guards the literality of the event. This was no hallucination: "They *all* saw him, and were troubled" (Mark 6: 50). He soon settled their troubled minds: "But straightway (immediately: so He hastened to calm their fears: He does so still) Jesus spake unto them, saying, Be of good cheer; it is I; be not afraid". This was not the only occasion on which the disciples "supposed it had been a spirit" (Mark 6: 49). See Luke 24: 37. In Matthew 9: 2, we have the "good cheer" of **conversion:** "Son, be of good cheer; thy sins be forgiven thee"; in Mathew 14: 27 and Mark 6: 50, we have the "good cheer" of **companionship:** "Be of good cheer; it is I; be not afraid"; in John 16: 33, we have the "good cheer" of **conflict:** "In the world ye shall have tribulation: but be of good cheer: I have overcome the world". On the earthly level, it's always reassuring to hear the voice of someone we know and trust when we're faced with troubles and difficulties. How much more so when it is the voice of Christ:

> *It is Thy perfect love that casts out fear;*
> *I know the voice that whispers, "It is I";*
> *And in the well-known words of heavenly cheer*
> *I find the joy that bids each sorrow fly.*

Paul proved this at Corinth: "Then spake the Lord to Paul in the night by a vision, Be not afraid, but speak, and hold not thy peace: for I am with thee" (Acts 18: 9-10). Mary proved this in the garden: "Jesus saith unto her, Mary. She turned herself, and saith unto him, Rabboni" (John 20: 16).

The words, "***It is I;*** be not afraid", are literally, '*I am,* be not afraid'. This was the title used by God in the Old Testament: "Thus shalt thou say unto the children of Israel, **I AM** hath sent me unto you" (Exodus 3: 14). The Lord Jesus is God Himself. He still speaks to His people. We hear His voice through reading and pondering the Word of God.

ii) He spoke to Peter, vv.28-31. Wm.MacDonald suggests that when Peter heard the well-known and well-loved voice of the Master, his affection and enthusiasm bubbled over: "Lord if it be thou, bid me come to thee on the water" (v.28). Was it a case of 'impetuous Peter?' (Compare Matt. 17: 4; Luke 9: 33). If so, then he was soon to discover that enthusiasm by itself was not enough. Perhaps, however, we should not regard Peter's 'if' as a sign of small faith, but a bold request as a mark of great trust. Peter sensed that Jesus' commands are His enablements, that He gives strength for whatever He orders" (Wm.MacDonald). What happened next is a picture of coming events in Peter's life. We can look at it like this

- On the lake. See Matthew 14: 28-31. *He began well*: "he walked on the water"; *he began to sink*: "when he saw the wind boisterous...and beginning to sink; *he was saved*: "immediately Jesus stretched forth his hand, and caught him"

- In Jerusalem. See Luke 22: 33, 54, 57 etc., John 21: 15-17. *He began well*: "I am ready to go with thee...to death"; *he began to sink*: he saw the storm and "followed afar off...he denied him"; *he was saved*: the man who denied the Lord three times by a fire, said, "Thou knowest that I love thee" three times by another fire.

- At Antioch. See Galatians 2: 11-14. *He began well*: see Acts 10-11 which records his visit to the house of Cornelius, a Gentile, at Caesarea, and the subsequent vindication of his ministry to the Gentiles there; *he began to sink*: he saw the storm: "fearing them which were of the circumcision" (Gal 2: 12); *He was saved*: he later wrote of "the true grace of God wherein ye stand" (1 Pet 5: 12), and described Paul as "our beloved brother" (2 Pet. 3: 15).

We should add that the storm did not always cause Peter to sink! See Acts 4: 21, 5: 18 etc. But bearing in mind that he was able to walk on the water so long as he kept his eyes on the Lord Jesus, and that he only began to sink when he "saw the wind boisterous", how important for us to look constantly "unto Jesus the author and finisher of (our) faith" (Heb. 12: 2). Elijah would agree wholeheartedly: notice what happened to him when he looked in the wrong direction (1 Kings 19: 3). Jezebel could certainly be likened to a storm! The lesson is clear: 'the minute we become occupied with ourselves or our circumstances, we begin to sink. Then we must cry to Christ for restoration and for divine enablement' (Wm.MacDonald). Although the Lord has to say sometimes to us, "O thou of little faith, wherefore didst thou doubt?" (v.31), like David, we all have good cause to say thankfully, "He restoreth my soul" (Psalm 23: 3). Many of us can say, "When I said, My foot slippeth; thy mercy, O LORD, held me up" (Psalm 94: 18).

C) His presence during the remainder of the voyage, vv.32-33
"And when they were come into the ship, the wind ceased. Then they that were in the ship came and worshipped him, saying, Of a truth thou art the Son of God". We should notice:

i) The wind ended, v.32. It has been pointed out that 'the storm is quieted when the lesson is over, not while they were walking on the water!' (supplied by Justin Waldron). In the words of the psalmist, "He maketh the storm a calm, so that the waves thereof are still… so he bringeth them to their desired haven" (Psalm 107: 29-30).

ii) The disciples worshipped, v.33. Up to this point, only God Himself, the devil and the demons had called the Lord Jesus "the Son of God" (cf. 3: 17; 4: 3; 8: 29). At the end of the first Galilean storm, they said, "What manner of **man** is this" (Matt. 8: 27). But now, "Of a truth thou art **the Son of God".** According to Mark, "they were sore amazed in themselves beyond measure, and wondered. For they considered not the miracle of the loaves: for their heart was hardened (meaning, according to W.E.Vine, 'dull in perception)" (Mark 6: 51-52). Putting Matthew and Mark together, we might conclude that it was only at this point that the disciples fully recognised His true identity. But Andrew Wilson makes the valid point that it "was not a case of them not knowing who He was before this. It was rather a case of them needing a fresh vision of Christ's power to remind them of who He was": hence, "***Of a truth*** thou art the Son of God".

J.C.Ryle has a nice piece here: 'The event first recorded in these verses, is a beautiful emblem of the position of all believers, between the first and second advents of Jesus Christ. Like the disciples, we are now tossed to and fro by storms, and do not enjoy the visible presence of our Lord. Like the disciples, we shall see our Lord face to face again, though it may be a time of great extremity when He returns. Like the disciples, we shall see things changed for the better, when our Master comes to us. We shall no longer be buffeted by storms. There will be a great calm'.

4) HIS PERFECTION IN HEALING, vv.34-36
The lack of belief on the part of Peter and the other disciples contrasts

strangely with the way in which the inhabitants of Gennesaret received Him: "And when they were gone over, they came into the land of Gennesaret. And when the men of that place had knowledge of him (Mark says: "straightway they knew him"), they sent out into all that country round about (Mark says that they "*ran* throughout that whole region roundabout), and brought unto him all that were diseased; and besought him that they might only touch the hem of his garment: and as many as touched were made perfectly whole". We have already commented on "the border of His garment". See our note on 9: 21 in which we pointed out that like every pious Jew, the Lord Jesus wore a ribband of blue on the hem of His garment. This was a constant reminder to the **wearer** of the need for obedience and holiness. See Numbers 15: 38-41. The Pharisees enlarged the borders of their garments for the benefit of the **onlookers.** See Matthew 23: 5. But, as we noted at the time the woman with "an issue of blood" didn't touch **them!** The Lord Jesus was known for His purity, and for His ability to help and save. He said to the woman "thy **faith** hath made thee whole" (9: 22). Similarly here: the people's touch was the expression of their faith, but the healing was brought about by the power of the Lord Jesus, not by His garment.

Matthew emphasises that "as many as touched were made perfectly whole (*diasozo*, 'to save thoroughly')". In the words of John Heading, 'If there are those today who claim such powers, we would remind them that divinely-accomplished miracles were instantaneous, complete, and lasting. God does nothing less than this". All that the Saviour did was perfect. This is true in every way: He imparts "everlasting life" (John 3: 16); He is the "author of eternal salvation" (Heb. 5: 9); He has obtained "eternal redemption" (Heb. 9: 12); He promises an "eternal inheritance" (Heb. 9: 15). What a Saviour!

THE GOSPEL OF MATTHEW

"These are the things which defile a man"

Read Chapter 15: 1-20
The previous chapter concluded with the welcome given to the Lord Jesus by enthusiastic crowds in Gennesaret. They made full use of their opportunity: they "brought unto him all that were diseased; and besought him that they might only touch the hem of his garment: and as many as touched were made perfectly whole" (14: 35-36). This chapter commences, not with **warm enthusiasm**, but with **cold criticism.** We must ensure that we are not infected in this way. There is something vitally wrong when we are devoid of feeling for one another: see 1 Corinthians 12: 26. We are to "rejoice with them that do rejoice, and weep with them that weep" (Rom. 12: 15). The scribes and Pharisees were totally devoid of that spirit: "Then came to Jesus scribes and Pharisees, which were of Jerusalem, saying, Why do thy disciples transgress the tradition of the elders? for they wash not their hands when they eat bread" (vv. 1-2). In Mark's words: "And when they saw some of his disciples eat bread with defiled, that is to say, with unwashen hands, *they found fault*" (Mark 7: 2). There was nothing new in their fault-finding: see Matt. 9: 3; 9: 11; 12: 1-2; 12: 10. Bearing in mind their track record, these religious leaders had evidently come up from Jerusalem to Gennesaret with the specific purpose of criticising and condemning the Lord Jesus. It has been suggested that they had probably expected the Lord to go to Jerusalem for the Passover (cf. John 6:1-4: parallel with Matt. 14:13-21), and that when he did not do so, they went to Galilee (supplied by J.Waldron).

The passage may be divided as follows: *(1)* Pharisaical tradition (vv. 1-9): the Lord Jesus addresses the scribes and Pharisees; *(2)* public repudiation (vv. 10-11): the Lord Jesus addresses the multitude; *(3)* private explanation *(*vv. 12-20): the Lord Jesus addresses the disciples.

1) PHARISAICAL TRADITION, vv.1-9
We must notice *(a)* the accusation by the religious leaders (vv.1-2); *(b)* the answer of the Lord Jesus (vv.3-9).

a) The accusation by the religious leaders, vv.1-2
This was no polite enquiry: it was downright criticism: "Why do thy disciples transgress the tradition of the elders?" Let's concentrate first of all on the word "tradition" (*paradosis*). According to W.E.Vine, it means 'a handing down' or 'a handing on'. It is used in two quite different ways in the New Testament.

i) Here, it refers to "the tradition of the elders" (v.2) or "the tradition of men"; "your own tradition"; "your tradition (Mark 7: 7, 9, 13). See also Galatians 1: 14: "the traditions of my fathers"; Colossians 2: 8: "the tradition of men". (A different word is used in 1 Pet. 1: 18).

ii) Elsewhere, it refers to apostolic teaching: see 1 Cor. 11: 2: "Now I praise you. Brethren, that ye remember me in all things, and keep the ordinances ('traditions', RV) as I delivered them to you"; 2 Thess. 2: 15: "Therefore, brethren, stand fast, and hold the traditions which ye have been taught, whether by word, or our epistle"; 2 Thess. 3: 6: "Now we command you, brethren, in the name of our Lord Jesus Christ, that ye withdraw yourselves from every brother that walketh disorderly, and not after the tradition which he received of us".

In the first case, the "tradition" has no divine authority: in the second case, it is nothing less than the word of God. But the religious leaders had invested their own inventions with divine authority; they taught "for doctrines the commandments of men" (v.9). J.C.Ryle (writing on Mark) has a very telling comment here: 'The first step of the Pharisees, was to add their traditions to the Scriptures, as useful supplements. The second was to place them on a level with the word of God, and give them equal authority. The third was to honour them above the Scripture, and to degrade Scripture from its lawful position'.

Mark gives us a little more information about the "tradition of the elders", namely, "For the Pharisees, and all the Jews, except they wash their hands oft, eat not, holding the tradition of the elders. And when they come from the market, except they wash, they eat not. And many other things there be, which they have received to hold, as the washing of cups, and pots,

Matthew

brazen vessels, and of tables" (Mark 7: 3-4). So the Pharisees and scribes ceremoniously washed their hands and household utensils, not just on the grounds of hygiene (after all, we're all supposed to wash our hands before meals, aren't we?) but because they believed that failure to do so would make them unclean in God's sight. As we shall see, it all cloaked their disobedience to God's word. For the record, 'It was customary to cleanse oneself ritually before and after a meal by twice pouring cold water over the hands. The first water cleansed the hands; the second washed away the first water, which had become unclean' (J.Waldron).

b) The answer of the Lord Jesus, vv.3-9
The Good Shepherd would not allow criticism of His sheep by the religious leadership. He springs to their defence. In answering the critics, the Lord Jesus calls them "hypocrites" (v.7), charges them with "teaching for doctrines the commandments of men" (v.9). He provides a specific illustration (vv.3-6) before making a general application (vv.7-9). In the first place, their practices accommodated disobedience, and in the second they were devoid of reality. The Lord charged them with hypocrisy because:

i) Their practices amounted to disobedience, vv.3-6
Having said, "Why do ye also transgress the commandment of God by your tradition?" (v.3), the Lord contrasts God's precept (v.4) with their practice (vv.5-6), and shows how they had jettisoned the former in favour of the latter.

- **God's precept:** "For God commanded, saying, Honour thy father and mother: and, He that curseth father or mother, let him die the death" (v.4). The Lord Jesus cites Exodus 20: 12 and 21: 17. See also Leviticus 20:9; Deut. 27: 16). It is clear from the Lord's words which follow, that the fifth commandment, "Honour thy father and thy mother: that thy days may be long upon the land which the Lord thy God giveth thee" (Exodus 20: 12), involved financial support for parents where necessary. Lip-service alone did not fulfil the commandment. In this connection we should notice New Testament teaching that "if any provide not for his own, and specially for those of his own house, he hath denied the faith, and is worse than an infidel" (1 Tim. 5: 8). Younger readers of these notes might care to note that the command, "Honour thy father and thy mother", involves subjection to them. This is certainly not fashionable today, but the example of the Lord Jesus settles the matter: "He went down with them, and came to Nazareth, **and was subject unto them**" (Luke 2: 51). The Lord Jesus honoured His mother by making provision for her. See John 19: 26-27. In fact, at all times,

He 'magnified the law, and made it honourable', Isaiah 42: 21. We ought to add that in marriage, a man leaves "his father and his mother" (Genesis 2: 24), but he does not cease to honour them.

- Their practice. Sadly, the Jews had an 'opt-out' clause when it came to supporting parents, as a result of which, in the Saviour's words, "ye made the commandment of God of none effect by your tradition" (v.6). The Lord begins, "But *ye* say", in direct opposition to "***God*** commanded" (v.4), and continues: "Whosoever shall say to his father or his mother, It is a gift, by whatsoever thou mightest be profited by me; and honour not his father or his mother, he shall be free" (vv.5-6).

Mark gives us slightly more: "But ye say, If a man shall say to his father or mother, It is Corban, that is to say, a gift, by whatsoever thou mightest be profited by me; he shall be free. And ye suffer him no more to do ought for his father or his mother; making the word of God of none effect through your tradition, which ye have delivered: and many such like things ye do" (Mark 7: 11-13). Although this means leaving Matthew for a few moments, we ought to say that the word "Corban", as a Hebew word (*qorban*) is used in the Old Testament with reference to the Levitical and other offerings. See, for example, "If any man of you bring an offering (*qorban*) unto the Lord, ye shall bring your offering (*qorban*) of the cattle, even of the herd, and of the flock". In the New Testament, the word "treasury" (Matt 27: 6) is *'korbanas'*, meaning 'the place of gifts' (W.E.Vine). The teaching of the scribes and Pharisees gave a man freedom to exclude his parents from the support and help required by the fifth commandment, simply by saying, in the form of a vow, "Corban". In saying this, the man said in effect to his parents, 'The money (or whatever it was) that you expected me to give you has been dedicated as an offering to God'. In actual fact, he had no intention of giving it to God, or to anyone else, but so far as the people who hoped to receive it were concerned, it had become dedicated to God, and therefore they couldn't have it. In this way, they were "making the word of God of none effect by their tradition". It was a flagrant violation of the law. Since a simple form of words could remove the responsibility for caring for parents, it is not surprising that the Lord's next words were, "Ye hypocrites" (v.7).

Having demonstrated their hypocrisy in this way, the Lord Jesus goes further in saying that their flagrant disregard for God's law was symptomatic of a general malaise. They were hypocrites because:

ii) Their practices were devoid of reality, vv.7-9

There was tremendous emphasis on ceremony, but that was all. The Saviour frequently attacked the religious hypocrisy of the leadership in this way. For example, "Woe unto you, scribes and Pharisees, hypocrites! (other people would have called them 'rabbi' or 'teacher') For ye devour widows' houses, and for a **pretence** make long prayer" (Matt. 23: 14). James reminds us that, "Pure religion and undefiled before God and the Father, is this, To visit the fatherless and widows in their affliction, and to keep himself unspotted from the world" (James 1: 27). The religious leadership did neither.

The Lord Jesus summarises the situation by referring to Isaiah 29: 13, "well did Esaias prophesy of you, saying, This people draweth nigh unto me with their mouth, and honoureth me with their lips; but their heart is far from me. But in vain do they worship me, teaching for doctrines the commandments of men" (vv.8-9). It is worth noting the actual words in Isaiah 29: 13. The verse begins with "Wherefore" which alludes to the solemn context: the people had no desire to understand the Word of God, and their ability to do so had been withdrawn, but they still practised their formal religion. It was devoid of reality, and this only added to their guilt: **"Wherefor**e the Lord said, Forasmuch as this people draw near me with their mouth, and with their lips do honour me, but have removed their heart far from me (i.e. having no desire for His word), and their fear toward me is taught by the precept of men: Therefore, behold, I will proceed to do a marvellous work (judicially) among this people." There are solemn lessons for consideration here:

- **Orthodox religious behaviour can be hypocrisy.** The Lord Jesus prefaced His quotation from Isaiah with, "Ye hypocrites". The word "hypocrisy" is borrowed from the acting profession, and "a form of godliness" (2 Tim 3:5) without inward reality is nothing more than play-acting. It is still possible for the Lord's people today to say the right things, quote the right verses, and generally express what people expect them to say, but to have cold, disobedient hearts. The true organ of worship is the heart. If the heart is not involved, everything becomes mere pretence.

- **Traditions can become more important than Scripture.** "Their fear toward me is taught by the precept of men ('learned by rote', RV margin)" (Isaiah 29: 13). This was far removed from "the fear of the Lord", which "proceeds from the heart and is characterised by a devotion of the whole being to God" (E.J.Young).

We cannot ignore these lessons. It is sadly possible for even believers to have "a form of godliness" (2 Tim. 3: 5). We should notice that **disobedience to the word of God nullifies worship:** "In vain do they worship me". Hence, "If I regard iniquity in my heart, the Lord will not hear me" (Psalm 66: 18).

J.C.Ryle puts it as follows: 'It must not content us to take our bodies to church (he was an Anglican), if we leave our hearts at home'. Turning to 'private devotions', J.C.Ryle continues, 'It must not satisfy us to say good words, if our heart and our lips do not go together. What does it profit us to be fluent and lengthy, if our imaginations are roving far away, while we are upon our knees? - It profits us nothing at all. God sees what we are about, and rejects our offering. Heart-prayers are the prayers He loves to hear. Heart-prayers are the only prayers that He will answer'. The New Testament urges us to "draw near with a true heart" (Heb. 10: 22). A "true heart" says, "For me to live is Christ" (Phil. 1: 21). It is all too easy to become spiritual actors. As we have already noted, the word "hypocrisy" comes from the stage. But it was even worse than that: the Pharisees and scribes were not only devoid of reality, they actually violated the law. They were hypocrites indeed. Warren Wiersbe points out that God wants us to give Him our hearts, and not just lip service. We believe in the heart (Rom. 10: 9-10); love from the heart (Matt. 22: 37); sing from the heart (Col. 3: 16); obey from the heart (Rom. 6: 17); and give from the heart (2 Cor. 9: 7)'.

2) PUBLIC REPUDIATION, vv.10-11
The Lord Jesus now addresses the people, and publicly condemns the hypocrisy of their leaders: "And he called the multitude, and said unto them, Hear, and understand: not that which goeth into the mouth defileth a man; but that which cometh out of the mouth, this defileth a man". The reason for public condemnation is clear: the teaching and practices of the Pharisees were a public violation of God's Word, and must therefore be condemned publicly. This is why Paul withstood Peter "to the face" and reprimanded him "before them all" (Gal. 2: 11-14). When error is propagated publicly, whether by word or example, it must be dealt with publicly. The practices of the Pharisees were far more than petty foibles: they were a total misrepresentation of the truth.

As we can imagine, the Pharisees and their colleagues did not take kindly to the Saviour's teaching, and the disciples drew the Lord's attention to their displeasure - not that He was unaware of the situation! In the next section of the chapter, the Lord addresses their concern, and then, in response to

Peter's request, explains His teaching in v.11. Peter called it "this parable" (v15).

3) PRIVATE EXPLANATION, vv.12-20
These verses give the Lord's answers to two questions: "Then came his disciples, and said unto him, Knowest thou that the Pharisees were offended, after they heard this saying?...Then answered Peter and said unto him, Declare unto us this parable" (vv.12 and 15). We can summarise it as follows: *(a)* the disciples' concern (vv.12-14); *(b)* the Lord's concern (vv.15-20).

a) The disciples' concern, vv.12-14
"Then came his disciples, and said unto him, Knowest thou that the Pharisees were offended, after they heard this saying?" (v.12). It seems possible that the disciples were rather fearful at the way in which the Lord had dealt with the Pharisees, perhaps anticipating adverse consequences. The Lord's answer takes us back to 'the parable of the wheat and tares' (Matt. 13: 24-30: 36-43). The servants said, "Wilt thou then that we go and gather them (the tares) up? But he said, Nay; lest while ye gather up the tares, ye root up also the wheat with them. Let both grow together until the harvest". The scribes and Pharisees would have objected still further if the Lord had called them "tares" publicly, but this is exactly what they were - tares sown by the enemy, but more than that, they were "blind leaders of the blind": "Every plant which my heavenly Father hath not planted, shall be rooted up. Let them alone; they be blind leaders of the blind. And if the blind lead the blind, both shall fall into the ditch ('pit', RV)" (vv.13-14). It has been suggested that the Lord's words, "Let them alone", might well mean 'do not try to please those who are displeasing to God'. One form of blindness is certainly failure to differentiate between what is essential and what is unimportant.

b) The Lord's concern, vv.15-20
If the disciples were concerned over the reaction of the Pharisees, then the Lord was concerned over the disciples' lack of understanding. "Then answered Peter and said unto him, Declare unto us this parable (referring to v.11). And Jesus said, Are ye also yet ('still', JND) without understanding?" (vv.15-16). The Saviour evidently expected a higher level of spiritual intelligence from the disciples "Are ye also yet ('still') without understanding?" Compare John 14: 9. The writer of Hebrews evidently thought the same about his first readers: "For when for the time (by this time) ye ought to be teachers, ye have need that one teach you again which be the first principles

of the oracles of God" (Heb. 5: 12). The Saviour then emphasised *(i)* what does not defile a man (v.17); *(ii)* what does defile a man (vv.18-20).

i) What does not defile a man, v.17
Defilement is not contracted by what "**entereth in at the mouth**". In answering Peter's question, the Saviour makes it perfectly clear that it is not food passing through a person's digestive tract that makes them unclean in God's sight. After all, the food we eat doesn't convey sinful thoughts and ideas to our minds, it simply feeds the body. The words "out into the draught" mean, 'out into the drain or latrine', and simply refers to the discharge of waste from our bodies. Mark adds "purging all meats" (Mark 7: 19)" which is best explained by the following rendering: 'Perceive ye not, that whatsoever from without goeth into a man, it cannot defile him; because it goeth not into his heart, but into his belly, and goeth out into the draught? ***This he said, making all meats clean***". The emphasised words are unique to Mark. H.St. John comments as follows: 'In a single sentence, all the legal restrictions as to meats made by Moses, are swept aside for ever. In making this comment, Mark may well have had in mind Peter's vision on the housetop at Caesarea (Acts 10: 15)'.

ii) What does defile a man, vv.18-20
Defilement is contracted by "those things which proceed out of the mouth": they "come forth from **the heart**, and they **defile the man**" (v.18). The Lord now explains: "For out of the **heart** proceed evil thoughts, murders, adulteries, fornications, thefts, false witness, blasphemies". Mark has "evil thoughts, adulteries, fornications, murders, thefts, covetousness, wickedness, deceit, lasciviousness, an evil eye, blasphemy, pride, foolishness" (Mark 7: 21-22). Commenting on Mark, H.St.John observes, 'The thirteen forms of poison which issue forth from the human heart are of sad, supreme importance, but the passage of food through the human body is not!' In the words of the Lord Jesus, "These are the things which defile a man: but to eat with unwashen hands defileth not a man" (v.20).

The word "**heart"** refers to our inner life. The first three references to "heart" in the Bible disclose its significance. See Genesis 6: 5, where the word is used in connection with the **intellect,** Genesis 6: 6, where the word is used in connection with the **emotions** (grief is an emotion), and Genesis 8: 21, where the word is used in connection with **volition** (a posh word for 'will!') When the Bible says, "The heart of man is deceitful above all things, and desperately wicked" (Jer.17: 9), it is stating that sin has invaded and ruined man's intellect, man's emotions, and man's will. No wonder Solomon said, "Keep thy heart with all diligence; for out of it are the issues of life" (Prov. 4: 23).

Notice that the list is headed by "evil thoughts". As J.C.Ryle observes: 'Thoughts are the parents of words and deeds. Let us pray daily for grace to keep our *thoughts* in order'. The following are relevant at this point: "As a man thinketh in his heart, so is he" (Prov. 23: 7); "Whatsoever things are true, whatsoever things are honest, whatsoever things are just, whatsoever things are pure, whatsoever things are lovely...think on these things" (Phil. 4: 8). Notice the occurrence of "adulteries" and "fornications". The fact that the two words occur together, as they do elsewhere in the New Testament (e.g. 1 Corinthians 6: 9, Hebrews 13: 4), implies that they have different meanings. This is most important when dealing with the subject of divorce, particularly in Matthew 5: 32 and 19: 9.

"O woman, great is thy faith"

Read Chapter 15: 21-39
The three incidents described in this passage took place in two different parts of the country. The "coasts of Tyre and Sidon" (v.21), or "borders of Tyre and Sidon" (Mark 7: 24), lay some fifty miles north-west of the Sea of Galilee. The area was known as Phoenicia, and occupied the coast of Northern Syria. During their long history, the Phoenicians conducted a vast seaborne trade (including, it is said, tin from Cornwall), from which they supplied the East. Tyre was known as the 'Queen of the East'. From "the borders of Tyre and Sidon", the Lord Jesus then travelled south-east *en route* for the Sea of Galilee via "the coasts (borders) of Decapolis" (Mark 7: 31). This area lay to the east of the Sea of Galilee. 'Decapolis' means 'ten cities'. After the conquest of Palestine by the Romans, these cities were rebuilt and partly colonised by them. One of the ten cities was Gadara, reminding us that having been healed, the demoniac "began to publish in Decapolis how great things Jesus had done for him: and all men did marvel" (Mark 5: 20). It was here that the Lord healed "those that were lame, blind, dumb, maimed, and many others" (v.30), and fed "four thousand men, beside women and children" (v.38).

Both areas therefore had strong Gentile connections. The chapter contrasts the hypocrisy of the scribes and Pharisees, with their studious avoidance of ceremonial defilement (vv.1-20), with the willingness of the Lord Jesus to bestow blessing on 'unclean' Gentiles (vv.21-29), one of whom likened herself to a dog eating crumbs under the table (v.27).

The passage may be divided as follows: *(1)* helping a distraught mother" (vv.21-28): "she…worshipped him, saying, Lord, help me" (v.25); *(2)* healing various ailments (vv.29-31): "the multitude wondered, when they saw the dumb to speak, the maimed to be whole, the lame to walk, and the blind to see" (v.31); *(3)* feeding the multitude (vv.32-39); "And they did all eat, and were filled" (v.37). J.M.Flanigan puts it beautifully (as usual) in saying 'Crumbs from the Table: Bread in the Wilderness'.

1) HELPING A DISTRAUGHT MOTHER, vv.21-28

Mark tells us that having arrived in "the borders of Tyre and Sidon", the Lord Jesus "entered into an house, and would have no man know it: but he could not be hid" (Mark 7: 24). It would be wonderful if it could be said of every assembly, "he could not be hid" (Mark 7: 24), and "it was noised that he was in the house" (Mark 2: 1). There can be no doubt that the Lord Jesus went deliberately beyond His usual preaching area in order to meet the Syrophenician woman. Compare John 4: 3-4. We should now notice:

a) The region of Tyre and Sidon, v.21

"Then Jesus went thence, and departed into the coasts of Tyre and Sidon". (See Matt. 11: 22-23). The setting is important. While we must always carefully notice the **content** of the Lord's teaching, it is helpful to notice the **context** of His teaching. As noted, the Lord was in Gentile territory. The Lord evidently went to the area with the blessing of this woman and her daughter in view and, at the same time, to demonstrate that Jew and Gentile are blessed by God on exactly the same basis. According to Mark, the woman who "came and fell at his feet" was "a Greek, a Syrophenician by nation" (Mark 7: 26). The word "Greek" does not necessarily mean that she was a native of Greece: it is used with a wider sense in the New Testament, on some occasions referring to Gentiles in general, whether Greek citizens or not. "Syrophenician" simply means that she belonged to Phenice (or Phoenicia) in Syria. Matthew simply calls her, "a woman of Canaan" (v.22). Compare Numbers 13: 29.

We should add that it is not without significance that the Lord's statement, "Thou art Peter (*petros*), and upon this rock (*petra*) I will build My church", was made, not in Jerusalem, but in **Caesarea Philippi** (Matt. 16: 13-20), another place with strong Gentile connections, anticipating later New

Testament teaching that the church is not an extension of Israel. Ephesians chs. 2-3 should be carefully read in this connection.

b) The request by the mother, v.22
"And behold, a woman of Canaan came out of the same coasts, and cried (*kraugazo*) unto him, saying, Have mercy on me, O Lord, thou son of David; my daughter is grievously vexed with a devil". This was remarkable: a Gentile woman addresses Him as "son of David". "Son of David" is the royal title of the Messiah. See Matt. 1: 1; 21: 9, 15. As John Heading observes. 'the Lord's fame must have spread into this territory, and she accepted Him and His power without question'. We should notice the earnestness of her request. Mark emphasises this in saying that she "came and fell at his feet" (Mark 7: 25). The woman evidently recognised that only the Lord Jesus could rid her daughter of Satanic power. It is rather interesting that the two blind men, evidently Jews, who "followed him, crying (*krazo*), and saying, Thou son of David, have mercy on us", showed similar earnestness: they followed Him to "the house" (Matt. 9: 27-28). The earnestness of the blind men and the woman is a lesson to us all. "Blessed are they…that seek him with the whole heart" (Psalm 119: 2). See also Luke 18:1-8. While we must always look for new opportunities and better methods, it remains that the "effectual *fervent* prayer of a righteous man availeth much" (James 5: 16). Prayer is our most important weapon in the spiritual warfare.

c) The response of the Lord Jesus, vv.23-24
Initially, the Saviour seemed terribly unsympathetic. In fact, He appeared to completely ignore her: "he answered her not a word" (v.23). But worse, seemingly, was to follow, for when the irritated disciples said, "Send her away; for she crieth after us", He said (evidently to the disciples, although the woman was clearly listening), "I am not sent but unto the lost sheep of the house of Israel" (vv.23-24). This looked like the death-knell to all her hopes. There was nothing more to be said: the matter was closed. We shall see, of course, that the Saviour was *not* at all unsympathetic towards the woman. His apparent disinterest was all part of His desire for her blessing. But this could hardly be said about the disciples! With this in mind, we should note:

i) **The response of the Saviour.** She had called him "son of David", in which case, since He was Israel's Messiah, a Gentile woman had no claim upon Him, so "he answered her not a word" (v.23). The only people who could expect His help were "the lost sheep of the house of Israel" (v.24).

Their need was immense, they were "lost sheep" (Isaiah 53: 6), and they needed a shepherd's care (Matt. 9: 36), so there was no time for anybody else. After all, we could argue, the Lord Jesus was simply doing what He told His disciples to do: "Go not into the way of the Gentiles...But rather to the lost sheep of the house of Israel" (Matt. 10: 5-6). But was the Saviour really disinterested in the woman's case?

Watch this space!

ii) The response of the disciples. "Send her away; for she crieth (*krazo*) after us". We must try to be charitable. It is quite possible that the disciples had the interests of their busy Master in mind. A case of, "trouble not the Master" (Luke 8: 49). Compare Matthew 19: 13-15. On the other hand, they might have objected to her on racial grounds: she was a Gentile. Then, quite possibly, her persistence may have 'got under their skin'. Whatever the motives of the disciples, it reminds us of the need for patience and kindness in the Lord's service. Unsaved people (and sometimes, alas, the Lord's people) can 'get to us', and we begin to 'wish them somewhere else'. In dealing with people we must be 'constrained' (held fast) by "the love of Christ" (2 Cor. 5: 14).

d) The reply of the mother, v.25

"Then came she and worshipped him, saying, Lord, help me". Earlier, Peter had said, "Lord, save me" (14: 30). (Perhaps there's the beginning of a sermon here!). We must notice two important things here:

- **How she approached the Lord Jesus.** She "worshipped him". The word worship here (*proskuneo*) comes from two words: '*pros*, towards, and *kuneo*, to kiss' (W.E.Vine). It is widely used in the New Testament, and not always in connection with God and the Lord Jesus. Let's just say that she approached the Lord in the right way.

- **How she addressed the Lord Jesus.** Not now, "O Lord, thou son of David" (v.22), but simply (but significantly) as "Lord". Wm.MacDonald makes the insightful observation, 'If she couldn't come to Him as a Jew to her Messiah, she would come as a creature to her Creator'. She certainly addressed Him in the right way. But there is more: she condensed her request to the simple words, "Lord, help me". No long preamble: her earnestness brought her immediately to the point - she desperately needed His help. Do ***we*** approach God in prayer with a real sense of need?

e) The response of the Lord Jesus, v.26
"But he answered and said, It is not meet to take the children's bread, and cast it to the dogs". Mark gives us a little more: "But Jesus said unto her, Let the children first be filled: for it is not meet to take the children's bread, and to cast it unto the dogs" (Mark 7: 27). On a technical note the word rendered "dog" (*kunarion*) refers to 'a little dog, a puppy' (W.E.Vine) rather than to the homeless scavenging mongrels (*kuon*) which prowled the streets in search of food. (You find them in Matt.7: 6; Luke 16: 21; 2 Pet. 2: 22; Phil. 3: 2; Rev. 22: 15). There can be no doubt that the Lord is referring to Israel as "the children", and to the Gentiles as "dogs". It is also clear that the Lord Jesus did not intend to be rude or derogatory. By referring to "the dogs", He alluded to the **Jewish** conviction that they alone were entitled to benefit from God's goodness. The meal was for the children, not the dogs. But do notice the Saviour's words exactly: "Let the children **first** be filled", so the dogs would get their turn in due course! In this way, He tested the resolve and faith of the Syrophenician mother. But she was soon to prove the accuracy of the hymn

> *Judge not the Lord by feeble sense,*
> *But trust Him for His grace;*
> *Beneath a frowning providence*
> *He hides a smiling face.*

f) The reply of the mother, v.27
"And she said, Truth, Lord: yet the dogs eat of the crumbs which fall from their masters' table" or, as in Mark, "Yes, Lord: yet the dogs under the table eat of the children's crumbs" (Mark 7: 28). This was the language of faith. Whilst the woman knew only too well that she wasn't a member of the privileged Jewish nation, she believed that other people could be blessed through His mission to the Jews. There does seem to be a measure of spiritual intelligence in this: in the past Gentile women, such as Rahab and Ruth, had been brought into blessing by the God of Israel. They had been marvellously blessed by 'crumbs' from the table! (T.Miller). Moreover the woman recognised that something so small as a 'crumb' from the table was nevertheless completely sufficient to meet her need! (T.Miller). Wm MacDonald puts it very nicely indeed: 'While the unbelieving children had no hunger or the bread, here was a self-confessed dog who was crying out for it'. Her faith was rewarded. We should add that that Paul describes the Jewish teachers as "dogs" in saying: "Beware of dogs, beware of evil workers, beware of the concision" (Phil. 3: 2). The "dogs" have become

Jews! Not little dogs (*kunarion*), but 'the prowling dogs (*kuon*) of the east' (W.E.Vine).

g) The response of the Lord Jesus, v.28
"Then Jesus answered and said unto her, O woman, great is thy faith: be it unto thee even as thou wilt, And her daughter was made whole from that very hour". The 'frowning providence' (see above) now gives place to the 'smiling face'. The Lord Jesus had no intention of avoiding the woman, simply because she was a Gentile. His apparent disinterest made the woman declare her faith. He had scant regard for curiosity, but every regard for genuine faith, whether on the part of Jew or Gentile. This must have been a salutary lesson to the disciples, who had asked permission to send her packing (v.23).

The encounter with the Syrophenician woman reminds us of at least two most important facts:

i) *That salvation is available to all by faith.* The Gospel records make it clear that both Jews and Gentiles are blessed on the ground of faith. As to Jews: "Daughter...*thy faith* hath made thee whole" (Matt. 9: 22); "According to your faith, be it unto you" (Matt. 9: 29). As to Gentiles: speaking of a Roman centurion, "Verily I say unto you, I have not found so **great faith**, no, not in Israel" (Matt. 8: 10); "O woman, great is *thy faith*: be it unto thee even as thou wilt" (Matt. 15: 28). Paul puts it beautifully: "Is he the God of the Jews only? is he not also of the Gentiles? Yes, of the Gentiles also: seeing it is the same God, which shall justify the circumcision by faith, and uncircumcision through faith" (Rom. 3: 29-30).

ii) *That salvation is available to all without priority.* It is no longer a case of, "the dogs under the table eat of the children's crumbs" (Mark 7: 28), and that the Gospel is primarily for the Jews with the Gentiles scraping in where they can! We know that "salvation is of the Jews" (John 4: 22) and that, historically, the Gospel is to "the Jew first, and also to the Greek" (Rom. 1: 16), but the fact remains that, "God so loved the world, that he gave his only begotten Son, that whosoever believeth in him should not perish, but have everlasting life" (John 3: 16). The Jewish nation today is not specially favoured by the Gospel message. Israel's national future is assured, but this awaits the completion of the church, "where there is neither Greek nor Jew, circumcision nor uncircumcision, Barbarian, Scythian, bond nor free: but Christ is all in all" (Col. 3: 11).

Matthew

2) HEALING VARIOUS AILMENTS, vv.29-31

"And Jesus departed from thence, and came nigh unto the sea of Galilee; and went up into a mountain, and sat down there. And great multitudes came unto him, having with them those that were lame, blind, dumb, maimed (meaning 'crooked' or 'crippled'), and many others, and cast them down at Jesus' feet; and he healed them: insomuch that the multitude wondered, when they saw the dumb to speak, and maimed to be whole, the lame to walk, and the blind to see: and they glorified the God of Israel". The final words, "and they glorified the God of Israel", imply that the Lord was amongst Gentiles. Matthew's words, "Jesus...went up into a mountain, and sat down there" paint a regal picture. The King is present. Compare Psalm 2: 6. When the King reigns, the whole world will be at His feet, and He will solve every problem!

We might add that since Gadara was one of the 'ten cities' (Decapolis) in the area, the once demon-possessed man appears to have done a good job! See Mark 5: 19-20. That apart, the Lord was well-known by people from Decapolis (Matt. 4: 25).

Mark concentrates on one man: "And they bring unto him one that was deaf and had an impediment in his speech" and although, having given the man hearing and speech, the Lord "charged them that they should tell no man", the news spread rapidly: "But the more he charged them, so much the more a great deal they published it; and were beyond measure astonished, saying, He hath done all things well: he maketh both the deaf to hear, and the dumb to speak" (Mark 7: 31-37).

The miracles described here by Matthew gave these Gentiles a taste of "the powers of the world (age) to come" (Heb. 6: 5). We know that when the Lord Jesus returns to establish His kingdom "the eyes of the blind shall be opened, and the ears of the deaf shall be unstopped: then shall the lame man leap as an hart, and the tongue of the dumb sing" (Isaiah 35: 4-6), and while this passage has particular reference to the Jewish nation, we cannot doubt that all men will benefit in the same way.

3) FEEDING THE MULTITUDE, vv.32-39

We are all well aware that these verses describe the second of two similar miracles performed by the Lord Jesus, and that later He refers to both in the same breath (16: 9-10). On the previous occasion (14: 15-21) there were "about five thousand men, beside women and children" and on this occasion "four thousand men, beside women and children" (v.38). In the first case, the crowd was Jewish: in the second, bearing in mind the setting and the response of the multitude (v.31), it was probably a Gentile crowd.

It would be quite wrong to accelerate past these verses simply because we have already noted similar lessons in connection with the first of the two miracles. We must never forget past teaching. In the words of Peter: "Wherefore I will not be negligent to put you always in remembrance of these things, though ye know them, and be established in the present truth" (2 Pet. 1: 12). Here are four simple things to think about:

a) About the Saviour, v.32
On the previous occasion, the disciples approached the Lord. But here the Lord "called his disciples". He took the initiative, saying: "I have **compassion** on the multitude". We have already noted the literal meaning of compassion: 'to be moved as to one's inwards' (W.E.Vine). The Lord Jesus felt deeply for His hearers. He was concerned about them as people. It is one thing to deliver a lecture, but something quite different to really care about the audience. Paul puts it in familiar words: "Though I speak with the tongues of men and of angels, and have not charity, I am become as a sounding brass, or a tinkling cymbal" (1 Cor. 13: 1). The compassion of Christ embraced both the spiritual and material need of the multitude. Moreover, it was preventative ministry. He did not wait until the people had almost succumbed. He did something before it was too late. He exhibited care and concern for the whole man. John has some scathing words for anything less: "Hereby we have known love, because he has laid down his life for us... But whoso may have this world's substance, and see his brother having need, and shut up his bowels (*splanchnon*: "compassion" is *splanchnizomai*) from him, how abides the love of God in him?" (1 John 3: 16-18, JND).

b) About the crowd, v.32
"Then Jesus called his disciples unto him, and said, I have compassion on the multitude, because they continue with me now three days, and have nothing to eat: and I will not send them away fasting, lest they faint in the way". If you find it difficult to sit through a meeting, just remember this, although, in fairness, neither Matthew nor Mark mention teaching on this occasion, unlike the previous occasion (see Mark 6: 34). However, the fact that Matthew describes the Lord Jesus seated on a mountain (v.29), strongly suggests that He was teaching. The teachers sat in those days. See, for example, Luke 4: 20; 5: 3: Matt. 24: 3. J.C.Ryle is probably correct in saying that 'He

knew that the great majority were following Him from no other motive than idle curiosity, and had no claim whatever to be regarded as His disciples'. However, the fact remains that the crowd spent three days in the wilderness with the Lord Jesus, and if that wasn't enough, there was evidently no food provided. Priority was given to His work amongst the sick, rather than to eating. We should remember that Job said, "I have esteemed the words of his mouth **more than my necessary food**" (Job 23: 12). Jeremiah had a great appetite for God's word: "Thy words were found, and *I did eat them;* and thy word was unto me the joy and rejoicing of my heart" (Jer 15: 16). The Psalmist was equally enthusiastic about the Word of God: "O how I love thy law! it is my meditation all the day" (Psalm 119: 97).

c) About the disciples, v.33
"And his disciples say unto him, Whence should we have so much bread in the wilderness, as to fill so great a multitude?". This does not necessarily mean that the disciples had quickly forgotten the previous miracle. Had this been the case, we could have expected the Lord to immediately rebuke them. H.S.Paisley, writing on Mark, is probably right in saying that 'it appears to be a confession of the powerlessness of mere men to satisfy such a crowd, and their absolute dependence upon the Lord Himself…They realised that no man could supply the need. The solution lay with Him'. This is supported by their words, "From whence can a *man* satisfy these men with bread here in the wilderness?" (Mark 8: 4).

d) About the meal, vv.34-38
It has been nicely pointed out that while the disciples thought negatively (v.33), the Lord asked them what they did have: "How many loaves have ye?" (v.34). He thought positively! The existing resources, in themselves, were quite inadequate to meet the need of hungry men, but they proved more than sufficient in the Saviour's hands. If we are prepared to give Christ what we have, He will make more of it than we ever thought possible. Having "commanded the multitude to sit down on the ground", the Lord "took the seven loaves and the fishes, and gave thanks, and brake them, and gave to his disciples, and the disciples to the multitude. And they did all eat, and were filled; and they took up of the broken meat that was left seven baskets full".

We have already noted (in connection with the previous miracle of feeding) that the word "baskets" (*spuris*) refers to 'a reed basket, plaited, a capacious kind of hamper, sometimes large enough to hold a man (see Acts 9: 25)' (W.E.Vine), whereas in Matthew 14: 20 the word (*kophinos*) refers to a small wicker basket. It has been said, that the first was a Hebrew lunch-basket, and the second was a Gentile merchant's hamper. Interesting!

The Lord then "sent away the multitude, and took ship, and came into the coasts of Magdala" (v.39). In other words, He crossed the lake from east to west. The name Mary Magdalene will be familiar to us! Mark tells us that "he entered into a ship with his disciples, and came into the parts of Dalmanutha" (Mark 8: 10). Nothing is known of Dalmanutha, it remains unidentified, but it was presumably another name for the area.

THE GOSPEL OF MATTHEW

"Do ye not yet understand...?"

Read Chapter 16: 1-12

We have noticed that after the Lord had healed the man with the withered hand on the Sabbath day, "the Pharisees went out and held a council against him, how they might destroy him", and that "when Jesus knew it, he withdrew himself from thence" (Matt. 12: 14-15). The murderous intentions of the Pharisees were bad enough, but even worse followed when they accused Him of casting out "devils (demons)...by Beelzebub the prince of the devils" (12: 24). In a further attempt to discredit Him, the scribes and Pharisees then requested a sign (12: 38), following which the Lord "went out of the house, and sat by the sea side" (13: 1).

Our current chapter commences with a second similar attempt by the Pharisees, now accompanied by the Sadducees, to discredit the Lord Jesus: they "came and tempting desired him that he would shew them a sign from heaven" (v.1). Having answered them, the Lord, significantly, "left them and departed" (vv.2-4). Against the background of their unbelief, and having condemned their evil doctrine (vv.5-12), the Lord then announces, significantly, at Caesarea Philippi, that He would undertake something entirely new: "I will build my church", and just as the kingdom of heaven would not and could not be overthrown, so "the gates of hell" would not prevail against His church (v.18).

The chapter may be divided as follows: *(1)* the sign of Jonas (vv.1-4): "A wicked and adulterous generation seeketh after a sign; and there shall no sign be given unto it, but the sign of the prophet Jonas" (v.4); *(2)* the significance of leaven (vv.5-12); "not...the leaven of bread, but of the doctrine of the Pharisees and of the Sadducees" (v.12); *(3)* the start of the church (vv.13-20): "thou art Peter, and upon this rock I will build my church" (v.18); *(4)* the suffering at Jerusalem (vv.21-28): "From that time forth began Jesus to shew unto his disciples, how that he must go unto Jerusalem, and suffer many things" (v.21).

1) THE SIGN OF JONAS, vv.1-4
As noted at the end of our previous study, having fed "four thousand men, beside women and children, the Lord "took ship, and came into the coasts of Magdala" (15: 39) or, in Mark's words, "the parts of Dalmanutha" (Mark 8: 10). As we have already said, nothing is known of Dalmanutha, it remains unidentified, but was presumably another name for the area.

The compassion of the Saviour in dealing with the hungry crowds (15: 32) now gives place to confrontation: "The Pharisees also with the Sadducees came, and tempting desired him that he should shew them a sign from heaven" (16: 1). As Wm.Kelly observes, "It is an awful thing to find opposed parties with only one thing uniting them - dislike of Jesus; persons who could have torn each other to pieces at another time, but this is their gathering point - tempting Jesus". Their sole objective was to derail and condemn Him, whereas "the common people heard him gladly" (Mark 12: 37). Matthew emphasises the Lord's anger with the religious fraternity ("O ye hypocrites...A wicked and adulterous generation", vv.3-4), while Mark emphasises His deep sorrow: "And the Pharisees came forth, and began to question with him, seeking of him a sign from heaven, tempting him. And he sighed (groaned) deeply (*anastenazo*) in his spirit" (Mark 8: 11-12). The words "sighed deeply" translate an intensified form of the word "sighed" (*stenazo*) occurring in Mark 7: 34. According to W.E.Vine, it means a deeply-drawn sigh. Unbelief causes the Saviour deep sorrow. J.C.Ryle writes: "There was deep mourning in that sigh! It came from a heart which mourned over the ruin that these wicked men were bringing on their own souls".

As we have already noticed, this was the second request for a sign. See Matthew 12: 38-45, where the Saviour answered similarly. We should notice: *(a)* the object of the demand (v.1); *(b)* the Lord's declaration (vv.2-4); *(c)* the Lord's departure (v.4).

a) The object of the demand, v.1
There was no lack of evidence for His Messiahship. A most remarkable miracle had just been performed on the other side of Galilee, with at least four thousand witnesses! Although they asked for a "sign from heaven" (evidently something like the fire on Mount Carmel: 1 Kings 18), the Pharisees didn't really expect to get one: this much is clear from the words,

"seeking of him a sign from heaven, ***tempting him***" (Mark 8: 11). No doubt, they expected to return triumphantly from Magdala with the news that there was no evidence that Jesus of Nazareth was the Messiah. His claim was bogus. They failed to recognise that "The most significant token that God ever gave man was before them in the person of His Son, who eclipsed all other signs. But such is unbelief, that it can go into the presence of the full manifestation of God, can gaze at a light brighter than the sun at noonday, and there and then ask God to give a farthing candle" (Wm.Kelly). At first glance, Ahaz appears to have been superior to the religious leaders here. Having been told to "ask…a sign of the Lord thy God", he replied "I will not ask, neither will I tempt the Lord" (Isaiah 7: 11-12). It sounded good, but it was 'hypocritical piety' (M.F.Unger). Ahaz was already intent on forging an alliance with the Assyrians (2 Chron. 28:16). No wonder the Lord said to him, "If ye will not believe, surely ye shall not be established" (Isaiah 7: 9). The same could be said of the Pharisees and the Sadducees.

Whilst there were people who "believed in his name, when they saw the miracles which he did" (John 2: 23), the words which follow are deeply significant: "But Jesus did not commit Himself unto them". We sometimes say, 'Seeing is believing', but God looks for believing ***without*** seeing: "Blessed are they that have not seen, and yet have believed" (John 20: 29). See also 1 Peter 1: 8: "Whom having not seen, ye love; in whom, though now ye see him not, yet believing, ye rejoice with joy unspeakable and full of glory". Contrary to human logic, "Through faith we understand" (Heb. 11: 3).

b) The Lord's declaration, vv.2-4
He contrasts the ability of the Pharisees and Sadducees to discern the signs in the sky (vv.2-3) with their inability to discern "the signs of the times" (vv.3-4). As R.V.G.Tasker points out, the Lord's reference to the signs in "the sky" links up with the "sign from heaven" demanded here, but not designated in Matthew 12: 38.

i) The signs in the sky. "When it is evening, ye say, It will be fair weather: for the sky is red. And in the morning, it will be foul weather (*cheimon*, meaning 'winter' or 'winter storm') to day: for the sky is red and lowring (spelt 'lowering' in some Bibles). O ye hypocrites, ye can discern the face of the sky; but can ye not discern the signs of the times?" (vv.2-3). The word translated "lowring" (*stugnazo*) means 'to have a gloomy, sombre appearance' (W.E.Vine). It occurs in Mark 10: 22: "he was sad" or "his countenance fell" (RV).

*ii) **The "signs of the times".*** "O ye hypocrites, ye can discern the face of the sky; but can ye not discern the signs of the times? A wicked (*poneros*: as in 12: 39 where it is rendered "evil") and adulterous (in the sense of spiritually unfaithful to God) generation seeketh after a sign; and there shall no sign be given unto it, but the sign of the prophet Jonas" (vv.3-4). R.H.Mounce makes the telling observation that "they are hypocrites, because while pretending to pose a reasonable request they are in fact a wicked and adulterous generation". R.H.Mounce then quotes another writer: "to perform a miracle for 'an immoral generation' would be out of the question". When asked for a sign on the previous occasion, the Lord added "for as Jonas was three days and three nights in the whale's belly; so shall the Son of man be three days and three nights in the heart of the earth" (12: 40). In saying that they could not "discern the signs of the times", the Lord evidently referred to the fact that "the blind received their sight, and the lame walk, the lepers are cleansed, and the deaf hear, the dead are raised up, and the poor have the gospel preached unto them" (Matt. 11: 5). All pointed to the fact that the Messiah had come (Isaiah 35: 5-6; 61: 1-2). But the Pharisees and Sadducees were "blind leaders of the blind" (15: 14).

As before (see, again, 12: 38-45), this should be compared with the Lord's answer to the question, "What sign shewest thou unto us, seeing that thou doest these things?", to which He replied, "Destroy this temple, and in three days I will raise it up...But he spake of the temple of his body" (John 2: 18-21). We know that even this "sign" failed to bring the Jews to repentance and faith. They did not believe "the sign of Jonas the prophet". See Matt. 28: 11-15; Luke 16: 31. The Lord Jesus was "declared to be the Son of God... by the resurrection from the dead" (Rom 1: 4). Jonah had been a sign to his generation (Luke 11: 30) and the Lord Jesus would be a sign to the current generation. "As the Sadducees disbelieved in any form of resurrection, while the Pharisees believed in a final resurrection of the righteous only, mention of this 'sign' would be particularly appropriate" (R.V.G.Tasker).

In passing, it is worth noting that amongst David's mighty men were "the children of Issachar, which were men that had understanding of the times, to know what Israel ought to do" (1 Chron. 12: 32). People like that are most valuable! Paul certainly had "understanding of the times" (1 Thess. 5: 1). The Lord's "understanding of the times" was perfect (see, for example, Matt. 10: 16-23), and later He fully answered the disciples' questions, "Tell us, when shall these things be? And what shall be the sign of thy coming, and of the end of the world?" (Matt. 24: 3).

c) The Lord's departure, v.4

The section ends on a sad and ominous note: "And He left them, and departed". The multitudes on the other side of the lake went away blessed and fed (15: 37-38), but the Pharisees and Sadducees got nothing. But there is more to learn here. Wm.Kelly puts it clearly: "And what was this sign? The sign of one that disappeared from the earth; that, through the figure of death, passed away from the Jewish people, and after awhile was given back to them. It was the symbol of death and resurrection, and our Lord immediately acted upon it. He 'left them and departed'. He would pass under the power of death; He would rise again, and the message which Israel had despised, He would carry to the Gentiles".

2) THE SIGNIFICANCE OF LEAVEN, vv.5-12

While the disciples were concerned over their forgetfulness (v.5), the Lord Jesus was concerned over much more important matters. In the words of J.C.Ryle, "His mind was evidently pained with the false doctrines which he saw among the Jews, and the pernicious influence which they exercised. He seizes the opportunity to utter a caution: 'Take heed, and beware of the leaven of the Pharisees and of the Sadducees'" (v.6). The short encounter with these people here prompted the Lord Jesus to alert His disciples to "the doctrine of the Pharisees and of the Sadducees" (v.12). Mark gives us a little more information: "Take heed, beware of the leaven of the Pharisees, and of the leaven of Herod" (Mark 8: 15).

Before we think about "the leaven of the Pharisees...of the Sadducees...of Herod", we must notice that the disciples completely misunderstood Him. In this connection, the Lord deals with their lack of understanding in general (v.8-10), and then their lack of understanding in particular (vv.11-12).

a) Their lack of understanding in general, vv.8-10

They assumed that He was chiding them for failing to take sufficient bread for the voyage across Galilee (v.7). It is often pointed out that the disciples had "left the Jewish area for the lonely, half-Gentile eastern side of the country" and that they "had already set out when they discovered that they had forgotten to take bread with them. It would be difficult to find a Jewish baker on the other side" (supplied by J.Waldron).

It is hardly surprising that the Saviour reproved them in view of His proven ability to feed multitudes of people (vv.9-10). We, too, are apt to forget that, in Paul's words, "My God shall supply all your need according to his riches in glory by Christ Jesus" (Phil. 4: 19). Notice that the Saviour put four questions to them (vv.8-11). Mark supplies more information at this point. He records nine questions, and cites Isaiah 6: 9-10, which refers to the blindness and deafness of Israel. The Lord's disciples were just like the nation at large. See Mark 8: 17-21. It's worth pointing out that between the two occasions on which the Lord had to say "O thou of little faith" (14: 31) and "O ye of little faith" (16: 8), He was able to say to a Gentile woman "great is thy faith" (15: 28).

b) *Their lack of understanding in particular, vv.11-12*
As noted, the Lord Jesus mentioned three kinds of leaven: "Beware of the leaven of the Pharisees and of the Sadducees" (Matthew); "beware of the leaven of the Pharisees, and of the leaven of Herod" (Mark). Matthew alone tells us what the Lord Jesus meant by the word "leaven": "Then understood they how that he bade them not beware of the leaven of bread, but of the **doctrine** of the Pharisees and of the Sadducees" (v.12). God's figures of speech are always exact. In the Bible, leaven (yeast) is without exception a figure of evil, and the reason is not difficult to discover. Leaven has the property of converting sugar and allied substances, as starch, into alcohol and carbon dioxide. That is, it changes the character of those substances. When moist, as in contact with dough, it is a living organism. Leaven is therefore an apt symbol of pervasive evil. Sin has the same property: when it is unchecked, it will completely change a person's life and character. The *way* in which leaven works contributes to its significance as a picture of evil: "The kingdom of heaven is like unto leaven, which a woman took, and *hid* in three measures of meal, till the whole was leavened" (Matt. 13: 33). It begins its work as something small and unseen, but acts with deadly power and efficiency.

The Scriptures have a great deal to say about this subject. For example, the feast of passover and the feast of unleavened bread are never divided in the Bible: see Exodus 12: 13-15; Deuteronomy 16: 1-8; Mark 14: 12; Luke 22: 1, 7; 1 Corinthians 5: 7-8. Redeemed people must be holy people. Since leaven is a picture of sin, its presence was strictly forbidden in every sacrifice which speaks of the Lord Jesus. See Exodus 23: 18, "Thou shalt not offer the blood of my sacrifice with leavened bread". Compare Leviticus 2: 11. The use of leaven was commanded on two occasions in the book of Leviticus (in the law of the peace offering, 7: 13; and in the feast of weeks, 23: 17), but in both cases it refers to the nature of God's people rather than to the sinless character of Christ. A detailed study of the subject will be amply rewarded.

We must now ascertain the precise meaning of the expressions, "leaven of the Pharisees...leaven of the Sadducees....leaven of Herod".

a) The leaven of the Pharisees
This was religious hypocrisy. See Luke 12: 1: "Beware of the leaven of the Pharisees, which is hypocrisy". The Lord Jesus sums it up elsewhere: "They say, and do not" (Matt. 23: 3). In fact, the hypocrisy of the Pharisees is fully disclosed by the Lord Jesus in Matthew ch.23. For example, "Woe unto you, scribes and Pharisees, hypocrites! for ye pay tithe of mint and anise and cummin, and have omitted the weightier matters of the law, judgment, mercy and faith" (v.23). We must beware of this in our own lives: God expects *total* compliance with His Word. A further illustration from Matthew ch.23 will suffice: "Woe unto you, scribes and Pharisees, hypocrites! for ye make clean the outside of the cup and of the platter, but within they are full of extortion and excess" (v.25). In this case their hypocrisy lay in the discrepancy between what they said, and what they were. We must beware of religious hypocrisy. For example, assemblies noted for their orthodox practices have been known to founder on the rocks of bitterness, selfishness and division.

b) The leaven of the Sadducees
If the "leaven of the Pharisees" was legalism, then the "leaven of the Sadducees" was liberalism. As Wm.Kelly observes, the Sadducees "were the free-thinkers of the day". They were given to doctrinal error. "The same day came to him the Sadducees, which say that there is no resurrection" (Matt. 22: 23). But that was not all: "the Sadducees say that there is no resurrection, neither angels, nor spirits" (Acts 23: 8.) The Sadducees were rationalists, and therefore the forerunners of our modern higher critics and theologians who attempt to explain away, or completely deny, anything in Scripture that cannot be reduced to the slide rule of human logic. We must beware of false teaching. The Lord Jesus answered the Sadducees: "Ye do err, not knowing the scriptures, nor the power of God" (Matt. 22: 29).

J.C.Ryle has a splendid piece on the leaven of the Pharisees and the leaven of the Sadducees. Here is part of his discourse: "Let us remember that we live in a world where Pharisaism and Sadduceeism are continually striving for the mastery of the church of Christ. Some want to add to the Gospel, and some want to take away from it; some would bury it, and some would pare it down to nothing; some would stifle it by heaping on additions, and some would bleed it to death by subtraction from its truths. Both parties agree only in one respect: both would kill and destroy the life of Christianity, if they succeeded in having their own way. Against both errors let us watch and pray, and stand upon our guard...Let our principle be 'the truth, the whole truth, and nothing but the truth': nothing added to it, and nothing taken away". Follow that!

c) The leaven of Herod
For completeness, we must note Mark's reference to "the leaven of Herod" (Mark 8: 15). This evidently refers to worldliness, although the emphasis is often placed on the danger of political aspirations. J.C.Ryle relates it to "the worldliness and scepticism of the courtiers of Herod". Herod the Great (see Matt. 2: 1) and his successors endeavoured to ingratiate themselves with the Jews, particularly in the costly enterprise of building a new temple in Jerusalem. They also introduced the Greek and Roman games to Palestine, and these were accompanied by all sorts of evil practices. Whilst these were a great grief to the strict Jews, a great many gave them support. "The leaven of Herod" carries a warning against evil living.

"Thou art the Christ, the Son of the living God"

Read Matthew 16: 13-20
As we have noted, Matthew ch.16 may be divided as follows: *(1)* the sign of Jonas (vv.1-4); *(2)* the significance of leaven (vv.5-12); *(3)* the start of the church (vv.13-20); *(4)* the suffering at Jerusalem (vv.21-28).

1) THE SIGN OF JONAS, vv.1-4
Having told the sign-seeking Pharisees and Sadducees that "A wicked and adulterous generation seeketh after a sign", the Lord added "and there shall no sign be given unto it, but the sign of the prophet Jonas", after which "he left them and departed" (v.4). See John 1:11.

2) THE SIGNIFICANCE OF LEAVEN, vv.5-12
Following this incident, the Lord warned His disciples to "Take heed and beware of the leaven of the Pharisees and of the Sadducees" (v.6), and they eventually "understood...that he bade them not beware of the leaven of bread, but of the doctrine of the Pharisees (legalism) and of the Sadducees (liberalisim)" (v.12).

3) THE START OF THE CHURCH, vv.13-20
These verses contain the first reference in the New Testament to the church: "And I say also unto thee, That thou art Peter, and upon this rock I will build my

church; and the gates of hell shall not prevail against it" (v.18). The second reference to the church is also in Matthew's Gospel: "And if he neglect to hear them, tell it unto the ***church:*** but if he neglect to hear the ***church,*** let him be unto thee as an heathen man and a publican" (Matt. 18: 17). These are the only occurrences of the word in the Gospels. This section of the chapter can be considered as follows: *(A)* the time of the announcement (v.13); *(B)* the place of the announcement (v.13); *(C)* the identity of the Founder (vv.13-17); *(D)* the work of the Founder (v.18); *(E)* the authority of Peter (v.19).

A) THE TIME OF THE ANNOUNCEMENT, v.13
The announcement was made at significant time. The immediate background is provided by vv.1-12. The Lord Jesus had censured the religious leadership, represented by the Pharisees and Sadducees (vv.1, 6). "A wicked and adulterous generation seeketh after a sign; and there shall no sign be given unto it, but the sign of the prophet Jonas. ***And he left them, and departed***" (v.4). These are significant words! He left the Pharisees with their religious hypocrisy, and he left the Sadducees with their doctrinal error, warning His disciples: "Take heed and beware of the leaven of the Pharisees and of the Sadducees" (vv.6,11). Now, shortly after, He announced, for the first time, something ***totally new.*** "I will build my ***church***". Whilst embracing the Jew, it was ***not*** based on Judaism. So far as Judaism was concerned, He had "left them and departed". This in no way cancels the promises made to the Patriarchs. God has not abandoned His earthly people. Romans 9-11 make this abundantly clear.

B) THE PLACE OF THE ANNOUNCEMENT, v.13
The announcement was made in a significant place - at Caesarea Philippi. This was the most northerly point reached by the Lord in His journeys, and marked the boundary between Jewish and Gentile territory. It was therefore at a place ***where Jewish and Gentile territory met,*** that the Lord Jesus made the first ever statement about the church, in which Jew and Gentile are made "***one new man***". Formerly named Panium (after the god, Pan), Caesarea Philippi is now known as Banias. (The 'P' has become a 'B'). It was enlarged by Herod Philip, who named the place after Caesar and himself.

C) THE IDENTITY OF THE FOUNDER, vv.13-17
The Lord introduces His teaching about the commencement of the church by asking two questions: *(i)* "Whom do ***men*** say that I the Son of man am?", to which the disciples gave various answers (vv.13-14); *(ii)* "But whom say ***ye*** that I am?", to which Peter replied, "Thou art the Christ, the Son of the

living God" (vv.15-16). The answer to the second question was the result of a revelation from God concerning Christ (v.17), and led to a revelation from Christ concerning the church (v.18) together with a revelation from Christ concerning Peter (v.19). At this point, we should notice the contrast between *(a)* human speculation (vv.13-14) and *(b)* divine revelation (vv.15-17).

a) Human speculation, vv.13-14

"Whom do **men** say that I the Son of man am?" This does not mean that the Lord Jesus was unaware of their opinion. He "needed not that any should testify of man: for he knew what was in man" (John 2: 25). He never required information. He asked questions to make a point. The Lord's intention was evidently to contrast the **error** of human perception, with the **truth** of divine revelation. If we want to know the truth about Christ, we do not go to men ("Whom do **men** say that I the Son of man am?"): we listen to God ("Blessed art thou, Simon Bar-Jona: for flesh and blood hath not revealed it unto thee, but **my Father** which is in heaven"). Notice the title, "Son of man". He constantly used this title. For example, "The foxes have holes... but the **Son of man** hath not where to lay his head" (Matt. 8: 20). The title emphasises His ideal manhood, and therefore His right to dominion: "And I saw in the night visions, and behold, one like the Son of man came with the clouds of heaven...and there was given him dominion and glory and a kingdom, that all people, nations, and languages should serve him" (Dan. 7: 13-14). See also Revelation 7: 15.

Notice the answer given by the disciples: "And they said, Some say thou art John the Baptist: some, Elias; and others, Jeremias, or one of the prophets" (v.14). Men answered according to the wisdom of "**flesh and blood**" (v.17). But **why** did they answer in this way? Those who suggested that He was **John the Baptist** possibly did so because He preached the same message: "Repent". Note the words of Herod: "This is John the Baptist; he is risen from the dead; and therefore mighty works do shew forth themselves in him" (Matt. 14: 1-2). Those who suggested that He was **Elias** possibly did so because He performed miracles. There had been none since the days of Elijah and Elisha. The Jews expected Elijah to come: "Why then say the scribes that Elias must first come?" (Matt.17: 10). Those who suggested that He was **Jeremias** possibly did so because He showed the same compassion. Jeremiah has been described as 'cast in bronze but melted in tears'. He is known as 'the weeping prophet'. The eyes of the Lord Jesus were, at times, filled with tears. Those who suggested that He was **one of the prophets** possibly did so because He appealed to the same authority.

Matthew

The prophets said, "Thus saith the Lord", and the Lord Jesus appealed time and time again to the Scriptures. This leads to:

b) Divine revelation, vv.15-17

"But whom say *ye* that I am?" or "But *ye*, who do *ye* say that I am?" (v.15, JND). This leads, as we have noted, to: *(i)* a revelation from God concerning Christ (vv.16-17); *(ii)* a revelation from Christ concerning the church (v.18); *(iii)* A revelation from Christ concerning the role of Peter (v.19).

"And Simon Peter answered and said unto him, Thou art the Christ, the Son of the living God". Notice what *men* said about the Lord Jesus (v.14), what *Peter* said about Him (v.16), and what *God* said about Him (Matt.17: 5). We should note the following:

- *"Thou art the Christ".* Peter had now proved the accuracy of his brother's report: "One of the two which heard John speak, and followed him, was Andrew, Simon Peter's brother. He first findeth his own brother Simon, and saith unto him, We have found the Messias, which is, being interpreted, the Christ" (John 1: 41). The Old Testament clearly taught that the Christ would be the Son of God. See, for example, Psalm 2: "his anointed (v.2)... thou art my Son" (v.7).

- *"The Son of the living God".* Notice the emphasis on "Son of the *living* God". That is, as opposed to lifeless idols, of which Pan was one. See above. Quite often, the expression, "the living God", occurs against an idolatrous background. Compare 1 Thess. 1: 9, "Ye turned to God from idols, to serve the *living* and true God", citing Jeremiah 10: 10 with its idolatrous context. See also 1 Kings 17: 1; Acts 14: 15. (This is not, however, always the case: see, for example, Matthew 26: 63). The Lord Jesus is the "Son of God". That is, having all the character and nature of God. The title, "the Son of the *living God*", emphasises that "as the Father hath life in himself; so hath he given to the Son to have life in himself" (John 5: 26). Through Him divine life has been imparted to every believer, so that they are called "the children of the living God" (Rom. 9: 26), possessing "the Spirit of the living God" (2 Cor. 3: 3) and meeting locally as "the church of the living God" (1 Tim.3: 15). Having come to the "living stone" (*lithos*), believers, "as living stones (*lithos*), are built up a spiritual house, an holy priesthood, to offer up spiritual sacrifices, acceptable to God by Jesus Christ" (1 Pet. 2: 4-5).

Peter's answer was not the result of native wisdom, or of careful deduction;

it was the result of divine revelation. "Blessed art thou, Simon (meaning 'hearing') Bar-Jona (meaning 'son of Jona': Jona being the Greek form of Johanan, meaning, 'God is gracious'), for flesh and blood (see John 6: 63: "the flesh profiteth nothing") hath not revealed it unto thee but **my Father** which is in heaven" (v.17). Compare Matt.11: 27. It follows that men, religious or otherwise, who deny the deity of the Lord Jesus, whether publicly or privately, are destitute of the Spirit, and destitute of the truth. They have no knowledge of God at all. Peter's confession was not made on the spur of the moment: he voiced a God-given conviction formed as he "witnessed his Master's mighty works and listened to the words of eternal life that fell daily from His lips". In it all, "the 'living God'...had been leading him to see that Jesus was indeed His Son" (R.V.G.Tasker). This reminds us that throughout Scripture, God takes the initiative in revealing Himself, through Christ, to men and women.

D) THE WORK OF THE FOUNDER, v.18
The Lord Jesus refers to His work in connection with the church as follows: *(a)* He is the foundation of the church; *(b)* He is the builder of the church; *(c)* He is the owner of the church; *(d)* He provides the security of the church.

a) He is the foundation of the the church
"And I say also unto thee, That thou art Peter, and upon **this** rock I will build my church; and the gates of hell shall not prevail against it". We must address the question: why does the Lord Jesus introduce the concept of the church at **this point?** We have noted the significance of the background, but why at **this point** in the conversation. Is it not to emphasise that there cannot possibly be failure? "On this **rock** (the truth of His deity as "the Son of the living God") I will build my church". This emphasises the solid, immoveable, immutable foundation on which the church rests. In saying, "this rock", the Lord Jesus uses a divine title. See Deuteronomy 32: "He is the **Rock**, his work is perfect" (v.4); "Jeshurun...lightly esteemed the **Rock** of his salvation"(v.15); "Of the **Rock** that beget thee thou art unmindful" (v.18); "How could one chase a thousand...except their **Rock** had sold them" (v.30); "Their rock is not as our **Rock**" (v.31). The security of the church does not rest on men - even the best of men - but on the Son of God. After all, John the Baptist, Elijah, and Jeremiah were all great men, but they all had deficiencies. How much more, popes, prelates, archbishops, and moderators!

We must take time to notice the actual words of the Lord Jesus: "Thou art

Peter, and upon this rock I will build my church". The name Peter ("thou art **Peter**") translates a masculine word (*petros*). It describes a detached stone or boulder, and refers to a stone that can be thrown or easily moved. See John 1: 42: "Thou art Simon the son of Jona: thou shalt be called Cephas, which is by interpretation, A stone". But the word "rock" ("and upon this **rock**") translates a feminine word (*petra*). It describes a mass of rock and occurs in the following: "a wise man...built his house upon a **rock**...it was founded upon a **rock**" (Matt. 7: 24-25); "his own new tomb, which he had hewn out of the **rock**" (Matt. 27: 60); "the **rocks** rent" (Matt. 27: 51). The word is used of the Lord Jesus elsewhere in the New Testament: "they drank of that spiritual **Rock** that followed them: and that **Rock** was Christ" (1 Cor. 10: 4); "a stone of stumbling and **rock** of offence" (1 Pet. 2: 8). The absurdity of Peter being the rock is stressed in v.23! He made that clear himself: see 1 Peter 2: 4-5.

It should be noted that the Lord said, "Upon **this rock**". He did not say, directly, 'Upon Me', but referred rather to the truth confessed by Peter: "Thou art the Christ, the Son of the living God." The church is built on the fact that He is "the Christ, the Son of the living God". Notice too, that it is **not** built on Christ as 'Son of man', but on Christ as '**Son of God**'. It is also worth noting the connection between the words *petros* and *petra*. We have differentiated between them, but the fact that the Lord Jesus used them closely together in one statement, "thou art Peter, and upon this rock I will build my church", is not without significance. There is a vital connection between a stone and a rock. A stone derives from the rock! There is a vital connection between Christ and His people. Believers are "built upon the foundation of the apostles and prophets, Jesus Christ himself being the chief corner stone" (Eph. 2: 20). We must remember that the apostles and prophets are not the foundation: they **laid** the foundation. See 1 Cor. 3: 11.

b) He is the builder of the church
The Lord Jesus is the builder. The tense should be noted: "I **will** build my church". The Lord had not yet commenced the work. He did not do so until the day of Pentecost, and then "**the Lord** added to the church daily such as should be saved" (Acts 2: 47). This is most important. In the parable of the wheat and tares, the Lord Jesus is specifically named as the Sower. "He that soweth the good seed is the Son of man; the field is the world: the good seed are **the children of the kingdom**" (Matt. 13: 37-38). We can sow the seed, but only the Lord Jesus can sow the "children of the kingdom". Similarly, He alone is the builder. Compare Ephesians 2: 21 "**In whom**

(Jesus Christ) all the building fitly framed together groweth unto an holy temple in the Lord: *in whom* ye also are *builded* together for an habitation of God through the Spirit". (It is worth noting that when it comes to the local church, building work is entrusted to preachers and teachers: see 1 Cor. 3: 10). Most certainly, "*a greater than Solomon is here*". Solomon built the temple. It was a wonderful edifice, but its builder had to say: "Behold, the heaven and the heaven of heavens cannot contain thee; how much less this house that *I have builded?*" (1 Kings 8: 27). Sadly, his temple was ultimately destroyed. But the church, "an holy temple in the Lord" (Eph. 2: 21), built by the Lord Jesus, will *never* be destroyed. The Lord Jesus is not only "greater than Solomon": He is "greater than *the temple*". The temple was the place where God dwelt: the Lord Jesus *is* God! The Jews said to the Lord Jesus, with reference to Herod's temple, "Forty and six years was this temple in building" (John 2: 20). The Lord Jesus has been building His church for two thousand years! His disciples drew His attention to the vast stones of the temple in Jerusalem: "Master, see what manner of stones and what buildings are here!". The Saviour answered, "Seest thou these great buildings? There shall not be left one stone upon another, that shall not be thrown down" (Mark 13: 1-2). (Compare Genesis 11: 4; Daniel 4: 30). But the stones in His temple, the church, will never be "thrown down!"

It has been nicely said (T.Miller) that as the Builder of the church, the Lord Jesus fully 'counted the cost' of His great enterprise. It will never be said of Him, "This man began to build, and was not able to finish". He knew the cost, and paid it all. Similarly, He is well able to keep His own against every mighty foe that "cometh" (Luke 14: 28-31): "the gates of hell" will not prevail against His church.

c) He is the owner of the church
"I will build *my* church". It belongs to *Him*! The expression "my church" suggests its preciousness to Christ, and takes us to Ephesians 5: 25, "Christ also loved the church, and gave himself for it". Its character is conveyed by the word "church" (*ekklesia*) meaning 'called-out'. The church comprises people 'called-out' in a variety of ways, including men and women from Jewish and Gentile backgrounds. Hence, "Give none offence, neither to the Jews, nor to the Gentiles, nor to the church of God" (1 Cor. 10: 32).

d) He provides the security of the church
The church enjoys divinely-given security: "And the gates of hell shall not prevail against it". In Scripture "gates" stand for power and authority, for

government and administration: we find, for example, Lot in the gate of Sodom, Boaz in the gate of Bethlehem, and the husband of the virtuous woman in the gate of the city. Since *hades* ("hell", AV) refers to 'the region of the departed spirits of the lost' (W.E.Vine), that is, to their **temporary** residence pending final judgment, the Lord is clearly stating that for His church death with its terrible consequence has no power. The word "prevail" means 'to be strong against', and it is strongly implied here that nothing could be stronger. According to the *Linguistic Key to the Greek New Testament*, it means 'to overpower, to have strength against, to gain mastery over'. The message is therefore clear: The very power to which all unregenerate men are subject, and which receives them all, will not prevail against the church. Believers, who comprise the church, will not enter hades. Its power against them has been annulled. In the words of William Kelly: 'The death of the Christian is in the hands of Christ".

We must notice, finally, the Lord's teaching in connection with the particular role of Peter where we have:

E) THE AUTHORITY OF PETER, v.19
The Lord Jesus taught that "whosoever shall confess me before men, him will I confess also before my Father which is in heaven" (Matt.10: 32: see also Luke 12: 8). He now applies that principle. Peter had confessed *Him*: now *He* confesses Peter.

Quite obviously, there is an important connection here with the foregoing teaching. The Lord builds: that is **His work**. Peter was to use keys: that was **his work**. We should notice in this connection that this was Peter's **particular** ministry. The plural "ye" occurs in v.15, and the plural "they" in v.20: But Peter is here addressed **alone**: "And I will give unto **thee** the keys of the kingdom of heaven: and whatsoever *thou* shalt bind on earth shall be bound in heaven: and whatsoever *thou* shalt loose on earth shall be loosed in heaven". This particular work was therefore peculiar to Peter. What was that work?

Peter did not have 'the keys of the church'. Keys are not used for building! Keys are used for opening, and for closing. Peter was given "the keys of the kingdom of heaven". We could say that he opened the way to God and to heaven. This stands in direct contrast to the religious leaders: "But woe unto you, scribes and Pharisees, hypocrites! For ye **shut up the kingdom of heaven against men:** for ye neither go in yourselves, neither suffer ye them that are entering to go in" (Matt. 23: 13). Compare Luke 11: 52, "Woe unto you, lawyers! For ye have taken away **the key of knowledge**: ye entered not in yourselves, and them that were entering ye hindered". But Peter, with "the key of knowledge", would enable men and women to enter "the kingdom of heaven". Peter could not build the church, that is the Lord's work **alone,** but he was given the privilege of declaring, on two special occasions, how men and women could experience the blessings of divine rule in their hearts and lives. The very expression "kingdom of heaven" (or "kingdom of God": notice how both expressions are used in 19: 23-24) is indicative of divine rule. Through Peter's preaching, men and women heard how they could enter the "kingdom of heaven", and having responded to the message, they were added by the Lord to the church. "Keys" are associated with authority: see Isaiah 22: 22 (cited in Rev. 3: 7), "And the key of the house of David will I lay upon his shoulder; so he shall open, and none shall shut; and he shall shut, and none shall open". (As C.I.Scofield points out, this did not involve "the determination of the eternal destiny of souls. The keys of death and the place of departed spirits are held by Christ alone, Rev. 1: 18"). The question therefore arises: when did Peter use these "keys?"

Bearing in mind that the church comprises Jews and Gentiles, it was Peter who first brought before Jew and Gentile, in that order, the glorious opportunity of entering God's kingdom. He did this on two momentous occasions.

- To the **Jew** on the day of Pentecost in Acts 2. "Repent, and be baptised every one of you in the name of Jesus Christ for the remission of sins, and ye shall receive the gift of the Holy Ghost. For the promise is to you, and to your children, and to all that are afar off, even as many as the Lord shall call. And with many other words did he testify and exhort, saying, Save yourselves from this untoward generation. Then they that gladly received his word were baptised: and the same day there were added unto them about three thousand souls" (Acts 2: 37-41). Through Peter's preaching men and women entered "the kingdom of heaven": something that Pharisees, scribes and lawyers could never accomplish. Peter used "the keys" in Jerusalem. He used the "key of knowledge", which was, "Whosoever shall call on the name of the Lord shall be saved" (Acts 2: 21).

- To the **Gentile** at Caesarea in Acts 10. "Through his name whosoever believeth in him shall receive remission of sins" (Acts 10: 43). "Forasmuch then as God gave them the like gift as he did unto us, who believed on the

Lord Jesus Christ; what was I, that I could withstand God? When they heard these things, they held their peace, and glorified God, saying, Then hath God also to the Gentiles granted repentance unto life" (Acts 11: 18). Peter used "the keys" at Caesarea (not, in this case, Caesarea Philippi).

Quite clearly, the words that follow, "and whatsoever ***thou*** shalt bind on earth shall be bound in heaven: and whatsoever ***thou*** shalt loose on earth shall be loosed in heaven", are connected with the preaching of Peter. Notice, again, the singular: "thou". We should notice the tense here. According to the *Linguistic Key to the Greek New Testament,* the original reads, literally, 'Whatsoever thou shalt bind on earth ***will have been bound*** in heaven: and whatsoever thou shalt loose on earth ***will have been loosed*** in heaven'. It is a case of carrying out heaven's decisions, rather than heaven ratifying human decisions.

Bearing in mind the personal commission to Peter, the words 'binding' and loosing' evidently have particular reference to those two occasions. But why 'binding' and 'loosing?' The figure of binding is used in connection with preparation for judgment. See Acts 22: 4; Matthew 13: 30; 22: 13. 'Binding' and 'loosing' are also mentioned in Matthew 18: 18 . In this case 'binding' again refers to judgment in the sense of church discipline (excommunication). Loosing, obviously, is the reverse: restoration after repentance. See 1 Cor. 5: 4-5; 2 Cor. 2: 6-8.

- Peter preached 'binding' and 'loosing' on the day of Pentecost, when he "opened the door of Christian opportunity to Israel" (C.I.Scofield). As to ***binding:*** "And it shall come to pass that every soul, which will not hear that prophet, shall be destroyed from among the people" (Acts 3: 23). Peter proclaimed the sentence, already passed by heaven, on those who reject the word of God. As to ***loosing:*** "Repent and be baptised every one of you in the name of Jesus Christ for the remission of sins" (Acts 2: 38). Peter proclaimed the blessing, already decided in heaven, on those who received the word of God.

- Peter preached 'binding' and 'loosing' at Caesarea when the Gentile audience was told that God had ordained the Lord Jesus to be "the Judge of quick and dead" and that "To him give all the prophets witness, that through his name whosoever believeth in him shall receive remission of sins" (Acts 10: 42-43). Men are bound or loosed in connection with their rejection or acceptance of salvation.

Chapter 16

"Then charged he his disciples that they should tell no man that he was Jesus the Christ" (v.20). This was judicial. Israel had rejected her Messiah, and further opportunity – for the present – was withdrawn. This, together with the verse following, represents what J.S.Stewart calls "the watershed of the Gospels" (quoted by Wm.MacDonald). The revelation of the commencement of the church is therefore preceded and followed by reference to the Lord's rejection by Israel. Before Him lay the cross, and He brings this before His disciples in the final section of this chapter.

"Whosoever will save his life shall lose it"

Read Matthew 16: 21-28
As we have already suggested, this chapter may be divided as follows: *(1)* the sign of Jonas (vv.1-4); *(2)* the significance of leaven (vv.5-12); *(3)* the start of the church (vv.13-20); *(4)* the suffering at Jerusalem (vv.21-28).

1) THE SIGN OF JONAS, vv.1-4
Having told the sign-seeking Pharisees and Sadducees that "A wicked and adulterous generation seeketh after a sign", the Lord added "and there shall no sign be given unto it, but the sign of the prophet Jonas", following which "he left them and departed" (v.4). See John 1:11.

2) THE SIGNIFICANCE OF LEAVEN, vv.5-12
Following this incident, the Lord warned His disciples to "Take heed and beware of the leaven of the Pharisees and of the Sadducees" (v.6), and they eventually "understood…that he bade them not beware of the leaven of bread, but of the doctrine of the Pharisees and of the Sadducees" (v.12).

3) THE START OF THE CHURCH, vv.13-20
The Lord's rejection by the nation, so clearly expressed in Chapter 12 where the Pharisees "held a council against him, how they might destroy him (v.14), and accused him of casting out demons "by Beelzebub the prince of the devils (demons)" (v.24), following which, significantly, He "went…out of the house (13: 1)…departed into the coasts of Tyre and Sidon (15: 21)…left them and departed" (16: 4), forms the background to His announcement, "I will build my church; and the gates of hell shall not prevail against it" (16: 18).

Having said this, "Then charged he his disciples that they should tell no man that he was Jesus the Christ ('that he was the Christ', JND)" (16: 20). As Wm. Kelly rightly observes, "Forbidding the disciples to tell that He was the

Christ is the turning point in Christ's ministry". He had been "rejected as the Christ - the Messiah, the Anointed of Jehovah. He is refused by Israel, and He accepts the fact". Before Him lay the cross, and He brings this before His disciples in the final section of this chapter. We come, therefore, to:

4) THE SUFFERING AT JERUSALEM, vv.21-28

These verses contrast vividly with the preceding section. Although He is the Christ, the Son of God, He had come to die, and Matthew emphasises that the Lord's reference here to His death and resurrection marks a new stage in His teaching: "From that time forth began Jesus to shew unto His disciples, how that he must go unto Jerusalem, and suffer many things of the elders and chief priests and scribes, and be killed, and be raised again the third day" (v.21). Compare: "From that time Jesus began to preach, and to say, Repent: for the kingdom of heaven is at hand" (4: 17). The two verses (4: 17; 16: 21) taken together are immensely significant: they signal the commencement and conclusion of the Lord's public offer of the kingdom to Israel.

These verses therefore signify the beginning of a new testimony based, not on His acceptance as King, but on His death and resurrection. It was therefore necessary to adjust the disciples' thinking. Peter had said, "Thou art the Christ". He anticipated the kingdom. But the Lord now shows that He - Israel's Messiah - would go to Jerusalem, not to be crowned, but to be crucified. Parallel passages are found in Mark 8: 31-38 and Luke 9: 21-26.

This section of the chapter may be divided as follows: *(A)* the Lord's immediate future (vv.21-23); *(B)* the disciples' ongoing future (vv.24-26); *(C)* the Lord's ultimate future (vv.27-28).

A) The Lord's immediate future, vv.21-23

It should be noted that while the Lord anticipated His death, this was far from Peter's mind. These verses therefore present a contrast between the way in which the Lord saw the future (v.21) and the way in which Peter saw the future (vv.22-23).

a) How the Lord saw the future, v.21

Hitherto, the Lord Jesus had made veiled references to His coming death. See for example: "the days will come, when the bridegroom shall be taken from them (that is from the disciples, called "the children of the bridechamber"), and then shall they fast" (9: 15); "For as Jonas was three days and three nights in the whale's belly; so shall the Son of man be three days and three nights in the heart of the earth" (12: 40). Now he foretells His death in unmistakable terms.

It may be worth pointing out that both Mark and Luke tell us that in predicting His coming suffering the Lord Jesus described himself as the "Son of man": "And he began to teach them, that the Son of man must suffer many things" (Mark 8: 31); "The Son of man must suffer many things" (Luke 9: 22). Matthew does not use this title at this particular point. Significantly, he alone records Peter's statement in full, "Thou art the Christ, the Son of the living God" (v.16), and then tells us that the Lord said, "and upon this rock I will build my church" (v.18). Mark and Luke, who emphasise His title as "Son of man", say nothing about the church. The church is built on Christ as "the Son of the living God" rather than on "the Son of man", which describes the Lord Jesus in His relationship with earth. Returning now to the immediate passage, we should note the following:

i) **The necessity for His death and resurrection.** "From that time forth began Jesus to shew unto His disciples, how that he *must* go unto Jerusalem, and suffer many things...and be killed, and be raised again the third day". Compare John 3: 14: "And as Moses lifted up the serpent in the wilderness, even so *must* the Son of man be lifted up". (The occurrences of "must" in the Gospels make a profitable study). The Lord was "delivered by the determinate counsel and foreknowledge of God" (Acts 2: 23). Amongst the necessity for the Lord's death and resurrection is the fact that "the scripture cannot be broken" (John 10: 35). Hence "Christ died for our sins according to the scriptures...he was buried, and...rose again the third day according to the scriptures" (1 Cor. 15: 3-4), to which we must add that He must die and rise from the dead because salvation was not possible in any other way. We sing:

> *There was no other good enough*
> *To pay the price of sin.*
> *He only could unlock the gate*
> *Of heaven, and let us in.*

Further, "he must go to Jerusalem...and be killed, and raised again the third day" because it was essential for the establishment of the kingdom as well as the church. As we have seen, the kingdom had not been abandoned, but its public manifestation had been deferred until God's eternal purpose for the church is accomplished. But the foundation on which the kingdom will be established is the death and resurrection of the King.

In this connection, we should notice that in his parallel record, Mark adds something omitted elsewhere: "And he spake that saying **openly**" (Mark 8: 32). This is important. It expresses the certainty and conviction of the Lord Jesus. Compare John 18:19-21.

*ii) **The certainty of His death and resurrection.*** The Lord Jesus did not deal in assumptions and speculations. Suffering did not come as a surprise to Him. There was never any question about the matter. "The Son of man **shall** be betrayed into the hands of men: and they **shall** kill him, and the third day he **shall** be raised again" (Matt. 17: 22-23); "Behold, we go up to Jerusalem, and the Son of man **shall** be betrayed unto the chief priests and unto the scribes, and they **shall** condemn him to death, and **shall** deliver him to the Gentiles to mock, and to scourge, and to crucify him: and the third day he **shall** rise again" (Matt. 20: 18-19).

*iii) **The foreknowledge of His death and resurrection.*** The fact that He knew in advance what was shortly to happen, did not deter the Lord from making the journey to Jerusalem, and emphasises His resolution and determination. Peter tells us that the Lord Jesus was fully aware of the cruel death that awaited Him. He refers to "the prophets" who "inquired and searched diligently…searching what, or what manner of time the Spirit of Christ which was in them did signify, when it testified beforehand ('testifying beforehand', JND) the sufferings of Christ, and the glory that should follow", and continues "who verily was foreordained (as the Lamb of God) before the foundation of the world" (1 Pet. 1: 10-11, 20).

*b) **How Peter saw the future, vv.22-23***
"Then Peter took him, and began to rebuke him (*epitimao*: an intensive word with 'overtones of persistence and vehemence'), saying, Be it far from thee, Lord; this shall not be unto thee" (v.22) or "[God] be favourable to thee, Lord; this shall in no wise be unto thee" (JND). This might be literally rendered: 'God be propitious to thee'. The RV margin has 'God have mercy on thee'; Luther translates with 'God forbid'; Lightfoot with 'Nay, verily' or 'away with the thought'. The whole idea horrified Peter. He did not look at the future in that way at all. As we have noticed, Peter thought in terms of the ***crown***, not in terms of the ***cross***. (Peter's perception was completely altered by the time He came to write his first letter where he refers to suffering and

glory in that order). We must now listen to the Lord's reply: "But he turned, and said unto Peter, Get thee behind me, Satan (compare Matt. 4: 10): for thou art an offence (or 'stumblingblock') unto me: for thou savourest not (from *phroneo*, to think: hence 'mindest not', RV) the things that be of God, but those that be of man" (v.23). (Compare v.17 where "the things" of man – "flesh and blood" - are contrasted with "the things of God - "my Father"). The Lord perceived a snare laid for him by Satan. According to Mark, "But when he had turned about and looked on His disciples (as if to warn them against saying the same as Peter), he rebuked Peter, saying, Get thee behind me, Satan..." (Mark 8: 33).

It hardly seems possible that this is the very man who said, "Thou art the Christ, the Son of the living God" (v.16). In the words of R.V.G.Tasker, citing 1 Pet.2: 8, "the Rock had become (to Peter) a stone of stumbling, and a rock of offence". The man who had soared to spiritual heights ("Thou art the Christ, the Son of the living God"), now makes a grave blunder, reminding us of the warning, "let him that thinketh he standeth take heed lest he fall" (1 Cor.10: 12). We must all take heed.

The name, "Satan", means 'adversary'. In attempting to dissuade the Lord Jesus from suffering and death, Peter had unwittingly become a channel for Satanic opposition. Bearing in mind that the Lord had taken "flesh and blood" in order "that through death he might destroy him that had the power of death, that is, the devil; and deliver them who through fear of death were all their lifetime subject to bondage" (Heb.2: 14-15), it is not surprising that Satan should endeavour to prevent the Lord's death, since that would mean the end of his dominion. Whilst it seemed very noble of Peter to speak in this way, he little knew what he was actually doing. As Wm.Kelly observes, "was it not for Peter that He was going there (to the cross)? Had Peter thought of this, would he have said, 'Be it far from thee, Lord"?. The Amplified Version puts it as follows: "Get behind me, Satan, For you do not have a mind intent on promoting what God wills, but what pleases men!" We must not think that by calling Peter "Satan", the Lord implied that the apostle, like Judas (John 6: 70; 13: 27), was indwelt and controlled by Satan: rather that Peter's actions and words were what could be expected of Satan.

B) The disciples' ongoing future, vv.24-26
The Lord now explains the position of His disciples with reference to His rejection. They would not, as yet, be associated with Him in the glory of

His kingdom: they must first share the suffering of His rejection: "Then said Jesus unto his disciples, If any man will come after me, let him deny himself, and take up his cross, and follow me" (v.24). We should notice that the Lord does not say here, 'If any man will come *to* me', but "If any man will come *after* me". Mark particularly mentions the fact that the Saviour addressed non-disciples and disciples alike (Mark 8: 34). Whether saved or unsaved people are involved., the cost of following Christ needs to be spelt out in detail. The introductory word, "Then", links the Lord's sufferings at the hands of men with the suffering of those who follow Him. He would be rejected by the world (v.21) - and so would they.

i) **"Let him deny himself".** (Initially, Peter denied Him). This is in the aorist tense: an action involving a definite decision. Moses is a good illustration: He "refused to be called the son of Pharaoh's daughter (so **position in Egypt** did not attract him); choosing rather to suffer affliction with the people of God, than to enjoy the pleasures of sin for a season (so **pleasure in Egypt** did not attract him); esteeming the reproach of Christ greater riches than the treasures in Egypt (so **prosperity in Egypt** did not attract him): for he had respect unto the recompence of the reward" (Heb. 11: 24-26). Do remember that the Lord does not require something of His disciples which He has not supplied Himself. He 'denied Himself': see, for example Phil. 2: 1-8.

ii) **"Let him...take up his cross".** (Initially, Peter forsook Him). Again, the aorist tense. A man carrying his cross was potentially dead. That man did not come back. He was severing his connection with this world. He had no future in this world. R.H.Mounce puts it clearly: "For a person to carry his or her cross means to accept the sentence of death on all personal ambitions and goals". The truth is expounded in Galatians 2: 20; 5: 24; 6: 14.

iii) **"Let him...follow me".** (Initially, Peter "stood with them", John 18: 18). This is in the continuous tense. It means, in general, that we go where He leads. It means that we listen when He speaks. It means that we obey when He commands. It means, in particular, bearing in mind the context, "not merely that He is going to the cross, but they must be prepared to follow Him there" (Wm. Kelly).

With this in mind, the Saviour spells out the alternatives. Notice that He does not describe discipleship as a hobby or pastime, but as life itself:

a) "Whosoever will save his life", v.25a

As already noticed, the Lord's teaching here is applicable to both unregenerate men and to disciples. "For whosoever will save his life (*psuche*) shall lose it". This is explained in v.26, "For what is a man profited, if he shall gain the whole world, and lose his own soul (*psuche*)? Or what shall a man give in exchange for his soul (*psuche*)?" We can put our own interests first. That is, opt out of the reproach of Christ and, in His own words, "be ashamed of me and of my words in this adulterous and sinful generation". In the **short term**, we may appear to do extremely well out of it, and "gain the whole world". But in **the long term,** we will do extremely badly: the whole of life is lost, because there has been nothing for God. See 1 Corinthians 3: 15. What is more, we cannot have life back for a second attempt, for "what shall a man give in exchange for his soul? ('in exchange for his life?')". This will be made terribly clear when Christ returns: "for the Son of man shall come in the glory of his Father with his angels; and then he shall reward every man according to his works" (v.27). Or, according to Mark, "Whosoever therefore shall be ashamed of me and of my words in this adulterous and sinful generation; of him also shall the Son of man be ashamed, when he cometh in the glory of His Father with the holy angels" (Mark 8: 38). Luke has: "of him shall the Son of man be ashamed, when he shall come in his own glory, and in his Father's, and of the holy angels" (Luke 9: 26).

John Heading points out that 'The rich man in Luke 16: 19 gained his life but then lost it in *hades*. The rich farmer gained more and more as great profit, but lost his soul in one night having laid up treasure for himself (Luke 12: 16-21). The rich young man in Matthew 19: 16-22 had "great possessions", but as far as we can assess he lost his own soul, going away sorrowful'. John Heading adds, "Believers also cannot trifle with their lives, for "ye are not your own...ye are bought with a price" (1 Cor. 6: 19-20).

b) "Whosoever shall lose his life", vv.25b-26

"And whosoever will lose his life for my sake shall find it". Mark has, "but whosoever shall lose his life for my sake and the gospel's, the same shall save it" (Mark 8: 35). That is, we can put Christ's interests first, and respond to His words, "Follow me". In the **short term**, we may appear to do extremely badly out of it. After all, by human standards, there doesn't seem to be much future in heeding His words, "let him deny himself, and take up his cross". But in the **long term**, there could be no better way to use our lives. See Philippians 1: 21 ("For to me to live is Christ, and to die is gain"); 3: 4-8 ("But what things were gain to me, those I counted loss for

Christ. Yea, doubtless, and I count all things but loss for the excellency of the knowledge of Christ Jesus my Lord: for whom I have suffered the loss of all things, and do count them but dung, that I may win Christ"). This will be made abundantly clear when Christ returns, see 2 Timothy 4: 6-8. In the words of C.T.Studd:

> *Oh let my love with fervour burn,*
> *And from the world now let me turn;*
> *Living for Thee, and Thee alone,*
> *Bringing Thee pleasure on Thy throne;*
> *Only one life, 'twill soon be past:*
> *Only what's done for Christ will last.*

It has also been said:
> *Live for self, you live in vain;*
> *Live for Christ, you live again;*
> *Live with Him – with Him you reign;*
> *Pass it on.*

We should add that believers who are prepared to 'lose' their lives now will enjoy an unsurpassed quality of life *now*, let alone in the future. Eternal life is a quality of life: "This is life eternal, that they might know thee the only true God, and Jesus Christ, whom thou hast sent" (John 17: 3).

C) The Lord's ultimate future, vv.27-28
The final verses of the chapter refer to the public return of Christ to earth to reign. This is clear from the Lord's title, "the Son of man". The Lord Jesus does not here develop truth concerning the heavenly calling of the church. He told His disciples, "I have yet many things to say unto you, but ye cannot bear them now. Howbeit when he the Spirit of truth is come, he will guide you into all truth" (John 16: 12-13). The unique calling, character, and destiny of the church were ultimately revealed through the apostle Paul, particularly in the letter to the Ephesians. Rewards for faithful service now will be bestowed at the judgment seat of Christ, and displayed in Christ's kingdom.

How beautifully then the Lord Jesus adjusted the disciples' thinking. Peter had said, "Thou art the Christ", only to discover that His Master anticipated a cross rather than a crown. But "Christ crucified" (1 Cor.1: 23) would most certainly be 'Christ glorified!' This would take place not so soon as Peter anticipated, but the Lord Jesus will be glorified on earth none the less when

He comes "in the glory of his Father with his angels" (v.27). See Matthew 24: 30; 26: 64; 2 Thess. 1: 7-10. The words, "in the glory of his power (Father)", rather than 'in His own glory', suggest that His coming, amongst other things, will be the Father's public answer to His beloved Son's public sufferings.

But could His disciples be certain about His coming? In order to assure them that the future was secure, the Lord Jesus gave them a preview: "Verily I say unto you, There be some standing here, which shall not taste of death, till they see the Son of man coming in his kingdom" (v.28), and this was explained some six days later when "Jesus taketh Peter, James, and John his brother, and bringeth them up into an high mountain apart, and was transfigured before them: and his face did shine as the sun, and his raiment was white as the light" (17: 1-2). Peter was in no doubt that the three apostles saw "the Son of man coming in his kingdom" on the 'mount of transfiguration': "For we have not followed cunningly devised fables, when we made known unto you the power and coming of our Lord Jesus Christ (that is, His second coming), but were eyewitnesses of his majesty" (2 Pet. 1: 16).

THE GOSPEL OF MATTHEW

"Jesus...was transfigured before them"

Read Chapter 17: 1-13
The introduction to this chapter lies at the end of Chapter 16: "Verily I say unto you, There be some standing here, which shall not taste of death, till they see the Son of man coming in his kingdom" (v.28). Mark has, "till they have seen the kingdom of God (compare Luke 9: 27) come with power" (Mark 9: 1-3). By using the expression, "come with power" (JND 'in power'), the Lord Jesus emphasised the public inauguration of the kingdom, as opposed to its present character in which it "cometh not with outward show" (Luke 17: 20-21). They did not have long to wait! Matthew continues, "And after six days Jesus taketh Peter, James, and John his brother, and bringeth them up into an high mountain apart, and was transfigured before them: and his face did shine as the sun, and his raiment was white as the light" (17: 1-2).

Whilst Matthew and Mark say, "And after six days" (Matt 17: 1; Mark 9: 2), Luke says "***About*** an eight days after these sayings" (Luke 9: 28). In all probability, Luke is counting inclusively, that is, he is including the day of the conversation and the day of the transfiguration. Commentators point out that six is the number of man, and that after 'six days' of human failure, Christ will inaugurate His kingdom. Similarly, eight is the number associated with a new beginning, and the inauguration of the kingdom will be a new beginning in human affairs.

Clearly the Lord Jesus did not infer that some in His audience would not die until He returned to establish His kingdom. He meant, rather, that they would see beforehand His glory as King (Matt. 16: 27). Peter confirmed the connection between the return of Christ and His transfiguration in writing: "For we have not followed cunningly devised fables, when we made known unto you the power and coming of our Lord Jesus Christ (that is, His second coming), but were eye-witnesses of his majesty. For he received from God the Father honour and glory, when there came such a voice to him from the excellent glory, This is my beloved Son, in whom I am well pleased. And this voice which came from heaven we heard, **when we were with Him in the holy mount"** (2 Pet. 1: 16-18).

Bearing this in mind, the chapter may be divided as follows: *(1)* the Lord's transfiguration on the mount (vv.1-9); (2) the Lord's clarification of Elijah's coming (vv.10-13); *(3)* the Lord's explanation of deficient power (vv.14-21); *(4)* the Lord's anticipation of His death and resurrection (vv.22-23); *(5)* the Lord's participation in payment of the tribute (vv.24-27).

1) THE LORD'S TRANSFIGURATION ON THE MOUNT, vv.1-9

Of these verses it may be truly said, "the well is deep!" All we can do is to make some suggestions for further study and meditation. We must at least consider: *(a)* the men He chose (v.1); *(b)* the majesty He displayed (v.2); *(c)* the ministry of Moses and Elijah (v.3); *(d)* the mistake of Peter (vv.4-8); *(e)* the mandate to the disciples (v.9).

a) The men He chose, v.1

Peter, James and John were given the privilege of witnessing the transfiguration, just as they had already witnessed the raising of Jairus' daughter (Mark 5: 41) and would witness His suffering in Gethsemane (Matt. 26: 36-37). We know from Scripture that all three suffered for their loyalty to Christ: for Peter, see John 21: 18-19; for James, see Acts 12: 1-2; for John, see Rev 1: 9. The Lord Jesus spoke about the suffering of Peter (John 21: 18-19), and of James and John (Matt 20: 20-23), and gave them here the assurance that nothing could thwart His ultimate triumph. We must not forget that although it often appears that God is losing ground against the forces of evil, the time is coming when "great voices in heaven" will proclaim that the "kingdoms of this world are become the kingdoms of our Lord, and of his Christ; and he shall reign for ever and ever (or 'The kingdom of the world of our Lord and of his Christ is come', JND)" (Rev 11: 15).

b) The majesty He displayed, vv.1-2

In this connection, we should notice *(i)* why it was displayed; *(ii)* where it was displayed; *(iii)* when it was displayed; *(iv)* how it was displayed.

i) Why it was displayed.

The context provides the answer. Preceding chapters have stressed the rejection of the Lord Jesus. He had come "unto his own, and his own received him not". For example, "the Pharisees went out and held a council against him, how they might destroy him" (Matt. 12: 14).

Matthew

The murderous intentions of the Pharisees were followed by the accusation that He cast out "devils (demons)...by Beelzebub the prince of the devils" (12: 24). In a further attempt to discredit Him, the scribes and Pharisees then requested a sign (12: 38), following which, significantly, the Lord "went out of the house (an apt picture of Israel), and sat by the sea side (an apt picture of the Gentile nations)" (13: 1). The religious leaders did not lessen their hostility: in Chapter 15, they accused His disciples of transgressing "the tradition of the elders" (v.2), and were "offended" at the Lord's reply (v.12): in Chapter 16, they masked their true intentions by asking, again, for "a sign from heaven" (v.1), which led the Saviour to warn His disciples against "the leaven of the Pharisees and of the Sadducees" (v.11).

Moreover, the Saviour anticipated the time when the murderous desire of the Pharisees would be fulfilled (Matt. 16: 21). The nation would ultimately reject their King with the cry "We have no king but Caesar" (John 19: 15), and mock Him with the words, "If he be the King of Israel, let him come down from the cross, and we will believe him" (Matt. 27: 42). But two disillusioned and dispirited disciples were told, "Ought not Christ to have suffered these things, and to enter into his glory?" (Luke 24: 26). The day will come when God will say, "Yet have I set my king upon my holy hill of Zion" (Psalm 2: 6). The Lord's transfiguration foreshadows His glory on earth. The fact that "his face did shine as the sun" has strong Messianic connections: "But unto you that fear my name shall the Sun of righteousness arise with healing in his wings" (Mal. 4: 2). The fact that "his raiment was white as the light" suggests His moral gory: "raiment" is indicative of character. See, for example, Rev. 19: 8.

*ii) **Where it was displayed**.* It was on "an high mountain apart". The identity of the mountain is uncertain. Tradition assigns the transfiguration to Tabor (approximately 1800 feet), but others feel that it was more likely to have been Hermon (approximately 9000 feet), which was nearer Caesarea Philippi. The important thing to remember is that we can only enjoy the glory of Christ when we rise above the level of this world in order to be alone with Him. How necessary to be "apart" with Him!.

*iii) **When it was displayed**.* In all probability (although we are not specifically told), the transfiguration took place at night. Luke tells us that "Peter and they that were with him were heavy with sleep" and continues, "And it came to pass, that on **the next day,** when they were come down from the hill ('mountain', JND)" (Luke 9: 32, 37). If so, then it is very appropriate that the glory of Christ should be seen against the background of this world's darkness. His glorious kingdom will be established in a very dark world.

iv) How it was displayed. Matthew and Mark say, "And he was transfigured before them". The word here *(metamorphoo)* stresses change from within, and stands in direct contrast to outward change alone. Compare 2 Cor 11: 14; "For such are false apostles, deceitful workers, **transforming themselves** *(metaschematizo)* into the apostles of Christ". The use of *metamorphoo* is therefore most important: the essential and intrinsic glory of Christ shone through His body, and through His clothing. The same word is used of believers in Rom 12: 2 ("transformed") and 2 Cor 3: 18 ("changed"). Both passages emphasise that the change is effected from within: it is not cosmetic. Moses radiated the glory of God which he beheld in the tabernacle, (Exodus 34: 29-35), but the Lord Jesus displayed His own glory.

Luke alone tells us that the transfiguration took place as the Lord prayed: "And as he prayed, the fashion of his countenance was altered, and his raiment was white and glistering" (Luke 9: 29). It is significant that He "went up into a mountain to pray. And as he prayed..." So often we intend to pray, and then do something else! Luke emphasises the Lord's prayer life. He presents Him as the perfect, dependent man. The word "glistering" *(astrapto)* is used of lightning in Luke 17: 24, and has been explained as, 'to emit flashes of light, to shine or glister as lightning' (quoted by J.C.Ryle). Mark refers particularly to the Lord's clothing: "His raiment became shining, exceeding white as snow; so as no fuller (laundryman) on earth can white them" (Mark 9: 3).

c) The ministry of Moses and Elijah, v.3
"And, behold, there appeared unto them Moses and Elijah talking with him". Their presence is deeply significant, and can be understood in different ways:

i) **The role of Moses and Elijah.** Moses was the lawgiver: "the law was given by Moses" (John 1: 17). Elijah was the great prophet of the Old Testament. They stood therefore for the law and the prophets respectively. But we find them here in the presence of the very Christ who fulfilled both the law and prophecy: "But now the righteousness of God without the law is manifested, being witnessed by **the law** and **the prophets**" (Rom 3: 21). Moses and Elijah had occupied places of vast importance, and considerable drama. Both occupied centre stage. We have only to think of Moses on

Mount Sinai and Elijah on Mount Carmel. But now, on another mountain, **Christ is pre-eminent**.

ii) The service of Moses and Elijah. Scripture records only one blot on the record of **Moses'** service: he failed to sanctify God in the eyes of the children of Israel: see Num 20: 10-12; Psalm 106: 32-33. He was replaced, after forty years, by Joshua. Scripture records only one blot on the record of **Elijah's** service. He became a complaining servant: "I have been very jealous for the Lord God of hosts...they seek my life, to take it away" (1 Kings 19: 14). He was replaced after "forty days and forty nights" by Elisha. **But the perfect Servant needed no replacement**. There was no failure in His service.

iii) The desires of Moses and Elijah. Moses was the man who would have loved to *live,* and enter the land, but he died. Elijah was the man who desired to *die* (1 Kings 19: 4), but he has never died! Both are found in the company of the Lord Jesus who said, "I am he that liveth and was dead ('became dead', JND); and, behold, I am alive for evermore, Amen" (Rev. 1: 18).

iii) The departure of Moses and Elijah. Matthew simply says, "Moses and Elias talking with him" (compare Mark 9: 4), but Luke goes further: "they spake of his decease (his exodus) which he should accomplish at Jerusalem" (Luke 9: 31). Both Moses and Elijah left this world in a remarkable way. **Moses:** "So Moses the servant of the Lord died there in the land of Moab according to the word of the Lord. And *he* buried him in a valley in the land of Moab over against Beth-Peor: but no man knoweth of his sepulchre unto this day" (Deut 34: 5-6). **Elijah** "went up by a whirlwind into heaven" (2 Kings 2: 11). But they did not speak of the exodus of either Moses or Elijah: "They spake of *his* decease (*exodus:* the same word occurs in 2 Pet 1:15 and Heb 11: 22) which he should accomplish at Jerusalem". (The Bible also refers to His *eisodos,* His 'coming in', Acts 13: 24).

Unlike the Lord Jesus, neither Moses nor Elijah accomplished their own departure! The Lord Jesus was in perfect control of His own death ("his decease...which *he* should accomplish"). His death could not be hastened, and it could not be delayed. It must take place at the appointed time, and in the appointed place ("which he should accomplish *at Jerusalem*").

iv) The representative position of Moses and Elijah. Bearing in mind that the mount of transfiguration provides a picture of the coming kingdom, Moses and Elijah, both glorified, have a representative role. However, we must begin with the Lord Jesus:

- **Christ will be pre-eminent in the coming kingdom.** His face will "shine as the sun" and His raiment will be "white as the light". He will come "with power and great glory" (Matt. 24: 30)

- **Moses was in glory via death, and Elijah was in glory apart from death** (they "appeared in glory", Luke 9: 31), reminding us that when the Lord comes, "the dead in Christ shall rise first: then we which are alive and remain shall be caught up together with them in the clouds, to meet the Lord in the air: and so shall we ever be with the Lord" (1 Thess 4: 16-17). What will we all talk about? The great theme of conversation in the kingdom will be the work of Christ: we will "speak of *his* decease". See Rev 5: 9-10.

- **Peter, James and John can also be regarded as representative men.** Unlike Moses and Elijah, they are not glorified, and describe Israel on earth during the millennial reign.

- **The multitude at the foot of the mountain represent the nations of the world** which will benefit from the power of Christ.

d) The mistake of Peter, vv.4-8
"Then answered Peter, and said unto Jesus, Lord, it is good for us to be here: if thou wilt, let us make here three tabernacles; one for thee, and one for Moses, and one for Elias" (v.4). Luke gives us a little more detail: "But Peter and they that were with him were heavy with sleep: and when they were awake ('having fully woke up', JND), they saw his glory, and the two men that stood with him. And it came to pass, as they departed from him, Peter said unto Jesus, Master, it is good for us to be here: and let us make three tabernacles; one for thee, and one for Moses, and one for Elias: not knowing what he said" (Luke 9: 32-33), or according to Mark, "For he wist not what to say; for they were sore afraid" (Mark 9: 6). Norman Crawford speaks for us all in saying that the 'sleep of Peter, James and John under such circumstances is very difficult for us to understand'. Only Luke refers to the sleep of the disciples here. They also slept in Gethsemane (Luke 22: 45-46). We should notice:

i) What Peter said. He unwittingly placed Moses and Elijah on the same level as the Lord Jesus: "let us make here three tabernacles; one for thee, and one for Moses, and one for Elias" (v.4), with Luke adding, "not knowing what he said". But we must not be too severe on Peter. He did put the Lord first, and he rightly understood the significance of the occasion. It was most certainly a picture of the coming kingdom (Matt. 16: 28), and Peter came to the conclusion that it had actually arrived. He therefore concluded that Israel had reached that happy stage prefigured by the Old Testament feast of tabernacles. This was the "feast of ingathering at the year's end" (Exodus 34: 22), when the children of Israel were to dwell in booths, and anticipated deliverance from all enemies. It was a time of rejoicing (Lev 23: 40) after national regathering (the feast of trumpets) and repentance (the day of atonement).

Peter, having glimpsed the glory of the Lord Jesus, said, "it is good for us to be here", but what will *we* say when we behold His glory, and enjoy the fulfilment of the Lord's desire for His people: "Father, I will that they also whom thou hast given me, be with me where I am; that they may behold my glory" (John 17: 24)?

*ii) **What God said.*** "While he yet spake, behold, a bright cloud (compare Rev. 10: 1) overshadowed them (apparently referring to the Lord, Moses and Elijah, and the three disciples): and behold a voice out of the cloud, which said, This is my beloved Son, in whom I am well pleased ('In whom I have found all my delight', JND); hear ye him" (v.5). Bearing in mind that the transfiguration scene depicts the coming kingdom, this has added significance. When the Lord Jesus was on earth, and down to the present day, men failed to recognise that He was the Son of God, and refused to obey His voice. They will do both when He reigns.

Quite clearly, it was no ordinary cloud: "And there came a voice out of the cloud". Peter writes, "There came such a voice to him from the excellent glory" (2 Pet 1: 17), or 'Such a voice being uttered to Him *by* the excellent glory' (JND). In the Old Testament, the cloud was the symbol of God's presence. See, for example, Exodus 19: 9, "And the Lord said unto Moses, Lo I come unto thee in a thick cloud"; Exodus 40: 34-38, "Then a cloud covered the tent of the congregation, and the glory of the Lord filled the tabernacle...the cloud of the Lord was upon the tabernacle by day, and fire was on it by night". We can now understand why the disciples "fell on their face, and were sore afraid" (v.6) and why, in Luke's words, they "feared as they entered into the cloud" (Luke 9: 34). Although not a Biblical expression, it is often called the 'Shekinah cloud', meaning 'God dwelling'.

Notice the speed with which God spoke: it was while Peter was speaking! Peter was allowed to go no further for two reasons. *In the first place,* as we have already noticed, he had unwittingly infringed the pre-eminence of Christ; "Let us make **three** tabernacles..." *In the second place,* in assuming that the kingdom had been established, he had forgotten the Lord's teaching, a few days previously, in connection with His death: "From that time forth began Jesus to shew unto his disciples, how that he must go unto Jerusalem, and suffer many things of the elders and chief priests and scribes and be killed, and be raised again the third day" (Matt. 16: 21). Hence the voice of God, "This is my beloved Son; **hear him**".

iii) What the Lord said. "And Jesus came and touched them, and said, Arise, and be not afraid. And when they had lifted up their eyes, they saw no man, save Jesus only" (vv.7-8). In Mark's words, "And suddenly, when they had looked round about, they saw no man any more, save Jesus only with themselves" (Mark 9: 8). Luke says, "And when the voice was past, Jesus was found alone" (Luke 9: 36). It is delightful to notice that the Lord did not censure Peter or engage in any recrimination: simply, "Arise, and be not afraid".

e) The mandate to the disciples, v.9
"And as they came down from the mountain, Jesus charged them, saying, tell the vision to no man, until the Son of man be risen from the dead". Mark reads similarly (Mark 9: 9). The disciples obviously obeyed: "they kept it close, and told no man in those days any of those things which they had seen" (Luke 9: 36). There was no visible glory now, but "the Lord of glory" (1 Cor. 2: 8) was there! The Lord Jesus waited the Father's time. He did not seek publicity; He left the time of His exaltation and glory in His Father's hands. This is the fifth and final injunction to silence in Matthew's Gospel (8: 4; 9: 30; 12: 16; 16: 20; 17: 9).

2) THE LORD'S CLARIFICATION OF ELIJAH'S COMING, vv.10-13
The disciples' question, "Why then say the scribes that Elias must first come?" (v.10), arose out of the prophet's appearance on the mount of transfiguration (v.3). The words "first come" evidently refer to his coming before the establishment of the kingdom, in accordance with the prophecy, "Behold, I will send you Elijah the prophet before the coming of the great and dreadful day of the Lord: and he shall turn the heart of the fathers to the children, and the heart of the children to the fathers, lest I come and smite the earth with a curse" (Mal. 4: 5-6). The question here is understandable. If their Master was the long-awaited Christ, where was Elijah?

Matthew

It is of more than passing interest to notice that Malachi mentions Moses immediately before he mentions Elijah. See Malachi 4: 4. Both were on the mount of transfiguration. It was through **Moses** that the covenant was **made:** it was through **Elijah** that the covenant was **restored** (1 Kings 18: 30-31 etc). Elijah called the people **back to God.**

The coming of "Elijah the prophet" raises some interesting questions. For example, was this prophecy fulfilled in the coming of John the Baptist, or does it still await fulfilment? If the prophecy has been partially fulfilled in John, but awaits complete fulfilment, are we to expect Elijah himself, and does the Bible tell us anything more about his coming?

These issues were fully dealt with in our Malachi studies (December 2000/ March 2001), and we concluded, notwithstanding the problems posed by the words, "I will send you Elijah before the coming of the great and dreadful day of the Lord" and "he shall turn the heart of the fathers to the children, and the heart of the children to the fathers", that the prophecy was fulfilled in John the Baptist. Zacharias, the father of John, was told, "he shall go before him (the Lord) in the spirit and power of Elias, to turn the hearts of the fathers to the children, and the disobedient to the wisdom of the just, to make ready a people prepared for the Lord" (Luke 1: 17). John was certainly not the reincarnation of Elijah. This was something he categorically denied! (See John 1: 21).

The Lord Jesus made it very clear when commending John behind his back (something we ought to do more!) that "all the prophets and the law prophesied until John. And if ye will receive it, this is Elias, which was for to come", adding, "he that hath ears to hear, let him hear" (Matt. 11: 13-15). The Lord's answer to His disciples in our current passage evidently confirms this: "Elias truly shall first come (or, 'Elias indeed comes first', JND), and restore all things. But I say unto you, That Elias is come already, and they knew him not, but have done unto him whatsoever they listed. Likewise shall also the Son of Man suffer of them. Then the disciples understood that he spake unto them of John the Baptist" (vv. 11-13). The rendering, 'Elias indeed comes first' (JND) does not necessarily place his coming in the future, and it is significant that in Mark's record, the words "Elias verily cometh first, and restoreth all things" (Mark 9: 12) are rendered 'Elias indeed, having first come, restores all things' (JND).

The conclusion that the ministry of John the Baptist fulfilled the Old

Testament prophecy is certainly not accepted by all, but to insist that Elijah will return to earth at the end-time raises more questions than it answers! The disciples understood the Lord's reply (v.13), "which means they had obtained a satisfactory answer to their question" (Justin Waldron). There we must leave it.

"This kind goeth not out but by prayer and fasting"

Read Chapter 17: 14-27
In our previous study, we suggested that this chapter may be divided as follows: *(1)* the Lord's transfiguration on the mount (vv.1-9); (2) the Lord's clarification of Elijah's coming (vv.10-13); *(3)* the Lord's explanation of deficient power (vv.14-21); *(4)* the Lord's anticipation of His death and resurrection (vv.22-23); *(5)* the Lord's participation in payment of the tribute (vv.24-28).

1) THE LORD'S TRANSFIGURATION ON THE MOUNT, vv.1-9
Years later Peter wrote: "For we have not followed cunningly devised fables, when we made known unto you the power and coming (the second coming) of our Lord Jesus Christ, but were eyewitnesses of his majesty. For he received from God the Father honour and glory, when there came such a voice to him from the excellent glory, This is my beloved Son, in whom I am well pleased. And this voice which came from heaven we heard, when we were with him in the holy mount" (2 Pet.1:16-18). There could not be a better commentary! The best commentary on the Bible is the Bible!

2) THE LORD'S CLARIFICATION OF ELIJAH'S COMING, vv.10-13
In answering the disciples' question, "Why then say the scribes that Elias must first come?" (v.10), the Lord Jesus replied, "Elias truly shall first come, and restore all things ('Elias indeed comes first and will restore all things', JND)" (v.11), confirming the accuracy of the prediction, and then continued, "But I say unto you that Elias is come already, and they knew him not, but they have done unto him whatsoever they listed. Likewise shall the Son of man suffer of them. Then the disciples understood that he spake unto them of John the Baptist" (vv.12-13). The messenger had been murdered, and the Messiah he heralded would be murdered too. Whilst not all would agree, there certainly seems to be good ground to believe that the Lord explained to His disciples that the Old Testament prophecy (Malachi 4: 5-6) had been fulfilled in John the Baptist.

3) THE LORD'S EXPLANATION OF DEFICIENT POWER, vv.14-21

As we have seen, the Lord Jesus "received from God the Father honour and glory, when there came such a voice to him from the excellent glory, This is *my beloved Son,* in whom I am well pleased" (2 Pet. 1: 17, quoting Matt. 17: 5). Not only so, the Lord Jesus is also God's "only begotten Son (*monogenes*)". The expression is used five times of the Lord Jesus: John 1: 14, 18; John 3: 16, 18; 1 John 4: 9. Now, another father speaks about his son, "Lord, have mercy on my son" (v.15), and Luke gives a fuller account of the father's request: "Master, I beseech thee, look upon my son; for he is *mine only child* (*monogenes*)" (Luke 9: 38). The contrast could not be greater. The mount of glory and transfiguration gives place to the valley of grief and tragedy. Our experience is often the same: sacred moments alone with Christ, quickly give place to the harsh realities of life. We contemplate the glory of Christ, and then the misery caused by Satan. The preview of the millennial kingdom, when Satan will be absent, is followed by a picture of this present age, in which Satan is most certainly present. But the same Lord, who was "transfigured" (v.2) before Peter, James and John, "came down from the mountain" (v.9) to the remaining nine beleaguered and perplexed disciples. When the spiritual battle rages, "the Lord of glory" (1 Cor 2: 8) is with us!

As J.C.Ryle points out, 'The Lord Jesus did not tarry long on the mountain. His communion with Moses and Elias was very short. He soon returned to His accustomed work of doing good to a sin-stricken world. In His life on earth, to receive honour and have visions of glory was the exception. To minister to others, to heal all who were oppressed by the devil, to do acts of mercy to sinners, was the rule'. Whilst we must never lose sight of coming glory, we must not become 'visionaries'. It has been nicely said that:

> A vision without a task makes a visionary,
> And a task without a vision makes for drudgery,
> But a task and a vision makes a missionary!

Having established the connection with the previous verses, we can now outline our present passage. We must note the following: *(a)* the cry of the father (vv.14-15); *(b)* the condition of the son (v.15); *(c)* the criticism of the disciples (v.16); *(d)* the cure by the Lord Jesus (vv.17-18); *(e)* the concern of the disciples (vv.19-21).

a) The cry of the father, vv.14-15

"And when they were come down to the multitude, there came to him a certain man, kneeling down to him, and saying, Lord, have mercy on my son". Mark tells us that "when he came to his disciples, he saw a great multitude about them, and the scribes questioning with them" (Mark 9: 14). Luke, who constantly draws our attention to human detail, concentrates on the deep feelings of the man. See Luke 9: 38. The details are well worth emphasising:

i) He stresses the man's deep concern. He **"cried out"**. According to W.E.Vine, some manuscripts have *anaboao* here, meaning an intensive cry. It is used of the Lord's cry on the cross: "And about the ninth hour Jesus cried with a loud voice" (Matt 27: 46). The word "beseech" *(parakaleo)* here is a stronger word than "ask" *(aiteo).*

ii) He stresses that the demon-possessed boy was the man's **"only child"**. This emphasises the man's depth of feeling. It is Luke who tells us that Jairus "had one only daughter" (8: 42) and that the dead man at Nain was "the only son of his mother" (7: 12).

Whilst we rightly pray for "all men" (1 Tim 2: 1), our prayers for those close to us do have additional weight and feeling, and the Saviour understands this perfectly. He is not unmindful of our deep concern for family members. J.C.Ryle reminds us that 'the child of many prayers shall seldom be cast away...He may think fit to prove our faith by keeping us long waiting. But so long as a child lives, and a parent prays, we have no right to despair about that child's soul'.

b) The condition of the son, v.15

"He is a lunatick (*seleniazo,* literally 'to be moon struck', an epileptic: epilepsy was supposed to be influenced by the moon), and sore vexed ('suffereth grievously', RV): for ofttimes he falleth into the fire, and oft into the water". Luke provides further details: "Lo, a spirit taketh him, and he suddenly crieth out; and it teareth him that he foameth again; and bruising him hardly departeth from him" (Luke 9: 39). Mark describes the spirit as "a dumb spirit...foul spirit...dumb and deaf spirit" and adds, with Matthew, "ofttimes it hath cast him into the fire, and into the waters, to destroy him" (Mark 9: 17, 22, 25).

All these things remind us that Satan is intent on inflicting harm and injury upon men and women, and in particular, upon young people. Mark tells us that the demon had been active since the boy's earliest days: in answering the Lord's question, "how long is it ago since this came unto him?", the father replied, "Of a child" (Mark 9: 21). The incidence of juvenile delinquency today is striking evidence of Satan's power in early life. Most horrifying crimes have recently been committed by children. "The devil, we may be quite sure, loses no time in endeavouring to influence the minds of young people. He begins with them even 'of a child'" (J.C.Ryle).

c) The criticism of the disciples, vv.16-17

"And I brought him to thy disciples, and they could not cure him" (v.16). The father expected help from the disciples, which is a salutary reminder that men and women expect something of us too. We may not be expected to expel demons (!), but we are expected to have answers to people's problems. The very same disciples who a short time before had been given "power against unclean spirits, to cast them out" (Matt. 10: 1; Luke 9: 1) were confronted with a case too hard for them. They had evidently lost the power given to them. When they asked, "Why could not we cast him out?" (v.19), the Lord replied bluntly, "**Because of your unbelief**" (v.20). As Justin Waldron points out, "The disciples' experience here resembles that of Gehazi (2 Kings 4: 31 ff)".

More about this in due course, but first of all, to whom was the Lord referring in replying, "O faithless and perverse generation, how long shall I be with you? how long shall I suffer you?" (v.17). He could hardly be addressing the disciples who, although lacking in faith as we have seen (vv.19-20), could not be described as a "faithless and **perverse** (meaning 'distorted' or 'twisted') generation". He could hardly be addressing the father alone since he had done all that he could. The words, "how long shall I be with you? how long shall I suffer you?" make it clear that He was referring to the nation of Israel who would reject Him, and from whom He would withdraw. According to Mark, "when he came to his disciples, he saw a great multitude about them, and the scribes questioning with them…And he asked the scribes, What question ye with them?" Having then listened to the father of the boy ("one of the multitude"), the Saviour "answered **them** (RV/JND), and saith, O faithless generation…." (Mark 9: 14-19). The suggestion that the Lord is therefore referring to the unbelief of the people generally is supported by the fact that He was quoting from the Old Testament: "They have corrupted themselves…they are a perverse and crooked generation…they are a very froward ('perverse', JND) generation, children in whom is no faith" (Deut. 32: 5, 20).

d) The cure by the Lord Jesus, vv.17-18

The words, "bring him hither to me (v.17) strike a happier note. As G.Campbell Morgan puts it: "But now let us observe the action of the King... Oh the majesty of that word of Jesus! What confidence He had in His own ability". It was entirely justified: "And Jesus rebuked the devil (demon); and he departed out of him: and the child was cured from that very hour" (v.18). The Lord's disciples had failed to exercise the power imparted to them in dealing with the case: now He deals with it directly. It is worth pointing out that Mark 9: 21-24 should be read at this juncture. These verses end with the well-known words, "If thou canst believe, all things are possible to him that believeth. And straightway the father of the child cried out, and said with tears, Lord, I believe; help thou mine unbelief". This stands in direct contrast to the people generally, and the religious leaders particularly. As we have seen, they are described as "a faithless generation". We should notice additional details given by Luke:

i) The determination of the demon. Yes, even in the presence of Christ: "And as he was yet a coming, the devil threw him down, and tare him" (Luke 9: 42). Demon power was particularly evident when the Saviour came to "destroy ('undo', JND) the works of the devil" (1 John 3: 8), and this will be repeated before His second coming. It is worth remembering that God's work will always be attended by Satanic activity. See 1 Cor 16: 9, "For a great door and effectual is opened unto me, *and there are many adversaries*". In this case, it was the demon's 'last throw'. Defeat stared him in the face: "And they brought him to him. And *seeing him* the spirit immediately tore him" (Mark 9: 20, JND), reminding us that at the end-time, the devil will rage and do his worst, but he "knoweth that he hath but a short time" (Rev. 12: 12).

ii) The deliverance of the boy. The Lord "healed the child, and delivered him again to his father" (Luke 9: 42). The boy was no longer in the possession of the "strong man" (Luke 11: 21-22). Mark joins Matthew in making it clear that his deliverance was complete: "the child was cured *from that very hour*" (Matt. 17: 18); "I charge thee, come out of him, *and enter no more into him*" (Mark 9: 25-27). There was no question of repossession. Satan's power over the boy was broken for ever. In his death, the Lord Jesus, "destroyed him that had the power of death, that is, the devil; and delivered them who through fear of death were all their lifetime (like this boy) subject to bondage" (Heb. 2: 14-15). The words, "delivered him again to his father" (only Luke says this) are particularly lovely bearing in mind that the boy was his father's "only child".

Matthew

e) The concern of the disciples, vv.19-21

"Then came the disciples to Jesus apart, and said, Why could not we cast him out?", to which the Saviour replied, "Because of your unbelief: for verily I say unto you, If ye have faith as a grain of mustard seed (said to be the smallest of all seeds), ye shall say unto this mountain, Remove hence to yonder place; and it shall remove; and nothing shall be impossible unto you. Howbeit, this kind (referring to demons) goeth not out, but by prayer and fasting". Notice that something so small in itself would remove something so vast – a mountain! According to R.V.G.Tasker, "to 'remove mountains' meant in Jewish idiom 'to remove difficulties'. The meaning of the verse is that strong faith can accomplish the seemingly impossible, for the faith of the man is drawing upon divine resources". We have an example in the book of Zechariah 4: 6-7. Zerubbabel's "great mountain" was, undoubtedly, the difficulties and opposition encountered in the Lord's work. See Ezra 4 & 5. We all have 'great mountains'. We all wish that they could become "a plain"! Our "great mountain" can only be overcome as we trust God to empower us by the Holy Spirit: hence Zechariah was told, "Not by might, nor by power, but by my spirit, Saith the Lord of hosts" (Zech. 4: 6).

If the disciples had lost their spiritual power because their faith had failed, then their faith had failed because it had not been nourished by prayer and self-denial (fasting). We must carefully note the Lord's searching words here: "Howbeit, this kind goeth not out, but by prayer and fasting" (v.21). H.S.Paisley *(What The Bible Teaches - Mark)* puts it well: "They, like us, may have depended on past successes, instead of depending alone on God (Mark 6: 7,13). The early church, when feeling human weakness and Satanic power, found grace in the prayers of faith (Acts 4: 24-33). And the greatest need of the churches of God today, is for a revival of prayer and dependence upon God for real power in testimony". John Heading makes the point that "Prayer is continual contact of the heart with God; fasting is the continual lack of contact with the world. Even things normally regarded as necessary may have to be dispensed with if they hinder effective service (Matt. 19: 29)".

This raises very serious issues. It must be true that a great deal of our ineffectiveness and weakness is attributable to unbelief. Whilst, theoretically, we gladly acknowledge with Abraham that "what he (God) had promised, he was able also to perform" (Rom 4: 21), in practice we don't expect very much. We have almost persuaded ourselves that since these are the "last days", and the Lord's coming is near, this is "the day of small things" (a misapplication of Zechariah 4: 10). We must ask ourselves if we really do believe that "the gospel is the power of God unto salvation" (Rom 1: 16), and that "whatsoever we ask, we receive of him, because we keep his commandments, and do those things which are pleasing in his sight" (1 John 3: 22). (Compare John 15: 7, "If ye abide in me, and my words abide in you, ye shall ask what ye will, and it shall be done unto you"). We must ask ourselves if we do have the confidence "that, if we ask any thing according to his will, he heareth us" (1 John 5: 14) and that He "is able to do exceeding abundantly above all that we ask or think, according to the power that worketh in us" (Eph.3: 20). When it seemed inevitable that the ship bound for Italy would founder, Paul was confident: "Sirs, be of good cheer; for *I believe God,* that it shall be even as it was told me" (Acts 27: 25). James warns: "If any of you lack wisdom, let him ask of God…but let him ask in faith, nothing wavering. For he that wavereth, is like a wave of the sea, driven with the wind, and tossed" (James 1: 5-6).

4) *THE LORD'S ANTICIPATION OF HIS DEATH AND RESURRECTON, vv.22-23*

"And while they abode in Galilee, Jesus said unto them, The Son of man shall be betrayed into the hands of men: and they shall kill him, and the third day he shall be raised again. And they were exceeding sorry ('they were greatly grieved', JND)". Mark gives us further details: "they departed thence, and passed through Galilee; and he would not that any man should know it. For he taught his disciples, and said unto them, The Son of man is delivered into the hands of men, and they shall kill him; and after that he is killed, he shall rise the third day. But they understood not that saying, and were afraid to ask him" (Mark 9: 30-32). We must add Luke's account: "But while they wondered every one at all things which Jesus did, he said unto his disciples, Let these sayings sink down into your ears: for the Son of man shall be delivered into the hands of men. But they understood not this saying, and it was hid from them, that they perceived it not: and they feared to ask him of that saying" (Luke 9: 43-45). On a practical note, it is so important for us to allow God's word to "to sink down" into *our* ears! We must take heed *how* we hear (Luke 8: 18). There are at least three things to notice as we piece together the three accounts:

i) **The connection with the preceding miracle.** Men and women "wondered every one at all things which Jesus did" (Luke 9: 43) but the disciples were not to be carried away on 'the crest of the wave'. He therefore warns them of His impending death.

ii) The content of the Saviour's statement. "The Son of man (He became "the Son of man" in order to die) shall be betrayed into the hands of men" (Matt. 17: 22) or 'The Son of man is *about* to be delivered up into [the] hands of men' (JND). They had heard the same thing from His lips little more than a week before (Matt. 16: 21), and Peter, James and John had heard at least something of His conversation with Moses and Elijah when they "spake of his decease (exodus) which he should accomplish at Jerusalem" (Luke 9: 31). Did Judas remember his words? It was through *him* that the Saviour was "betrayed into the hands of men". At the same time, we must never forget that the Lord Jesus was "delivered by the determinate counsel and foreknowledge of *God*" (Acts 2: 23).

iii) The conflict in the disciples' minds. On the first occasion that the Lord Jesus spoke to His disciples about His death, Peter "began to rebuke him", and was himself rebuked by the Saviour (Matt. 16: 22-23; Mark 8: 31-33). On another occasion, James and John could only think of sitting "one on thy right hand, and the other on thy left hand, in thy glory" (Mark 10: 32-37). The disciples were evidently unable to reconcile, or had no wish to reconcile, *their expectation* of the kingdom, with *His expectation* of suffering, death, and resurrection. The disciples would ultimately learn that there could be no kingdom apart from His death and resurrection. He must die for the sins of the subjects of that kingdom, before they could ever enjoy its blessings. It is the cause of ceaseless wonder to us that He made no attempt to avoid His death. How much He loved us!

5) THE LORD'S PARTCIPATION IN PAYMENT OF THE TRIBUTE, vv.24-27

This incident is only recorded by Matthew, and it has been suggested that it was of particular interest to him since he was a tax-collector! Against this it should be remembered that Matthew collected taxes for the Romans, and that the tax here was payable in connection with the temple. According to R.V.G.Tasker, this tax, levied upon every male Jew above the age of nineteen for the costly maintenance of the temple and upkeep of its services, was based on the instructions given to Moses in Exodus 30: 11-16. "The tax consisted of half-a-shekel, called a *didrachma* or 'double-drachma in v.24 where it is translated 'tribute money' in the AV and 'half-shekel in the RV. But as the *didrachma* was not in current coinage, it was customary for two persons to combine and pay a full shekel, called a *statar* in v.27, where it is translated 'a piece of money' in the AV and 'a shekel' in the RV". R.V.G.Tasker continues by suggesting that the "tax-collectors in the present story…may have accosted Peter, because Jesus, having been away from Capernaum for a considerable time, was somewhat behind in His payment. Peter therefore assured them that Jesus is no tax-dodger; and he clearly intends to bring the matter to His Master's attention at the earliest opportunity".

The Lord anticipated ('prevented', AV) this, and posed the question: "What thinkest thou, Simon? Of whom do the kings of the earth take custom (*tele*: indirect local taxes collected at custom-houses by *telonai* 'publicans') or tribute (*kensos*, a direct capitation tax levied on persons and paid direct to the imperial treasury)? Of their own children, or of strangers?" (v.25), to which Peter replied, "Of strangers" (v.26). The Lord then pointed out that He cannot therefore be subject to taxation. After all, the temple was His "Father's house" (John 2: 16), and He was the Son of God! It follows that He, above all people, was excluded from temple tax! But do notice how the Saviour continues: "Notwithstanding, lest we should offend them (*skandalizo*, meaning, amongst other things, 'anything that arouses prejudice'), go thou to the sea, and cast an hook, and take up the fish that first cometh up; and when thou hast opened his mouth, thou shalt find a piece of money: that take, and give unto them for me and thee" (v.27). He provided for Peter too!

It has been pointed out that the Lord showed His dominion here over fish, over animals in Matthew 21: 1-7, and over fowls in Matthew 26: 34, 74-75. As Wm.MacDonald observes, "The miracle was astounding, yet it is narrated with utmost restraint. Christ's omniscience is seen in the following: *(i)* He knew which one of all the fish in the Sea of Galilee had a stater in its mouth; *(ii)* He knew the location of that one fish; *(iii)* He knew that it would be the first fish that Peter would catch".

This incident provides a lesson for us all. While we must not compromise doctrine and morality under any circumstances, nevertheless we should studiously avoid giving unnecessary offence to believers and non-believers. So far as believers are concerned, see, for example, 1 Cor. 8: 13: "Wherefore if meat (that is, meat offered to idols) make my brother to offend (*skandalizo*: 'be a fall-trap to my brother'), I will eat no flesh while the world standeth". So far as unbelievers and believers are concerned, see 1 Corinthians 10: 32 where Paul uses a different word but maintains the same principle: "Give none offence (*aproskopos*), neither to the Jews, nor to the Gentiles, nor to the church of God". Declining to support, shall we say, some local charitable appeal, might not enhance our testimony in the street, especially if the collector lives next door!

Matthew

A nice piece supplied by Justin Waldron points out that the Lord's provision of the temple tax here reminds us that He "did many things for Peter, healing his mother-in-law (Mark 1: 29-34), enabling him to walk on water (Matt. 14: 22-33), healing Malchus' ear (Matt. 26: 47-56), and delivering him from prison (Acts 12: 1-17)". Warren Wiersbe adds, "No wonder Peter wrote, 'Casting all your care upon Him: for he careth for you' (1 Pet. 5: 7)".

THE GOSPEL OF MATTHEW

"These little ones which believe"

Read Chapter 18: 1-14
In introducing his comments on this chapter, G. Campbell Morgan (*The Gospel According to Matthew*) notes that the passage "falls into two parts; the Master's instruction, first concerning greatness, and secondly concerning forgiveness. The first part was His answer to their question, 'Who then is greatest in the kingdom of heaven?' (Campbell Morgan quotes the RV here). Then He merged His teaching concerning greatness into His teaching concerning forgiveness, the attitude of His people towards wrongdoing".

We will follow Campbell Morgan's chapter division as follows: *(1)* greatness in the kingdom (vv.1-14); *(2)* forgiveness amongst brethren (vv.21-35). The former (greatness in the kingdom) may be divided into two sections: *(a)* imitating children (vv.1-4); *(b)* injuring children (vv.5-14). As William Kelly (*Lectures on Matthew*) rightly observes, "Starting from a little child whom He sets in the midst, He carries the thought of the little one all through this part of His discourse". The latter (forgiveness amongst brethren) may also be divided into two sections: *(a)* dealing with offences (vv.15-20); *(b)* displaying forgiveness (vv.21-35). We should notice the Lord's words here, "If thy brother shall sin **against thee**" (v.15), and Peter's question "How often shall my brother sin **against me**, and I forgive him?" (v.21).

1) GREATNESS IN THE KINGDOM, vv.1-14
The connection with the previous chapter has been delightfully spelt out by J.M.Flanigan (*Behold your King*): "Notice how the chapter commences, 'At the same time...' Literally it is, 'In that hour'. The Master had, in that hour, just demonstrated what true greatness really was. Though He was Sovereign over all and Lord of the Temple, He had just waived His rights, and concedes to pay tribute money. He could have resisted, but, as He explained to Peter, 'Lest we should offend them...', and in humility He had

provided the tribute money for Himself and for Peter. This was greatness indeed. It was in that hour that the disciples brought their query about greatness in the kingdom".

As already noted, these verses may be divided as follows: *(A)* imitating children (vv.1-4); *(B)* injuring children (vv.5-14).

A) Imitating children, vv.1-4
"At the same time came the disciples unto Jesus, saying, Who is the greatest in the kingdom of heaven?" (v.1). We know from Mark that the question was asked at Capernaum (Mark 9: 33), so Matthew is quite right (of course) in saying "At the same time", since it was at Capernaum that the Lord provided the temple tax for Himself and Peter (Matt. 17: 24). Mark and Luke also tell us that the question arose out of a dispute amongst the disciples: "they had disputed among themselves, who should be the greatest" (Mark 9: 33-34: Luke 9: 46). The disciples were concentrating their attention on the crown, whereas the Saviour had been speaking to them about the cross (Matt. 17: 22-23; Mark 9: 30-32; Luke 9: 44-45).

Possibly the dispute arose from the fact that Peter, James and John had been selected to accompany the Lord Jesus on the 'mount of transfiguration'. However, the fact remains that we are often far more concerned with our own interests, rather than the interests of the Saviour who died for us. Their selfishness must have grieved Him, and our forgetfulness and self-centredness must grieve Him too.

The Lord Jesus taught His disciples that true greatness lay in humility. "And Jesus called a little child unto him, and set him in the midst of them. And said, Verily I say unto you, Except ye be converted, and become as little children, ye shall not enter into the kingdom of heaven. Whosoever therefore shall humble himself as this little child, the same is greatest in the kingdom of heaven" (vv.2-4). Mark tells us that the Lord took the child "in his arms" (Mark 9: 36). He deals with two matters here:

- *Entering the kingdom demands humility, v.3.* "Except ye be converted, and become as little children, ye shall not enter into the kingdom of heaven".

- *Elevation in the kingdom demands humility, v.4.* "Whosoever therefore shall humble himself as this little child, the same is greatest in the kingdom of heaven".

The order, obviously, is important. In the words of R.V.G.Tasker, "It would be idle to discuss who is greatest in the kingdom of heaven, while there is still uncertainty about the qualifications for entering it". Preachers have pointed out from time immemorial that the Lord Jesus refers here, not to childishness, but to childlikeness. But far more is implied. The Lord's words should be carefully noted: **not** 'Except ye become as little children', **but** "Except ye be **converted** (or 'turned': from *strepho,* meaning 'to turn'), and become as little children, ye shall not enter into the kingdom of heaven". The word "converted" here is best understood in the passive sense, since it is not something that men and woman can accomplish themselves. It is in fact nothing less than new birth, something divinely accomplished (John 3: 3-6). The consequence of being "converted" is to "become as little children".

R.V.G.Tasker points out that the words, "Whosoever therefore shall humble himself as this little child, the same is greatest in the kingdom of heaven", do not mean 'humbles himself as this little child humbles himself', but 'humbles himself until he is *like* this little child'. A little child has no idea that he is great, and so in the kingdom of heaven the greatest is he who is least conscious of being great". Compare Matthew 19: 14. Moreover, a child is not rated of great importance by others from the point of view that his or her opinion counts for little, if anything, and there is no maturity in thought and behaviour. Hence the humility in becoming as a "little child".

We cannot leave this without saying that, as always, the Lord Jesus is the perfect example of His own teaching. He "humbled himself…Wherefore God also hath highly exalted him, and given him a name which is above every name" (Phil. 2: 8-9). He perfectly exemplifies Peter's injunction, "Humble yourselves therefore under the mighty hand of God, that he may exalt you in due time" (1 Pet. 5: 6).

Having used "a little child" to illustrate His teaching, the Saviour takes the opportunity to speak about the way in which children should be treated. So:

B) Injuring children, vv.5-14
It is worth pointing out that in these verses, emphasis is placed on the result for the world generally, following the maltreatment of "these little ones which believe", together with the recompence incurred by the particular people responsible for maltreating them. The key expressions are, "Woe unto the world because of offences!…but woe (particularly) to that man by whom the offence cometh!" (v.7). The recompence for acting in this way is fearful: "Cast

into everlasting fire…cast into hell (*geenna*) fire" (vv.8-9). The perpetrators of harm are unregenerate men and women. In the second section of the chapter (vv.15-35), emphasis is placed on relationships between believers. The key expressions are "thy brother" (v.15); "the church" (v.17); "my brother" (v.21); "his brother" (v.35), not to mention "For where two or three are gathered together in my name, there am I in the midst of them" (v.20). Judgment is pronounced in both cases, but with a vast difference between them!

Not all agree on the precise identity of the children to whom the Lord refers in these verses. We should therefore ask -

- Does He refer to those who have "become as little children" (v.3), that is, to the man or woman who "shall humble himself *as* this little child" (v.4). In other words, does the Lord refer to *all believers*, albeit describing them as either "a little child" (v.5) or "these little ones" (vv.6,10,14)?

- Does He refer to young believers in the usually accepted sense of the expression? It could be argued that since the word translated "little child…little children" (*paidion*), see vv.2-5, is applied to various categories in the New Testament, including "the youngest believers in the family of God, 1 John 2: 13, 18" (W.E.Vine), the Lord's teaching here embraced more than actual children. Very clearly, the context makes it clear that the "little children" to which John refers are far more than literal children! The argument that the use of *paidion* ("little child…little children) in vv.2-5, and *mikros*, meaning 'little' ("little ones") in vv.6, 10, 14 indicates two different categories, is hardly tenable. The words, "And whoso shall receive one such little child (*paidion*) in my name receiveth me" (v.5) and, "But whoso shall offend one of these little ones (*mikros*) which believe in me" (v.6), clearly refer to the same individuals. We should add that the two words used here to describe these children arise from the circumstances in which they occur. In the first place, the Lord's people are seen from His point of view (v.5), and in the second, bearing in mind the Lord's words, "Woe unto the *world* because of offences!" (v.7), from the world's point of view (vv.6-14). They are insignificant in the world's eyes: *mikros* is the opposite of *megas*, meaning "great".

- Does He refer to children like the "little child" whom He called "and set…in the midst of them" (v.2)? In other words, is the Lord still referring to *actual children*? It has to be said that this does appear to be the case, with the qualification that he is referring particularly to "these little ones

which believe in me" (v.6). J.M.Flanigan is surely right in saying, "Here is assurance, if assurance were needed, that even little ones may believe on the Saviour. We must never discourage, or offend, or despise them in their simplicity".

The view adopted in these notes (without being at all dogmatic: we must not forget the 'learning curve') is that the Lord's words, "these little ones ***which believe in me"*** (v.6), settle the matter, and that He is referring to believing children. Confirmation might well be found in the Saviour's words: "Suffer little children (*paidion*), and forbid them not to come unto me: for of such is the kingdom of heaven" (Matt. 19: 14).

Bearing this in mind, we should notice the following: *(a)* the privilege of receiving them (v.5); *(b)* the punishment for offending them (vv.6-9); *(c)* the preciousness bestowed upon them (vv.10-14).

a) The privilege of receiving them, v.5
"And whoso shall receive one such little child in my name receiveth me". Parallel passages are found in Mark 9: 33-37 and Luke 9: 46-48, but with a different emphasis. If Matthew emphasises that the Lord began by teaching that His disciples were to be as little children, then Mark and Luke emphasise that whilst helping a child doesn't seem to be the work of a great leader - we naturally expect something far more dramatic and sensational from leaders - greatness in God's sight means that we must be humble enough to help a little child.

The principle enunciated by the Lord Jesus here is seen again, under different circumstances, in His 'Olivet Discourse': "inasmuch as ye have done it unto one of the least of these my brethren, ye have done it unto me" (Matt. 25: 40). This reminds us that kindness displayed to the Lord's people is far in advance of 'charitable work' or 'the milk of human kindness'. It is serving Christ Himself. Hence His words, "whoso shall receive one such little child ***in my name*** receiveth me". The humblest service is crowned with the highest dignity. Everything done for the benefit of others is regarded as being done for Christ, and for the Father who sent Him. Conversely, damage done to God's people, is damage done to Christ. See Acts 9: 4-5. (Compare Zechariah 2: 8). This follows:

b) The punishment for offending them, vv.6-9
The immense seriousness of offending believing children is stressed in two

ways: *(i)* it is preferable to die than to sin in this way (v.6); *(ii)* it is punishable by eternal judgment (vv.7-9).

i) It is preferable to die than to sin in this way, v.6. "But who shall offend one of these little ones which believe in me, it were better (*sumphero*, meaning 'profitable') for him that a millstone were hanged about his neck and that he were drowned in the depth of the sea". It is immensely serious to stumble a believing child. The word "offend" (*skandalizo*) means 'to put a snare or stumbling-block in the way'. Originally it meant 'the name of the part of a trap to which the bait is attached' (W.E.Vine). The Lord's meaning is clear: it is better to die now, or to be put to death, than to become guilty of stumbling "one of these little ones".

J.C.Ryle expands this in making *a general application*: "we put offences or stumbling-blocks in the way of men's souls whenever we do anything to keep them back from Christ - or turn them out of the way of salvation - or to disgust them with true religion. We may do it directly, by persecuting, ridicule, opposing, or dissuading them from decided service for Christ; we may do it indirectly, by living a life inconsistent with our religious profession, and by making Christianity loathsome and distasteful by our own conduct. Whenever we do anything of the kind, it is clear, from our Lord's words, that we commit a great sin". While the Lord Jesus is evidently speaking particularly about the way in which wicked men can stumble believing children, we do well to heed J.C.Ryle ourselves. Sadly, it is not unknown for young believers to be stumbled by the unspiritual conduct of older Christians. The effect on young people in the assembly when discord and divisions occur, with all their accompanying accusations and counter-accusations, is devastating.

On a technical point, the "millstone" ('a great millstone', RV), was certainly sufficiently heavy to take anybody attached to it into "the depth of the sea". W.E.Vine points out that the Lord was not referring to one of the two stones comprising a hand-mill (*mulos*), but to a much larger stone 'turned by an ass' (*mulos onikos*).

ii) It is punishable by eternal judgment, vv.7-9. "Woe to the world because of offences! For it must needs be that offences come; but woe to that man by whom the offence cometh". The twice-repeated "woe" is nothing less than a divine pronouncement. In the words of Robert H. Mounce, "It is a terrible thing that in the world there are influences that cause people to lose their faith. The temptations that lead astray will always be with us, but woe to the person through whom they come". It is generally said that the first "woe" is a cry of lamentation, and that the second "woe" takes on the nature of a curse.

The Lord deals particularly with the *individual* responsible: "woe to *that man* by whom the offence cometh". In this solemn connection, He refers to two alternatives: either 'entering into life', or being "cast into everlasting fire...into hell fire": "Wherefore if thy hand or thy foot offend thee (actions and behaviour), cut them off, and cast them from thee: it is better for thee to *enter into* life halt or maimed, rather, than having two hands or two feet to be *cast into everlasting fire.* And if thine eye offend thee (desire and covetousness), pluck it out, and cast it from thee: it is better for thee to *enter into life* with one eye, rather than having two eyes to be *cast into hell fire*". (vv.8-9). Compare Matthew 5: 29-30. It should be carefully noted that the very things which the Lord describes as a stumbling-block (an offence, AV) to others (vv.6-7) are in fact a stumbling-block to *the offender himself* ("if thy hand or thy foot offend *thee*...if thine eye offend *thee*", vv.8-9). Self-judgment is vital!

While H.A.Ironside, together with others, espouses the view that the Lord was referring here to physical mutilation - "Better to mutilate oneself by cutting off a hand or a foot than to be guilty of using either physical member to point or lead one of these children astray" - it seems far more likely, as we suggested in connection with Matthew 5: 29-30, that the Lord is urging His disciples to strike at the very root of anything that would produce unholy actions. E.H.Plumptre (Ellicott's Commentary) takes this view: "The bold severity of the phrase (he is commenting on Matthew 5: 29-30) excludes a literal interpretation. The seat of the evil lies in the will, not in the organ of sense or action, and the removal of the instrument might leave the inward taint unpurified".

There was to be no quarter in dealing with potential sin. This is emphasised in the New Testament epistles. See Romans 13: 14 ("make not provision for the flesh, to fulfil the lusts thereof"); Colossians 3: 5 ("Mortify therefore your members which are upon the earth; fornication..."); Romans 6: 13 ("Neither yield ye your members as instruments of unrighteousness unto sin"); 1 Cor. 6: 20 ("Glorify God in your body"). We are indebted to our contributor Gareth Armstrong for pointing out that Job dealt with his eyes in this way: "I made a covenant with mine eyes: why should I think upon a maid?" (Job 31: 1).

While the Lord Jesus is evidently addressing His disciples here: "it is better (good) for *thee*…it is better (good) for *thee*…", there can be no doubt that He is describing, as noted above, two different classes of people:

- *Those who will "enter into life"*. That is, those who will enter into the blessings and benefit of *eternal* life. Bearing in mind that the Saviour continues by describing eternal judgment, the words "enter into life" evidently refer, not to life *now*, but rather to life in *eternity*, which will be enjoyed by the very people who have been "converted, and become as little children". Conversion involves a new attitude to sin and sinful tendencies. The New Testament is very clear about this: "Know ye not that the unrighteous shall not inherit the kingdom of God? Be not deceived: nether fornicators, nor idolaters, nor adulterers, nor effeminate, nor abusers of themselves with mankind, nor thieves, nor covetous, nor drunkards, nor revilers, nor extortioners, shall inherit the kingdom of God. And such were some of you: but ye are washed, but ye are sanctified, but ye are justified in the name of the Lord Jesus, and by the Spirit of our God" (1 Cor. 6: 9-11).

We should carefully notice the way in which the Lord describes their entry "into life", having dealt ruthlessly on earth with sin, "it is good (*kalos*, meaning intrinsically good) for thee to enter into life lame or maimed" (v.8 JND). It is rather striking that the Lord should describe the entry "into life" in this way - as something 'goodly…fair…beautiful' (the extended meaning of *kalos*). Perhaps we could say that Peter refers to the same thing in speaking of an 'abundant entrance' into "the everlasting kingdom of our Lord and Saviour Jesus Christ" (2 Pet. 1: 11).

- *Those who will be "cast into everlasting fire"*. If the people who will enter "into life" are "converted" people - people who have turned (the meaning of conversion) from sin - then those who will be "cast into everlasting fire… into hell fire" are those who have *not* been converted, and their lives make it quite clear that this is the case.

c) The preciousness bestowed upon them, vv.10-14
The Lord Jesus completes this part of His discourse by giving His disciples three reasons why the disciples should not "despise (*kataphroneo*, 'to think or look down upon') one of these little ones" (v.10): *(i)* because angels are concerned for their welfare (v.10); *(ii)* because the Lord Jesus in concerned for their welfare (vv.11-13); *(iii)* because the Father is concerned for their welfare (v.14).

i) ***Because angels are concerned for their welfare***: "I say unto you, That in heaven their angels do always behold the face of my Father which is in heaven" (v.10). While it has been suggested that the expression "their angels" refers to spirits of departed children (Wm.Kelly), it seems more likely that the Lord is referring here to the ministry of angels later described by the writer to the Hebrews: "Are they not all ministering spirits, sent forth to minister (to do service) for them who shall be heirs of salvation" (Heb. 1: 14). See also Acts 12: 7. G. Campbell Morgan has this to say: "Jesus said to these men who were going to be in His Kingdom, and who wanted to know about greatness; Do not forget that the angels do not despise the children. They watch them and guard them, and stand in heaven's court for them". But this is not the highest reason for not despising "one of these little ones". An even more weighty reason follows:

ii) ***Because the Lord Jesus is concerned for their welfare.*** "For the Son of man is come to save that which was lost. How think ye? if a man have an hundred sheep, and one of them is gone astray, doth he not leave the ninety and nine, and goeth into the mountains (or 'doth he not leave the ninety and nine on the mountains', JND), and seek that which is gone astray? And if so be that he find it, verily I say unto you, he rejoiceth more of that sheep, than of the ninety and nine which went not astray" (vv.11-13). It should be noted that although v.11 is omitted in the Revised Version, it is included by J.N.Darby, but with a marginal note. In context, the Lord Jesus is not referring here to lost sinners, but to "one of these little ones which believe in me" (v.6). Robert H. Mounce makes the point that whereas in Luke "the parable of the lost sheep is used to justify Jesus' practice of ministering to tax collectors and sinners (i.e. religious outcasts, cf. Luke 15: 1-7), in Matthew the parable serves to teach God's concern lest a single member of the flock, however insignificant, wander from the truth". What rejoicing when a backslider is restored! But not all are restored ("***if*** so be he find it"). But even this is not the highest reason for not despising "one of these little ones". A third reason follows:

iii) ***Because the Father is concerned for their welfare***. "Even so it is not the will of your Father which is in heaven, that one of these little ones should perish" (v.14). It should be carefully noted that the word "perish" (*apollumi*) signifies 'not of extinction but ruin, loss, not of being, but of well-being' (W.E.Vine). We know, of course, that He is "not willing that any should perish, but that all should come to repentance" (2 Pet. 3: 9).

Wm.MacDonald, who suggests that in vv.5-6, "the Lord Jesus glides almost imperceptibly from the subject of a natural child to a spiritual child", an alternative view to the position taken in these notes, nevertheless sums up the section succinctly: "If they are important enough to engage angels, and the Lord Jesus, and God the Father, then clearly we should never despise them, no matter how unlovely or lowly they might appear".

"There am I in the midst of them"

Read Chapter 18: 15-35
In our previous study we suggested that this chapter may be divided as follows: *(1)* greatness in the kingdom (vv.1-14); *(2)* forgiveness amongst brethren (vv.21-35).

1) GREATNESS IN THE KINGDOM, vv.1-14
We noted that this section of the chapter may be divided into two sections: *(A)* imitating children (vv.1-4); *(B)* injuring children (vv.5-14), and that William Kelly (*Lectures on Matthew*) rightly observes, "Starting from a little child whom He sets in the midst, He carries the thought of the little one all through this part of His discourse". In dealing with the disciples' question, "Who is the greatest in the kingdom of heaven?", the Lord Jesus, with a little child in His arms (Mark 9: 36), taught them two lessons: *(a) entering the kingdom demands humility*: "Except ye be converted, and become as little children, ye shall not enter into the kingdom of heaven" (v.3); *(b) elevation in the kingdom demands humility*: "Whosoever therefore shall humble himself as this little child, the same is greatest in the kingdom of heaven" (v.4).

We also noted that while, in the Lord's own words, the 'little children' or "little ones" in these verses, are described as "these little ones which believe on me" (v.6), commentators understand His exact meaning in different ways. Some writers define the children here as 'spiritual children'. See, for example, Wm.MacDonald: "In these verses, the Lord Jesus glides almost imperceptibly from the subject of a natural child to a spiritual child". Robert H. Mounce defines them as "the 'average members' of the local congregation!" R.V.G.Tasker has "the weaker and more sensitive brethren!". However, it does seem that the Lord is referring, as noted above, simply to believing children: "these little ones which believe on me". The Saviour speaks about *(a)* the privilege of receiving them (v.5); *(b)* the punishment for offending them (vv.6-9); *(c)* the preciousness bestowed upon them (vv.10-14). This brings us to:

2) FORGIVENESS AMONG BRETHREN, vv.15-35

This section of the chapter may also be divided into two sections: *(A)* dealing with offences (vv.15-20); *(B)* displaying forgiveness (vv.21-35). We should notice the Lord's words here, "If thy ***brother*** shall sin ***against thee***" (v.15), and Peter's question "How often shall my ***brother*** sin ***against me***, and I forgive him?" (v.21).

A) Dealing with offences, vv.15-20

Having warned His disciples against stumbling "one of these little ones which believe in me" (v.6), the Lord Jesus looks at the subject from the opposite point of view and outlines the correct response of a believer who has been offended: "Moreover if thy brother shall trespass against thee…" (v.15). In dealing with offending "the little ones which believe in me", we noticed that reference is made to "the world" generally and to "that man by whom the offence cometh" particularly (v.7). The Lord's references to "everlasting fire" and "hell fire" are proof positive that He is not referring to converted people. But this is not the case in our current passage. The Lord now deals with the question of relationships between believers: "if thy ***brother*** shall trespass against thee…thou hast gained thy ***brother***… tell it unto the ***church***…if he neglect to hear the ***church***…where two or three are ***gathered together in my name***, there am I in the midst of them" (vv.15, 17, 20). We should notice: *(a)* the circumstances (v.15); *(b)* the confidentiality (v.15); *(c)* the confirmation (v.16); *(d)* the culmination (v.17); *(e)* the consequences (vv.17-20).

a) The circumstances, v.15

"If thy brother shall ***trespass*** against thee…" The word "trespass" (*hamartano*) means 'to sin', literally 'a missing of the mark' (W.E.Vine). Very clearly then, the Lord Jesus refers to a serious ***personal*** matter. Moral failure or erroneous doctrine, where "a little leaven leaveneth the whole lump" (1 Cor. 5: 6; Gal 5: 9), are immensely serious, but that is not the subject here. Neither is it a question of a believer being "overtaken in a fault" (Gal. 6: 1). It has to be said that things are often said and done amongst the Lord's people which are best overlooked, and that is the end of the matter. Believers sometimes take offence too quickly over small matters, and 'fly off the handle' at the smallest criticism or observation from a fellow-believer! On the other hand, tale-bearing, character-assassination, and deliberate misrepresentation are very different matters (read Leviticus 19: 16; Proverbs 16: 28; 26: 20, 22; Galatians 5: 15), and Christians can certainly "trespass" against each other in this way.

b) The confidentiality, v.15

"If thy brother trespass against thee, go and tell him his fault between thee and him *alone*: if he shall hear thee, thou hast gained thy brother". The Lord is evidently referring here to Levitcus 19: 17: "Thou shalt not hate thy brother in thine heart: thou shalt in any wise rebuke thy neighbour, and not suffer sin upon him ('lest thou bear sin on account of him', JND)". Bearing in mind that the word "fault" (*elencho*) means 'to convict, reprove, rebuke' (W.E.Vine), this may be translated, "go, reprove him between thee and him alone" (JND). Not go and complain about your brother's conduct to someone else. Not go around, lobbying other people in order to 'drum up' support for your cause. Not ostracise the offending brother. Not 'giving as good as you get'. But go and see him (or her) privately, raise the matter, make your complaint, not to humiliate or destroy him, but in order to 'gain' (*kerdaino*) your brother. The object is to win your brother who "by being told privately of his offence, and by accepting the representations, is won from alienation and from the consequences of his fault" (W.E.Vine). But, as Wm.MacDonald rightly points out, "The trouble is that we don't do this. We go to everyone else and gossip about it. Then the matter spreads like wildfire and strife is multiplied". We are not always very good when it comes to confidentiality!

We mustn't think that Paul ignored the Lord's teaching here when he "withstood" Peter "to the face", and "said unto Peter before them all..." (Gal. 2: 11, 14). Peter had set a bad example publicly (Gal. 2: 12-13), and the matter had to be adjusted publicly. But a private matter must not be turned into a 'blow by blow' news item for all in the assembly, and beyond the assembly, to digest. Let it be said clearly, that the object of the visit described here is the resumption of good relationships. "Behold, how good and how pleasant it is for brethren to dwell together in unity" (Psalm 133: 1).

c) The confirmation, v.16

"But if he will not hear thee, then take with thee one or two more, that in the mouth of two or three witnesses every word may be established". Robert H. Mounce is surely right in saying that "If that does not clear up the problem, the next step is to take one or two others along, not to prove the other's guilt, but **to help in reconciliation**". At the same time, "it provides competent testimony, as required by the Scripture, 'that in the mouth of two or three witnesses every word may be established'...No one can measure the trouble that has plagued the church through failure to obey the simple rule that a charge against another person must be supported by the testimony of two or three others. In this respect, worldly courts often act more righteously than Christian churches or assemblies" (Wm. MacDonald).

The Lord refers here to Deuteronomy 19: 15, "One witness shall not rise up against a man for any iniquity, or for any sin, in any sin that he sinneth: at the mouth of two witnesses, or at the mouth of three witnesses, shall the matter be established". Robert H. Mounce confirms his observation above by saying that the purpose of this quotation "in the New Testament setting is not to establish a conviction, but to settle a dispute".

d) The culmination, v.17
"And if he shall neglect to hear them, tell it unto the church: but if he neglect to hear the church, let him be unto thee as an heathen man and a publican". According to W.E.Vine the words "neglect to hear" translated one word (*parakouo*), primarily signifying 'to overhear, hear amiss or imperfectly… then…to hear without taking heed'". We must take the opportunity to say that this is the second reference to the church in Matthew's Gospel.

- The first reference concerns the founding and building of the **universal church**. That is, "the church, which is his body, the fulness of him that filleth all in all" (Eph. 1: 22-23). The Lord Jesus said, "thou art Peter, and upon this rock (the truth confessed by Peter) I will build my church" (Matt. 16: 18), and we noted that this declaration was made against the background of His national rejection. Having described the nation as "a wicked and adulterous generation" which "seeketh after a sign", the Lord "left them and departed" (Matt. 16: 4), and, shortly afterwards, He announced the commencement of the church.

- The second reference (twice in v.17) concerns a **local church**, or, to use R.V.G.Tasker's thoroughly recommended language, 'the local congregation'. If the reason for introducing the universal church in Matthew 16: 18 is clear, then so are the reasons for introducing the local church here. As we have observed on several occasions in our 'Matthew studies', the Lord Jesus did not **develop** the subject of the church, whether in its universal or local aspects, in view of the inability of the disciples to understand at the time: "I have yet many things to say unto you, but ye cannot bear them now, Howbeit when he, the Spirit of truth, is come, he will guide you into all truth" (John 16: 12-13). But the question of maintaining good relationships between believers in the local church (the local congregation), and dealing with fractured relationships, is so important that the Saviour dealt with this subject Himself. Experience has shown how right He was! Many companies of God's people have foundered, not on the rocks of wrong doctrine, and certainly not under fierce opposition (this only serves to strengthen the testimony), but on the rocks of personal antagonism and severed or strained relationships. How necessary it is to "stand fast in one spirit, with one mind striving together for the faith of the gospel" (Phil. 1: 27). Do remember that "the little foxes...spoil the vines" (Song of Solomon 2: 15). The trouble is that the "little foxes" sometimes turn into roaring lions!

Returning now to the text in our passage, it could be said that in the circumstances described, the local church is the final court of appeal: "And if he shall neglect to hear them, tell it unto the church". It is hardly necessary to point out that the Lord does not say 'tell it to the bishop' or 'tell it to the synod'. He does not refer to the governing body of a 'Christian denomination'. The local church (local assembly or congregation) is invested with importance and responsibility. It is to be hoped that the person responsible for 'trespassing' (sinning) against his brother will "hear the church". It is also to be hoped that the 'offended brother' will relate the case with deep grief. There was nothing gleeful or enthusiastic about Paul when he wrote to the assembly at Corinth about their misdemeanours: on the contrary, he wrote "out of much affliction and anguish of heart... with many tears" (2 Cor. 2: 4). There were also tears in his eyes when he wrote to the Philippians: "many walk, of whom I have told you often, and now tell you even weeping, that they are the enemies of the cross of Christ" (Phil. 3: 18).

Speaking generally, it has been known for believers to resort to the law of the land in attempting to settle disputes between them. This happened at Corinth: "Dare any of you, having a matter against another, go to law before the unjust, and not before the saints?...I speak to your shame. Is it so, that there is not a wise man among you? No, not one that shall be able to judge between his brethren? But brother goeth to law with brother, and that before unbelievers...Why do ye not rather take wrong? Why do ye not rather suffer yourselves to be defrauded?" (1 Cor. 6: 1, 5-7). This is not the time or place to expound this passage, but we should at least notice that rather than imperil the entire testimony by 'washing our dirty linen in public', believers should accept the situation, however distasteful: "Why do ye not rather take wrong? Why do ye not rather suffer yourselves to be defrauded?" In this context, the word "defrauded" means robbed, cheated, possibly of money or property" (J.Hunter, *What the Bible Teaches*).

e) The consequences, vv.17-20

The balance of the present section describes procedure should the guilty party not "hear the church". "If he shall neglect to hear the church, let him be unto thee as an heathen man and a publican" (v.17). Wm.MacDonald can hardly be bettered here: "If the defendant refuses to admit his wrong before the church, then he is to be considered as 'a Gentile (*ethnikos*: AV 'heathen man'; JND 'one of the nations') and a tax collector. The most obvious meaning of this expression is that he should be looked upon as being outside the sphere of the church; that is, he should be excommunicated. Though he be a true believer, he is not living as one. Therefore he should be taken at his profession and treated accordingly. Though still in the universal church, he should be barred from the privileges of the local church". This may seem severe, but on reflection, how can a believer who refuses to be reconciled to his brother against whom he has sinned, and who refuses to listen to the judgment, advice and exhortation of the local church, possibly remain "in fellowship"? This would turn the Lord's supper into a farce: see 1 Cor. 10: 16-17. Paul deals with the matter of excommunication on account of sinful behaviour, particularly immorality, in 1 Cor. 5: 1-13. It should be pointed out that the purpose of such disciplinary action is the restoration and well-being of the person concerned: see 1 Cor. 5: 5. In this particular case, repentance having taken place, Paul later urged the assembly at Corinth to forgive him and restore him to assembly fellowship: see 2 Cor. 2: 6-8.

The Lord Jesus makes three important points in connection with the disciplinary action by the local church:

i)　It has already been determined in heaven, v.18: "Verily I say unto you, Whatsoever ye shall bind on earth shall be bound in heaven: and whatsoever ye shall loose on earth shall be loosed in heaven". The Lord Jesus said exactly the same (apart from the use of "thou" in the place of "ye") in Matthew 16: 19, where He referred to the preaching of the Gospel, as explained in the relevant notes. In the current passage, 'binding' again refers to judgment in the sense of church discipline (excommunication). Loosing, obviously, is the reverse: restoration after repentance. See 1 Cor. 5: 4-5; 2 Cor. 2: 6-8. Again, according to the *Linguistic Key to the Greek New Testament,* the original reads, literally, 'Whatsoever thou shalt bind on earth **will have been bound** in heaven: and whatsoever thou shalt loose on earth **will have been loosed** in heaven'. It is "the church on earth carrying out heaven's decisions, not heaven ratifying the church's decision".

Matthew

ii) It is carried out with united prayer, v.19: "Again I say unto you, That if two of you (that is, the smallest possible number) shall **agree** on earth as touching any thing that they shall **ask**, it shall be done for them of my Father which is in heaven". It would be quite wrong to use this as a 'blank cheque' and to assume that anything and everything is available as long as we are united in our request. John steers us away from such a notion by saying, "And this is the confidence that we have in him, that, if we ask any thing **according to his will**, he heareth us" (1 John 5: 14). In the case of church discipline, the Lord Jesus has clearly revealed His will in this very passage. However, cases of this nature can be perplexing in the extreme, and it does therefore seem that the Lord is referring here to a request for wisdom in the circumstances, reminding us that "if any of you lack wisdom, let him ask of God, that giveth unto all men liberally, and upbraideth not; and it shall be given him" (James 1: 5).

iii) It is carried out with the Lord's presence and sanction, v.20: "For where two or three are gathered together in my name ('unto my name', JND), there am I in the midst of them". This verse is quoted *ad lib* (an abbreviation of *ad libitum*) amongst the Lord's people, and the last thing we would wish to do is to rob believers of the reassurance and joy that it brings them. However, as with any passage in the scriptures, the context points to the correct interpretation, and Wm.MacDonald expresses this admirably: "It does not refer primarily to the composition of a New Testament church in its simplest form. Neither does it refer to the general prayer meeting. It refers to a meeting when the church seeks to effect the reconciliation of two Christians who have been separated by some sin. Of course, it may be legitimately **applied** (our italics) to all meetings of believers where Christ is the gathering Centre, but a specific type of meeting is in view here". In this connection, it has been pointed out that 1 Corinthians 5: 3-5 describes a meeting of the church for the same purpose: "For I verily, as absent in body, but present in spirit, have judged already, as though I were present, concerning him that hath so done this deed, in the name of our Lord Jesus Christ, when ye be **gathered together**, and my spirit, **with the power of our Lord Jesus Christ**, to deliver such an one unto Satan for the destruction of the flesh, that the spirit may be saved in the day of the Lord Jesus".

B) Displaying forgiveness, vv.21-35
These verses can be simply divided as follows: *(a)* the question (v.21); *(b)* the answer (v.22); *(c)* the illustration (vv.23-35).

a) The question, v.21

Peter had evidently been giving some thought to the Lord's teaching. Having heard the Lord say, "if thy brother shall trespass against thee, go and tell him his fault between thee and him alone: if he shall hear thee, thou hast gained thy brother" (v.15), he asks the question, "Lord, how oft shall my brother sin against me, and I forgive him? Till seven times?" (v.21). In the words of Wm. Kelly: "We had instruction how we were to act in the case of a personal trespass. But Peter raises another question. Supposing my brother sins against me over and over, how often am I to forgive him?"

It should be said that Peter's question must have been based on the assumption that in each hypothetical case he had gone to his brother and reproved him, following which there had been repentance and restoration of fellowship. This must be the case. Sins can never be forgiven without repentance. They cannot be passed over in silence. But even on this basis, is there a limit to forgiveness? In Peter's words, "Till seven times?" According to Robert H. Mounce, "Rabbinic literature taught that 'if a man sins once, twice, or three times, they forgive him: if he sins a fourth time, they do not forgive him'", and adds, "Going beyond the accepted limit, Peter asks, 'Would seven times be enough' (Phillips)".

b) The answer, v.22

"Jesus saith unto him, I say not unto thee, Until seven times: but, Until seventy times seven". John Heading (*What the Bible Teaches - Matthew*) suggests that it is possible that the Lord's reply alludes to "the 'sevenfold' vengeance that would have been taken against a man who murdered Cain (Gen. 4: 15)", and Lamech's boast that "he would be avenged 'seventy and sevenfold', going far beyond the number associated with Cain (Gen. 4: 24)". It is worth pointing out that according to the Hebrew text, Lamech does say "seventy and sevenfold" which is seventy-seven. According to Basil F. C. Atkinson, the Septuagint Greek version has 'seventy times seven'. Perhaps we should simply say that the Lord is evidently referring here to **unlimited forgiveness**. If you want to press "seventy times seven" (490), you may wish to think in terms of Daniel's 'seventy weeks' prophecy (Dan. 9: 24-27). These are weeks of years, and therefore cover 490 years which is the period determined "to finish the transgression, and to make an end of sins, and to make reconciliation for iniquity, and to bring in everlasting righteousness, and to seal up the vision and prophecy, and to anoint the most Holy" (Dan. 9: 24). In forgiving and restoring His people, God thinks in terms of 'seventy times seven'.

c) The illustration, vv.23-35
This speaks for itself. We have been marvellously forgiven ourselves (vv.23-27); we are therefore to show forgiveness to others (vv.24-35).

i) The extent of our forgiveness by God, vv.23-27.
Just look at the man's debt: "ten thousand talents". It is thought that the verb "brought" (*prosago*) could mean 'brought from prison' (v.24). According to W.E.Vine (in his *Expository Dictionary of New Testament Words* published in 1940), "the vastness of the sum...(£2,400,000), indicates the impossibility of the man's clearing himself, by his own efforts, of the guilt which lies upon him before God". (W.E.Vine is preaching the Gospel from the passage!). In saying to the king, "Lord, have patience with me, and I will pay thee all" (v.26), the debtor was stating the impossible. 'A talent is the same as 6,000 denarii, and one denarius is about a labourer's wages for a day's work (Matt. 20: 2)' (supplied by Justin Waldron). This well describes our position without Christ: hopelessly in debt to God. But there is good news for the man - marvellous news: "Then the lord of that servant was moved with compassion, and loosed him, and forgave him the debt" (v.27). And there is marvellous news for us too. Just listen to this: "God for Christ's sake hath forgiven you" (Eph. 4: 32).

ii) The exercise of our forgiveness to others, vv.28-35.
Enter another debtor, owing the newly-forgiven man a comparatively small sum: "an hundred pence (denarii)" (v.28): less than five pounds. There is no question of the creditor going and telling him "his fault" (v.15). He takes his fellow-servant "by the throat, saying, Pay me that thou owest" (v.28). The half-throttled fellow-servant uses almost the same words as the merciless man had previously used himself (v.29), but to no avail: he is consigned to the debtors' prison. The consequences follow: "Then said his lord...O thou wicked servant, I forgave thee all that debt, because thou desiredst me: shouldest not thou also have had compassion on thy fellowservant, even as I had pity on thee?" (vv.32-33). The word "tormentors" (literally 'torturers', v.34) refers, in applying the illustration, to 'retributive judgment' (W.E.Vine).

The Lord Jesus makes the application: "so likewise shall my heavenly Father do also unto you, if ye from your hearts forgive not every one his brother their trespasses" (v.35). Peter got his answer, and Paul adds: "And be ye kind one to another, tenderhearted, forgiving one another, even as God for Christ's sake hath forgiven you" (Eph. 4: 32). After all:

He little knows of God or heaven,
Who never breathes the word 'Forgiven'.

THE GOSPEL OF MATTHEW

"What...God hath joined together, let not man put asunder"

Read Chapter 19: 1-15
The Lord now leaves Galilee and commences what is evidently His final journey to Jerusalem. His stay in Capernaum (on the north-west shore of the lake) commenced with the enquiry about "tribute money" (17: 24), and concluded with His teaching in connection with greatness in the kingdom (18: 1-14) and forgiveness amongst brethren (18: 15-35). "And...when Jesus had finished these sayings, he departed from Galilee, and came into the coasts of Judaea beyond Jordan". The initial stages of His journey to Jerusalem took Him through Perea, "the area of Judaea that lay east of the Jordan" (Robert H. Mounce). "In great and customary grace He makes time for the multitudes that follow Him, and He heals their sick (v.2)" (J.M.Flanigan).

This brings us to the first of the two major sections in our passage: *(1)* His concern for the security of marriage (vv.3-12); *(2)* His concern for the salvation of children (vv.13-15). The passage exposes hardness of heart on the part of both the Pharisees (v.8), and, alas, the Lord's own disciples (v.13). A parallel passage is found in Mark 10: 1-16. But we must listen first to J.C.Ryle: "It is difficult to overrate the importance of these two subjects: the well-being of nations, and the happiness of society, are closely connected with right views upon them. Nations are nothing but a collection of families. The good order of families depends entirely on keeping up the highest respect for the marriage tie, and on the right training of children".

1) HIS CONCERN FOR THE SECURITY OF MARRIAGE, vv.1-12
At one time, when divorce and remarriage was a comparative rarity, the problem was largely academic. That is not so today: recent statistics suggest that 50% of marriages will end in the divorce court. Whilst the 50% divorce rate certainly does not apply to believers, there is, sadly, an

increasing incidence of broken marriages amongst the Lord's people. Whilst it is therefore important to stress the seriousness of divorce, it is equally important to stress the seriousness of marriage.

This section of the chapter may be divided as follows: *(a)* the subtlety of the Pharisees (v.3); *(b)* the teaching of the Lord Jesus (vv.4-9); *(c)* the conclusion of the disciples (vv.10-12).

a) The subtlety of the Pharisees, v.3
"The Pharisees also came unto him, tempting him, and saying unto him, Is it lawful for a man to put away his wife for every cause?" The words, "tempting him", make it clear that this was a 'catch question'. (Subtlety can be defined as 'slyness in design').

i) If the Lord Jesus had answered, 'No, it is not lawful for a man to put away his wife', the Pharisees would have gleefully quoted Deuteronomy 24: 1-2, "When a man hath taken a wife, and married her, and it come to pass that she find no favour in his eyes, because he hath found some uncleanness in her; then let him write her a bill of divorcement, and give it in her hand, and send her out of his house. And when she is departed out of his house, she may go and be another man's wife".

ii) On the other hand, if the Lord Jesus had answered, 'Yes, it is lawful for a man to put away his wife', the Pharisees would have gleefully quoted Genesis 2: 24, "Therefore shall a man leave his father and his mother, and shall cleave unto his wife: and they shall be one flesh".

There seemed to be no way out of this impasse: the Lord's enemies had apparently put Him in an impossible position. But their attempt to out-wit and out-manoeuvre Him utterly failed. His answer satisfied both passages. (We should note that, undaunted, the Pharisees, with the Herodians, later faced the Lord Jesus with another apparent dilemma, only to be silenced again. See Mark 12: 13-17. He proved to be complete master of the situation on both occasions). Notice now the principle on which He dealt with the Pharisees' question:

b) The teaching of the Lord Jesus, vv.4-9
The Saviour silenced His enemies by *explaining* both passages. For their purposes, the Pharisees were prepared to set one Bible passage against another. They would do just anything to achieve their end. But their attempt

to defeat the Lord Jesus fell apart when the relevant Scriptures were carefully explained. This is most important. When two passages appear to contradict each other, or others tell us that there is a contradiction, *careful study will resolve the problem.* This must involve reference to the context in which any statement is made, and the time at which it is made. It must also involve recognition that all Scripture must be interpreted with reference to God's original, and unchanged, purposes. This will now become very clear as we listen to the Lord's teaching. We should notice three major points here: *(i)* the institution of marriage by God (vv.4-6); *(ii)* the introduction of divorce through Moses (vv.7-8); *(iii)* the instruction on divorce by Christ (v.9).

i) The institution of marriage by God, vv.4-6

The Lord Jesus answered the Pharisees by emphasising God's clearly-stated intention for marriage: "He answered and said unto them, Have ye not read (could that be said of us?), that he which made them at the beginning made them male and female, and said, For this cause shall a man leave (*kataleipo*, to leave behind) father and mother, and shall cleave (*proskollao*, to glue or cement together) to his wife: and they twain shall be one flesh? Wherefore they are no more twain, but one flesh. What therefore God hath joined together, let not man put asunder". In passing, do notice that the Lord cited Genesis 1: 27 as well as Genesis 2: 24. This, in itself, clearly answers any suggestion of evolution. The Lord Jesus confirms the creation of Adam and Eve, which is not at all surprising when we remember that, "All things were made by him; and without him was not anything made that was made" (John 1: 3).

Returning to the particular subject of the passage, it should be noted that the words, "let not *man* put asunder" are not qualified. "It is left open whether the reference is to one of the two parties concerned, or an intruder who may seek to wreck the marriage, or to an official who would pronounce a decree of divorce" (Harold St. John, *An Analysis of the Gospel of Mark*). The Lord's words, "Moses, because of the hardness of your hearts, suffered you to put away your wives, *but from the beginning it was not so"* (v.8) confirm the divine purpose for continuity in marriage.

The fact that Paul cites Genesis 2: 24 in speaking "concerning Christ and the church" (Eph. 5: 31-32), is indicative of the intended permanence and indissolubility of marriage. This standard has never been revoked. Marriage is regarded as a solemn covenant before God. See Proverbs 2:

17 and Malachi 2: 14. God has made His mind perfectly clear on the subject of divorce: "For the Lord, the God of Israel, saith that he hateth putting away" (Mal. 2: 16). It should be the desire of every believer to fulfil God's revealed will in relation to marriage, and therefore **divorce should never be contemplated.**

There is a most important principle here: God's **original purposes** stand unchanged, whatever may happen subsequently. We must always therefore go back to the beginning when settling any question. Notice how Paul applied this principle in Galatians 1: 8-9. He settles the whole question of justification by faith, as opposed to righteousness by the law, on exactly the same basis. Read, for example, Romans 4.

ii) The introduction of divorce through Moses, vv.7-8
While, as we have seen, the Lord Jesus cited God's original and unchanged purpose for marriage, the fact remains that in answer to their question, "Why did Moses then command to give a writing of divorcement, and to put her away?", the Lord replied: "Moses, because of the hardness of your hearts (one word, *sklerokardia*) suffered you to put away your wives: but from the beginning it was not so". Moses did not "command" divorce: he permitted it. The word, "hardness", indicates 'a hard, even inhuman, character' (W.E.Vine). We should therefore notice:

- That in the Old Testament, divorce, though not envisaged in the divine ideal for marriage, was allowed in order to save an unfortunate woman from a loveless marriage. See Deuteronomy 24: 1-2. The woman was then free to marry, and there is no reference to this being an "abomination before the Lord", and "causing the land to sin" (Deut. 24: 4). As H.St.John rightly observes, "It was not the highest that could have been given, it was the best that Israel was fit to receive". Sufficient to say that the child of God lives, not by the best possible solution for unregenerate man, but by the highest standard taught in Genesis 2: 24. Without entering into the detail of Deuteronomy 24: 1-2, it can at least be said that the circumstances described must refer to the very earliest stage of a marriage.

- That this provision had been evidently abused, and men were divorcing their wives at the slightest whim. Hence the question, "Is it lawful for a man to put away his wife **for every cause?**" (v.3). The school of Shammai (those who followed Rabbi Shammah) allowed divorce only on the ground of adultery. The school of Hillel (those who followed Rabbi Hillel, with his more liberal views) allowed divorce for the most amazing reasons. J.C.Ryle: cites Lightfoot's Horae Hebraicae on Matthew 5: 31. 'The school of Hillel saith, If a wife cooks her husband's food ill by over-salting it, or over-roasting it, she is to be put away'. Edersheim notes that the same liberal school allowed divorce on the grounds that a man had found another woman more attractive than his wife. Others allowed a man to divorce his wife for spinning in the streets, or if she spoke disrespectfully about his parents in his presence. The mind boggles!

iii) The instruction on divorce by Christ, v.9
In view of the abuse of Deuteronomy 24: 1-2, the Lord Jesus adjusts the Mosaic provision by restating the divine ideal, and the consequences of its transgression: "And I say unto you, Whosoever shall put away his wife, excepting it be for fornication, and **shall marry another**, committeth adultery: and whoso marrieth her which is put away doth commit adultery". We must listen to Mark here: Whosoever shall put away his wife, and **marry another**, committeth adultery against her. And if a woman shall put away her husband, and be **married to another**, she committeth adultery" (Mark 10: 11-12). We must also listen to Luke: "Whosoever putteth away his wife and marrieth another committeth adultery: and **whosoever marrieth her that is put away from her husband,** committeth adultery" (Luke 16: 18). Mark and Luke admit no exception. Only Matthew has "excepting it be for fornication". Paul sets out the position very clearly indeed: "The law hath dominion over a man as long as he liveth. For a woman which hath an husband is bound by the law to her husband **as long as he liveth;** but if the husband be dead, she is loosed from the law of her husband. So then **if while her husband liveth,** she be married to another man, she shall be called an adulteress; but **if her husband be dead,** she is free from that law; so that she is no adulteress, though she be married to another man" (Rom. 7: 2-3).

Since the Lord Jesus is clearly amending the Mosiac law, we must recognise that He had every authority to do so. In this connection, His exact words should be carefully noted: "He saith unto them, Moses because of the hardness of your hearts, suffered you to put away your wives: but from the beginning it was not so. And **I say unto you...**". See also 5: 31-32: "It hath been said, Whosoever shall put away his wife, let him give her a writing of divorcement: **But I say unto you...**" This clearly expresses the Lord's authority, and it is worth noting that while the words **"saith the Lord of hosts"** punctuate the last book in the Old Testament, they are replaced by *"I say unto you"* in the first book of the New Testament. The Lord who **speaks** from heaven in Malachi, is **present on earth** in Matthew.

There is, however, the question of the so-called 'exception clause': "And I say unto you, Whosoever shall put away his wife, **except it be for fornication,** and shall marry another, committeth adultery: and whoso marrieth her that is put away doth commit adultery". See also Matthew 5: 31-32. One thing is perfectly clear, these verses (Matt. 5: 32; 19: 9) allow divorce on one ground only: immorality. Not mental cruelty, incompatibility, desertion, irretrievable breakdown, irrecoverable brain damage, or any other reason. **The only ground is immorality**. If otherwise than immorality (to be precise, "fornication"), then the husband who puts away his wife and remarries becomes guilty of adultery (19: 9): the woman who has been wrongly put away and then remarries, is caused to commit adultery (Matt. 5: 32): the person who marries the wife wrongly put away also commits adultery (Matt. 5: 32; 19: 9).

But 'immorality' must be qualified. The precise word is "fornication". This is the word used by the Lord Jesus in Matthew, and it is here that able men divide. There are two major camps:

i) *That "fornication" includes immorality of all kinds*: pre-marital and post-marital, and therefore includes adultery. It is unfortunate that W.E.Vine, in his excellent *Expository Dictionary of New Testament Words*, should say 'in Matthew 5: 32 and 19: 9, it stands for, and includes, adultery'. If the Lord Jesus meant adultery as the one ground of divorce, then it is surprising that He did not say so.

ii) *That "fornication" must be distinguished from "adultery"*, and refers to pre-marital unchastity alone. The fact that **only Matthew**, writing **for Jews**, includes the 'exception clause', gives support for the view that a man could only divorce his wife if there had been evidence of pre-marital unchastity. Under the Jewish betrothal laws, a betrothed maiden was regarded as a wife, although - technically - this was not actually the case. This is clear from Deuteronomy 22: 23-34 ("betrothed to an husband.... his neighbour's wife"), and illustrated in Matthew 1: 18-20, where Joseph is called "her husband", and Mary, "thy wife....his wife", even "before they came together". There is, therefore, a particularly Jewish context to Matthew 5 and Matthew 19, which is inapplicable in Mark and Luke, where there is no 'exception clause'.

In further support for this view, it is often stated that where the word "fornication" is used *alone,* it signifies immorality generally, but where it is used with adultery, it refers specifically to pre-marital unchastity as opposed to post-marital infidelity. See Matthew 5: 32, Matthew 19: 9, 1 Corinthians 6: 9, and Hebrews 13: 4 (AV "whoremongers': JND 'fornicators').

There can therefore be no question of divorce for the believer. In the words of H.S.Paisley, "The ideal for a broken marriage is not divorce, but reconciliation in the spirit of forgiveness". In cases where a husband or wife is deserted, and under current English law, a divorce can be obtained by the guilty party after two years, the innocent party must remain single. In the sight of God, the original marriage remains valid.

It is also important to remember that whilst we speak of 'Christian marriage', there is in fact no such thing. Marriage is connected with creation, not Christianity, and this must be borne in mind when dealing with *any* divorce question.

iii) The conclusion of the disciples, vv.10-12
"His disciples say unto him, If the case of the man be so with his wife, it is not good to marry" (v.10). Wm.MacDonald leaves us in no doubt about the disciples' meaning: "When the disciples heard the Lord's teaching on divorce, they proved themselves to be creatures of extremes by adopting the absurd position that if divorce is obtainable on only one ground, then it would be better not to marry at all". He further explains that in saying "all men cannot receive this saying save they to whom it is given" (v.11), the Lord did not mean that "all men cannot understand the meaning of what follows, but rather that they cannot live a continent life unless they are called to it". Only certain people are called to a celibate life. The Lord Jesus then described three types of eunuchs (v.12), two involuntary (those "so born from their mother's womb" and those "made eunuchs of men", and one voluntary (those "which have made themselves eunuchs for the kingdom of heaven's sake"). Wm.MacDonald describes the third category nicely: "They have no physical impairment. Yet in dedication to the King and His kingdom, they willingly forego the marriage relationship in order to give themselves to the cause of Christ without distraction, As Paul wrote later: 'He that is unmarried careth for the things that belong to the Lord, how he may please the Lord' (1 Cor. 7: 32)".

Having said this, the Lord Jesus adds, "He that is able to receive it (that is, marriage), let him receive it". In summary, the disciples had said, "If the case of the man be so with his wife, it is not good to marry" (v.10), to which the Saviour, having said that there are exceptions, replies that in general it *is* good to marry.

2) HIS CONCERN FOR THE SALVATION OF CHILDREN, V13-15

As J.M.Flanigan observes: "It seems so fitting that immediately following all this they bring little children to Him. It is well known that so often when there is divorce, the real casualties of the breaking up of the marriage are the children". We should notice the following: *(a)* the attitude of the parents (v.13); *(b)* the attitude of the disciples (v.13); *(c)* the attitude of the Lord Jesus (vv.14-15).

a) The attitude of the parents, v.13

"Then were there brought unto him little children (*paidion*: as in 18: 2-5), that he should put his hands on them, and pray". Mark has: "And they brought young children (*paidion*) to him, that he should touch them" (Mark 10: 13). Luke has "And they brought unto him also infants (*brephos*, a suckling), that he would touch them" (Luke 18: 15). All three have *paidion* when it comes to "Suffer little children (or 'Suffer the little children) to come unto me". J.C.Ryle is so right in saying: "We must never allow ourselves to suppose that little children's souls may be safely let alone. Their characters for life depend exceedingly on what they see and hear during their first seven years". Ryle continues: "The boys and girls of every family should be taught as soon as they can learn, should be brought to public worship as soon as they can behave with propriety, should be regarded with affectionate interest as the future congregation, which will fill our places when we are dead". This much will meet with ready agreement by every spiritually minded parent. But that does not mean that we must agree with him over his teaching on infant baptism! It is very important to read with discernment!

b) The attitude of the disciples, v.13

"The disciples rebuked them". The same word (*epitimao*) is used all in three Gospels. We could be charitable and suggest that in all probability, they were thinking, misguidedly, of their Master's best interests. 'We mustn't allow Him to be bothered with such trivialities'. But if that was their reason, the Lord Jesus was not impressed: Mark tells us that "he was much displeased (JND 'indignant')" (Mark 10:14). We may conclude that His displeasure arose, **firstly**, from their assumption that He would not wish to be bothered by children, and, **secondly**, from their failure to remember recent-given teaching: "Whosoever shall receive one of such children in my name receiveth me: and whosoever shall receive me, receiveth not me, but him that sent me" (Mark 9: 37). H.St.John makes a telling comment that "Many Protestant Churches are either merely marking time, or even withering at the roots, because Christ's little ones are neglected, and the chief energies of their members are devoted to adults. Rome is wiser". Whilst that could be regarded as a sweeping statement, it is worth serious consideration. After all, generally speaking, children are the only age group today, at least in the U.K., who will listen to the Gospel.

c) The attitude of the Lord Jesus, vv.14-15

Notice two things here. **Firstly,** what He said: ""Suffer little children, and forbid them not, to come unto me: for of such is the kingdom of heaven ('kingdom of God', Mark 10: 15; Luke 18: 16)" (v.14). Mark adds, "Verily I say unto you, Whosoever shall not receive the kingdom of God as a little child, he shall not enter therein" (Mark 10: 15). See also Luke 18: 17. The lesson is clear: The Saviour is not teaching that we must become **childish**, but **childlike**. That is, to enter God's kingdom, we must have the simple faith and trust of a little child: absolute, implicit confidence in Him. **Secondly,** what He did: "And he laid his hands on them, and departed thence" (v.15) or "he took them up in his arms, and put his hands upon them, and blessed them" (Mark 10: 16). Isaiah had said, "Behold, the Lord God will come with strong hand, and His arm shall rule for him...He shall gather the lambs with his arm, and carry them in his bosom" (Isaiah 40: 10-11). The **arm** that rules is the **arm** that gathers the lambs. But here the Saviour uses **both arms!** The message is clear for all involved in Gospel work amongst children: He has infinite love and concern for them. A child can truly sing:

> *Jesus, when He left the sky,*
> *And for sinners came to die,*
> *In His mercy passed not by*
> *Little ones like me.*
>
> *Twas for them His life He gave,*
> *To redeem them from the grave;*
> *Jesus able is to save*
> *Little ones like me.*

"Who then can be saved"

Read Chapter 19: 16-30
In commenting on this chapter, F.B.Hole (*The Gospels and Acts*) suggests that "we may summarise vv.10-26 by stating that the Lord shed His light upon marriage, children and possessions: three things that occupy so much of our lives in this world, and in each case the light He shed overturned the thoughts which previously the disciples had entertained, see vv.10, 13, 25".

Our current passage may be divided into two related paragraphs: *(1)* a man who had everything (vv.16-26), but he had nothing: he did not respond to the Saviour's demand, "come and follow me" (v.21); *(2)* men who had nothing (vv.27-30), but they had everything: they had responded to the Saviour's demand: "we have forsaken all, and followed thee" (v.27). Parallel passages are found in Mark 10: 17-31; Luke 18: 18-30.

1) A MAN WHO HAD EVERYTHING, vv.16-26
In the previous paragraph, the Lord said, "Suffer little children...to come unto me: for of such is the kingdom of heaven" (v.14), but He now has to say that "a rich man shall hardly enter into the kingdom of heaven" (v.23) Mark tells us that the Saviour said, "Whosoever shall not receive the kingdom of God as a little child, he shall not enter therein" (Mark 10: 15) and Luke reads similarly (Luke 18: 17). Now we have a man who would not "receive the kingdom of God as a little child". The children went away "blessed" but this man "went away grieved" (Mark 10: 16, 22).

The incident related here is usually entitled 'The Rich Young Ruler'. Matthew tells us that he was a "young man" and that "he had great possessions" (v.22). Mark notes his "great possessions" (Mark 10: 22), and Luke says that he was "very rich" (Luke 18: 23). Luke also tells us that he was "a certain ruler" (Luke 18: 18). The word rendered "ruler" (*archon*) does not necessarily imply that he was a ruler of a synagogue: it is more likely that he was a government official.

The details given have been used to good effect in Gospel preaching. At the same time, we must not overlook lessons for ourselves. We can summarise these verses as follows: *(a)* the question he asked (v.16); *(b)* the answer he received (vv.17-19); *(c)* the submission he made (v.20); *(d)* the action he must take (v.21); *(e)* the decision he made (v.22); *(f)* the lesson that followed (vv.23-26)

Chapter 19

a) The question he asked, v.16
"And, behold, one came and said unto him, Good Master, what good thing shall I do that I may have eternal life?" The Lord Jesus deals with his form of address first (v.17a), and then with his actual question (vv.17b-19).

Matthew simply says "one came", but Mark tells us that he "came...running" (Mark 10: 17). He was evidently enthusiastic and genuinely expectant, quite the reverse of the Pharisees who "came unto him, tempting him, and saying unto him, Is it lawful for a man to put away his wife for every cause" (v.3). He had not come to ask a 'catch question'. Mark tells us that he "kneeled to him", which was something the proud Pharisees would never do. This man recognised the authority and superiority of the Lord Jesus.

If this was the attitude of a man who, so far as we can judge, never entered the kingdom of God, how much more enthusiasm, expectancy and submission, should be exhibited by all who follow Christ! But having said this, we must notice his evident concern about eternal life. Bearing in mind his position in life, this might have been the last question he wished to address. After all, he was *young* (vv.20, 22); he was *healthy* (he could run, (Mark 10: 17) he was *influential*, a ruler (Luke 18: 18); he was *rich*: "very rich" (Luke 18: 23); he was *moral*: "all these things (the commandments) have I kept from my youth up" (v.20). He had 'everything going for him', including morality. But he was concerned about eternal life, and evidently felt that all his advantages gave no assurance that it belonged to him. Sadly, however, his concern in itself was not sufficient. In the words of J.C.Ryle, "We must never forget that good feelings alone in religion are not the grace of God. We may know the truth intellectually; we may often feel pricked in conscience, we may have religious affections awakened within us, and have many anxieties about our souls, and shed many tears: but all this is not conversion. It is not the genuine saving work of the Holy Ghost".

b) The answer he received, vv.17-19
As noted above, this falls into two parts *(i)* the Lord's response to the address, "Good Master" (according to the scholars, the reading here should be simply "Master" or 'Teacher', see JND: but Mark and Luke have "Good Master" without question); *(ii)* the Lord's reply to the question, "what good thing shall I do, that I may have eternal life?"

i) The Lord's response to the address, "Why callest thou me good? there is none good but one, that is, God". In saying, "Good Master" (*didaskalos*, meaning 'teacher'), the young man used an expression unique in Scripture. N.Crawford (*What the Bible Teaches - Luke*) quotes A.Plummer: "There is no instance in the whole of the Talmud (the Jewish civil and canonical law) of a rabbi being addressed as 'Good Master'; the title was absolutely unknown among the Jews". Wm.Kelly makes the point that the "man had no idea that the one to whom he was speaking was God Himself. He merely went to Him as a good man". H.A.Ironside concurs: "In addressing the Lord as 'Good Master', the young man evidently meant to do Him honour, but Jesus points out that only God is good. All men are sinners (Rom. 3: 12). Therefore, if Jesus were only a man, He would not be good, in this absolute sense. If truly good, then He is God". There can be little doubt that in making the point, the Lord Jesus was laying the foundation for saying, "go and sell that thou hast, and give to the poor...and come and follow me" (v.21). The first commandment was, "Thou shalt have no other gods before me" (Exodus 20: 3). The Lord Jesus, therefore, had every right to the man's total allegiance.

ii) The Lord's reply to the question, "what good thing shall I do, that I may have eternal life?" Any gospel preacher worthy of the name would have answered the question by pointing out that none of us can do anything in order to gain eternal life. According to Mark, the young man asked, "Good Master, what shall I *do* that I may *inherit* eternal life" (Mark 10: 17). See also Luke 18: 18. The question itself is something of a paradox: it is not usual for a man to work for an inheritance, and it is *totally impossible* for a man to work for eternal life! The Scriptures speak for themselves: "the wages of sin is death; but *the gift of God* is eternal life, through Jesus Christ our Lord" (Rom. 6: 23); "For by grace are ye saved through faith; and that not of yourselves: it is the gift of God: not of works, lest any man should boast" (Eph. 2: 8-9). When the Lord Jesus was asked, "What shall we *do*, that we might work the works of God?", He answered: "this is the work of God, that ye *believe* on him whom he hath sent" (John 6: 28-29). When the Philippian jailor cried, "Sirs, what must I *do* to be saved?". Paul and Silas answered, "*Believe* on the Lord Jesus Christ, and thou shalt be saved" (Acts 16: 30-31).

However, the Lord Jesus did not answer in this way on this occasion. The young man had asked, "what good thing shall I *do*, that I may have eternal life?", and the Lord Jesus gave him a straight answer: "if thou wilt enter into life, keep the commandments". The law promised life to those who kept it (Lev. 18: 5; Gal. 3: 12) but, as H.A.Ironside points out, "this declaration was designed to show the man his inability to obtain life on that ground". Then, in answering his further question, "Which?", the Lord continued: "Thou shalt do no murder, Thou shalt not commit adultery, Thou shalt not steal, Thou shalt not bear false witness; honour thy father and thy mother; and, Thou shalt love thy neighbour as thyself" (vv.18-19), to which the young man replied, "All these things have I kept from my youth up: what lack I yet?" This brings us to:

c) The submission he made, v.20
"The young man saith unto him, All these things have I kept from my youth up: **what lack I yet?"** In fact, he might have said, in Paul's words, "touching the righteousness which is in the law, blameless (not, however, 'sinless')" (Phil. 3: 6). Here are two often-suggested answers to his question:

i) That the young man is typical of so many who have little conception of their sinfulness and guilt in the sight of God ("All these things have I kept from my youth up: what lack I yet?"): "so utterly ignorant is he of the spirituality of God's statutes, that he never doubts that he has perfectly fulfilled them. He seems thoroughly unaware that the commandments apply to the thoughts and words, as well as to the deeds, and that if God were to enter into judgment with him, he could 'not answer him one of a thousand' (Job 9: 3)" (J.C.Ryle). This is, of course, absolutely correct. However, the Lord Jesus did not actually go on to tell him that whilst he had kept the specified commandments outwardly, he had not kept them inwardly.

ii) That the Lord Jesus made no reference to the tenth commandment, "Thou shalt not covet", because it was here that the man failed, and had the Saviour included it, he would not then have been able to say, "All these things have I kept from my youth up". However, this is not specifically stated. As we shall see, his failure lay in another direction. In any case, the tenth commandment actually says, "Thou shalt not covet thy neighbour's house, thou shalt not covet thy neighbour's wife, nor his manservant, nor his maidservant, nor his ox, nor his ass, nor anything that is thy neighbour's" (Exod. 20: 17).

While we should certainly consider the answers above, it has to be said that the Saviour did not contradict the young man. He takes his submission at face value. But it was not the whole story, and we should carefully notice that while there are differences (but not contradictions) in the three accounts (Matthew alone has "Thou shalt love thy neighbour as thyself"; Mark alone has "defraud not"), all tell us that the Lord quoted those commandments which are **manward** in application. This is clear from the 'terminal summary': "Thou shalt love thy neighbour as thyself". He did **not** refer, as He did when dealing with the "lawyer", to "the first and great commandment": "Thou shalt love the Lord thy God with all thy heart, and with all thy soul, and with all thy mind" (Matt. 22: 35-38). This is what the young man 'lacked', and the Lord Jesus now answers his question, "All these things have I kept from my youth up: **what lack I yet?**", on the ground of his failure to love the Lord with all his "heart...soul...mind".

d) The action he must take, v.21
At this point, we really must bring in Mark to tell us **how** the Lord answered him, before allowing Matthew to tell us **what** the Lord said to him;

i) How the Lord answered him. "Then Jesus, beholding him, loved him" (Mark 10: 21). This is unique to Mark. It wasn't a sudden, fleeting, emotion. "Then Jesus, **beholding him**, loved him". J.C.Ryle comments beautifully: "We must never forget that Jesus feels love and compassion for the souls of the ungodly. Without controversy, He feels a peculiar love for those who hear His voice and follow Him. They are His sheep, given to Him by the Father, and watched with special care. They are His bride, joined to Him in an everlasting covenant, and dear to Him as part of Himself. But the heart of Jesus is a wide heart. He has abundance of pity, compassion, and tender concern even for those who are following sin and the world. He who wept over unbelieving Jerusalem is still the same".

ii) What the Lord said to him. "If thou wilt be perfect (*teleios*: 'complete', or 'attain the goal'), go and sell that thou hast, and give to the poor, and thou shalt have treasure in heaven: and come and follow me" (v.21), or "One thing thou **lackest** (here is the Lord's answer to the question, "what lack I yet"): go thy way, sell whatsoever thou hast, and give to the poor, and thou shalt have treasure in heaven: and come, take up the cross, and follow me" (Mark 10: 21). See also Luke 18: 22. The Lord Jesus answered the young man on the ground of his own confession. He had said, "all these things have I kept from my youth up: what lack I yet?" (v.20). But was this really the case? The man had said that he had fulfilled the commandments cited, including "Thou shalt love thy neighbour as thyself". But what will he do now in view of the Lord's words, "go thy way, sell whatsoever thou hast, and give to the poor?" His response made it very clear that he had not kept that commandment. He did not 'love his neighbour as himself'. Moreover, bearing in mind that the Lord Jesus is God ("there is none good, but one, that is, God"), He abrogated the first commandment: "Thou shalt have no other gods before me" (Exodus 20: 3). The law stated that "thou shalt love the Lord thy God with all thine heart, and with all thy soul, and with all thy might" (Deut 6: 5) and while Lord loved **him** (Mark 10: 21), it could not be said that he loved the Lord.

We must notice that the Lord Jesus spelt out the man's position very clearly. Eternal life meant identification with Him: "follow me". That meant two things. It **meant surrender of possessions:** "go and sell that thou hast, and give to the poor, and thou shalt have treasure in heaven. But more than even that, it meant **surrender of self:** "follow me". Mark makes the point with greater force: "come, take up the cross, and follow me" (Mark 10: 21). The significance of the cross has been explained as follows: "The old cross is a symbol of death. It stands for the abrupt violent end of a human being. The man in Roman times who took up his cross and started down the road had already said good-bye to his friends. He was not coming back. He was not going to have his life redirected; he was going to have it ended. The cross made no compromise, modified nothing, spared nothing; it slew the man completely and for good. It did not try to keep on good terms with its victim. It struck swift and hard, and when it had finished its work the man was no more....God offers life, but not an improved old life. The life He offers is life out of death. It stands on the far side of the cross. Whoever would possess it must pass under the rod. He must repudiate himself and concur in God's just sentence against him" (Extracted from *The Modern Smooth Cross*: author unknown).

e) The decision he made, v.22
"But when the young man heard that saying, he went away sorrowful: for he had great possessions". "Thus the great refusal was made; he kept his wealth, his town and country houses, and his seat on the council; but he had flung away the one key that would have opened to him the gates of life eternal" (H.St.John, writing on Mark). "The man had become the victim of his riches" (quoted by J.Waldron). He counted the cost, and it was too high. The Lord Jesus taught, "And whosoever doth not bear his cross, and come after me, cannot be my disciple" (Luke 14: 27). We must all face this test. The Lord Jesus does not say to every one of **us,** "go and sell that thou hast, and give to the poor", but He might say, 'Put Me before your plans for the future', or, 'Put my service before all that overtime'. He is God. Do we love Him with all our "heart...soul...mind?" It should be said that rich men are not universally censured in Scripture. See, for example Matt.27: 57. Paul

does not condemn the possession of riches, but urges rich believers not to trust in their riches (1 Tim. 6: 17).

f) The lesson that followed, vv.23-26
The Lord Jesus now draws a lesson from the refusal of the young man to sell his possessions, and follow Him: "Verily I say unto you (the disciples), That a rich man shall hardly ('a rich man shall with difficulty', JND) enter into the kingdom of heaven. And again I say unto you, It is easier for a camel to go through the eye of a needle, than for a rich man to enter into the kingdom of God" (vv.23-24). According to Mark, His disciples needed some help before they could grasp His teaching, so the Saviour explained his original statement ("a rich man shall hardly enter into the kingdom of heaven") by inserting additional wording: "Children, how hard it is ('how difficult it is', JND) for them that **trust in riches** to enter into the kingdom of God!" (Mark 10: 24). The oft-quoted words, "It is easier for a camel to go through the eye of a needle, than for a rich man to enter into the kingdom of God", refer to the eye of a domestic needle, rather than to a postern gate. The usual explanation appears to be based on Shakespeare (!): "It is as hard to come, as for a camel to thread the postern of a needle's eye" (Richard II). The word used by Matthew and Mark comes from the verb *rhapto,* to sew. (W.E.Vine). Luke uses a different word (*belone*), and reveals his profession. He refers to a surgeon's needle!

This recalls the Lord's teaching in Matthew 6: 19-21, and Paul's ministry on the subject in 1 Timothy 6: 5-10, 17-19. Note particularly, "For the love of money is the root of all evil: which while some coveted after, they have erred from the faith, and pierced themselves through with many sorrows... Charge them that are rich in this world, that they be not highminded, nor trust in uncertain riches, but in the living God, who giveth us richly all things to enjoy" (1 Tim. 6: 10, 17).

The Lord's answer evidently shocked the disciples: "When his disciples heard it, they were exceedingly amazed, saying, Who then can be saved?" (v.25). They reasoned as follows: 'If a rich man cannot be saved, then who can?' This will sound strange to us, until we remember that wealth, with all its advantages, was regarded as divine favour. Material advantages gave wealthy people spiritual advantages. They were able to give more generously for a start. Everybody else were 'also-rans'. But "Salvation is of the Lord" (Jonah 2: 9). Through divine grace, "The brother of low degree rejoiceth in that he is exalted", and, "the rich, in that he is made low" (James 1: 9-10). The words of the Lord Jesus are an encouragement to every servant of God: "With men this is impossible; but with God all things are possible" (v.26).

2) MEN WHO HAD NOTHING, vv.27-30

"Then answered Peter and said unto him, Behold, we have forsaken all, and followed thee; what shall we have therefore? (v.27). Peter has attracted a lot of criticism for saying this, but the Lord does not condemn him. We can see Peter's mind working: 'Unlike that rich young ruler who declined to forsake his riches and follow the Master, we have forsaken everything and followed Him. But to what end?' The Lord replied, "Verily I say unto you, That ye which have followed me, in the regeneration when the Son of man shall sit in the throne of his glory, ye also shall sit upon twelve thrones, judging the twelve tribes of Israel. And every one that hath forsaken houses, or brethren, or sisters, or father, or mother, or wife, or children, or lands, for my name's sake, shall receive an hundredfold, and shall inherit everlasting life" (vv.28-29). While "the saints shall judge the world" (1 Cor.6: 2), "the twelve" will have the unique responsibility of "judging the twelve tribes of Israel". Wm.MacDonald rightly points out that "Rewards in the New Testament are closely linked with positions of administration in the millennium...they are *awarded* at the judgment seat of Christ, but *manifested* when the Lord returns to earth to reign".

While Matthew emphasises future rewards, Mark refers to present ("in this time") and future recompence ("in the world to come"). See Mark 10: 29-30. The expressions, "the regeneration" (*palingenesia*: 'the inception of a new state of things', W.E.Vine), and "the world (age) to come", have particular reference to the millennial age: that much is clear from Matthew 19. Mark has some significant inclusions: *(i)* "for my sake, and the gospel's"; *(ii)* "shall receive an hundredfold now in this time...with persecutions" (Mark 10: 29-30). Both remind us that Mark emphasises the **work** of the Servant. That is why the book commences and concludes with reference to the Gospel. Mark's two inclusions emphasise the work, and the difficulties of the work. Matthew emphasises the glory of the coming kingdom, and therefore omits "persecutions".

Malcolm Horlock (*Precious Seed, February 2010*) points out that with the words, "shall inherit everlasting life" (v.29), 'the section has come full circle, for they clearly link back to the rich young ruler's question in verse 16, "what good thing shall I do, that I may have eternal life?" Indeed, Luke closes his account of the incident at this point (Luke 18: 30), as a story complete in itself: wholehearted commitment to Christ brings eternal life'.

The wording of the Lord Jesus requires careful attention. He does not say, 'And every one that hath forsaken houses, **and** brethren, **and** sisters, **and** father, **and** mother, **and** wife, **and** children, for my name's sake'. Some leave one thing, some another thing: hence "every one that hath forsaken houses, **or** brethren, **or** sisters, **or** father, **or** mother, **or** wife, **or** children, **or** lands, for my name's sake". But look at the recompence according to Mark: "But he shall receive an hundredfold now in this time, houses, **and** brethren, **and** sisters, **and** mothers, **and** children, **and** lands" (Mark 10: 30). Notice that the Lord Jesus does not say, "and **fathers**, and **wives**". Hopefully, the reason for the latter omission will be obvious, but what about the former?!

The Lord closed His discourse with, "But many that are first shall be last; and the last shall be first" (v.30). This could refer to those, like the rich young ruler, who were first in life, but were the least important to God, as opposed to the disciples whose association with Christ put them in a most inferior position in this world, but who were most important to God. This will become evident "in the regeneration, when the Son of man shall sit in the throne of his glory". Or, and perhaps more likely in view of the word "but", it could well be a warning to the disciples: Peter had said, "Behold, we have forsaken all, and followed thee". But many a servant of God has stumbled after making a promising start. Of so many it has to be said, "Ye did run well; who did hinder you?" (Gal. 5: 7).

It has been suggested that the statement that "many that are first shall be last; and the last first" is illustrated by the parable in the next chapter. Watch this space!

THE GOSPEL OF MATTHEW

"Whatsoever is right I will give you"

Read Chapter 20: 1-16
The opening word of this chapter makes it clear that the Lord is continuing His teaching at the end of the previous chapter. This is most apparent when we omit the chapter division: "But many that are first shall be last; and the last shall be first. *For* the kingdom of heaven is like unto a man that is an householder..." (Matt. 19: 30 - 20: 1). But that isn't all. Having completed the parable of the labourers in the vineyard, the Lord Jesus adds the explanatory note: "*So* the last shall be first, and the first last: for many be called, but few chosen" (20: 16). This literary device is called an *inclusio*.

Having established the link between the two chapters, and before we give our attention to the details of the opening parable, an overall glance at Chapter 20 will reveal four main sections. They may be summarised as follows: *(1)* service in the vineyard (vv.1-16); *(2)* suffering at Jerusalem (vv.17-19); *(3)* seeking preferential treatment (vv.20-29); *(4)* sight for blind men (vv.30-34).

1) SERVICE IN THE VINEYARD, vv.1-16
It might be helpful to deal with these verses in the following way: *(a)* the purpose of the parable; *(b)* the context of the parable; *(c)* the details of the parable; *(d)* the lesson of the parable.

a) The purpose of the parable
As we have noticed, the parable opens with the little word "for", and is immediately followed by the little word "so", and Malcolm Horlock (*Precious Seed, February 2010*) points out that "these verbal links tell us plainly that the purpose of the parable is to explain, to illustrate, and to amplify" the Lord's words that "many that are first shall be last; and the last shall be first" (19: 30) and, reversing the order, "the last shall be first, and the first last". (20:16). In Malcolm Horlock's words, "Clearly these two sayings are meant to function as the bookends of the parable... any satisfactory interpretation

of the parable must harmonise with the saying (i.e. in verses v.1 & 16), and any satisfactory interpretation of the saying must harmonise with the parable". This is a good way to test any aspect of Bible teaching. Context is so important. This follows:

b) The context of the parable
We do not have to look far for the context of the parable. Another little word points us in the right direction: "***But*** many that are first shall be last; and the last shall be first" (19: 30). The Lord's words here come after Peter had said, "Behold, we have forsaken all, and followed thee (unlike 'the rich young ruler'); what shall we have therefore?" (19: 27), to which the Lord had replied: "Verily I say unto you, That ye which have followed me, in the regeneration when the Son of man shall sit in the throne of his glory, ye also shall sit upon twelve thrones, judging the twelve tribes of Israel. And everyone that hath forsaken houses, or brethren, or sisters, or father, or mother, or wife, or children, or lands, for my name's sake, shall receive an hundredfold, and shall inherit everlasting life" (19: 28-29).

The Lord's teaching is clear: all who 'follow' Him (v.28), and all who 'forsake' possessions and people to do so (v.29), will be rewarded. However, this does not mean that the rewards will all be equal, and so the Lord adds, "***But*** many that are first shall be last; and the last shall be first" (19: 30). Having illustrated this in the parable, He restates the point, albeit in a different order: "***So*** the last shall be first, and the first last" (20: 16). Very clearly, the context of the parable points to its significance. The parable refers to reward for labour, and its whole point is to highlight the way in which the labourers were paid at the end of the day. So: "when even was come, the lord of the vineyard saith unto his steward, Call the labourers, and give them their hire. ***Beginning from the last unto the first***" (v.8). As Malcolm Horlock so rightly points out, here "the words 'last' and 'first' become all-important…'the first' quite literally becomes 'the last', and 'the last' quite literally becomes 'the first'".

c) The details of the parable
Speaking generally, the parable, as we will see (hopefully!), demonstrates ***the way*** in the rewards will vary. Should you argue that all the workers received the same rate of pay, do remember that while they all received the same amount, and in that sense their pay did ***not*** vary, not all the workers worked for the same length of time. So, proportionately, their pay varied considerably. But more than that, it demonstrates ***why*** the rewards will vary. The 'Lord of the vineyard' in ***our*** case has good reasons for rewarding His

labourers in the way described here. The details are more than interesting: they are immensely significant. We should notice:

i) **The employer of the labourers**. He is called the "householder. The word (*oikodespotes*) is translated "the goodman of the house" (v.11), and "the master of the house" (Matt. 10: 25). He is also called "the lord of the vineyard" (v.8). Very clearly, he owned the vineyard, and he had authority over the vineyard. It was "his vineyard" (vv.1, 2). Perhaps the Lord is saying to *us*, "Son, go work to day in *my* vineyard" (Matt. 21:28).

ii) **The work of the labourers**. They are employed in a vineyard. We are not specifically told that it was the season of grape harvest, but at that particular time of the year (the end of September) workers were in great demand. There is, of course, one reason, and one reason only, for planting a vineyard: "He looked that it should **bring forth grapes**" (Isaiah 5: 2). Leaving aside its particular reference to Israel (see Matt. 21: 33-46), every servant of the Lord is involved in the business of obtaining fruit for 'the Lord of the vineyard'. We can *apply* the figure to Gospel work, of which Paul said, "now I would not have you ignorant brethren (the believers at Rome), that oftentimes I purposed to come unto you...that I might have some fruit among you, even as among other Gentiles" (Rom. 1: 13). We can *apply* the figure to assembly work. After all, each assembly should be like a fruitful vineyard: "the fruit of the Spirit is love, joy, peace, longsuffering, gentleness, goodness, faith, meekness, temperance" (Gal. 5: 22-23). How much we need to cultivate the 'assembly vineyard!' Which ever way we apply the details here, one thing is perfectly clear: the labourers in the vineyard and the "lord of the vineyard" were one in object and desire.

iii) **The hiring of the labourers**. This took place at various times during the day: "early in the morning" (v.1)...about the third hour" (v.3)...about the sixth and ninth hour (v.5)...about the eleventh hour" (v.6).

- At 6 a.m. The "householder...went out early in the morning" (v.1). That is, he went down to the Jobcentre (the marketplace), presumably, at the commencement of the Jewish day. It is most important to note the terms on which the "householder" hired his labourers: "when he had agreed with the labourers for a penny a day, he sent them into his vineyard" (v.2). According to W.E.Vine, the word "agreed" (*sumphoneo*) means literally, 'to sound together'. The "householder" and the "labourers" were in harmony over the rate of pay: "a penny (denarius) a day". The two parties "entered into a binding agreement, everything being conducted in the most business-like manner. There was a contract with very clear terms, specifying both a stipulated sum and a stipulated period; 'a denarius a day'" (M.Horlock). We are told that "one denarius was a reasonable wage at that time" (Wm. MacDonald). "This vineyard owner was certainly not out to short-change or to exploit the men who worked for the whole day" (M.Horlock).

- **At 9 a.m.** The householder reappears in the marketplace at "the third hour". He needed more workers, and they were readily available. "He saw others standing idle in the marketplace. And said unto them; Go ye also into the vineyard, and whatsoever is right I will give you. And they went their way" (vv.3-4). On a technical note, the word "idle" (*argos*) doesn't mean that they were 'malingerers in the market place' ("lewd fellows of the baser sort", Acts 17: 5, AV), but simply men who were inactive because they were not yet employed. The point to notice is that, unlike the first batch of labourers with their stipulated terms of employment, these men had no specific agreement. As Wm.MacDonald says, 'They went to work with nothing but his word that he would give them what was right". They evidently trusted the householder, and took him at his word that he would give them "whatsoever is right". Imagine that happening today! Even some marriages only proceed once a pre-nuptial agreement is in place!

- **At 12 noon and 3 p.m.** Lo and behold, it happened again! "Again he went out about the sixth and ninth hour, and did likewise" (v.5). But that wasn't the end of the story:

- **At 5 p.m.** The "householder" returns yet again to the marketplace: "And about the eleventh hour he went out, and found others standing idle, and saith unto them, Why stand ye here all the day idle? They say unto him, Because no man hath hired us. He saith unto them, Go ye also into the vineyard: and whatsoever is right, that shall ye receive" (vv.6-7). However, it should be said that according to scholars, the words "and whatsoever is right, that shall ye receive" are omitted from many manuscripts. According to J.N.Darby, 'the clause is doubtful'. It does seem, therefore, that the men who were hired at "about the eleventh hour" went straight to work without any assurance from the "householder" that they would be paid at all. Much as we look askance at such deviations from the Authorised Version, it has to be said that the omission of any rate of pay, or even the assurance of pay, is a vital part of the parable. These men went to the vineyard in complete faith. They hadn't even been told "whatsoever is right I will give you". "They were content to depend entirely on his character. Lacking any promise of recompence, they had no legal comeback, even if, in the event, the man chose to pay them nothing at all" (M.Horlock). This differs considerably from the householder's words at 9 a.m., 12 noon and 3 p.m., let alone what was agreed at 6 a.m.

Oh, by the way, does the Lord have to say to us, "Why stand ye here all the day idle?" Do remember the proverb (that is, the English proverb) that 'Satan finds work for idle hands to do'. People who are busy in the assembly don't usually pose much of a threat to its well-being! Perhaps we ought to add that, in our case (mark this), the fact that "no man hath hired us" (nobody has given us anything to do), is no excuse for standing "all the day idle". Just take a good look round: it won't be long before you spot opportunities for assembly service. How about a little 'job creation?'

iv) *The summoning of the labourers*. "So when even was come, the lord of the vineyard saith unto his steward, Call the labourers, and give them their hire, beginning from the last unto the first" (v.8). This was strictly in accordance with the law. See Leviticus 19: 13; Deut. 24: 14-15. This "householder" was obviously quite different to the men described by James: "Behold, the hire of the labourers who have reaped down your fields, which is of you kept back by fraud, crieth: and the cries of them which have reaped are entered into the ears of the Lord of sabaoth" (James 5: 4).

One day, perhaps soon, the Lord Jesus will return to "call the labourers" and to "give them their hire". In Paul's words, "For we must all appear before the judgment seat of Christ; that every one may receive the things done in his body, according to that he hath done, whether it be good or bad" (2 Cor. 5: 10). Paul anticipated this with great joy: "I have fought a good fight, I have finished my course, I have kept the faith: henceforth there is laid up for me a crown of righteousness (a rightly-adjusted crown of reward), which the Lord, the righteous judge, shall give me at that day: and not to me only, but unto all them also that love his appearing" (2 Tim. 4: 7-8).

v) *The reward of the labourers*. "Call the labourers, and give them their hire, beginning from the last unto the first. And when they came that were hired about the eleventh hour, they received every man a penny. But when the first came, they supposed that they should have received more; and they likewise received every man a penny" (vv.8-10). It will not escape notice that there were two surprises:

- **The precedence**. The men hired at "the eleventh hour" were rewarded before the men hired "early in the morning". The men who commenced work at 5 p.m are called "these last" (v.12) whereas the men who began at 6 a.m. are called "the first" (v.10), but the wages were paid, not on the basis of 'first come, first served', but 'last come, first served'. Quite obviously the 6 a.m. 'shift' knew exactly what the 5 p.m. 'shift' were getting!

- **The payment**. All the workers received one denarius ("every man a penny"). It isn't surprising that the men who had worked all day should have "supposed that they should have received more" than the men who evidently worked for just one hour. Malcolm Horlock paints the picture: "We can almost see them while they stood waiting in the queue, rubbing their hands together, tapping their noses and whispering, 'Therefore what shall we have?'". Well, perhaps they didn't use Peter's exact words (Matt. 19: 27), but the parable does say that they "supposed that they should have received more", which certainly implies that they expected, like Peter and his colleagues, to be well-rewarded. After all, if the late-comers got one denarius for one hour's work, it was to be fully expected that twelve hours work would receive a most handsome reward.

We are not altogether surprised at the reaction of those labourers who, having "borne the burden and heat of the day" (v.12), reached the head of the queue, only to discover that that their pay did not exceed the remuneration of the men who worked for just one hour. No wonder, we might say, that "they murmured against the goodman of the house, saying, These last have wrought for but one hour, and thou hast made them equal unto us, which have borne the burden and heat of the day" (vv11-12). Peter didn't put it quite like that, but he did say, "Behold, we have forsaken all, and followed thee" (19: .27).

vi) The explanation to the labourers. "But he ('the lord of the vineyard') answered one of them (presumably their spokesman), and said, Friend, I do thee no harm: didst thou not agree with me for a penny? Take that thine is, and go thy way: I will give unto this last (referring to either all the labourers who commenced "about the eleventh hour", or to the last one of them) even as unto thee. Is it not lawful for me to do what I will with mine own? Is thine eye evil, because I am good?" (vv.13-15). We should notice the following:

- **The lord of the vineyard's demeanour**. "*Friend,* I do thee no wrong" (v.13). The word "friend" here (*hetairos*) signifies 'comrade, companion, partner' and 'is used as a term of kindly address' (W.E.Vine). It is to be distinguished from the word *philos* which was a term of endearment. See, for example, John 11: 11, "Our friend Lazarus sleepeth". The "lord of the vineyard" answered courteously. A lesson here!

- The lord of the vineyard's integrity. "Friend, I do thee no wrong: didst not thou agree with me for a penny?" (v.13). He had honoured in full the agreement made with them "early in the morning" (vv.1-2). He had been a man of his word. Another lesson here!

- The lord of the vineyard's generosity. "Take that thine is, and go thy way: I will give unto this last even as unto thee" (v.14). As Malcolm Horlock observes: "Essentially the man was saying, 'To you I am fair and just; to them I am generous and good'". Wm.MacDonald is worth quoting here: "The farmer knew that all these men needed the money. Doubtless they had families who were waiting for food. So the farmer paid them according to their need rather than greed. No one received less than he deserved, but all received what they needed for themselves and their families". It can all be summed up in one word - "Grace". Andrew Wilson puts it nicely: "The landowner was not depriving the early workers of anything they had agreed upon. Out of the goodness of his heart he was simply giving more to the late workers than they really deserved".

- The lord of the vineyard's prerogative. "Is it not lawful for me to do what I will with mine own?" It is a case of "Shall not the Judge of all the earth do right?" (Gen. 18: 25). J.M.Flanigan puts it clearly: "the Lord of the vineyard in which we labour has sovereign rights, which must not, dare not, be questioned by the labourers. He does what He wills, and He is neither accountable nor answerable to any man for what He does. Happy is that labourer today who serves in the consciousness of the sovereignty of the Lord of the harvest". It is not ours to question His will when, for example, some servants of God see bountiful blessing upon their labours, while other equally-faithful and devoted servants of God have little encouragement in this way. God is sovereign, and His goodness to others should not leave us with a jealous or grudging spirit. This is the meaning of the words, "Is thine eye evil, because I am good?" (v.15). (The NIV has 'or are you envious because I am generous'). This can be illustrated from Deuteronomy 15: 9, "Beware that there be not a thought in thy wicked heart, saying, The seventh year, the year of release is at hand; and *thine eye be evil* against thy poor brother, and thou givest him nought". It should also be said that the expression "evil eye" occurs with reference to "greed of gain" (J.Heading). See, for example, Prov. 28: 22; Matt. 6: 23.

While all these are important points, they do not convey what is evidently the main lesson of the parable. God is certainly sovereign in calling and using His servants, but unlike Nebuchadnezzar (Dan. 5: 19) He does not practice 'random choice'. This brings us to:

d) The lesson of the parable

In 'real terms' the labourers hired at 5 p.m. received a great deal more than those hired at 6 a.m. The former received one *denarius* an hour, but the latter received only one *pondion* an hour (a *'pondion'* was one-twelfth of a denarius). Work it out! So why did 'the lord of the vineyard' put a higher value on the latecomers? The answer lies in the difference between the attitude of the two sets of labourers:

- The men hired at 6 a.m. ("the first", v.10) worked for 'the lord of the vineyard' because they had negotiated an acceptable contract of employment, and were therefore most unhappy when others received more than the 'going rate'. They were motivated by reward, whereas

- The men hired at 5 p.m ("the last", v.12) "simply got on with the work, willing to leave the question of any reward entirely to the master" (M.Horlock). Unlike the men hired first thing in the morning, who were more concerned about their rights, they did not say, to use Peter's words, "what shall we have therefore?"

The Lord does promise rewards to His servants. See, for example, Hebrews 6: 10: "For God is not unrighteous to forget your work and labour of love, which ye have shewed toward his name, in that ye have ministered to the saints, and do minister"; 1 Peter 5: 1-4: "The elders which are among you I exhort…Feed the flock of God which is among you…And when the chief Shepherd shall appear, ye shall receive a crown of glory that fadeth not away". We are certainly encouraged by the prospect of reward, but that should not be our motivation. Paul sets an example for us all in saying, "For the love of Christ constraineth us; because we thus judge, that if one died for all, then were all dead: and that he died for all, that they which live should not henceforth live unto themselves, but unto him which died for them, and rose again" (2 Cor. 5: 14-15).

We should also say that the parable warns against "watching other workers and measuring ourselves by them" (supplied by Justin Waldron). Paul makes this very point: "Therefore judge nothing before the time, until the Lord come, who both will bring to light the hidden things of darkness, and will make manifest the counsels of the hearts: and then shall every man have praise of God" (1 Cor. 4: 5).

Wm.MacDonald sums it up like this: "Some who thought they would be first will be last because their service was inspired by pride and selfish ambition ("what shall we have therefore?"). Others who served out of love and gratitude will be highly honoured". In the words of John Phillips, "The parable illustrates the truth that while all true disciples will be rewarded, the order of rewards will be determined by the spirit in which the disciple served". Here then is the meaning of the parable, and the meaning of the Lord's words, "So the last shall be first, and the first last" (v.16). Wm.Kelly suggests that the words, the "first shall be last , and the last first" emphasises "the failure of man", whereas "the last shall be first, and first last" emphasises that there is no failure in the sovereignty of God. But perhaps it is all part of the *inclusio*!

The final words, "for many be called, but few chosen", are omitted in some Greek texts. They are omitted by the RV, but included by JND (with a marginal note). Having pointed out that these words "are not found in many ancient manuscripts", R.V.G.Tasker submits that they are "ill-suited to the present context, for *all* the labourers in the vineyard were 'chosen'". The words are, of course, strictly relevant in Matt. 22: 14. John Heading's suggestion that in the current context, the "many" refers to the service of all believers, and the "few" refers to "those who have no ulterior motives and aspirations in their hearts", is decidedly unsatisfactory.

"Whosoever will be chief among you, let him be your minister"

Read Chapter 20: 17-34
In our previous study, we suggested that this chapter may be divided in the following way: *(1)* service in the vineyard (vv.1-16); *(2)* suffering at Jerusalem (vv.17-19); *(3)* seeking preferential treatment (vv.20-29); *(4)* sight for blind men (vv.30-34).

1) SERVICE IN THE VINEYARD, vv.1-16
The "bookends" (M.Horlock) of the parable of the vineyard labourers are easily recognisable: "many that are first shall be last; and the last shall be

first...the last shall be first, and the first last" (19: 30; 20: 16). The "bookends" can only be rightly interpreted by the parable, and the parable can only be rightly interpreted by the "bookends". The entire section, including the "bookends", flows out of the Lord's teaching that "every one that hath forsaken houses, or brethren, or sisters, father or mother, or wife, or children, or lands, *for my name's sake*, shall receive an hundredfold, and shall inherit eternal life. *But* many that are first shall be last; and the last first" (19: 29-30). The principal purpose of the parable is to illustrate that some people are motivated by reward ("they supposed that they should have received more", v.10) rather than unquestioning faith in 'the lord of the vineyard'. In the words of John Phillips, quoted in our previous study, "The parable illustrates the truth that while all true disciples will be rewarded, the order of rewards will be determined by the spirit in which the disciple served". When Peter said, "Behold, we have forsaken all, and followed thee; what shall *we have* therefore" (19: 27), the Lord did not publicly rebuke him for focusing on reward, but He certainly didn't let the matter drop! He dealt with it indirectly, and in a way that makes it applicable to us all.

Sadly, as we shall see, the lesson seems to have fallen on deaf ears in at least some cases: "Grant that these my two sons may sit, the one on thy right hand, and the other on the left, in thy kingdom" (v.21). Like the 'twelve-hour shift' in the parable (v.10), and Peter (19: 27), James and John were still thinking about a handsome reward for their labour. But the Lord Jesus was occupied with something quite different. This brings us to:

2) SUFFERING AT JERUSALEM, vv.17-19
This is the third occasion in Matthew's Gospel on which the Lord Jesus spoke to His disciples about His death and resurrection. See Matthew 16: 21; 17: 22-23. Do notice that the Lord "took the twelve disciples apart in the way", reminding us that, like them, we can best hear His voice when we are away from the hustle and bustle of everyday life. See 1 Kings 19: 12; Psalm 46: 10. As we noted in connection with the first of the three occasions (Matt. 16: 21), up to that point the Lord Jesus had made veiled references to His coming death. See for example: "the days will come, when the bridegroom shall be taken from them (that is from the disciples, called "the children of the bridechamber"), and then shall they fast" (9: 15); "For as Jonas was three days and three nights in the whale's belly; so shall the Son of man be three days and three nights in the heart of the earth" (12: 40). But in Matthew 16, the Lord Jesus foretold His death in unmistakable terms. He did so again in Matthew 17, and in the present verses He gives

His disciples a more detailed account of His coming sufferings. According to Luke, the disciples "understood none of these things: and this saying was hid from them, neither knew they the things which were spoken" (Luke 18: 34). As J.C.Ryle observes, 'The blindness of the disciples about our Lord's crucifixion and suffering is, at first sight, very extraordinary. But we must remember that they were all Jews, and trained from their infancy to expect a Messiah in glory and majesty, but not in suffering and humiliation'. This is certainly confirmed in the next section in our chapter. See vv.20-21.

Very clearly, the Lord Jesus did not make the journey to Jerusalem with a vague notion that something unpleasant might happen. There was no question about His suffering. "Behold, we go up to Jerusalem; and the Son of man **shall** be betrayed…they **shall** condemn him to death, and **shall** deliver him to the Gentiles…he **shall** rise again". This is far more than a premonition of disaster. As our contributor Justin Waldron rightly points out, "Nothing came as a surprise to Him". The fine detail proclaims His omniscience. The Lord's foreknowledge predated His incarnation. Peter tells us that "the Spirit of **Christ"** was in the prophets, and that He **"testified beforehand** the sufferings of Christ, and the glory that should follow" (1 Pet. 1: 11-12). It is deeply significant that the Holy Spirit should be called here "the Spirit of Christ". Amongst other things, this emphasises that the Lord Jesus was thoroughly aware of His sufferings long before His incarnation. But that is not all: Peter describes the Lord Jesus as "a lamb without blemish and without spot: who verily was **foreordained before the foundation of the world**…" (1 Pet. 1: 19-20). The Lord's foreknowledge was eternal.

When we think of His foreknowledge we must also think of His fortitude: "Behold, we go up to Jerusalem" (v.18), knowing all that lay before Him. We should add that Mark tells us specifically at this point that "Jesus **went before** them…" (Mark 10: 32). We all take measures to avoid suffering, but the Lord Jesus went deliberately to Jerusalem. His journey began with the words, "he stedfastly set his face to go to Jerusalem" (Luke 9: 51). Compare Isaiah 50: 7, "I set my face like a flint". Like His ancestor David, the Lord Jesus was "a mighty valiant man" (1 Sam. 16: 18). We must now notice:

a) What Judas would do
"The Son of man shall be betrayed unto the chief priests and unto the scribes", v.18. ***This was exactly fulfilled***: "And while he yet spake, lo, Judas, one of the twelve, came and with him a great multitude…from the chief priests and elders of the people. Now he that betrayed him gave them

a sign, saying, Whomsoever I shall kiss, that same is he: hold him fast... Then came they, and laid hands on Jesus, and took him" (Matt. 26: 47-50)

b) What the Jews would do
"They shall condemn him to death, and shall deliver him to the Gentiles", vv.18-19. *This was exactly fulfilled.* Having heard the Lord say "Hereafter shall ye see the Son of man sitting on the right hand of power, and coming in the clouds of heaven", the high priest, with his "rent...clothes", cried "He hath spoken blasphemy...What think ye?", to be answered, "He is guilty of death" (Matt. 26: 62-66). The following day, "all the chief priests and elders of the people took counsel against Jesus to put him to death: and when they had bound him, they led him away and delivered him to Pontius Pilate the governor" (Matt. 27: 1-2). Although the Sanhedrin could condemn men to death, the Roman authorities would not allow the Jewish leaders to carry out the sentence. They reserved the right to do that themselves.

c) What the Romans would do
"Mock...scourge...crucify him", v.19. ***This was exactly fulfilled***: "Then released he (Pilate) Barabbas unto them: and when he had scourged Jesus, he delivered him to be crucified...Then the soldiers of the governor took Jesus into the common hall, and gathered unto him the whole band of soldiers. And they stripped him, and put on him a scarlet robe. And when they had platted a crown of thorns, they put it upon his head, and a reed in his right hand: and they bowed the knee before him, and mocked him, saying, Hail, King of the Jews!" (Matt. 27: 26-30). They then "crucified him" Matt. 27: 35). Crucifixion was not a Jewish form of punishment. It originated with the Phoenicians and was later adopted by the Greeks and Romans. It was commonly used with slaves, foreigners, and criminals of the lowest class.

d) What the Lord would do
"The third day he shall rise again", v.19. *This was exactly fulfilled*. In the words of "angel of the Lord" (Matt. 28: 6), "He is not here: for he is risen, as he said. Come, see the place where the Lord lay" (Matt. 28: 6).

> *How didst Thou humble Thyself to be taken,*
> *Led by Thy creatures, and nailed to the cross!*
> *Hated of men, and of God, too, forsaken,*
> *Shunning not darkness, the curse, and the loss.*

Chapter 20

How hast Thou triumphed, and triumphed with glory,
Battled death's forces, rolled back every wave!
Can we refrain, then, from telling the story?
Lord, Thou art Victor o'er death and the grave.

3) SEEKING PREFERENTIAL TREATMENT, vv.20-29
We will divide these verses as follows: *(a)* the desire of James and John (vv.20-23); *(b)* the displeasure of the disciples (vv.23-28)

a) The desire of James and John, vv.20-23
James and John, not to mention the other disciples, evidently had no conception of events at the end of the journey to Jerusalem. The Lord Jesus was well aware that they were using their mother as a spokeswoman! He addressed His answer, not to their mother (Salome: compare Matt. 27: 56 with Mark 15: 40), but to them: "Then came to him the mother of Zebedee's children **with her sons**, worshipping him, and desiring a certain thing of him. And he said unto her, What wilt thou? She saith unto him, Grant that these my two sons may sit, the one on thy right hand, and the other on thy left, in thy kingdom. But Jesus answered and said, Ye know not what ye ask. Are **ye** able to drink of the cup that I shall drink of, and to be baptized with the baptism that I am baptized with? **They** say unto him, **We** are able" (vv.20-22). It all smacks of the early shift in the parable: "they supposed that they should have received more" (v.10). James and John (and mother) were wholly occupied with their position in the coming kingdom. The Lord's anticipation of suffering and death (vv.17-19) does not seem to have registered with them at all. We should notice:

i) Ambition for position. Mark's record strongly emphasises this: "Master, **we** would that thou shouldest do for us whatsoever **we** shall desire" (Mark 10: 35). Compare the Lord's words in Gethsemane: "And he said, Abba, Father, all things are possible unto thee, take away this cup from me, nevertheless not what I will, but what thou wilt" (Mark 14: 36). James and John evidently wished to capitalise on the Lord's recent promise: "Verily, I say unto you, That ye which have followed me, in the regeneration, when the Son of man shall sit upon the throne of his glory, ye also shall sit upon twelve thrones, judging the twelve tribes of Israel" (19: 28). But previous teaching had been forgotten: "Whosoever therefore shall humble himself as this little child, the same is greatest in the kingdom of heaven" (Matt. 18: 1-4). Sadly, the argument continued to rumble on: see Luke 22: 24-27, and then read John 13. The lesson in Philippians 2 is not quickly learnt:

"In lowliness of mind let each esteem other better than themselves" (Phil. 2: 3). But notice too:

ii) Assurance of the kingdom. James and John were at least convinced that their Master was going to reign, and they were right! The dying thief was equally convinced: "Lord, remember me when thou comest into thy kingdom ('in thy kingdom', JND)" (Luke 23: 42). He will sit "upon the throne of his father David, and upon ***his kingdom***, to order it, and to establish it with judgment and with justice, from henceforth even for ever" (Isaiah 9: 7). See also, for example, Matthew 25: 31, 1 Corinthians 15: 24-28. It has to be said, however, that James and John were probably thinking of something much sooner!

iii) Anticipation of suffering. "Ye know not what ye ask. Are ye able to drink of the cup that I shall drink of, and to be baptized with the baptism that I am baptized with? They say unto him, We are able" (v.22). (According to scholars, the references here to baptism do not appear in the oldest manuscripts, and they are therefore omitted by JND/RV, but they are certainly present when it comes to Mark 10: 38-39). The Lord's cup and the Lord's baptism must refer in this instance to His suffering at the hands of men. This much is clear from His words: "Ye shall drink indeed of my cup, and be baptized with the baptism that I am baptized with" (v.23). The confident, "We are able", was little understood at the time. But the Saviour took them at their word: see Acts 12: 2 and Revelation 1: 9. It must be said that in the final analysis they were "able".

Quite obviously, the Saviour did not refer here to His sufferings as our sin-bearer on the cross. None could share those sufferings, and therefore the "cup that I drink of" cannot be the same cup that the Lord anticipated in Gethsemane (Matt 26: 39, 42; Mark 14: 36; Luke 22: 42). The words "baptized" and "baptism" mean what they always mean in Scripture - to immerse. As J.Heading observes in connection with Mark 10: 38-39, "The symbol of immersion was fitting to describe the depths into which the Lord went under the waters of suffering". Attention is drawn to the figures used by the Lord Jesus: "Are ye able to drink of the ***cup*** that I shall drink of, and to be baptized with the baptism that I am baptized with?" In the first case, the element is ***in the person***, and in the second case, the person is ***in the element***. Perhaps the two figures represent inward and outward suffering. Or perhaps the cup represents the determination with which the Saviour entered upon His sufferings - to take a cup is a deliberate act, whilst the baptism represents the ferocity of His enemies.

iv) Allocation of reward. "But to sit on my right hand, and on my left is not mine to give, but it shall be given to them for whom it is prepared of my Father" (v.23). This refers, not of course to the Lord's position at the "right hand of the throne of the Majesty in the heavens" (Heb. 8: 1), but to the time when "the Son of man shall come in his glory…then shall he sit upon the throne of his glory: and before him shall be gathered all nations" (Matt. 25: 31-32). We must not overlook the words, "for whom it is ***prepared***". (Compare Matthew 25: 41 with John 14: 2-3: what a difference!). Rewards will not be awarded on the basis of whim and fancy, but on the basis of perfect equity.

Now notice the wisdom of the Lord Jesus. Had He said, 'Yes' to James and John, imagine the feelings of the other disciples. They were indignant enough as it was! Had He said, 'No', that would have implied that someone other than James and John would be given that position - and may well have provoked the other disciples to say, 'There you are, serve you right for asking!' When the Lord said, "It shall be given to them for whom it is prepared of my Father", He was not excluding James and John: neither was He agreeing to their request. All who are faithful will reign with Him: see 2 Timothy 2: 12.

b) *The displeasure of the disciples, vv.23-28*
We will divide these verses in the following way: *(a)* greatness explained (vv.24-27); *(b)* greatness exemplified (v.28).

a) Greatness explained, vv.24-27
The disciples were highly indignant with James and John (probably because they coveted the same position) for asserting themselves in this way. You can almost hear them muttering, 'Who do they think they are…what a nerve… trying to get the best place for themselves…' The Lord Jesus therefore found it necessary to explain again, as He had already done in Mark 9: 34-35, that authority and leadership belong only to those who are willing to be "servant of all". This is totally contrary to practice elsewhere. In every other sphere, people govern by rank: it is a man's position rather than his character, that counts: "Ye know that the princes of the Gentiles exercise dominion (an intensive word: the RV has 'lord it'), and they that are great exercise authority upon them (the Roman Empire was sufficient example of that). But it shall not be so among you…" (vv.25-26). In Christ's kingdom, greatness lies in humility and service: "but whosoever will be great among you, let him be your minister (*diakonos*); and whosoever will be the chief among you, let him be your servant (*doulos*)" (vv.26-27). The man who

says, 'You must do what I say because I'm on the oversight', or because 'I'm a ministering brother' (whatever that is!), has no right to be heard. True leadership amongst God's people rests with people who have *moral* authority. This is why God places such value on shepherds. (Shepherding is given a most important place in both Old and New Testaments: it makes a most profitable study). The eastern shepherd leads the flock, and is able to do so effectively because the sheep recognise his care and concern for them. The man who is willing to devote time and energy to the humblest tasks, has the allegiance of the flock.

b) Greatness exemplified, v.28
The Lord Jesus is the greatest example of His own teaching. If it is true that "whosoever will be great among you, let him be your minister" (v.26), then the Lord Jesus has every right to unrivalled greatness because He has undertaken the greatest service of all, for "even…the Son of man came not to be ministered unto (to be served), but to minister (to serve), and to give his life a ransom for many" (vv.28). This explains why John heard the great proclamation, "Behold, *the Lion* of the tribe of Juda…hath prevailed to open the book", only to discover that "in the midst of the throne and of the four beasts, and in the midst of the elders, stood *a Lamb*, as it had been slain" (Rev. 5: 5-6). The figures of lion and lamb seem mutually exclusive, until we remember that the Lamb who died on behalf of all men has the moral right, as the Lion, to execute judgment on all men.

It is important to compare Matthew 20: 28 with 1 Timothy 2: 6. In the first case, the Lord Jesus gave His life, "a ransom *for many*". In the second case, He gave His life, "a ransom *for all*". In the first case, the Lord Jesus died in *the place* of many. In the second case, He died *on behalf* of all. W.E.Vine points out that the word translated "ransom" (*lutron*) in Matt. 20: 28 and Mark 10: 45 is connected with the preposition *anti*, which has vicarious significance and means 'in the stead of'. In 1 Tim. 2: 6, the word translated "ransom" (*antilutron*) is connected with the preposition *huper* meaning 'on behalf of'. "Thus the three passages consistently show that while the provision was universal, for Christ died for all men, yet it is actual for those only who accept God's conditions, and who are described in the Gospel statements as 'the many'" (W.E.Vine).

The incident that now follows illustrates still further the Lord's teaching that "whosoever will be chief among you, let him be your servant" (v.27). The 'Son of David', none other than the Messiah, interrupts His journey to

Jerusalem (having evidently crossed the Jordan from Perea: see 19: 1) in order to meet the need of two blind beggars. So:

4) SIGHT FOR BLIND MEN, vv.29-34

These verses are quite sufficient in themselves for a single study. They describe the last miracle recorded in Matthew's Gospel. Compare Mark 10: 46-52; Luke 18: 35-43. Matthew differs from Mark and Luke in two particulars: he puts the miracle at the *departure* from Jericho, as opposed to the *arrival* at Jericho, and specifies *two* blind men. The first problem is usually explained by the fact that there was an old Jericho and a new Jericho. The first was 'a ruined village, dating back to the times of Joshua': the second was located 'near to the mouth of the Wady Kelt' (H.St.John). The miracle therefore evidently took place between the two. The second problem is usually explained by recognising that there were two men, but that 'Bartimaeus, being more earnest in his plea for mercy, is given the prominent place' (H.S.Paisley). Let's just notice four things:

a) The recognition by the blind men, v.30

"Have mercy on us, O Lord, thou son of David". Mark tells us that when Bartimaeus "heard that it was Jesus of Nazareth, he began to cry out, and say, Jesus, thou son of David, have mercy on me" (Mark 10: 47). He recognised that "Jesus of Nazareth" was the long-awaited King. He was blind, but he could see far more than most people! Mary was told, "He shall be great, and shall be called the Son of the Highest: and the Lord God shall give unto Him the throne of His father David" (Luke 1: 32). The very title, 'Son of David', emphasises His right to reign.

b) The resolution of the blind men, v.31

"The multitude rebuked them, because they should hold their peace: but they cried the more saying, Have mercy on us, O Lord, thou son of David". The two men would not be deterred. They were in earnest. The Gospel preacher will capitalise on this!

c) The response to the blind men, vv.32-34

"And Jesus stood still, and called them, and said, What will ye that I shall do unto you? They said unto him, Lord, that our eyes may be opened. So Jesus had compassion on them, and touched their eyes; and immediately their eyes received sight". There is plenty here for the Gospel preacher! These men knew their need - the Lord's compassion (His heart was touched by their need) - the Lord's personal contact - they received sight immediately.

Add the fact that Mark tells us that the multitude said to Bartimaeus, "Be of good comfort, rise: he calleth thee". It must have been like music to his ears! Add as well Mark's note that nothing was allowed to get in the way: "And he, casting away his garment, rose, and came to Jesus" (Mark 10: 49-50). Add still further Mark's note that the Lord said, "Go thy way; thy faith hath made the whole" (Mark 10: 52), and Luke's account: "Receive thy sight: thy faith hath saved thee" (Luke 18: 42). What more does the Gospel preacher want?

c) *The response of the blind men, v.34*
"They followed him". Mark and Luke expand this simple statement. Luke says, that Bartimaeus "followed, glorifying God: and all the people, when they saw it, gave praise unto God" (Luke 18: 43). Mark tells us that the Saviour said, "Go *thy way*", but that Bartimaeus "followed Jesus in *the way*" (Mark 10: 52). The word "followed" here is in the imperfect tense, which means that he kept on following. Bartimaeus said in effect, '*My* way' is '*Thy* way'.

Can *we* say that?

THE GOSPEL OF MATTHEW

"Behold, thy King cometh unto thee"

Read Chapter 21: 1-22

The final stage of the Lord's journey to Jerusalem, involved a seventeen mile ascent of more than 3,000 feet from Jericho through desolate country. While the Lord entered Jerusalem to the cry "Hosanna to the son of David: Blessed is he that cometh in the name of the Lord; Hosanna in the highest" (v.9), He was well aware that He would be "betrayed unto the chief priests and unto the scribes" who would "condemn him to death, and…deliver him to the Gentiles to mock, and to scourge, and to crucify him" (20: 18-19). The Jewish leadership would say, in effect, "This is the heir; come let us kill him" (v.38). But the Saviour did not deviate. As we noted in our previous study, His perfect foreknowledge was accompanied by amazing fortitude.

We should notice that Matthew 21 refers to each of the Lord's first three days in Jerusalem:

- *The first day.* "And when he was come into Jerusalem" (v.10) Mark (and only Mark) tells us that the Lord "entered into Jerusalem, and **into the temple**: and when he had looked round about upon all things, and now the eventide was come, he went out unto Bethany with the twelve" (Mark 11: 11).

- *The second day.* "And Jesus went into **the temple of God**, and cast out all them that sold and bought in the temple" (v.12). "And he left them, and went out of the city into Bethany; and he lodged there" (v.17). See also Mark 11: 12-19; Luke 19: 45-46.

- *The third day.* "Now in the morning as he returned into the city…And when he was come into **the temple**…" (vv.18, 23). For the Lord's departure from the temple on the third day, see Matt. 24: 1. See also Mark 11: 20 - 13: 1; Luke 20: 1. Luke speaks generally about the Lord's ministry during this period. See, again, Luke 20: 1, together with Luke 21: 37-38.

Amongst other things, we should notice the significant fact that the Lord Jesus did not spend a night in Jerusalem: He went to Bethany. See Mark 11: 11-12 (end of the first day); Matt. 21: 17 (end of the second day). Compare Mark 14: 3. There was a family home there that He loved to visit, and where He was always welcome. "Jesus loved Martha, and her sister, and Lazarus" (John 11: 5). He knew that He would be rejected at Jerusalem: He knew that He was a welcome guest in Bethany. The world is just like Jerusalem - it doesn't want Him. But our hearts and homes should be just like the household in Bethany!

Matthew 21 may be divided as follows: : *(1)* the acquisition of the ass (vv.1-7); *(2)* the arrival in Jerusalem (vv.8-11); *(3)* the purging of the temple (vv.12-17); *(4)* the cursing of the fig tree (vv.18-22); *(5)* the authority of the Lord Jesus (vv.23-32); *(6)* the antagonism of the leaders (vv.33-46).

1) THE ACQUISITION OF THE ASS, vv.1-7
"And when they drew nigh unto Jerusalem, and were come unto Bethphage, unto the mount of Olives..." (v.1). Mark has, "And when they were come unto Jerusalem, unto Bethphage and Bethany (meaning 'house of figs' or 'house of dates') at the mount of Olives..." (Mark 11: 1). Luke 19: 29 reads similarly. Bethany was a village about two miles from Jerusalem on the eastern slopes of the Mount of Olives. According to Leon Morris, the location of Bethphage is not known for certain, but clearly it was nearby. Some say that it was a suburb of Jerusalem, being regarded as the outer limit of the city.

There is a great amount of significant information packed into these verses. It has been nicely said (Bernard Osborne) that we have here:

a) A manifestation of His deity
"Go into the village over against you, and straightway ye shall find an ass tied, and a colt with her..." (v.2). There was no doubt about the whereabouts of the animal. Not, simply, 'ye shall find an ass in the village', but "**straightway ye shall find an ass tied**". Mark has "as soon as ye be entered into it" (Mark 11: 2), and Luke, "at your entering" (Luke 19: 30), and "tied." The Lord displayed divine omniscience. Luke tells us that the two disciples "went their way, and found even as he had said unto them" (Luke 19: 32). It is not without significance that Luke continues with reference to the destruction of Jerusalem (19: 39-44). The Lord's omniscience not only included the precise whereabouts of an animal, but the precise manner of a city's destruction:

"For the days shall come upon thee, that thine enemies shall cast a trench about thee, and compass thee round, and keep thee on every side..." At the same time, the acquisition of the ass was:

b) An indication of His poverty
"Ye shall find an ass tied, and a colt with her...loose them, and bring them unto me" (v.2). They had to borrow an ass. The Lord had nothing. "Though he was rich...he became poor" (2 Cor. 8: 9), even though He owned "the cattle upon a thousand hills" (Psalm 50: 10). The Saviour's entry to Jerusalem would be devoid of all grandeur. Not for Him the massed legions and splendid chariots drawn by fine horses. He entered His capital city "meek, and sitting upon an ass, and a colt the foal of an ass" (v.5). He was the true 'pauper prince'. The acquisition of the ass was:

c) An assertion of His authority
i) In relation to the disciples. The Lord said "go" (v.2) and "say" (v.3), and the disciples "**went**, and did as Jesus had commanded them (v.6). Mark tells us that they "**said** unto them even as Jesus had commanded them" (Mark 11: 6). This is true discipleship. They didn't say, 'We know of a better place to find a colt', or, 'We'll think of an answer if somebody asks questions'. They simply did and said what the Lord wanted - and it worked out perfectly (of course). For the sake of completeness, we must add two further details from Luke:

ii) In relation to the owners. "And if any man ask you, Why do ye loose him? thus shall ye say unto him, Because **the Lord** hath need of him". When the owners asked, "Why loose ye the colt", the disciples answered as instructed, and brought the animal to the Lord (Luke 19: 31-34). Do we respond in the same way when the Lord "hath need" of our property? In this case it was help with transport. Just substitute 'car' for "ass", and you have the up to date lesson!

iii) In relation to the colt. It was "a colt...whereon yet never man sat" (Luke 19: 30), but Mark tells us that the Lord "sat upon him" (Mark 11: 7). What is more, the animal didn't bolt when faced with the noise and activity of the crowds. Compare Mark 1: 13, "And was with the wild beasts". The Lord Jesus never surrendered His authority over creation.

d) A fulfilment of prophecy
"All this was done, that it might be fulfilled which was spoken by the prophet,

saying, Tell ye the daughter of Zion, Behold, thy King cometh..." (vv.4-5). The Lord entered Jerusalem in fulfilment of Zechariah 9: 9: "Rejoice greatly, O daughter of Zion; shout, O daughter of Jerusalem; behold, thy King cometh unto thee: he is just, and having salvation; lowly, and riding upon an ass, and upon a colt the foal of an ass". The context of the Zechariah passage is most significant. The preceding verses (vv.1-8) predict the victorious march south of Alexander the Great, with all his power and pomp. But Jerusalem's King would come in a totally different way - "Behold, *thy* King cometh unto thee...lowly, and riding upon an ass". But the following verses (vv.10-17) tell us that He will ultimately be a world-conqueror beyond all the dreams of Alexander! The exact and minute fulfilment of Zechariah 9: 9 guarantees the exact and minute fulfilment of Zechariah 9: 10-17!

It might be worth mentioning that the Lord rode on *one* animal, but came with *two.* Having shut up their calves, the Philistines attached the "milch kine" to the cart carrying the ark, and set them off to Israel. They "went along the highway, lowing as they went", all the way to Beth-shemesh (1 Sam. 6: 1-12). But the Lord did not separate mother and foal! Both the she-ass and her colt came together!!

2) THE ARRIVAL IN JERUSALEM, vv.8-11

All four Gospel writers record the Lord's arrival in Jerusalem. See Matthew 21: 4-11; Mark 11: 7-10, Luke 19: 35-38; John 12: 12-16. Sir Robert Anderson, head of Scotland Yard during the reign of Queen Victoria, and author of *The Coming Prince*, proves arithmetically that the Lord's arrival in Jerusalem coincided exactly with the expiry of sixty-ninth "week" of Daniel's 'seventy-week' prophecy: "Know, therefore, and understand, that from the going forth of the commandment to restore and rebuild Jerusalem, unto Messiah the Prince, shall be seven weeks, and threescore and two weeks... and after threescore and two weeks shall Messiah be cut off" (Dan. 9: 25-26). We must notice that this event is unique in the life of the Lord Jesus. Thus far, He had always withdrawn from public notice. Here, and only here, He **calls public attention to Himself,** and does so at a time when Jerusalem was packed with thousands of visiting Jews, who had come to celebrate the Passover. H.St.John (writing on Mark) explains: "He had repeatedly charged His disciples to keep silence as to His miracles and as to His Messiahship. Here, for the first time, He deliberately set the stage for a scene in which He Himself would be the central figure, thus **forcing men to accept or to reject His claim**". His public arrival in Jerusalem was followed by his public crucifixion at Calvary. We cannot separate the two. "He over-ruled things in such a way that the eyes of all Jerusalem were fixed upon Him, and when He died, He died before many witnesses" (J.C.Ryle). This is most important. The Gospel rests on solid historical fact. Paul stressed this to Agrippa: "For the king knoweth of these things...for I am persuaded that none of these things are hidden from him; **for this thing was not done in a corner**" (Acts 26: 26).

The Lord's entry into Jerusalem was certainly "not done in a corner". "And a very great multitude spread their garments in the way; others cut down branches from the trees, and strawed them in the way. And the multitudes that went before, and that followed, cried, saying, Hosanna to the son of David: Blessed is he that cometh in the name of the Lord blessed be the kingdom of our father David, that cometh in the name of the Lord: Hosanna in the highest" (vv.8-9). Casting garments before someone was a sign of subjection: see 2 Kings 9: 13. The crowds thought that the long-awaited Messiah was about to establish His kingdom, and that the time had come for deliverance from the Roman occupation. "Hosanna" means, 'Save now'.

The multitudes were evidently convinced that Psalm 118: 25-26 was in process of fulfilment: "Save now, I beseech thee, O LORD! O LORD, I beseech thee, send now prosperity. Blessed be he that cometh in the Name of the LORD: we have blessed you out of the house of the LORD". While this Psalm describes the coming glory and triumph of Israel's great Deliverer, it also describes His prior rejection: "The stone which the builders refused is become the head stone of the corner" (Psalm 110: 22). (This verse is quoted in v.42). But the crowds in Jerusalem failed to recognise that their Messiah must suffer before He reigned. Had this not been the case, His subjects could have no forgiveness of sins.

The nation will repeat the cry, properly, when He **does** come to reign, see Matthew 23: 39, and it will be then that Jacob's prophecy will be fulfilled: "The sceptre shall not depart from Judah...until Shiloh come; and unto him shall the gathering of the people be: binding his **foal** unto the vine, and his **ass's colt** unto the choice vine..." (Gen. 49: 10-11). The colt depicts repentant Israel's subjection to her Messiah.

The level of tumult and excitement can be gauged from the word "moved" (*seio*) which is usually used in connection with earthquakes. Having heard the cry, "Hosanna to the son of David" (a title, as opposed to a name), the question is asked, "Who is this?", that is, who bears this title? (v.10), with the answer, "This is Jesus the prophet of Nazareth of Galilee" (v.11). There can be little doubt that they were thinking of Deuteronomy 18: 18, "I will raise them up a Prophet from among their brethren". The question, "Who is this?", will be asked again: "**Who is this** that cometh from Edom, with dyed garments from Bozrah? this that is glorious in his apparel, travelling in the greatness of his strength?", with the answer, "I that speak in righteousness, mighty to save" (Isaiah 63: 1). Jerusalem will then ring with the cry: "Lift up your heads, O ye gates; and be ye lift up, ye everlasting doors; and the King of glory shall come in" (Ps 24: 7-10). There will be no misunderstanding then. They will not say then, "This is Jesus the prophet of Nazareth of Galilee". He will be recognised as "the King of glory".

3) THE PURGING OF THE TEMPLE, vv.12-17
Deuteronomy 14: 24-27 made provision for those who had long distances to travel, but as usual, this facility had been totally abused. Jews from all parts of the Roman Empire came to Jerusalem, but the temple there had its own currency, and foreign money had to be changed into the right coinage. The *bureaux de change* were open for business. Instead of being a place of prayer and worship, the temple had become a profitable opportunity for enterprising businessmen. Not altogether fair trading either: "ye have made it a den of thieves" (v.13). We can well imagine the sharp practices of the currency dealers. The Lord Jesus cited Isaiah 56: 7 and Jeremiah 7: 11 in saying, "Is it not written, My house shall be called of all nations the house of prayer? but ye have made it a den of thieves". This is particularly incisive: the temple will be called "an house of prayer for *all people*" (Isaiah 56: 7), but the nation of *Israel* had turned it into "a den of thieves".

The Lord Jesus had evidently done exactly the same thing at the beginning of His public preaching: see John 2: 13-21, but the traders were soon back, and it was 'business as usual'. His standards had not diminished during the intervening period, but theirs had evidently deteriorated: whilst both occasions refer to the actual trading, Matthew (together with Mark and Luke) emphasises their dishonesty and corruption: "ye have made it a den of thieves"

The word "temple" is also used to describe a Christian's body. See 1 Corinthians 6: 19-20. The words have a slightly different meaning. In Matthew 21, it means 'outer temple' or the entire building (*hieron*), and in 1 Corinthians 6, it means 'inner temple' (*naos*). The temple in Jerusalem should have been the place where God was honoured and worshipped (see Psalm 29: 9), but it was used for other purposes. The believer's body is "the temple of the Holy Ghost" and must not, therefore, become defiled by evil practices. The word temple is also used in relation to the church in its totality (see Ephesians 2: 21), and of the local assembly (see 1 Corinthians 3: 16-17). The local assembly must not become degraded either: it is not the place for 'Bring and Buy Sales', 'Flower Festivals', or anything else in that category.

With the eviction of the businessmen, the temple became a place of blessing: "the blind and the lame came to him *in the temple*; and he healed them". Matthew calls this "the wonderful things that he did". It also became a place of praise: "the children" were heard "crying *in the temple*", and saying, "Hosanna to the son of David" (v.15). Every assembly ought to be like that: a place of blessing and a place of praise. Remember that Paul said to the Corinthians, "Know ye not that ye are the *temple* of God? (1 Cor. 3: 16).

But this had no effect on the religious leaders: "the chief priests and scribes...were sore displeased, and said unto him, Hearest thou what these say?, to be told, "Yea; have ye never read, Out of the mouth of babes and sucklings hast thou perfected praise" (vv.15-16). The Lord was quoting from Psalm 8: 2, which teaches that God has deliberately by-passed proud arrogant men, and revealed Himself to people with no claim to wisdom or preferment. *That is just where we come in too:* "For ye see your calling, brethren, how that not many wise men after the flesh, not many mighty, not many noble, are called: but God hath chosen the foolish things of the world, to confound the wise; and God hath chosen the weak things of the world, to confound the things which are mighty...that no flesh should glory in His presence" (1 Cor. 1: 26-29). The Lord evidently referred to Psalm 8: 2 on another occasion: He prayed, "I thank thee, O Father, Lord of heaven and earth, because thou hast hid these things from the wise and prudent, and *hast revealed them unto babes*. Even so, Father: for so it seemed good in thy sight" (Matt. 11: 25-26).

We should add that the words "sore displeased" (v.15) led to something worse. Mark tells us that "the scribes and chief priests...sought how they might destroy him: for they feared him, because all the people were astonished at his doctrine" (Mark 11: 18). See also Luke 19: 48. The concluding verse of this section has prophetic overtones: "And he *left them*, and *went out of the city* into Bethany; and lodged there" (v.17). He left them in more senses than one. It was a symbolic act. Mark tells us

Matthew

that "when ***even was come***, he ***went out of the city***" (Mark 11: 19). This too has prophetic overtones. For the nation, "even" had certainly come. He is still rejected by the religious world, but He finds a warm welcome in the hearts of His people. Paul prayed that the believers at Ephesus might be "strengthened with all might by his Spirit in the inner man; that Christ may dwell ('make a home in your hearts') by faith" (Eph. 3: 16-17). May all our hearts be like Bethany!

4) THE CURSING OF THE FIG TREE, vv.18-22
It should be carefully noted that Matthew and Mark differ in relating this incident. Mark tells us that "on the morrow, when they were come ***from Bethany***, he was hungry" and finding no figs, He said, "no man eat fruit of thee hereafter for ever" (Mark 11: 12-14). Mark then tells us that the Lord entered the temple "and began to cast out them that sold and bought in the temple" and "when even was come, he went out of the city". The following morning, "as they passed by, they saw the fig tree dried up from the roots" (Mark 11: 20). Matthew evidently condenses the incident, the words, "Now in the morning as he returned into the city" (vv.18-19) referring to the Lord's return to Jerusalem in order to purge the temple, and the words "How soon is the fig tree withered away" (v.20) referring to the return to Jerusalem the following day.

We must never forget the true humanity of the Lord Jesus. We must never forget either, that whilst He was, and is, a ***true*** man, He was not, and is not, a ***mere*** man. It was genuine hunger, just as genuine weariness made Him sit on the well at Sychar. Quite obviously, hunger, thirst and tiredness are not evidence of a sinful nature. Having stated the obvious, although it is not quite so obvious to some people, we can now proceed to notice something else. The Lord Jesus used the occasion to teach an important lesson. He was hungry in another sense as well: He looked for fruit in His people. The fig tree is used in Scripture as a symbol for Israel. See Hosea 9: 10, and the Lord's teaching in Luke 13: 6-9. He had every right to expect His people to give Him the pleasure and joy to which He was entitled as their Messiah. But there was, "nothing...but leaves" (v.19). The Lord then uttered the solemn words, "Let no fruit grow on thee henceforward for ever" (v.19). We know that Israel will revive nationally, see Matt. 24: 32-33, but for centuries the nation has been under the solemn curse.

Whilst we must bear in mind the meaning of the incident, we must not overlook its practical application. What does He find in our lives?

Chapter 21

> *Nothing but leaves! Sad memory weaves*
> *No vail to hide the past:*
> *And as we trace our weary way*
> *And count each lost and misspent day,*
> *We sadly find at last -*
> *Nothing but leaves! nothing but leaves!*

On a technical note, the fig tree produces fruit before it produces leaves. Since there were leaves, there ought, therefore, to have been fruit, even though the ordinary fig season had not arrived. These early figs were called 'first-ripe figs'. This explains the rather perplexing statement: "he came, if haply he might find any thing thereon: and when he came to it, he found nothing but leaves; for the time of figs was not yet" (Mark 11: 13). This is deeply significant in itself. The tree, so to speak, made pretensions of fruit, but there wasn't any! This was precisely the situation with Jewish religion, and particularly so with the temple. Plenty of pretension, but no fruit! There was no fruit on the tree, and the Lord said, "Let no fruit grow on thee henceforward for ever": there was no fruit in the temple, and the Lord said, "Behold, your house is left unto you desolate" (Matt. 23: 38).

But there is more. The Lord used the disciples' observation, "How soon is the fig tree withered away!" (v.20), to teach the importance of believing prayer. "Verily I say unto you, If ye have faith, and doubt not, ye shall not only do this which is done to the fig tree, but also if ye shall say unto this mountain, Be thou removed, and be thou cast into the sea; it shall be done. And all things, whatsoever ye shall ask in prayer, believing, ye shall receive" (vv.21-22). It is generally thought that "this mountain" is the Mount of Olives, and "the sea" is the Dead Sea, but the Lord "did not mean that the disciples would be able to move mountains in a concrete sense, but...is speaking figuratively and hyperbolically" (supplied by Justin Waldron). We have a good example in Zechariah 4: 7 where Zerubbabel's great mountain was, undoubtedly, the difficulties and opposition encountered in the Lord's work. We should notice that the Saviour postulates 'believing prayer': "If ye have faith, and doubt not...whatsoever ye shall ask in prayer, believing, ye shall receive". It has been rightly pointed out that asking 'in faith' must mean acceptance of God's will: "And this is the confidence that we have in him, that, if we ask any thing according to his will, he heareth us" (1 John 5: 14). See also 1 John 4: 22.

Matthew

"They will reverence my son"

Read Chapter 21: 23-46

In our previous study, we suggested that this chapter may be divided as follows: *(1)* the acquisition of the ass (vv.1-7); *(2)* the arrival in Jerusalem (vv.8-11); *(3)* the purging of the temple (vv.12-17); *(4)* the cursing of the fig tree (vv.18-22); *(5)* the authority of the Lord Jesus (vv.23-32); *(6)* the antagonism of the leaders (vv.33-46).

1) THE ACQUISITION OF THE ASS, vv.1-7
Amongst other things we noticed that the Lord entered Jerusalem in the manner predicted by Zechariah: "Rejoice greatly, O daughter of Zion; shout, O daughter of Jerusalem; behold, thy King cometh unto thee: he is just, and having salvation; lowly, and riding upon an ass, and upon a colt the foal of an ass" (Zech. 9: 9).

2) THE ARRIVAL IN JERUSALEM, vv.8-11
The Lord entered Jerusalem to the ringing cry, "Hosanna to the son of David: Blessed is he that cometh in the name of the Lord; Hosanna in the highest" (v.9). Their loud 'hosannas' (meaning 'save now') related to deliverance from Roman occupation. They failed to recognise that their Messiah must suffer before He reigned. He had come to "save his people from their sins" (Matt. 1: 21).

3) THE PURGING OF THE TEMPLE, vv.12-17
Having evicted the businessmen, the temple became a place of blessing and a place of praise: "the blind and the lame came to him *in the temple*; and he healed them" (v.14), and "the children" were heard "crying *in the temple*", and saying, "Hosanna to the son of David" (v.15).

4) THE CURSING OF THE FIG TREE, vv.18-22
While we must not forget the important lesson regarding believing prayer (vv.21-22), the barren fig tree represented barren Israel. The Lord had every right to expect His people to give Him the pleasure and joy to which He was entitled as their Messiah. But there was, "nothing...but leaves" (v.19). What about us? This bring us to:

5) THE AUTHORITY OF THE LORD JESUS, vv.23-32
If on the occasion of the Lord's previous visit to the temple, "the blind and

the lame came to him" (v.14), on the third visit "the chief priests and elders of the people came unto him" (v.23). The displeasure of the "chief priests and scribes" on the previous occasion (v.15) had clearly brought them to the conclusion that the Lord Jesus must be silenced.

A great deal of this third day was taken up with answering a series of questions, of which the first was, "By what authority doest thou these things? and who gave thee this authority?" (v.23). Very clearly, the chief priests and elders were convinced that He had no official authority, and were persuaded that if He could be forced to admit this in front of the people, it would both discredit Him, and justify His arrest. They certainly had no interest in ascertaining whether or not His teaching was right, or if He had been right in cleansing the temple. They regarded Him as a rival who must be eliminated.

The Lord's answer demonstrates that He was Master of the situation. He was never outwitted by the catch questions of His enemies, and there can be little doubt that this was a catch question. He would be faced with another one later in the day. See Matthew 22: 17. The Lord's reply is in two parts: *(a)* he answers them with a question (vv.24-27); *(b)* he answers them with a parable (vv.28-32).

a) *The question, vv.24-27*
"And Jesus answered and said unto them, I also will ask you one thing, which if ye tell me, I in like wise will tell you by what authority I do these things. The baptism of John, whence was it? From heaven, or of men" (vv.24-25). This was highly embarrassing for His questioners. John had the authority of the Old Testament Scriptures. He made it perfectly clear that, as the scriptures had predicted (Isaiah 40: 3; Mal. 3: 1), he baptized in preparation for the coming of the Lord (John 1: 22-27), who was none other than Jehovah Himself (Isaiah 40: 3). The Lord Jesus therefore needed no authority. He **was** the authority!

The Lord's question therefore left them in an impossible situation. Either answer to the Lord's question would have landed them in deep trouble. "If we shall say, From heaven; he will say unto us, Why did ye not then believe him? But if we shall, Of men; we fear the people; for all hold John as a prophet" (vv.25-26). David Gooding puts it like this: 'To admit that John's baptism was of God and obligatory on everyone, would have been to own in front of the people that they were in rebellion against God by refusing to be baptised, and to accept the Messiah to whom John had testified'. Their only way out of the dilemma was to say 'we do not know', to which the Saviour replied, "Neither tell I you by what authority I do these things" (v.27). But He had made the point very clearly indeed!

b) The parable, vv.28-32
This parable is only recorded by Matthew. It emphasises the guilt of the religious leaders in rejecting the message of John the Baptist. R.V.G.Tasker points out, "the first son who says he will not go and work in his father's vineyard, but afterwards changes his mind and goes, corresponds to the publicans and sinners, who though at first they were very far from righteous, later repented as a result of the preaching of John the Baptist. The second son, who as soon as he receives the order promises with a good deal of gush that he will go and work, but who in the end never goes at all, stands for the professedly religious, whose self-righteousness prevents them from responding to any call to repentance. Unconscious of the need for forgiveness they are among those satirized elsewhere by the Lord Jesus as 'the ninety and nine just persons, which need no repentance'". We must not miss the lessons from the command, "Son, go work to day in my vineyard" (v.28). Every word is important: "**Son...go...work...today...my vineyard**". As Justin Waldron points out, the second son's response, "I go, sir: and went not" (v.29) "reminds us of the Israelites' response to the reading of the law: "All that the LORD hath said will we do, and be obedient" (Ex. 24: 7). But events proved otherwise. We should note the expression "kingdom of God" (v.31), one of only five such references in Matthew. The words "before you" (v.31) may mean that in divine mercy of God, the door remained open at that time for the religious leaders to enter "the kingdom of God" (v.31).

6) THE ANTAGONISM OF THE LEADERS, vv.33-46
Their rejection of John the Baptist (v.32) makes an appropriate introduction to the parable of the wicked husbandmen. The "husbandmen" had rejected John, together with his predecessors (vv.34-36), and they were now in the process of rejecting the Son (v.37) as well. The "chief priests and Pharisees" certainly grasped the meaning of the parable: "they perceived that he spake **of them**" (v.45).

The New Testament parable of the vineyard (see also Mark 12: 1-12; Luke 20: 9-19) has its counterpart in the Old Testament: "Now I will sing to my well-beloved a song of my beloved touching his vineyard. My beloved hath a vineyard in a very fruitful hill" (Isaiah 5: 1-7). There is no doubt about the meaning of the passage: "For the vineyard of the Lord of hosts is **the house of Israel**..." (v.7). The entire chapter should be read carefully. The "wild grapes" (literally 'stinking grapes') are identified in vv.8, 11, 18, 20, 21, 22, with the introductory words, "Woe unto them that..."

Isaiah 27 refers to Israel in the future as a vineyard: "In that day sing ye unto her, A vineyard of red wine. I the LORD do keep it: I will water it every moment: lest any hurt it, I will keep it night and day" (vv.2-3); "Israel shall blossom and bud, and fill the face of the world with fruit" (v.6). This will only happen after God has cleansed and purged the nation. Notice the expressions, "By this, therefore, shall the iniquity of Jacob be **purged**" (v.9), and, "When the boughs thereof are withered, they shall be broken off: the women come and **set them on fire**" (v.11). John 15 is now compulsory reading: especially vv.2, 6. Psalm 80: 8-19 also describes Israel as a vineyard: "Return, we beseech thee, O God of hosts: look down from heaven, and behold, and visit this vine; and the vineyard which thy right hand hath planted" (vv.14-15). These Old Testament passages give us the key to this parable. The following should be noted:

a) The reason for planting a vineyard
There is course, one reason, and one reason only, for planting a vineyard. "He looked that it should **bring forth grapes**" (Isaiah 5: 2). The parable of Jotham (Judges 9: 7-21) emphasises the point: "Then said the trees unto the vine, Come thou, and reign over us. And the vine said unto them, **Should I leave my wine**, which cheereth God and man, and go to be promoted over the trees?" (vv.12-13). There can, therefore, be no doubt about the reason for Israel's national existence. God intended His people to be a fruitful vineyard, that is, to bring Him joy and pleasure. Micah sums it up like this: "What doth the LORD require of thee, but to justly, and to love mercy, and to walk humbly with thy God" (Micah 6: 8). But God had to say, "Israel is an empty vine, he bringeth forth fruit unto himself" (Hosea 10: 1). There was nothing for Him. See also Ezekiel 15: 1-8.

All this should provoke serious thought. We are here for precisely the same reason as Israel. Listen to the True Vine: "Ye have not chosen me, but I have chosen you, and ordained you, that ye should go and **bring forth fruit**" (John 15: 16). Each assembly should also be like a fruitful vineyard. See Galatians 5: 22. How much pleasure do we, as individuals, bring to God? How much pleasure does the assembly with which we are associated, bring to God?

b) The role of the husbandmen

The word 'husbandman' simply means someone who works on the land. The Greek word *georgos* has given us the English name 'George'. If the vineyard itself represents Israel, then the husbandmen represent the leaders and rulers who should have cared for Israel and ensured that it fulfilled its God-given purpose. Ezekiel calls them "shepherds" (Ezek. 34: 2-10). The Lord Jesus calls them "the builders" (v.42). Israel had lost its kings and princes, but the leadership was vested in the chief priests, scribes and elders. There had been little, if any, change in the character of the "husbandmen" over the years. Zephaniah describes the leadership as follows: "Her princes within her are roaring lions; her judges are evening wolves...her prophets are light and treacherous persons: her priests have polluted the sanctuary, they have done violence to the law" (Zeph. 3: 3-4). Nothing had changed in six hundred and fifty years. The Lord was obliged to say, "Woe unto you, scribes and Pharisees..." (Matt. 23: 13, 14, 15, 23, 24, 25, 27, 29).

Israel's leadership was particularly culpable before God: the nation was barren. Let every assembly leader beware. Paul taught that the local assembly is "God's husbandry" (*georgion*, meaning 'God's tillage' or 'God's cultivated field'). An elder is "the steward of God" (Titus 1: 7), and therefore responsible to ensure that the assembly brings pleasure to Him.

c) The resistance to the owner

The "householder" (v.33) or "lord" (v.40), compare Matthew 20 vv.1, 8, had every right to expect fruit. Israel owed its very existence to God. They were a slave-nation in Egypt: **He** delivered them. They were strangers to the desert: **He** led them. They were totally untrained for warfare: **He** fought their battles. **He** gave them Canaan, "the land that floweth with milk and honey" (Exodus 3: 8 etc). In the words of the parable: "There was a certain householder, which planted a vineyard, and hedged it round about, and digged a winepress in it, and built a tower, and let it out to husbandmen, and went into a far country" (v.33). But "when the time of the fruit drew near, he sent his servants to the husbandmen, that they might receive the fruits of it. And the husbandmen took his servants, and beat one, and killed another, and stoned another" (vv.34-35). It is a very solemn picture. The husbandmen resisted and rejected the rights and objectives of the owner. They wanted to live completely for themselves: they did not miss the owner for one moment: they were utterly opposed to his claims. Jeremiah gives an apt commentary: "What iniquity have your fathers found in me, that they are gone far from me...Neither said they, Where is the LORD that brought us up out of the land of Egypt, that led us through the wilderness...?" (Jer. 2: 4-8).

But just how seriously do *we* take God's claims on our lives? We are happy to say, "The LORD hath done great things for us; whereof we are glad" (Psalm 126: 3), but do we realise that He has absolute rights over our lives as Lord and Sovereign? It is sadly possible for even Christians to live with little reference to God and His Word, and with little acknowledgement of the Lordship of Christ. Believers are not to "live unto themselves, but unto him which died for them, and rose again" (2 Cor. 5: 15).

d) *The resolve of the owner*
He persisted. "Again, he sent other servants more than the first: and they did unto them likewise" (v.36). The book of Jeremiah emphasises God's longsuffering: "Since the day that your fathers came forth out of the land Egypt unto this day, I have even sent unto you all my servants the prophets, daily rising up early, and sending them" (Jer. 7: 25). (There are eleven similar references in Jeremiah). The New Testament contributes to the subject as follows: "God, who at sundry times and in divers manners, spake in time past unto the fathers by *the prophets*..." (Heb. 1: 1) To put it mildly, they were not well received. They were often regarded as a downright nuisance - or an absolute menace - or worse. Take, for example, Jeremiah: "Now it came to pass, when Jeremiah had made an end of speaking all that the LORD commanded him to speak unto all the people, that the priests and the prophets and all the people took him, saying, Thou shalt surely die" (Jer. 26: 8). Stephen charged the Jewish council (the Sanhedrin): "which of the prophets have not your fathers persecuted" (Acts 7: 52).

The prophets called the nation back to God, only to be faced by downright opposition from its leaders. But rather than repossessing the vineyard immediately by force, He made a final appeal. In the words of the parable: "But last of all he sent unto them his son, saying, They will reverence my son" (v.37), or "Having yet therefore one son, his well-beloved, he sent him also last unto them, saying, They will reverence my son" (Mark 12: 6). Put another way, "God, who...spake in time past unto the fathers by the prophets, hath *in these last days* spoken unto us *by his Son*" (Heb. 1: 3).

The Lord Jesus is now speaking of Himself, and the language of the parable demands particularly careful consideration. As we have noted above, Mark (and Luke) gives a fuller account of the Lord's words here, and we should take the opportunity to notice the details as given in Mark 12: 6:

- **"Having yet therefore one son"**. That is, he was the heir. Everything now depended on the mission of that son. The husbandmen were quite correct: "This is the heir". Hebrews 1 continues by saying of the Lord Jesus, "whom he (God) hath appointed *heir* of all things" (v.2). Every purpose of God centres on Christ.

- **"His well-beloved"**. The Lord Jesus said in prayer, "thou lovedst me before the foundation of the world" (John 17: 24). He is 'the Son of his (God's) love' (Col. 1: 13, JND). Closely connected with this is the expression, "only begotten". It is a term which conveys deepest love and intimacy. See, for example, John 1: 18.

- **"They will reverence my son"**. See Psalm 2: "Thou art my Son, this day (referring to the incarnation) have I begotten thee" (v.7). This is a statement of His deity. The title, "Son of God", conveys absolute equality with God. The Lord Jesus has the very nature, character and attributes of God Himself. He is, therefore, worthy of our deepest reverence. They had said, "By what authority doest thou these things? and who gave thee this authority?" (v.23). Here is the answer: **He is God's "beloved son"**. But Israel would say, "And when we shall *see* him, there is no beauty that we should desire him" (Isaiah 53: 2). This follows:

e) The rejection of the Son

"But when the husbandmen saw the son, they said among themselves, This is the heir; come, let us kill him, and let us seize on his inheritance. And they caught him, and cast him out of the vineyard, and slew him" (vv.38-39). The Jewish leadership had virtually said, "come, let us kill him", the previous day. See Luke 19: 47. The significance of these words would not have been lost on His audience, for the Lord Jesus used the very words of Joseph's brethren in Gen. 37: 18-20: "Come now, therefore, and let us slay him". Joseph was the well-beloved son, his dreams proclaimed his glorious future, and he was hated by his brethren. Although rejected by his brethren, he ultimately became pre-eminent in Egypt. Although "cast...out of the vineyard", the Lord Jesus remains "the heir of all things". Hence the apostolic preaching: "Ye denied the Holy One and the Just...and killed the Prince of life, whom God hath raised from the dead...whom the heaven must receive until the times of restitution of all things" (Acts 3: 13-26).

The parable gives us further evidence of the Lord's perfect foreknowledge. Once again, He anticipates His own suffering and death.

f) The result of his rejection

"When the lord therefore of the vineyard cometh, what will he do unto those husbandmen? They say unto him, He will miserably destroy those wicked men, and will let out his vineyard unto other husbandmen, which shall render him the fruits in their seasons. Jesus saith unto them, Did ye never read in the scriptures, The stone that the builders rejected, the same is become the head of the corner: this is the Lord's doing, and it is marvellous in our eyes?" (vv.40-42). We should notice:

i) **The result for them.** "He will miserably (*kakos*) destroy those wicked (*kakos*) men". The double use of *kakos* leads to the rendering, 'evil (as they are) he will evilly destroy them' (W.E.Vine). And He did. In A.D.70, the Roman armies brought Israel's national life to an end amidst the most fearful suffering and bloodshed. Matthew 21: 43 expands the words, "and will let out his vineyard unto other husbandmen", as follows: "Therefore say I unto you, **The kingdom of God** shall be taken from you, and given to a nation bringing forth the fruits thereof". The "vineyard" is "the kingdom of God" in the sense that Israel as a nation was the place of divine rule. But that rule had been rejected. "The kingdom of God" is now operative in the hearts and lives of believers. What God did not receive from His earthly people, He now receives from those who have been "delivered from the power of darkness, and translated...into the kingdom of his dear Son" (Col. 1: 13). Peter describes them as "a chosen generation, a royal priesthood, an holy nation, a peculiar people", who "shew forth the praises of him who hath called you out of darkness into his marvellous light" (1 Pet.2: 9).

ii) **The result for Him.** "The stone that the builders rejected, the same is become the head of the corner: this is the Lord's doing, and it is marvellous in our eyes" This cites Psalm 118: 22-23. Thus God has reversed man's verdict. His resurrection and ascension proclaims that He is central to every divine purpose, and "it is marvellous in our eyes". The Psalmist (Psalm 118: 10-12) describes a concerted attempt to destroy him, followed by victory and vindication. Whilst, in context, this quotation refers to Christ's coming glory in Israel, we cannot forget that He will have His rightful place in every sphere, for "God also hath highly exalted him, and given him a name which is above every name: that at the name of Jesus every knee should bow... and that every tongue should confess that Jesus Christ is Lord, to the glory of God the Father" (Phil. 2: 9-11). Peter quoted the same Psalm in the presence of the Jewish leaders. He addressed them as follows: "Be it known unto **you all,** and to all the people of Israel, that by the name of Jesus Christ of Nazareth, whom ye crucified, whom God raised from the dead, even by him doth this man stand here before you whole. This is the stone which was set at nought of **you builders,** which is become the head of the corner" (Acts 4: 5-11). Peter also **wrote** about Christ as the "living stone". See 1 Peter 2: 4-8.

Not only so, but the "stone...set at nought" by the builders would execute judgment on them: in the Lord's words, "Whosoever shall fall upon this stone shall be broken (all who challenged the Lord Jesus were 'broken' in argument): but on whomsoever it shall fall, it will **grind him to powder**" (v.44). Israel was 'ground to powder'. Compare Daniel 2: 34-35. The words, "Whosoever shall fall upon this stone shall be broken" are clearly explained in Isaiah 8: 13-15, "Sanctify the LORD of hosts himself; and let him be your fear, and let him be your dread. And he shall be for a sanctuary; but for a stone of stumbling and a rock of offence to both the houses of Israel...And many among them shall stumble and fall, and be broken, and be snared, and be taken".

But the "husbandmen" were true to character: "they sought to lay hold on him" (v.46). Their fear of a public outcry if they had dared to deny the authority of John the Baptist (v.26) was accompanied by their fear of a public outcry should they have apprehended the Lord Jesus: "they feared the multitude, because they took him for a prophet" (v.46). Mark's account ends with the significant words, "they **left him**, and went **their** way" (Mark 12: 12).

THE GOSPEL OF MATTHEW

"Is it lawful to give tribute to Caesar, or not?"

Read Chapter 22: 1-22
As we have seen, a large part of the Lord's third day in Jerusalem was evidently given to question and answer sessions. In the first place, His enemies questioned Him, and in the second, He questioned them. It can be put like this;

i) He answered questions
The Lord was asked four questions. The questioners and the questions differed in each case:

- *the first* was a *personal* question, and posed by "the chief priests and elders": "By what authority doest thou these things? and who gave thee this authority?" (21: 23).

- *the second* was a *political* question, and posed by the Pharisees and Herodians: "Is it lawful to give tribute unto Caesar, or not?" (22: 17).

- *the third* was a *doctrinal* question, and posed by the Sadducees: "In the resurrection whose wife shall she be of the seven?" (22: 28).

- *the fourth* was an *ethical* question, and posed by a lawyer: "Master, which is the great commandment in the law?" (22: 36).

In the Old Testament, "the queen of Sheba heard of the fame of Solomon concerning the name of the LORD" and "came to prove him with hard questions". She was not disappointed: "And Solomon told her all her questions: there was not any thing hid from the king, which he told her not", leading her to say, "It was a true report that I heard in mine own land of thy acts and of thy wisdom. Howbeit I believed not the words, until I came, and mine eyes had seen it: and behold, the half was not told me: thy wisdom

Matthew

and thy prosperity exceedeth the fame which I heard" (1 Kings 10: 1-7). And now, a thousand years later, "behold, a **greater than Solomon** is here!" (Matt. 12: 42). He told His questioners 'all their questions', and while the Pharisees and Herodians "marvelled...and went their way" (v.22), and "the multitude...were astonished at his doctrine" (v.33), it had no lasting effect on them.

It is delightful to notice that nothing had changed in twenty years. At the age of twelve, the Lord Jesus was found in the same temple, "sitting in the midst of the doctors, both hearing them, and asking them questions. And all that heard him were astonished at his understanding and answers" (Luke 2: 46-47). Even at that early age, it was clear that He possessed "all the treasures of wisdom and knowledge" (Col. 2: 3, AV). (It is worth adding that other translations do not necessarily alter the sense of this quotation).

ii) He asked questions
The Lord then asked the Pharisees two questions. They answered the first: "What think ye of Christ? whose son is he?", but were unable to answer the second: "If David then call him Lord, how is he his son?". The question and answer sessions ended with silence: "And no man was able to answer him a word, neither durst any man from that day forth ask him any more questions" (vv.41-46).

Bearing this in mind, Matthew ch.22 may be divided as follows: *(1)* they refused His invitation (vv.1-14); *(2)* they questioned His allegiance (vv.15-22); *(3)* they challenged His doctrine (vv.23-33); *(4)* they tested His discernment (vv.34-40; *(5)* He silenced their unbelief (vv.41-46).

1) THEY REFUSED HIS INVITATION, vv.1-14
The opening section of this chapter continues the Lord's answer to the questions, "By what authority doest thou these things? and who gave thee this authority?" (21: 23). As we have noted, the Lord answered their questions by referring to His herald, John the Baptist, and then to His own identity as the Heir.

- In the first case, John had made it perfectly clear that he baptized in preparation for the coming of the Lord (John 1: 22-27), who was none other than Jehovah Himself (Isaiah 40: 3). He had scriptural authority for preaching and baptizing in this way. He had come as the Scriptures had predicted (Isaiah 40: 3; Mal. 3: 1). But the religious leaders did not believe him (21: 25, 32).

- In the second case, the Lord Himself made it perfectly clear that He was none other than the "son" of the "householder" who owned the vineyard or, to put it in different words, the "heir" of the "lord" of the vineyard. But in the parable, the "husbandmen" (the chief priests and Pharisees) "caught him, and cast him out of the vineyard and slew him" (21: 37-39). The religious leaders listened to the parable, and 'bit the bullet': "they perceived that he spake of them".

The parable of the 'marriage feast' extends 'the parable of the wicked husbandmen'. It amplifies the statement, "the kingdom of God shall be taken from you, and given to a nation bringing forth the fruits thereof" (21: 43). The connection is clear. In answering the question, "When the lord of the vineyard cometh, what will he do unto those husbandmen?", the chief priests and Pharisees were obliged to answer, "He will miserably destroy those wicked men, and will let out his vineyard unto other husbandmen, which shall render him the fruits in their season" (21: 40-41). In the present parable, having "sent forth his armies, and destroyed those murderers, and burned up their city", the king despatches his servants to gather "as many as ye shall find", bidding them "to the marriage" (22: 7-9). The passage should be compared with Luke 14: 16-24. There are similarities and dissimilarities, and the circumstances in each case point to two different occasions.

The two parables here are complementary. The first parable centres on the rights of "a certain householder" (21: 33), and the second on the invitation by "a certain king" (22: 2). Notice too that both parables concern a son. In the first case, the "householder" sent his son (21: 37), and in the second, the "king" invited people to the wedding of his son (22: 3). In the first case people refused to *give* something, and in the second people refused to *accept* something. The lesson is clear: men and women refuse to *give* what God wants *from them*, and they refuse to *accept* what God wants *to give to them.*

The parable of the wedding feast has two component parts which can be entitled: *(a)* the call to attend (vv.2-10), *(b)* the condition of attendance (vv.11-14).

a) The call to attend, vv.2-10

While the Gospel preacher will find plenty of good material here (and even more in the similar parable in Luke 14: 16-24), it has been rightly said by Alva J.McClain (*The Greatness of the Kingdom*), and others before him, that the parable of the marriage feast clearly sets out the offer to the nation of Israel, with its subsequent rejection and the consequences.

- The ***first*** call in the parable (vv.2-3) was issued by the Lord through His disciples (Matt. 10: 1-15; Luke 10: 1-9), and directed exclusively to the chosen nation, when it was officially rejected (v.3). In the Lord's own words, "The kingdom of heaven is like unto a certain king, which made a marriage (*gamos*) for his son, and sent forth his servants (bondservants) to call them that were bidden to the wedding (*gamos*): and they would not come". The word rendered "marriage" and "wedding" can refer either to the wedding ceremony or to the wedding feast. Hence the renderings 'marriage feast' (RV) or 'wedding feast' (JND) in both cases.

Any attempt to introduce the church here ought to be firmly resisted. The context of the parable does not point at all in that direction. No reference is made to the bride. We could say, speaking generally, that a marriage feast is the epitome of joy, and that the figure is used with that in mind. However, it does seem quite legitimate to go further and say that the king convenes the feast in honour of his son, inviting the guests to share his joy. But, sadly, the nation (like so many today) refused to honour the king's son: "they would not come" (v.3). The Lord Jesus said, "ye will not come to me, that ye might have life" (John 5: 40). See also Matthew 23: 37.

- The ***second*** call in the parable (vv.4-7) announced that the dinner was now "prepared", and "all things are ready" (v.4). In the words of Alva McClain, "This is surely a reference to the Lord's finished work of redemption at Calvary. Such a call could not have gone forth until after the resurrection. But again the call was rejected, this time by actions which help to identify it in Biblical history: some Jews would turn away with contemptuous indifference, according to the parable, while others would mistreat and kill the messengers (v.6). This points to the post-Pentecostal offer, as described in the book of Acts, when the officials of Israel did exactly that. During the Gospel period not an official disciple of Christ was killed by the Jews, but during the period of the Acts the terrible persecution and killing of the messengers began".

Attention is drawn to the Lord's words, "But they made light of it, and went their ways, one to his farm, another to his merchandise" (v.5). The words "they made light of it" mean that they 'did not care about it' or were 'negligent of it' (J.Heading). We could say that they did not take the invitation seriously. The word *ameleo,* meaning 'to be careless, not to care' (W.E.Vine), occurs in 1 Timothy 4: 14 ("Neglect not the gift that is in thee"); Heb. 2: 3 ("How shall we escape, if we neglect so great salvation"); 2 Pet. 1: 12 ("I will not be negligent to put you always in remembrance of these things"). It also occurs in Hebrews 8: 9 ("I regarded them not, saith the Lord"). On the one hand we have passive opposition, "they...went their ways, one to his farm, another to his merchandise" (v.5), and on the other, active antagonism: "and the remnant took his servants, and entreated them spitefully, and slew them" (v.6). We must now listen to the solemn words of J.C.Ryle: "Open sin may kill its thousands; but indifference and neglect of the Gospel kill their tens of thousands. Multitudes will find themselves in hell, not so much because they openly broke the ten commandments, as because they made light of the truth. Christ died for them on the cross, but they neglected Him". As H.A.Ironside observes, "In order to be lost for ever it is not necessary to be opposed to Christ. It is not necessary to say deliberately, 'I reject Jesus'. Just neglect Him and you will never get in to the feast".

There is no further call for this generation of Israel, but judgment falls: the king sends forth his armies, destroys the murderers, and burns their city - a parabolic prediction of the awful destruction of Jerusalem in AD 70 (v.7). In Paul's words, "wrath is come upon them to the uttermost" (1 Thess. 2: 16). The Roman soldiers are called "his armies", that is, the king's armies, or interpreting the parable, the **King's** armies. Compare Isaiah 10: 5.

- The **third** call in the parable (vv.8-10) was issued, **not** to those "that were bidden to the wedding" (v.3), **but** to "as many as ye shall find" in "the highways (*diexodous ton hodon:* literally 'the partings of the highways'). In the words of "the king", "The wedding (*gamos*) is ready, but they which were bidden were **not worthy**. Go ye therefore into the highways and as many as ye shall find, bid to the marriage (*gamos*)". It is said that the Greek word *diexodos* (meaning, literally, according to Vincent, 'a way out through') refers to "the place where a street reaches the city boundary and debouches into open country, i.e the end of the street, a square outside or on the edge of the city. Many people always gathered here, especially beggars, robbers, the unclean. It is obvious that Jesus is speaking prophetically about the Gentiles" (supplied by J.Waldron). The best commentary on this is found in Acts 13: 45-46: "Then Paul and Barnabas waxed bold, and said, It was necessary that the word of God should first have been spoken to you: but seeing ye put it from you, and judge yourselves **unworthy** of everlasting life, lo, we turn to the Gentiles". It has been pointed out, they did not **express** the opinion that they were "unworthy of everlasting life" for they thought the exact reverse, but by their **conduct** they condemned themselves: they had deliberately and solemnly rejected the gospel, and thus shown that they were not fitted to enter into everlasting life (Alfred Barnes).

"So those servants went out into the highways, and gathered together all as many as they found, both bad and good: and the wedding (some manuscripts have *numphon* here, referring to the room) was furnished with guests" (v.10). All were welcome, and "bad and good" came, in response to the invitation, to honour the son. William Kelly puts it beautifully: on one hand "a dying thief, or a woman that was a sinner", and on the other, a "Lydia or a Cornelius". It is a question of "whosoever (irrespective of who they are and what they are) shall call on the name of the Lord shall be saved" (Acts 2: 21).

b) The condition of attendance, vv.11-14

These are solemn verses. They illustrate the fact that "the Lord knoweth them that are his" (2 Tim. 2: 19). "And when the king came in to see the guests, he saw there a man which had not on a wedding garment" (v.11). The Lord does not say, 'he saw there a "bad" man amongst all the "good guests"', but a man without "a wedding garment". As William Kelly helpfully observes, "The servants did not look for such garments outside: they were not worn on the highways (*that is, before they responded to the invitation*), but within at the wedding feast (*that is, after they had responded to the invitation*)". (Our italics). There does not appear to be any foundation for the popular view that 'wedding garments' were supplied by the host. According to R.V.G.Tasker, this idea was "a guess of Augustine but...is unsupported by any evidence". It has been said that "the wedding garment was not some unusual festive garment, but clean washed clothes" (supplied by J.Waldron).

In the **immediate context**, the Lord Jesus is speaking to "the chief priests and Pharisees" (21: 45 - 22: 1), and the man without the "wedding garment" must therefore represent the religious leadership, to whom the Saviour referred in saying, "That except your righteousness shall exceed the righteousness of the scribes and Pharisees, ye shall in no case enter into the kingdom of heaven" (Matt. 5: 20). In this connection we should read Matthew 23 in its entirety. It was of these very people that Paul wrote: "I bear them record that they have a zeal of God, but not according to knowledge. For they being ignorant of God's righteousness, and going about to establish their own righteousness, have not submitted themselves unto the righteousness of God. For Christ is the end of the law for righteousness to every one that believeth" (Rom. 10: 3-4). They preferred their "own righteousness" to the righteousness "which is through the faith of Christ, the righteousness which is of God by faith" (Phil. 3: 7-9). The man in the parable professes to honour the king and the king's son, but thinks that he can do so on his own terms. On inspection, he is completely out of place. He is still in the "filthy rags" (Is. 64: 6) of his own righteousness. He does not have what we might call "the garments of salvation" (Isaiah 61: 10). The Gospel preacher has plenty of material here!

It should be noted that while the man is addressed as "Friend" (v.12), the word (*hetairos*), which also occurs in Matt. 20: 13; 26: 50, means 'a comrade, companion, partner', and 'is to be distinguished from *philos*, which is a term of endearment' (W.E.Vine). The fact that the man is "speechless" reminds us that "every mouth" will "be stopped" (Rom. 3: 19). The expression "outer darkness" must mean total exclusion from God of whom it is said, "God is light, and in him is no darkness at all" (1 John 1: 5). 2 Thess. 1: 9, 2 Pet. 2: 17, and Jude v.13 should be read in this solemn connection.

The Lord concludes the parable with the words, "For many are called, but few are chosen" (v.14). It goes without saying that this statement is explained by the preceding parable. The "many" must be those who are invited to the wedding feast, both Jews (v.3) and Gentiles (v.9). In the case of the former, it could be said that the "many" refused to come (v.3) and "made light of it, and went their ways" (v.5). In the case of the latter, it is specifically said, "as many as ye shall find, bid to the marriage" (v.9). The "few" must be those that responded to the invitation, and while "the wedding was furnished with guests", the good attendance was only "few" when compared with the total invited. The Saviour was once asked, "Lord, are there few that be saved?" to which He replied, "strive to enter in at the strait gate; for many, I say unto you, will seek to enter in (once the door is shut), and shall not be able" (Luke 13: 23-24). The words, "few are chosen" indicate that left to themselves, no one would respond to the invitation. This does not make God unjust. "God is only unfair if He gives *less* than what is right or what we deserve – not if, in grace, He gives *more* than what is deserved – even to a select few" (Andrew Wilson). John 6: 37 is now compulsory reading: "All that the Father giveth me shall come unto me; and him that cometh unto me I will in no wise cast out". We should add that those who are "chosen" will display the fact

Matthew

in their lives. See 1 Thess. 1: 4 where the word "knowing" (*oida*) means to know by observation.

2) THEY QUESTIONED HIS ALLEGIANCE, vv.15-22
While Mark and Luke place this question immediately after the parable of the vineyard, Matthew inserts the parable of the wedding feast between the two. These verses are easily divided: *(a)* the question (vv.15-17); *(b)* the answer (vv.18-22).

a) The question, vv.15-17
In this connection, we must notice *(i)* the purpose intended (v.15) *(ii)* the parties involved (v.16); *(iii)* the tactics employed (vv.16-17).

i) The purpose intended, v.15. "Then went the Pharisees and took counsel how they might **entangle** (*pagideuo*, to ensnare) **him in his talk"**. Mark has, "to catch (*agreuo*, to take by hunting) him in his words" (Mark 12: 13), and Luke, "that they might take hold of his words, that so they might deliver him unto the power and authority of the governor" (Luke 20: 20). But it was all to no avail: "they could **not take hold of his words before the people**" (Luke 20: 26).

ii) The parties involved, v.16. "And they (the Pharisees) sent out unto him their disciples with the Herodians". Luke has, "And they watched him, and sent forth spies, which should feign themselves just men" (Luke 20: 20). It seems quite incredible to us that they should send "spies", 'secret agents' (J.Heading), in an attempt to discredit the omniscient Christ! This was not the first time that these unlikely bed-fellows had teamed up against Christ. See Mark 3: 6. The Pharisees and Herodians were usually sworn enemies. They were people of totally different persuasions. But here, they form an alliance against Christ. It is quite amazing what people will do in their hatred for Him. Pilate and Herod were enemies until they, too, became friends in their common hatred of the Lord Jesus. See Luke 23: 6-12.

iii) The tactics employed, vv.16-17. First of all, they tried to catch the Lord 'off guard' with a few compliments (v.16), and then they asked an apparently harmless question: "Tell us therefore, What thinkest thou? Is it lawful to give tribute unto Caesar or not?" (v.17). They are perfect examples of the man in Proverbs 26: 24-25, "He that hateth dissembleth with his lips, and layeth up deceit within him; when he speaketh fair, believe him not; for there are seven abominations in his heart".

The trap was very cleverly prepared. If the Saviour replied, 'Yes, it is lawful to give tribute to Caesar', the Pharisees would have branded Him a traitor to the Jewish cause. If He had replied, 'No, it is not lawful to give tribute to Caesar', the Herodians would have branded him a rebel against Roman authority, and gone hot-foot to the governor (Luke 20: 20). Either answer would have meant big trouble. But the question presented no difficulty to divine omniscience.

b) The answer, vv.18-22

Genuine questions (see, for example, John 3: 4; 4: 11-12) received clear answers, but those who asked catch-questions only succeeded in getting caught themselves! They attacked the Lord Jesus with a two-edged sword, only to find themselves on the receiving end! This follows: "But Jesus perceived their wickedness ("craftiness", Luke 20: 23), and said, Why tempt ye me, ye hypocrites? Shew me the tribute money. And they brought unto him a penny. And he said unto them, Whose is this image and superscription? They say unto him, Caesar's. Then saith he unto them, Render therefore unto Caesar the things which are Caesar's; and unto God the things that are God's" (vv.18-21). No doubt the Pharisees and Herodians thought they had engineered a situation from which escape was impossible. But they were wrong! And they were silenced: "When they heard these words, they marvelled, and left him, and went their way" (v.22). Later, they turned the Lord's answer into a deliberate lie. See Luke 23: 2.

The "penny" *(denarion)* was a silver coin minted in Rome. It was used in every part of the Roman Empire, and was the coinage in which tax (in this case, a poll-tax: from *kensos:* Latin, *tributum capitis)* must be paid. John Heading observes that the "image on the coin will be developed into a larger image in that future day (Rev.13: 1-10), with life being given to it so that it will be worshipped: this shows the ultimate development of world politics".

The Saviour's exact answer is important: He did not say, 'give' *(didomi),* but 'give back' *(apodidomi:* AV "render") to Caesar. We owe something to the State in return for the benefits that we receive from the State. This includes the payment of taxes. The Bible does not encourage political agitation. Christians are expected to obey the law, and act as good citizens. Read Romans 13: 1-7 and 1 Peter 2: 13-14. Whilst this does not normally create problems for us, many of God's people have had to face unacceptable demands by the State. Witness the demands made on Daniel and his three colleagues. Early Christians were required, with everybody else, to worship

Caesar. The alternatives were quite clear: either compromise, or obey God, and take the consequences. Many paid the ultimate price. It is not outside the bounds of possibility that we may have to face the same situation. It is worth asking ourselves the question, 'What would *I* do if 'Caesar' should ask for something that belongs to God alone? After all, to be forewarned is to be fore-armed.

"What think ye of Christ? whose son is he?"

Read Chapter 22: 23-46
As we have noted more than once, a large part of the Lord's third day in Jerusalem was evidently given to question and answer sessions. In the first place, His enemies questioned Him (21: 23; 22: 17; 22: 28; 22: 36), and in the second, He questioned them (22: 41-46). We could put it differently, and say that the Lord Jesus answered their questions by asking *them* questions:

- They asked Him a *personal* question: they questioned His authority (21: 23), which He answered by questioning them about the authority of John the Baptist (21: 25), leading to the parables of the two sons and of the wicked husbandmen (21: 28-46).

- They asked Him a *political* question: they questioned His allegiance (22: 17), which He answered by questioning them about "the image and superscription" on the "tribute money" (22: 20).

- They asked Him a *doctrinal* question: they questioned His doctrine (22: 28), which He answered by questioning their knowledge of the Scriptures: "But as touching the resurrection of the dead, have ye not read that which was spoken unto you by God, saying, I am the God of Abraham, and the God of Isaac, and the God of Jacob?" (22: 31-32).

- They asked Him an *ethical* question: they questioned His discernment (22: 35-36), and having answered the lawyer's question, the Lord tested their discernment with two questions (22: 41-46). They achieved 50% (hardly a pass-mark) in answering the first question, and 0% in answering the second!

However, in introducing the chapter, we did say that the passage may be divided as follows: *(1)* they refused His invitation (vv.1-14); *(2)* they questioned His allegiance (vv.15-22); *(3)* they challenged His doctrine (vv.23-33); *(4)* they tested His discernment (vv.34-40; *(5)* He silenced their unbelief (vv.41-46).

1) THEY REFUSED HIS INVITATION, vv.1-14
Those that were bidden to "the marriage (feast) of the king's son" refused the invitation in the first place, and in the second, either "made light of it" or "took his servants (the king's servants), and entreated them spitefully, and slew them", with dire consequences (vv.1-7). The Lord was well aware that the Jewish nation would reject the invitation, but this would not mean that the wedding would not be "furnished with guests". He knew that God would "visit the Gentiles, to take out of them a people for his name" (Acts 15: 14). But nobody, Jew or Gentile, would enjoy divine blessing unless they were clothed in "the garments of salvation" (Isaiah 61: 10).

2) THEY QUESTIONED HIS ALLEGIANCE, vv.15-22
We need say nothing here, except to beware when 'Caesar' (call it 'the State', if you like) exceeds its divinely-given brief (Rom.13: 1-7) and wants what belongs to God. In such cases, we would have to say, "We ought to obey God rather than men" (Acts 5: 29). This sounds fine in theory, but the apostles 'nailed their colours to the mast' in the teeth of opposition, and got beaten for their pains (Acts 5: 40). This brings us to:

3) THEY CHALLENGED HIS DOCTRINE, vv.23-34
In these verses, we have *(a)* the Sadducees' question, which is quite self-explanatory (vv.23-28); *(b)* the Lord's answer (vv.29-32); *(c)* the people's response (vv.33-34). It has been said that "this is the only clash between the Jesus and the Sadducees reported in the Gospels. Jesus did not speak so sharply against them as He did against the Pharisees, for the Sadducees were not hypocrites but openly said what they thought" (supplied by Justin Waldron).

a) The Sadducees' question, vv.23-28
"The same day came to him the Sadducees, which say that there is no resurrection…" (v.23). The Sadducees were rationalists. They did not believe in resurrection. They did not believe in angels or spirits either. See Acts 23: 8. In practice, they limited the Scriptures to the Pentateuch.

Like the Pharisees and Herodians, the Sadducees had constructed a catch-question. "Master, Moses said, If a man die, leaving no children, his brother shall marry his wife, and raise up seed unto his brother. Now there were with us seven brethren: and the first, when he married a wife, deceased, and, having no issue, left his wife unto his brother: likewise the second also, and the third, unto the seventh. And last of all the woman died also. Therefore in the resurrection whose wife shall she be of the seven? For they all had her" (vv.24-28).

The question was based upon the law of levirate marriage (the requirement of a man to marry the widow of a brother who had died without children; from the Latin *levir*, a husband's brother). See Deut. 25: 5; Ruth 4: 5, 10. (The perpetuation of a man's name was an important matter in Jewish life). The Sadducees made their point quite clearly by saying, in effect, 'Look, if there is such a thing as resurrection (and we don't believe there is), then it's going to be very embarrassing for people who've married more than once!'

We can only speculate about the reason for asking this question at this particular time. Quite possibly the Sadducees thought that this was an opportunity to succeed where their arch-rivals, the Pharisees, had failed. It would have been a real 'feather in their cap' if they could have silenced the Saviour. But they were dealing with the "greater than Solomon!"

b) *The Lord's answer, vv.29-32*
We should notice that the Lord prefaced His answer by saying, "Ye do err, not knowing the scriptures, nor the power of God" (v.29). In answering the question, the Lord therefore does three things:

i) **He addresses their basic error**. The Lord deals, first of all, with the root problem: "Ye do err, not knowing the scriptures, nor the power of God?" All error begins here: lack of knowledge and lack of faith. They did not understand the Word of God, and they did not believe in the power of God. It was a significant combination. Our knowledge of the Word of God will be totally ineffective without the faith that expects the fulfilment of His word. Incidentally, our English word, 'planet' comes from the Greek word (*planao*) rendered "err".

ii) **He answers their particular question.** The Lord points out, secondly, that when husbands and wives are raised from the dead, they will no longer be husbands and wives. "For in the resurrection they neither marry, nor are given in marriage, but are as the angels of God in heaven" (v.30). Marriage belongs to this life only. Death dissolves marriage, and resurrection introduces an entirely new life from which earthly relationships will be absent.

Luke gives us the Lord's answer in greater length: "The children of **this world** marry, and are given in marriage: but they which shall be accounted worthy to obtain **that world,** and the resurrection from (among) the dead, neither marry, nor are given in marriage: neither can they die any more: for they are equal unto the angels (remember, the Sadducees did not believe in angels); and are the children of God, being the children of the resurrection" (Luke 20: 34-36). Perhaps it is worth saying that the Lord's answer is reassuring to Christians who have remarried after the death of a spouse. The King James Study Bible has an excellent note here: "For Christians, the life to come will be something incomprehensively superior to the present one. The fellowship of marriage, as high an ideal as it is in Scripture, will be surpassed by the depth and diversity of new life in the presence of God".

iii) He applies the Word of God. The Lord proves, thirdly, that the Sadducees' doctrine was wrong by referring to the very part of Scripture that they accepted: "But as touching the resurrection of the dead, have ye not read that which was spoken unto you by God, saying, I am the God of Abraham, and the God of Isaac, and the God of Jacob? God is not the God of the dead, but of the living" (vv.31-32). See Exodus 3: 6. Luke has, "Now that the dead are raised, even Moses shewed at the bush, when he calleth the Lord the God of Abraham, and the God of Isaac, and the God of Jacob. For he is not a God of the dead, but of the living: for all live unto him" (Luke 20: 37-38). As H.S.Paisley observes (writing on Mark): "If death had ended the existence of Abraham, Isaac and Jacob, He never could have said, 'I am (at that moment) their God'". The patriarchs had died, but they were alive.

This is, of course, the great subject of 1 Corinthians 15. The chapter's teaching surrounds two questions: "How say some among you that there is no resurrection of the dead?" (v.12), and "How are the dead raised up? and with what body do they come?" (v.35). Paul spells out the frightening implications if there is "no resurrection of the dead". **Firstly,** "then is Christ not risen". **Secondly,** "and if Christ be not risen, then is our preaching vain, and your faith is also vain…your faith is vain; ye are yet in your sins. Then they also that are fallen asleep in Christ are perished. If in this life only we have faith in Christ, we are of all men most miserable" (vv.13-19).

c) The hearers' response, vv.33-34
There was a mixed reaction to the Lord's answer to the Sadducees: "and when the **multitude heard** this, they were astonished (*ekplesso*) at his doctrine (see also Matt. 7: 28; 13: 54; 19: 25), but when the **Pharisees**

had heard that he had put the Sadducees to silence, they were gathered together" (Matt. 22: 33-34).

i) The response of the multitude, v.33. "And when the ***multitude*** heard this, they were astonished at his doctrine". As we noted in our previous study, in every way the Lord Jesus was "greater than Solomon". God gave Solomon "wisdom and understanding exceeding much, and largeness of heart" (1 Kings 4: 29), and that wisdom was tested by the queen of Sheba who came "to prove him with hard questions" (1 Kings 10: 1). Pharisees and Herodians, Sadducees and, finally, as we shall see, a lawyer (v.35), came to Christ with ***their*** "hard questions", but the "greater than Solomon" answered them all. In the adapted language of 1 Kings 10: 3, He 'told them all their questions'. The queen of Sheba listened to the king, saw his achievements and glory, and "there was no more spirit in her". Having listened to the way in which the Lord Jesus answered the Pharisees, the multitude followed suit: "they were astonished at his doctrine".

ii) The response of the Pharisees, v.34. "But when the ***Pharisees*** had heard that he had put the Sadducees to silence, they were gathered together". The word "silence" (*phimoo* from *phimos* meaning a muzzle) is rendered "speechless" in v.12. Compare 1 Cor. 9: 9, "Thou shalt not muzzle (*phimoo*) the mouth of the ox that treadeth out the corn". As R.V.G.Tasker points out that gathering of the Pharisees was not so much to gloat over the "discomfiture of their opponents, but to conspire further against Jesus", adding that the language is strikingly similar to the wording of Psalm 2, "the rulers take counsel together, against the LORD, and against his anointed" (v.2).

4) THEY TESTED HIS DISCERNMENT, vv.34-40
In these verses, we have ***(a)*** the lawyer's question, which is in itself quite self-explanatory, although the motive behind the question is suspect (vv.35-36); ***(b)*** the Lord's answer (vv.37-40).

a) The lawyer's question, vv35-36
"Then one of them, which was a lawyer, asked him a question, tempting him, and saying, Master, which is the great commandment in the law?" We ought to say that according to W.E.Vine (quoting from Hastings Bible dictionary), lawyers, scribes and doctors (Luke 2: 46; 5: 17) were "terms used synonymously, and did not denote three distinct classes". The word "scribe" (*grammateus*) denotes 'a man of letters', a student of Scripture,

whereas the word "lawyer" (*nomikos*) denotes a man who had devoted himself "mainly, though by no means exclusively, to the study of the law".

Putting Matthew and Mark together here, it appears that the lawyer posed "a ***test*** question ('tempting him') because, it would seem, they hoped that Jesus in His reply would say something unorthodox and startling, which would render Him liable to a charge of blasphemy. But if this were so, the questioner was destined to be sadly disappointed, for the answer given by Jesus proved to be orthodoxy itself" (R.V.G.Tasker). However, according to Mark, the man was so suitably impressed by the Lord's reply, that he responded by saying, "Master, thou hast said the truth", causing the Lord Jesus to say, "Thou art not far from the kingdom of God" (Mark 12: 32-34). The occasion on which the Lord quoted the same two commandments to the lawyer in Luke 10: 25-27 is evidently quite different from the circumstances described by Matthew and Mark.

We are told that "the Jews found 613 commandments in the law, one for each of the letters in the Ten Commandments. The 613 commandments consisted of 248 positive commands ('thou shalt') and 365 negative commands ('thou shalt not'). The positive and negative commands were subdivided into greater and lesser, according to importance. This often coincided with the more difficult or easier to obey" (supplied by J. Waldron).

b) The Lord's answer, vv.37-40
"Jesus said unto him, Thou shalt love (*agapao*) the Lord thy God with all thy heart, and with all thy soul, and with all thy mind. This is the first and great commandment. And the second is like unto it, Thou shalt love (*agapao*) thy neighbour as thyself. On these two commandments hang all the law and the prophets". The Lord Jesus answered with a combination of Deuteronomy 6: 5 and Leviticus 19: 18.

i) **Love for God** involves the totality of our being. The words, "all thy heart", refer to our undivided affection for Him, and "all thy soul" to our undiminished desire and determination to do His will. See Acts 4: 32; Eph. 6: 6 (*psuche*, 'soul': AV has "heart"); Phil. 1: 27 (*psuche*, 'soul': AV has "mind"); Heb. 12: 3 (*psuche*, 'souls': AV has "minds"). The words, "all thy mind" (*dianoia*) refer to our unreserved recognition of His word: it involves our submission to Him intellectually. Referring to Mark 12: 30, Jameson, Fausset and Brown have "thou shat love the Lord thy God with all thy heart (**sincerely**), and with all thy soul (**fervidly**), and with all thy mind (**intelligently**), and with all thy strength (**energetically**)". ('Fervidly' means 'impassionately, very warm in zeal').

Matthew

ii) **Love for others.** We need only to read Romans 13: 8-10, "Owe no man anything, but to love one another: for he that loveth another hath fulfilled the law. For this, Thou shalt not commit adultery...kill...steal...bear false witness...covet; and if there be any other commandment, it is briefly comprehended in this saying, namely, Thou shalt love thy neighbour as thyself. Love worketh no ill to his neighbour: *therefore love is the fulfilling of the law".*

5) HE SILENCED THEIR UNBELIEF, vv.41-46
The Lord Jesus now puts two questions to the Pharisees, and waits for their answers: *(a)* the first question (vv.41-42); *(b)* the second question (vv.43-46).

a) The first question, vv.41-42
"While the Pharisees were gathered together, Jesus asked them, saying, What think ye of Christ? Whose son is he? They say unto him, The son of David". Mark combines the two questions: "How say the scribes that Christ is the son of David?" (Mark 12: 35). The Pharisees answered correctly. God had said, "I have made a covenant with my chosen. I have sworn unto David my servant, Thy seed will I establish for ever, and build up thy throne to all generations" (Psalm 89: 3-4). See also Isaiah 9: 6-7. This was generally known: "Hath not the scripture said, That Christ cometh of the seed of David, and out of the town of Bethlehem, where David was?" (John 7: 41-42). Although correct, the answer was nevertheless incomplete, and the Lord goes further by asking a counter-question based on Psalm 110: 1.

c) The second question, vv.43-45
"How then doth David in spirit ('in Spirit', JND) call him Lord, saying, The Lord said unto my Lord, Sit thou on my right hand, till I make thine enemies thy footstool? If David then call him Lord, how is he his son?" Notice that Luke has "And David himself saith *in the book of Psalms*, the Lord said unto my Lord..." (Luke 20: 42).

The Lord is making the point that if the long-awaited Messiah would be David's son by birth, then the fact that God says to Him, "Sit thou on my right hand, till I make thine enemies thy footstool", implies that having encountered his enemies, who "slew him" (21: 39), He had risen from the dead and ascended to God's right hand.

We must look at the Lord's teaching here in three ways: *(i)* Christ is David's son; *(ii)* Christ is David's Lord; *(iii)* Christ is David's son and David's Lord.

- **Christ is David's son.** As we have seen, the blind men at Jericho recognised this: "Have mercy on us. O Lord, **thou son of David**" (Matt. 20: 30-31), and the "multitudes...cried, saying, Hosanna to **the son of David!"** (Matt. 21: 9). The scribes were, of course, perfectly correct. David was "a prophet, and knowing that God had sworn with an oath to him, that of **the fruit of his loins**, according to the flesh, he would raise up Christ to sit on his throne; he, seeing this before, spake of the resurrection of Christ..." (Acts 2: 30-31). The covenant with David seemed vulnerable at times, particularly during the reign of Athaliah, who thought that she had destroyed "all the seed royal of the house of Judah" (2 Chron. 22: 10), but the royal line was preserved (v.11), and Christ was born, as the prophet Micah anticipated (5: 2), in the city of David (Luke 2: 4). Mary was told, "behold, thou shalt conceive in thy womb, and bring forth a son, and shall call his name JESUS. He shall be great, and shall be called the Son of the Highest: and the Lord God shall give unto him the throne of **his father David"** (Luke 1: 31-32).

- **Christ is David's Lord.** But David knew, through the Holy Spirit, that although the promised Messiah would be descended from him, He was none other than his Sovereign Lord (*Adon*), and therefore lived before He was born: "The Lord said unto **my Lord,** Sit thou at my right hand, until I make thine enemies thy footstool" (Psalm 110: 1). This Psalm records the divine welcome enjoyed by the Lord Jesus at His ascension. "For David is not ascended into the heavens: but he saith himself, The Lord said unto my Lord, sit thou on my right hand...Therefore let all the house of Israel know assuredly, that God hath made that same Jesus, whom ye crucified, both **Lord and Christ"** (Acts 2: 34-36). The Psalm has been described as an 'enthronement oracle' (D.Kidner). Psalm 109 is a most appropriate introduction to Psalm 110. While in Psalm 109, David describes a harrowing personal experience, the language is well-suited to the experience of the Lord Jesus. See vv.1-5. We should notice v.25: "I am become also a reproach unto them: when they looked upon me they shaked their heads". Compare Matt. 27: 39. This Psalm describes the suffering of the Lord Jesus at the hand of His adversaries. In Psalm 109, He is "Benoni", meaning, 'Son of my sorrow'. In Psalm 110, He is "Benjamin", meaning, 'Son of my right hand'. See Gen. 35: 18.

The words rendered "Lord" are quite different: "The Lord (*Jehovah*) said unto my Lord (**Adon,** singular)..." The name 'Jehovah' describes the covenant-keeping, immutable God: the title 'Adon' means the 'Sovereign Lord, Master, Possessor, Proprietor' (Newberry) which is, of course, a title of absolute deity.

Notice that the Lord Jesus settles some important questions about Psalm 110. He settles the *authorship* of the Psalm; "*David* himself said...". He settles the *inspiration* of the Psalm; "David himself said by the *Holy Ghost*" (Mark 12: 36). He settles the *subject* of the Psalm; it refers to Christ. He settles the *deity of Christ*; He is "Adonai". But we must not leave this without a question. Can *we* say with David, "*My* Lord"?

- **Christ is David's son and David's Lord.** The answer to the Lord's question ("David therefore calleth him Lord, how is he then his son?") lies in one word: *"Emmanuel*; which being interpreted is, God with us" (Matt.1: 23). In His *humanity*, He is David's Son. In his *deity*, He is David's Lord. He was "made of the seed of David, *according to the flesh*; and declared to be (not 'made') the *Son of God* with power..." (Rom.1: 3-4). He is the "child...born", but He is also the "Son...given" (Isaiah 9: 6). He is "*the root and offspring of David*" (Rev. 22: 16). 'He is both earlier and later, before David and after him, the Maker of the Ages and the Ancient of Days' (Harold St. John).

The Pharisees responded with a deafening silence! "And no man was able to answer him a word, neither durst any man from that day forth ask him any more questions" (v.46). Mark ends this section with the words, "And the common people heard him gladly" (Mark 12: 37). Perhaps they were thoroughly sickened by their religious leaders, and welcomed teaching which was stamped with authority and truth. (Compare Matt. 7: 28-29; Mark 11: 18). The scribes and Pharisees were on the receiving end for a change! We can say with certainty from what follows (23: 1-39) that they did not 'hear him gladly', but do *we* hear Him gladly?

THE GOSPEL OF MATTHEW

"They say, and do not"

Read Chapter 23: 1-22
In this chapter, Matthew continues his account of the Lord's third day in Jerusalem by giving us a detailed account of His description and denunciation of the scribes and Pharisees. Mark and Luke give us only a brief summary of His discourse. See Mark 12: 38-40; Luke 20: 45-47. The 'Olivet Discourse' (Matt. 24: 1 - 25: 46) follows.

The chapter may be divided into three clear sections: *(1)* the Lord's description of the religious leaders (vv.1-12); *(2)* the Lord's denunciation of the religious leaders (vv.13-36); *(3)* the Lord's distress over Jerusalem (vv.37-39).

1) HIS DESCRIPTION OF THE RELIGIOUS LEADERS, vv.1-12
In this section of the chapter we should notice *(a)* the discrepancy between their doctrine and practice, (vv.1-3); *(b)* their denial of the sole authority of God's Word (v.4); *(c)* their desire for recognition by men (vv.5-12). The Lord draws attention to their insincerity (v.3), their legality (v.4), their hypocrisy (v.5), their publicity (v.6), their flattery (v.7), and to the cure of all these ills (v.12).

a) The discrepancy between their doctrine and practice, v.1-3
"Then spake Jesus to the multitude, and to his disciples, saying, The scribes and the Pharisees sit (according to Campbell Morgan, 'have seated themselves') in Moses' seat: all therefore whatsoever they bid you observe, that observe and do; but do ye not after their works: for they say, and do not". The same group of people are described in the parable of the two sons, saying, "I go, sir, and went not" (21: 30). Notice that the Lord addresses His disciples as well as His wider audience. We must take steps to ensure that the censure in this chapter does not apply in *our* case. The Lord's discourse is a cautionary warning to *us as well.*

The word rendered "seat" here (*kathedra*), from which we get our word 'cathedral', is reproduced in the Latin *ex cathedra,* with its Popish associations. The scribes and the Pharisees pretended that they had the authority of Moses. It is said that "Moses' seat" was "a piece of furniture from which they taught in the synagogue" (supplied by Justin Waldron - not the furniture, just the information!). Our contributor Justin Waldron continues by pointing out that Ezra was so different. He was "a ready scribe in the law of Moses" and "prepared his heart to seek the law of the LORD, and to ***do it***, and to teach in Israel statutes and judgments" (Ezra 7: 6, 10). There was no dichotomy between doctrine and practice in Ezra's life.

There was no such dichotomy either in the life of the Lord Jesus. Luke commences the book of Acts by reminding Theophilus "of all that Jesus began both to ***do*** and ***teach***" (Acts 1: 1). He taught "as one that had authority" (Mark 1: 22), and "went about doing good" (Acts 10: 38). He was the perfect exemplar of His own ministry. This is attested by the highest possible authority: "Thou hast ***loved*** righteousness, and ***hated*** iniquity" (Heb.1: 9); "By his knowledge shall my ***righteous*** servant justify many" (Isa. 53: 11). Our teaching may be right, but are ***we*** right? Talk must be exemplified in walk! It was for this reason that Timothy was told, "Take heed unto ***thyself***, and unto the ***doctrine***" (1 Tim. 4: 16). Paul had the moral right to say this to Timothy: he practised what he preached: "Ye know...after what manner I have been with you at all seasons, serving the Lord with all humility of mind...and how I kept back nothing that was profitable unto you, but have taught you publickly, and from house to house" (Acts 20: 18-20). It would be disastrous if people said to us, 'what you are saying is drowned by what you are doing'.

b) *Their denial of the sole authority of God's Word, v.4*
"For they bind heavy burdens, and grievous to be borne, and lay them on men's shoulders; but they themselves will not move them with one of their fingers". The "heavy burdens" comprised the welter of rabbinical ordinances which had been given parity - in some cases, more than parity - with the Word of God. They taught "for doctrines the commandments of men" (Matt. 15: 9). In our previous study, we noted that "the Jews found 613 commandments in the law, one for each of the letters in the Ten Commandments. The 613 commandments consisted of 248 positive commands ('thou shalt') and 365 negative commands ('thou shalt not'). The positive and negative commands were subdivided into greater and lesser, according to importance".

No wonder the Lord Jesus described these as "heavy (*barus*) burdens, and grievous to be borne". But, even worse, the "tradition" of the scribes and Pharisees made "the commandment of God of none effect" (Matt. 15: 6). They had some very convenient 'opt-out' clauses, leading the Saviour to say, "Ye hypocrites, well did Esaias prophesy of you, saying, This people draweth nigh unto me with their mouth, and honoureth me with their lips; but their heart is far from me" (Matt. 15: 7-8).

The Lord Jesus did not "bind heavy burdens, and grievous to be borne, and lay them on men's shoulders". He said, "Come unto me, all ye that labour and are heavy laden, and I will give you rest. Take my yoke upon you, and learn of me; for I am meek and lowly in heart: and ye shall find rest unto your souls. For my yoke is easy, and my burden is light" (Matt. 11: 28-30). As we noted in this connection, to be 'yoked' with the Lord Jesus "is to have a very gentle (AV "meek") and humble-minded Teacher, who is never impatient with those who are slow to learn, and never intolerant with those who stumble" (R.V.G.Tasker). Unlike the heavy burdens imposed by the scribes and Pharisees, those who submit to His "yoke" find that "his commandments are not grievous (meaning 'burdensome')" (1 John 5: 3). But under their religious leaders, the Jewish people "fainted ('they were harassed', JND), and were scattered abroad, as sheep having no shepherd" (Matt. 9: 36).

Believers are to "bear...one another's burdens (*baros*)*,* and so fulfil the law of Christ" (Gal. 6: 2), referring to the burden of anxiety felt by a saint who has fallen. The spiritual weakness of fellow-believers should be a matter of personal - mutual - concern. The word "burdens" here *(baros)*, denotes a weight. Its use always suggests something heavy and burdensome. See, for example, Matthew 20: 12, "which have borne the burden and heat of the day". Here (Gal. 6: 2), it is a *crushing* burden: in Gal. 6: 5 it is a burden that can be *carried* (a burden of responsibility). The scribes and Pharisees would not lift a finger to help the people they burdened with their 'do's and don'ts', but *we* are to help fellow-believers in every possible way.

c) Their desire for recognition by men, vv.5-12
"But all their works they do for to be seen of *men*". They loved to parade their religion. What a contrast to the Lord Jesus who was the very "mystery of *godliness*" (1 Tim. 3: 16). Whilst the scribes and Pharisees loved to "have glory of *men*" and to be "seen of *men*" (Matt. 6: 2, 5), He could say, "the Father hath not left me alone; for I do always those things that please *him*" (John 8: 29).

i)   They loved to wear the right clothes, v.5. "They make broad their phylacteries, and enlarge the borders of their garments". W.E.Vine explains the word 'phylactery' (only mentioned here) as follows: "it denotes…a small strip of parchment, with portions of the Law written on it (contained in a leather pouch); it was fastened by a leathern strap either to the forehead or to the left arm over against the heart, to remind the wearer of the duty of keeping the commandments of God in the head and in the heart". The words, "thou shalt love the LORD thy God with all thine heart, and with all thy soul, and with all thy might" were, amongst other things, to be bound "for a sign upon thine hand, and they shall be as frontlets between thine eyes" (Deut. 6: 4-8; cp. Exodus 13: 16). See also Deuteronomy 11: 18, "Therefore shall ye lay up these my words in your heart and in your soul, and bind them for a sign upon thine hand, that they may be as frontlets between your eyes". "The Pharisees broadened their phylacteries to render conspicuous their superior eagerness to be mindful of God's law" (W.E.Vine). But it was pure show. God's Word was far from their hearts and souls.

The reference to the "borders (*kraspedon*) of their garments" is explained by Numbers 15: 38-39, "Speak unto the children of Israel, and bid them that they make them fringes in the borders of their garments throughout their generations, and that they put upon the fringe of the borders a ribband of blue: and it shall be unto you for a fringe, that ye may look upon it, and remember all the commandments of the LORD, and do them; and that ye seek not after your own heart and your own eyes, after which ye use to go a whoring". The "fringes in the borders of their garments" were therefore to remind the wearers of the need for personal godliness, certainly not to parade their supposed virtues! The woman with "an issue of blood twelve years…said within herself, If I may but touch *his* garment, I shall be whole" (Matt. 9: 20-21). It is noteworthy that the woman did *not* touch the garments of the scribes and Pharisees: the Lord Jesus was known for His purity, and for His ability to help and save.

Amongst many other commendable things in Richard Collings' wise and balanced answer to the question, 'Does the Bible specify a dress code for the meetings?' (*Precious Seed*, November 2011), is the following: "If we dress in order to attract attention to ourselves (be that positive or negative attention), or to show off our affluence, or to rebel against authority, then we are amiss. In the meetings, Christ and God ought to be the centre of attention, not us, and therefore we should avoid wearing anything that would make us the focus of interest…There is one form of dress code the New

Testament does stipulate for us all, 'Yea, all of you be subject one to another, and be clothed with humility: for God resisteth the proud, and giveth grace to the humble' (1 Pet. 5: 5)".

ii) They loved to sit in the right seats. v.6. "They...love the uppermost rooms ('the chief place', JND) at feasts, and the chief seats ('the first seats', JND) in the synagogues". That is, prominence on social and religious occasions. Perhaps we should say that there is a vast difference between having an important place, and coveting such a position. The 'platform', especially the 'conference platform', can be a dangerous place. However, the "uppermost rooms at feasts, and the chief seats in the synagogues", had no appeal for the Lord Jesus. When popularity threatened, "he withdrew himself into the wilderness, and prayed" (Luke 5: 16). He willingly awaited the Father's time when it came to His glory and exaltation: He "made himself of no reputation, and took upon him the form of a servant, and was made in the likeness of men: and being found in fashion as a man, he humbled himself, and became obedient unto death, even the death of the cross. Wherefore God also hath highly exalted him, and given him a name which is above every name..." (Phil. 2. 7-11).

Since "in all things" He has "the preeminence" (Col.1: 18), there should be no place in our hearts for the pharisaical spirit of Diotrephes of whom John said, "I wrote unto the church: but Diotrephes, who loveth to have the preeminence among them, receiveth us not" (3 John v.9).

iii) They loved to be addressed in the right way, vv.7-11. "They love... greetings in the markets, and to be called of men, Rabbi, Rabbi" (v.7). The word "Rabbi", from "a word *rab*, primarily denoting 'master' in contrast to a slave,...is used as a courteous title of address" (W.E.Vine). As is so often the case, the Bible explains itself on this point: "They said unto him, Rabbi, (which is to say, being interpreted, Master) where dwellest thou" (John 1: 38). "Master" here translates *didaskalos,* meaning "Teacher". See also John 20: 16, "She (Mary Magdalene) turned herself, and saith unto him, Rabboni; which is to say, Master (*didaskalos*). "Rabboni" means 'my great master' (W.E.Vine). But we don't have to go beyond the present verses to get the point: "be not ye called Rabbi: for one is your Master (*kathegetes*, a guide, although other manuscripts have *didaskalos*, a teacher), even Christ" (v.8).

It is one thing to be a teacher, but quite another to glory in being a teacher. James warns against this: "My brethren, be not many masters (*didaskalos*, teachers), knowing that we shall receive the greater condemnation" (James 3: 1). Whilst James is certainly not attempting to dissuade anyone who aspires to teach, he does warn them that this ministry carries heavy responsibility. Let all who set their sights on public preaching and teaching take careful note! It isn't quite so glamorous as it looks! The greater the privilege, the greater the responsibility. The Lord now drives the point home in three ways, and "a threefold cord is not quickly broken" (Eccl. 4: 12).

- "But be ye not called Rabbi: for one is your Master (see above), even Christ; and all ye are brethren (*adelphos*)" (v.8). Wm.MacDonald puts it very clearly indeed: "The obvious meaning of the Saviour's words is that in the kingdom of heaven, all believers form an equal brotherhood, and that there is no place for distinctive titles, setting one above another. Yet think for a moment of the pompous titles that are found in Christendom today: Reverend, Very Reverend, Right Reverend, Most Reverend, Father, Padre, Doctor, and a host of others". Perhaps we should add 'ministering brother' and 'accredited teacher'. That brings it nearer home! We must never forget that we are all disciples at the feet of Christ.

- "And call no man your father upon the earth: for one is your Father, which is in heaven" (v.9). It is hardly necessary to say that the Lord Jesus is not referring here to the family circle, but to relationships amongst His people. The Father is the source of every blessing bestowed upon us. We owe everything to Him. See James 1: 17.

- "Neither be ye called masters (*kathegetes*, a guide): for one is your Master (*kathegetes*), even Christ" (v.10). According to R.V.G.Tasker, the word (*kathegetes*) means "a guide, or instructor occupying a position of authority, such as a master at a school or a professor in a university. The word in modern Greek means 'professor'". (This does not imply that Christians should not become professors in their chosen subject!). We rightly recognise such qualifications in the world, but amongst the Lord's people the holders of such academic qualifications are simply "brethren" (v.8) without further distinction. Believers, including those who have responsibility for leading the Lord's people, look to the Lord alone for guidance and direction.

There is no room for self-assertion or pride of place. In the Lord's own words here: "He that is greatest among you shall be your servant. And whosoever shall exalt himself shall be abased: and he that shall humble himself, shall be exalted" (vv.11-12).

2) HIS DENUCIATION OF THE RELIGIOUS LEADERS, vv.13-36

The Lord's faithful exposure of their behaviour is punctuated with the words, "Woe unto you, scribes and Pharisees, hypocrites!" (vv. 13, 14, 15, 23, 25, 27, 29). The Lord Jesus had every right to censure the scribes and Pharisees, for He was "without partiality, and without hypocrisy", and therefore perfectly embodied the "wisdom that is from above" (James 3: 17).

Having already urged the disciples to beware of "the leaven of the Pharisees, which is hypocrisy" (Luke 12.1), He now exposes their hypocrisy by highlighting the following: *(a)* they precluded blessing (v.13); *(b)* they pretended to pray (v.14); *(c)* they procured proselytes (v.15); *(d)* they perverted vows (vv.16-22); *(e)* they perverted tithing (vv.23-24); *(f)* they professed purity (vv.25-26); *(g)* they publicly impressed others (vv.27-28); *(h)* they perpetuated past sin (vv.29-36).

a) They precluded blessing, v.13

"Woe unto you, scribes and Pharisees, hypocrites! For ye shut up the kingdom of heaven against men: for ye neither go in yourselves (they refused to enter themselves), neither suffer ye them that are entering to go in". Wm.MacDonald calls this "obduracy and obstructionism" and points out that "religious leaders are often the most active opponents of the gospel of grace". The Lord Jesus opened the kingdom to men, urging them to repent and to enter into it. See Matthew 7: 13-14. But "by insisting on works of the law as the sole ground of acceptance with the God", the scribes and Pharisees were "standing in the way of others who wished to accept it on the only two conditions that are essential, namely, repentance and faith" (R.V.G.Tasker).

Perhaps we should ask ourselves if our conduct or attitude is stumbling others in any way.

b) They pretended to pray, v.14

"Woe unto you, scribes and Pharisees, hypocrites! For ye devour widows' houses, and for a pretence make long prayer: therefore ye shall receive the greater damnation". It should be said that this verse is not found in "the best manuscripts" (AV margin), and that it is omitted by JND/RV (with a marginal note in both cases). However there is no dispute about its inclusion by Mark (12: 40) and Luke (20: 47). Devouring "widows' houses" was deliberate transgression of God's Word: "Ye shall not afflict any widow, or fatherless child" (Exodus 22: 22). The prophets constantly thundered against this

Matthew

inequity in Israel (see, for example, Malachi 3: 5), and **we** must not forget the teaching of 1 Cor. 12: 25-26. James tells us that "pure religion and undefiled before God and the Father, is this, To visit the fatherless and **widows** in their affliction, and to keep himself unspotted from the world" (James 1: 27). What they did was utterly deplorable, but worse follows: "and for a pretence make long prayer". Religious deceit is most offensive to God. See, again, Matthew 15: 8. With all their long prayers, they were covetous and greedy at heart. We must never forget that "the Lord is a God of knowledge, and by him actions are weighed" (1 Sam. 2: 3). The words "therefore ye shall receive greater damnation" or 'a severer judgment' (Luke 20: 47, JND), indicate that there are degrees of punishment, just as there are degrees of reward.

The word "pretence" (*prophasis*) is rendered "cloke" in 1 Thess. 2: 5 ("nor with a pretext for covetousness", JND); John 15: 22 ("now they have no cloke for their sin") and "colour" in Acts 27: 30 ("the shipmen...had let down the boat into the sea, under colour as though they would have anchors out of the foreship"). Perhaps men in the assembly should ask themselves if there is a discrepancy between their public prayers and their private practices. What about our attitude to widows?

The Lord Jesus prayed from a pure heart. He could say in prayer, "Father, I thank thee that thou hast heard me, and I knew that thou hearest me always" (John 11: 41-42). But these people fell into the category of Psalm 66: 18.

c) They procured proselytes, v.15
"Woe unto you, scribes and Pharisees, hypocrites! For ye compass sea and land to make one proselyte, and when he is made, ye make him twofold more the child of hell than yourselves". "The motive was utterly selfish, the building up of their own sect. Judaism was torn with sects, schisms and schools, each Rabbi having his personal following of disciples. These Rabbis were both jealous and zealous, ever seeking converts to their own particular party. They would stop at nothing to make a convert..." (J.M.Flanigan). They had no interest in making Gentiles children of God, only in gaining followers for themselves.

R.V.G.Tasker observes that "It is well known that those who exchange one religion for another are more likely to show an intemperate zeal for their new religion than those who have experienced no such drastic change. So the converts of the Pharisees tended to become even more Pharisaic than the Pharisees themselves". The result was that "the *con*verted became the *per*verted" (R.V.G.Tasker), and a man in this category became "twofold more the child of hell (*geenna*)" than the scribes and Pharisees themselves.

Perhaps we should ask ourselves if we are more concerned with building up our party position than in the spiritual welfare of others.

The Lord Jesus said, "If the Son therefore shall make you free, ye shall be free indeed" (John 8: 36).

d) They perverted vows, vv.16-22

They were completely illogical as well. They placed emphasis on lesser things, and totally ignored the binding authority of greater things. The Lord calls them "blind guides" (v.16) and addresses them as "fools and blind" (vv.17, 19). Instead of being, as they thought, "a guide to the blind" (Rom. 2: 19), they were, as noted, "blind guides". He gives three instances of their hypocrisy which arose out of the subtle distinctions that they made between the temple and its gold (v.16), the altar and the gift upon the altar (v.18), and heaven and the throne of God in heaven (v.22).

i) The temple and its gold, vv.16-17. "Woe unto you, ye blind guides, which say, Whosoever shall swear by the temple, it is nothing; but whosoever shall swear by the gold of the temple, he is a debtor! Ye fools and blind: for whether is greater, the gold, or the temple that sanctifieth the gold?" The word "fools" (*moras*) means, primarily, 'dull' or 'sluggish', hence 'stupid or 'foolish'. It refers to heart and character (W.E.Vine). Very clearly, the scribes and Pharisees had engineered a 'get-out' clause in their oaths. To swear by the temple was *not* binding, but to swear by the gold of the temple *was* binding. The Lord reverses their standard of judgment by pointing out that the greater hallows the lesser.

ii) The altar and the gift upon the altar, vv.18-19. "Whosoever shall swear by the altar, it is nothing; but whosoever shall swear by the gift that is upon it, he is guilty. Ye fools and blind: for whether is greater, the gift, or the altar that sanctifieth the gift?" In their view, to swear by the altar was *not* binding, but to swear by the gift on the altar *was* binding. Once again, the Lord points out that the greater hallows the lesser.

The Lord then restates the point: "Whosoever therefore shall swear by the altar, sweareth by it, and by all things thereon. And whoso shall swear by the temple, sweareth by it, and by him that dwelleth therein" (vv.20-21). The last words, "by him that dwelleth therein" emphasises that while temple and gold, and altar and sacrifices, are inseparable, in both instances it is, at the same time, a case of swearing by God. This brings us to:

iii) Heaven and the throne of God in heaven, v.20. "And he that shall swear by heaven, sweareth by the throne of God, and him that sitteth thereon". As noted in connection with Matthew 5: 34-36, the scribes and Pharisees taught that "if swearing was not to a false proposition, and did not profane the actual name of God, there was no need to regard oaths as binding' (R.V.G.Tasker). No wonder the Lord said, "But let your communication be, Yea, yea; Nay, nay: for whatsoever is more than these cometh of evil" (Matt. 5: 37).

The duplicity of the religious leaders fed through, as we will see, to their tithing: "mint, and anise, and cumin" took precedence over "judgement, mercy, and faith" (v.23), three characteristics seen perfectly in the life of the Lord Jesus.

"Woe unto you, scribes and Pharisees, hypocrites!"

Read Chapter 23: 23-39
In our previous study, we suggested that this chapter may be divided into three sections: *(1)* the Lord's description of the religious leaders (vv.1-12); *(2)* the Lord's denunciation of the religious leaders (vv.13-36); *(3)* the Lord's distress over Jerusalem (vv.37-39).

1) HIS DESCRIPTION OF THE RELIGIOUS LEADERS, vv.1-12
In describing the scribes and Pharisees, the Lord highlighted: *(a)* the discrepancy between their doctrine and practice, (vv.2-3); *(b)* their denial of the sole authority of God's Word (v.4); *(c)* their desire for recognition by men (vv.5-12).

2) HIS DENUNCIATION OF THE RELIGIOUS LEADERS, vv.13-36
Earlier in His ministry, the Lord had warned His disciples against emulating the hypocrisy of the Pharisees: "beware ye of the leaven of the Pharisees, which is hypocrisy" (Luke 12: 1). He now faithfully identifies various forms of hypocrisy, introducing each case with either "Woe unto you, scribes and Pharisees, hypocrites!" (vv. 13, 14, 15, 23, 25, 27, 29), or "woe unto you, ye blind guides" (v.16). Since He was "without partiality, and without hypocrisy" (James 3. 17), He had every right to censure the scribes and Pharisees in this way.

Chapter 23

The Lord's description of their hypocrisy may be summarised as follows: *(a)* they precluded blessing (v.13); *(b)* they pretended to pray (v.14); *(c)* they procured proselytes (v.14); *(d)* they perverted vows (vv.16-22); *(e)* they perverted tithing (vv.23-24); *(f)* they professed purity (vv.25-26); *(g)* they publicly impressed others (vv.27-28); *(h)* they perpetuated past sin (vv.29-36).

a) They precluded blessing, v.13
"But woe unto you, scribes and Pharisees, hypocrites! for ye shut up the kingdom of heaven against men: for ye neither go in yourselves, neither suffer ye them that are entering to go in". As we have already noticed, "by insisting on works of the law as the sole ground of acceptance with God", the scribes and Pharisees were "standing in the way of others who wished to accept it on the only two conditions that are essential, namely, repentance and faith" (R.V.G.Tasker). Perhaps we should ask ourselves if our conduct or attitude is stumbling others in any way.

b) They pretended to pray, v.14
"Woe unto you, scribes and Pharisees, hypocrites! for ye devour widows' houses, and for a pretence make long prayer: therefore ye shall receive greater damnation". Religious deceit is most offensive to God. With all their long prayers, they were covetous and greedy at heart. The word "pretence" (*prophasis*) is rendered "cloke" in 1 Thess. 2: 5 ("nor with a pretext for covetousness", JND); John 15: 22 ("now they have no cloke for their sin") and "colour" in Acts 27: 30 ("the shipmen...had let down the boat into the sea, under colour as though they would have cast anchors out of the foreship"). Perhaps men in the assembly should ask themselves if there is a discrepancy between their public prayers and their private practices. What about our attitude to widows?

c) They procured proselytes, v.15
"Woe unto you, scribes and Pharisees, hypocrites! For ye compass sea and land to make one proselyte, and when he is made, ye make him twofold more the child of hell than yourselves". They had no interest in making Gentiles children of God, only in gaining followers for themselves. Perhaps we should ask ourselves if we are more concerned with building up our party position than in the spiritual welfare of others.

d) They perverted vows, vv.16-22
"Woe unto you, ye blind guides, which say, Whosoever shall swear by the

temple, it is nothing; but whosoever shall swear by the gold of the temple, he is a debtor! Ye fools and blind: for whether is greater, the gold, or the temple that sanctifieth the gold?..." Very clearly, they had engineered a 'get-out' clause in their oaths. To swear by the temple was *not* binding, but to swear by the gold of the temple *was* binding. This was completely illogical, let alone utterly deceitful. They placed emphasis on lesser things, and totally ignored the binding authority of greater things. Perhaps we should ask ourselves if we are completely transparent in what we say. Far better to let our "communication be Yea, yea; Nay, nay: for whatsoever is more than these cometh of evil" (Matt 5: 37).

As we shall now see, the duplicity of the religious leaders in this way fed through to their tithing:

e) They perverted tithing, vv.23-24
"Woe unto you, scribes and Pharisees, hypocrites! for ye pay tithe of mint, and anise (or 'dill'), and cummin, and have omitted the weightier matters of the law (in contrast to such light-weight things as tithed herbs), judgment, mercy, and faith: these ought ye to have done, and not to leave the other undone" (v.23). Earlier in His ministry, in a Pharisee's house, the Lord Jesus had made the same point: "But woe unto you, Pharisees! for ye tithe mint and rue and all manner of herbs, and pass over judgment and the love of God: these ought ye to have done, and not to leave the other undone" (Luke 11: 42). The Lord Jesus displayed "the weightier matters of the law" perfectly in His life. There was certainly no "leaven of the Pharisees" in Him!

According to Leviticus 27: 30, 32 and Deuteronomy 14: 22-23, tithes were to be paid on the produce of the land (corn, oil, new wine, and fruits), and on cattle. But in their misplaced zeal, the Pharisees had extended these commandments to include garden herbs. It has been said that tithing was "meant to be a joyful offering of love, but this calculation of one tenth of all the stalks of garden herbs made a burdensome mockery of it". (Leon Morris). The Pharisees were going beyond what was required, and we must make sure that we do not do the same. The Lord Jesus did not censure the practice of tithing "mint, and anise, and cummin", but he *did* censure the way in which they emphasised the trivial at the expense of the important. We must not fall into the same snare. It is sadly possible in assembly life to insist on a rigid form of words and procedure, and at the same time to show little, if any, love, tenderness and understanding towards needy brothers and sisters, and especially to those who need spiritual help and guidance.

The Old Testament makes this very point in relation (note this) to the levitical offerings: "Wherewith shall I come before the LORD, and bow myself before the high God? shall I come before him with burnt-offerings, with calves of a year old? Will the LORD be pleased with thousands of rams, or with ten thousands of rivers of oil...He hath shewed thee, O man, what is good; and what doth the LORD require of thee, but to do justly, and to love mercy, and to walk humbly with thy God? (Micah 6: 6-8). See also Zechariah 7: 9, "Thus speaketh the LORD of hosts, saying, Execute true judgment, and shew mercy and compassions every man to his brother".

The Pharisaical practice of emphasising the trivial at the expense of the important is vividly illustrated in the Lord's words: "Ye blind guides which strain at a gnat, and swallow a camel" (v.24), or "who strain out the gnat, but drink down the camel" (JND). Sifting for gnats refers to filtering wine in order to remove them. It has been said that both gnats and camels were unclean creatures. The camel is certainly listed as unclean in Leviticus 11: 4, and we are told that the Jews regarded insects as "creeping things" (Lev. 11: 41), and therefore unclean. The gnat and camel are examples of the smallest and largest respectively of the unclean creatures. The smallest thing was given exaggerated attention among them, while they disregarded the greatest.

f) They professed purity, vv.25-26
We must notice the fourfold contrast between things 'outside' and things 'within' in vv.25-28: "Woe unto you, scribes and Pharisees, hypocrites! for *(i)* ye make clean the **outside** of the cup and of the platter, but **within** they are full of extortion and excess. *(ii)* Thou blind Pharisee, cleanse first that which is **within** the cup and platter, that the **outside** of them may be clean also. Woe unto you, scribes and Pharisees, hypocrites! *(iii)* For ye are like unto whited sepulchres, which indeed appear beautiful **outward**, but are **within** full of dead men's bones, and of all uncleanness. *(iv)* Even so ye also **outwardly** appear righteous unto men, but **within** ye are full of hypocrisy and iniquity".

So far as the "cup and...platter" are concerned, the noun "extortion" (v.25), translated "ravening" in Luke 11: 39, means 'pillage, plundering, robbery' (W.E.Vine). An example of the Pharisees "extortion" (*harpage*) occurs in v.14, "ye devour widows' houses". The word "excess" (v.25) means 'want of self-control, incontinence' (*akrasia*).

Matthew

In another connection, Ananias and Sapphira cleaned "the outside of the cup" in laying part of the proceeds of sale at the feet of the apostles. It looked good. But it masked inward evil, leading Peter to say to Ananias, "why hast thou conceived this thing in thine heart? thou hast not lied unto men, but unto God" (Acts 5: 1-11).

g) They publicly impressed others, vv.27-28

"Woe unto you, scribes and Pharisees, hypocrites! for ye are like unto whited sepulchres, which indeed appear beautiful outward, but are within full of dead men's bones, and of all uncleanness. Even so ye also outwardly appear righteous unto men, but within ye are full of hypocrisy and iniquity". His omniscience in this way is evidence of His deity. "He knew what was in man" (John 2: 25).

It is said that "whited sepulchres" refers to the fact that "In the month Adar, the month before the Passover, graves were whitewashed so that pilgrims would not defile themselves accidentally (cf. Luke 11: 44)" (supplied by Justin Waldron). Others suggest that this refers to "ornamental plastering of the walls of the more ornate sepulchres which would make them appear beautiful" (quoted by R.V.G.Tasker).

The Lord Jesus was transparently holy inwardly and outwardly. He said, "thy law is within my heart" (Psalm 40: 8). God, who required "truth in the inward parts" (Psalm 51.6), found it uniquely in His Son. He had the moral right to reprove the inward sin of the scribes and Pharisees. There was no "leaven of the Pharisees" in Him!

Like ourselves sometimes, sadly, they had forgotten that David had said, "Behold, thou desirest truth in the inward parts" (Psalm 51: 6), and "O Lord, thou hast searched me and known me. Thou knowest my downsitting and mine uprising; thou understandest my thought afar off" (Psalm 139: 1-2). See also 1 Sam. 16: 7. He is thoroughly aware of our inward and outward lives. The Pharisees could hardly say with David, "Search me, O God, and know my heart; try me, and know my thoughts; and see if there be any wicked way in me, and lead me in the way everlasting" (Psalm 139: 23-24). But do **we**?

What about **our** inner lives? We would be justly indignant if someone told us that we were "full of hypocrisy and iniquity" (v.28), or "full of ravening and wickedness" (Luke 11: 39), but could it be said of **us** that "this people draweth nigh unto me with their mouth, and honoureth me with their lips:

but their *heart* is far from me" (Matt. 15: 8)? While we usually apply the Lord's censure here to a lack of inward reality, He continues by specifically mentioning other forms of evil: "out of the heart proceed evil thoughts, murders, adulteries, fornications, thefts, false witness, blasphemies: these are the things which defile a man: but to eat with unwashen hands defileth not a man" (Matt. 15: 18-20).

h) They perpetuated past sin, vv.29-36
This is the most solemn of the charges made here by the Lord Jesus. It carries the most fearful condemnation and promises terrifying judgment, leading to the Lord's lament over the city of Jerusalem (vv.37-39). We should notice the following:

i) They repudiated the past. The scribes and Pharisees adopted a superior attitude. They claimed to have greater enlightenment than their forebears: "Woe unto you, scribes and Pharisees, hypocrites! Because ye build the tombs of the prophets, and garnish (*kosmeo*, to adorn) the sepulchres of the righteous, and say, If we had been in the days of our fathers, we would not have been partakers with them in the blood of the prophets" (vv.29-30). They said, in effect, 'we have come a long way since the old days: we would never have done what our fathers did'.

As a token of their professed superiority they had built "tombs of the prophets" and garnished "the sepulchres of the righteous". It all looked very commendable. One generation was endeavouring to make amends for the crimes of previous generations. But it was a veneer. We must notice:

- *Their unchanged nature*. "Wherefore ye be witnesses unto yourselves, that ye are children ('sons', JND) of them which killed the prophets" (v.31). They were certainly the sons of the fathers in a literal sense, but the Lord Jesus uses the word in another way: they were the sons of their fathers in character. They claimed to be different from their fathers, but in actual fact they were exactly the same. "The murderous lust that had led to the persecution of so many of God's prophets in the past was still in their blood" (R.V.G.Tasker). The family characteristics were unmistakable. The Lord's words which follow, "Fill ye up then the measure of your fathers" (v.32), are evidently ironical, and mean either 'Make up what was lacking in your father's guilt', or, 'Go on till you reach the degree of guilt your fathers reached' (R.V.G.Tasker). The latter seems the more likely, reminding us that like the Amorites, their iniquity was "not yet full" (Gen. 15: 16).

- ***Their unqualified condemnation***. "Ye serpents, ye generation of vipers, how can ye escape the damnation of hell?" (v.33). John the Baptist had used similar language in describing the Pharisees and Sadducees: "O generation of vipers, who hath warned you to flee from the wrath to come? Bring forth therefore fruits meet for repentance" (Matt. 3: 7-8), and the Lord Jesus had described the Pharisees as a "generation of vipers, how can ye, being evil, speak good things?" (Matt. 12: 34). The reason for such strong condemnation here lay in the utter hypocrisy of the scribes and Pharisees. Their professed superiority over the fathers was pure cant: they were following their fathers' example exactly. Earlier in the very same day they had "sought to lay hands on him" (21: 46). Wm.MacDonald calls it "outward homage, inward homicide" and adds, "The Lord knew that at the very time they were decorating the graves of the prophets, they were plotting His death". Their unqualified condemnation must be linked with:

- ***Their unavoidable punishment***. "How can ye escape the damnation of hell?" (v.33). The word "hell" here (*geenna*) refers to "the lake of fire" (Rev. 20: 14). Other solemn references to eternal judgment are found in Matt. 18: 8 ("everlasting fire"); Matt. 18: 9 ("hell fire"); Mark 9: 43 ("the fire that never shall be quenched").

ii) *They would repeat the past*. They would do exactly the same as their predecessors. "Wherefore, behold, I send unto you prophets, and wise men, and scribes: and some of them ye shall kill and crucify; and some of them ye shall scourge in your synagogues, and persecute them from city to city. That upon you may come all the righteous blood shed upon the earth, from the blood of righteous Abel unto the blood of Zacharias son of Barachias, whom ye slew between the temple and the altar. Verily I say unto you, All these things shall come upon this generation" (vv.34-36). Attention is drawn to the following:

- ***Continuing testimony***. "Wherefore, behold, I send unto you prophets, and wise men, and scribes" (v.34). As J.M.Flanigan points out, "in spite of all these indictments, God would yet send them prophets, wise men and scribes". The apostles were certainly in this category. Like the Old Testament prophets, they reproved the nation's sin, and called men and women to repentance: "Him, being delivered by the determinate counsel and foreknowledge of God, ye have taken, and by wicked hands have crucified and slain...Repent, and be baptized every one of you in the name of Jesus Christ for the remission of sins" (Acts 2: 23, 38). See also Matthew 10: 41.

Like wise men in the Old Testament they declared the mind and will of God (see Matt. 13: 52). Like scribes in the Old Testament, of which Ezra is an example, they understood and applied God's Word.

We should notice that the Lord Jesus said, "behold, *I send* unto you prophets, and wise men, and scribes". This implies His deity. The God who sent "prophets, and wise men, and scribes" in the past would do so again. The Lord does not actually refer here to His own rejection, but Stephen did so in the same context (see Acts 7: 51-52).

- **Continuing opposition.** The treatment of faithful servants of God in the past would be repeated. They had endured "trial of cruel mockings and scourgings, yea, moreover of bonds and imprisonment" and had been "stoned...sawn asunder...tempted...slain with the sword" (Heb. 11: 36-37), and it would happen again: "And some of them ye shall kill and crucify; and some of them ye shall scourge in your synagogues, and persecute them from city to city" (v.34). The Lord Jesus warned His disciples of coming persecution: "They shall put you out of the synagogues: yea, the time cometh, that whosoever killeth you will think that he doeth God service" (John 16: 2).

We should remember that suffering is the norm for the believer: "Unto you it is given in the behalf of Christ, not only to believe on him, but also to suffer for his sake" (Phil. 1: 29); "all that will live godly in Christ Jesus shall suffer persecution" (2 Tim. 3: 12).

- **Cumulative guilt.** "That upon you may come all the righteous blood shed upon the earth, from the blood of righteous Abel unto the blood of Zacharias son of Barachias, whom ye slew between the temple and the altar. Verily I say unto you, All these things shall come upon this generation" (vv.35-36). They would complete the sum of the nation's sin by killing, crucifying, scourging and persecuting the servants of Christ. Stephen charged them with this, and referred to the crowning crime of all in betraying and murdering "the Just One": "ye do always resist the Holy Ghost: as your fathers did, so do ye. Which of the prophets have not our fathers persecuted? and they have slain them which shewed before the coming of the Just One; of whom ye have been now the betrayers and the murderers" (Acts 7: 51-52). Stephen himself was numbered amongst those who would be killed (v.34). The nation, particularly its leaders, would face divine judgment, not only because of their own guilt in rejecting the Lord's servants, but because that in doing so they had ignored their own history. This enhanced their guilt. Daniel made this very point to Belshazzar: "thou...hast not humbled thine heart, though thou knewest all this (the lessons learnt by Nebuchadnezzar)" (Dan. 5: 22). Divine judgment fell some forty years later in A.D.70, but "this generation" (v.36) may well have an extended meaning and embrace future judgment as well.

It is usually said, bearing in mind that 2 Chronicles is the last book in the Hebrew Bible, that the "blood of righteous Abel" (compare Heb.11: 4) and "the blood of Zacharias son of Barachias" refer to the first and last murder in the Old Testament. See Genesis 4: 8-10; 2 Chron. 24: 21. However, because Zacharias (or Zechariah) was the son of Jehoiada (notice what he said in 2 Chron. 24: 22: compare Stephen in Acts 7: 60), some commentators say that the omission of Barachias' name in Luke 11: 51 suggests that a copyist dealing with Matthew made a mistake, and mixed up the prophet Zacharias, whose father was Barachias, or Berechiah (Zech. 1: 1), with the priest in 2 Chron. 24: 21. Since, however, there is no textual evidence that there was a mistake in this way, the matter remains unexplained. Perhaps the prophet Zechariah was killed in this manner. However, it has been suggested that since Jehoiada was outstanding in his godliness, he was known as the 'the blest of the Lord', the meaning of the name Barachias.

3) *THE LORD'S DISTRESS OVER JERUSALEM, vv.37-39*
We must notice two principal things here: *(a)* the Lord's sorrow (v.37); *(b)* the Lord's sentence (vv.38-39).

a) *The Lord's sorrow, v.37*
He did not speak dispassionately in saying "Verily I say unto you, All these things shall come upon this generation" (v.36). To the contrary, He was deeply moved: "O Jerusalem, Jerusalem, thou that killest the prophets, and stonest them which are sent unto thee, how often would I have gathered thy children together, even as a hen gathereth her chickens under her wings, and ye would not!" (v.37). As Campbell Morgan observes, "That is the very heart of sin - 'Ye would not'; the human will set against the will of God...had they but come to Him, He could have gathered the whole of them from the impending judgment of evil...His purpose was not to pronounce a curse but to bring blessing...This was His purpose, 'I would', and this was their sin, 'ye would not'". But they refused to come: "ye will not come to me, that ye might have life" (John 5: 40). It caused the Saviour deep distress. And us?

b) The Lord's sentence, vv.38-39

"Behold, your house is left unto you desolate". It must be so: the Messiah of Israel had been rejected: the King was about to leave: "And Jesus went out, and departed from the temple" (24: 1). It would be so: "There shall not be left here one stone upon another, that shall not be thrown down" (24: 2). But that was not the end. It could not be the end for, if otherwise, "how then shall the scriptures be fulfilled?" No, it could not be the end. We listen to His closing words in the temple: "Ye shall not see me henceforth, *till* ye shall say, **Blessed is he that cometh in the name of the Lord**" (v.39).

THE GOSPEL OF MATTHEW

"All these are the beginning of sorrows"

Read Chapter 24: 1-14

While the earlier part of the Lord's third day in Jerusalem was spent in the temple (21: 23; 24: 1), at least some of the later part was spent on the mount of Olives (24: 3). Mark specifically tells us that the Lord "sat upon the mount of Olives over against the temple" (Mark 13: 3), whereas Luke is evidently speaking generally in saying, "in the day time he was teaching in the temple; and at night he went out, and abode in the mount that is called the mount of Olives" (Luke 21: 37). We cannot apportion the time between the two locations, but it was clearly a very busy day throughout. Perhaps we could say that the Lord's time was spent in the following way: *(i) answering questions* (21: 23 - 22: 46); *(ii) accusing the leaders* (23: 1-39); *(iii) anticipating the future* (24: 1 - 25: 46). Our next few studies in Matthew's Gospel will be devoted to the third of these. Chapters 24 & 25 comprise what is known as 'The Olivet Discourse' (see also Mark 13: 1-37; Luke 21: 5-38), in which the Saviour describes future events, culminating with His return "in the clouds of heaven with power and great glory" (24: 30). But that is not all. It is often said that the Scriptures never describe future events in a vacuum. The Lord's return is always presented as an incentive to godly living and faithful service. 'The Olivet Discourse' is no exception. The disciples were told, "Watch therefore: for ye know not what hour your Lord doth come" (24: 42); "be ye also ready" (24: 44); "Watch therefore, for ye know neither the day nor the hour wherein the Son of man cometh" (25: 13). Faithful servants will receive commendation and reward (25: 21, 23).

Having said this, it is important to go further and ascertain *(a)* the period involved; *(b)* the people involved.

a) The period involved
Although Luke refers additionally to events which would shortly take place

(see Luke 21: 20-24), Matthew, Mark and Luke, all describe events which will take place *after* the Lord Jesus descends "from heaven with a shout", when "the dead in Christ shall rise first" and "we which are alive and remain shall be caught up together with them in the clouds to meet the Lord in the air" (1 Thess. 4: 16-17). Events in 'The Olivet Discourse' commence with the "beginning of sorrows" (v.8) and continue to "the end" (v.14). In the Old Testament, the latter part of this period is called "the time of Jacob's trouble" (Jer. 30: 7). In the New Testament, it is called "the great tribulation" (Rev. 7: 14, RV/JND). We should say at this juncture that the Lord Jesus did not dwell on the sufferings of His earthly people dispassionately. Like Jeremiah centuries before, He wept over Jerusalem (Luke 19. 41), and shortly before leaving the temple, He expressed His deep sorrow at her suffering (Matt. 23: 37). Judgment is "his strange work" (Isaiah 28: 21). He "delighteth in mercy" (Micah 7: 18).

The period covered by 'The Olivet Discourse' becomes clear from the questions put by Peter, James, John, and Andrew (Mark 13: 3): "Tell us, when shall these things be? and what shall be the sign of thy coming *(parousia)*, and of the end of the world?" (v.3). See also Mark 13: 4 and Luke 21: 7.

The first question, "when shall these things be?", must refer to the Lord's teaching that "there shall not be left here one stone upon another, that shall not be thrown down" (v.2). The Lord's answer to this particular question is only given by Luke (21: 20-24), and we know that His prophecy was duly fulfilled in the siege and destruction of Jerusalem by the Romans in A.D.70. Without giving any further details, Luke then refers to the "Son of man coming in a cloud with power and great glory" (Luke 21: 27), whereas Matthew and Mark concentrate entirely on end-time events, of which the siege and destruction of Jerusalem in A.D.70 was a shadow. At the end-time, the Jewish people will experience unparalleled suffering: "For then shall be great tribulation such as was not since the beginning of the world to this time, no, nor ever shall be" (v.21). Jerusalem will again be surrounded by enemies with no apparent prospect of deliverance, at which point the Lord will "go forth, and fight against those nations, as when he fought in the day of battle". See Zechariah 14: 1-4. Matthew, with Mark, gives the Lord's full answer to the questions, "what shall be the sign of thy coming, and of the end of the world?"

b) The people involved
We cannot fail to notice that the context of this discourse is entirely Jewish.

Matthew

In the setting of this passage, the disciples represent Messiah's faithful witnesses at the end-time. The discourse begins with reference to the temple and the Mount of Olives. In Mark's record, the Lord refers to 'sanhedrims' and 'synagogues' (Mark 13: 9, JND). The Lord then refers to the "abomination of desolation, spoken of by Daniel the prophet", standing "in the holy place" (v.15), and to "them that be in Judaea" (v.16). He refers to the "sabbath day" (v.20). There is no reference to the church, with its unique character and unique hope, and the four disciples (Mark 3: 4), referred to throughout as "ye" and "you", are addressed as representatives of the Jewish nation. In view of this, we *must* interpret the passage with reference to the coming of Christ as Israel's Messiah, to deliver His earthly people and establish His millennial kingdom.

With this in mind, Matthew ch.24 may be divided as follows: *(1)* the setting of the discourse (vv.1-3); *(2)* the subject of the discourse (vv.4-31); *(3)* the significance of the discourse (vv.32-51). In the last section, the Lord Jesus emphasises the necessity for watchfulness and readiness: "Watch therefore...Therefore be ye also ready" (vv.42, 44).

1) THE SETTING OF THE DISCOURSE, vv.1-3

Its setting is most significant. "And Jesus went out, and departed from **the temple**: and his disciples came to him to shew him the buildings of **the temple**. And Jesus said unto them, See ye not all these things? Verily I say unto you, There shall not be left here one stone upon another, that shall not be thrown down. And as he sat upon the **mount of Olives**, the disciples came unto him privately..." As we have noted, Mark tells us that "as he sat on the **mount of Olives**, over against **the temple**, Peter and James and John and Andrew asked him privately" (Mark 13: 3). Both the temple and the mount of Olives play an important part at the end-time. The discourse anticipates the time when the Lord will "suddenly come to his temple" (Mal. 3: 1), and "his feet shall stand...upon the mount of Olives" (Zech. 14: 4). The fact that the Lord went from the temple to the mount of Olives may well have significance: the location of His rejection gives place to the location of His return (T.Miller).

As His heavenly people (Heb. 3: 1), we gladly anticipate the Lord's return to take us to our heavenly home (1 Thess. 4: 17-18), but do we gladly anticipate His return to earth in order to establish His kingdom (Matt. 24:30)? We should rejoice that our Saviour will return triumphantly, not only to the world, but to the very city which rejected Him.

A) *The temple*
In his excellent commentary on Luke *(What the Bible Teaches)*, Norman Crawford (p.335) refers to the description of the temple given by the Jewish historian Josephus. "It stood on a massive base of masonry in which some of the stones were enormous, and had marble columns standing more than forty feet high. It was adorned with many costly gifts from princes and wealthy private individuals. Josephus tells us of one such gift from Herod the Great, a golden vine with bunches of grapes as high as a man's head. Herod had boasted that the temple was built for permanence and would outlast the pyramids, but he could not have been more wrong".

Matthew records the Lord's final words in the temple "Behold, **your house** (notice: not 'God's house') **is left unto you desolate.** For I say unto you, Ye shall not see me henceforth, till ye shall say, Blessed is he that cometh in the name of the Lord. And Jesus went out, and departed from the temple" (23: 38-39). That same temple would be utterly destroyed: "there shall not be left here one stone upon another, that shall not be thrown down" (v.2). But at the end-time, another temple will witness the most fearful idolatry in human history: "When ye therefore shall see the abomination of ('that causeth') desolation, spoken of by Daniel the prophet, stand in the holy place..." (v.15). Compare Dan. 9: 27; 2 Thess. 2: 3-4; Rev. 11: 1. Shortly after this, "the Lord, whom ye seek (see their ironical question: Mal. 2: 17), shall suddenly come to **his temple"** (Mal. 3: 1-4).

B) *The mount of Olives*
This, too, is most significant. The Lord Jesus will return to the Mount of Olives. He actually ascended from Bethany on the eastern slopes of the mount (Luke 24: 50), and the watching disciples were told by the angels, "This same Jesus, which is taken up from you into heaven, shall so come in like manner as ye have seen him go into heaven. Then returned they unto Jerusalem from **the mount called Olivet**" (Acts 1: 11-12). While only His disciples saw Him ascend, His return will be public: "Then shall the LORD go forth, and fight against those nations, as when he fought in the day of battle. And his feet shall stand in that day upon **the mount of Olives**, which is before Jerusalem on the east; and the mount of Olives shall cleave in the midst thereof toward the east and toward the west" (Zech.14: 3-4). This brings us to:

2) *THE SUBJECT OF THE DISCOURSE, vv.4-31*
The "great prophet" (Luke 7: 16) speaks with divine omniscience. The Lord

Matthew

Jesus differed from all other prophets in that they described the future as it was revealed to them, but He predicted the future because *He controlled it!* It is therefore most significant that Revelation 6, which describes "the beginning of sorrows", commences: "And I saw when *the Lamb* opened one of the seals" (v.1). The future of the world lies, not in the mailed fist, but in the pierced hand of the Lord Jesus!

The disciples had asked, "What shall be the sign of thy coming, and of the end of the world ('the completion of the age?', JND)?". The Lord's answer covers a period which can be divided into three sections: *(A) its commencement* (vv.4-14); *(B) its crisis* (vv.15-28); *(C) its conclusion* (vv.29-31). It concludes, of course, with the return of the Lord Jesus. For the prophetic students, the period represents the final "week" (seven years) of Daniel's 'seventy-week' prophecy (Daniel 9: 24-27). We can look at it like this: events at *the beginning* of the "week" (vv.4-14); events commencing in *the middle* of the "week" (vv.15-28); events at *the end* of the "week" (vv.29-31).

A) The commencement of the end of the age, vv.4-14

We could call this section, in the words of the Lord Jesus Himself, "the beginning of sorrows" (v.8). It answers to events in Revelation chs.6-7. The section may be divided into two parts, each of them being a warning: *(a)* what would happen *in the world* (vv.4-8); *(b)* what would happen *to His disciples* (vv.9-14). The former (vv.4-8) relates to events in Revelation 6: 1-8, and the latter (vv.9-14) to events in Revelation 6: 9 - 7: 17.

a) What will happen in the world, vv.4-8

He tells them what would happen in the religious world, in the political world, and in the physical world.

i) In the religious world, vv.4-5.

"Take heed that no man deceive you. For many shall come in my name, saying I am Christ ('I am the Christ', JND); and shall deceive many". This is true, of course, of the present day. We have probably heard, in our own lifetime, of people claiming to be Christ. John wrote about the subject: "Even now there are many antichrists; whereby we know that it is the last time. They went out from us, but they were not of us" (1 John 2: 18-19). Quite evidently, this will happen with increasing frequency at the end-time. Notice how Luke puts it: "Many shall come in my name, saying, I am Christ; and the time draweth near: go ye not therefore after them" (Luke 21: 8). In the middle of the period, that is, after three and a half years have elapsed, the false Christ will emerge, and will sit "in the temple of God, shewing himself that he is God" (2 Thess. 2: 4).

ii) In the political world, vv.6-7. "And ye shall hear of wars, and rumours of wars: see that ye be not troubled: for all these things must come to pass ('must take place', JND), but the end shall not be yet. For nation shall rise against nation, and kingdom against kingdom". There have been "wars and rumours of wars" since time immemorial, but this anticipates, as we shall see, universal bloodshed.

iii) In the physical world, v.7. "And there shall be famines, and pestilences, and earthquakes, in divers places". Earthquakes (including Indian Ocean in 2004, Haiti in 2010, Christchurch in 2011, off Japan in 2011, not to mention so many others in recent years) and famines (Ethiopia, Somalia, Eritrea) occur with increasing regularity and intensity. But they will occur with unprecedented intensity in the end-time.

Further details of "the beginning of sorrows" are given in Revelation ch.6. This chapter describes the first series of judgments on wicked men. Two further series follow: the "trumpet judgments" (Rev. 8-9), and the "vial" or 'bowl' judgments, (Rev. 16-18), but all fail to bring men to repentance (Rev.16: 21). The hitherto unseen Judge then appears at the head of heaven's armies to execute irresistible judgment on all who oppose Him. See Revelation ch.19.

In Revelation ch.6, John describes four successive world conditions, each of which is represented by a horse and rider:

The white horse, v.2. This represents peaceful conquest. The rider carries a bow, that is, he has the ability to deliver destruction through the air, but the bow is not used. It answers to the "peace and safety", which will give place to "sudden destruction" (1 Thess. 5: 3).

The red horse, vv.3-4. This represents universal bloodshed: "Power was given to him that sat thereon to take peace from the earth, and that they should kill one another: and there was given unto him a great sword". Compare this with the Lord's words: "For nation shall rise against nation, and kingdom against kingdom" (v.7).

The black horse, vv.5-6. This represents universal famine (or shortage of food - perhaps deliberately regulated), the result of universal warfare. Staple food is sold at famine prices, but luxury items are untouched. Compare this with the Lord's words: "there shall be famines" (v.7).

The pale horse, vv.7-8. The rider is identified in the passage: "his name that sat on him was Death, and Hell followed with him". Death is the result of famine and the two grim riders have power to "kill with sword...hunger... death (perhaps signifying plague)...beasts of the earth". The "four sore judgments" in Ezekiel 14: 21 ("the sword and the famine, and the noisome beast, and the pestilence") are mentioned here. The Lord Jesus refers to "famines, and pestilences" (see v.7).

b) What will happen to His disciples, vv.9-14

The Saviour was concerned for the welfare of His disciples at this time. They must be warned about the perplexities, pressures and perils that lay ahead. They would be **victims**, and **victors.** As **victims**, their lot would be one of suffering and death at the hands of men. They would be "hated of all nations" (v.9). But as **victors**, their faithfulness, and their fearless and extensive preaching of the "gospel of the kingdom...for a witness unto all nations" (v.14), would burst all bonds. Then, as now, the messengers may be bound, but not the message. See 2 Timothy 2: 9. We should say again that while we cannot ignore lessons for the present time, in the setting of this passage, the disciples represent Messiah's faithful witnesses at the end-time. Notice that Mark also refers to the Lord's promise of the Holy Spirit's help for His servants. See Mark 13: 11. The Lord had already referred to this in Matthew 10: 19-20.

i) Their persecution, vv.9-10. "Then shall they deliver you up to be afflicted, and shall kill you: and ye shall be hated of all nations (Gentile hatred of the Jewish witnesses) for my name's sake" (v.9). Mark expands this: "But take heed to yourselves: for they shall deliver you up to councils ('sanhedrims', JND); and in the synagogues ye shall be beaten: and ye shall be brought before rulers and kings for my sake, for a testimony against them...And ye shall be hated of all men for my name's sake..." (Mark 13: 9, 13). The Lord had already warned His disciples of coming persecution and antagonism. See Matt. 10: 17-18.

This would involve betrayal and hatred: "And then shall many be offended (*skandalizo*, meaning 'stumbled'), and shall betray one another, and hate one another" (v.10). Mark expands this as follows: "Now the brother shall betray the brother to death, and the father the son; and children shall rise up against their parents, and shall cause them to be put to death" (Mark 13: 12). H. S. Paisley (writing on Mark 13) sums up: "A period of persecution, betrayal and hatred is predicted. These will be arranged by religious leaders, political dictators and domestic relations". The Lord had already warned His disciples of this as well. See Matt. 10: 21-22.

Christ's witnesses will face martyrdom, and after describing events under the first four seals, Revelation 6 continues with reference to these martyrs under the fifth seal: "I saw under the altar the souls of them that were slain for the word of God, and for the testimony which they held" (Rev. 6: 9). Notice their cry, "How long, O Lord, holy and true, dost thou not judge and avenge our blood on them that dwell on the earth?" (Rev. 6: 10-11). This is not a *Christian* cry! These are not Christians, but faithful witnesses (the true 'Jehovah's Witnesses') on earth after the church has gone.

iii) Their problems, vv.11-12. "And many false prophets shall rise, and deceive many. And because iniquity shall abound, the love of many shall wax cold"

- *Firstly*, "many false prophets shall rise, and deceive many" (v.11). Compare v5, "For many shall come in my name, saying, I am Christ; and shall deceive many". This is expanded later in the discourse: "Then if any man shall say unto you, Lo, here is Christ; or there; believe it not. For there shall arise **false Christs**, and **false prophets,** and shall shew great signs and wonders; insomuch that, if it were possible, they shall deceive the very elect. Behold I have told you before" (vv.23-25). Paul refers to this in his Thessalonian correspondence: "Even him whose coming is after the working of Satan with all **power and signs and lying wonders,** and with all deceivableness of unrighteousness in them that perish: because they received not the love of the truth, that they might be saved. And for this cause God shall send them strong delusion, that they should believe a (the) lie" (2 Thess. 2: 9-11). Men who will not believe the truth, will ultimately "believe a (the) lie". The Lord Jesus said, "I am come in my Father's name (that is, without attempting to either publicise Himself or make a name for Himself), and ye receive me not; if another shall come in his own name, him ye will receive" (John 5: 43).

- *Secondly*, "and because iniquity *(anomia)* shall abound, the love of many ('the love of the most', JND margin) shall wax cold" (v.5). The marginal note suggests that the Lord refers here to empty profession. Compare Matthew 13: 20-21.

*iii) **Their perseverance, v.13.*** "But he that shall endure unto the end, the same shall be saved". The context demands that "the end" refers to the termination of the period of suffering and persecution prior to the return of the Lord Jesus to earth. See v.3 ("what shall be the sign of Thy coming, and of **the end** of the world (age)"; see v.6 ("all these things must come to pass, but **the end** is not yet"); see v.14 ("And this gospel...shall be preached in all the world for a witness unto all nations; and then shall **the end** come").

We have, therefore, to identify **who** will "endure unto the end". Quite clearly, there will be many martyrs: see, again, Revelation 6: 9-11; compare 12: 11 and 20: 4. But Luke 21: 17-19 is most specific: "And ye shall be hated of all men for my name's sake. But there **shall not a hair of your head perish** (so this cannot refer to the twelve disciples!). In your patience possess ye your souls". Salvation here, therefore refers to preservation from death. Compare Rom.11: 26, "And so all Israel shall be saved". Salvation from sin rests upon the work of Christ, not on enduring "unto the end".

Later in this discourse, the Lord Jesus refers to the "elect" (v.22). We meet them again, all 144,000 of them (the true 'Jehovah's Witnesses'), in Revelation 7: 1-8, where they are sealed with the "seal of the living God" (strongly suggesting divine preservation). They are preserved from the demon "locusts" (Rev. 9: 3-4), and accompany the Lamb on mount Zion in His millennial reign (Rev. 14: 1). These are the people who will "endure unto the end".

*iv) **Their preaching, v.14.*** "And this gospel of the kingdom shall be preached in all the world for a witness unto all nations: and then shall the end come". Very clearly, the persecution is a direct result of the preaching. H.S.Paisley, again, sums up the position most helpfully: "The gospel always means 'good news', and has its foundations upon the death and resurrection of Christ, but its content differs in various ages. The message to be preached here is unique and should not be confused with the gospel of the grace of God of this present age. It is a message concerning the coming Messianic Kingdom on earth and the imminent advent of the King Himself".

The preaching will be undertaken by the 144,000 Jewish witnesses (Rev. 7: 1-8) and the result of their testimony is described in the same chapter: "a great multitude, which no man could number, of all nations, and kindreds, and people, and tongues" (vv.7-9).

Chapter 24

Having dealt with *(a) the commencement* of the end of the age (vv.4-14), in our next two studies we will consider *(b) the crisis* at the end of the age (vv.15-26); *(c) the coming* at the end of the age (vv.27-31).

"For then shall be great tribulation"

Read Chapter 24: 15-26
In our first study of the Lord's 'Olivet Discourse', we suggested that Matthew 24 may be divided as follows: *(1)* the setting of the discourse (vv.1-3); *(2)* the subject of the discourse (vv.4-31); *(3)* the significance of the discourse (vv.32-51). In the last section, the Lord Jesus emphasises the necessity for watchfulness and readiness: "Watch therefore... Therefore be ye also ready (vv.42, 44).

1) THE SETTING OF THE DISCOURSE, vv.1-3
As we have already noted, the setting of the discourse is most significant. "And Jesus went out, and departed from *the temple*: and his disciples came to him to shew him the buildings of *the temple*. And Jesus said unto them, See ye not all these things? Verily I say unto you, There shall not be left here one stone upon another, that shall not be thrown down. And as he sat upon the *mount of Olives*, the disciples came unto him privately..." Or, in Mark's words, "as he sat on the *mount of Olives*, over against *the temple*, Peter and James and John and Andrew asked Him privately" (Mark 13: 3). Both the temple and the mount of Olives play an important part at the end-time. The discourse anticipates the time when the Lord will "suddenly come to his temple" (Mal. 3: 1), and "his feet shall stand...upon the mount of Olives" (Zech. 14: 4).

2) THE SUBJECT OF THE DISCOURSE, vv.4-31
The disciples asked, "when shall these things be? And what shall be the sign of thy coming, and of the end of the world? ('the completion of the age', JND)" (v.3). We noted in our previous study, that this section of the discourse may be divided into three parts *(A)* the commencement of the end of the age (vv.4-14); *(B)* the crisis at the end of the age (vv.15-26); *(C)* the coming at the end of the age (vv.27-31).

A) The commencement of the end of the age, vv.4-14
As already noted, this section can be rightly called, in the words of the Lord Jesus Himself, "the beginning of sorrows" (v.8). It answers to events in Revelation chs.6-7. The section can be divided into two parts, each of them

being a warning: *(a)* What would happen *in the world* (vv.4-8); *(b)* what would happen *to His disciples* (vv.9-14).). The former (vv.4-8) relates to events in Revelation 6: 1-8, and the latter (vv.9-14) to events in Revelation 6: 9 - 7: 17. This brings us to:

B) The crisis at the end of the age, vv.15-26

The Lord Jesus now passes from events in the first half of Daniel's 'seventieth week' (Dan. 9: 27), that is, the period of "the beginning of sorrows", to events in the second half of the 'week', that is, the three and a half years in which Satan will display his power as never before, only to be utterly defeated at the end of the period. A parallel passage is found in Mark 13: 14-23. Luke refers more particularly to the siege and destruction of Jerusalem in A.D.70. See Luke 21.20-23.

Having said, "and then shall the end come" (v.14), the Lord outlines events leading to "great tribulation, such as was not since the beginning of the world, no, nor ever shall be" (v.21). His teaching should be read and studied in conjunction with Revelation chs.11-13. We must notice *(a)* "the abomination of desolation" (v.15); *(b)* the "great tribulation" (vv.16-22); *(c)* the deception (vv.23-26).

a) "The abomination of desolation", v.15

"When ye therefore shall see the abomination of desolation, spoken of by Daniel the prophet, stand in the holy place..." Perhaps this can be best explained by asking, and answering, a series of questions as follows:

i) **What is an "abomination?"** The word (*bdelugma*) means 'an object of disgust'. It occurs in Luke 16: 15, "that which is highly esteemed among men is abomination in the sight of God". It occurs again in Revelation 17: 4-5; 21: 27, where it has strong idolatrous associations, and this concurs with the way in which the word "abomination" (*shiqquts,* meaning 'a detestable thing') is used in the Old Testament to describe idols. See, for example, 1 Kings 11: 5: "Solomon went after... Milcom the abomination of the Ammonites... Solomon built an high place for Chemosh the abomination of Moab". A different word (*toebah)* is also translated "abomination", and used extensively in a variety of ways (see, for example Leviticus 18: 26-29) including idolatry (see, for example Deut.7: 25-26).

The 'times of the Gentiles' (Luke 21: 24) commenced with an idol (Daniel 3: 1), and will end with the most sophisticated idol of all time. "And he (the second "beast" alias "the false prophet") had power to give life ('breath', JND) unto the image of the beast, that the image of the beast should both speak, and cause that as many as would not worship the image of the beast should be killed" (Rev. 13: 14-15).

ii) **Where will the *"abomination"* stand?** It will stand "in the holy place". This assumes the rebuilding of the temple, and this is confirmed in 2 Thessalonians 2: 4 ("he, as God, sitteth in the temple of God, shewing himself that he is God"). Compare Daniel 12: 11: "And from the time that the daily sacrifice shall be taken away, and the abomination that maketh desolate set up, there shall be a thousand two hundred and ninety days"; Daniel 9: 27: "And he shall confirm that covenant with many for one week; and in the midst of the week he shall cause the sacrifice and oblation to cease, and for the overspreading of abominations he shall make it desolate", possibly meaning that the idol will be placed on the wing or pinnacle of the temple: "And the abominations (idols) of the desolator shall be on the pinnacle (i.e. of the temple')" (JND margin). It should be noted that Daniel 11: 31 ("They shall pollute the sanctuary of strength, and shall take away the daily sacrifice, and they shall place the abomination that maketh desolate") refers to "the act of Antiochus Epiphanes (in 168 BC), the prototype of the man of sin, who sacrificed a sow upon the altar, and entered the holy of holies" (C.I.Scofield).

iii) **What will the *"abomination"* portray?** It will be "an image to the beast, which had the wound by a sword, and did live" (Rev. 13: 14-15). In His discourse, the Lord Jesus has now reached a point in prophecy (which is history written in advance) where a Jewish temple exists in Jerusalem, in which, as we have seen, sacrifices will commence, and then end (Daniel 12: 11 and 9: 27) in favour of unrivalled worship of a world-wide emperor called, amongst other things, either "the beast" (Rev. 17: 8, 13) or "that man of sin" (2 Thess. 2: 3). This requires further explanation.

The fact that John saw the "beast rise up out of the sea" (Rev. 13: 1), strongly suggests that he is a Gentile. He is a world ruler, and is described as having "seven heads and ten horns". We are told what the "seven heads and ten horns" represent: "The seven heads are seven mountains…and there are seven kings: five are fallen, and one is, and the other is not yet come; and when he cometh, he must continue a short space. And the beast which was, and is not, even he is the eighth, and is of the seven, and goeth into perdition. And the ten horns which thou sawest are ten kings, which have received no kingdom as yet; but receive power as kings one hour with the beast" (Rev. 17: 9-12).

The heads are therefore representative of something successive. That is, successive world empires. The fact that "the beast" has seven heads indicates that he combines within himself the genius of past empires. Compare Revelation 13: 1-2 where "the beast" has the features of "a leopard...a bear...a lion" referring to Greece, Medo-Persia and Babylon respectively (see Dan. 7: 4-6).

- *"Five are fallen".* The Bible empires with their kings are those of Egypt (Pharaoh), Assyria (Sennacherib), Babylon (Nebuchadnezzar), Medo-Persia (Cyrus), and Greece (Alexander).

- *"One is".* That is, it existed at the time of writing. It is, of course, Rome, with its Caesars.

- *"And the other is not yet come".* When it does come, this kingdom will be of short duration. In fact, only three and half years. The kingdom of "the beast" will be the seventh, and at the same time, it will be the eighth. That is, whilst he commences as a human ruler, he will become a superhuman ruler. The words, "which had the wound by a sword, and did live", mark the transition from human to superhuman. He will be assassinated, and will be raised by Satanic power, so counterfeiting the resurrection.

The horns represent something contemporary. "The beast" will have a ten part kingdom. This answers to the "ten toes" of the image in Daniel 2, and, again, to the "ten horns" in Daniel 7. In the latter passage, the same beast of Revelation 13 is described as a "little horn, before whom there were three of the first horns plucked up by the roots: and behold, in this horn were eyes like the eyes of a man, and a mouth speaking great things" (Dan. 7: 8).

The fact that in both Daniel 2 and Revelation 7, there is an evident connection with the Roman Empire, suggests that "the beast" will be from the Western world.

iv) Who will place the "abomination" in the temple? It will be placed in the temple by the second "beast" described in Revelation 13 (see vv.11-18), otherwise known, as already noted, as "the false prophet". (See 16: 13

& 19: 20). For the sake of clarity, we will call him by this name ("the false prophet"), and retain the title "the beast" when referring to the first "beast" of Revelation ch.13.

The fact that John saw the second "beast (or 'false prophet') coming up out of the earth" (Rev. 13: 11) strongly suggests that he will be of Jewish origin. Like the "beast", he will be satanically inspired: "he spake as a dragon" (Rev. 13: 11). Like the "beast", he will have world-wide power. His very title also suggests Jewish origin. The fact that he places the image of "the beast" in the rebuilt temple at Jerusalem suggests that he will be the final Jewish ruler who will command obedience and worship to "the beast". Bearing this in mind, it is apparent that he does not claim Messiahship for himself, but claims it for "the beast", otherwise known, not only as "that man of sin...the son of perdition... that Wicked" (2 Thess. 2: 3, 8), but also as "antichrist" (1 John 2: 18). The whole objective of the "false prophet" is to glorify "the beast". Perhaps we should say, in passing, that Paul's description of "the beast" in 2 Thessalonians is as frightening as John's description in Revelation 13. Paul describes him as "that man of sin ('man of lawlessness')": he is the incarnation of evil: totally without law. Moreover, he is "the son of perdition (indicative of his destiny: fitted for destruction) ... that Wicked (lawless one)...".

Daniel 11, which describes the ebb and flow of kingdoms to the north and south of Israel in both past and future, describes the activities of "the king" in vv.36-39. He is evidently situated between the northern and southern kingdoms of Syria and Egypt respectively (that is, in Israel), and will "neither regard the God of his fathers, nor the desire of women, nor regard any god: for he shall magnify himself above all". The passage continues: "But in his estate (i.e. in the place of God) shall he honour the god (lower case, as in RV/JND) of forces (or 'fortresses'); and a god whom his fathers knew not shall he honour...thus shall he do in the most strong holds with a strange god, whom he shall acknowledge and increase with glory..." This evidently fits the second "beast", or "false prophet", of Revelation 13, and confirms his Jewish ancestry: "neither regard the God of his fathers, nor the desire of women". See Luke 1: 28.

Since the work of the "false prophet" will be, as we have seen, to direct universal worship to "the beast", it will be the beast himself who "opposeth and exalteth himself above all that is called God or that is worshipped; so that he as God sitteth in the temple of God, shewing himself that he is God" (2 Thess. 2: 4). Quite obviously, he will not sit in the temple permanently, but his false claims will be perpetuated in the image of him placed in the temple by the "false prophet".

But why will he sit "in the temple of God?" Put another way, why will he not occupy St.Peter's at Rome, or Canterbury Cathedral, or sit in Mecca or Medina? The answer is clear. The "beast" will know that God had said that "the mountain of the LORD'S house shall be established in the top of the mountains, and shall be exalted above the hills; and all nations shall flow into it", and that "out of Zion shall go forth the law, and the word of the LORD from Jerusalem" (Isaiah 2: 2-4). He will know too that God had said of "the man whose name is The BRANCH" that "he shall build the temple of the LORD: even he shall build the temple of the LORD; and he shall bear the glory, and shall sit and rule upon his throne..." (Zech. 6: 12-13). The "beast" will therefore endeavour to render the promises and purposes of God null and void, only to be utterly destroyed himself. It should also be noted that he will put down "all that is called God, or that is worshipped" (2 Thess. 2: 4), including the amalgam of all world religion represented by the "scarlet woman" (Rev. 17: 1-18).

To sum up: the world will be governed by a trinity of evil: "the dragon", "the beast", and the "false prophet".

- ***"The dragon"*** will answer to the Father: he gives to "the beast" his "power and his seat and great authority" (Rev. 13: 2). That is, the dragon has the powers of initiative and design: "they worshipped the dragon which gave power unto the beast".

- ***"The beast"*** will answer to the Son: he will accomplish the purpose of the dragon. It will be through him that "the dragon" achieves his objectives. "The beast" (so called, not because he looks like one, but because he will act like one) will also be worshipped (Rev. 13: 4, 8).

- ***"The false prophet"***, that is, the second "beast" (see above) of Revelation 13, will answer to the Holy Spirit: it will be through his power that "the beast" is worshipped (Rev. 13: 12, 15). The "false prophet" is not himself worshipped.

With the exception of "the elect" (vv.22, 24), and only as allowed by God, Satan's power will be total: "***all*** the world wondered after the beast... power was given him over ***all*** kindreds, and tongues and nations. And ***all*** that dwell upon the earth shall worship him... causeth the ***earth*** and ***them which dwell*** *therein* to worship the first beast...deceiveth them that ***dwell on the earth***...causeth ***all***, both small and great, rich and poor, free and bond, to receive mark in their right hand, or in their foreheads" (Rev. 13: 3, 7, 8, 11, 14, 16).

v) Why is the image called "the abomination of desolation?" The title of the image reflects its effect: it is "the abomination causing desolation" (Mark 13: 14, JND margin). The word 'desolation' (*eremosis*) means 'to lay waste'. As a result of the establishing of the image, and the worship paid to it, desolation will occur. The worship given to the image will bring the most fearful judgment upon Israel. This brings us to:

b) The "great tribulation", vv.16-22
"When ye therefore shall see the abomination of desolation...stand in the holy place, then let them which be in Judaea flee into the mountains...For then shall be great tribulation, such as was not since the beginning of the world to this time, no, nor ever shall be. And except those days should be shortened, there should no flesh be saved: but for the elect's sake those days shall be shortened".

i) The reason for the "great tribulation". The connection between "the abomination of desolation" and the "great tribulation" is clear from the passage. As already noted, the latter is the result of the former. As F.A.Tatford observes, "All the descriptions given in the Scriptures of this dread time show that it will be a period of unprecedented horrors, during which the Jews will suffer torment and hardships unspeakable, as God pours out upon them His unmitigated wrath for their wrongdoing". He will use Satan's malign power to bring His people to repentance. It has been said that, when the Lord resumes direct dealings with the nation, He will fully answer their cry, "His blood be on us, and on our children" (Matt. 27: 25), and that in the "great tribulation" He will deal with Israel on its own admission of responsibility.

ii) The source of the "great tribulation". God is the source of the great tribulation. Hence the words, "power was given unto him to continue forty and two months...and it was given unto him to make war with the saints" (Rev. 13: 5, 7). Revelation 12: 13-17 make it clear that Satan will be allowed to initiate this awful period of persecution, and Revelation 13 describes how he will carry it out.

iii) The scope of the "great tribulation". While, at this time, the entire world will be subject to divine wrath (see, for example, Revelation 16: 1-21), the "great tribulation" will encompass Israel in particular. God will employ the forces of "the beast" to destroy the idol-worshipping Jew, and he will endeavour to eliminate the nation in its entirety. In this connection, attention is drawn to the following: "For thus saith the Lord, we have heard a voice of trembling, of fear, and not of peace...Alas! for that day is great, so that none is like it; it is even the time of Jacob's trouble" (Jer. 30: 5-7); "And at that time shall Michael stand up, the great prince which standeth for the children of thy people: and there shall be a time of trouble such as never was since there was a nation even to that same time" (Dan. 12: 1); "Behold the day of the Lord cometh and thy spoil shall be divided in the midst of thee. For I will gather all nations against Jerusalem to battle; and the city shall be taken, and the houses rifled, and the women ravished, and half the city shall go forth into captivity" (Zech. 14: 1-4); "And when the dragon saw that he was cast unto the earth, he persecuted the woman which brought forth the man child...And the dragon was wroth with the woman, and went forth to make war with the remnant of her seed, which keep the commandments of God, and have the testimony of Jesus Christ" (Rev. 12: 13-17).

iv) *The survivors of the "great tribulation".* "Except those days should be shortened, there should no flesh be saved: but for the elect's sake those days shall be shortened" (v.22). The Lord Jesus used the word "shortened", not in the sense of lessening the appointed period (three and a half years, as we shall see when dealing with the duration of the great tribulation), but in the sense of limiting it to that period. Notice how the passages above continue: "It is even the time of Jacob's trouble, but he shall be **saved** out of it" (Jer. 30: 7); "And at that time thy people shall be **delivered**, every one that shall be found written in the book (the 'elect')" (Dan. 12: 1); "Then shall the **Lord go forth**, and fight against those nations, as when He fought in the day of battle. And His feet shall stand in that day upon the mount of Olives, which is before Jerusalem on the east" (Zech. 14: 3-4). In the context of Matthew 24, the "elect" are elect Jews: "And I will bring forth a seed out of Jacob, and out of Judah an inheritor of my mountains; and mine elect shall inherit it, and my servants shall dwell there....mine elect shall long enjoy the work of their hands" (Isaiah 65: 9, 22).

v) *The duration of the "great tribulation".* "And except those days should be shortened..." We have observed that "the beast" will "continue for a short space" (Rev. 17: 10). That "short space" is defined as "forty and two **months**" (Rev. 13: 5), and "a thousand two hundred and threescore **days**" (Rev.11: 3; 12: 6). Daniel 7 puts the same period as "a time and times and the dividing of time" (Dan. 7: 25). Looked at in every way, the period is three and half years. That is, the second half of the seventieth week in the prophecy of Daniel 9, when "in the midst of the week he shall cause the sacrifice and oblation to cease" (v.27).

c) The deception, vv.23-26
"Then if any man shall say unto you, Lo, here is Christ, or there; believe it not. For there shall arise false Christs and false prophets, and shall shew great signs and wonders". This is amplified by Paul: "Even him whose coming is after the working of Satan with all power and signs and lying wonders, and with all deceivableness of unrighteousness in them that perish: because they received not the love of the truth, that they might be saved. And for this cause God shall send them strong delusion, that they should believe a (the) lie" (2 Thess. 2: 9-11).

If men "believed not the truth", they will ultimately "believe a lie". The Lord Jesus said, "I am come in my Father's name (that is, without attempting to either publicise Himself or make a name for Himself), and ye receive me not; if another shall come in his own name, him ye will receive" (John 5: 43).

However, God's purposes do not end here: "The LORD said unto my Lord, Sit thou at my right hand *until* I make thine enemies thy footstool" (Psalm 110: 1). Having dealt with *(a) the commencement* of the end of the age (vv.4-14), and *(b) the crisis* at the end of the age (vv.15-26), in our next study we will consider *(c) the coming* at the end of the age (vv.27-31). Unlike the "false Christs" and "false prophets", who advertise their presence with "great signs and wonders" and who are said to be in "the desert" and "secret chambers", the coming of the Son of man will be sudden and public, for "every eye shall see him". In His own words, "For as the lightning cometh out of the east, and shineth even unto the west; so shall also the coming of the Son of man be" (Matt. 24: 27). His title here, "Son of man", proclaims His moral right to rule over the world.

"They shall see the Son of man coming in the clouds of heaven"

Read Chapter 24: 27-31
In our first study of the Lord's 'Olivet Discourse', we suggested that Matthew 24 may be divided as follows: *(1)* the setting of the discourse (vv.1-3); *(2)* the subject of the discourse (vv.4-31); *(3)* the significance of the discourse (vv.32-51). In the final section (vv.32-51), the Lord Jesus applies the prophecy

by a series of illustrations emphasising the necessity for watchfulness and readiness.

1) THE SETTING OF THE DISCOURSE, vv.1-3

Matthew tells us that the Lord Jesus "departed from *the temple*" and "sat upon the *mount of Olives.* Mark tells us that the disciples asked their questions "as he sat on the *mount of Olives*, over against *the temple* (Mark 13: 3). This is most significant: both the temple and the mount of Olives play an important part at the end-time. The discourse anticipates the time when the Lord will "suddenly come to his temple" (Mal. 3: 1), and "his feet shall stand...upon the mount of Olives" (Zech. 14: 4).

2) THE SUBJECT OF THE DISCOURSE, vv.4-31

The disciples asked, "when shall these things be? And what shall be the sign of thy coming, and of the end of the world? ('the completion of the age', JND)" (v.3). As we have noted, this section of the discourse may be divided into three parts *(A)* the commencement of the end of the age (vv.4-14); *(B)* the crisis at the end of the age (vv.15-26); *(C)* the coming at the end of the age (vv.27-31).

A) The commencement of the end of the age, vv.4-14

As already noted, we can call this section, in the words of the Lord Jesus Himself, "the beginning of sorrows" (v.8). It answers to events in Revelation chs.6-7. The section can be divided into two parts, each of them being a warning: *(a)* what would happen *in the world* (vv.4-8); *(b)* what would happen *to the disciples* (vv.9-14). The former (vv.4-8) relates to events described in Revelation 6: 1-8, and the latter (vv.9-14) in connection with events described in Revelation 6: 9 - 7: 17.

B) The crisis at the end of the age, vv.15-26

In these verses, the Lord Jesus passes from events in the first half of Daniel's 'seventieth week' (Dan. 9: 27), that is, the period of "the beginning of sorrows", to events in the second half of the 'week', that is, the three and a half years in which Satan will display his power as never before, only to be utterly defeated at the end of the period. Having said, "and then shall the end come" (v.14), the Lord outlines events leading to "great tribulation, such as was not since the beginning of the world, to this time no, nor ever shall be" (v.21), involving *(i)* "the abomination of desolation" (v.15); *(ii)* the "great tribulation" (vv.16-22); *(iii)* the deception (vv.23-26). This brings us to:

C) The coming at the end of the age, vv.27-31

Whilst the "Great Tribulation" appears to be a triumph for the forces of evil, it is completely under divine control. The last word in human history belongs to "the Lord, and...his anointed" (Psalm 2: 2). The Lord Jesus now describes events at the end of this dark period in human history.

"For as the lightning cometh out of the east, and shineth even unto the west (compare Psalm 103: 12); so shall also the coming of the Son of man be. For wheresoever the carcase is, there will the eagles (or vultures) be gathered together" (vv.27-28). His coming will be "instantly and clearly visible to all" (Wm.MacDonald): compare the statements in v.26. W.E.Vine suggests that "just as these birds of prey gather where the carcase is, so the judgments of God will descend upon the corrupt state of humanity", but there seems good reason to take these words literally (see Rev. 19: 17-18; Ezek. 39: 4).

The Lord Jesus described three things in this connection: *(a)* the cosmic disturbances (v.29); *(b)* the coming of the Son of man (v.30); *(c)* the gathering of the elect (v.31). Parallel passages are found in Mark 13: 24-27; Luke 21: 25-28. He will come as the great Creator (v.29); the glorious King (v.30); the gracious Shepherd (v.31).

a) The cosmic disturbances, v.29

The Lord will come as the great Creator. "Immediately after the tribulation of those days shall the sun be darkened, and the moon shall not give her light (note the scientifically correct order: no sunlight and therefore no moonlight), and the stars shall fall from heaven (a startling statement: but notice that the Lord did *not* say 'fall from heaven upon the earth'), and the powers of the heavens shall be shaken". W.E.Vine defines "the powers of the heavens" as 'the natural forces of the heavens and heavenly bodies'.

The Lord Jesus is quoting from the Old Testament: "Behold, the day of the LORD cometh, cruel both with wrath and fierce anger, to lay the land desolate: and he shall destroy the sinners thereof out of it. For the stars of heaven and the constellations thereof shall not give their light: the sun shall be darkened in his going forth, and the moon shall not cause her light to shine. And I will punish the world for their evil, and the wicked for their iniquity" (Isaiah 13: 9-11). Similar passages occur in Isaiah 24: 23, Ezekiel 32: 7-8, Joel 2: 10, 31; 3: 15.

The literality of these statements is largely confirmed in Luke 21: 25-26, where the Lord Jesus distinguishes between celestial and terrestrial disturbances: "And there shall be signs in the sun, and in the moon, and in the stars; and upon the earth (as distinct from the heavenly luminaries) distress of nations, with perplexity; the sea and the waves roaring; men's hearts failing them for fear, and for looking after those things which are coming on the earth; for the powers of the heavens shall be shaken". See also Acts 2: 19-20: "And I will shew wonders in heaven above, and signs in the earth beneath: blood and fire, and vapour of smoke: the sun shall be turned into darkness, and the moon into blood, before that great and notable day of the Lord come". It is worth adding that we should take something as literal if it makes good sense to do so. See, for example, Revelation 8: 7-12.

Our knowledge of the solar system, and beyond, has been enhanced by observation and, in some cases, by exploration. But human wisdom pales before divine power. The mighty hand that made "the greater light to rule the day, and the lesser light to rule the night...the stars also", now darkens both sun and moon, and causes the stars to "fall from heaven". He will make the "lights in the firmament of the heaven" serve His purpose. He has done so before; see Joshua 10; 12-14; Judges 5: 20. There was "darkness over all the land (earth)" when the Lord Jesus bore divine judgment on the cross: there will be darkness again when He comes to execute divine judgment. Men last saw the Lord prior to darkness: they will next see the Lord after darkness (T.Miller). This follows:

b) The coming of the Son of man, v.30

The Lord will come as the glorious King. "And then shall appear the sign of the Son of man in heaven: and then shall all the tribes of the earth mourn, and they shall see the Son of man coming in the clouds of heaven with power and great glory". The "sign of the Son of man in heaven" is explained by the Lord Himself in Matthew 26: 64: "Hereafter shall ye see **the Son of man sitting on the right hand of power** (referring to God in all His power: see Psalm 110: 1-3: compare Heb. 8: 1), and coming in the clouds of heaven". We should notice:

i) **The title at His coming.** "Son of man". This is rather more than a statement of His humanity, although that is most certainly included. It is a statement of His right to reign on earth. This Man has the right to reign. It belongs to no other. After four world empires have run their course, it will be "One like the Son of man" who will be given "dominion, and glory, and a kingdom, that all people, nations, and languages should serve him" (Dan. 7: 13-14). The Jews recognised this title as a statement of deity: see Matt. 26: 64; Acts 7: 56-57.

*ii) **The manner of His coming.*** He will come "in the clouds of heaven" and "with power and great glory":

- *"In the clouds of heaven"*. Compare Revelation 1: 7 ("Behold, he cometh with clouds, and every eye shall see him"); Revelation 14: 14: ("And I looked, and behold a white cloud, and upon the cloud one sat like unto the Son of man, having on his head a golden crown, and in his hand a sharp sickle"). He will make "the clouds his chariot" (Psalm 104: 3). His coming will be as irresistible and as overwhelming as the clouds on which He rides. "Gird thy sword upon thy thigh, O most mighty, with thy glory and thy majesty. And in thy majesty ride prosperously because of truth and meekness and righteousness; and thy right hand shall teach thee terrible things" (Psalm 45: 3-4). The ensuing 'battle' will be over immediately. He simply said (but how profound) "I am (he)" in Gethsemane, and His enemies "went backward, and fell to the ground" (John 18: 6). He will speak again, and the combined military forces of the world with their ruler, the beast, will be utterly destroyed (2 Thess. 2: 8, referring to Isaiah 11: 4; Rev. 19: 15, 21).

- *"With power and great glory"*. This is amplified particularly in Revelation 19 and Zechariah 14: "And I saw heaven opened, and behold a white horse; and he that sat on him was called Faithful and True, and in righteousness he doth judge and make war...And he hath on his vesture and on his thigh a name written, KING OF KINGS, AND LORD OF LORDS" (Rev. 19: 11-16); "Then shall the LORD go forth, and fight against those nations, as when he fought in the day of battle. And his feet shall stand in that day upon the mount of Olives which is before Jerusalem on the east, and the mount of Olives shall cleave in the midst thereof toward the east and toward the west...and the LORD my God shall come, and all the saints with thee." (Zech. 14: 3-5).

*iii) **The reaction to His coming.*** "And then shall all the tribes of the earth ('land', JND) mourn..." This *may* refer particularly to the Jewish nation. See Zechariah 12: 10-14, "They shall look upon me whom they have pierced, and they shall mourn for him, as one mourneth for his only son, and shall be in bitterness for him, as one that is in bitterness for his firstborn". But, at the same time, the entire world will see Him: "Behold, he cometh with clouds, and every eye shall see him, and they also which pierced him: and all kindreds of the earth shall wail because of him" (Rev. 1: 7).

c) The gathering of the elect, v.31
The Lord will come as the gracious Shepherd. "And he shall send his angels with a great sound of a trumpet, and they shall gather together his elect from the four winds, from one end of heaven to the other". This is the last of three references to the elect Jew; see vv.23-24. They constitute the "all Israel" of Romans 11.26. The Messiah will come "with strong hand, and his arm shall rule for him", but He will also "feed his flock like a shepherd: he shall gather the lambs with his arm" (Isaiah 40: 10-11).

Some teach that the apparent similarity between Matthew 24: 30-31 and 1 Thessalonians 4: 13-17 supports the view that both passages refer to the same event, leading to the conclusion the church will pass through the 'great tribulation'. After all, it is argued, both passages speak about the Lord's coming, both speak about clouds, both mention angels and a trumpet sound, and both speak about the gathering of God's people. We have already noted, however, that the 'Olivet Discourse' is particularly concerned with the Jewish nation, and that the 'great tribulation' will encompass Israel in particular. See Jeremiah 30: 5-7; Daniel 12: 1; Zechariah 14: 1-4; Revelation 12: 13-17. In this connection we should notice:

i) "He shall send his **angels**…and **they** shall gather together his elect". In the case of the church, "the Lord **himself** shall descend from heaven with a shout" (1 Thess. 4: 16). In the case of Israel, angels are involved. In the case of the church, the Lord will speak with "the voice of the **archangel**", or 'with archangel's voice' (JND). Scholars tell us that "the shout" and "the voice of the archangel" are one and the same. It can be translated, 'The Lord himself shall descend from heaven with a shout, in (*en*) the voice of the archangel', or 'in archangel's voice'.

ii) "He shall send his angels with a great **sound of a trumpet**". This was foretold in the Old Testament: "And it shall come to pass in that day, that the LORD shall beat off (the land will become a threshing-floor) from the channel of the river (referring to the Euphrates) unto the stream of Egypt (the extent of the land promised to Abraham), and ye shall be gathered one by one, O ye children of Israel. And it shall come to pass in that day, that **the great trumpet shall be blown**, and they shall come which were ready to perish in the land of Assyria, and the outcasts in the land of Egypt, and shall worship the LORD in the holy mount at **Jerusalem**" (Isaiah 27: 12-13). It should be noted that the people gathered here, following the sound of the trumpet, "worship the LORD in the holy mount at Jerusalem", but the people summoned by the Lord Jesus when He descends with "the voice of the archangel, and with the trump of God" (1 Thess. 4: 16) will be "caught up" and "ever be with the Lord" in His "***Father's house***" (John 14: 2), so that we can sing:

> *There at our Saviour's side,*
> *Heaven is our home!*
> *We shall be glorified,*
> *Heaven is our home!*
> *There with the good and blest,*
> *Those we've loved most and best,*
> *We shall for ever rest –*
> *Heaven is our home.*

iii) "They shall ***gather together his elect".*** We must remember that in this passage "his elect" are Jews. "And I will bring forth a seed out of Jacob, and out of Judah an inheritor of my mountains; and mine ***elect*** shall inherit it, and my servants shall dwell there....mine ***elect*** shall long enjoy the work of their hands" (Isaiah 65: 9, 22); "And at that time thy people shall be ***delivered***, every one that shall be found written in the book (the 'elect')" (Dan. 12: 1).

So far as the church is concerned, it will be a case of meeting "the Lord in the air" (1 Thess. 4: 17). But while the gathering of the Jewish 'elect' will certainly be accomplished by divine power, it will not involve transportation through the air (a rapture). This is confirmed by such passages as Isaiah 49: 18-23: "Lift up thine eyes round about, and behold: all these gather themselves together, and come to thee...***I will lift up mine hand*** to the Gentiles, and ***set up my standard*** to the people: and ***they*** shall bring thy sons in ***their*** arms, and thy daughters shall be carried upon ***their*** shoulders. And kings shall be thy nursing fathers, and their queens thy nursing mothers." This is ***not*** at variance with Matthew 24: 31, "And he shall send ***his angels*** with a great sound of a trumpet, and ***they*** shall gather together his elect from the four winds, from one end of heaven to the other". The exiles will be gathered by angelic power, but ***Gentiles*** will be the vehicle through which it will be accomplished.

iv) "They shall gather together his elect from ***the four winds, from one***

end of heaven to the other". The Lord Jesus refers here to passages in Deuteronomy and Nehemiah. Having been told that if they disobeyed the Lord, the nation would be scattered "from the one end of the earth even unto the other" (Deut. 28: 64), Moses went on to say that following repentance the Lord would "return and gather thee from all the nations, whither the LORD thy God had scattered thee" and "If any of thine be driven out unto the outmost parts of heaven ('the farthest parts under heaven', NKJV), from thence will the LORD thy God gather thee, and from thence will he fetch thee" (Deut. 30: 2-4). Nehemiah quoted this in prayer: "Remember, I beseech thee, the word that thou commandest thy servant Moses, saying, If ye transgress, I will scatter you abroad among the nations: but if ye return unto me...though there were of you cast out unto the uttermost part of the heaven, yet will I gather them from thence, and will bring them unto the place that I have chosen to set my name there" (Neh. 1: 8-9). According to Isaiah 11: 11-12, "the LORD...shall set up an ensign for the nations, and shall assemble the outcasts of Israel, and gather together the dispersed of Judah from the four corners ('wings') of the earth". Andrew Wilson (*Matthew's Messiah*) helpfully points out that Jeremiah 49: 32, 36 prove that the words "four winds" refer to the four compass points.

Andrew Wilson also points out that "Isaiah 13: 5 and Deuteronomy 4: 32 both further prove that the 'end of heaven' is simply a Hebraic way of saying 'the ends of the earth'". He adds, "Matthew 24: 31 is therefore a hark-back to God's promise to eventually gather ***Israel*** from its Dispersion among the nations....it refers to ***Israel's*** regathering to its ancient land - ***not*** to Christians being caught up into the air".

v) The Lord Jesus does not refer here to the resurrection of dead Jews. The passage concerns living Jews. But Paul refers to "we which are alive and remain" ***and*** to "them which are asleep" (1 Thess. 4: 15).

The immediate hope of the believer is the fulfilment of the Lord's promise, "I will come again, and receive you unto myself; that where I am, there ye may be also" (John 14: 3). But while we gladly "wait for his Son from heaven... which hath delivered us from the wrath to come" (1 Thess.1: 10), we should also gladly anticipate His ***public*** return, when "every eye shall see him". He will then be vindicated in the world which rejected Him, and we should therefore "love His appearing" (2 Tim. 4: 8).

Oh, the joy to see Thee reigning,
Thee, my own beloved Lord!
Every tongue Thy Name confessing,
Worship, honour, glory, blessing,
Brought to Thee with one accord;
Thee, my Master and my Friend,
Vindicated and enthroned,
Unto earth's remotest end
Glorified, adored, and owned!

"Watch therefore"

Read Chapter 24: 32-51
As we have noted in our previous three studies of the Lord's 'Olivet Discourse', Matthew 24 may be divided as follows: **(1)** the setting of the discourse (vv.1-3); **(2)** the subject of the discourse (vv.4-31); **(3)** the significance of the discourse (vv.32-51).

1) THE SETTING OF THE DISCOURSE, vv.1-3
Matthew tells us that the Lord Jesus "departed from **the temple**" and "sat upon the **mount of Olives**", and the location of the discourse is most significant in view of the fact that both the temple and the mount of Olives play an important part at the end-time. The discourse anticipates the time when the Lord will "suddenly come to his temple" (Mal. 3: 1), and "his feet shall stand...upon the mount of Olives" (Zech. 14: 4).

2) THE SUBJECT OF THE DISCOURSE, vv.4-31
The disciples asked, "when shall these things be? And what shall be the sign of thy coming, and of the end of the world? ('the completion of the age', JND)" (v.3). As we have noted more than once, this section of the discourse may be divided into three parts **(a)** the commencement of the end of the age (vv.4-14); **(b)** the crisis at the end of the age (vv.15-26); **(c)** the coming at the end of the age (vv.27-31). This brings us to

3) THE SIGNIFICANCE OF THE DISCOURSE, vv.32-51
In the final section of the chapter, the Lord Jesus applies the prophecy using several illustrations to emphasise the necessity for watchfulness and readiness. Coming events must influence present conduct. But whilst we must always seek appropriate lessons for ourselves in every part of Scripture, these particular verses do refer to the period immediately prior to the Lord's

coming as "the Son of man" (vv.39, 44). The Lord Jesus addresses His disciples representatively here: "So likewise *ye*, when *ye* shall see all these things...Watch therefore: for *ye* know not what hour *your* Lord may come... Therefore be *ye* also ready" (vv.33, 42, 44). If the disciples were meant personally they would still be alive now!

These verses may be divided as follows: *(a)* the indication of His coming (vv.32-33); *(b)* the certainty of His coming (vv.34-35); *(c)* the suddenness of His coming (vv.36-41); *(d)* the expectation of His coming (vv.42-44); *(e)* the conduct in view of His coming (vv.45-51).

a) The indication of His coming, vv.32-33
"Now learn a parable of the fig tree; When his branch is yet tender, and putteth forth leaves, ye know that summer is nigh: so likewise ye, when ye shall see all these things, know that it is nigh, even at the doors". The RV has '*he* is nigh', the difference in translation arising from the fact that "the Greek verb *estin* can mean either 'it is' or 'he is'" (J.Heading).

In the Old Testament, the fig tree is one of the figures used to describe Israel. For example, "I found Israel like grapes in the wilderness; I saw your fathers as the firstripe in the *fig tree* at her first time" (Hos. 9: 10); "He hath laid my vine waste, and barked my *fig tree*" (Joel 1: 7). The figure is carried over into the New Testament: "And when he (the Lord Jesus) saw a *fig tree* in the way, he came to it, and found nothing thereon, but leaves only, and said unto it, Let no fruit grow on thee henceforward for ever. And presently the fig tree withered away" (Matt. 21: 18-19); "Behold, these three years I come seeking fruit on this *fig tree*, and find none: cut it down...Lord, let it alone this year also, till I shall dig about it, and dung it: and if it bear fruit, well: and if not, then after that thou shalt cut it down" (Luke 13: 6-9). As a nation, Israel had become fruitless, and in consequence had "withered away" and been 'cut down'. Absence of fruit had brought divine judgment on Israel, but the renewal of spiritual life, with all the attendant events at the end-time ("all these things"), will be indicative of the Lord's near return. "So likewise ye, when ye shall see all these things come to pass, know ye that the kingdom of God is nigh at hand" (Luke 21: 31). There will be "time (delay) no longer" (Rev. 10: 6).

But in what sense are we to understand the Lord's reference to life in the fig tree? While it is perfectly true that the State of Israel was proclaimed in

1948, and national life has flourished ever since, the Lord is surely referring here to **spiritual life.** The nation existed when the Lord Jesus was present two thousand years ago, but there was no fruit for Him, and nothing for God. The 'tender branch' and the 'leaves' suggest new spiritual life, and John Heading points us in the right direction in saying that "The leaves speak of the experiences of the Jewish remnant during the great tribulation". The preaching of the 144,000 Jewish witnesses (Revelation 7: 1-17) will be nothing less than "leaves" on "the fig tree", indicating that the long winter of suffering and persecution is about to give place to the summer of divine blessing and fruitfulness.

In his parallel passage, Luke expands the Lord's statement: "And he spake to them in parables; Behold the fig tree, and all the trees; when they now shoot forth, ye see and know of your own selves that summer is now night at hand" (Luke 21: 29-30). If, as we have suggested above, "the fig tree" represents the nation of Israel then, by the same rule, "all the trees" must represent the Gentile nations, in whom there will certainly be spiritual life at the same time. See Revelation 7: 9-17.

b) The certainty of His coming, vv.34-35

"Verily I say unto you, This generation shall not pass, till all these things be fulfilled. Heaven and earth shall pass away, but my words shall not pass away". We cannot fail to notice the contrast between the impermanence of "this generation", the impermanence of "heaven and earth", and the permanence of the Lord's teaching.

i) The impermanence of the current generation.

We should notice two important things here:

- **Firstly,** that the Jewish nation will exist when He returns. It will not be obliterated. The Egyptians attempted to curtail the growth of the nation (Exodus 1: 16), and Haman endeavoured to eradicate it entirely (Esther 3: 8-9), but the nation survived, and will continue to survive. While God's people will experience "A time of trouble, such as never was since there was a nation even to that same time", the passage continues by saying "thy people **shall be delivered**, every one that shall be found written in the book" (Dan. 12: 1). Jeremiah writes similarly: "We have heard a voice of trembling, of fear, and not of peace...Alas! for that day is great, so that there is none like it; it is even the time of Jacob's trouble, but he **shall be saved out of it**" (Jer. 30: 5, 7).

- **Secondly**, that the Jewish nation will be changed. This is clear from the words, "This generation shall not pass, *till* all these things be fulfilled". The word, "generation" (*genea*) has a wider significance in Scripture than its modern use where it refers to a life span of, say, thirty or forty (or more) years. According to W.E.Vine, the word can mean "a family, or successive members of a genealogy (Matt. 1: 17), or of a race of people, possessed of similar characteristics, pursuits, etc (of a bad character): Matt. 17: 17; Mark 9: 19; Luke 9: 41; Luke 16: 8; Acts 2: 40". But there will be a change. The nation will no longer be "a faithless and perverse generation" (Luke 9: 41) or a "crooked and perverse nation (*genea*)" (Phil. 2: 15). The Lord will put His "law in their inward parts, and write it in their hearts; and will be their God, and they shall be my people" (Jer. 31: 33).

ii) The impermanence of creation. "Heaven and earth shall pass away" Peter writes about this: "the heavens and the earth which are now, by the same word (the "same word" which brought them into existence) are kept in store, reserved unto fire against the day of judgment and perdition of ungodly men...the heavens shall pass away with a great noise, and the elements shall melt with fervent heat, the earth also and the works that are therein shall be burned up" (2 Pet. 3: 7, 10).

iii) The permanence of the Lord's word. "Heaven and earth shall pass away, but *my words shall not pass away"*. The Lord's teaching bears the stamp of His own eternity. His words will "not pass away" because *He* will never "pass away". Just listen to this: "And, Thou, Lord, in the beginning hast laid the foundation of the earth; and the heavens are the works of thine hands: they shall perish; but thou remainest; and they all shall wax old as doth a garment; and as a vesture shalt thou fold them up, and they shall be changed: but thou art the same, and thy years shall not fail" (Heb. 1: 10-12). His word can be trusted because *He* is unchanging and unchangeable. Everything He says will "be fulfilled" (v.34). Abraham was "fully persuaded that, what he (God) had promised, he was able also to perform" (Rom. 4: 21), and this is equally applicable to the Lord Jesus, who is, of course, God manifest in the flesh.

c) The suddenness of His coming, vv.36-41
Having spoken of His coming (v.30) and made it clear that revival of spiritual life in the nation will indicate that His coming "is near, even at the doors" (v.33), the Saviour continues, "But of that day and hour knoweth no man, no, not the angels of heaven, but my Father only" (v.36). We must pause

here, and ponder two things: *(i)* the time of His coming; *(ii)* the knowledge of His coming, to which we must add *(iii)* the unexpectedness of His coming (vv.37-41).

i) **The time of His coming**. "But of that **day and hour** knoweth no man". It has often been said that with the emergence of "the beast" and the "false prophet", and particularly with the placing of "the abomination of desolation…in the holy place", godly men and women will be able to estimate the time of the Lord's return "with power and great glory" (v.30). They will know that He will return at the end of three and a half years. The period is expressed in months ("forty and two months", Rev. 13: 5), in days (1,260 days, Rev. 12: 6) and in the formula "a time, and times, and half a time" (Rev. 12: 14). But as John Heading rightly points out, while "they will be able to deduce when the end will come…the exact 'day and hour' may still be unknown.

ii) **The knowledge of His coming**. "But of that day and hour knoweth no man, no, not the angels of heaven, *but my Father only"* (v.36). Mark adds to this: "But of that day and that hour knoweth no man, no, not the angels which are in heaven, *neither the Son,* but the Father" (Mark 13: 32). This is explained by Acts 1: 7, "It is not for you to know the times or the seasons (that is, the precise timetable for future events), which *the Father hath put in his own power*". In Psalm 110, God addresses His Son: "Sit thou at my right hand, *until* I make thine enemies thy footstool". The Lord Jesus was content to leave the time of His vindication on earth to the Father, just as He left His exaltation and glory to the Father two thousand years ago. See Philippians 2: 5-11. His part, as the Perfect Servant, was obedience "unto death", but "*God* hath highly exalted him". It is significant that the words, "neither the Son", are omitted by Matthew. They are appropriate in Mark, the Gospel of the Servant. The fact that He refers to Himself as "the Son", and therefore in complete possession of every divine attribute, proves that this verse is not a denial of His absolute deity and omniscience. The Scriptures cannot contradict themselves.

iii) **The unexpectedness of His coming**. "But as the days of Noe were, so shall also the coming of the Son of man be. For as in the days that were before the flood they were eating and drinking, marrying and giving in marriage, until the day that Noe entered into the ark, and knew not until the flood came, and took them all away; so shall also the coming of the Son of man be. Then shall two be in the field; the one shall be taken, and the other left. Two women shall be grinding at the mill; the one shall be taken, and the other left" (vv. 38-41).

Although not all agree, the fact that "the flood came", and "took...away" people who were completely oblivious of their danger and 'carrying on as normal', although they had the witness of Noah, does seem to point clearly to the identity of the people who will be "taken" when the Lord Jesus returns to earth. Like the antediluvians, the people concerned will be "taken" in judgment. In the larger context of the 'Olivet Discourse' and the immediate context of the Flood, the words "one shall be taken, and the other left" refer, not to 'the rapture' (1 Thess. 4: 16-17), but to "the end of the world (age)", when "The Son of man shall send forth his angels, and they shall gather out of his kingdom all things that offend, and them which do iniquity" (Matt. 13: 41).

Some very conservative and highly respected commentators suggest that the Lord Jesus is in fact referring to 'the rapture' here and point out that different words are used in the text. They rightly note that the word *airo* is used in v.39, "**took** them all away" whereas the word *paralambano* is used in vv.40-41, "one shall be **taken**", and point out that very often in the New Testament this is translated "receive" (see, for example, John 14: 3), concluding that those who are "taken" in vv.40-41 are taken, not for judgment, but for blessing. However, the word *paralambano* is not always used in this way. For example, "Then the soldiers **took** (*paralambano*) Jesus into the common hall...And they stripped him, and put on him a scarlet robe" (Matt. 27: 27-28); "And they **took** (*paralambano*) Jesus, and led him away" (John 19: 16).

William Kelly points out that "when the Son of Man thus comes in judgment upon living men here below, it will not be, as when the Romans or others took Jerusalem, indiscriminate slaughter or captivity; but whether in the open country or the duties at home, whether men or women, there will be righteous discernment of individuals". It will be discriminatory judgment: "Then shall two be in the field, the one shall be taken and the other left; two women shall be grinding at the mill, the one shall be taken and the other left" (vv.40-41). See, again, Matthew 13: 41. It is worth saying that while this will not necessarily take place at the moment the Lord Jesus appears to destroy the armies which will besiege Jerusalem (Zech. 14: 1-4), bringing about the end of the period the "great tribulation", it is part of the process, as we have already noticed, of gathering "out of his kingdom all things that offend, and them which do iniquity" (Matt. 13: 41).

This is a good opportunity to remind ourselves that before the Flood came, Enoch was taken to heaven: "By faith Enoch was translated that he should not see death; and was not found, because God had translated him: for before his translation he had this testimony, that he pleased God" (Heb. 11: 5). But, like Enoch, Noah also "walked with God" (Gen. 5: 22; 6: 9), and he was preserved through the Flood and emerged from the ark to live in a new and cleansed earth. Similarly, the Lord's people today - His church - will, like Enoch, be taken to heaven before the flood of divine judgment engulfs the world, but God will have a people on earth, a godly remnant who will look for the coming of the Messiah, and who having passed through the floods of divine judgment, will enjoy the millennial blessings that follow.

d) *The expectation of His coming, vv.42-44*
Whilst the world will be caught unawares by the coming of "the Son of man" (men will be totally deceived by the satanic "lie", 2 Thess. 2: 11), the godly remnant of that day will be required to exercise constant vigilance. "Watch therefore: for ye know not what hour your Lord will come. But know this, that if the goodman of the house had known in what watch the thief would come, he would have watched, and would not have suffered his house to be broken up. Therefore be ye also ready: for in such an hour as ye think not, the Son of man cometh".

In their context, these verses do refer to the need for vigilance in view of the coming of "the Son of man". While the words "son of man" appear on numerous occasions (93) in connection with Ezekiel, they stress, on one hand, his frailty when compared with the glory of the Lord, and on the other, the Lord's grace in using him. To think that He would use such a frail vessel as the "son of man!" The title is used of the Lord Jesus, and by the Lord Jesus, rather differently. It emphasises, of course, His perfect humanity, but more than that, His ideal humanity. He has the right to reign because He is the perfect man! Hence, "I saw in the night visions, and, behold, one like the Son of man came with the clouds of heaven…and there was given him…a kingdom, that all people, nations, and languages, should serve him; his dominion is an everlasting dominion, which shall not pass away, and his kingdom that which shall not be destroyed" (Dan. 7: 13-14). The title "Son of man" therefore has particular reference to His reign on earth, but how marvellous that the very Son of man, who will reign, came "to seek and to save that which was lost" (Luke 19: 10) and was "lifted up" at Calvary (John 3: 14)!

As our heading states, these verses emphasise the need for expectation. The disciples were not to be like the "goodman of the house" (elsewhere translated "master of the house" or "householder") who bemoaned the fact that his house had been burgled ("broken up" means, literally, 'dig through' and refers here to thieves breaking into a house), and exclaimed, 'If only I knew they were coming!'

While, in its immediate context, this refers to the Lord's return to establish His kingdom, the lesson is most certainly applicable *now.* How awful if the Lord suddenly came, and *we* had to say, 'If only I had expected Him!' We should live in expectation of the Lord's coming. It should never be, for us, as "a thief in the night" (1 Thess. 5: 2). In fact, when the Lord's coming is described in this way, it is always in connection with judgment. See, for example, Revelation 16: 15. It is therefore solemn to notice that the church at Sardis ran the risk of being caught unprepared by the second coming of Christ in exactly the same way that unsaved people will! See Revelation 3: 3. Are *we* waiting and watching for our Lord's return? Does it have to be said to *us,* "Awake thou that sleepest?" (Eph. 5: 14).

e) The conduct in view of His coming, vv.45-51
The Lord Jesus has illustrated the need for readiness in view of His coming, with reference to the "goodman of the house" (vv.43-44). He now illustrates the need for faithfulness in view of His coming with reference to stewardship. A similar passage occurs in Luke 12: 42-48. In its context, the lesson must be that "the coming of the Son of man will be unexpected and many will be caught unprepared...Some, apostate Jews, evil and false shepherds of Judaism, will abandon hopes of His coming and turn to things material, carnal, and sensual, to their everlasting ruin (see, again 2 Thess. 2: 11-12). The Lord of the faithful steward will reward him, and in context, that reward will be a place of responsibility and rule in the kingdom" (J.M.Flanigan).

There are lessons for ourselves here. Readiness will promote faithfulness. Notice the expressions, "his lord" (vv.45-46), "My lord" (v.48), and "the lord of that servant" (v.50). But there is an important difference; only the "faithful and wise servant" recognised his lordship in practice. We too must beware: "And why call ye me, Lord, Lord, and do not the things which I say?" (Luke 6: 46).

As always, the Lord Jesus is the model of His own ministry. He is, above all, the "faithful and wise servant". With Him there was never even the possibility of failure. As the One faithful and obedient unto death, he has the moral authority to urge others to be "faithful unto death" (Rev. 2: 10). He embodied perfectly, and at all times, "the wisdom that is from above" (James 3: 17). He, most certainly, gives God's household "meat in due season" and does so as the Head of the church. He will be "ruler over all". Every knee will bow to Him. Of Him, in a unique sense, it can be rightly said, "Blessed is that servant". This, surely, is the essence of God's expressed delight, "'Behold my servant, whom I uphold, mine elect, in whom my soul delighteth" (Isaiah 42: 1).

The Lord's figure is timeless in application. He refers to the **requirements** of the servant; he is "faithful and wise": to the **responsibility** of the servant; he is made "ruler over all his household": to the **reliability** of the servant: when the lord returns, he finds the servant "so doing": to the **reward** of the servant; he is made ruler over "all his goods". Here, then, is a servant in complete submission to an appreciative lord. The "Lord of all" (Acts. 10: 36) is no less appreciative of faithful service, as is clear in His call to serve, and by His assured compensation: "If any man serve me, let him follow me; and where I am, there shall also my servant be: if any man serve me, him will my Father honour" (John 12: 26).

The "evil servant" is also rewarded. He did not expect the lord's return, he had no regard for the lord's servants, and paid no regard to the lord's interests. His conduct belied his profession. He was a hypocrite, and joined his colleagues in endless remorse (v.51). "By their fruits ye shall know them" (Matt. 7: 20).

This does not bring us to the end of 'the Olivet Discourse'. It continues in the next chapter.

THE GOSPEL OF MATTHEW

"Behold, the bridegroom cometh"

Read Chapter 25: 1-13
In introducing all four studies in Matthew 24, under the general title 'Olivet Discourse', we suggested that the chapter may be divided as follows: *(1)* the setting of the discourse (vv.1-3); *(2)* the subject of the discourse (vv.4-31); *(3)* the significance of the discourse (vv.32-51). In dealing with the final section of the chapter (vv.32-51), we noticed that the Lord Jesus applies the prophecy using several illustrations to emphasise the necessity for watchfulness and readiness. Having 'marked, learned, and inwardly digested' these important lessons, we added that this did not bring us to the end of 'the Olivet Discourse', and that it continued in Chapter 25.

The division between the two chapters does not disguise the fact that the Lord is continuing His discourse. This is clear from the opening words of Chapter 25: "***Then*** shall the kingdom of heaven be likened unto ten virgins, which took their lamps, and went forth to meet the bridegroom" (v.1). The end of the discourse is clearly marked: "And it came to pass, when Jesus had ***finished all these sayings***." (26: 1).

The Lord's coming in glory is common to both chapters: "For as the lightning cometh out of the east, and shineth even unto the west, so shall also the ***coming*** of the Son of man be" (24: 27); "they shall see the Son of man ***coming*** in the clouds of heaven with power and ***great glory***" (24: 30); "But as the days of Noe were, so shall also the ***coming*** of the Son of man be" (24: 37). See also vv.39, 42, 44. "Behold, the bridegroom ***cometh***...ye know neither the day nor the hour wherein the Son of man ***cometh*** (25: 6, 13); "after a long time the lord of those servants ***cometh***" (25: 19); "When the Son of man shall ***come*** in his ***glory***" (25: 31).

Matthew 25 has three constituent parts: *(1)* the parable of the virgins (vv.1-13); *(2)* the parable of the talents (vv.14-30); *(3)* the judgment of the nations (vv.31-46). While the first two sections commence with the words, "Then shall the kingdom of heaven be likened unto ten virgins" (v.1) and "For the kingdom of heaven is as a man travelling into a far country" (v.14) respectively, the last section of the chapter is not a parable. It commences with the words, "When the Son of man shall come in his glory...then shall he sit upon the throne of his glory" (v.31). The two parables (vv.1-13; vv.14-30), like those in the previous chapter, emphasise the impact that the Lord's return in "the clouds of heaven with power and great glory" should have on His people at the end-time, but in the words of E.W.Rogers, "its main principles (he is referring to the parable of the ten virgins) apply throughout the whole period from the time the Lord returned to heaven till the time that He comes back again to earth. Its principles apply to us of the present calling; its principles will apply to the godly after the church has been taken away" (quoted by J.M.Flanigan). But as J.M.Flanigan rightly observes, "this parable is essentially a warning and exhortation for those who wait for the Son of Man. Believers today wait for the Son of God, their Bridegroom and Saviour. 'Son of Man' is a title associated with Israel and with judgment, rather than with the Bride, the Church".

1) THE PARABLE OF THE VIRGINS, vv.1-13
The Lord Jesus is, of course, the "glorious Bridegroom of our hearts", and we gladly sing of Him in that way:

> *Thou glorious Bridegroom of our hearts,*
> *Thy present smile a heaven imparts;*
> *Oh, lift the veil, if veil there be,*
> *Let every saint Thy beauties see!*
>
> C.H.Spurgeon

Nevertheless, this parable must be understood in its proper context. As already noted, the previous chapter refers to the Lord's return in glory, and events described in this chapter are preparatory for His millennial reign. See v.34. Since the entire chapter is essentially part of the Olivet Discourse, it does not directly refer to either the rapture or the judgment seat of Christ, although we cannot over-emphasise that *the principles* in the parable are applicable to the Lord's people today.

In summary, the Lord Jesus returns as the Bridegroom, not to claim His bride, but *with* His bride. "When Christ, who is our life shall appear, then shall ye also appear with him in glory" (Col. 3: 4). "He will come "to be glorified *in his saints*, and to be admired in *all them that believe*" (2 Thess. 1: 10). While "the marriage of the Lamb" (Rev. 19: 7), will take place in heaven", the "marriage supper of the Lamb" (Rev. 19: 9) will take place on earth, and it is to this that the Lord refers in the parable: "then they that were ready went in with him to the marriage" (v.10, AV), or "to the marriage feast" (RV). Those who wait for the Bridegroom are described as virgins. They must not be confused with the bride (who is not mentioned here), and do not, therefore, represent the church and Christendom, as some suggest, or the supposed division between spiritual and unspiritual Christians. The virgins are not further identified in the parable, but they are evidently people who profess to be waiting for the return of the Messiah.

The parable describes Israel's expectation of Messiah's return, but as Archie Payne (*When the King Comes*) points out, "The period of waiting, being a period of tribulation, will seem prolonged, and weariness and lassitude will set in, so that many slumber and sleep". But the time has now come, and the midnight cry rings out, "Behold, the bridegroom cometh; go ye out to meet him". But the nation which should have been ready to meet Him is divided. In some cases, lamps were "going out" (v.8, JND), perhaps the result of the pressure of circumstances at the time. In other cases, lamps were burning: they needed trimming but they did not need lighting! There was light in the darkness fuelled by Spirit-given assurance that the King was coming. Their testimony, and its result, is described in Revelation 7, and their reward, "these are they which follow the Lamb whithersoever he goeth", is described in Rev. 14: 4. In the language of Matthew 25, "'they...went in with him to the marriage feast" (v.10, RV).

At the 'wedding feast', and beyond, the 'wise virgins' will hear the bride address the Bridegroom in adoring wonder: "Yea, he is altogether lovely. This is my beloved, and this is my friend, O daughters of Jerusalem" (S. of S. 5: 16).

With this in mind, we must now address the details of the parable. They may be summarised as follows: *(a)* awaiting the bridegroom (vv.1-5); *(b)* announcing the arrival (v.6); *(c)* asking for oil (vv.7-9); *(d)* attending the feast (v.10); *(e)* applying for entry (vv.11-12); *(f)* applying the lesson (v.13).

Chapter 25

a) Awaiting the bridegroom, vv.1-5

While these verses can be regarded as a general introduction to the parable, they serve to introduce us to the waiting people. We should notice *(i)* the common description (v.1): they are all called "virgins"; *(ii)* the important difference (vv.2-4): they fall into two categories, the "wise" and the "foolish". It may be significant that there were "ten virgins". Ten is the number of human responsibility. The word "Then", suggests that "This is not a parable which is true of the kingdom of heaven at any other time: it is only true of the kingdom of heaven *then*" (T.Miller).

i) Their common description. "Then shall the kingdom of heaven be likened unto ten **virgins**" (v.1). While they obviously had something in common, for they were all virgins (some commentators prefer 'maidens'), there were vital differences between them, to the extent that the Bridegroom refused five of them admission to the marriage feast with the words, "I know you not" (v.12).

The very term "virgin" supposes uprightness and purity of life. The true 'Jehovah's Witnesses' of Revelation 7 are seen in Revelation 14 where they are described as "they which were not defiled with women: for they are virgins" (Rev. 14: 4). It could therefore be said that so far as outward observation was concerned, all ten virgins were indistinguishable. The five without oil could not be distinguished from the five with oil in terms of morality and uprightness of life. Paul could well speak for them in saying, "If any other man thinketh that he hath whereof he might trust in the flesh, I more… touching the righteousness which is in the law, blameless" (Phil. 3: 4-6).

The "lamps" remind us of the "more sure word of prophecy; whereunto ye do well that ye take heed, as unto a light (*luchnos,* meaning a lamp) that shineth in a dark ('murky' or 'squalid') place" (2 Pet. 1: 19). While, admittedly, the word here (*luchnos*) differs from the word translated "lamps" in our current passage (*lampas*), it remains that the lamps are crucial in enabling people to find their way in the darkness, and that men and women in the end-time will need the word of God to lighten their pathway in the dark days of the tribulation.

ii) Their important difference. "And five of them were wise, and five were foolish. They that were foolish took their lamps ('torches', RV margin), and took no oil with them: but the wise took oil in their vessels with their lamps" (vv.2-4). It should be said that the word "lamps" (*lampas*) 'denotes a torch…

frequently fed, like a lamp, with oil from a little vessel used for the purpose... they held little oil and would frequently need replenishing" (W.E.Vine). We should notice the difference in priority: "They that were foolish took ***their lamps*** ('torches', RV margin), ***and took no oil*** with them: but the wise ***took oil*** in their vessels ***with their lamps"***. In the first case it is "lamps...oil"; in the second "oil...lamps"

While all ten virgins "took their lamps, and went forth to meet the bridegroom" (v.1), indicating their interest in him and acting as though they desired to meet him, five evidently had no true expectation. Their lamps were going out ("gone out", AV), and they made no provision for the moment of his arrival. On the other hand, five evidently recognised that their "vigil may be long" and that "he may not come as soon as may have been expected, and there must be provision for the waiting" (Campbell Morgan). The burning lamps of the five 'wise virgins' indicates that they really were waiting for the bridegroom to come. There was no real expectation on the part of the others. It was empty profession. Genuine interest and spiritual reality is "wise". Empty profession is "foolish". While all "slumbered (usually said to mean 'drowsy') and slept", five were ready for his coming, and five were not.

This was exactly the situation at the ***first coming*** of the Lord Jesus. There were people with oil in their lamps. Simeon was one: he was "just and devout...and the Holy Ghost was upon him. And it was revealed unto him by the Holy Ghost, that he should not see death before he had seen the Lord's Christ. And he came by the Spirit into the temple". (Luke 2: 25-27). Anna was another and she "spake of him to all them that ***looked*** for redemption in Jerusalem" (Luke 2: 38). Later, Joseph of Arimathaea was another (Luke 23: 51). But while the religious leaders had their lamps and were able to tell Herod "where Christ should be born", they hadn't the slightest interest in Him (Matt. 2: 4-6). They had no oil in their lamps.

We must take the opportunity to say that ***we*** should not 'slumber and sleep'. John Heading (*What the Bible Teaches - Matthew*) puts it nicely: "This is not the state of those who are watching for the coming of the Lord: "Therefore let us not sleep, as do others: but let us watch" (1 Thess. 5: 6), but if there is failure, we need the exhortation, "It is high time to awake out of sleep" (Rom. 13: 11)...In the Old Testament, David certainly did not sleep when there was important work before him (Psalm 132: 4), and the One who keeps Israel never slumbers (Psalm 121: 3).

b) Announcing the arrival, v.6

"And at midnight there was a cry made, Behold, the bridegroom cometh; go ye out to meet him". It is worth stressing again that the Lord Jesus refers here, *not* to the marriage, *but* to the marriage feast, and that when He returns to earth it will not be *for* His bride, but *with* His bride. In this connection we should notice that according to Revelation 19: 7, "the marriage of the Lamb is come, and his wife hath made herself ready". The following questions must be asked, and answered:

i) **Why will it be "the marriage of the Lamb?"** Or, for that matter, the "marriage supper *of the Lamb*". The centre of attraction is *not* the bride, but the **Bridegroom!** Hence, as already noted, "**He** shall come to be glorified in his saints, and to be admired in all them that believe" (2 Thess. 1: 10). Again, it is called "the marriage of the Lamb" because His blood was shed in order to make her His bride: he "loved the church, and gave himself for it" (Eph. 5: 25). No wonder we sing:

> *The bride eyes not her garment,*
> *But her dear bridegroom's face:*
> *I will not gaze at glory,*
> *But on my King of grace;*
> *Not at the crown He giveth,*
> *But on His pierced hand:*
> *The Lamb is all the glory,*
> *Of Emmanuel's land.*

Anne R. Cousins

ii) **Why will "his wife make herself ready?"** Not ready for "the Lamb!" She is already "His **wife**". But ready to be *displayed* by the Lamb as the bride who will reign with Him.

iii) **Why wait until then to be displayed by the Lamb?** Surely it will be to show to the world that after the vile harlot of Revelation chs. 17-18, God has something infinitely pure and beautiful to display. The beauty of the bride will be displayed against the background of the degradation of the harlot. Hence the words, "And after these things I heard a great voice of much people in heaven, saying, Alleluia; Salvation, and glory, and honour, and power, unto the Lord our God: for true and righteous are his judgments: for he hath judged **the great whore**, which did corrupt the earth with her fornication, and hath avenged the blood of his servants at her hand" (Rev. 19: 1-2).

Accompanied then by His bride, the Lord will come. For Israel, it will indeed be "at midnight". With Jerusalem surrounded by enemies, and the nation about to be annihilated (Zech. 14: 1-2), "then shall the LORD go forth, and fight against those nations...And his feet shall stand upon the mount of Olives which is before Jerusalem" (Zech. 14: 1-4). Then the 'wise virgins' will cry "Lo, this is our God; we have waited for him, and he will save us: this is the LORD: we have waited for him, we will be glad and rejoice in his salvation" (Isa. 25: 9).

c) Asking for oil, vv.7-9
"Then all those virgins arose, and trimmed their lamps. And the foolish said unto the wise, Give us of your oil; for our lamps have gone out. But the wise answered, saying, Not so; lest there be not enough for us and you: but go ye rather to them that sell, and buy for yourselves".

There can be no doubt that oil is one of several pictures in the Bible of the Holy Spirit. Men were anointed with oil in the Old Testament, signifying that God had set them apart for their particular service and empowered them to undertake their work. When Saul was anointed to be king, Samuel said, "the Spirit of the Lord shall come upon thee" (1 Sam. 10: 1, 6). When David was appointed king in his place we are told that "Samuel took the horn of oil, and anointed him in the midst of his brethren: and the Spirit of the Lord came upon David from that day forward" (1 Sam. 16: 13). The book of Zechariah provides a further example. Having seen "a candlestick all of gold, with a bowl upon the top of it, and his seven lamps thereon, and seven pipes to the seven lamps, which are upon the top thereof: and two olive trees by it", the prophet was told, "This is the word of the Lord unto Zerubbabel, saying, Not by might, nor by power, but by My Spirit, saith the Lord of hosts" (Zech. 4: 2-6).

The 'wise virgins' enjoyed the power and enlightenment of the Holy Spirit, whereas the 'foolish virgins' did not. As already noted, the 'wise virgins' "trimmed their lamps": they did not need to light them! The word "trim" has the idea of adornment or to make presentable. Adjustments had to be made in view of the coming of the bridegroom, a lesson that we all need to remember in view of the coming of the Lord to take us home to heaven. But the 'foolish virgins' could clean and polish their lamps *ad infinitum*, but all their effort would be in vain - their lamps were "going out" (RV/JND), and they had no reserves on which to draw. In a word, they were not ready, in the same way that "if any man have not the Spirit of Christ, he is none of his" (Rom. 8: 9).

This raises a technical problem. Does this imply that the five "foolish virgins" were once in possession of the Holy Spirit, but no longer? The answer must be that the parable does not state that the 'virgins' were **themselves** indwelt by the Spirit (something, in any case, peculiar to the present 'church' dispensation), but rather that they all had, at one time, oil in **their lamps**. Five of them continued to live in the good of the Holy Spirit's witness to the return of Christ, and five of them failed to "endure unto the end", displaying their lack of reality.

Moreover, the Holy Spirit cannot be communicated to others. While there is no question of a limited supply of the Holy Spirit, either at the end-time, as here, or for ourselves today, for "God giveth not the Spirit by measure" (John 3: 34), the possession of the Holy Spirit is a personal matter. Hence the advice, "go ye rather to them that sell, and buy for yourselves" (v.9). It has been pointed out that while the Holy Spirit cannot be purchased, "the Bible does use the literary figure of buying salvation without money and without price (Isa. 55: 1)" (Wm.MacDonald). As H.A.Ironside points out, "The wise could not impart to them, but directed them to the source of supply". R.V.G.Tasker makes the observation that 'This uncompromising refusal is followed by the semi-ironical injunction 'go ye rather to them that sell, and buy for yourselves'. As it was now after midnight, it is not surprising that the purchase could not be made in time!"

d) Attending the feast, v.10
"And while they went to buy, the bridegroom came; and they that were ready went in **with him** to the marriage ('marriage feast', RV): and the door was shut". In an earlier parable, the Lord Jesus had said, "be ye also ready: for in such an hour as ye think not the Son of man cometh" (24: 44). There is a solemn contrast here. On the one hand, the Lord refers to **entry:** "they went in **with him** to the marriage", and to great joy. On the other, the Lord refers to **exclusion**: "and the door was shut", with consequent sorrow.

Unlike our wedding receptions (or 'wedding breakfasts'), Eastern marriage feasts last for a long time, but this 'wedding feast' will last for a thousand years! "The marriage feast is a fitting designation of the joy and blessing of Christ's earthly kingdom" (Wm. MacDonald).

e) Applying for entry, vv.11-12

"Afterward came also the other virgins, saying, Lord, Lord, open to us. But he answered and said, Verily I say unto you, I know you not". This, surely, is clear proof of their true spiritual status, and must be compared with the equally solemn words of the Lord Jesus earlier: "Not every one that saith unto me, Lord, Lord, shall enter into the kingdom of heaven; but he that doeth the will of my Father which is in heaven. Many will say to me in that day, Lord, Lord, have we not prophesied in thy name? And in thy name have cast out devils? And in thy name done many wonderful works? And then will I profess unto them, I never knew you: depart from me, ye that work iniquity" (Matt. 7: 21-23).

f) Applying the lesson, v.13

"Watch therefore, for ye know not the day nor the hour wherein the Son of man cometh". While, according to scholars, the words "wherein the Son of man cometh" are evidently omitted from 'the best manuscripts' (see RV/JND), there can be no doubt that the Lord's coming as "the Son of man" is the context of the entire 'Olivet Discourse'. Wm.Kelly's observation that "if the words "Son of man" were really to be read here, it would be hard indeed to account for them", is based on a very flimsy foundation.

The New Testament reminds us that "the time is short (not, 'time is short', but "*the* time is short): it remaineth, that both they that have wives be as though they had none: and they that weep, as though they wept not; and they that rejoice, as though they rejoice not; and they that buy, as though they possessed not; and they that use this world, as not abusing it (over-using it): for the fashion of this world passeth away" (1 Cor. 7: 29-31). James urges us to be like the 'wise virgins': "Be patient therefore, brethren unto the coming of the Lord...Be ye also patient; stablish your hearts: for the coming of the Lord draweth nigh" (James 5: 7-8).

In the words of Campbell Morgan, "The wise virgins are such as have no eyes, no thought, no care for anything except the Bridegroom, and the hour of His approach".

Is that true of us?

"Well done, thou good and faithful servant"

Read Chapter 25: 14-30

As we have already noticed, the division between Chapters 24 and 25 does not disguise the fact that the Lord is continuing His 'Olivet Discourse'. This is clear from the opening words of Chapter 25: "***Then*** shall the kingdom of heaven be likened unto ten virgins, which took their lamps, and went forth to meet the bridegroom" (v.1). The end of the discourse is clearly marked: "And it came to pass, when Jesus had ***finished all these sayings***." (26: 1).

We have also noted that Matthew 25 has three clearly marked constituent parts: *(1)* the parable of the virgins (vv.1-13); *(2)* the parable of the talents (vv.14-30); *(3)* the judgment of the living nations (vv.31-46). Attention is drawn to the sequence of the three passages:

- In the first case, the Lord Jesus is *"the bridegroom"* (vv.1, 5, 6), coming, not for His bride, but with His bride. There is a division: on the one hand, five 'wise virgins', and on the other, five 'foolish virgins'. The parable deals with joy in the kingdom.

- In the second case, the Lord Jesus is the *"man"* (v.14), representative of government and authority. He leaves as the "man", but he returns as the "lord" (vv.19, 20, 21, 22, 23, 24, 26). There is a division: on the one hand, industrious men, and on the other, an indolent man. The parable deals with fitness to rule in the kingdom, or preparation for rule.

- In the third case, the Lord Jesus is *"the King"* (vv.34, 40), exercising authority over all the nations of the earth. There is a division: on the one hand (the right hand), the sheep, and on the other (the left hand), the goats. The passage deals with the presence of Gentiles in the kingdom.

1) THE PARABLE OF THE VIRGINS, vv.1-13

As we have already noted above, the Lord Jesus returns as the Bridegroom, not to claim His bride, but **with** His bride. He will come "to be glorified ***in his saints***, and to be admired in ***all them that believe***" (2 Thess. 1: 10). While "the marriage of the Lamb" (Rev. 19: 7), will take place in heaven", the "marriage supper of the Lamb" (Rev. 19: 9) will take place on earth, and it is to this that the Lord refers in the parable: "then they that were ready went in with him to the marriage" (v.10, AV), or "to the marriage feast" (RV). The ten virgins must not be confused with the bride. They represent Jews waiting for their Messiah. They can be compared with John the Baptist who, in different circumstances, likened himself to "the friend of the bridegroom": "He that hath the bride is the bridegroom: but the friend of the bridegroom, which standeth and heareth him, rejoiceth greatly because of the bridegroom's voice..." (John 3: 29).

It has been nicely said that "Our Lord, in the great forecast of His return, immediately follows the parable of the Virgins with the parable of the Talents: that is, the command, 'Watch!' is immediately balanced and reinforced by the command, 'Work!'".

2) THE PARABLE OF THE TALENTS, vv.14-30

Since both chapters refer to the Lord's coming in glory (24: 30; 25: 31), all three sections of our current chapter must be *interpreted* in the context of His return to earth. But that does not mean that we cannot *apply* the Lord's teaching to ourselves, particularly in the case of the parable of the talents which embodies important principles of labour and reward. While like other 'kingdom parables', it refers to Israel's accountability, and its setting in the Olivet Discourse clearly emphasises its relation to the end-time, this must not blunt its practical keen edge for us today. We must learn from every part of God's Word, and it has been well said that whilst all Scripture is not *about* the church, all Scripture is *for* the church.

With this in mind, we must now address the details of the parable. They may be broadly summarised as follows: *(a)* responsibility at his departure (vv.14-15); *(b)* trading in his absence (vv.16-18); *(c)* reckoning at his coming (vv.19-30).

a) Responsibility at his departure, vv.14-15
"For the kingdom of heaven is as a man travelling into a far country (or 'For it is as when a man going into another country', RV; 'going away out of a country', JND), who called his own servants, and delivered unto them his goods. And unto one he gave five talents, to another two, and to another one; to every man according to his several ability; and straightway took his journey". Presumably the expression "his *own* servants (bond-servants)" stresses their special allegiance to him.

Since the parable commences with a man departing (*apodemeo*) for "a far country", and ends with the same man (now called "the lord of those servants") returning "after a long time" (v.19), we are certainly justified in highlighting lessons for ourselves. Like the parable of the pounds (Luke 19: 11-27), the parable of the talents can be said to span the time from the ascension of Christ to His return, and that, like the parable of the pounds, it sets out principles of labour and reward which are applicable both at the present time (the church age), and during the period between the rapture of the church and the Lord's return to earth to establish His kingdom.

While, however, there are points of similarity between the parable of the talents here and the parable of the pounds, there are distinct differences. For example the parable of the pounds was given to correct the idea that "the kingdom of God should immediately appear" (Luke 19: 11), whereas a long period lay ahead. The parable of the talents stresses rather that the "long time" is drawing to a close, which is in keeping with the overall teaching of the 'Olivet Discourse'. But more particularly, the parable of the talents stresses the diversity of ability ("to every man according to his ability") whereas the parable of the pounds stresses common responsibility (each servant had one pound and was told, "Occupy till I come"). The parable of the talents stresses that lesser ability does not lessen personal responsibility.

The "man travelling into a far country" called "his own servants, and delivered unto them his goods". They were to husband his resources, reminding us that we are all to be "good stewards of the manifold grace of God" (1 Pet. 4: 10). But more was involved than looking after the man's property on a repair and maintenance basis. The servants were to be concerned with expansion. This involved trading (v.16). With this in mind we must notice that certain amounts were given to the servants out of the man's "goods", but not indiscriminately: it was "to every man according to his several ability" (v.15). This can be illustrated from Paul's writings; "the manifestation of the Spirit is given to every man to profit withal. For to one (with certain "ability") is given by the Spirit the word of wisdom (a "talent"); to another (with certain "ability") the word of knowledge (a "talent") by the same Spirit…to another… to another…to another" (1 Cor. 12: 7-10). The word "talent" does not mean here, as it does today, ability ('he is very talented person'), but an amount out of the man's possessions (his "goods"). Presumably the talents represent the value of the goods. "Ability" is thus evidently something entirely separate from the "talents" (Campbell Morgan).

It should be said that this is not natural ability but rather divinely-given ability: "unto every one of us is given grace according to the measure of the gift of Christ" (Eph. 4: 7). This is not to say that the Lord does not use natural ability, but in the New Testament, "gifts" are divinely bestowed. They are spiritual gifts. In Paul's words, "I laboured more abundantly than they all: yet not I, but the grace of God which was with me" (1 Cor. 15: 10).

Well, what have **we** been given in trust? What talents have been committed to **us** by the "Lord of all?" Or, putting it differently, if, as scribes being "instructed unto the kingdom of heaven" we are going to be like the "householder, which bringeth out of his treasure things new and old" (Matt. 13: 52), what will we have to tell our fellow men? Campbell Morgan defines "the goods of the absent Lord" as follows: "His revelation of God and of man; His provision for man's great need; His perpetual call; His mediation; His dynamic for paralysed souls". The fact that the number of talents entrusted varies from case to case cannot mean that some understand one aspect of divine truth and others something else, but rather that different servants have differing levels of appreciation.

b) Trading in his absence, vv.16-18
While all three servants received "talents" (albeit in varying amounts), they responded differently. In two cases, there was industry (vv.16-17) and in one case there was indolence (v.18).

i) Industry. "Then he that received the five talents went and traded with **the same** (compare 2 Tim. 2: 2, "the things that thou hast heard of me… **the same** commit thou…"), and made them other five talents. And likewise he that had received two, he also gained other two" (vv.16-17). It could be said of these servants that they were "always abounding in the work of the Lord" (1 Cor. 15: 58), and that they were found "redeeming the time" (Eph. 5: 16). All of which reminds us that the Lord Jesus was the most industrious Servant of all. He traded in divine truth, and diminished "not a word" (Jer. 26: 2). The claims on His time were so great that His relatives said, "He is beside himself" (Mark 3: 21).

ii) Indolence. "But he that received one went and digged in the earth, and hid his lord's money" (v.18). The wording is most significant: "hid his **lord's money**". This could not be said of the assembly at Thessalonica: "For from you sounded out the **word of the Lord** (it was **His** word) not only in Macedonia and Achaia, but also in every place your faith to Godward is spread abroad; so that we need not to speak any thing". The word "you" ("For from you") is plural. So they **all** 'rolled up their sleeves' and got involved in this great work of evangelising the area. They certainly did not hide their "lord's money!" They fulfilled, for their part, the great commission, "Go ye therefore, and teach all nations, baptizing them in the name of the Father, and of the Son, and of the Holy Ghost; teaching them to observe all things whatsoever I have commanded you" (Matt. 28: 19-20). The Thessalonians certainly did not hide their "lord's money" in "***the earth***", where it was 'out of sight and out of mind!' Sadly, it is possible for believers to bury their "lord's money" so effectively, that nobody knows what has been committed to them. Even worse, the indolent servant buried his "lord's money" quite deliberately. He had no intention of trading like his colleagues (v.16).

c) *Reckoning at his coming, vv.19-30*
Amongst other things, we should notice the following *(i)* the return; *(ii)* the report; *(iii)* the reward; *(iv)* the rebuke.

i) The return
"After a long time the lord of those servants cometh, and reckoneth with them" (v.19). It has been said that "it is in the very nature of a trust that a reckoning-day must come, when a report on how the trust has been exercised has to be rendered". In New Testament language, "we must all appear before the judgment seat of Christ; that every one may receive the things done in his body, according to that he hath done, whether it be good or bad" (2 Cor. 5: 10). The "long time" should not cause *us* to say, "My lord delayeth his coming" so that His return takes place "in a day when he looketh not for him, and in an hour that he is not aware of" (Matt. 24: 48-50).

ii) The report
"He that had received five talents came and brought other five talents, saying, Lord, thou deliveredest unto me five talents: behold, I have gained beside them five talents more...He also that had received two talents came and said, Lord, thou deliveredst unto me two talents: behold, I have gained two other talents beside them" (vv.20, 22). This raises an important question: 'If the talents represent, not ability imparted *to* the Lord's servants, but truth deposited *with* them, how does it increase? Truth does not evolve: it is "the faith which was ***once delivered*** unto the saints" (Jude v.3). The answer must be that while truth in itself does not increase, the number of people who possess and enjoy it can and does increase. See Acts 19: 20, "So mightily grew the word of God and

prevailed". The 'gain' might be in terms of souls saved, and it might be in terms of believers' spiritual growth (2 Pet. 3: 18).

We can therefore say that through the 'trading' of these two servants, the interests of their lord had been extended. Without forgetting the immediate context of the parable, the return of the Lord "in power and great glory" (24: 30), but remembering that its principles are applicable to ourselves, these verses serve to remind us that "every one of us shall give account of himself to God" (Rom. 14: 12). We might well sing:

> *Must I go - and empty handed?*
> *Thus my dear Redeemer meet?*
> *Not one day of service give Him,*
> *Lay no trophy at His feet?*

We must notice that both servants called him "Lord". But so did the third servant! (v.24). But, clearly, there is a big difference between them. The first two servants, called him "Lord" with justification, but this was certainly not true in the case of the third servant, reminding us that the "Lord of all" said, "And why call ye me, Lord, Lord, and do not the things which I say?" (Luke 6: 46).

iii) The reward
To both the 'five-talent servant' and the 'two-talent servant', the lord said, "Well done, good and faithful servant; thou hast been faithful over a few things, I will make thee ruler over many things: enter thou into the joy of thy lord" (vv.21, 23). We should notice what the lord says to his servants, what he does for them, and what it will mean for them:

- He **addresses them** as "good and faithful" **servants** who had been "faithful over a **few things**". The word "good" (*agathos*) means 'beneficial in its effect' (W.E.Vine). We must notice that both men, although trading with different amounts, are rewarded in the same way. One does not receive a higher commendation than the other. To put it simply, the 'big preacher' (no disrespect or criticism intended) does not receive a greater reward than the faithful Sunday School teacher or the faithful personal worker. Both are equally commended and equally rewarded.

We are reminded, however, that "it is required in stewards, that a man be found faithful" (1 Cor. 4: 2). God counted Paul faithful (1 Tim. 1: 12), and at the end of his life, the apostle declared that he had "kept the faith" (2 Tim. 4: 7). The expression "a few things" does not mean that they were either inconsiderable or inconsequential, but that they seemed so inconspicuous when compared with the vast reward bestowed by "the lord of those servants" (v.19). Compare Romans 8: 18, "For I reckon that the sufferings of this present time are not worthy to be compared with the glory which shall be revealed in us"; 2 Corinthians 4: 17, "For our light affliction (how about that!), which is but for a moment, worketh for us a far more exceeding and eternal weight of glory".

- He **advances them** to **rulers** over "**many things**". From servants to rulers! Compare Matthew 19: 28, "Verily I say unto you, That ye which have followed me, in the regeneration when the Son of man shall sit in the throne of his glory, ye also shall sit upon twelve thrones, judging the twelve tribes of Israel". But, in principle, this is no exception: humble unostentatious service always leads to exaltation. See, for example, 1 Pet. 5: 5.

- He **expresses his joy**: "enter thou into the joy of **thy** lord". He acknowledges that they were quite justified in addressing him as "Lord". For obvious reasons, this is not said to the third man. While we could understand this to be the bliss of heaven ("in thy presence is fulness of joy; at thy right hand there are pleasures for evermore", Psalm 16: 11), the passage does seem to refer to the lord's personal joy, reminding us that the Lord Jesus will be "anointed with the oil of gladness" above His "fellows" (Heb. 1: 9). Since the writer refers here to the Lord's reign ("Thy throne, O God is for ever and ever") the "oil of gladness" refers to His joy in the kingdom. His will be the greatest joy, but His servants will share 'the joy of their Lord!' See also Hebrews 12: 2.

iv) The rebuke

"Then he which had received the one talent came and said, Lord, I knew thee that thou art a hard man, reaping where thou hast not sown, and gathering where thou hast not strawed ('scattered', RV): and I was afraid, and went and hid thy talent in the earth: lo, there thou hast that is thine. His lord answered and said unto him, Thou wicked and slothful servant", and took him up on his own assessment: "thou knewest that I reap where I sowed not. And gather where I have not strawed ('scattered', RV): thou oughtest therefore to have put my money to the exchangers ('bankers', RV; 'money-changers', JND), and then at my coming I should have receive my own with usury ('interest', RV)" (vv.24-27).

Matthew

All three servants called him "Lord", but the first two understood the title in a completely different way from the third. In fact, they totally disproved the third man's assessment. It was certainly not a "hard man" (v.24) who said, "Well done, good and faithful servant" (vv.21, 23) He gladly gave far more than he gained. In fact the first two servants kept what they gained (v.28), and were given even more (v.29). The third servant hadn't squandered his talent on a risky enterprise, or spent it on himself. He hadn't acted in the unseemly way and begun to "smite his fellowservants, and to eat and drink with the drunken" (Matt. 24: 49). He had simply done nothing, and that earned him the censure "thou wicked and slothful servant", as opposed to "thou good and faithful servant" in the first two cases. This is certainly a warning to **us**. We can be "wicked and slothful servants for "to him that knoweth to do good, and doeth it not, to him it is **sin**" (James 4: 17).

But exactly who is the "wicked and slothful" servant in the parable? We must now endeavour to ascertain his spiritual status. This is not altogether an easy task. It could be argued (and has been argued in an article published in "The Word") that he was one of the lord's "own servants" (v.14), and that "to no unbeliever is any such trust ever committed". Furthermore, that "if the first two servants are regenerate, and the third is not" then "so far from our Lord's aim being attained, there is no warning to a child of God at all". Still further, that "if the third servant is a lost soul, and the 'outer darkness' is eternal destruction, then salvation by works is established; for his whole condemnation rests on his not having multiplied his talent, and on that alone". Moreover, it is argued that "all three servants are judged together, on one spot and at one time, proving it to be the Judgment Seat of Christ: unbelievers are not judged until the Great White Throne, a thousand years later". Finally, it is argued that "while the faithful servants share the full blaze of the coming Kingdom, the slothful servant is expelled into the 'outer darkness' of the Parousia clouds, and gnashing his teeth over lost opportunities, loses the Kingdom".

We must say in reply, that the parable concerns the review and assessment of service, not at the judgment seat of Christ, but at the coming of the Lord to earth in glory. While, as we have seen, the parable serves to illustrate unchanging **principles** of labour and reward, and therefore provides important lessons for believers today, it refers particularly to servants of God on earth immediately prior to the millennial reign of Christ. The context is "the kingdom of heaven", which refers to the sphere of profession (see, for example, Matt. 13:

31, 33). This was the case with the ten virgins (vv.1-13), and it is the case here. The man passes as a servant, but he has no concept of the master he professes to serve (vv.24-25). In fact, his excuses are downright insulting. He makes no attempt to trade on behalf of his master (v.27). While, as some observe, the word "wicked" is used in the New Testament of a believer (1 Cor. 5: 13), the "outer darkness" and "weeping and gnashing of teeth (indicating extreme suffering)", can hardly refer to anything other than divine judgment on an unregenerate man. Compare Matthew 8: 12.

While the subject is absorbing, H.A.Ironside rightly says that "Nothing is gained by quibbling as to the exact dispensational place of this lesson.... The important thing is to see that we use aright what we have received of the Lord". This is a good note to conclude our study, and do so with reference to what Wm.MacDonald calls "the fixed law in the spiritual realm": "unto every one that hath shall be given, and he shall have abundance: but from him that hath not shall be taken away even that which he hath" (v.29). Wm.MacDonald continues: "Those who desire to be used for God's glory are given the means to do it. The more they do, the more they are enabled to do for Him. On the other hand, we lose what we don't use. Atrophy is the reward of indolence".

"Before him shall be gathered all nations"

Read Chapter 25: 31-46
As we have already noticed in recent studies, Matthew 25 continues the Lord's 'Olivet Discourse' which commences in the previous chapter, and deals with events associated with the return of the Lord Jesus to earth "with power and great glory" (24: 30).

We have also noted that Matthew 25 has three clearly marked constituent parts: *(1)* the parable of the virgins (vv.1-13); *(2)* the parable of the talents (vv.14-30); *(3)* the judgment of the living nations (vv.31-46). Attention is drawn again to the sequence of the three passages:

- In the first case, the Lord Jesus is *"the bridegroom"* (vv.1, 5, 6), coming, not for His bride, but with His bride. There is a division: on the one hand, five 'wise virgins', and on the other, five 'foolish virgins'. The parable deals with joy in the kingdom (v.10), and exclusion from the kingdom (vv.11-12).

- In the second case, the Lord Jesus is the *"man"* (v.14), representative of government and authority. He leaves as the "man", but he returns as the "lord" (vv.19, 20, 21, 22, 23, 24, 26). There is a division: on the one hand, industrious men, and on the other, an indolent man. The parable deals with preparation for rule in the kingdom (vv.21, 23), and, again, exclusion from the kingdom (v.30).

- In the third case, the Lord Jesus is *"the King"* (vv.34, 40), exercising authority over all the nations of the earth. There is a division: on the one hand (the right hand), the sheep, and on the other (the left hand), the goats. The passage deals with the presence of Gentiles in the kingdom, and, for the third time, exclusion from the kingdom.

1) THE PARABLE OF THE VIRGINS, vv.1-13

As we have already noted above, the Lord Jesus returns as the Bridegroom, not to claim His bride, but **with** His bride. He will come "to be glorified *in his saints*, and to be admired in *all them that believe*" (2 Thess. 1: 10), and his saints will "appear *with him* in glory" (Col. 3: 4). While "the marriage of the Lamb" (Rev. 19: 7), will take place in heaven, the "marriage supper of the Lamb" (Rev. 19: 9) will take place on earth, and it is to this that the Lord refers in the parable: "then they that were ready went in with him to the marriage" (v.10, AV), or "to the marriage feast" (RV). The ten virgins represent Jews waiting for their Messiah. There is a striking correspondence between the two classes of people in attendance when the Lord Jesus first came (the "chief priests and scribes" on the one hand, and Simon and Anna on the other), and the two classes in attendance when He returns (the 'foolish' and 'wise virgins').

2) THE PARABLE OF THE TALENTS, vv.14-30

If the parable of the virgins concludes with the word "Watch" (v.13), then the parable of the talents could be said to carry the command 'Work'. While like other 'kingdom parables', the parable of the talents must be *interpreted* in relation to Israel, and its setting in the Olivet Discourse clearly emphasises its relation to the end-time, this does not mean that we cannot *apply* the Lord's teaching to ourselves. The parable embodies important and timeless principles of labour and reward, reminding us that we can profit from every part of God's Word, whatever its immediate context.

3) THE JUDGMENT OF THE LIVING NATIONS, vv.31-46

It has been nicely said that "As the Bridegroom, He has rejoiced over His bride; as Messiah, He has delivered and judged His people Israel; and now, as the universal Lord (we might well say, 'universal King' here), He calls the nations before Him for judgment" (Archie Payne, *When the King Comes*). In considering these verses we should give attention to the following: *(a)* the setting of the judgment (v.31); *(b)* the splendour of the Judge (v.31); *(c)* the separation by the Judge (vv.32-33); *(d)* the sovereignty of the Judge (v.34). *(e)* the sanction of the Judge, (vv.34-40); *(f)* the sentence by the Judge (vv.41-46).

a) The setting of the judgment, v.31

It will take place "When the Son of man shall **come in his glory**, and all the holy angels with him". The judgment of the living nations will take place after the Lord has been "revealed from heaven with his mighty angels, in flaming fire, taking vengeance on them that know not God, and that obey not the gospel of our Lord Jesus Christ" (2 Thess. 1: 7-8). This is described in Revelation 19: 11-21. Having utterly defeated the armies of the world, He will deal with the nations they represent. With this in mind, we should carefully distinguish between three future sessions of judgment, of which this is the second. They are, in chronological order:

- ***The judgment seat of Christ***: "For we must all appear before the judgment seat of Christ" (2 Cor. 5: 10).

- ***The judgment of the living nations.*** This is described here: "When the Son of man shall come in his glory, and all the holy angels with him, then shall he sit upon the throne of his glory: and before him shall be gathered all nations".

- ***The judgment of the wicked dead:*** "And I saw a great white throne, and him that sat on it" (Rev. 20: 11).

In passing, we must also distinguish between "the day of Christ" (referring to heaven and reward), the "day of the Lord" (referring to earth and judgment), and the "day of God" (referring to the eternal state). Returning to our current subject, we can look at the three sessions of judgment in the following way:

- ***As to people.*** The judgment seat of Christ concerns believers of the church age; the judgment of the living nations is self-explanatory, and so is the judgment of the wicked dead.

- **As to place.** The judgment seat of Christ will take place *in heaven*; the judgment of the living nations will take place *on earth*; the judgment of the wicked dead will take place *in space.*

- **As to period.** The judgment seat of Christ will take place **after the rapture**: see 1 Corinthians 4: 5, "Therefore judge nothing before the time, until the Lord come, who both will bring to light the hidden things of darkness, and will make manifest the counsels of the hearts: and then shall every man have praise of God"; the judgment of the living nations will take place **prior to the Millennium**; the judgment of the wicked dead will take place **after the Millennium**.

- **As to purpose.** The judgment seat of Christ is concerned with **the reward of the saints**; the judgment of the living nations is concerned with **place in the kingdom**; the judgment of the wicked dead is concerned with the **final sentence on sinners**.

b) The splendour of the Judge, v.31

"When the Son of man shall come *in his glory*, and all the holy angels with him, then shall he sit upon *the throne of his glory*". This is none other than the very "Son of man" who came "to seek and to save that which was lost" (Luke 19: 10), and who said "as Moses lifted up the serpent in the wilderness, even so must the **Son of man** be lifted up" (John 3: 14). He also said, "When ye have lifted up the **Son of man**, then shall ye know that I am he, and that I do nothing of myself; but as my Father hath taught me, I speak these things" (John 8: 28). (This was fulfilled on the day of Pentecost when thousands of the very people who cried "Crucify him" were brought to believe on Him as "both Lord and Christ", A.W.Pink). The world last saw "the Son of man" on a cross with all its shame and brutality. The world will next see Him sitting upon "the throne of his glory". The ancient prophesy will then be fulfilled: "I saw in the night visions, and, behold, one like the Son of man came with the clouds of heaven...And there was given him dominion, and glory, and a kingdom, that all people, nations, and languages, should serve him: his dominion is an everlasting dominion, which shall not pass away, and his kingdom that which shall not be destroyed" (Dan. 7: 13-14).

In the garden of Gethsemane, the Lord Jesus declined to summon "More than twelve legions of angels" (Matt. 26: 53), but He will "come in his glory, and *all* the holy angels with him". If one angel destroyed 185,000 Assyrians in one night (Isaiah 37: 36), we cannot begin to estimate the immense fire power at the Lord's command when He comes "with *all* the holy angels!" See also Matthew 16: 27. At His birth, the angels went "away...*into* heaven" (Luke 2: 15). At His revelation, they will come with Him "*from* heaven" (2 Thess. 1: 7).

We should also note the expression, "the throne of his glory". This is His millennial throne, to which He referred in saying: "To him that overcometh will I grant to sit with me in my throne, even as I also overcame, and am set down with my Father in his throne" (Rev. 3: 21). His words, "sit with me in my throne", refer to the coming of the Lord to reign: "When Christ, who is our life shall appear, then shall ye also appear with him in glory" (Col. 3: 4). The saints will be on 'public display', with not a single hint of embarrassment!

c) *The separation by the Judge, v.32-33*
"And before him shall be gathered all nations: and he shall separate them one from another, as a shepherd divideth his sheep from the goats ('the sheep from the goats', JND): and he shall set the sheep on his right hand, but the goats on the left". We are reminded that as now, so then: the "good shepherd" knows His sheep! "Sheep and goats are often herded together, however the character of the two animals are different. A shepherd would separate the animals in the evening before enclosing them in their pens" (supplied by Justin Waldron).

It should be said at this point that the customary title given to this passage, 'The Judgment of the Living Nations', could be slightly misleading! Bearing in mind that the Lord's people will be "hated of *all nations* for my name's sake" (Matt. 24: 9), it is hardly likely that men and women will be gathered by nationality, and that some *nations* in their entirety will be classed as "sheep" and others as "goats". Campbell Morgan puts it clearly: "It is a separation on the basis of character....In that hour the distinction between Frenchmen, Englishmen, Germans, and others will be secondary...The first process of the King will be thus to gather together, and then to institute a new separation, not between tribes and families and nationalities as in the past, but between those whom he designates sheep and goats". In other words, it will not be the nations that will be separated, but the individuals in those nations. The case of Rahab illustrates the point. She gave shelter and protection to the men of Israel, and all in her house were saved when Jericho fell with the complete destruction of all the other inhabitants. She then entered the kingdom (Joshua 6: 21-25). It should also be said that "nations are ultimately resolved into individuals, and, as individuals, enjoy either blessing or the eternal torments of the lost" (Archie Payne).

These verses remind us that "the Father judgeth no man, but hath committed all judgment unto the Son...And hath given him authority to execute judgment also, because he is the Son of man" (John 5: 22, 27). C.I.Scofield makes the interesting observation that "'Son of man' is His racial name as the representative Man...as 'Son of David' is distinctively His Jewish name, and 'Son of God' His divine name". His title "Son of man" indicates, not only His true humanity, but His perfect humanity. David tells us that God made man "a little lower than the angels" and made "him to have dominion over the works of thy hands" (Psalm 8: 5-6), and therefore the Lord's title, "Son of man", refers to His universal headship and His perfect humanity. His perfection therefore qualifies Him to "execute judgment" in the same way that when "no man was found worthy to open and read the book, neither to look thereon", because all men were subject to the judgments in the book, John was told, "Weep not: behold, the Lion of the tribe of Juda, the Root of David, hath prevailed to open the book, and to loose the seven seals thereof" (Rev. 5: 5). God "has appointed a day (so He has a timetable), in the which he will judge the world (*oikoumene*: the 'inhabited earth' but referring to its inhabitants) in righteousness **by that man** whom he hath ordained; whereof he hath given assurance unto all men, in that he hath raised him from the dead" (Acts 17: 31).

Here, the living nations are assembled before His throne on earth, as noted, before the Millennium. As we will see, the Judge divides the nations with reference to their treatment of His "brethren" (v.40) during the dark days of the "great tribulation" (Matt. 24: 21). His "brethren"' are the remnant of Israel "which keep the commandments of God, and have the testimony of Jesus Christ" (Rev. 12: 17), of whom the Lord said, "Then shall they deliver you up to be afflicted, and shall kill you: and ye shall be hated of all nations for my name's sake" (Matt. 24: 9). The division of the nations between "ye blessed" and "ye cursed" (vv.34, 41), is the final fulfilment of Genesis 12: 3, "And I will bless them that bless thee, and curse him that curseth thee".

d) *The sovereignty of the Judge, vv.34*
"Then shall the **King** (the first occasion on which the Lord Jesus explicitly refers to Himself as a King) say unto them on his right hand..." Another king ("the son of David, king in Jerusalem") said, "Where **the word of a king** is

there is power: and who may say unto him, What doest thou? (Eccl. 8: 4). Isaiah saw "the King, the **LORD of hosts**" (Isaiah 6: 5). What power!

Matthew's Gospel commences with the enquiry, "Where is he that is born king of the Jews" (Matt. 2: 2), and ends with that same King on a cross: "And sitting down they watched him there; and set up over his head his accusation written, THIS IS JESUS THE KING OF THE JEWS" (Matt. 27: 36-37). But He is the "King of Israel" (John 1: 49), the "King of nations" (Rev. 15: 3, JND), and the "KING OF KINGS, AND LORD OF LORDS" (Rev. 19: 16). He is "the prince (singular: *archon*, meaning 'Ruler') of the kings (plural) of the earth" (Rev. 1: 5).

The title "King of nations" (Rev. 15: 3, JND) is particularly applicable here since "before him shall be gathered all nations" (v.32). The power of the King will be readily recognised: "Forasmuch as there is none like unto thee, O LORD; thou art great, and thy name is great in might. Who would not fear thee, O King of nations? for to thee doth it appertain: forasmuch as among all the wise men of the nations, and in all their kingdoms, there is none like unto thee" (Jer. 10: 6-7). God's people today can rejoice, as they will in the future, that "The LORD hath prepared his throne in the heavens; and his kingdom ruleth over all" (Ps 103.19). They can say, "Sing praises to God...For God is the King of all the earth: sing ye praises with understanding. God reigneth over the heathen: God sitteth upon the throne of his holiness" (Psalm 47: 6-8).

e) The sanction of the Judge, vv.34-40
These verses comprise three stanzas: *(i)* blessing bestowed (vv.34-36); *(ii)* surprise expressed (vv.37-39); *(iii)* explanation given (v.40).

i) Blessing bestowed, vv.34-36. "Then shall the King say unto them on his right hand, Come, ye blessed of my Father, inherit the kingdom prepared for you from the foundation of the world: for I was an hungred, and ye gave me meat: I was thirsty, and ye gave me drink: I was a stranger, and ye took me in: naked, and ye clothed me: I was sick and ye visited me: I was in prison, and ye came unto me". At the close of the end-time, God's earthly people "will be faced by a tremendous combine of nations under the leadership of the Beast. The sufferings of the people during that period are described as being without parallel in the history of mankind (Dan. 12: 1)" (Archie Payne). While the entire nation will be involved, the expression "my brethren" evidently refers to the godly remnant who will bear witness for God during this terrible period. J.M.Flanigan explains that the Lord's millennial kingdom "will be a righteous kingdom into which only the righteous (v.34) will enter, and the purpose of this judgment is to separate from the nations those who have responded to the message of the remnant, the gospel of the kingdom...Many Gentiles will have heard and believed that message, 'a great multitude, which no man could number, of all nations, and kindreds, and people, and tongues' (Rev. 7: 9). They will 'have washed their robes, and made them white in the blood of the Lamb' (Rev. 7: 14). Scattered among the nations, they have received and befriended the godly remnant of preachers, and their attitude to them is accounted as their attitude to the King Himself". This is not a case of salvation by works. Those blessed in this way have displayed their faith by their works.

The "right hand" is synonymous with blessing and honour. See, for example, Psalm 110: 1. The "kingdom prepared for you from the foundation of the world" is the kingdom described in Daniel 7: 13-14. There can be little doubt that these people will constitute "the nations of them that are saved" who will "walk in the light" of "that great city, the holy Jerusalem" which John saw "descending out of heaven from God" (Rev. 21: 24 cf. vv.10-11). Later generations in the millennial kingdom will rebel and be destroyed (Rev. 20: 7-10).

ii) Surprise expressed, vv.37-39. "Then shall the righteous answer him, saying, Lord, when saw we thee an hungred, and fed thee? Or thirsty, and gave thee drink? When saw we thee a stranger, and took thee in? or naked, and clothed thee? Or when saw we thee sick, or in prison, and came unto thee?" While some suggest that the Gentiles involved seem unconscious of any relationship between the godly remnant and the Lord, hence their questions, this is hardly tenable. What they did not understand was the way in which the Lord identified Himself *so personally* with His suffering people.

iii) Explanation given, v.40. "And the king shall answer and say unto them, Verily I say unto you, Inasmuch as ye have done it unto one of the least of these my brethren, ye have done it unto me". God had said of Israel, "he that toucheth you toucheth the apple of his eye" (Zech. 2: 8), The "King" is deeply appreciative of kindness bestowed upon "these my brethren", and deeply sensitive to their hurt. As already noted, at the beginning of the 'Olivet Discourse', the Lord had foretold the sufferings of His witnesses (Matt. 24: 9), but He now identifies Himself with them in their suffering, just as He had done when His people were hounded and persecuted by Saul of Tarsus: "Saul, Saul, why persecutest thou me?" (Acts 9: 4).

The future setting of the passage must not make us overlook the current need to help and befriend suffering and disadvantaged saints. "Remember them that are in bonds, as bound with them" (Heb. 13: 3). Correct words are not good enough. See 1 John 3: 17-18. The Lord's words are certainly applicable today: "Inasmuch as ye have done it unto one of the least of these my brethren, ye have done it unto me".

f) The sentence by the Judge, vv.41-46
These verses also comprise three stanzas: *(i)* cursing bestowed (vv.41-43); *(ii)* surprise expressed (v.44); *(iii)* explanation given (v.45-46).

i) Cursing bestowed, vv.41-43. "Then shall he say also unto them on the left hand, Depart from me, ye cursed, into everlasting fire, prepared for the devil and his angels: for I was an hungred, and ye gave me no meat: I was thirsty, and ye gave me no drink: I was a stranger, and ye took me not in: naked, and ye clothed me not: sick and in prison, and ye visited me not". If the "sheep" are told "**Come**, ye **blessed** of my Father, inherit the kingdom **prepared for you** from the foundation of the world" (v.34), then the "goats" are told, "**Depart** from me, ye **cursed**, into everlasting fire, **prepared for the devil** and his angels" (v.41).

As Wm.MacDonald points out, "the kingdom is said to have been prepared for the righteous from the foundation of the world (v.34), whereas hell is said to have been prepared for the devil and his angels (v.41). God's desire is that men should be blessed; hell was never intended for the human race (judgment is God's "strange work", Isaiah 28: 21). But if man willfully refuses life, he necessarily chooses death". The words, "Depart...into everlasting fire" strongly suggests the eternal judgment of the "lake of fire" rather than the intermediate *hades.*

ii) Surprise expressed, vv.44. "Then shall they also answer him, saying, Lord when saw we thee an hungred, or athirst, or a stranger, or naked, or sick, or in prison, and did not minister unto thee?"

iii)   Explanation given, v.45-46. "Then shall he answer them, saying, Verily I say unto you, Inasmuch as ye did it not to one of the least of these, ye did it not to me. And these shall go away into everlasting punishment: but the righteous into life eternal". It should be carefully noted that the words "everlasting" and "eternal" translate the same word (*aionios*). The punishment here is therefore "not temporary...but final, and, accordingly, the phraseology shows that its purpose is not remedial but retributive" (W.E.Vine).

From all this we now turn to events leading to "the King of the Jews" hanging upon a cross. But how wonderful that the Lord revealed beforehand that His coming betrayal, suffering and death were not the end, and that He would return to "sit upon the throne of his glory".

THE GOSPEL OF MATTHEW

"She hath wrought a good work on me"

Read Chapter 26: 1-16
In the words of J.C.Ryle, "We now approach the closing scene of our Lord Jesus Christ's earthly ministry. Hitherto we have read of His sayings and doings: we are now about to read of His sufferings and death. Hitherto we have seen Him as the great Prophet, we are now about to see Him as the great High Priest".

But there is more. Matthew's Gospel begins with the words, "The book of the generations of Jesus Christ, the son of David, the son of Abraham" (Matt. 1: 1), and in our first study we noted that Matthew refers to Him as "the son of David" before "the son of Abraham". In this connection, we explained that David is mentioned first, because it is Matthew's purpose to emphasise **the kingship of Christ.** In fact, the New Testament commences with "Jesus Christ, the son of David" and ends with "I am the root and offspring of David" (Rev. 22: 16). It is noteworthy that in Matthew's following genealogy, only David is mentioned as having office: he is "David **the king**" (v.6).

Referring again to the order of the names, we noted that the title "the son of David, the son of Abraham", is an appropriate introduction to the Gospel. The "son of David" was **Solomon**, and the glory and strength of his kingdom is proverbial. The expression, "son of David", therefore points to a glorious reign. The Lord Jesus is "greater than Solomon", and so He will ultimately "sit upon the throne of his glory" (Matt. 25: 31). Matthew **Chapters 1-25** are occupied with the King and His kingdom. The "son of Abraham" was **Isaac**, and he was placed on the altar. The expression, "son of Abraham", therefore points to the Lord's death and resurrection, and Matthew **Chapters 26-28** are occupied with these closing scenes of His life on earth. It should be noted that Matthew does not record the ascension. He emphasises His earthly kingdom.

Matthew

But there is still more. As we commence to read these closing three chapters, humanity was about to perpetrate its darkest crime, but at the same time, God was about to display His deepest love. We notice that the Lord reminded His disciples that "after two days is the feast of Passover" (v.2) leading us to exclaim in Tersteegen's words:

> *The Lamb was slain! let us adore,*
> *And all His gracious mercy own,*
> *And prostrate now and evermore*
> *Before His pierced feet fall down:*
> *Serve without dread, with reverence love*
> *The Lord, whose boundless grace we prove.*

Matthew 26: 1-16 may be divided as follows: *(1)* the feast that prefigures Him (vv.1-2); *(2)* the death they planned for Him (vv.3-5); *(3)* the love poured out to Him (vv.6-13); *(4)* the value they placed upon Him (vv.14-16).

1) THE FEAST THAT PREFIGURES HIM, vv.1-2

Having completed His 'Olivet Discourse' ("When Jesus had finished all these sayings": compare 7: 28; 11: 1; 13: 53; 19: 1), then comes a pause, a hush as of a shadow falling upon the spirit, and quietly the words fall from the lips of the greatest of all Prophets - His last prophecy: "Ye know that after two days is the feast of the Passover, and the Son of man is betrayed (delivered up, JND) to be crucified" (Archie Payne). As Justin Waldron points out, "He wants it to be clearly understood that it was not the crafty plans of the Sanhedrin (vv.3-4), but the Lord's will and word that decided the time of His arrest and death".

This was the fourth Passover (they were held in April, our reckoning) during the public ministry of the Lord Jesus. Only John mentions the first two: see 2: 13, 23 (A.D.27), 6: 4 (A.D.28), the third is not mentioned at all (A.D.29), and all four Evangelists mention the fourth (A.D.30). It was to be the most momentous of all passover feasts. The Saviour said, "With desire have I desired to eat *this* passover with you before I suffer" (Luke 22: 15). He knew exactly what was to happen. But although cognizant of all that lay before Him, He "was not rebellious, neither turned away back" (Isaiah 50: 5). Israel's calendar began with the death of the lamb (Exod. 12: 2), and our spiritual life begins with "the precious blood of Christ, as of a lamb without blemish and without spot" (1 Pet. 1: 19). The true 'Passover Lamb' was soon to die. He was about to accomplish "eternal redemption" (Heb. 9: 12).

We must notice that the feasts of Passover and Unleavened Bread are never divided in Scripture: "After two days was the feast of the passover, and of unleavened bread" (Mark 14: 1); "Now the feast of unleavened bread drew nigh, which is called the Passover" (Luke 22: 1); "Christ our passover is sacrificed for us: therefore let us keep the feast (not referring to the Lord's supper)…with the unleavened bread of sincerity and truth" (1 Cor. 5: 7-8). Since in Scripture, leaven is always a picture of evil (including Matt. 13: 33) in its various forms, we learn that godliness and purity are required in the lives of those redeemed by the blood of Christ.

At the same time, we cannot escape the fact that at the very time the Jewish people were symbolically proclaiming their separation from evil (in the Bible, as noted above, 'leaven' is always a picture of evil), their leaders were planning the greatest evil in their entire history.

The words "after **two days** is the feast of the passover" (see also Mark 14: 1) have perplexed not a few in view of the fact that John has "Jesus **six days** before the Passover came to Bethany" where Mary took "a pound of spikenard, very costly, and anointed the feet of Jesus" (John 12: 1-8). It has been suggested that the two passages describe two separate, though similar, incidents, but even so it is difficult to escape the overall similarity between John and Matthew with Mark.

The problem is easily resolved. The fact that Matthew 26 commences with the Lord's declaration that "after two days is the feast of the Passover" whereas John 12 commences with "Jesus six days before the Passover came to Bethany", makes it clear that His anointing as related by Matthew (and Mark) took place four days before the Lord told His disciples definitely that in two days He would be crucified. Having recorded the Lord's prediction, two days before the passover, of His coming death (v.1-2), and noted the intention of the religious leaders to take Him "by subtilty, and kill him" (vv.3-5), Matthew takes us back four days to show how this would take place: having witnessed the anointing of the Lord Jesus, Judas had gone to "the chief priests" to negotiate His betrayal. As A.W.Pink points out, "Judas protested against Mary's extravagance and the Lord rebuked him (John 12: 4-8), and it was immediately afterward that the traitor went and made his awful pact with the priests. In Matthew's words, "**Then** one of the twelve, called Judas Iscariot, went unto the chief priests" (v.14). Compare Mark 14: 10. As G.Campbell Morgan points out, the Lord said, "after two days is the feast of the passover, and the Son of man is betrayed to be crucified",

Matthew

whereas the religious leaders said, "Not on the feast day", and events four days previously showed who would be right (the Lord referred to His burial, v.12), and who would be wrong. During the intervening four days, Judas had thirty pieces of silver in his pocket as he watched for a suitable opportunity to betray the Lord, and then events at the Passover forced his hand: it was there that He realised that the Lord was fully aware of his intentions (vv.21-25). Judas had to act.

2) THE DEATH THEY PLANNED FOR HIM, vv.3-5

"Then assembled together the chief priests, and the scribes, and the elders of the people, unto the palace (*aule* meaning 'court', perhaps a courtyard used as a meeting-place) of the high priest, who was called Caiaphas" (v.3). This was evidently an official meeting of the Sanhedrin. Caiaphas, appointed by the Romans, was in office between A.D.18-36. We are told that there were twenty-eight high priests between 37 B.C and A.D. 67. The Jewish Council, with its 71 members, "took counsel together in order that they might seize Jesus by subtilty and kill him (this was not the first time that they had met with this in view: see John 11: 47); but they said, Not in the feast" (vv.4-5, JND). The A.V. has "and *consulted* that they might take Jesus by subtilty", but they did not consult the Scriptures! (T.Miller). But their plans to postpone the death of the Lord Jesus until after the Passover crowds had dispersed could not prevail over the divine programme. He was "delivered by the determinate counsel and foreknowledge of God" (Acts 2: 23), and there is deep significance in the words, "then came the day of unleavened bread, when the passover ***must*** be killed" (Luke 22: 7). His death could not be either hastened (Luke 4: 28-30; John 8: 59; 10: 31, 39), or delayed.

J.C.Ryle puts it nicely: "They thought to have put Him to death privily, and without observation; and instead, they were compelled to crucify Him publicly, and before the whole nation of the Jews. They thought to have silenced His disciples, and stopped their teaching; and instead, they supplied them with a text and a subject for evermore. So easy is it for God to cause 'the wrath of man to praise him' (Psalm 76: 10)".

Luke tells us that "the chief priests and scribes sought how they might kill him; for they feared the people" (Luke 22: 2). They feared men, rather than God. Mark tells us that the "chief priests and scribes sought how they might take him, by craft, and put him to death" (Mark 14: 1). All three synoptic writers therefore emphasise that it was the ***religious*** world that was intent on His death, and very little, if anything, has changed in two thousand years.

Organised religion has no place for Christ. We live in the "perilous times" anticipated by the apostle Paul, when men will have "a form of godliness, but denying the power thereof" (2 Tim. 3: 5). J.C.Ryle (he was a nineteenth century Anglican bishop) puts it like this: "high offices in the church do not preserve the holders of them from blindness and sin".

3) THE LOVE POURED OUT TO HIM, vv.6-13
"Now when Jesus was in Bethany, in the house of Simon the leper, there came unto him a woman having an alabaster box of very precious ointment, and poured it on his head, as he sat at meat" (vv.6-7).

When the children of Israel were given details of their coming redemption from Egypt, "the people bowed the head and worshipped" (Exod. 12: 27). Centuries later, the Lord Jesus announced His death as the Passover Lamb (v.2), and a godly woman expressed her love and devotion to Him. Remembrance of "Christ our Passover" should be accompanied by purity of life ("unleavened bread"), and worship. We must consider the following:

a) The place, v.6
Luke records a similar event (Luke 7: 36-50), but although on both occasions the host was a man named Simon, it is quite clear that two separate incidents are described. Whilst Matthew and Mark do not tell us the name of the woman who anointed the Lord Jesus (John tells us that it was Mary the sister of Martha and Lazarus, John 12: 1-3), we do know that the incident took place in the house of "Simon **the leper**". It seems highly unlikely that he was a leper at the time, and much more likely that he was then cured of leprosy, reminding us of the Lord's ability to cleanse us from the disease of sin, then taking residence in our hearts and lives, just as He was in residence in the house of Simon the leper. He loves to be in the lives of those He has blessed.

H.St.John (writing on Mark) observes, "it is remarkable that it took place in a leper's house". He continues, "In this country, we carry our kings to the noblest temple that the nation owns, and there the highest dignitary in the church pours out the coronation oil and crowns the sovereign. The King of Glory was anointed...in a place that suggests disease and poverty. (Bethany means, 'the house of the poor')". Others say that it means 'the house of dates'. As A.W.Pink (*Exposition of the Gospel of John*) observes, "what makes Bethany so attractive is that He seemed to find in the little company there a resting place in His toilsome path. It is blessed to know that there was one oasis in the desert, one little spot where He who 'endured the contradiction of sinners against himself' could retire from the hatred and antagonism of His enemies".

b) The act, v.7

"There came unto him a woman having an alabaster box of very precious ointment, and poured it on his head as he sat at meat". John Heading *(What the Bible Teaches - Matthew)* gives details: "The 'alabaster box' (Greek, *alabastron*) was made of marble-like stone found near Alabastron in Egypt: usually it was shaped like a flask with a long sealed neck. The neck was broken to gain access to the perfume or ointment". Mark tells us that it was "ointment of spikenard very precious" (Mark 14: 3), a fragrant oil procured from the stem of an Indian plant. Alternatively, it is described as "ointment of **pure nard,** very costly" (JND), probably suggesting that it was absolutely genuine, and not adulterated in any way. There are other explanations: see W.E.Vine's *Expository Dictionary of New Testament Words*. Its value can be gauged from the fact that it could have been sold for "more than three hundred pence" (Mark 14: 5). The labourers in Matthew 20: 2 contracted to work for "a penny a day", so the "ointment of spikenard" was worth at least three hundred days' work! Quite probably, the woman had acquired the spikenard over a long period of time, and we are told that Hebrew girls kept it for their wedding day. The spikenard was most valuable, a treasured possession. We must now notice what follows:

"She poured it on his head, as he sat at meat", or "she brake the box, and poured it on his head" (Mark 14: 3). John notices that she anointed the Lord's feet (John 12: 3) "for as the Son of God it was fitting that this disciple should take her place in the dust before Him!" (A.W.Pink). She gave her most treasured possession to the Saviour without reservation. She did it as an act of pure devotion. She was not commanded to do so, and certainly no pressure was exerted on her. **She did it because she loved Him.** Within hours wicked men would be congratulating themselves on a marvelous opportunity to rid themselves of the despised Nazarene (vv.14-15), but at Bethany a devoted woman expressed her love, and it was precious to Christ: "she hath wrought a good work upon me" (v.10). "Before an enemy's hand is laid upon Him, love's hands first anoint Him!" (A.W.Pink). We should notice that she didn't say a word, but the expression of her love was no less precious. What an encouragement for assembly sisters! (T.Miller).

We cannot anoint the Lord Jesus with "very precious ointment", but we can bring to Him the worship and appreciation of our grateful hearts. True worship is never cheap: it flows out of prayerful reading and meditation. We must have something to offer. We cannot "appear before the Lord empty" (Deut. 16: 16). But although the ointment was most valuable, its fragrance would have remained undetected if it had never been poured out. We often sing and speak about our love for Him, but do we actually **tell Him** that we love Him? This is called 'ministering to the Lord' in Acts 13: 2, where the word "ministered" (*leitourgia*) refers to priestly work: compare Hebrews 8: 2, 6; 9: 21. By anointing the Lord Jesus, this woman was 'ministering' to the Lord. We 'minister' to unsaved men and women by preaching the Gospel, and we 'minister' to one another as Christians in various ways, but how often do we 'minister' to the Lord?'

c) The criticism, vv.8-9
It was all too much for some disciples: "But when his disciples saw it, they had indignation (they 'murmured against her', Mark 14: 5), saying, To what purpose is this waste? For this ointment might have been sold for much, and given to the poor". We have already noticed that it was valued at "more than three hundred pence" (Mark 14: 5). Do notice that Matthew tells us specifically that the criticism came from the disciples. They were evidently led in this by Judas who had seemingly poisoned their minds (John 12: 4). The disciples were of the opinion that this expenditure was misdirected, and it is worth remembering that devotion to Christ can sometimes attract criticism from fellow-Christians whose hearts are not filled with the same love, and who sometimes accuse others of 'taking things a bit too far'.

But there is no "waste" in love for Christ. Giving Him our best is never "waste". Think of the joy that the woman brought to Christ that night in Bethany. The highest thing in life is to love Him. It is sadly possible to be so busy serving and helping other people, that we forget to express our love for Christ Who "hath loved us, and hath given himself for us" (Eph. 5: 2). "It is more important to be in love with the Lord of the work than with the work of the Lord" (*Choice Gleanings*, 17th May 2012).

d) The commendation, vv.10-11
Notice how the Saviour answered the critics: "Why trouble ye the woman? For she hath wrought a good work **upon me**" (v.10). The word "good" (*kalos*) could be rendered 'beautiful'. The word denotes that which is intrinsically good, and so, goodly, fair, beautiful..." (W.E.Vine). The disciples may have regarded the woman's devotion as extravagant waste, but the Lord described it as 'beautiful'. The disciples had a unique opportunity: "For ye

Matthew

have the poor always with you: but me ye have not always" (v.11). The woman had taken what was probably the last opportunity she would ever have on earth to show the Lord just how much she loved and appreciated Him. We too have the opportunity to bring joy to Christ in a hostile world. Soon that unique opportunity will be gone: there will be no hostile observers in heaven! Amongst other things, this ought to deepen our desire to shew our love for the Lord Jesus in remembering Him in the breaking of bread. Any Lord's day might be the last!

e) The reason, v.12
"For in that she hath poured this ointment out on my body, she did it for my burial" or "She is come aforehand to anoint my body to the burying" (Mark 14: 8). See also John 12: 7. Unlike the disciples, she seemed to know that His death was imminent. In the midst of His sufferings, the fragrance of the ointment would remain, and still be about His body when they took Him down from the cross. Nicodemus "brought a mixture of myrrh and aloes" in preparation for His burial (John 19: 39). Other women came later to the tomb with "sweet spices" (Mark 16: 1). But Mary anointed Him **before** His death. A.W.Pink draws attention to the Lord's words, "against the day of my burying hath she kept this" (John 12: 7), and points out that "the devotion of Mary was prompted by no sudden impulse, adding that the word "kept" means 'diligently preserved' and is used by the Lord in John 17: 12, 15.

f) The memorial, v.13
"Verily I say unto you, Wheresoever this gospel shall be preached in the whole world, there shall also this, that this woman hath done, be told for a memorial of her". What happened in the house of Simon the leper is a "memorial" to her faith. She, alone, understood and accepted that the Saviour would die, and in love for Him, she anointed His body "for my burial". This is why the Lord Jesus particularly associates her act of love with the Gospel. It was an outstanding example of faith. Mary of Bethany gave her best to Christ, no sacrifice was too great for Him, but Judas Iscariot was willing to exchange Him for money.

4) THE VALUE THEY PLACED ON HIM, vv.14-16
"Then one of the twelve, called Judas Iscariot, went unto the chief priests, and said unto them, What will ye give me, and I will deliver him unto you? And they covenanted with him (*histemi*, meaning to place, or weigh: 'they weighed unto him', RV) for thirty pieces of silver. And from that time he sought opportunity to betray him". Mark has: "And Judas Iscariot, one of the twelve, went unto the chief priests, to betray him unto them. And when

they heard it, they **were glad**, and promised to give him money. And he sought how he might conveniently betray him" (Mark 14: 10-11). See also Luke 22: 3-6. According to M.R.Vincent, the "thirty pieces of silver" were "shekels of the sanctuary, of standard weight, and therefore heavier than the ordinary shekel"

"Thirty pieces of silver". This was the value of a slave gored by an ox (Ex. 21: 32), and here is another Servant, soon to be surrounded by the "strong bulls of Bashan" (Psalm 22: 12), and soon to cry, "they pierced my hands and my feet (Psalm 22: 16). Unwittingly, they fulfilled Zechariah 11: 12, and this time it was the value of the divine Shepherd: "And I said unto them, If ye think good, give me my price; and if not forebear. So they weighed for my price thirty pieces of silver". It was a shameful insult, and more offensive than if they had paid nothing at all.

The actions of Judas Iscariot are a terrible warning of the "lengths a man may go to in a false profession of religion" (J.C.Ryle). He continues: "It is impossible to conceive a more striking proof of this painful truth, than the history of Judas Iscariot. If ever there was a man who at one time looked like a true disciple of Christ, and bade fair to reach heaven, that man was Judas. He was chosen by the Lord Jesus Himself to be an apostle. He was privileged to be a companion of the Messiah, and an eye-witness of His mighty works, throughout His earthly ministry…He was so like his fellow disciples that they did not suspect him of being a traitor. And yet this man turns out at last a false-hearted child of the devil - departs entirely from the faith - assists our Lord's deadliest enemies, and leaves the world with a worse reputation than anyone since the days of Cain".

Paul says, "Examine yourselves, whether ye be in the faith; prove your own selves" (2 Cor. 13: 5).

Thirty pieces of silver for the Lord of life they gave:
Thirty pieces of silver - 'twas only the price of a slave.
But it was the priestly value of the holy Son of God,
And they weighed it out in the temple - the price of the Saviour's blood.

Thirty pieces of silver lay in Iscariot's hand,
Thirty pieces of silver, and with the aid of an armoured band
They brought Him forth, the Saviour, the blessed Son of God,
At midnight from the Garden, where His sweat had been like blood.

Thirty pieces of silver burned on the traitor's brain:
Thirty pieces of silver, but, oh, it was hellish gain.
'I have sinned and betrayed the guiltless', he cried with feared breath,
And flung them down in the Temple, and rushed to a madman's death.

Thirty pieces of silver lay in 'the house of God':
Thirty pieces of silver but, oh, 'twas the price of blood!'
And so for a field to bury the stranger in, they gave
The price of their own Messiah, who lay in a borrowed grave.

It may not be for silver, it may not be for gold,
And yet by tens of thousands is the precious Saviour sold.
Sold - for a godless friendship, Sold - for a selfish aim,
Sold - for a fleeting trifle, Sold - for an empty name.

Sold - in the mart of science, Sold - in the seat of power,
Sold - at the shrine of fortune, Sold - in pleasure's bower.
Sold - where the awful bargain none but God's eye can see,
Then ponder my soul the question, 'shall he be sold by thee?'

Sold! - O God, what a moment! Stifled is conscience's voice:
Sold! - but the weeping angel records the dreadful choice.
Sold! - but the price of the Saviour to a living coal shall turn
With the pangs of remorse for ever, deep in the soul to burn.

How much do we value Him?

"Ye are bought with a price: therefore glorify God in your body, and in your spirit, which are God's" (1 Cor. 6: 20).

"He sat down with the twelve"

Read Chapter 26: 17-35
When the Lord Jesus instituted the Lord's supper, He said, "this do in **remembrance** of me" (Luke 22: 19; 1 Corinthians 11: 24). It was instituted at the very time of **national remembrance.** Israel was celebrating the passover, of which God said, "Thou shalt therefore sacrifice the passover unto the LORD thy God…that thou mayest **remember** the day when thou camest forth out of the land of Egypt all the days of thy life" (Deut. 16: 1-3). The proximity of the two acts of remembrance could not have been closer:

"And ***as they were eating*** (the passover), Jesus took bread, and blessed it, and brake it, and gave it to the disciples, and said, Take, eat; this is my body" (v.26). But whilst there are points of similarity, there are points of striking dissimilarity, and one of these is very clear from the above verses. In the case of the passover, Israel was to remember "***the day*** when thou camest forth out of the land of Egypt": in the case of the Lord's supper, the Lord Jesus said, "This do in remembrance ***of me***". It is worth making the point that we do not meet together to remember ***our*** blessings, wonderful though they are, but to remember the Lord Jesus Himself.

The passage before us may be divided as follows: *(1)* the preparation for the Passover (vv.17-19); *(2)* the identification of the betrayer (vv.20-25); *(3)* the institution of the supper (vv.26-30); *(4)* the reaction of the disciples (vv.31-35).

1) THE PREPARATION FOR THE PASSOVER, vv.17-19

"Now the first day of the feast of unleavened bread, the disciples came to Jesus, saying unto him Where wilt thou that we prepare for thee to eat the passover?" The disciples evidently had ***His*** interests in mind. This was the fourth passover during the public ministry of the Lord Jesus. As we noted in our previous study, only John mentions the first two: see 2: 13, 23 (April A.D.27), 6: 4 (A.D.28). The third is not mentioned at all (A.D.29), and all four Evangelists mention the fourth (A.D.30). We have already noticed the connection between the feasts of passover and unleavened bread: see our preceding study. Whilst the feast of unleavened bread commenced on the fifteenth day (see Leviticus 23: 6), the actual Passover Feast on the fourteenth day was also to be eaten without leaven, and the Jews therefore linked the two feasts. Hence the words, "the first day of unleavened bread, when they killed the passover" (Mark 14: 12).

The disciples' question, "Where wilt thou that we prepare for thee to eat the passover?" was in response to the Lord's request, "Go and prepare us the passover, that we may eat" (Luke 22: 8). Humanly speaking, this was a very difficult task. Jerusalem was thronged with visitors, and suitable accommodation was in very short supply. But there was no problem so far as the Lord was concerned, "Go into the city to such a man, and say unto him, the Master saith, My time is at hand; I will keep the passover at thy house with my disciples". The Lord's words, "The Master saith, My time is at hand" (He was fully aware of coming events) are unique to Matthew. The way in which He describes Himself ("The Master saith") seems to suggest that the owner of the house would immediately recognise Him. According to H.A.Ironside, "Tradition says that it was in the home of John Mark that the last Passover was held by the Saviour". Perhaps some support for this might be found in Acts 12: 12. But this is incidental. The Lord indicated that as the Passover Lamb He was about to die (Luke 22:15).

Matthew gives us a brief summary of events, but Mark and Luke are much more detailed. Here is Mark's account: "And the first day of unleavened bread, when they killed the passover, his disciples said unto him, Where wilt thou that we go and prepare that thou mayest eat the Passover? And he sendeth forth two of his disciples (Peter and John, Luke 22: 8), and saith unto them, Go ye into the city, and there shall meet you a man bearing a pitcher of water (men did not usually carry pitchers of water): follow him. And wheresoever he shall go in, say ye to the goodman of the house, The Master saith, Where is the guest-chamber, where I shall eat the passover with my disciples? And he will shew you a large upper room furnished and prepared: there make ready for us" (Mark 14: 12-15). See also Luke 22: 7-12.

While we are now studying Matthew's Gospel, we really ought to do a little revision and briefly refer to our studies in Mark and Luke.

i) Finding the place. "There shall meet you a man carrying a pitcher of water: follow him" (Mark 14: 13). The disciples were not given the address, and told to go straight there! The Lord did not say, 'and there you will meet a man', but, "there shall a man *meet you*". This emphasises, once again, that the Lord was in complete control of the situation. He planned beforehand. One of the reasons was security. Had he given the address, Judas would have been able to alert the authorities, who could then have quietly arrested the Lord Jesus and avoided "an uproar among the people" (v.5). In any case, had the actual address been given, it would have become yet another religious shrine by now! The Lord is not interested in popular shrines, but He is deeply interested in quiet 'upper rooms' where His people gather.

Notice too that it was an unnamed man. Not one of the "wise...mighty... noble" (1 Cor. 1: 26). Harold St.John has a delightful comment here: he refers to the man with the pitcher as "one who humbled himself to do a woman's work" (that is, in the Middle East), and adds "only such men can carry the water with which the feet of disciples can be cleansed (referring to John 13: 5) and can conduct them to the place where the living streams are flowing (John 13: 1-16)". We should add that preachers and commentators often suggest that the unnamed man, like the unnamed servant in Genesis

24, is a picture of the Holy Spirit. Without attempting to press the details too far, it is certainly true that the Holy Spirit does lead the saints to the place where they can meet the Lord!

ii) Addressing the owner. In addressing the "goodman of the house", which translates one word (*oikodespotes*) meaning 'the master of the house', the disciples were to say, "The Master (meaning 'Teacher') saith, Where is the guest-chamber, where I shall eat the passover with my disciples?" (Mark 14: 14). The disciples were to refer, not to 'a teacher', but to 'The Teacher'. Nicodemus acknowledged that He was "a teacher come from God" (John 3: 2), to which the Lord replied, "Art thou a master ('the teacher', JND/RV) of Israel, and knowest not these things" (John 3: 10). So we have, in John 3, "a teacher" who knew everything, and 'the teacher' who was strikingly deficient in knowledge!

iii) Describing the room. "And he will shew you a large upper room furnished and prepared: there make ready for us" (Mark 14: 15). These words have supplied the material for many sermons! Here are some of the points made by preachers over many years.

- ***It was "a large room".*** The upper room was a place of divine appointment, and a place of activity where they "made ready the Passover" as commanded by the Lord. Every assembly should be like this. In the words of Norman Crawford (writing on Luke), "The large room suggests to us that in it there was room for the Lord Himself and His own. In an assembly there is room for Him, His Spirit and His word, and all His people who are willing to submit to its authority and be led by the Holy Spirit (i.e., as they follow the man with the 'pitcher of water'). There is room for the New Testament priesthood to function in all its liberty, and room for the gifts in all their variety.'

- ***It was an "upper room".*** W.E.Vine defines this as "a chamber, often over a porch, or connected with a roof, where meals were taken and privacy obtained". The expression, "upper room" (one word, *anogeon*) means, simply, 'above ground'. As N.Crawford observes, "It is tragic when a local testimony comes down to the level of the world". It happened at Corinth, "For ye are yet carnal: for whereas there is among you envying, and strife, and divisions, are ye not carnal, and **walk as men?**" (1 Cor. 3: 3).

- ***It was a prepared room.*** Disorders in the assembly at Corinth obliged Paul to write: "But let a man examine himself, and so let him eat of that bread, and drink of that cup" (1 Cor. 11: 28). We must always "make ready" before assembly gatherings.

But we can also apply the description of the "upper room" in a personal way. Our lives should be like "*a large* upper room": we should not self-centred and narrow-minded. There should be a "largeness of heart" (1 Kings 4: 29) that embraces the needs of others. Our lives should be like "a large **upper** room": see Colossians 3: 2, "Set your affections on things above, not on things on the earth". Our lives should be like a **prepared** room. They have already been "furnished and prepared" with divinely-given gifts and ability, but we must ensure that we are "prepared unto every good work" (2 Tim. 2: 21).

2) THE IDENTIFICATION OF THE BETRAYER, vv.20-25

"Now when the even was come, he sat down with the twelve. And as they did eat, he said, Verily I say unto you, that one of you shall betray me" (vv.20-21). According to John Heading, "This was the legal hour in the beginning of the fourteenth day of the month Nisan". That is, at 18.00 hours.

"And as they sat and did eat, he said, Verily I say unto you, that one of you shall betray me. And they were exceeding sorrowful, and began every one of them to say unto him, Lord, is it I" (vv.21-22). As John Heading points out, "It seems strange that all of them ('every one of them') could not trust their own hearts". It has often been noted that whilst the eleven disciples said, "**Lord**, is it I?", Judas said, "**Master** (Rabbi), is it I", Matthew 26: 22, 25. Judas never said, "Lord".

We must carefully note the Lord's reply: it illustrates divine sovereignty and human responsibility: "He that dippeth his hand with me in the dish, the same shall betray me (see Psalm 41: 9). The Son of man goeth as it is written of him: but woe unto that man by whom the Son of man is betrayed! It had been good for that man if he had not been born" (vv.23-24). The co-existence of divine sovereignty and human responsibility is apparent in Acts 2: 23. Even though the Lord's betrayal had been predicted (see Psalm 41: 9, cited in John 13: 18), the responsibility of Judas remained: he could not escape the consequences of his deed. In connection with Judas, notice John 6: 70-71, where the word "devil" (*diabolos*) rightly occurs: usually "devil" means 'demon' (*daimon* or *daimonion*). Other relevant passages are found in John 13: 2; 17: 12; Luke 22: 3. Whilst, in the mercy of God, there will be no such "Woe" for us, we must nevertheless ensure that **we** are not disloyal to the Saviour

"Then Judas, which betrayed him, answered and said, Master, is it I? He said unto him, Thou hast said" (v.25). "Hypocritically he repeats the others' question (v.22) so as to arouse no suspicion" (supplied by Justin Waldron). The identification of Judas as the betrayer (see John 13: 21-30) raises the question of his presence or otherwise at the institution of the Lord's supper (vv.26-29). John gives additional details (John 13: 21-30). We must note the words, "he was troubled in spirit, and testified, and said, Verily, verily, I say unto you, that one of you shall betray me" (John 13: 21). We should notice that "having received the sop (morsel)", Judas "went immediately out" (John 13: 30). This suggests that he was not present when the Lord's supper was instituted, with apparent confirmation by the use of the imperfect tense used in 1 Corinthians 11: 23, 'the same night in which he was **being betrayed**'. But Luke records the institution of the supper, and continues, "But, behold, the hand of him that betrayeth me is with me on the table. And truly the Son of man goeth, as it was determined..." (Luke 22: 19-23). The difficulty is not easily resolved. The matter is covered in a very comprehensive answer by Wm.Hoste in 'Bible Problems and Answers'.

The matter is not quite so clear as some people think, but even so, the presence of Judas at the supper, if this was the case, cannot sanction participation by unsaved people today. There have been occasions when assemblies have been unaware of the true spiritual status of a person 'in fellowship'. There is some similarity in the case of Judas. It is, of course, quite a different matter to deliberately admit an unsaved person to the fellowship of the assembly.

3) THE INSTITUTION OF THE SUPPER, vv.26-30
When dealing with the subject in our Mark and Luke studies, we briefly noted the references to the institution of the Lord's supper as part of the overall passage (Mark 14: 12-26; Luke 22: 1-23), and then devoted an entire session to the institution of the Lord's supper (Mark 14: 22-24; Luke 22: 19-20). We will now note the details given by Matthew, and more comprehensive notes on the subject are attached. They are almost identical to those issued in connection with our Mark and Luke studies. With this in mind, we must briefly notice:

a) The time, v.26
"And as they were eating" (that is, as they were eating the Passover), the Lord Jesus said, "With desire I have desired to eat **this** passover with you before I suffer" (Luke 22: 15). He was thoroughly aware of His coming

suffering. The Saviour's words, "*this* passover", indicate its importance. It marked the end of an era, and the commencement of something entirely new. One act of remembrance was giving place to another. The Lord's supper commemorates the reality of which the Passover was a picture. Within a matter of hours, the Lord Jesus was to die as "the Lamb of God". In Paul's words, "Christ our passover is sacrificed for us" (1 Cor. 5: 7). For centuries, Israel had kept the passover in remembrance of their deliverance from Egypt: now, another Lamb was to die in order to deliver men and women from worse bondage. His death "as of a lamb without blemish and without spot" had been "foreordained before the foundation of the world" (1 Pet. 1: 19-20), and announced by John the Baptist: "Behold the Lamb of God, which taketh away the sin of the world" (John 1: 29).

b) The symbols, vv.26-28
"Jesus took bread, and blessed it, and brake it, and gave it to the disciples, and said, Take, eat; this is my body. And he took the cup, and gave thanks, and gave it to them, saying, Drink ye all of it; for this is my blood of the new testament, which is shed for many for the remission of sins". The subject is expanded in the accompanying study, but attention is drawn to the following:

In connection with **the bread**, we should notice that Luke uses the words "gave thanks (*eucharisteo*)" (Luke 22: 19) where Matthew and Mark say "blessed" (*eulogeo*, meaning 'to speak well of'). Do notice that in Matthew, "*it*" is in italics. The Saviour did not bless the bread! According to Luke, having said, "This is my body", the Lord Jesus continued with the words, "which is given for you: this do in remembrance of me".

In connection with **the cup**, we should notice that while Matthew and Mark have "this is my blood of the new testament, which is shed for **many**", Luke has "shed for **you**". Matthew alone adds "for the remission (meaning 'a dismissal, release') of sins". The "new testament" (or covenant) is discussed in the accompanying study.

It is worth pointing out that Luke refers to **two** cups (Luke 22: 17, 20), the first of which was part of the **passover ceremony**. Having said, "with desire I have desired to eat this passover with you before I suffer", the Lord Jesus continued, "I will not any more eat thereof, until it be fulfilled in the kingdom of God. And he took the cup (that is, the Passover cup) and gave thanks, and said, Take this, and divide it among yourselves" (Luke 22: 15-17). Matthew and Mark refer to the passover ceremony with the simple statement, "And as they were eating" (JND in both gospels). The Lord Jesus "took bread" and instituted the first part of the "Lord's supper" (1 Cor. 11: 20) whilst eating the passover meal, and the second part of the "Lord's supper" after the passover meal was concluded. Hence the expressions, "Likewise also the cup *after* supper" (Luke 22: 20) and, "when he had supped" (1 Cor. 11: 25). Having passed the Passover cup to the disciples, the Lord Jesus then said, "I will not drink of the fruit of the vine, until the kingdom of God shall come" (Luke 22: 18). He had already said virtually the same when eating the Passover (Luke 22: 16), which brings us to:

c) The kingdom, v.29
"But I say unto you, I will not drink henceforth of this fruit of the vine, until the day when I drink it new (*kainos*) with you in my Father's kingdom", or, "in the kingdom of God" (Mark 14: 25). J.N.Darby's marginal note is significant: "not 'anew', but 'in a new way, or, of a new kind'". There seems little doubt that both references, to eating and to drinking, refer to the celebration of the passover in the millennial kingdom (Ezek. 45: 21). As Wm.Macdonald rightly points out, "the wine would then have a new significance, it would speak of the joy and blessedness of His glorious kingdom". In the meantime, His people would remember "Christ our Passover…sacrificed for us" (1 Cor. 5: 7) in the bread and wine of the Lord's supper.

d) The hymn, v.30
"And when they had sung an hymn, they went out into the Mount of Olives". It is generally thought that it is most likely that this was the closing Psalm of the Passover, Psalm 118. It was evidently the usual custom to sing the Hallel Psalms at the Passover (Psalms 113-118). Psalm 118 includes the following: "The LORD is on my side, I will not fear what men can do unto me" (v.6); "I shall not die, but live, and declare the works of the LORD" (v.17); "The stone that the builders refused is become the headstone of the corner" (v.22); "bind the sacrifice with cords, unto the horns of the altar" (v.27). However, we are not told here what the Lord and His disciples actually sang. There is divine wisdom in this: if the words had been recorded by the Gospel writers, they would have become a standard formula, and repeated on every occasion that believers meet for the Lord's supper!

4) THE REACTION OF THE DISCIPLES, vv.31-35
These verses may be simply divided as follows: *(A)* the Lord's prediction (vv.31-32); *(B)* the disciples' protest (vv.33-35).

A) The Lord's prediction, vv.31-32

"Then saith Jesus unto them, All ye shall be offended (*skandalizo*, meaning 'stumbled') because of me this night: for it is written, I will smite the shepherd, and the sheep of the flock shall be scattered abroad. But after that I am risen again, I will go before you into Galilee". It is unwise to condemn the disciples. Christ is still "a rock of offence" (1 Pet. 2: 8), and "the offence of the cross" (Gal. 5: 11) remains. Opposition and ridicule can stumble us too. We may not say in so many words, "I know not this man of whom ye speak" (Mark 14: 71), but lack of positive testimony amounts to the same thing. We must notice:

a) The effect of the Shepherd's death

i) The Scripture quoted. The Lord Jesus refers here to Zechariah 13: 7 which reads, "Awake, O sword, against my shepherd, and against the man that is my fellow, saith the LORD of hosts: smite the shepherd, and the sheep shall be scattered: and I will turn my hand upon the little ones". We must notice the Lord's exact words: "for it is written" (v.31). He did not say, 'for the Scripture is fulfilled'. The Zechariah passage describes Israel's rejection of Messiah, and its fearful consequences. Divine judgment still rests upon the nation, and will intensify to unprecedented levels in the coming tribulation. The Lord Jesus therefore **applied** the prophecy, just as Peter **applied** Joel 2: 28-32 on the day of Pentecost: "*but this is that* which was spoken by the prophet Joel". Incidentally, we must notice the expression, "the man that is my fellow". The word "man" here, means 'a strong man'. The word "fellow" has been variously translated, 'the man of my union'; 'a man co-equal with me'; 'the man my equal'. He is the **Divine Shepherd**. He is "equal with God" (Phil 2: 6). He said, "I and my Father are one" (John 10: 30).

ii) The Shepherd smitten. It is important, again, to notice the Lord's exact words. While He referred to Zechariah 13: 7, He actually amended the passage from "Awake, O sword, against my shepherd...smite the shepherd, and the sheep shall be scattered", to "*I will smite* the shepherd, and the sheep of the flock shall be scattered" (v.31). The Saviour emphasised that He would be "stricken, smitten **of God**, and afflicted" (Isaiah 53: 4).

iii) The sheep scattered. This is exactly what happened. After the Lord's arrest, "all the disciples forsook him, and fled" (Matt. 26: 56). Only Peter and another disciple followed the Lord to the high priest's palace, and only John "stood by the cross of Jesus" (John 19: 26). Compare John 16: 32. But the scattered sheep would be regathered:

b) The effect of the Shepherd's resurrection

"But after that I am risen again, I will go before you into Galilee" (v.32). This appears to have been completely unnoticed by the disciples. When the women brought news of the resurrection, "their words seemed to them as idle tales, and they believed them not" (Luke 24: 11). See also Mark 16: 11-14. In the words of J.C.Ryle, "How much comfort professing Christians miss by carelessness and inattention...how many truths we read yearly in the Bible, and yet remember them no more than if we had never read them at all". It is rather sobering to notice that the Lord's enemies *did* remember His words: "We remember that that deceiver said, while he was yet alive, After three days I will rise again" (Matt. 27: 63). We must now notice:

i) The Shepherd risen. The Lord Jesus had no doubts about His resurrection: "But after that I am risen". The chief priests and Pharisees called Him, "that deceiver". But "neither was any deceit in His mouth" (Isaiah 53: 9). The message of the angels was clear: "He is not here: for he is risen, *as he said*" (Matt. 28: 6.) In this particular passage, the Lord anticipates His resurrection as "that great shepherd of the sheep" (Heb. 13: 20). So:

ii) The sheep regathered. "I will go before you into Galilee". Compare Matthew 28: 7. The words, "go before" are the words of a shepherd. See John 10: 4, "and when he putteth forth his own sheep, *he goeth before them*". The Lord Jesus regathered the sheep after His resurrection by appearing to groups and individuals at different times and in different places. But it was in Galilee that He taught fishermen to become shepherds, see John 21: 10-16. It is rather lovely to note that rather than censuring the disciples over their coming failure, the Saviour gives them hope.

B) The disciples' protest, vv.33-35

"Peter answered and said unto him, Though all men shall be offended because of thee, yet will I never be offended" (v.33), and having heard the Lord say, "this night, before the cock crow, thou shalt deny me thrice", he renewed his protest: "though I should die with thee, yet will I not deny thee" (vv.34-35). We must not forget that whilst he was evidently the most vocal of the disciples, "Likewise also said all the disciples" (v.35). Mark alone emphasises the intensity of Peter's profession: "But he spake the more vehemently" (Mark 14: 31). By the way, Peter did not die *with* the Lord Jesus, but he did die *for* Him (John 21: 18-19).

As J.C.Ryle observes, "Their loud professions were all forgotten. The present danger swept all their promises of fidelity clean away. So little do we know how we shall act in any particular position until we are placed in it! So much do present circumstances alter our feelings!" He continues: "Let us learn to pray for humility. 'Pride goeth before destruction, and a haughty spirit before a fall' (Prov.16: 18). There is far more wickedness in our hearts than we know. We never can tell how far we might fall, if once placed in temptation... 'Let him that thinketh he standeth take heed lest he fall' (1 Cor. 10: 12); 'He that trusteth his own heart is a fool' (Prov. 28: 26). Let our daily prayer be, 'Hold Thou me up, and I shall be safe' (Psalm 119: 117)".

Although the Lord predicted Peter's denial, He did not do so with acrimony and anger, witness His words at this time (only recorded by Luke): "Simon, Simon, behold, Satan hath desired to have you (**plural:** all the disciples), that he may sift (you) as wheat: **but** I have prayed for thee (**singular:** Peter personally), that thy faith fail not: and when thou art converted, strengthen thy brethren" (Luke 22: 31-34). The repeated name, "Simon, Simon", conveys the deep feeling of the Lord Jesus. Norman Crawford observes that "the sifting by Satan himself, not by one of his emissaries, is an experience that few believers have encountered. Let us remember this when we concentrate on Peter's failure!" The words, "I have prayed for **thee**" anticipate the particular trial that Peter would face. We must not think for one moment that the Lord's prayer was unanswered. His courage failed, but not his faith! He **was** turned again ("converted", AV) to the extent that he publicly charged the nation: "Ye denied the Holy One and the Just, and desired a murderer to be granted unto you: and killed the Prince of life" (Acts 3: 14-15). And he **did** 'strengthen his brethren': just read his two epistles!

"Jesus took bread"

Read Matthew 26: 26-28; 1 Corinthians 11: 23-29
"And as they were eating (the Passover), Jesus took bread, and blessed *it*, and brake it, and gave it to the disciples, and said, Take, eat; this is my body. And he took the cup, and gave thanks, and gave it to them, saying, Drink ye all of it; for this is my blood of the new testament, which is shed for many for the remission of sins".

A comparison of the three accounts in the Gospels (see Matt. 26: 26-28; Mark 14: 22-24; Luke 22: 15-20) shows that while Matthew and Mark have "Take, eat; this is my body", Luke has the additional words "This is my body **which is given for you: this do in remembrance of me"** (Luke 22: 19).

Chapter 26

Again, Matthew and Mark have "this is my blood of the new testament, which is shed for *many*", whereas Luke has "This cup is the new testament in my blood, which is shed for *you*". Matthew alone has "for the remission of sins". We should also notice that while, in connection with the bread, Matthew and Mark say "blessed" (*eulogeo*, meaning 'to speak well of'), Luke uses the words "gave thanks" (*eucharisteo*). Do notice that in Matt. 26: 26, the word "it" is in italics, indicating that it is not in the original text: the Lord did not bless the bread!

Assembly fellowship is expressed in various ways, and in particular by participation in "the Lord's supper". Paul uses this expression in 1 Cor. 11: 20 to describe what we commonly call the "breaking of bread", which is also a thoroughly Biblical expression: see Acts 20: 7. It was not optional: the Lord Jesus said, "This do in remembrance of me" (Luke 22: 19; 1 Cor.11: 24). But He expects more than reluctant compliance. If we love someone, it follows quite naturally that we will do all in our power to please them (see Gen. 29: 20, "And Jacob served seven years for Rachel; and they seemed unto him but a few days for the love he had to her"), and our love for Christ should not be an exception to this rule. The Lord Jesus said, "If ye love me, keep my commandments...he that hath my commandments, and keepeth them, he it is that loveth me" (John 14: 15, 21).

Before considering various aspects of "the Lord's supper", we ought to examine the expressions, "the Lord's supper", and "the Lord's table". We will make this the first of two major points in this study. So:

1) CONFUSION REGARDING THE NAME OF THE SUPPER

a) *"The Lord's supper"*
i) It is "the **Lord's** supper". The Greek word (*kuriakos*) "signified pertaining to a lord or master" (W.E.Vine). "The word was used in the papyri in the sense of belonging to the Caesar, or Imperial" (The Linguistic Key to the Greek New Testament). Since it is *His* "supper", and He is the divine Host, we cannot do as we please or say what we like.

ii) It is "the Lord's *supper*". Whilst, as we know, it was instituted "when even was come" (Matt. 26: 20, Mark 14: 17, JND), it is the type of meal rather than the time of day which is particularly important. See Rev. 3: 20, "I will come in to him, and *sup* with him, and he with me". Supper was a long meal, the main meal of the day, when members of the family and their

551

guests spent time in conversation and reflection. It was unhurried, and more leisurely than other meals. The "Lord's supper" is therefore an occasion when believers gather to spend time in praise and worship as they are 'occupied alone with Him'.

b) "The Lord's table"

Whilst our hymnology often uses this expression in relation to "the Lord's supper", or "breaking of bread", it really means something quite different. In 1 Cor. 10: 21, Paul uses the expression in connection with **fellowship with God**: "Ye cannot drink the cup of the Lord, and the cup of devils (demons): ye cannot be partakers of the Lord's table, and of the table of devils (demons)". In the Old Testament, the "Lord's table" was the altar (see Mal. 1: 7, 12), and the sacrifices on the altar are described as "the bread of thy God" (see Lev. 21: 8 etc). The altar was the place of fellowship with God, and this was expressed particularly in the peace offering, in which God, the priests, and the offerer and his family, all participated (see 1 Cor. 10: 18, "Behold Israel after the flesh: are not they which eat of the sacrifices partakers of the altar?"). We were brought into fellowship with God on faith in Christ. It was then that we took our place at "the Lord's table". Moreover, we are **always** there, and we will **never leave it!** While Paul certainly **alludes** to "the Lord's supper" in describing our place at "the Lord's table", he reverses the order of the emblems. The "cup of blessing" is placed first, because it is the **basis** of fellowship with God, and the bread second, where it is used as a symbol of fellowship between believers. Whilst "the Lord's supper" is essentially a time when we remember the Lord Jesus, it also expresses the principal benefits of "the Lord's table", namely, our fellowship with God, and with each other. It has been nicely said (T.G.Baker) that the highest expression of "the Lord's table" is "the Lord's supper".

It might be helpful to notice that the Lord's teaching in John 6: 53-56 does not refer to "the Lord's supper". His words, "Whoso eateth my flesh, and drinketh my blood, hath eternal life", refer to salvation. The children of Israel had to appropriate the manna to stay alive in the wilderness, and men and women have to appropriate Christ in order to possess eternal life. See John 6: 47-51, "I am the living bread which came down from heaven: if any man eat of this bread, he shall live for ever…"

2) CIRCUMSTANCES SURROUNDING THE INSTITUTION OF THE SUPPER

"For I have received of the Lord that which also I delivered unto you, That the Lord Jesus, *the same night in which he was betrayed*, took bread" (1 Cor. 11: 23).

i) It was Passover night. "This is that night of the Lord" (Exodus 12: 42). But it was no ordinary Passover night. The Lord Jesus said, "With desire I have desired to eat *this* passover with you before I suffer" (Luke 22: 15). He was thoroughly aware of His coming suffering, witness His words, "before I suffer". The Saviour's words, "*this* passover", indicate its importance. It marked the end of an era, and the commencement of something entirely new. Within a matter of hours, He was to die as "the Lamb of God". In Paul's words, "Christ our passover is sacrificed for us" (1 Cor. 5: 7). For centuries, Israel had kept the passover in remembrance of their deliverance from Egypt: now, another Lamb was to die in order to deliver men and women from worse bondage.

ii) It was 'night' in another sense. "The night in which he was betrayed". The imperfect tense suggests the rendering, 'the night in which he was being betrayed'. Judas was about his treachery, possibly at that very moment. The fact that the Lord Jesus instituted "the Lord's supper" at this time is, in itself, quite amazing. Mankind was committing its foulest crime, and it would have been perfectly reasonable for the Lord Jesus to have completely severed all connection with the human race. But in infinite grace He still valued the love and devotion of "His own" (John 13: 1), and instituted the "supper" by which they could meet to remember Him.

We must now consider the following. It will be helpful to have 1 Corinthians 11 open, with particular reference to vv.23-29, and it is important to notice that Paul's information was not second hand. He received it by direct revelation: "*I received of the Lord* that which also I delivered unto you, That the Lord Jesus, the same night in which he was betrayed, took bread" (v.23).

A) THE WAY IN WHICH THE LORD'S SUPPER WAS INSTITUTED
"And when He had given thanks" (1 Cor. 11: 24). This is far from a simple statement of fact. The Lord Jesus was about to suffer in a manner, and to a degree, that was totally unparalleled. In fact, it was in a manner and to a degree that no other person *could* ever suffer. He spoke about His body, and later about His blood, and He *gave thanks!* The Bible does not record the Saviour's words, for the same reason that we do not know what the Lord and His disciples sang before they "went out into the Mount of Olives" (Mark 14: 26). There is divine wisdom in this: if the Saviour's words had

been recorded by the Gospel writers, they would have become a standard formula, and repeated on every occasion that believers meet for the Lord's supper! But we do know that earlier He said, "Now is my soul troubled; and what shall I say? Father save me from this hour: but for this cause came I unto this hour. Father **glorify Thy Name**" (John 12: 27-28). We also know that in His 'high-priestly' prayer, He said, "I have glorified thee on the earth: I have finished the work which thou gavest me to do" (John 17: 4). Perhaps, therefore, the Lord Jesus 'gave thanks' because He knew that God would be glorified through His death (compare John 11: 4, where God was glorified through the death of Lazarus), and that has certainly happened. Men and women, teenagers, boys and girls, saved because He suffered at Calvary, can sing:

> *To God be the glory, great things He hath done;*
> *So loved He the world that He gave us His Son.*

We also know that "for the **joy** that was set before him", the Lord Jesus "endured the cross, despising the shame" (Heb. 12: 2), and this could be another reason for His thanksgiving here.

B) THE REASON FOR WHICH THE LORD'S SUPPER WAS INSTITUTED

"This do in remembrance of **me**" (1 Cor. 11: 24). The Passover was instituted "that thou mayest remember **the day** when thou camest forth out of the land of Egypt" (Deut. 16: 1-3). But here, it is, "In remembrance of **me**". Hence the emphasis in 1 Corinthians 11: "This is **my** body...this cup is the new testament in **my** blood...in remembrance of **me** (twice)...the **Lord's** death... this cup of the **Lord**...the body and blood of the **Lord**...the **Lord's** body". We ought to notice that the Lord Jesus did not say, 'This do **in memory** of me', but "**in remembrance** of me". It is not a case of remembering someone that we had forgotten, but doing something quite deliberate. In the words of W.E.Vine, "The word (*anamensis*) denotes a bringing to mind, and here an affectionate calling of the Person to mind".

People would have the greatest difficulty in complying, if any one of us was to make that request. Perhaps the first thing they would remember would be most uncomplimentary. Possibly they would have the greatest difficulty in remembering anything about us very clearly, and in any case, we might not really be worth a great deal of thought at all! **But this is the Lord Jesus**, and He will occupy the minds and hearts of His people for eternity! His command, "This do in remembrance of me", does not impose limitations: to the contrary, it opens vast horizons, and the well-known hymn describes the range:

> *Jesus! my Shepherd, Saviour, Friend,*
> *My Prophet, Priest, and King,*
> *My Lord, my Life, my Way, my End,*
> *Accept the praise I bring.*

C) THE SYMBOLS WITH WHICH THE LORD'S SUPPER WAS INSTITUTED

a) The bread

"The Lord Jesus...took **bread:** and when he had given thanks, he brake it, and said, Take, eat; this is my body, which is broken for you" (1 Cor. 11: 23-24). J.N.Darby renders this: 'This is my body, which (is) for you'. The bread is a picture, or symbol, of His body. It could not possibly be His actual body, since He was bodily present at the time. The doctrines of transubstantiation and consubstantiation are blasphemous nonsense. The bread is a powerful reminder to believers that whilst the Lord Jesus was a perfect man, He was not a mere man. He is "Jesus the Son of God" (Heb. 4: 14), possessing perfect humanity and perfect deity, not as a dual personality, but as "Emmanuel, which being interpreted is, God with us" (Matt. 1: 23). "The Word became flesh and dwelt among us" (John 1: 14, JND). Every time we 'break bread', we confess the doctrine of the Incarnation, and therefore the doctrines of Christ's stainless humanity and absolute deity. What a privilege!

The first mention of bread in Scripture occurs in Gen. 3: 19, "In the sweat of thy face shalt thou eat bread..." Bread there denotes an **unfinished** work. When the Lord Jesus "took bread", He anticipated His **finished** work. Bread in Scripture is connected with life: for example, "bread which strengtheneth man's heart" (Psalm 104: 15). But to Him it was connected with death.

But there is more. The bread tells us about the purpose of the Incarnation. The Lord Jesus said, "This is my body, **which (is) for you**" (JND). Peter refers to this, "Who his own self **bare our sins in his own body on the tree**" (1 Pet. 2: 24). The words, "his own self", and, "his own body" refer respectively to His deity and to His humanity. The Son of God 'became flesh' in order to die for us at Calvary.

It is worth mentioning that the brother who actually breaks the bread at "the Lord's supper" does so purely to help the gathered saints: "to enable the believers to break it decently and without difficulty" (W.E.Vine). He does not break the bread as their representative, but purely as their servant. We 'break bread' when we break off our individual piece. It is "the bread which *we* break": see 1 Corinthians 10: 16, where Paul refers to "the Lord's supper" in dealing with "the Lord's table".

b) The cup

"He took the *cup*, when he had supped (i.e. when the Passover meal had ended), saying, This cup is the new testament in my blood: this do ye, as oft as ye drink it, in remembrance of me" (1 Cor. 11: 25). We know, of course, what was in the cup - "this fruit of the vine" (Mat. 26: 29) - but the Saviour said, "this cup", rather than, 'this wine'. The word "cup" is often used in Scripture as a symbol of judgment and death. See Psalm 75: 8 ("For in the hand of the Lord there is a *cup*, and the wine is red; it is full of mixture, and he poureth out the same: but the dregs thereof, all the wicked of the earth shall wring then out, and drink them"); Isaiah 51: 17, 22 ("Awake, awake, stand up, O Jerusalem, which hast drunk at the hand of the Lord the *cup* of his fury: thou hast drunken the dregs of the *cup* of trembling, and wrung them out…"); Ezekiel 23: 32-33 ("Thus saith the Lord God, Thou shalt drink of thy sister's *cup* deep and large…Thou shalt be filled with drunkenness and sorrow, with the *cup* of astonishment and desolation, with the *cup* of thy sister Samaria").

The Lord Jesus Himself said, "O my Father, if it be possible, let this cup pass from me" (Matt. 26: 39). See also Matt. 20. 22, "Are ye able to drink of the cup that I shall drink of?" The cup reminds us, eloquently, that the blood of the Lord Jesus was shed under divine judgment.

But there is more. "This cup is the **new testament** (covenant) in my blood" (1 Cor. 11: 25). The 'old covenant' was the law, under which God **demanded** righteousness, with the words, "*Thou* shalt…*Thou* shalt not". Transgression carried a solemn penalty: "Cursed is every one that continueth not in all things which are written in the book of the law to do them" (Gal. 3: 10). But under the 'new covenant', God **imparts** righteousness, with the words, "*I* will". See Heb. 8: 8-12. When the 'old covenant' was instituted, animal blood was shed (see Heb. 9: 20), but the 'new covenant' rests upon "the precious blood of Christ" (1 Pet. 1: 19). When we take the cup, we are reminded of "him that loved us, and washed us from our sins in his own blood" (Rev. 1: 5). The cup reminds us that "without shedding of blood is no remission" (Heb. 9: 22).

The first reference to wine in Scripture occurs in Gen. 9: 21, "And he (Noah) drank of the wine, and was drunken". Wine is associated there with something dishonourable. When the Lord Jesus "took the cup", He anticipated something sacred and honourable beyond words, His own precious blood. Wine in Scripture is associated with joy: see, for example, Psalm 104: 15, "wine that maketh glad the heart of man". But to Him it symbolised suffering and sorrow beyond compare.

D) THE DURATION FOR WHICH THE LORD'S SUPPER WAS INSTITUTED
"For as often as ye eat this bread, and drink this cup, ye do shew the Lord's death *till he come"* (1 Cor. 11: 26). We must notice:

a) Its celebration
"For as **often** as ye eat this bread..." Whilst there is no specific command, it was evidently the practice in New Testament times to 'break bread' on "the first day of the week". W.E.Vine is worth quoting *in extenso*: "The narrative in Acts 20 is instructive and significant. Concerning the apostle's journey to Jerusalem via Troas, it is recorded that he 'hasted, if it were possible for him, to be at Jerusalem the day of Pentecost' (v.16 RV). In spite of this, he 'tarried seven days' at Troas (v.6 RV), after arriving there on the second day of the week (our Monday). 'And upon the first day of the week (the seventh day of the stay), when we were gathered together to break bread, Paul discoursed with them, intending to depart on the morrow' (v.7 RV). Clearly, he stayed all the week so as to be with them for the Lord's supper on the recognised day, trusting the Lord as to arriving at Jerusalem as he hoped. There is obviously a divine purpose in the mention of these details of time. 'As oft as', therefore, does not mean that it is left to the saints to choose any time they like. It simply means 'every time that', i.e. on each occasion".

Two things emerge very clearly from the narrative in Acts 20: **firstly**, that the early believers 'broke bread' on the first day of the week and **secondly**, they broke bread in association with an established testimony. It was undertaken corporately, as an assembly activity. Notice the expressions, "come together", in 1 Cor. 11: 17, 18, 20, 33. W.E.Vine continues, "Moreover, what is of paramount importance lies in the repeated 'in remembrance of me'. Where the hearts of the saints are thus attracted to Christ, the gathering to partake of the Lord's supper will have such *a soul-stirring effect, that such an arrangement as a fortnightly or monthly fulfilment will be out of the question"*.

Matthew

b) Its proclamation

"Ye do **shew** the Lord's death". The word "shew" *(katangello)* is used of preaching, see for example, Acts 4: 2, 13. 5. The act of 'breaking bread', is "a silent proclamation of the fact, significance and efficacy of the Lord's death" (W.E.Vine). We sing:

> *No gospel like this feast,*
> *Spread for us, Lord, by Thee;*
> *No prophet nor evangelist*
> *Preach the glad news so free.*

c) Its anticipation

"Till He come". (1 Cor. 11: 26). The Lord Jesus is coming back. He said so: "If I go and prepare a place for you, *I will come again*, and receive you unto myself; that where I am, there ye may be also" (John 14: 3). The "Lord's supper" takes us back to His first coming with all its shame and suffering, and it takes us forward to His second coming with all its glory and victory. One day, we will no longer take the bread and the cup at "the Lord's supper": there will be no necessity to do so, for "we shall be like him; for we shall **see him**" as he is" (1 John 3: 2).

It would be quite wrong to leave the subject without taking careful note of the solemn warning in 1 Cor. 11: 27-29, "Wherefore, whosoever shall eat this bread, and drink this cup of the Lord, unworthily, shall be guilty of the body and blood of the Lord. But let a man examine himself, and so let him eat of that bread, and drink of that cup. For he that eateth and drinketh unworthily, eateth and drinketh damnation (judgment) to himself, not discerning the Lord's body". We "eat of this bread, and drink this cup of the Lord, unworthily", when our lives are inconsistent with our profession at "the Lord's supper". We must ensure that we are right in ourselves, right with our fellow-believers, and right with God. Otherwise we are "guilty of the body and blood of the Lord", that is, we dishonour Him by treating His work at Calvary with indifference. **"Let a man examine himself".**

"If it be possible, let this cup pass from me"

Read Chapter 26: 36-56

With 'unshod feet' (Ex. 3: 5), we now enter the garden of Gethsemane. "Then cometh Jesus with them unto a place called Gethsemane" (v.36). A short while before, the disciples had pledged their allegiance to the Lord Jesus.

In Peter's words, "Though I should die with thee, yet will I not deny thee", to which Matthew adds, "Likewise also said all the disciples" (26: 35). Their allegiance was now about to be sorely tested.

It may come as a surprise to learn that the words 'the garden of Gethsemane' do not occur in Scripture! Matthew refers to "a *place* (*chorion*, meaning 'a region' or 'piece of land') called Gethsemane" and Mark uses the same word in saying, "a *place* which was named Gethsemane" (Mark 14: 32). Luke refers to "the place" (*topos*) (Luke 22: 40), and John to "a garden" (John 18: 1).

These verses may be divided into two main paragraphs: *(1)* the Lord's agony in Gethsemane (vv.36- 46); *(2)* the Lord's arrest in Gethsemane (vv.47-56).

1) THE LORD'S AGONY IN GETHSEMANE, vv.36-46

According to C.I.Scofield, Gethsemane means 'oil-press', whereas Morrish's Bible Dictionary opts for 'wine-press'. Hastings Bible Dictionary gives the location as "on the western slope of the Mount of Olives above the Kidron". Like David in rejection centuries before (2 Sam. 15: 23), the Lord "went forth with his disciples over the book Cedron, where was a garden, into the which he entered, and his disciples" (John 18: 1). The "first man Adam" (1 Cor. 15: 45-47) was found in a garden: "And the Lord God planted a garden eastward in Eden; and there he put the man whom he had formed" (Gen. 2: 8). The "last Adam (the head of the new creation, never to be succeeded or replaced)…the second man" (on the principle, "He taketh away the first, that he may establish the second", Heb. 10: 9), was also found in a garden. Adam was expelled from the garden of Eden as a consequence of sin: the Lord Jesus entered the garden of Gethsemane to face the consequences of sin. Adam sweated (Gen. 3: 19) because **he rebelled against** the will of God; the Lord Jesus sweated "as it were great drops of blood" (Luke 22: 44) because **He submitted** to the will of God.

We must reverently observe the Lord's sorrow of heart and agony of spirit *(a)* in the presence of His disciples (vv.36-38): *(b)* in the presence of His Father (vv.39-46).

a) In the presence of His disciples, vv.36-38

"Then cometh Jesus with them unto a place called Gethsemane, and saith unto his disciples, Sit ye here, while I go and pray yonder. And he took with him Peter and the two sons of Zebedee, and began to be sorrowful and very heavy. Then saith he unto them, My soul is exceedingly sorrowful, even unto death: tarry ye here, and watch with me". The words, "Sit ye here, while I go and pray yonder" are strikingly similar to the way in which Abraham spoke to his young men, "Abide ye here with the ass: and I and the lad will go yonder and worship" (Gen. 22: 5).

The Lord Jesus, who "*began* to preach" (4: 17), and "*began*...to shew unto his disciples, how that he must suffer" (16: 21), now "*began* to be sorrowful and very heavy". This is the third occasion on which these three disciples alone accompanied the Lord, see Mark 5: 37; Matt. 17: 1. Bearing in mind that Scripture later refers to the suffering of all three disciples, perhaps the Lord Jesus took them with Him on each of these three occasions, *(a)* to display His absolute power over death, *(b)* to display His glory in the coming kingdom, and *(c)* to display His complete submission to the Father's will in the face of death itself. Put another way, they saw His grace, His glory, and His grief.

The Lord Jesus was soon to bear the immense burden of God's wrath in respect of sin. We cannot begin to imagine His inner anguish as He approached the cross. Matthew tells us what the three disciples *saw*: He "began to be sorrowful and very heavy" (v.37). He also tells us what the three disciples *heard:* He said "My soul is exceedingly sorrowful, even unto death" (v.38). Mark has, He "began to be sore amazed, and to be very heavy; and saith unto them, My soul is exceedingly sorrowful unto death" (Mark 14: 33-34). We must reverently notice that our Lord was:

i) **"Sorrowful", v.37.** The verb here (*lupeo*) signifies pain, grief, distress. The depth of His sorrow will become apparent when He uses the same word with a prefix (*perilupos*) meaning, "exceeding sorrowful" (v.38). He was, indeed, "a "man of sorrows, and acquainted with grief" (Is. 53: 3). While, in context, this refers to His sorrow at the ravages of sin in the lives of men and women, how great was His sorrow in Gethsemane at the prospect before Him.

ii) **"Very heavy", v.37.** See also Mark 14: 33. The RV has 'sore troubled'. The expression (*ademoneo*) also occurs in connection with Epaphroditus: he was "full of heaviness" ('sore troubled', RV)" (Phil. 2: 26). The word implies "a restless, distracted, shrinking from some trouble or thought of trouble which nevertheless cannot be escaped" (A.H.McNeile). According to G. Campbell Morgan, "Nothing can be definitely said as to its derivation. It may have come from two words. Most probably it has come from one that means 'away from home'. It means more than that, of course; but that is its root idea, that of desolating loneliness".

iii) "Exceeding sorrowful, v.38. As noted above, the expression translates yet another intensive word *(perilupos)*. It means, literally, 'surrounded by sorrow' or 'overwhelmed with distress" (The Expositor's Greek Testament), or, in the words of G. Campbell Morgan, 'My soul is the centre of surging sorrows'. The intensity of His distress is emphasised by the words, "exceeding sorrowful ***unto death***". The Lord Jesus saw no relief for His distress, knowing that it must lead to death itself. In the words of David, "the sorrows of death compassed me" (Psalm 18: 4). The Saviour was "obedient unto death, even the death of the cross" (Phil. 2: 8).

Mark uses the words, "***sore amazed***" (Mark 14: 33). This translates one intensive word *(ekthambeo)* which is used only in Mark's Gospel. See Mark 9: 15 ("greatly amazed"); 16: 5 ("they were affrighted"); 16: 6 ("be not affrighted"). W.E.Vine points out that the word was "frequently associated with terror as well as astonishment". The word "denotes being in the grip of a shuddering horror in the face of the dreadful prospect before him" (C.E.B.Cranfield).

In Gethsemane, the Lord Jesus faced the unutterable horror of Calvary, where God "made him to be sin for us, who knew no sin; that we might be made the righteousness of God in him" (2 Cor. 5: 21). We reverently gaze upon 'The sinless One, for us made sin', as He contemplates the work before Him.

The Lord's request, "tarry ye here, and watch with me", is amplified in v.41: "Watch and pray that ye enter not into temptation: the spirit indeed is willing, but the flesh is weak. The Lord Jesus could say, "the prince of this world cometh, and hath nothing in ***me***" (John 14: 30). ***He*** could not fail, but He knew the weakness of His disciples.

b) In the presence of His Father, vv.39-46
The Lord Jesus prayed three times. He "offered up prayers and supplications with strong crying and tears unto him that was able to save him from (out of) death, and was heard in that he feared ('because of his piety', JND)" (Heb. 5: 7).

i) The first prayer, vv.39-41
We must notice two things here: the Lord's sorrow (v.39); the disciples' sleep (vv.40-41).

Matthew

- The Lord's sorrow. "And he went a little farther, and fell on his face, and prayed, saying, O my Father, if it be possible, let this cup pass from me; nevertheless not as I will, but as thou wilt" (v.39). Mark has, "he...prayed that, if it were possible, the hour might pass from him. And he said, Abba, Father, all things are possible unto thee; take away this cup from me: nevertheless not what I will, but what thou wilt" (Mark 14: 35-36). Luke tells us that "He was withdrawn from them about a stone's cast, and kneeled down, and prayed" (Luke 22: 41). For a thought-provoking exposition of this verse, see Norman Crawford, (*What the Bible Teaches - Luke*). It is Luke who tells us that "there appeared an angel from heaven, strengthening him. And being in an agony He prayed more earnestly: and his sweat was as it were great drops of blood falling down to the ground" (Luke 22: 43-44). Luke uses a medical term *(thrombos)* meaning 'thick clots of coagulated blood'. The physical evidence of our Lord's inner suffering points to depths of agony utterly beyond human comprehension.

His words, "O my Father, if it be possible, let this cup pass from me; nevertheless not as I will", do not suggest in any way that His will was opposed to the Father's will: they tell us, rather, that He desired only that the Father's will should be done. The Lord said, "if it be possible, let this cup pass from me", with the knowledge that it was ***not*** possible (see v.39; John 12: 27)), and that was exactly what He wished to convey. His address, "O my Father", reveals that He did not resent the will of His Father. This is even more emphatic in Mark: "Abba, Father, all things are possible unto thee; take away this cup from me: nevertheless not what I will, but what thou wilt" (Mark 14: 36). This is unique to Mark. The words, "Abba Father", also occur in Romans 8: 15 and Galatians 4: 6. It was a term used only by members of the family, and it is said that slaves were forbidden to address the head of the family by this title. W.E.Vine explains that "Abba" was a word used by children and betokened unreasoning trust, whilst "father" expressed an intelligent understanding of the relationship. "The two together express the love and intelligent confidence of the child". It is therefore deeply moving to hear the Saviour say, "Abba, Father" in the midst of His deep distress in Gethsemane.

In referring to "this cup", the Lord used a scriptural figure denoting divine judgment, something He did not deserve. See, for example, Psalm 75: 8, Isaiah 51: 17, Jeremiah 25: 15, Habakkuk 2: 16. The deep sorrow of the Lord Jesus in Gethsemane, 'in prospect of sin's burden', did not deter Him: "The cup which my Father hath given me, shall I not drink it?" (John 18: 11).

- **The disciples' sleep**. "And he cometh unto the disciples, and findeth them asleep, and saith unto **Peter**, What, could ye not watch with me one hour? Watch and pray, that ye enter not into temptation: the spirit indeed is willing, but the flesh is weak" (vv.40-41). (Does this mean that the Saviour had been praying for an hour?). The disciples had slept on the 'mount of transfiguration' (Luke 9: 32): now they slept in the garden of Gethsemane. The injunction, "Watch and pray, that ye enter not into temptation", was so relevant. The Lord's betrayal and arrest was imminent: their loyalty to Him was about to be tested. Victory lay in watching and praying. Defeat lay in self-confidence. Prayer and alertness go together. Wm.MacDonald has a searching piece here: "We dare not condemn them when we think of our own prayer lives; we sleep better than we pray, and our minds wander when they should be watching. How often the Lord has to say to us as He said to Peter, 'could ye not watch with me one hour? Watch and pray, that ye enter not into temptation'". For other connections between "watch" and "pray", see Ephesians 6: 18, Col. 4: 2.

ii) The second prayer, vv.42-43

"He went away again the second time, and prayed, saying, O my Father, if this cup may not pass from me, except I drink it, thy will be done. And He came and found them asleep again: for their eyes were heavy". Mark adds, "neither wist they what to answer him" (Mark 14: 40), suggesting that the disciples were ashamed. The Lord's second prayer makes the depth of the Saviour's obedience *even more apparent*. In the first prayer He said, "if it be possible, let this cup pass from me: nevertheless not as I will, but as thou wilt" (v.39). Now he prays, "if this cup may not pass from me, except I drink it, thy will be done". In accomplishing His Father's will, the Lord Jesus displayed unswerving obedience."Though he were a son, yet learned he obedience (that is, the cost of obedience) by the things which he suffered" (Heb. 5: 7).

iii) The third prayer, vv.44-45

"And he left them, and went away again, and prayed the third time, saying the same words". Then cometh he to his disciples and saith unto them, Sleep on now, and take your rest: behold the hour is at hand, and the Son of man is betrayed into the hands of sinners". "Three" suggests a limit. Paul "besought the Lord thrice" that the "thorn in the flesh" might depart from him (2 Cor. 12: 7-9).

It has been suggested that there is a short interval between the words "Sleep on now, and take your rest" (v.45) and, "Rise, let us be going: behold he is at hand that doth betray me" (v.46). We must notice that the Saviour did not censure His disciples. In grace and tenderness, He allowed them to sleep. "For he knoweth our frame; he remembereth that we are dust" (Psalm 103: 14). At the same time, we can understand the Saviour's words here with reference to His victory in Gethsemane. He had faced, and overcome, the dreadful prospect of Calvary, and was now ready to face its fearful reality. He therefore says to the disciples, "Sleep on now, and take your rest". G. Campbell Morgan has a nice piece here: "He came back to them, His own triumph won, when they were still drowsy, and opened their eyes as He came perchance, and He quietly said to them, 'There is a little time left, sleep on now'. And they went back to sleep as He watched over them. He kept the lone vigil over those sleeping men until presently He saw the flash of the torches, for Judas was coming, and then He put His hand upon them and said, 'Arise, let us be going'. What passed through His soul in those hours we do not know. Nothing but love for those men, those drowsy men whom He had to rebuke, was in His heart".

With divine resolution, divine omniscience, and divine dignity, He goes to meet His betrayer. There is no attempt to flee, and no hint of panic: "Rise, let us be going: behold he is at hand that doth betray me" (v.46). This brings us to:

2) *THE LORD'S ARREST IN GETHSEMANE, vv.47-56*
The "Spirit of Christ" (1 Pet. 1: 11) was in Isaiah when he wrote: "I was not rebellious, neither turned away back" (Isaiah 50: 5). Now, with divine resolution and assurance, like David before Him (1 Sam. 17: 45-47), He faces "a great multitude with swords and staves, from the chief priests and the elders of the people". They are led by "Judas, one of the twelve" (v.47). We must notice here: *(a)* the false kiss (vv.47-50); *(b)* the flashing sword (vv.51-53); *(c)* the fulfillment of Scripture (vv.54-56); *(d)* the forsaking by the disciples (v.56).

a) The false kiss, vv.47-50
The Lord Jesus had said, with divine omniscience, "Rise, let us be going: behold he is at hand that doth betray me" (v.46). The passage continues, "And while he yet spake, lo, Judas…came" (v.47). The betrayer acted without hesitation: "Now he that betrayed him gave them a sign, saying, Whomsoever I shall kiss (*phileo*), that same is he: hold him fast. And forthwith he came to Jesus, and said, Hail (literally, 'Rejoice'), Master; and kissed him (*kataphileo*)" (vv.48-49). The details should be noted:

i) Judas was "one of the twelve", v.47. This carries a chilling note, and we have already weighed the implications of the expression in connection with v.14-16, "Then one of the twelve, called Judas Iscariot, went unto the chief priests...And from that time he sought opportunity to betray him". Here is J.C.Ryle again: "The actions of Judas Iscariot are a terrible warning of the lengths a man may go to in a false profession of religion". See, again, 2 Corinthians 13: 5, "Examine yourselves, whether ye be in the faith; prove your own selves". On an equally solemn note, it is terribly possible for us to profess love for Christ, and actually address Him to that effect in word or song, but at the same time to be utterly disloyal to Him in life and conduct.

ii) Judas "came, and with him a great multitude with swords and staves", v.47. The religious leaders evidently expected armed resistance, and showed that they had totally misunderstood His mission. He had not come "to destroy men's lives, but to save them" (Luke 9: 56). His ministry fulfilled the ancient prophecy, "He shall not strive, nor cry; neither shall any man hear his voice in the streets. A bruised reed shall he not break, and a smoking flax shall he not quench" (Matt. 12: 17-21). A few hours later, He made the matter very clear to Pilate: "My kingdom is not of this world: if my kingdom were of this world, then would my servants fight, that I should not be delivered to the Jews: but now is my kingdom not from hence" (John 18: 36).

iii) Judas had given them "a sign", v.48. Contrary to artistic impressions, there was no halo surrounding the head of the Lord Jesus, neither did His face glow with heavenly glory. He had to be identified by Judas, otherwise it could be a case of mistaken identity in the gloom of the garden. We must remember that the Lord Jesus was "found in fashion as a man". (Phil. 2: 8). The word, "fashion" (*schema*) refers to the outward and perceptible appearance of the Lord Jesus. His mode of appearance, though very God, was that of a man.

iv) Judas said, "Hail, master; and kissed him", v.49. As we have already observed, Judas never called Him "Lord". Here we have the traitor's kiss: "And as soon as he was come, he goeth straightway to him, and saith, Master, master; and kissed him (*kataphileo*, to kiss fervently)" (Mark 14: 45). This was the most infamous kiss in history. Solomon tells us that "the kisses of an enemy are deceitful" (Prov. 27: 6). When Jacob kissed Isaac, it was a deceiver's kiss (Gen. 27: 26-27). When Orpah kissed Naomi, it was an irresolute kiss (Ruth 1: 14). When Joab kissed Amasa, it was a murderer's kiss (2 Sam. 20: 9-10). But Judas betrayed the Son of God. The Gospel writers record just two occasions on which the Lord Jesus was kissed: He was kissed by the woman in Luke 7: 36-50. She kissed His feet out of deep love for Him (see v.45). He was kissed by Judas for thirty pieces of silver. Judas could have identified the Lord Jesus in some other way, but perhaps the kiss was intended to convey the impression that all was well, and so reduce the possibility of flight. If so, he had completely failed to recognise the Lord's omniscience, perhaps even failed to recognise that He was the Son of God.

Matthew tells us how the Lord Jesus addressed Judas: "Friend, wherefore art thou come?" (v.50). John Heading explains: "This particular word (*hetairos*)... does not involve affection, rather companionship, reflecting the fact that Judas, as one of the twelve, had accompanied the Lord for several years in His ministry". Luke tells us something else that the Lord said to Judas: "Betrayest thou the Son of man with a kiss?" (Luke 22: 48). John gives us further details, emphasising the Lord's deity even in these circumstances (John 18: 3-9).

We must not forget that one day, heaven will command earth's rulers to "**Kiss the Son**, lest he be angry and ye perish from the way" (Psalm 2: 12).

b) The flashing sword, vv.51-53
"And, behold, one of them that were with Jesus (we know it to have been Peter, John 18: 10) stretched out his hand, and drew his sword, and struck a servant (we know it to have been Malchus, John 18: 10) of the high priest's, and smote off his ear" (v.51). Only Luke, the medical man, tells us that the man's ear was restored. Luke and John tell us that it was the right ear (Luke 22: 50-51; John 18: 10).

The Lord's words to Peter, "Put up again thy sword into his place: for all they that take up the sword shall perish with the sword" (v.52), remind us, sadly, that Christians have taken up arms in the name of Christ, with dire results. We must note in this connection that the sword of governmental justice is quite different (Rom. 13: 4). Paul describes the Christian warfare in Ephesians 6, and specifies the weapons required. In fact, the entire incident, with its associated teaching, reminds us that "the weapons of our warfare are not carnal, but mighty through God to the pulling down of strongholds" (2 Cor.10: 3-4).

The Lord Jesus did not need to be defended. No power on earth could have arrested Him against His will. Matthew refers to the angelic fire-power at His disposal: "Thinkest thou that I cannot now pray to my Father, and he shall presently give me more than twelve legions of angels?" (v.53). If **one** angel slew 185,000 Assyrian soldiers in one night (2 Kings 19: 35), just think what 72,000 angels ("twelve legions" of them) would have done! But He did not need the angelic host to deliver Him. This is very clear from John's account of the arrest: "As soon as he had said unto them, I am (he), they went backward, and fell to the ground" (John 18: 6). **"I AM"** (Exodus 3: 14) had spoken! Not only so, the Lord Jesus did not ask to be defended: See John 18: 11, "Put up thy sword into the sheath: the cup that my Father hath given me, shall I not drink it?"

It can be said that the Lord *did* use a sword. In fact, it was precisely the same sword that He will use in the future. See Revelation 19: 15-21. In Gethsemane, He used the sword (His voice) quite moderately: "they went backward, and fell to the ground" (John 18: 6). At Armageddon, He will use that same sword without mercy.

c) The fulfillment of scripture, vv.54-56
He declined the help of "more than twelve legions of angels" because, in His own words, "how then shall the scriptures be fulfilled, that thus it must be?" (v.54). Then, having recorded the Saviour's words, "Are ye come out as against a thief with swords and with staves for to take me?", Matthew observes. "But all this was done, that the scriptures of the prophets might be fulfilled" (vv.55-56). In this connection, we should notice *(i)* their assessment of Him: "a thief" (v.55); *(ii)* His assessment of Himself: a teacher (v.55).

i) Their assessment of Him. "Are ye come out as against a *thief* with swords and staves for to take me?" The Lord Jesus taught that "the thief cometh not, but for to steal, and to kill, and to destroy" (John 10: 10). They treated Him as a thief, but in actual fact *they* were the thieves. They had come "to kill, and to destroy". Significantly, in this connection, "the chief priests, and captains of the temple, and the elders", were also present (Luke 22: 52).

ii) His assessment of Himself. "I sat daily with you *teaching* in the temple, and ye laid no hold on me". They knew full well why He had not been arrested in the temple. See v.2 with Luke 22: 6. They dared not act publicly, and were reduced to effecting a clandestine arrest. Luke adds here, "but this is your hour, and the power of darkness" (Luke 22: 53). We should note that the apostles followed the Lord's example: "And **daily** in the **temple**, and in every house, they ceased not to **teach** and preach Jesus Christ" (Acts 5: 42).

But all was in fulfilment of Scripture, and "the scripture cannot be broken" (John 10: 35). As noted above, Matthew is commenting, rather than quoting, in saying, "But all this was done, that the scriptures of the prophets might be fulfilled" (v.56) Whilst this statement appears to refer to the prophetic scriptures generally, rather than to any one particular scripture, it could refer to Isaiah 53: 7, 12. He was certainly "numbered with the transgressors" in Gethsemane as well as at Calvary, for they came "out as against a thief".

d) The forsaking by the disciples, v.56
"Then all the disciples forsook him, and fled". As H.S.Paisley (writing on Mark) notes that "the fearless composure of the Servant is contrasted with the failing courage of the eleven disciples. God had said of Him: 'he shall not fail nor be discouraged' (Isaiah 42: 4)". As Wm.MacDonald so rightly observes, "If their cowardice was inexcusable, ours is more so. They had not yet been indwelt by the Holy Spirit: we have". The Lord's own words were fulfilled: "All ye shall be offended because of me this night: for it is written, I will smite the shepherd, and the sheep of the flock shall be scattered abroad" (v.31).

Years later, Paul commented on his trial at Rome: "At my first answer no man stood with me, but **all men forsook me**...Notwithstanding the Lord stood with me, and strengthened me" (2 Tim. 4: 16-17). The Lord who stood with Paul and strengthened him, understood Paul's position perfectly. He had been there Himself. "We have not an high priest which cannot be touched with the feeling of our infirmities; but was in all points tempted like as we are, yet without sin" (Heb. 4: 15).

"He is guilty of death"

Read Chapter 26: 57-75
These verses describe **two** trials in the high priest's palace. The Lord Jesus was on trial in the upper hall of the palace (vv.57-68), and Peter was on trial in the courtyard below (vv.69-75).

1) THE LORD JESUS ON TRIAL, vv.57-68
"And they that had laid hold on Jesus led him away to Caiaphas the high priest, where the scribes and the elders were assembled" (v.57). While the religious trial of the Lord Jesus took place before Caiaphas (he is not

mentioned by name by either Mark or Luke), we know that He was taken first to Annas, the father-in-law of Caiaphas: "Then the band and the captain and officers of the Jews took Jesus, and bound him, and led him away to Annas first; for he was father in law to Caiaphas, which was the high priest that same year (John 18: 12-13). It is interesting to note that **both** were high priests when John the Baptist commenced to preach (Luke 3: 2). Annas had originally been high priest, but had been deposed by the Romans, who replaced him with Caiaphas. However, the Jews still recognised Annas as the rightful incumbent (see Acts 4: 6). John also tells us that "Caiaphas was he, which gave counsel to the Jews, that it was expedient that one man should die for the people" (John 18: 14 referring to John 11: 47-52). Caiaphas thought in terms of deliverance from the anger of Rome, but God had something quite different in mind!

All four Gospels tell us that the Lord Jesus was taken immediately to "the high priests's palace" and tried, and that He was then subjected to sickening abuse (Matt. 26: 57-68; Mark 14: 53-65; Luke 22: 54-65, John 18: 12-14, 9-24). It is also evident that after the "chief priests, and elders, and all the council" (v.59) had condemned the Lord Jesus, they separated, and met again early in the morning, and that Matthew 27: 1 ("When the morning was come, all the chief priests and elders of the people took counsel against Jesus to put him to death"), Mark 15: 1 and Luke 22: 66-71 refer to a second meeting of the Jewish leadership. One commentator (cited by J.C.Ryle), referring to Luke 22: 66-71, suggests that "it is not improbable that the high priest should again put the same questions to the Lord as he had done the night before, both to see whether He would stand by what He had said, and also that such members of the Council as had been absent might hear His answers".

Though he was unaware of it at the time, Peter also went to his trial. "But Peter followed him afar off unto the high priest's palace, and went in, and sat with the servants, to see the end (the outcome)" (v.58). Perhaps Peter remembered his promise, "If I should die with thee, I will not deny thee in any wise" (Mark 14: 31), and endeavoured to redeem himself after fleeing with the rest of the disciples. John gives additional details here (John 18: 12-16). J.C.Ryle observes that "there was no wisdom in this act. Having once forsaken his Master and fled, he ought to have remembered his own weakness, and not to have ventured into danger again. It was an act of rashness and presumption. It brought on him fresh trials of faith, for which he was utterly unprepared". Whilst this is true, we must not forget that the man who denied the Lord Jesus three times by a fire, was recommissioned by another fire. See John 21: 15-17. We must also remember that Peter had a private interview with the risen Lord, but since it was a personal matter between Peter and Christ, no details are given. See Luke 24: 34; 1 Corinthians 15: 5. We do know that the man who "followed...afar off", became strong enough to be a martyr. See John 21: 18-19.

Perhaps we too have "followed....afar off", and found warmth at the fires of this world, whilst Christ is maligned and rejected. Perhaps, unlike Peter who actively disassociated himself from the Lord Jesus, we have passively disassociated ourselves from Him, only to find ourselves faced with the situation described in Jeremiah 1: 17, "Be not dismayed at their faces, lest *I confound thee before them*". The world is hostile to Christ, and will therefore be hostile to all who follow Him, but we are urged to "go forth therefore unto him without the camp, bearing his reproach (Heb. 13: 13). But failure in loyalty to Christ does not mean irretrievable breakdown. The very man who "followed...afar off" later wrote, "If ye be reproached for the name of Christ, happy are ye; for the spirit of glory and of God resteth upon you: on their part he is evil spoken of, but on your part he is glorified" (1 Pet. 4: 14).

We should now notice *(a)* the evidence for the prosecution (vv.59-61); *(b)* the statements by the defendant (vv.62-64); *(c)* the verdict (vv.65-68).

a) The evidence for the prosecution, vv.59-61
i) The accusers, v.59. "Now the chief priests, and elders, and all the council, sought for witness against Jesus to put him to death; and found none". The "council" refers to the Sanhedrin, the Great Council of Jerusalem, consisting of 71 members, including Gamaliel (Acts 5: 34), who taught Saul of Tarsus (Acts 22: 3), possibly instilling in him hatred for the Lord Jesus. They had already settled the outcome of the trial, and looked only for supporting evidence. Nicodemus would have been silenced for the second time had he dared to ask, "Doth our law judge any man, before it hear him, and know what he doeth?" (John 7: 50-53). The hearing was biased from its very commencement. But no proper charge could be laid against the Accused. John 18: 19-24 give further details.

We could write over these and following verses, the words of the Lord Jesus Himself: "But this cometh to pass, that the word might be fulfilled which is written in their law, They hated me without a cause" (John 15: 25). We have now reached the point where the hatred of the religious leadership reached its height. His faithful exposure of their hypocrisy incited utter hatred, and they now appeared to have succeeded in gaining mastery over Him They little knew that they had only been successful in arresting Him because He had deliberately put Himself in their grasp. He was "delivered by the determinate counsel and foreknowledge of God" (Acts 2: 23), and the religious leaders could only do, in the words of the praying church at Jerusalem "whatsoever thy hand and thy counsel determined before to be done" (Acts 4: 24-28).

In passing, we should note two lessons here. **Firstly,** that we must avoid pre-judging people without first ascertaining the facts. See Deuteronomy 17: 2-7. There is always a temptation to condemn someone out of hand on the flimsiest of evidence, particularly if we don't like them in the first place! **Secondly,** we must behave in a manner which gives "none occasion to the adversary to speak reproachfully" (1 Tim. 5: 14). No valid charge could be brought against the Lord Jesus. They tried to prove His guilt, but only succeeded in proving His utter righteousness

ii) The accusations, vv.59-61. They "sought false witness against Jesus, to put him to death; but found none; yea, though many false witnesses came, yet found they none. At last came two false witnesses, and said, This fellow said, I am able to destroy the temple of God, and to build it in three days". The whole process was a complete farce! The Biblical rule of evidence (Deut. 17: 6; 19: 15-21) was totally disregarded. Mark is even more explicit: "For *many* bare false witness against him, but their witness agreed not together. And there arose certain, and bare false witness against him saying, We heard him say, I will destroy this temple that is made with hands, and within three days I will build another made without hands. But neither so did their witness agree together" (Mark 14: 55-59). The testimony of the individual witnesses was false, and the testimony of the witnesses collectively was contradictory. "The proceedings lacked every feature proper to a judicial trial at law. It was begun and ended during the darkness of a single night; the judges searched eagerly for hostile witnesses but when they were found, the hirelings contradicted one another, and the bench made no protest" (H.St.John). Just imagine what counsel for the defence in a modern court would have done with that kind of evidence. The prisoner would have been quickly acquitted. But this Prisoner stood alone: nobody spoke for Him, or pointed out the total injustice of the proceedings. His accusers displayed their parentage: their father, the devil, was 'the father of lies' (John 8: 44).

Matthew, together with Mark, record only one of the many false accusations

(Matt: 26: 61; Mark 14: 58). In Mark's words, "We heard him say, I will destroy this temple that is made with hands, and within three days I will build another made without hands". This was a misquotation. The Lord actually said, "Destroy this temple, and in three days I will raise it up" (John 2: 19-22). The Lord's refererence there to "the temple of his body", was turned by the "false witnesses" into a threat against the temple. As H.St.John points out, the misquotation "might be due to careless listening, but it seems to drip with malice". A similar charge was levelled at Stephen. To threaten the temple was regarded as blasphemy. See Acts 6: 13.

There are at least two lessons for ourselves here. **Firstly,** we will have to contend with misquotation and misrepresentation (see, for example, Romans 3: 8), sometimes, sadly, even amongst fellow-believers. There are always people ready to seize on a remark or statement, and twist its meaning, either by failure to listen carefully, or because they are looking for an opportunity to score a point. J.C.Ryle observes, "Lies and false reports are among Satan's choicest weapons. When he cannot deter men from serving Christ, he labours to harass them and makes Christ's service uncomfortable". **Secondly,** we must ensure that we accurately and faithfully quote other people. Do remember that you can quote someone quite accurately, but completely alter their meaning by changing their tone of voice, or by putting a different emphasis on certain words and expressions!

b) *The statements by the defendant, vv.62-64*
The high priest was evidently quite exasperated by the miserable failure of the witnesses for the prosecution. The trial seemed in jeopardy. Let the prisoner incriminate Himself. "And the high priest arose, and said unto him, Answerest thou nothing? What is it which these witness against thee? But Jesus held his peace" (vv.62-63). After all, there was no need for Him to answer the charges against Him. There was no factual charge to answer! Notice too, that the ancient prophecy was in course of fulfillment: "He was oppressed, and he was afflicted, yet he opened not his mouth: he is brought as a lamb to the slaughter, and as a sheep before her shearers is dumb, so he openeth not his mouth" (Isaiah 53: 7). As T.Miller points out, 'Our salvation lies in His silence'.

In deepening exasperation, Caiaphas asks a direct question, which leads to two statements by the Lord Jesus:

*i) **That He is the Son of God.*** In response to the question, putting the

Lord Jesus on oath, "I adjure thee ('to lay under the obligation of an oath') by the living God, that thou tell us whether thou be the Christ, the Son of God" (v.63), the Lord replied, "Thou hast said" (v.64). That is, Caiaphas was correct, He was indeed "the Christ, the Son of God", and although the high priest did not believe this for one moment, it would be proven: "nevertheless I say unto you, Hereafter shall ye see the Son of man sitting on the right hand of power, and coming in the clouds of heaven" (v.64). It seems likely that the high priest's question was asked in deepest irony. To quote Mark's record: "Art thou (a bound captive in poverty and shame) the Christ, the Son of the Blessed?" They must have waited with bated breath for His reply, and it came with absolute clarity: "I am" (Mark 14: 61-62). A further confirmation of His deity is given in the statement which follows:

ii) That He is the Son of man. He stood before His religious judges in humiliation and shame, but the bound prisoner would return in highest glory and honour: "I say unto you (plural), Hereafter shall ye (plural) see the Son of man sitting on the right hand of power (referring to God in all His power: Stephen saw Him "standing on the right hand of God"), and coming in the clouds of heaven" (v.64). The Lord referred here, as His accusers knew only too well, to Psalm 110: 1 ("The LORD said unto my Lord, Sit thou at my right hand, until I make thine enemies thy footstool") and to Daniel 7: 13-14 ("I saw in the night visions, and, behold, one like to the Son of man came with the clouds of heaven, and came to the Ancient of Days, and they brought him near before him. And there was given him dominion, and glory, and a kingdom").

In summary, the Lord Jesus, *(i)* confirmed that He was the Son of God, and *(ii)* assured His accusers that the nation would see His claim proved. Compare Revelation 1: 7, "Behold, he cometh with clouds; and every eye shall see him, and they also which pierced him; and all kindreds of the earth shall wail because of him". See also Matthew 24: 30, "They shall see the Son of man coming in the clouds of heaven with power and great glory". The Lord's words, ye shall "see the Son of man sitting on the right hand of power", and Stephen's words, "I see...the Son of man standing on the right hand of God" (Acts 7: 56), had the same result (Matt. 26: 65-68; Acts 7: 57-59)

c) The verdict, vv.65-68
"Then the high priest rent his clothes, saying, He hath spoken blasphemy; what further need have we of witnesses? Behold, now ye have heard his blasphemy. What think ye? They answered and said, He is guilty of death".

Matthew

Blasphemy carried the death penalty (Lev. 24: 16: John 10: 33). Preachers have been heard to say that by rending his clothes, the high priest forfeited his ministry, but this is not supported by passages usually quoted (Lev. 10: 6; 21:10). It was meant to convey intense sorrow, but the high priest was actually 'playing to the gallery'. In truth, he was delighted that at long last he had grounds, he thought, for an accusation

Although the Lord Jesus stood condemned by the high priest, no account was taken of the evidence to support His claim. Later, Peter charged the Jews as follows: "Jesus of Nazareth, a man approved of God among you by miracles and wonders and signs which God did by Him in the midst of you, *as ye yourselves also know*..." (Acts 2: 22). But the power of unbelief is greater than any evidence. They hated Him, and were determined to get rid of Him as quickly as possible.

The shameful treatment that followed contrasts with the honour and glory that surrounds the Saviour now in heaven, and which will be seen when He returns to earth. "Then did they spit in his face, and buffeted him (*kolaphizo*: to buffet with the fist); and others smote him with the palms of their hands, saying (with deepest irony), Prophesy unto us, thou Christ, Who is he that smote thee?" (vv.67-68). Mark notes that "the **servants** did strike him with the palms of their hands" (Mark 14: 65). All dignity and decency were flung to the winds, and Luke adds the disgusting detail that the Lord's captors played an obscene game of 'blind man's buff' with Him (Luke 22: 64). By spitting in the Lord's face, His captors both fulfilled Scripture (Isaiah 50: 6), and shewed their utter contempt (Deut. 25: 9). The employment of the word "prophesy" may indicate that the Lord was accused of being a false prophet. As such He should die (Deut. 18: 20). But although "oppressed and...afflicted, yet he opened not his mouth" (Isaiah 53: 7).

Whilst all this was happening, another trial was taking place. While, as we have already noticed, the Lord Jesus was on trial in the upper hall of the palace (vv.57-68), Peter went on trial in the courtyard below (vv.69-75).

2) PETER ON TRIAL, vv.69-75
Peter had said, "Though all men shall be offended because of thee, yet will I never be offended", to which the Lord had replied, "Verily I say unto thee, That this night, before the cock crow (twice, Mark 14: 30), thou shalt deny me thrice" (26: 33-34). As H.S.Paisley observes (writing on Mark): "The denial of Peter in the courtyard coincided with the confession of Christ

before His accusers. The perfect Servant witnessed a good confession, in contrast to the denial of an imperfect one". J.C.Ryle is so right to remind us "how far and how shamefully a great saint may fall". He catalogues the "special privileges" and "special mercies" shown by the Lord Jesus to Peter, including deliverance from drowning in the sea of Galilee, and then comments, "These things are written to show the church of Christ what human nature is, even in the best of men. They are intended to teach us that, even after conversion and renewal of the Holy Ghost, believers are compassed with infirmity and liable to fall". We cannot fail to remember the words, "Let him that thinketh he standeth, take heed lest he fall" (1 Cor. 10: 12).

The inclusion of Peter's denial and ultimate restoration, illustrates the Lord's perfect knowledge of His servants, and His personal interest in every one of them. The Lord Jesus allowed Peter to pass through the most harrowing experiences, not to punish him for his brash self-confidence but, by a process of refining, to deepen his love and make him more useful than he had ever been before. Hence the Saviour's words, "And when thou art converted, strengthen thy brethren" (Luke 22: 32). The Lord still takes a personal interest in each one of His children, with the same objects in view.

Once again, we must notice *(a)* the evidence for the prosecution (vv.69,71,73); *(b)* the statements by the defendant (vv.70,72,74; *(c)* the verdict (v.75)

a) The evidence for the prosecution, vv.69,71,73
Bearing in mind the Lord's words, "Verily I say unto thee, That this night, before the cock crow, thou shalt deny me thrice" (26: 34), we must note.

i) The first accusation. "Now Peter sat without in the palace ('was beneath in the palace', Mark 14: 66): and a damsel came unto him, saying Thou also wast with Jesus of Galilee" (v.69). Luke makes it quite clear that the girl was not mistaken: she "earnestly looked upon him" (Luke 22: 56). Peter, presumably to avoid further examination, then "went out into the porch; and the cock crew" (Mark 14: 68). Only Mark mentions the first cock-crowing. But he did not escape as simply as that:

ii) The second accusation. "And when he was gone out into the porch, another maid saw him, and said unto them that were there, This fellow was also with Jesus of Nazareth" (v.71). Although Mark tells us that "a maid ('*the*' maid, JND) saw him again, and began to say to them that stood by,

This is one of them" (Mark 14: 69), Matthew calls her "***another*** maid", so it doesn't seem to have been the same maid after all!

iii) The third accusation. "And after a while came unto him them that stood by, and said to Peter, Surely thou also art one of them; for thy speech bewrayeth thee" (v.73). Mark expands this: "And a little later, they that stood by said again to Peter, Surely thou art one of them: ***for thou art a Galilean, and thy speech agreeth thereto***" (Mark 14: 70). Perhaps one of the bystanders had a vested interest in Peter. See John 18: 26.

b) The statements by the defendant, vv.70,72,74
i) The first denial. "But he denied before them all, saying, I know not what thou sayest" (v.70). Mark expands this: "I know not***, neither understand I*** what thou sayest" (Mark 14: 68). ***The Lord Jesus*** made no attempt to plead ignorance: He affirmed that the high priest was correct in calling Him "the Christ, the Son of God" (v.63).

ii) The second denial. "And again he denied with an oath, I do not know the man" (v.72). ***The Lord Jesus***, under oath, answered the high priest truthfully (vv.63-64). Luke tells us that Peter responded to the second accusation with the words, "***Man,*** I am not" (Luke 22: 58). There is no contradiction, Matthew, Mark and Luke are all covered by John: "***they*** said therefore unto him, Art not thou also one of his disciples?" (Jn. 18: 25).

iii) The third denial. "Then began he to curse and to swear, saying, I know not the man. And immediately the cock crew" (v.74). ***The Lord Jesus*** was subject to cursing and swearing (vv.67-68). According to H.S.Paisley, Peter was not guilty of "profane cursing…but rather…placed himself under a curse from God if he were lying, and under an oath, as in court, to establish the truth of his denial". This may relieve Peter of the charge of 'cursing and swearing' in our modern sense, but it does not make the situation any less serious. If anything, it makes it worse.

c) The verdict, v.75
There can be no doubt about this. He was guilty, on his own admission. "And Peter remembered the word of Jesus, which said unto him, Before the cock crow, thou shalt deny me thrice. And he went out, and wept bitterly". According to J.C.Fenton (in a piece supplied by Justin Waldron), "It may be that we are meant to contrast the repentance of Peter with the despair of Judas (Matt. 27: 4). Paul similarly speaks of two kinds of sorrow: 'For

godly sorrow worketh repentance unto salvation not to be repented of: but the sorrow of the world worketh death' (2 Cor. 7: 10)"

The bold fisherman who had said, "Though all men shall be offended because of thee, yet will I never be offended" (26: 33), remembered "the word that Jesus had said unto him...And when he thought thereon, he wept" (Mark 14: 72). Matthew says, "And he went out, and wept bitterly", and so does Luke (Luke 22: 62). "The backslider in heart shall be filled with his own ways" (Prov. 14: 14). Luke also tells us that "the Lord turned, and looked upon Peter" (Luke 22: 61). John evidently records only the first two denials, "but in kindness to his friend omits any reference to oaths or curses" (Harold St.John).

But **we** mustn't sit in judgment on Peter. He represents a large number of people who ought to be faithful to Christ, but who dodge the issue when they're put on the spot. Paul said to Timothy, "Be not thou therefore ashamed of the testimony of our Lord, nor of me his prisoner: but be thou a partaker of the afflictions of the gospel according to the power of God" (2 Tim.1: 8).

THE GOSPEL OF MATTHEW

"Barabbas, or Jesus which is called Christ?"

Read Chapter 27: 1-26
As we have seen, Matthew 26: 57-67 describe the religious trial of the Lord Jesus. This was followed by His civil trial, described in Matthew 27: 11-26. These trials were totally unjust, and in both cases the charges and verdict bore no relation to the evidence. Jew and Gentile were united in rejecting Christ. This was recognised at the prayer meeting of the church at Jerusalem: "For of a truth, against thy holy child Jesus ('thy holy servant Jesus', JND), whom thou hast anointed, both Herod and Pontius Pilate, with the Gentiles, and the people of Israel were gathered together, for to do whatsoever thy hand and thy counsel determined before to be done" (Acts 4: 27-28).

The narrative in Matthew 27: 1-26 is punctuated by references to "the chief priests and elders" (vv.1, 3, 12, 20). (Similar references are not lacking in the other Gospel records). With this in mind we will divide the passage as follows: *(1)* they delivered the Lord to Pilate (vv.1-2); *(2)* they dismissed the remorse of Judas (vv.3-10); *(3)* they denounced the Lord before Pilate (vv.11-14); *(4)* they demanded the Lord's destruction (vv.15-26).

1) THEY DELIVERED THE LORD TO PILATE, vv.1-2
"When the morning was come, all the chief priests and elders of the people took counsel against Jesus to put him to death: and when they had bound him, they led him away, and delivered him to Pontius Pilate the governor". Little did Pilate know that the Prisoner would become "a Governor, that shall rule...Israel" (Matt. 2: 6: Micah 5: 2). We can contrast that "morning" (v.1) with another a few days later: "But when the morning was now come, Jesus stood on the shore" (John 21: 4). The expressions, "they...bound him"; "they led him away"; "they... delivered him" do not signify the mastery of His enemies, but His deliberate submission to their will:

Chapter 27

> *How didst Thou humble Thyself to be taken,*
> *Led by Thy creatures, and nailed to the cross!*
> *Hated of men, and of God, too, forsaken,*
> *Shunning not darkness, the curse, and the loss!*

At the end of the religious trial, they said "he is guilty of death" (Matt. 26: 66), but the sentence required confirmation and execution by the civil authority. See John 18: 31. By contrast, Stephen was stoned to death by the Jews without any apparent reference to the civil authority. E.H.Plumptre (Ellicott's Commentary) explains: "Then (in the case of the Lord Jesus)... the Roman procurator was present in Jerusalem. Now (in the case of Stephen) all restraint was removed, and fanaticism had full play". Pilate's usual headquarters were at Caesarea, but since the Jews often turned their festivals into demonstrations, he was present at his official residence in Jerusalem.

John records the utter hypocrisy of the religious leaders: "Then they led Jesus from Caiaphas unto the hall of judgment: and it was early; and they themselves went not into the judgment hall, lest they should be defiled; but that they might eat the passover" (John 18: 28). They were more interested in religious observance than moral conduct.

2) *THEY DISMISSED THE REMORSE OF JUDAS, vv.3-10*

They 'couldn't care less' about the remorse of Judas. After all, they had got what they wanted. They said, "What is that to us? see thou to that" (v.4). These verses are unique to Matthew's Gospel. We should notice *(a)* the unavailing remorse of Judas (vv.3-5); *(b)* the unfeeling response of the religious leaders (vv.6-10).

a) The unavailing remorse of Judas, vv.3-5

"Then Judas, which had betrayed him, when he saw that he was condemned, repented himself, and brought again the thirty pieces of silver to the chief priests and elders, saying, I have sinned in that I have betrayed the innocent blood. And they said, What is that to us? see thou to that. And he cast down (*rhipto*, to hurl) the pieces of silver, and departed, and went and hanged himself". Pilate also referred to the Lord Jesus in similar terms: he referred to "the blood of this just person" (v.24). For "innocent blood" see Deut. 19: 10, 13; 1 Sam. 19: 5; Psalm 94: 21. According to Wm.Kelly, "Manifestly Judas did not expect such an end for Jesus. He had known the Lord in imminent peril before; he had seen Him, when the people took up stones to cast at

Him, hiding Himself, going through the midst of them and passing on His way...But Judas was deceived, whatever his calculations may have been; he yielded to covetousness; he bargained for the blood of Jesus. To his horror, he found it but too true. And Satan, who had led him on by his love of money, leaves him without hope - in black despair".

G.Campbell Morgan calls this "a too late repentance" and "a too late restitution". We must take careful note of Judas' words: "I have sinned", and listen to J.C.Ryle: "It is possible for a man to feel his sins and be sorry for them - to be under strong convictions of guilt, and express deep remorse - to be pricked in conscience, and exhibit much distress of mind - and yet, for all this, not to repent with his heart. Present danger, or the fear of death, may account for all his feelings, and the Holy Ghost may have done no work whatever on his soul". The word used of Judas, "repented himself" (*metamelomai*) signifies 'to be remorseful' rather than a complete change of mind or attitude (H.A.Ironside).

Luke calls the thirty pieces of silver, "the reward of iniquity" (Acts 1: 18). We know that Judas "went and hanged himself" (v.5), but Luke "takes up the narrative...and records a further mishap to his body" (James Anderson). Wm.MacDonald, and others suggest that Judas "hanged himself on a tree" and "that the rope (or branch) broke, and that his body was hurled over a precipice, causing it to be disemboweled". What happened to his soul is even more terrible: he went "to his own place" (Acts 1: 25). Judas and the "man of sin" have at least one thing in common. Both are called "the son of perdition" (John 17: 12; 2 Thess. 2: 3), indicating their eternal destiny.

We cannot leave this without noticing the response of "chief priests and elders": "What is that to us? see thou to that". The Lord's "innocent blood" meant nothing to them, but believers can sing, with deep reverence and deep appreciation:

> *Precious, precious blood of Jesus,*
> *Shed on Calvary;*
> *Shed for rebels, shed for sinners,*
> *Shed for thee!*

b) The unfeeling response of the religious leaders, vv.6-10
Having said, "What is that to us?", the "chief priests and elders", without any feeling, "took the silver pieces, and said, "It is not lawful to put them into

the treasury, because it is the price of blood. And they took counsel, and bought with them the potter's field to bury strangers in. Wherefore that field was called, The field of blood, unto this day" (vv.6-8). Luke tells us that the "field is called in their proper tongue, Aceldama, that is to say, The field of blood" (Acts 1: 19). James Anderson calls this, "Luke's usual precision" in recording "the proper name of the potter's field once it had been bought". This fulfilled the parable enacted by Zechariah (see Zech. 11: 7-14): "And the LORD said unto me, Cast it unto the potter: a goodly price that I was prised at of them. And I took the thirty pieces of silver, and cast them to the potter in the house of the Lord" (Zech. 11: 13).

Campbell Morgan draws attention to the fact that men often "attempt to cleanse money by putting it to charitable uses. Mark the irony of the whole situation, how the people named the thing correctly, even when the priests tried to hide it. The priests said, 'A field to bury strangers in'. The people said, 'the field of blood'".

Matthew's record appears to differ slightly from Zechariah's prophetic parable, but we must bear in mind that Zechariah was acting the parable in the first person whereas Matthew applies the prophetic truths set out in the parable. According to Deuteronomy 23: 18, dishonourable money must not remain in the temple, and it was probably to this command that the chief priests referred in saying "It is not lawful for to put them (the silver pieces) into the treasury, because it is the price of blood" (v.6). The words "cast them to the potter" (Zech. 11: 13) seem to be at variance with "they...bought with them the potter's field, to bury strangers in" (v.7). However, the difficulty disappears when we understand that the words, "cast them to the potter", mean that the silver, having been cast down in the temple by Judas, went to the potter in payment for his field. A "potter was one of the lowliest of the common labourers, a worker whose products were so trifling in value that they could be replaced with little expenditure" (M.F. Unger). So much for the buying power of thirty pieces of silver! How much do *we* value Him?

But there is an apparent difficulty here: "Then was fulfilled that which was spoken by *Jeremy* the prophet, saying, And they took the thirty pieces of silver, the price of him that was valued, whom they of the children of Israel did value; and gave them for the potter's field (the place from which he extracted the clay to make pots), as the Lord appointed me" (vv.9-10). We can be certain, of course, that Matthew had *not* made a mistake in his quotation. We can also be sure that this was *not* a copyist's error. According to Wm.

Hoste (*Bible Problems and Answers*), "The probable explanation is the one cited by Lightfoot, that Jeremiah, as considerably the longest of the prophets, had the first place among them, and so his name came to be used for the volume of the the prophetic writings. He quotes the learned David Kimchi as his authority". Wm.Hoste also notes that it is possible that the words "spoken by Jeremy the prophet" may refer to "some well known word of the prophet", comparable to the words of the Lord Jesus, "It is more blessed to give than to receive" (Acts 20: 35), which are not recorded in the Gospels.

3) THEY DENOUNCED THE LORD BEFORE PILATE, vv.11-14

"And Jesus stood before the governor; and the governor asked him, saying, Art thou the King of the Jews? And Jesus said unto him, Thou sayest", that is, 'what thou sayest is true'. At first glance, this seems a sudden and unexpected question, but we know from Luke (23: 2) and John (18: 29-32), that it was prompted by Jewish accusations: "We found this fellow perverting the nation, and forbidding to give tribute to Caesar, saying that he himself is Christ a King" (Luke 23: 2). These were all carefully worded political accusations, and the first two were blatant lies. Far from "perverting the nation", the Lord Jesus "departed...into a mountain himself alone" when "he perceived that they would come and take him by force, to make him a king" (John 6: 15). When asked, "Is it lawful to give tribute unto Caesar, or not?", He answered, "Render therefore unto Caesar the things which are Caesar's, and unto God the things that are God's" (Matt. 22: 17-21). A far cry from, "forbidding to give tribute to Caesar!"

Matthew, bearing in mind his emphasis on the Lord's Messiahship, focuses on the third charge mentioned by Luke: "saying that he himself is Christ a King" (Luke 23: 2). This evidently astonished and intrigued Pilate. It was the first he had heard of a Jewish King! But was He really a king? Hence the incredulity in his question, "Art thou (a bound and abused Jewish prisoner) the King of the Jews?" (v.11).

The Saviour made no attempt to vindicate Himself: "And when he was accused of the chief priests and elders, he answered nothing, Then said Pilate unto him, Hearest thou not how many things they witness against thee? And he answered him to never a word; insomuch that the governor marvelled greatly" (vv.12-14). Centuries before, Isaiah had said, "He was oppressed, and he was afflicted; yet he opened not his mouth: he is brought as a lamb to the slaughter, and as a sheep before her shearers is dumb, so he openeth not his mouth" (Isaiah 53: 7). See also 1 Peter 2: 23. The Lord

Jesus "committed himself (committed His cause, or, committed the matter) to Him that judgeth righteously".

At this point, or a little later, having heard that the Lord Jesus was from Galilee, Pilate sent Him to Herod. See Luke 23: 6-12. This is not mentioned by the other three Gospel writers. Notice that even here, the "chief priests and scribes stood and vehemently accused him" (Luke 23: 10). Significantly, "the same day Pilate and Herod were made friends together: for before they were at enmity between themselves". Luke alone records Pilate's report: "Ye have brought this man unto me, as one that perverteth the people; and, behold, I, having examined him before you, have found no fault in this man, touching those things whereof ye accuse him; no, nor yet Herod: for I sent you to him; and, lo, nothing worthy of death is done unto him" (Luke 23: 13-16).

We should also notice that while the Lord Jesus was called the "King of the Jews" at the beginning (Matt. 2: 2) and end of His life (Matt. 27: 11, 37), He will next be seen on earth as "KING OF KINGS, AND LORD OF LORDS" (Rev. 19: 16).

4) THEY DEMANDED THE LORD'S DESTRUCTION, vv.15-26
Peter summed up the passage as follows: "The God of Abraham, and of Isaac, and of Jacob, the God of our fathers, hath glorified his Son Jesus; whom ye delivered up, and denied him in the presence of Pilate, when he was determined to let him go. But ye denied the Holy One and the Just, and desired a murderer to be granted unto you; and killed the Prince of life, Whom God hath raised from the dead; whereof we are witnesses" (Acts 3: 13-15). It was "the chief priests and elders" that "**persuaded the multitude that they should ask Barabbas, and destroy Jesus**" (v.20). Attention is drawn to the following: *(a)* the custom (vv.15-16); *(b)* the choice (vv.17-18); *(c)* the concern (v.19); *(d)* the cry (vv.20-23); *(e)* the capitulation (vv.24-26).

a) The custom, vv.15-16
"Now at that feast the governor was wont to release unto the people a prisoner, whom they would. And they had then a notable prisoner, called Barabbas". According to Harold St.John, "Apart from the gospels and Josephus (the Jewish historian), we have no knowledge of the custom referred to: the boon may have been instituted in answer to Jewish pressure. In any case, the feast celebrated the exodus of Israel from the iron furnace, and such a concession would be a suitable sop to national feeling". He continues, "Pilate thought that he saw his opportunity; if he could release

Jesus, he would placate his own uneasy conscience and please the crowd at the same time. The priests were more shrewd then he, and knew that Pilate was a prisoner of his own past, caught like a fly in a spider's web. Hated by the Jews (see Luke 13: 1), feared by his own men, and under suspicion at the Roman court, the lot of Pontius Pilate was not an enviable one".

b) The choice, vv.17-18
The choice was clear: Christ or Barabbas. "Whom will ye that I release unto you? Barabbas, or Jesus which is called Christ? For he knew that for envy they had delivered him". Although Pilate proved weak, he was certainly not unintelligent. Like Joseph centuries before, "he knew that for envy they had delivered him" (v.18). Compare Genesis 37: 11. As N.Crawford (writing on Luke) observes, "The real crime in the eyes of the leaders of the Jews was that the common people listened to Christ's teachings. Envy stirred their hearts, and Pilate knew it". No doubt in suggesting Barabbas, Pilate wished to emphasise the contrast between the two. Barabbas was "a notable prisoner" (v.16). It seems quite likely that Pilate "wanted to play off the crowd against the chief priests and elders. He had know from the beginning that the latter had handed Jesus to him because of their aversion to Him caused by His growing influence with the people (cf. Mark 15: 10)" (supplied by Justin Waldron). But this strategy failed: see v.20. Barabbas means 'son of the father'. We know nothing at all about his earthly father, but there can be no doubt about his spiritual father. Satan's character is clearly visible in Barabbas. **But the Lord Jesus was also 'the Son of the Father'.** What a contrast!

i) Barabbas
- ***He was a rebel.*** He "lay bound with them that had made insurrection (rebellion) with him" (Mark 15: 7). Barabbas had dared to rebel against the Roman authorities.

Satan, the father of Barabbas, is also a rebel. It is evident, possibly from Isaiah 14: 12-15, and more probably from Ezekiel 28: 12-19, that Satan was once a person of great glory and eminence, but that he rebelled against God, and attempted to gain the highest place in the universe. When Adam and Eve were created, we find Satan in the garden of Eden, urging them to break God's one commandment, and become rebels themselves.

- ***He was a murderer.*** He "lay bound with them that had made insurrection with him, who had committed murder in the insurrection" (Mark 15: 7). Satan the father of Barabbas, is also a murderer. The Lord Jesus said of Satan, "he was a murderer from the beginning" (John 8: 44). See also 1 John 3: 8. This is clear from Genesis 3. God had said, "But of the tree of the knowledge of good and evil, thou shalt not eat of it: for in the day that thou eatest thereof thou shalt surely die" (Gen. 2: 17). By encouraging Eve and Adam, in that order, to transgress the one prohibition imposed by God (Gen. 3: 1-7), "death passed upon all men" (Rom. 5: 12). The human race is "dead in trespasses and sins" (Eph. 2: 1). Satan became responsible for the spiritual murder of Adam and Eve, and through them, of the entire human race. But he was "a murderer from the beginning" in another way. Read 1 John 3: 12.

- **He was a robber.** "Now Barabbas was a robber" (John 18: 40). Satan, the father of Barabbas, is also a robber. He robs people of their character, honesty, decency and morals. But more than that, he robs people of eternal life. See 2 Corinthians 4: 4. The Lord Jesus called the religious leaders, "thieves and robbers" (John 10: 1).

ii) The Lord Jesus Christ
- **He was obedient.** If Barabbas was guilty of insurrection, then the Lord Jesus fulfilled the ancient prophecy, "He shall not strive, nor cry; neither shall any man hear his voice in the streets" (Matt. 12: 19). If Satan, is "Lucifer, son of the morning", cried, "I will ascend…I will exalt my throne…I will…I will…I will" (Isaiah 14: 12-14), the Lord Jesus prayed, "not as I will, but as thou wilt" (Matt. 26: 39). He was "obedient unto death, even the death of the cross" (Phil. 2: 8).

- **He gave life.** If Barabbas was a murderer, then the Lord Jesus raised the dead. But more, if Barabbas *took* the life of others, then the Lord Jesus *gave* His own life. If Satan was "a murderer from the beginning" (John 8: 44), then the Lord Jesus "gave his life a ransom for all" (1 Tim. 2: 6). He still gives life: "I give unto them ('my sheep') eternal life; and they shall never perish" (John 10: 28). He is "the true God, and eternal life" (1 John 5: 20).

- **He was a benefactor.** If Barabbas was a robber, then the Lord Jesus "went about doing good" (Acts 10: 38.) It remains the case. "He that spared not his own Son, but delivered him up for us all, how shall he not **with him** also freely **give us all things?**" (Rom. 8: 32).

c) The concern, v.19
"When he was set down on the judgment seat, his wife (said to be Claudia

Procula) sent unto him, saying, Have thou nothing to do with that just man: for I have suffered many things this day in a dream because of him". This is unique to Matthew's Gospel. The word translated "judgment seat" (*bema*) is also used of the judgment seat of Christ" (see Rom. 14: 10; 2 Cor. 5: 10). But what a difference! The Lord will be "the righteous judge" in that day (2 Tim. 4: 8). Not so Pilate! We do not know whether the dream was the result of divine visitation, or that a "worried conscience brought about the unpleasant dream or nightmare" (John Heading). He continues by saying, "At least she was bold enough to interrupt the proceedings, though without recorded effect". She must have confirmed her husband's thoughts about the Prisoner who stood before him. He said, shortly afterwards, "I am innocent of the blood of this just person" (v.24).

d) The cry, vv.20-23
"But the chief priests and elders **persuaded the multitude** that they should ask Barabbas, and destroy (*apollumi*, to destroy utterly, not *katargeo*, to abolish) Jesus. The governor answered and said unto them, Whether of the twain will ye that I release unto you? They said, Barabbas. Pilate saith unto them, What shall I do then with Jesus which is called Christ. They all say unto him, Let him be crucified. And the governor said, Why, what evil hath he done? But they cried out the more, saying, Let him be crucified". Having "begun to put justice in the hands of the mob (v.21), Pilate could not withdraw" (Justin Waldron). This was the last of three assertions by Pilate that the Lord Jesus was innocent, prior to the mockery in "the common hall" (v.27). Luke gives all three: see Luke 23: 4, 14-16, 22. We learn from John 19: 4-15, however, that Pilate made a further attempt to release the Lord Jesus after He had been mocked by the soldiers. But to no avail.

In crying for His crucifixion, they unwittingly fulfilled the thousand-year old prophecy: "They pierced my hands and my feet". It has been pointed out that "the means of execution demanded by the people was not the normal Jewish method of execution, which was by stoning, nor Roman, which was by beheading. Death by crucifixion was reserved for the vilest criminals. Usually only slaves and foreigners suffered such a terrible end" (H.S.Paisley).

e) The capitulation, vv.24-26
"When Pilate saw that he could prevail nothing, but that rather a tumult was made, he took water, and washed his hands (see Deut. 21:6-7; Psalm 26: 6; 73: 13) before the multitude, saying, I am innocent of the blood of this just person: see ye to it" (v.24). Mark puts it like this: "And so Pilate, **willing to**

content the people, released Barabbas unto them, and delivered Jesus, when he had scourged him, to be crucified" (Mark 15: 15). Luke follows suit: "And Pilate gave sentence that it should *be as they required.* And he released unto them him that for sedition and murder was cast into prison, *whom they had desired*; but he delivered Jesus to *their will*" (Luke 23: 24-25).

Centuries before, Joseph told his brothers, "But as for you, ye thought evil against me; but God meant it unto good, to bring to pass, as it is this day, to save much people alive" (Gen. 50: 20). Seventeen hundred years later, Christ came, and was condemned to death. Little did they know that they were implementing the "determinate counsel and foreknowledge of God" (Acts 2: 23), and that through the death of Jesus of Nazareth, their own salvation was made possible. On the other hand, little did they know what they were saying in answering Pilate (v.25), "Then answered *all* the people and said, His blood be on us, and on our children". Compare Acts 5: 28; 18: 6. This was partly fulfilled in A.D.70 when Jerusalem was destroyed by the Romans. But that was only the beginning. Even worse was to follow, and still is to follow. Well might the women who followed Him to Calvary 'weep for themselves, and for their children' (Luke 23: 28).

"Then released he Barabbas unto them: and when he had scourged Jesus, he delivered him to be crucified" (v.26). Scourging was dreadful. John Heading writes: "The Roman method of scourging was to tie the victim in a bent position to a post, or to stretch him on a frame. The whip consisted of leather thongs, with sharp pieces of metal or bone attached: these lacerated the back and front of the victim's body, tearing the flesh with great wounds...Such sufferings reduced a man to a state of indescribable suffering, weakness and helplessness, while some men died under this torture". The Lord Jesus anticipated this in Isaiah 50: 6, "I gave my back to the smiters", and in Psalm 129: 3, "the plowers plowed upon my back; they made long their furrows".

The Lord Jesus "witnessed a good confession" before Pilate (1 Tim. 6: 13). For example, "He witnessed a good confession" *(i) by not losing His temper:* He remained calm under extreme provocation: "He answered him to never a word; insomuch that the governor marvelled greatly" (Matt. 27: 14); *(ii) by not concealing His identity:* "the governor asked him, saying, Art Thou the King of the Jews? And Jesus said unto him, "Thou sayest" (Matt. 27: 11); *(iii) by not hiding His mission:* "To this end was I born, and for this cause came I into the world, that I should bear witness unto the truth" (John 18: 37).

Are *we* making "a good confession" in these three ways?

"Mocked"

Read Chapter 27: 27-44

The word occurs three times in these verses. It sums up the way in which the Lord Jesus was treated by the soldiers: "they bowed the knee before him, and **mocked** him, saying, Hail, King of the Jews…And after that they had **mocked** him, they took the robe from off him, and put his own raiment on him, and led him away to crucify him" (vv.29, 31), and it sums up the way in which He was treated by the religious leaders: "Likewise also the chief priests **mocking** him, with the scribes and elders said, He saved others; himself he cannot save" (vv.41-42). The word 'mock' (*empaizo*), meaning, literally, 'to play like a child', means 'to sport, jest' (W.E.Vine). It is used here of the insults inflicted on him by the soldiers of the governor (vv.29, 31) and by the chief priests (v.41).

While the death of the Lord Jesus displays the greatness of God's love, it also displays the wickedness of the human heart. Notice the way in which this is emphasised by Matthew: "***they*** stripped him, and put on him a scarlet robe. And when ***they*** had platted a crown of thorns they put it upon his head… ***they*** bowed the knee before him…***they*** spit upon him…***they*** took the robe off from him, and put his own raiment on him, and led him away to crucify him…***they*** crucified him…And sitting down ***they*** watched him there" (vv.28-31, 35, 36). The whole passage reads like a solemn indictment. In fact, only a few weeks later, Peter publicly charged the Jews with their awful crime: "Him…ye have taken, and by wicked hands have crucified and slain" (Acts 2: 23); "Jesus…whom ye delivered up, and denied him in the presence of Pilate, when he was determined to let him go. But ye denied the Holy One and Just, and desired a murderer to be granted unto you; and killed the Prince of life" (Acts 3: 13-15).

The Lord Jesus was: *(1)* mocked by the soldiers (vv.27-31); *(2)* mocked by the religious leaders (vv.32-44). Put another way, He was mocked in the Praetorium ("the common hall", v.27, AV), and He was mocked at Golgotha (v.33).

Chapter 27

1) MOCKED BY THE SOLDIERS, vv.27-31
"Then the soldiers of the governor took Jesus into the common hall (*praitorion*), and gathered unto him the whole band of soldiers" (v.27). The parallel passage in Mark leaves *praitorion* untranslated: "And the soldiers led him away into the hall called Praetorium; and they called together the whole band". At the end of his life on earth, the Lord was "led" by soldiers (Mark 15: 16, 20). He will return to earth leading the "armies" of heaven (Rev. 19: 14).

The Praetorium, meaning 'palace', was the official residence of the governor of a province, in this case, the official residence of the Roman governor of Jerusalem. It has been identified with the castle of Antonia (see Acts 21: 34-37, 22: 24), which was occupied by the regular garrison. The "whole band", or cohort, numbered about six hundred men commanded by a tribune, and was a tenth part of a Roman legion. Luke does not mention the mockery by the Roman soldiers, and John gives a brief summary of this shameful event. See John 19: 1-3. Since the Lord Jesus had been called, "the King of the Jews", He was given a mock coronation by the Roman soldiers. He had been mocked as a prophet (Matt. 26: 68; Mark 14: 65); here, He was mocked as a king; on the cross, He was mocked as a priest (Luke 23: 34-37).

Since He was a king:

a) He must have royal robes
So "they stripped him, and **put on him a scarlet robe**" (v.28). According to Mark, "they **clothed him with purple**" (Mark 15: 17). Perhaps Harold St.John has the explanation when he calls it "a soldier's faded coat, kingly scarlet or imperial purple". But the "King of the Jews" will return as "King of kings", and the garment given Him in mockery will give place to "a vesture dipped in blood" bearing the title "KING OF KINGS, AND LORD OF LORDS" (Rev. 19: 13, 16). The blood on his garment then ("a vesture dipped in blood"), will signify the blood of His enemies. When the question is asked, as He later approaches Jerusalem from Edom, "Wherefore art thou red in thine apparel, and thy garments like him that treadeth the winefat?" (Isa 63: 2), He will reply: "I have trodden the winepress alone; and of the people there was none with me: for I will tread them in mine anger, and trample them in my fury; and their blood shall be sprinkled upon my garments, and I will stain all my raiment" (Isa 63: 3, fulfilled in Rev. 19: 1-3).

Since He was a king:

b) He must have a royal crown
So they "***platted...a crown of thorns***" (v.29). This is deeply significant. "Thorns" (see also Hebrews 6: 8) were a sign of the curse (Gen. 3: 17-18). On the cross, the Lord Jesus was "made a curse for us" (Gal. 3: 13). He was given a victor's crown (*stephanos*). This was usually a token of public honour, but the soldiers gave it to Him in mockery. Little did they know that His greatest victory would be accomplished at Calvary. He will wear crowns of royal dignity (*diadema*) when He returns at the head of the greatest army ever seen on earth (Rev. 19: 12). The mocking salutation, "Hail, King of the Jews!", will give place to fear: "Then shall all the tribes of the earth mourn, and they shall see the Son of man coming in the clouds of heaven, with power and great glory" (Matt. 24: 30).

Since He was a king:

c) He must have a royal sceptre
So they gave Him "***a reed***", placing it "in his right hand" (v.29). But even this was not sufficient mockery: having given Him the reed, they snatched it back and "smote him on the head" with it (v.30). The hand that held the reed, will hold "a rod of iron" (Rev. 19: 15). He will come "to judge and make war" (Rev. 19: 11). God will then say to His Son, "Ask of me, and I shall give thee the heathen for thine inheritance, and the uttermost part of the earth for thy possession. Thou shalt break them with a rod of iron" (Psalm 2: 8-9). See also Hebrews 1: 8. "But unto the Son he saith, Thy throne, O God, is for ever and ever: a sceptre of righteousness is the sceptre of thy kingdom".

Since He was a king;

d) He must have royal homage
So "they "***bowed the knee before him, and mocked him, saying, Hail, King of the Jews***" (v.29). This contrasts with the great statement by the apostle Paul: "Wherefore God also hath highly exalted him, and given him a name which is above every name: that at the name of Jesus, every knee should bow, of things in heaven (angels), and things in earth (men), and things under the earth (demons); and that every tongue should confess that Jesus Christ is Lord, to the glory of God the Father" (Phil. 2: 9-11).

Since He was a king:

e) *He must have royal anointing*
So they "***spit upon him***" (v.30). In doing so, the ancient prophecy was fulfilled: "I gave my back to the smiters, and my cheeks to them that plucked off the hair: I hid not my face from shame and spitting" (Isaiah 50: 6). He was spat upon by the Jews (26: 67), and by the Gentiles (27: 30). But if men anointed him with spittle, He is God's anointed King (Psalm 2: 2). See also Psalm 45: 7, "Thou lovest righteousness, and hatest wickedness: therefore God, thy God, hath anointed thee with the oil of gladness above thy fellows". The expression, "above thy fellows", evidently refers to His companions in the coming kingdom. His will be the greatest joy in the kingdom.

"And after that they had mocked him, they took the robe off from him, and put his own raiment on him, and led him away to crucify him" (v.31). Harold St.John writes: "The scene all happened long ago, but it still has the power to make the heart sick. When we have recovered our balance, by faith we see Him with a crown of pure gold set upon His head, arrayed in a garment of light, holding a rod of iron in his hand, with which He will rule the nations; for the rest, at the Name of Jesus, every knee shall bow and every tongue confess Him Lord" (*The Collected Writings of Harold St. John*).

2) MOCKED AT GOLGOTHA, vv.32-44
The contents of John 19: 4-15 should be read between the words "And after that they had mocked him, they took the robe off from him, and put his own raiment on him" and "led him away to crucify him" (v.31). The mockery in the hall over, and Pilate's final appeal drowned by the cry "away with him, away with him, crucify him" (John 19: 15), the Lord was led to Golgotha.

> *The Lamb of God to slaughter led,*
> *The King of glory see!*
> *The crown of thorns upon His head,*
> *They nail Him to the tree.*

With hushed spirits we must now notice: *(a)* the journey to Golgotha (v.32); *(b)* the crucifixion at Golgotha (vv.33-38); *(c)* the mockery at Golgotha (vv.39-44).

a) The journey to Golgotha, v.32

"And as they came out, they found a man of Cyrene, Simon by name: him they compelled to bear his cross". Matthew says no more here, but Mark tells us that Simon was "coming out of the country" and that he was "the father of Alexander and Rufus" (Mark 15: 21). As the procession left the city, with the Lord "bearing his cross" (John 19: 17), either His strength failed or, as much preferred by H.S.Paisley, "to the eyes of His guards it seemed He might not reach Golgotha, so they seized a passer-by at random, Simon by name, and he was compelled to carry the cross-beam the remainder of the way". However, whilst the Gospel writers do not tell us why the soldiers compelled Simon to bear His cross, we can be sure that there was divine purpose. Perhaps it enabled the Lord Jesus to turn and address the "daughters of Jerusalem" (Luke 23: 26-31). Attention is drawn to:

i) The cross He carried. According to historians, the victim was forced to carry, not the whole cross, but the cross-beam. The man was laid across this on the ground, and his hands tied or nailed to it. The cross-beam was then fixed to the upright post already in position, and the victim's feet attached to this post. Others say that the victim was crucified whilst the cross was on the ground, after which it was placed in its socket with a sickening thud, dislocating the victim's bones. See Psalm 22: 14. W.E.Vine (see his *Expository Dictionary of New Testament Words*) believed that the cross (*stauros*) was an upright stake (the meaning of the word) on which the victim was crucified with arms vertical.

ii) The carrier of His cross. As already noted, Mark alone tells us that Simon of Cyrene was "the father of Alexander and Rufus". (Simon was a Hebrew name, Alexander a Greek name, and Rufus a Latin name). As always, the inclusion of such details cannot be without significance. It could therefore be possible, though we cannot be sure by any means, that Simon of Cyrene (Cyrenaica in North Africa) is the same as "Simon that is called Niger (meaning 'black')" (Acts 13: 1), and that Rufus is the same as "Rufus, chosen in the Lord" (Rom. 16: 13). Perhaps the inclusion of this detail had particular significance for the first readers of this Gospel, or perhaps we have missed something!

b) The crucifixion at Golgotha, vv.33-38

"And when they were come unto a place called Golgotha (an Aramaic word), that is to say, a place of a skull…there they crucified him".

Chapter 27

i) Where they brought Him. "Golgotha...a place of a skull" (v.33). We should note that 'Calvary' is the Latin name for "Golgotha": it is used in Luke 23: 33 (AV), but not in the Greek text: it should be rendered "the place which is called Skull" (JND).

It is usually suggested that the place was called "Golgotha" because it resembled a skull in shape and appearance. But its typical significance is inescapable. What a picture of mankind! In the words of Harold St.John, "A skull is a human head shorn of its dignity and beauty, with no light in its eye-sockets, an empty vacuum in its brain-space, and with none of that grace of hair which is the sign of a man's strength and of a woman's glory" reminding us "that when a man rejects Jesus Christ, all the lights of the world die down; there is nothing left but a bony, grinning death's head". Paul puts it like this: "But we speak the wisdom of God in a mystery...which none of the princes of this world knew: for had they known it, they would not have crucified the Lord of glory" (1 Cor. 2: 7-8).

ii) What they gave Him. "They gave him vinegar to drink mingled with gall (not its only ingredient: see Mark 15: 23): and when he had tasted thereof, he would not drink" (v.34). This was the first of three drinks offered to the Lord Jesus at Golgotha. Here, and in Mark 15: 23, it was offered in compassion to ease the severity of His pain. But He would not allow Himself to be anaesthetized in any way. Compare Leviticus 10: 9. On the cross, the Lord was offered a second drink: "the soldiers also mocked him, coming to him, and offering him vinegar" (Luke 23: 36-37). Before He died, the Lord cried, "I thirst", and on this occasion, He "received the vinegar" (John 19: 28-30). See also Matthew 27: 47-49; Mark 15: 35-37; Psalm 69: 21.

iii) What they took from Him. "And they crucified him, and parted his garments, casting lots: that it might be fulfilled which was spoken by the prophet (see Psalm 22: 18), They parted my garments among them, and upon my vesture did they cast lots" (v.35). Further details are given in John 19: 23-34. We gather from the fact that they "made four parts, to every soldier a part", including, "the head-dress, the shoes, the outer garment, the girdle, and the inner garment" (John Heading), that the Lord Jesus was taken to Golgotha with a guard of four soldiers.

All four Gospel writers say without further detail, "they crucified him". Matthew alone notes that "sitting down they watched him there" (v.36) - to thwart any attempt to release Him. The words "him there" are profound! Little did the soldiers know what they were watching. The "princes of this world" had "crucified the Lord of glory" (1 Cor. 2: 8).

iv) What they wrote over Him. They "set up over his head his accusation written, THIS IS JESUS THE KING OF THE JEWS" (v.37). John tells us that the chief priests objected: "Write not, the King of the Jews; but that he said, I am the King of the Jews" leading John Heading (*What the Bible Teaches - John*) to say, "These men had thwarted Pilate three times when he wanted to release the Lord (18: 38, 19: 4-6, 19: 12), so by writing 'the King' in three languages, Pilate annoyed the Jews by making them read the title three times". We are told by Luke that the superscription was written "in letters of Greek, and Latin, and Hebrew" (Luke 23: 38: see also John 19: 20). Greek was the language of the cultural world; Latin was the language of the political world; Hebrew was the language of the religious world. He was rejected by all three.

v) Who was crucified with Him. "Then were there two thieves (*lestai*, robbers, brigands) crucified with him one on the right hand and another on the left" (v.38). Mark adds, "And the scripture was fulfilled which saith, And he was numbered with the transgressors" (Mark 15: 28), but see RV/ JND footnote. They treated Him like a thief in Gethsemane (see Matt. 26: 55), but on the cross, He was able to *give* freely to a man who had robbed others. See Luke 23: 39-43.

c) The mockery at Golgotha, vv.39-44
Matthew refers to the contempt of ignorant, religious and condemned sinners, i.e. *(i)* "they that passed by", suggesting, not a hilltop, but a roadway (vv.39-40); *(ii)* the chief priests...with the scribes and elders" (vv.41-43); *(iii)* "the thieves" (v.44).

i) "And they that passed by reviled him, wagging their heads, and saying, Thou that destroyest the temple, and buildest it in three days, save thyself. If thou be the Son of God, come down from the cross" (vv.39-40). The word "reviled" (Mark has "railed") translates *blasphemeo,* and needs no further comment. According to W.E.Vine, the word "wagging" (*kineo*) indicates that they nodded "their heads in the direction of the cross at this supposed ending of His career". Compare Isaiah 37: 22, Lam. 2: 15.

The false witnesses before the Sanhedrin had misquoted the Lord's words (Matt. 26: 60-61), and the 'passers by' followed suit. They insinuated that the

Lord had intimated that *He* would destroy the temple at Jerusalem, whereas He had actually intimated that *they* would destroy the temple of His body: "Destroy this temple, and in three days I will raise it up" (John 2: 19). John Heading makes the delightful observation that their words "save thyself" should "be taken in conjunction with 'cast thyself' (Matt. 4: 6), 'pity thyself' (Matt. 16: 22 margin), and 'show thyself' (John 7: 4). Instead, He humbled Himself, and gave Himself". John Heading adds, "He would neither keep Himself alive by a miracle at His temptation in the wilderness, nor here on the cross". On both occasions, the Lord's enemies said, "If thou be the Son of God" (Satan in Matt. 4: 6, and men in Matt. 27: 40). There can be little doubt, therefore, that the passers by were motivated by Satan.

ii) *"Likewise also the chief priests mocking him, with the scribes and elders*, said, He saved others; himself he cannot save. If he be the King of Israel, let him now come down from the cross, and we will believe him. He trusted in God; let him deliver him now, if he will have him: for he said, I am the Son of God" (vv.41-43). They were *not*, of course, quoting Psalm 22: 8, written a thousand years beforehand: rather Psalm 22: 8 was quoting *them*! Another example of the pin-point accuracy of God's word!

Quite unwittingly, and certainly not in the way they intended, the high priests and scribes were right in saying, "He saved others; himself He *cannot* save" (v.42). As H.A.Ironside observes, "They were declaring a tremendous fact: if He would save others, He could not save Himself". We hear Him say, "Now is my soul troubled; and what shall I say? Father, save me from this hour: but for this cause came I unto this hour" (John 12: 27). Behind all these taunts was another voice. The death of the Lord Jesus meant Satan's defeat, and through this, deliverance from his power became available to all. If the Lord Jesus had come down from the cross, all His enemies would have been utterly confounded, but there would have been no Gospel message, no forgiveness of sins, no eternal life, and no place for us in heaven.

> *Himself He could not save!*
> *He on the cross must die,*
> *Or mercy could not come*
> *To ruined sinners nigh;*
> *Yes, Christ the Son of God, must bleed,*
> *That sinners might from sin be freed.*

At the beginning of His ministry, Nathanael exclaimed, "Rabbi, Thou art the

Son of God; Thou art the **King of Israel**" (John 1: 49). Now, with the Lord Jesus on the cross, both titles were denied: "**If** thou be the **Son of God**, come down from the cross" (v.40); **If** he be the **King of Israel**, let him now come down from the cross, and we will believe him. He trusted in God; let him deliver him now, if he will have him: for he said, I am **the Son of God**" (vv.42-43). But wicked men will not have the last word: "Yet have I set **my king** upon My holy hill of Zion. I will declare the decree: the Lord hath said unto me, Thou art **my Son**; this day have I begotten thee" (Psalm 2: 6-7).

iii) "The thieves also, which were crucified with him, cast the same in his teeth" (v.44). According to Mark, they "**reviled** him" (Mark 15: 32). The word "reviled" (*oneidizo*) means to reproach: they heaped discredit upon Him. This was prior to the repentance of the one thief documented by Luke. See Luke 23: 39-43.

The actions of all three classes above can be summarised as follows: "Consider him that endured such contradiction of sinners against Himself" (Heb. 12: 3). The word "contradiction" (*antilogia*) means 'to speak against'. The same three classes of people all said essentially the same thing. It was "an unholy alliance" (Wm.MacDonald).

- *"They that passed by".* "Thou that destroyest the temple, and buildest it in three days, **save thyself**" (v.40).

- *"The chief priests...scribes and elders".* "He saved others; himself he cannot save. If he be the King of Israel, let him now **come down** from the cross, and we will believe him" (v.42).

- *"The thieves".* Luke tells us how they "reviled him". "If thou be the Christ, **save thyself**, and us" (Luke 23: 39).

But He did not save Himself, in order that we might be able to say, "But after that the kindness and love of God our Saviour toward man appeared, not by works of righteousness which we have done, but according to his mercy **he saved us**" (Titus 4: 5).

"Jesus...yielded up the ghost"

Read Chapter 27: 45-56
This sacred passage brings before us the Lord's death, when God "made

him to be sin for us, who knew no sin" (2 Cor. 5: 21), Matthew (with Mark) records His cry, uttered prophetically a thousand years before, "My God, my God, why hast thou forsaken me" (Psalm 22: 1).

The Lord Jesus hung on the cross at Golgotha for six hours. Whilst Matthew (27: 45), Mark (Mark 15: 33) and Luke (23: 44) all refer to the "sixth" and "ninth" hours (1200 and 1500 hours), Mark also records that He was crucified at the "third hour" (0900 hours). See Mark 15: 25. John does not mention either the time of His crucifixion or the "darkness over all the land" from "the sixth hour...unto the ninth hour".

During the first three hours, the Lord Jesus suffered at the hands of men: during the second three hours, He suffered, additionally, under divine judgment. "About those three hours we know nothing, save the words which escaped the lips of the Sufferer Himself" (G. Campbell Morgan). When the Saviour was born, "the glory of the Lord" surrounded the shepherds, and there was "with the angel a multitude of the heavenly host, praising God, and saying, Glory to God in the highest" (Luke 2: 8-14). When the Saviour died, there was "darkness over the whole land until the ninth hour". Amos had foretold that God would "darken the earth in a clear day", and make that day as "the mourning of *an only son*" (Amos, 8: 9-10). While the prophecy refers to Israel, its language is deeply significant. There could be no greater expression of sorrow. This was supernatural darkness. Mark does not say "*the* darkness": it was not ordinary darkness. As Norman Crawford (*What the Bible Teaches - Luke*) observes, "we should not rationalise it by talking about an eclipse of the sun, for although the sun was darkened (Luke 23: 45), it was not naturally, but supernaturally". Darkness was a sign of God's wrath. See Matthew 24: 29. It betokened "the day of the LORD" (Joel 2: 1-2). See, again, Amos 8: 8-9.

There is some debate over the extent of the darkness, and the word itself (*ge:* hence our words 'geology' and 'geography'), used by all three Evangelists, could be rendered either *"land"* (as in Matthew and Mark) or *"earth"* (as in Luke). On this basis, the darkness was either countrywide, or universal. However, God suspended the natural laws of the *universe* on at least two previous occasions (see Joshua 10: 12-14 and 2 Kings 20: 9-11), and it seems likely that the suffering and death of the Son of God would have involved universal darkness. J.C.Ryle has a most interesting paragraph on the darkness and the rent veil: "The darkness would strike even thoughtless Gentiles, like Pilate and the Roman soldiers. The rent veil would strike even Annas and Caiaphas and their unbelieving companions".

Matthew

We must now consider: *(1)* the loud voice (vv.46-50): the Lord cried twice "with a loud voice" (vv.46, 50); *(2)* the rent veil (vv.51-53): the rent veil (v.51) was followed by rent rocks (vv.51-53); *(3)* the bystanders' verdict (v.54); *(4)* the women viewing (vv.55-56).

1) THE LOUD VOICE, vv.46-50
The Lord Jesus cried twice "with a loud voice" (vv.46, 50) and we must ponder His cries with deep reverence, not forgetting that they are the cries of "the Son of God, who loved me, and gave himself for me" (Gal. 2: 20).

a) The first cry, vv.46-49
Matthew (with Mark) records what the Lord actually said (v.46), and what some of the bystanders thought He said (vv.47-49).

i) What the Lord actually said. "And about the ninth hour Jesus cried with a loud voice, saying Eli, Eli, lama sabachthani? That is to say, My God, my God, why hast thou forsaken me".

The Lord Jesus spoke seven times whilst upon the cross, but only Matthew and Mark record these particular words, and they are the *only* words that Matthew and Mark record. Matthew records them in Hebrew: "*Eli, Eli,* lama sabachthani". Mark records them in Aramaic, the actual language used by the Lord: "*Eloi, Eloi,* lama sabachthani". The seven sayings of the Lord Jesus were as follows:

- "Father, forgive them; for they know not what they do" (Luke 23: 34).

- "Today shalt thou be with me in paradise" (Luke 23: 43).

- "Woman, behold thy son!" (John 19: 26).

- "Eli, Eli, lama sabachthani" (Matt. 27: 46; Mark 15: 34).

- "I thirst" (John 19: 28).

- "It is finished" (John 19: 30). This is a single word in Greek (*tetelestai*).

- "Father, into thy hands I commend my spirit" (Luke 23: 46).

The second cry mentioned by Matthew (27: 50) and Mark (15: 37), is evidently the cry, "It is finished" (John 19: 30), which immediately preceded His words, "Father, into thy hands I commend my spirit" (Luke 23: 46).

The Lord's words, spoken originally in Aramaic, are interpreted: "My God, my God, why hast thou forsaken me?" As noted above, they are taken from Psalm 22: 1. The Psalm continues by giving the answer to the Lord's cry. Here is the complete passage: "My God, my God, why hast thou forsaken me? why art thou so far from helping me, and from the words of my roaring? O my God, I cry in the daytime, but thou hearest not; and in the night season, and am not silent. **But thou art holy, O thou that inhabitest the praises of Israel**" (vv.1-3).

In the words of J.C.Ryle, "There is a deep mystery in these words, which no mortal man can fathom... They were meant to express the real pressure on His soul of the enormous burden of a world's sins; they were meant to show how truly and literally He was our substitute - was made sin, and a curse for us, and endured God's righteous anger against a world's sin in His own person". He endured what we deserved. The Lord's words imply "that God had for the time withdrawn from him the sense and vision of His comfortable presence". God "put him to grief" on account of sin (Isaiah 53: 10). We must carefully note three things:

- *His sufferings were not the result of His own sin.* The words "**My** God, **my** God" emphasise that there was no **moral** reason for the Saviour's sufferings. He said, "I have set the LORD **always** before me" (Psalm 16: 8). He "loved righteousness and hated iniquity" (Heb. 1: 9 citing Psalm 45: 7). He never deviated in the slightest degree from the will of God.

There is a certain emphasis upon "thou". "Why hast **thou** forsaken me?" He was forsaken by men, yes: but why was He forsaken by God? The abandonment of the Lord at Calvary is all the more poignant when we remember David's words, "I have been young, and now am old: yet have I not seen the righteous **forsaken**, nor his seed begging bread... For the Lord loveth judgment, and **forsaketh not** his saints" (Psalm 37: 25. 28). There is, equally, a certain emphasis on "Why hast thou forsaken **me**?" Others might deserve to be forsaken, but not the Lord Jesus. We hear Him say, "But that the world may know that *I love the Father; and as the Father gave me commandment, even so I do*" (John 14: 31).

- *His sufferings did not imply that God did not love Him.* It is so important to notice that the Lord Jesus did not say, '***My Father, my Father***, why hast thou forsaken me?' The love and pleasure expressed at His baptism and on the mount of transfiguration, were undiminished at Calvary: "Therefore doth my Father ***love me***, because I lay down my life, that I might take it again" (John 10: 17).

- His sufferings were on account of God's holiness. "But Thou art holy..." (Psalm 22: 3). There is no bitterness, or criticism of God's dealings with Him. He was suffering as the sin-bearer on account of God's holiness. "For Christ also hath once suffered for sins, the just for the unjust that He might bring us to God" (1 Pet. 3: 18). The ultimate penalty of sin is the "second death" (Rev. 20: 12-15), that is, eternal separation from God. The Lord Jesus suffered the unimaginable reality of the "second death", that we might never have to experience it. He cried, "Why hast thou ***forsaken*** me", in order to say to us, "I will never leave thee, nor ***forsake*** thee" (Heb. 13: 5). The cry of the Lord Jesus expressed infinitely more than physical pain or mental anguish. The sinless Lamb of God endured the wrath of God at Golgotha. It was then that He "put away sin by the sacrifice of himself" (Heb. 9: 26), and became the propitiation for "the whole world" (1 John 2: 2).

ii) What they thought the Lord said. "Some of them that stood there, when they heard that, said This man calleth for Elias" (v47). This must refer to Jewish bystanders. It is highly unlikely that the Roman soldiers would have been familiar with the Old Testament. Since the Lord Jesus had cried with "a loud voice", their mistake seems quite inexplicable. It has been suggested that since darkness was a sign of the "day of the Lord" (Zeph. 1: 15), and that the Old Testament had predicted the coming of Elijah before the "great and terrible day of the Lord" (Mal. 4: 5), these bystanders had assumed that the Lord had called for Elijah. It has also been suggested that their words, "This man calleth for Elias", were just mockery, and this certainly seems to be confirmed by what follows: "Let be, let us see whether Elias will come to save him" (v.49). The Lord's cry, "Eli, Eli, lama sabachthani" was evidently followed immediately by the cry, "I thirst" (John 19: 28). This accounts for the fact that the man who "ran, and took a spunge, and filled it with vinegar" in answer to the second cry ("I thirst", John 19: 28-30), was unsuccessfully interrupted by the bystanders who mockingly waited to see if there would be an answer to the first cry.

b) *The second cry, v.50*
For the second time, Matthew (with Mark) says, "Jesus, when he had cried

again with a loud voice, yielded up the ghost". This was His triumphant cry, "***It is finished***" (John 19: 30), to be followed by "***Father, into thy hands I commend my spirit***" (Luke 23: 46). We must not miss the significance of the words, "Jesus, when he had cried again with a loud voice, ***yielded up the ghost***". It was an act of will in accordance with His own prediction, "I lay down my life, that I may take it again. No man taketh it from me, but I lay it down of myself. I have power to lay it down, and I have power to take it again" (John 10: 17-18).

2) THE RENT VEIL, vv.51-53

"And, behold, the veil of the temple was rent in twain from the top to the bottom" (v.51). In the Old Testament, God could only be approached through the veil. It was a picture of the Lord Jesus, who said "I am the way, the truth, and the life: no man cometh unto the Father, but by me" (John 14: 6). Without attempting a detailed study, we should note the veil's three colours (Exodus 26: 31): ***blue***, describing His heavenly nature: blue (sapphire) is the colour of the heavenly throne (Exodus 24: 10; Ezek. 1: 26); ***scarlet***, describing His earthly nature: the word "scarlet" comes from a Hebrew root meaning 'worm'; ***purple*** (combining blue and scarlet), speaking of "God....manifest in the flesh" (1 Tim. 3: 16). We should note its material, "fine twined linen", describing the absolute purity of the Lord Jesus, and we should note the fact that it portrayed the cherubim. These had four faces (Ezekiel 1: 6, 10)), each of which displayed a different aspect of God's throne, and depicted the Lord Jesus as portrayed in the four Gospels (Matthew, the lion; Mark, the ox; Luke, the man; John, the eagle). What a wonderful picture of the Lord Jesus!

But now that veil was "rent in twain" to show that men and women, previously excluded from the presence of God, could now approach Him on the basis of Christ's death at Calvary. The picture had become the reality. As J.C.Ryle observes, the "rending of the veil proclaimed the termination and passing away of the ceremonial law: it was a sign that the old dispensation of sacrifices and ordinances was no longer needed". It is through the Lord Jesus, not through a beautiful curtain, that we now approach God. See Ephesians 2: 18, and Hebrews 10: 19-20. ***He*** is the "new and living way" by which we draw near to God. We come "through the veil, that is to say, his flesh". It is not without significance that the veil was rent "from ***the top*** to the bottom". God Himself rent the veil to shew that the way into the presence of God is opened to every believer on the ground of the blood of Christ (Heb. 10: 19-25).

Only Matthew tells us that the rent veil was followed by rent rocks: "And, behold, the veil of the temple was rent in twain from the top to the bottom; and the earth did quake, and the rocks rent; and the graves were opened; and many bodies of the saints which slept arose, and came out of the graves after his resurrection, and went into the holy city, and appeared unto many". When the Lord returns to establish His kingdom, "the mount of Olives will cleave in the midst thereof toward the east and toward the west" (Zech. 14: 4).

We must notice that while the earthquake "which split great rocks and opened many tombs" evidently took place at the point of the Lord's death, it was not until *after* the Lord's resurrection that the occupants of these tombs were raised, went into Jerusalem, and "appeared unto many". As Robert Mounce observes, this is "usually explained as appropriate in view of Jesus' being 'the firstborn from among the dead' (Col. 1; 18; Rev.1: 5)". Since the resurrection of these believers ("saints") evidently took place at the same time or just after the Lord's own resurrection, it appears that Matthew relates this occurrence at this point in the narrative to emphasise the inseparable link between the death and resurrection of the Lord as it affects His people.

John Heading speaks for us all in saying, "this was no miracle akin to the bringing back to life of Jairus' daughter, of the widow of Nain's son, and of Lazerus, all of whom died again as a natural process. Rather, we feel that the divine work in vv.52-53 was the genuine resurrection of these saints as to their bodies, though how they entered heaven is not described. It was a pre-enactment of the resurrection of Christians at the rapture. Since Scripture provides no further light on this event, any suggestive interpretation by expositors must be somewhat speculative". C.I. Scofield is in agreement: "That these bodies returned to their graves is not said and may not be inferred". The question is addressed by Wm.Hoste and E.W.Rogers. See the attached addendum.

3) THE BYSTANDERS' VERDICT, v.54
"Now when the centurion, and they that were with him, watching Jesus, saw the earthquake, and those things that were done, they feared greatly, saying, Truly this was the Son of God". The Jews rejected His claim to be the Son of God, and taunted Him with it (vv.40, 43). They rejected the evidence of His life and teaching, but the Gentile centurion was convinced by the evidence of His suffering and death! Another earthquake caused another Roman official to fear as well. See Acts 16: 26-27.

Mark concentrates on the centurion's response particularly as he watched the Lord: "And when the centurion, which stood over against him, saw that he so cried out, and gave up the ghost, he said, Truly this man was the Son of God". See also Luke 23: 47. The absence of the definite article ('Truly this was Son of God') does not infer that the centurion demeaned the Lord: the definite article is also absent in Matthew 4: 3, 6. The way in which the Saviour died deeply impressed this man who, after all, must have watched many people die by crucifixion. He was undoubtedly accustomed to oaths and curses, but the Lord Jesus exhibited no bitter resentment against those who put Him on the cross. Rather, "Father, forgive them; for they know not what they do" (Luke 23: 34), and now, at the end, serene confidence, "Father, into thy hands I commend my spirit" (Luke 23: 46). In Peter's words, "Who, when He was reviled, reviled not again; when he suffered, he threatened not; but committed himself to him that judgeth righteously" (1 Pet. 2: 23).

4) THE WOMEN VIEWING, vv55-56
"And many women were there beholding afar off, which followed Jesus from Galilee, ministering unto him: among which was Mary Magdalene, and Mary the mother of James and Joses, and the mother of Zebedee's children (Salome, mother of James and John)". These godly women stood at first "by the cross" enabling the Lord to speak to Mary (see John 19: 25-27), but now, at the end of His sufferings, they were "beholding afar off". See also Mark 15: 40-41; Luke 23: 49.

According to Luke, the Lord Jesus was accompanied by "the twelve" and by "certain women, which had been healed of evil spirits and infirmities, Mary called Magdalene, out of whom went seven devils (demons), and Joanna the wife of Chuza, Herod's steward, and Susanna, and many others, which ministered unto him of their substance" (Luke 8: 1-3). John Heading (*What the Bible Teaches - Matthew*) has a nice piece on Mary Magdalene. "The record has been silent about Mary Magdalene since Luke 8: 2, but now she reappears in the narrative at the Lord's death and resurrection. Not all faithful souls are always in the limelight or noted by name, but her constant service is recognised in our verse 55 - she was 'unknown, and yet well known' (2 Cor. 6: 9)". "Mary the mother of James ('James the less') and Joses" is also known as "Mary the wife of Cleophas" (John 19: 25). "Cleophas" and "Alpheus" both represent the same Hebrew name, and therefore "James the less" (to distinguish him from James the brother of John), is in fact "James son of Alpheus". His brother is known either as "Joses" or "Judas" (Luke 6: 16, Acts 1: 13).

Matthew

He is also known as "Thaddaeus" (Mark 3: 18), and "Lebbaeus, whose surname was Thaddaeus" (Matt.10: 3).

While we do not have a great deal of information about these godly women, their "witness is in heaven" and their "record is on high" (Job 16: 19). That should be an encouragement to us all. When our earthly record is examined in heaven, there could be no better commendation than this: they "followed him" (Luke 23: 49), and "ministered unto him" (Luke 8: 3).

Addendum

"And, behold, the veil of the temple was rent in twain from the top to the bottom; and the earth did quake, and the rocks rent; and the graves were opened; and many bodies of the saints which slept arose, and came out of the graves after his resurrection, and went into the holy city, and appeared unto many" (vv.51-53).

1) Extracted from Bible Problems and Answers
"Matthew 27: 52-53 states that 'many bodies of the saints which slept arose, and came out of the graves after his resurrection, and went into the holy city, and appeared unto many'. Is it known what happened to these saints? Did they go to heaven with Christ or did they return to their graves?"

"We are not told in the Scriptures, but the resurrection of these saints in connection with that of our Lord leaves little doubt, I think, on the matter. Our Lord Himself was shewn after His resurrection 'not to all the people, but unto witnesses chosen before of God' (Acts 10: 41), to make it easier for the people at large to believe in the resurrection. He was the first-fruits. 'Many bodies of the saints arose…and went into the holy city, and appeared unto many'. They could not deny their own senses that they had seen their dead friends alive, and if so, why should not the testimony of the disciples be that Christ had risen? Under such circumstances, it seems very difficult to believe that the resurrection of these saints was anything but a true and lasting resurrection. I believe this was the first stage in the First Resurrection, of which the resurrection of the sleeping saints, when the Lord comes, will be the second stage, and the remaining saints who have died when He returns in glory the final stage. 'This is the first resurrection'. Had they returned to their graves, it might be said that He did, too. Surely they were part of that captivity which He led captive when he ascended on high" (Wm. Hoste). See page 259.

2) Extracted from Answers to Bible Problems
"Is anything recorded concerning those who rose from the dead when Christ gave up the Ghost on the cross? Matthew 27: 52-53". (Question 48).

Answer – "The resurrection of the individuals concerned took place after the resurrection of the Lord Jesus. He was the First-born of them that slept. When Scripture is silent as to details, it is well that the believer should be satisfied with what is written. The information here is scant. It was an evidence in the case of 'many', given to 'many' of the triumph which the Lord Jesus had effected over death, not only in respect of Himself, but also in respect of His own. They may have been people known in Jerusalem, who but recently had died and who appeared to those who were known by them. But this is not necessary. I do not suppose that, like Lazarus and others, they went back into a state of death again, else of what force is the phrase 'after His resurrection'? But we must be careful not to be wise above what is written" (E.W.Rogers). See page 26.

"He...laid it in his own new tomb"

Read Chapter 27: 57-66
The preceding verses (vv.44-56) brought before us the Lord's death, when God "made him to be sin for us, who knew no sin" (2 Cor. 5: 21). Matthew (with Mark) records His cry, uttered prophetically a thousand years before, "My God, my God, why hast thou forsaken me" (Psalm 22: 1). The final section of the chapter (vv.57-66) brings before us the Lord's burial. This is recorded by all four Gospel writers. His burial exactly fulfilled the prophecy (it could not be otherwise), "And (men) appointed his grave with the wicked, but he was **with the rich in his death**" (Isaiah 53: 9 JND).

The passage clearly divides into two sections *(1)* the devotion of His disciples (vv.57-61); *(2)* the hatred of His enemies (vv.62-66).

1) THE DEVOTION OF HIS DISCIPLES, vv.57-61
While Matthew mentions only Joseph of Arimathaea, whom he calls "Jesus' disciple" (v.57), we know that Nicodemus was also involved in the Lord's burial (John 19: 38-42). So two men were involved. There were also two women: "Mary Magdalene, and the other Mary" (v.61).

a) The two men, vv.57-60
John describes the role of both Joseph of Arimathaea and Nicodemus in

the Lord's burial, whereas Matthew only mentions Joseph. However, for the record, here is John's account of the involvement of both men: "And after this Joseph of Arimathaea, being a disciple of Jesus, but secretly for fear of the Jews, besought Pilate that he might take away the body of Jesus: and Pilate gave him leave. He came therefore, and took the body of Jesus. And there came also Nicodemus, which at the first came to Jesus by night, and brought a mixture of myrrh and aloes, about an hundred pound weight. Then took *they* the body of Jesus, and wound it in linen clothes with the spices, as the manner of the Jews is to bury. Now in the place where he was crucified there was a garden; and in the garden a new sepulchre, wherein was never man yet laid. There laid *they* Jesus therefore because of the Jews' preparation day; for the preparation was nigh at hand" (John 19: 39-42).

We must notice the following in connection with Joseph of Arimathaea. It has been pointed out that a man named Joseph was present when the Lord was born, and another man of the same name was present when He died. The first took care of the infant, and the second took care of His body. Joseph of Nazareth was a Galilean, a poor man, and a carpenter. Joseph of Arimathaea was a Judean ("a city of the Jews", Luke 23: 51, possibly Ramah, or Ramathaim-zophim, the birthplace of Samuel), a rich man, and a counsellor. He is in fact described as "an honourable counsellor ('a councillor of honourable estate', Mark 15: 43, RV), which also waited for the kingdom of God". The following should be noted:

- **His character**. Luke describes Joseph as "a counsellor...a good man, and a just" who "had not consented to the counsel and deed of them" (so he was a member of the Sanhedrin) and "who also himself waited for the kingdom of God" (Luke 23: 50-51). Richard Catchpole (Cheshunt, 7th July, 2004) points out that we have a threefold description of his character. **Selfward,** he was "a good man". The word "good" (*agathos*) signifies 'being good in character...is beneficial in effect' (W.E.Vine); **manward,** he was "just", and this was seen in his refusal to concur with the unjust way in which his fellow-counsellors in the Sanhedrin treated the Lord Jesus; **Godward,** he "waited for the kingdom of God". Compare Titus 2: 12-13: "soberly" ('a good man'); "righteously" ('just'); "godly" ('waiting for the kingdom of God').

- **His confidence**. At the beginning of his Gospel, Luke refers to Simeon who was "waiting for the consolation of Israel" (Luke 2: 25) and at the end of the Gospel he refers to Joseph who was "waiting for the kingdom of God"

(Luke 23: 51). In both cases the word "waiting" (*prosdechomai*) means to 'look with expectation' or 'wait with confidence'. We should add that the dying thief and Joseph of Arimathaea had nothing in common socially or morally, but they did have a common hope: both anticipated the coming kingdom. See Luke 23: 42, 51.

Joseph of Arimathaea was a relatively unknown man. We look in vain for information about him prior to the Lord's death and after the Lord's death, reminding us that there are many faithful servants of God of whom we know little or nothing at all. At the same time, he was the man for the moment. Isaiah had predicted that the Lord would "be with the rich in his death", but evening was imminent, and the Lord's relatives and disciples were far from rich. But God had His man, and the word of God was proved, yet again, to be completely reliable and accurate (Richard Catchpole). We must now notice what Joseph of Arimathaea did:

i) He asked for the Lord's body, vv.57-58
"When the even was come, there came a rich man of Arimathaea, named Joseph, who also himself was Jesus' disciple: he went to Pilate, and begged (*aiteo*, to ask: 'asked for', RV) the body of Jesus". Mark tells us that "Joseph...went in boldly unto Pilate, and craved (*aiteo*) the body of Jesus" (Mark 15: 42-43). See also Luke 23: 50-52; John 19: 38. Since the word *aiteo* is often used in petitioning a superior, the sense may be 'begged' (see Mark 15: 43, JND).

While John describes Joseph of Arimathaea as a "disciple of Jesus, but secretly for fear of the Jews" (John 19: 38), Joseph did not end that way. Beyond any shadow of doubt, it must have been difficult in the extreme for him to 'nail his colours to the mast', but he "emboldened himself and went in to Pilate and begged the body of Jesus" (Mark 15: 43, JND). As Norman Crawford (*What the Bible Teaches - Luke*) rightly says, "It took courage to come out publicly as a supporter of the rejected and crucified Christ. The death of the Saviour caused the disciples to forsake Him, but it caused Joseph to show his love and loyalty". Amongst other things, this would have enraged his colleagues on the Great Council at Jerusalem, and Wm.McDonald must be right in saying, "In burying the body of Jesus, Joseph would never be part of Judaism again". David Gooding makes the application: "We who like Joseph are left to live in a world where God's Son was crucified, might well ask ourselves what we have done or are doing to make it clear publicly where we stand in relation to the claims of Christ".

David Gooding points out, had the Lord's body "been flung into a mass grave along with other bodies, it would subsequently have been impossible to point to the empty tomb as clear evidence of the resurrection". As we have already noted, the burial of the Lord Jesus in Joseph's tomb had been predicted centuries before: "And he made his grave with the wicked, and with the rich in his death" or, "And (men) appointed his grave with the wicked (plural), but he was with the rich (singular: 'the rich one') in his death" (Isaiah 53: 9, JND). The reason follows: "because", unlike the thieves with whom He was crucified, "he had done no violence, neither was any deceit found in his mouth". His honourable burial was in accord with His moral beauty, whereas His enemies would have given Him a criminal's grave.

ii) He was given the Lord's body, v.58
"Then Pilate commanded the body to be delivered". This is one of several Scriptural answers to the so-called 'swoon theory' used to explain away the resurrection. Those who advocate this view say that the Lord Jesus never actually died, and therefore there was no resurrection. As J.C.Ryle points out, "He who knows the end from the beginning prevented the possibility of such objections being made (though some people persist): by His over-ruling providence He ordered things so that the death and burial of Jesus was placed beyond a doubt: Pilate gives consent to His burial: a loving disciple wraps the body in linen...the chief priests themselves set a guard over the place where His body was deposited. Jews and Gentiles, friends and enemies, all alike testify to the great fact, that Christ did really and actually die, and was laid in a grave".

We must notice the reference to the Lord's "body": Joseph "went to Pilate, and begged the body of Jesus. Then Pilate commanded the body to be delivered" (v.58). Joseph himself removed the Lord's body from the cross (Luke 23: 53). The Greek word (*soma*) means, "properly, a human body, a living thing, a Person, a temple in which the Holy Ghost could dwell" (Harold St.John, citing Abbott-Smith's *Lexicon*). The Lord's body could never see corruption (Psalm 16: 10). Mark's record reads as follows: "Joseph of Arimathaea...went in boldly unto Pilate, and craved the body of Jesus. And Pilate marvelled if he were already dead: and calling unto him the centurion, he asked him whether he had been any while dead. And when he knew it, he gave the body to Joseph" (Mark 15: 43-45). According to some manuscripts, the word "body" in v.45 ("he gave the body to Joseph") is *ptoma*, meaning 'a corpse', literally 'a fallen thing'. It is used in Matthew 24: 28, "For wheresoever the carcase (*ptoma*) is, there will the eagles be gathered together". Norman Crawford sets out the difference between the two words as follows, "to Joseph, the body of the Lord Jesus was precious, and not a mere corpse as it was to Pilate".

iii) He buried the Lord's body, vv.59-60
"And when Joseph had taken the body, he wrapped it in a clean linen cloth, and laid it in his own new tomb, which he had hewn out in the rock: and he rolled a great stone to the door of the sepulchre, and departed". Matthew, writing for Jews, omits reference to the anointing of the body since this would have been taken for granted by the first readers. Joseph "bought fine linen", while Nicodemus "brought a mixture of myrrh and aloes, about a hundred pound weight" (John 19: 39-40). As Norman Crawford observes, "This is the entire record of the service of Joseph for the Lord…Some serve God in a life of seventy years or more and others have a very short service, but if each has fulfilled his course, that is all that matters". At His birth, the Lord Jesus was laid "in a manger" (Luke 2: 7): at his death, He was laid "in a sepulchre" (Mark 15: 46). To the women who were "sitting over against the sepulchre", it must have seemed absolutely final. Even His body was beyond their reach in the rock-hewn tomb with the stone sealing the entrance. The sabbath now began, and the "Lord of the sabbath" (Matt. 12: 8) was in a tomb! But soon the sabbath would be over, and things would be so marvellously different!

J.M.Flanigan has a typically beautiful piece here: "A new tomb. A clean linen cloth. A great stone. These tell the story of the burial of the Saviour. It was a rock-hewn tomb in a garden. Joseph gave it as a free-will offering. Did he realise that it was but a loan? That it was only being borrowed? For three days only it would be needed and it would be returned to him. The interest on his loan would be that his name would be inscribed in each of the four Gospels and that all those who loved the Saviour would love him too for his reverent handling of their Beloved on the dark day of the crucifixion. And the Marys watched!"

We must notice the details given in connection with the sepulchre. The Gospel writers give us seemingly small and unimportant pieces of information about the tomb. Matthew tells us that it was "his own new tomb, which he had hewn out in the rock" (v.60). John describes it as "a new sepulchre" (John 19: 41). Luke tells us that it was a tomb "wherein never man before was laid" (Luke 23: 53). The details are important, and help to expose the folly of people who try to explain away the resurrection:

- ***It was a "new tomb"***, so there was no question of crumbling masonry enabling the body to be extracted from the tomb.

- ***It was "hewn out in the rock"***, so there was no question of an alternative exit, for example, at the rear of the tomb.

- ***It was a tomb "wherein never man before was laid"***, so there was no question of mixing up bodies.

All this reminds us that little details of Scripture must never be overlooked! There is no 'baggage' in the Bible! Nothing superfluous!

b) The two women, v.61
"And there was Mary Magdalene, and the other Mary, sitting over against the sepulchre". As already noted, there were just four people at the Lord's funeral, two men (John 19: 38-42) and two women (Matt. 27: 61). The two women were certainly not "sitting over against the sepulchre" in idle curiosity. Luke tells us that "the women also, which came with him from Galilee, followed after, and beheld the sepulchre, and how his body was laid. And they returned, and prepared (*hetoimazo*) spices and ointments…" (Luke 23: 56). They did not know that their careful preparation would not be actually needed. Neither did they know how they were going to gain access to the body (Mark 16: 3), but this did not deter them. They were faithful to the last! The word "prepared" (Luke 23: 56) is used in 2 Tim. 2: 21, "prepared (*hetoimazo*) unto every good work". We can show *our* love for the Lord Jesus by preparation in this way. Additionally, we must not overlook the example of these godly women in obeying God's word. They "rested the sabbath day, according to the commandment" (Luke 23: 56).

2) THE HATRED OF HIS ENEMIES, vv.62-66
These verses are unique to Matthew. "Now the next day, that followed the day of the preparation, the chief priests and Pharisees came together unto Pilate, saying, Sir, we remember that that deceiver said, while he was yet alive, After three days I will rise again" (vv.62-63). It may be worth noting that Matthew does not say 'Now on the sabbath', but "Now the next day, that followed the day of the preparation…" See also Mark 15: 42, "And now when the even was come, because it was the Preparation, that is the day before the sabbath" or "and when it was already evening, since it was [the] preparation, that is, [the day] before a sabbath…" (JND). So the Lord was crucified, ***not*** - obviously - on the sabbath day, ***nor*** on the preparation for

the sabbath, *but* on the day before the preparation for the sabbath. See the addendum.

The closing verses of the chapter display the hatred of the religious leaders for the Lord Jesus. They called him "that deceiver", and took every possible step to ensure that the memory of Him was irreparably damaged. But God 'makes the wrath of man to praise Him' (Psalm 76: 10). By acting as they did, the Lord's enemies unwittingly provided incontrovertible evidence of His resurrection, and therefore confirmation of His true identity. "Their seal, their guard, their precautions, were all to become witnesses, in a few hours, that Christ had risen...They were taken in their own craftiness (1 Cor. 3: 19): their own devices became instruments to show forth God's glory" (J.C.Ryle). We should now notice: *(a)* their petition (vv.62-64); *(b)* their precautions (vv.65-66).

a) Their petition, vv.62-64
We should notice *(i)* the people involved (v.62); *(ii)* the phraseology used (v.63); (iii) the plea made (v.64).

i) The people. "Now the next day, that followed the day of the preparation, the chief priests and Pharisees came together unto Pilate" (v.62). While it has been said that these two groups, which as a rule opposed each other, were united in their opposition to Christ, it is noteworthy that it was the religious leadership which petitioned Pilate. There was nothing new about this. It reminds us that the greatest opposition to the Gospel has often come from institutionalised religion. In this case, as in many cases, the religious world sought the help and support of the political world. Moreover, they descended upon Pilate on "the next day, that followed the day of the preparation". The very people who were punctilious in observing the sabbath were not averse to contravening their own rules if necessary.

ii) The phraseology. The chief priests and Pharisees said, "Sir, we remember that that deceiver said, while he was yet alive, After three days I will rise again" (v.63). What a contrast in their language:

- *They addressed Pilate as "Sir".* The word translated "Sir" (*kurios*) is better known to us as "lord". It is translated in the same way in Matthew 13: 27: "Sir, didst not thou sow good seed" (see also Matt. 21: 30), and used in detailing relationships between master and servant. See, for example, Matthew 10: 24-25; 18: 25-27, 31-32, 34. Pilate was treated with respect, something they had not always practised. See, for example, Matthew 27: 23. But:

- **They described the Lord Jesus as "that deceiver".** These men may have been referring to Matthew 12: 40 which was addressed to the Pharisees. It has often been pointed out that "It is remarkable that Jesus' enemies remembered His words and had apparently understood them (but not necessarily believed them), while His friends, to whom He had spoken so much more clearly about His resurrection (Matt. 16: 21, 17: 23; 20: 19), had not understood them" (Supplied by Justin Waldron). The disciples had questioned "one with another what the rising from the dead should mean (Mark 9: 10).

iii) The plea. "Command therefore that the sepulchre be made sure until the third day, lest his disciples come by night, and steal him away, and say unto the people, He is risen from the dead: so the last error shall be worse than the first" (v.64). The religious leaders were decidedly uneasy. Possibly they had been taken by surprise that the Lord's body had been interred in Joseph's new tomb. They would have expected His body be consigned to a criminal's common grave in the valley of Hinnom, a location which had become Jerusalem's garbage-dump where worms fed and fires burned. These men saw the possibility of even greater challenges to their authority. If the despised and hated Jesus of Nazareth had so seriously undermined their authority by His life and teaching, what would be the result if it was reported, however erroneously, that He had risen from the dead? Or, in the words of R.V.G.Tasker, "This imposter, they pointed out, had deceived the people quite enough by claiming to be Messiah, and it would be the crowning deception if they were to be further tricked into thinking that He was still alive". R.V.G. Tasker adds, "As events turned out, it was the priests and the Pharisees who proved to be the deceivers of the people, by their persistent assertion after the resurrection that the disciples of Jesus had stolen His body". See Matt. 28:11-15.

b) Their precautions, vv.65-66
"Pilate said unto them, Ye have a watch: go your way, make it as sure as ye can. So they went, and made the sepulchre sure, sealing the stone and setting a watch". On a technical point, the words "Ye have a watch" can be understood as an imperative: 'take a guard' or 'you can have a guard'. In which case the guard would comprise Roman soldiers. On the other hand, the words could be understood in the indicative sense, in which case the

meaning would be 'you have a guard of your own', that is, the temple guard, with the implication 'you'll need no help from me' (Robert H. Mounce). It does seem that Roman soldiers were involved. See Matthew 28: 11-15. G. Campbell Morgan feels that "Most probably it was the language of weary indifference, as though he had said 'Let me be done with this thing; take the guard and get away, and do anything you like'". Nevertheless, there is a certain irony in the words, "go your way, make it as sure as ye can". The soldiers, the stone and the seal all proved to be completely ineffective, for:

> *Vain the stone, the watch, the seal,*
> *Christ hath burst the gates of hell:*
> *Death in vain forbids Him rise!*
> *Christ hath opened paradise.*
> *Hallelujah!*

ADDENDUM

The words, "the next day, that followed the day of the preparation" (see also Mark 15: 42; Luke 23: 54; John 19: 14) should be born in mind in endeavouring to settle the precise meaning of the Lord's words, "so shall the Son of man be three **days** and three **nights** in the heart of the earth" (Matt. 12: 40). If the Lord Jesus was crucified on 'Good Friday', and left Joseph's tomb on 'Easter Sunday', how could He have been "three days and three nights in the heart of the earth?" As we noted at the time, the usual answer is that in Jewish reckoning any part of a day and night counts as a complete period, and this would certainly be the answer if it were a question of "three days", but the Lord did say "three days and three nights!" It has been argued that the words "that sabbath day was an **high day**" (John 19: 31) indicate 'something special and distinct from a ordinary sabbath', arising from the fact that the feast of unleavened bread commenced on the fifteenth day of the first month and was regarded as a Sabbath, irrespective of the day of the week on which it fell (Lev. 23: 7). If it fell on the sixth day of the week, "then two Sabbaths would follow one another" (J. Heading). On this basis, the Lord would have been crucified, ***not*** on 'Good Friday', ***but*** on Thursday.

However, we should make our own calculations, taking all the available information into account, including the fact that the Lord rose before Mary Magdalene arrived at the tomb "when it was yet dark" (John 20: 1).

THE GOSPEL OF MATTHEW

"He is not here: for he is risen, as he said"

Read Chapter 28: 1-15
When Paul preached at Corinth, he prioritised the death, burial and resurrection of the Lord Jesus: "I delivered unto you first of all, (that is, 'first of all' in importance) that which I also received, how that **Christ died for our sins** according to the scriptures; and that **he was buried**, and that **he rose again the third day** according to the scriptures; and that he was seen…" (1 Cor.15: 1-5). In each case, whether the death, burial, or resurrection of the Lord Jesus, everything took place "according to the scriptures". There were occasions when His life was threatened by the Jews. See, for example, Luke 4: 28-30; John 8: 58-59; 10: 30-31. Had the Lord Jesus died on any of these occasions, it would *not* have been "according to the scriptures". Had the Lord Jesus been buried in a common grave, that too would *not* have been "according to the scriptures. But Isaiah 53: 9 must be fulfilled, "And (men) appointed his grave with the wicked (plural: 'wicked people'), but he was with the rich (singular: 'rich man') in his death" (JND). We must never forget that God's word is "for ever…settled in heaven" (Psalm 119: 89), and "the scripture cannot be broken" (John 10: 35). Similarly, the Lord's resurrection was "according to the scriptures", and this is true in at least three ways:

i) It was "according to the scriptures" prophetically. See, for example, Psalm 16: 10-11: "Thou wilt not leave my soul in hell; neither wilt thou suffer thine Holy One to see corruption. Thou wilt shew me the path of life…" Having referred to this passage on the day of Pentecost, Peter explained to the crowds that it could not possibly refer to David since he was "both dead and buried", but "being a prophet", David "spake of the resurrection of Christ" (Acts 2: 25-32).

ii) It was "according to the scriptures" ceremonially. While the part played by the two birds in the cleansing of the leper (Lev. 14: 1-7) certainly prefigures the death, resurrection and ascension of the Lord Jesus, His

Chapter 28

resurrection was clearly anticipated in the Old Testament "feasts of the LORD" (Lev. 23: 2). Paul refers to the 'feast of firstfruits' (Lev. 23: 9-14) in 1 Cor. 15: 20, "But now is Christ risen from the dead, and become the firstfruits of them that slept". It is noteworthy that the 'sheaf of the firstfruits' was to be presented to God on "the morrow after the sabbath" (Lev. 23: 11) or, as Luke puts it, upon the first day of the week" (Luke 24: 1). The Lord's resurrection therefore fulfilled the 'typical teaching' of the Old Testament. As "the firstfruits of them that slept" the risen Lord Jesus is the guarantee of a harvest to follow (1 Cor. 15: 22-24).

iii) It was "according to the scriptures" typically. See, particularly, the experience of Jonah: "For as Jonas was three days and three nights in the whale's belly; so shall the Son of man be three days and three nights in the heart of the earth" (Matt. 12: 40). Another example can be found in the experience of Isaac. See Gen. 22: 1-13; Heb. 11: 17-19.

Matthew 28, together with the resurrection accounts in Mark, Luke and John, is therefore of tremendous importance. The chapter may be divided in the following way: *(1)* the arrival of the women (v.1); *(2)* the removal of the stone (vv.2-4); *(3)* the explanation by the angel (vv.5-8); *(4)* the meeting with the Saviour (vv.9-10); *(5)* the deceit of the religious leaders (vv.11-15); *(6)* the commissioning of the disciples (vv.16-20).

1) THE ARRIVAL OF THE WOMEN, v.1
"In the end of the sabbath, as it began to dawn toward the first day of the week, came Mary Magdalene and the other Mary to see the sepulchre". We should notice: *(a)* who came: it was "Mary Magdalene and the other Mary"; *(b)* when they came: it was "in the end of the sabbath, as it began to dawn toward the first day of the week"; *(c)* why they came: it was "to see the sepulchre".

a) Who came
Mary Magdalene, and Mary the mother of James and Joses (Matt. 27: 56), to which we must add Salome (Mark 16: 1) who was evidently the wife of Zebedee, and mother of James and John (see, again, Matt. 27: 56), all showed an intensity of devotion to their Master which was certainly not matched by the men. All three were at Golgotha, "beholding afar off" (Matt. 27: 56), and two of them, Mary Magdalene and Mary the mother of James and Joses, "beheld where he was laid" (Matt. 27: 61; Mark 15: 47). All three (perhaps four: Joanna is also mentioned, Luke 24: 10; see Luke

Matthew

8: 3) now come to the tomb, having "bought sweet spices, that they might come and anoint him" (Mark 16: 1). There was not a male disciple in sight! While they thought it was all over and their beloved Master was dead, with no expectation of His resurrection, we must not overlook the fact that they were still willing to give Him their very best, even in death. They had served Him in His life (Mark 15: 40-41): now they were prepared to serve Him in His death. It's well worth emphasising again that although we know very little about the ministry of the women prior to the Lord's death and resurrection, there is no doubting their "meek and quiet spirit, which is in the sight of God of great price" (1 Pet. 3: 4). Their ministry never 'hit the headlines', but it was "of great price". While the role of sisters in the assembly differs from the role of men, it is of tremendous value. No assembly can exist in good health without it.

How great is *our* devotion to Him? He died for us, and rose to be our living Lord and Saviour. Surely He is worthy of *our* deepest love and loyalty.

b) When they came
It was "In the **end of the sabbath** (a plural word, 'sabbaths'), **as it began to dawn toward the first day of the week**". This is best understood with reference to the Amplified Version: "Now after the sabbath (that is, after 6 p.m.), near dawn of the first day of the week" or, "The sabbath was over, and it was about daybreak on Sunday" (N.E.B.). According to Mark, they came "very early in the morning, the first day of the week...at the rising of the sun" (Mark 16: 2). They came with "sweet spices", which they had either purchased "when the sabbath was past" (Mark 16: 1) or had purchased before the sabbath and, having "rested the sabbath day according to the commandment", then came with them to the sepulchre (Luke 23: 56 - 24: 1). Harold St.John espouses the first explanation: "Mark first assures his readers that the sabbath was past, that is, that it was after 6 p.m. on Saturday evening. The shops then being open, the spices were bought and early next morning the women arrived at the tomb".

But Mark's timing, "when **the sabbath was past**" and, "**the first day of the week**", with Matthew's timing "**end of the sabbath**, as it began to dawn toward **the first day of the week**", are more than chronological references. A new epoch had opened.

- **"The sabbath"** was the sign of the old covenant. "Speak thou unto the children of Israel, saying, verily my sabbaths ye shall keep: for it is a sign between me and you throughout your generations; that ye may know that I am the LORD that doth sanctify you" (Exodus 31: 12-17). Like the law it represented, it demanded obedience, but proved "weak through the flesh" (Rom. 8: 3). This was made very clear through Ezekiel: "I gave them my statutes, and shewed them my judgments, which if a man do, he shall even live in them. Moreover also, I gave them my sabbaths, to be a sign between me and them, that they may know that I am the Lord that sanctify them. But....my sabbaths they greatly polluted" (Ezek.20:10-24). The sabbath made demands on human nature which human nature could not meet, and men stood condemned by it.

- *"The first day of the week"* is a constant reminder that men and women can now rest for salvation, not on sabbath-keeping, and their own efforts to keep the law, but on the work of the Lord Jesus Christ, crucified at Calvary and risen from the dead. The sabbath required men and women to **do something for God,** whilst the "first day of the week" emphasises what God **has done for men and women.** The thoughtful Israelite must have often wondered why the Lord required a "sheaf of the firstfruits" to be presented "on the morrow after the sabbath" (Lev.23: 10-11). After all, the weekly calendar was dominated by the sabbath! This was something quite exceptional! The New Testament, as we have seen, supplies the answer: "But now is Christ risen from the dead, and become **the firstfruits** of them that slept" (1 Cor.15: 20).

c) Why they came
Matthew simply says that they came "to see the sepulchre". But this was no sight-seeing visit. They came to "see the sepulchre" bearing "sweet spices" with which to "**anoint him**" (Mark 16: 1) or, in Luke's language "bringing the spices which they had prepared" (Luke 24: 1). Evidently, their intention was to embalm the body of the Lord Jesus, not knowing that He had said a thousand years before: "Therefore did my heart rejoice, and my tongue was glad; moreover also my flesh shall rest in hope: because thou wilt not leave my soul in hell, **neither wilt thou suffer thine Holy One to see corruption**" (Acts 2: 25-32 citing Psalm 16: 9-10). That is not to say that their intense devotion was unrecognised for, as Noman Crawford points out, "the devotion and faithfulness of these dear women was honoured by God in that the Lord appeared first to them".

The fact that the women had "bought sweet spices", and came with them on "the first day of the week" (Mark 16: 1-2), is most thought-provoking. What do *we* bring on the "first day of the week?" They had spent money purchasing the spices, and time preparing them. They then got up "very early in the morning" (Mark 16: 2) to anoint, as they thought, the Lord's body. It would be so lovely if the Lord Jesus could say of us as we remember Him, "I am come into my garden, my sister, my spouse: I have gathered my myrrh and my spice" (Song of Solomon 5: 1).

But Matthew's expression, "to see the sepulchre" is best understood by their question, "And they said among themselves, Who shall roll us away the stone from the door of the sepulchre?" (Mark 16: 3) They came to what they expected would be a sealed tomb. We should remember that it was not only a case of heaving the stone out of the way. The stone stood in a slot, from which it would have to be lifted - a task far greater than the combined strength of the women. Mark tells us that the stone was "very great" (Mark 16: 4). Perhaps they were unaware that the stone could not be moved without breaking an official seal, and that Roman soldiers were in attendance (Matt. 27: 62-66). But the expected problem had been solved for them: the stone was already rolled away!

2) THE REMOVAL OF THE STONE, vv.2-4
This happened before the arrival of the women, and these verses, which are unique to Matthew, are therefore an explanatory parenthesis, enabling him to continue, "And the angel answered and said unto the women, Fear not ye: for I know that ye seek Jesus, which was crucified. He is not here: for he is risen as he said" (vv.5-6). We should notice: *(a)* the descent of the angel (v.2); *(b)* the description of the angel (v.3); *(c)* effect of the angel (v.4).

a) The descent of the angel, v.2
"And, behold, there was a great earthquake: for the angel of the Lord descended from heaven, and came and rolled back the stone from the door, and sat upon it". Matthew begins with "*the* angel of the Lord" appearing to Joseph (1: 20, 24) in connection with the Lord's incarnation: now, evidently, the same angel appears to the women in connection with His resurrection. Not, '*an* angel of the Lord', but "*the* angel of the Lord". This was therefore an angel of highest rank. While in the Old Testament, "the angel of the LORD" was none other than the Son of God himself, this divine title is not used of Him in the New Testament.

An earthquake took place at the Lord's death, causing the Roman guards great fear" (Matt. 27: 54). Now, another earthquake takes place in connection with the Lord's resurrection, causing the Roman guards even greater fear (v.4). But, as John Heading points out, "the earthquake manifesting divine power over nature did not cause faith in the unbelievers who witnessed it". While it was not the earthquake that caused the removal of the stone from the entrance to the tomb, but the angel who descended from heaven, the power exerted by the angel was so vast that it reverberated through creation. This is clear from the narrative: "And, behold, there was a great earthquake: *for* the angel of the Lord descended from heaven, and came and rolled back the stone from the door, and sat upon it". The word "behold", together with the word "lo" (*idou* in both cases, and used four times in vv.2, 7, 9) is used to mark "the striking nature of the events" (R.H.Mounce).

As noted, only Matthew states that the angel "sat upon it", a "position that denotes victory over death, and an authority that superseded the authority of Rome by which the tomb was sealed" (Norman Crawford). We should add, although it should not be necessary, that the stone was *not* rolled away to let the Saviour out of the tomb, *but* to show that He was not there!

We must understand that the Lord Jesus did not rise from the dead with a new body. The body that was placed in Joseph's tomb was precisely the same body that came out of the tomb, otherwise it would not have been resurrection at all. It is tempting to say that His body had new qualities, enabling Him, amongst other things, to transcend natural laws, so that a rock-hewn tomb, and closed doors, did not interrupt His movements. But against this, the Lord manifested transcendence over natural laws before His death and resurrection. He walked on storm-tossed Galilee (Matt. 14: 25-26).

b) The description of the angel, v.3
"His countenance was like lightning (see Heb. 1: 7), and his raiment white as snow". So the "young man" at the tomb was an angel. "And entering into the sepulchre, they saw a young man sitting on the right side, clothed in a long white garment; and they were affrighted" (Mark 16: 5). Luke mentions "two men…in shining garments" (Luke 24: 4).

It has been suggested that the angel took character from the Lord whose resurrection he announced. The angel's face and raiment are described in similar terms to the Lord's face and raiment: "his face did shine as the sun, and his raiment was white as the light" (Matt. 17: 2). The angel reflected the glory and purity of the Lord Jesus.

The precise description given by the Gospel writers is very important since it emphasises that this was no vague impression, or figment of the imagination. It might also be worth mentioning that in the Bible, angels always appear as men. So, strictly speaking, we shouldn't call a girl an angel! Neither do angels have wings. They must not be confused with the cherubim (Ezekiel 1: 9) and seraphim (Isaiah 6: 2). The word "angel" means 'messenger'. So it was a message from God, conveyed by an angel, that the women heard on resurrection morning.

c) The effect of the angel, v.4
"And for fear of him the keepers did shake, and became as dead men". What would have been the effect if "twelve legions of angels" (Matt. 27: 53) had descended?! The religious leaders thought they had a dead man in a tomb guarded by living men, but the position was reversed: it became a living Man and a 'dead' guard! There is no message of reassurance to the guard. In fact, there is no word for them at all! But the angel had something delightful to say to the women. This brings us to:

3) THE EXPLANATION BY THE ANGEL, vv.5-8
"Fear not ye (like the guards): for I know that ye seek Jesus, which was crucified. He is not here: for he is risen, **as he said.** (See Matthew 26: 32) Come, see the place where the Lord lay" (vv.5-6). Luke also gives a fuller account: "Why seek ye the living among the dead? He is not here, but is risen: **remember how he spake unto you when he was yet in Galilee,** saying, the Son of man must be delivered into the hands of sinful men, and be crucified, and the third day rise again. And they remembered his words" (Luke 24: 5-8).

The privilege of becoming the first heralds of the Lord's resurrection was given to these devoted women: "And go **quickly,** and tell his disciples that he is risen from the dead; and behold, he goeth before you into Galilee; there shall ye see him: lo, I have told you. And they departed quickly from the sepulchre with fear and great joy (compare Matt. 2: 10); and did run to bring his disciples word" (vv.7-8). See also Mark 16: 6-8; Luke 24: 9-11. Both Matthew and Mark tell us that they obeyed implicitly: see Matthew 28: 8 ("quickly") and Mark 16: 8 ("quickly").

The message is unchanged. **"He is risen".** It is a message for every believer. It brings certainty and assurance to all we believe. Otherwise "then is our preaching vain, and your faith is also vain" (1 Cor. 15: 14). It brings comfort in the face of death: "For if we believe that Jesus died and **rose again**, even so them also which sleep in Jesus will God bring with him" (1 Thess. 4: 14). It is said that when the early Christians met each other they would say, 'The Lord is risen', with the response, 'The Lord is risen indeed'. "**He is risen**". It is the hallmark of the Gospel. The resurrection of the Lord Jesus Christ was the outstanding feature of apostolic preaching. They triumphantly proclaimed, "He is risen": "With great power gave the apostles witness of the resurrection of the Lord Jesus" (Acts 4: 33). The message of these verses remains for us: "Come, see...go...tell"

Mark tells us that the women "went out quickly and fled from the sepulchre; for they trembled and were amazed; neither said they anything to any man; for they were afraid" (Mark 16: 8). The last words must refer to anybody they met *en route* to the disciples with the message. They certainly told the disciples! See Luke 24: 9-10, 22-24.

4) THE MEETING WITH THE SAVIOUR, vv.9-10

"And as they went to tell his disciples, behold, Jesus met them, saying, All hail. And they came and held him by the feet, and worshipped him. Then said Jesus unto them, Be not afraid: go tell my brethren that they go into Galilee, and there shall they see me".

These verses are unique to Matthew. For their place in the order of events on resurrection morning, see the Addendum. John Heading points out, rather beautifully, that the obedience of the women "brought a reward beyond anticipation". They were met by the risen Lord! The Lord's greeting, "All hail" (*chariete,* plural) is derived from a verb meaning 'to rejoice'. In the singular (*chairo*) it was used in treachery by Judas (Matt. 26: 49) and in mockery by the soldiers (Matt. 27: 29), but now it is used triumphantly!

The words "came and held him by the feet, and worshipped him" (v.9) bring before us "humility, wonder, love and faith mingled as an act of worship" (J.Heading). The word "worship" (*proskuneo*) is "the most frequent word rendered 'to worship'. It is used of an act of homage or reverence" (W.E.Vine). These words should be compared with the Lord's words to Mary Magdalene, "Touch me not; for I am not yet ascended to my Father" (John 20: 17). In Matthew, the King is with His earthly people and therefore acknowledges an earthly relationship, but in John the Lord refers to a heavenly relationship based on His ascension. Matthew does not record the Lord's ascension.

We should also carefully notice what follows: "Then said Jesus unto them, be not afraid; go tell *my brethren* that they go into Galilee, and there shall they see me" (v.10). As G. Campbell Morgan points out, "While He values our adoring worship, He will always lift us from the attitude of prostration, and will send us about His business. To lie at His feet is a sacred and blessed thing; but to remain there is to miss the meaning of His Resurrection". Mary Magdalene was also told, "go to *my brethren*", but there the similarity ends: the Lord continued, "and say unto them, I ascend unto my Father, and your Father; and to my God, and your God" (John 20: 17). The Lord Jesus had referred to His disciples as "my disciples" (John 15: 8); "my sheep" (John 10: 26-27); "my friends" (John 15: 14), and now, "my brethren". R.V.G.Tasker points out that the words, "go tell my brethren that they go into Galilee, and there shall they see me", do not necessarily imply that He was commanding His brethren to go at once to Galilee where they would see Him (v.10). The very urgency of the message would seem rather to be an indication that the forthcoming reunion in Galilee would be an event of momentous significance". It is clear that His appearance in Galilee is the climax of Matthew's Gospel. This will be discussed in our final study.

5) THE DECEIT OF THE RELIGIOUS LEADERS, vv.11-15
We should notice *(a)* the honesty of the keepers (v.11); *(b)* the dishonesty of the religious leaders (vv.12-15). Again, these verses are unique to Matthew.

a) The honesty of the keepers, v.11
"Now when they (the women) were going, some of the watch came into the city, and shewed unto the chief priests (Pilate had seconded the watch to them) all the things that were done". Whether or not they believed the report, it had to be suppressed. So:

b) The dishonesty of the religious leaders, vv.12-15
"And when they were assembled with the elders, and had taken counsel, they gave *large money* (compare 26: 15: "thirty pieces of silver") unto the soldiers, saying, Say ye, His disciples came by night, and stole him away while we slept. And if this come to the governor's ears, we will persuade him, and secure you. So they took the money, and did as they were taught: and this saying is commonly reported among the Jews to this day".

All we need do in this connection is to quote the very pertinent comments of W.MacDonald: "But the purported 'explanation' raises more questions than it answers:

i) Why were the soldiers sleeping when they should have been on guard?
ii) How could the disciples have rolled the stone away without waking the soldiers?
iii) How could all the soldiers have fallen asleep at the same time?
iv) If they were asleep, how did they know that the disciples stole the body?
v) If the story was true, why did the soldiers have to be bribed to tell it?
vi) If the disciples had stolen the body, why had they taken time to remove the grave-clothes and fold the napkin (Luke 24: 12; John 20: 6-7)?".

How the chief priests and elders proposed to deal with Pilate is not known. Perhaps even they did not know! As Leonard Sheldrake (*A Plant of Renown*) rightly observes, "They dared not question the disciples concerning stealing His body from the tomb. When all those who paid the soldiers to circulate this report had the disciples in the temple before them, why did thy not bring up the serious charge of breaking the Roman seal and stealing His body?" The 'father of lies' (John 8: 44) can be decidedly illogical. It has been said that "history is the version of past events that people have decided to agree upon" (Napoleon Bonaparte)

6) THE COMMISSIONING OF THE DISCIPLES, vv.16-20

Our final study in Matthew's Gospel will follow.

ADDENDUM

The order of events on resurrection morning

The order of events during the early part of resurrection day are evidently as follows: *(1) The women,* including Mary Magdalene, come early to the sepulchre (Matt. 28: 1; Mark 16: 1-2; Luke 24: 1; John 20: 1). *(2) Mary Magdalene* immediately runs to Peter and John (alone) with the message, "They have taken away the Lord out of the sepulchre, and we know not where they have laid him" (John 20: 2). She did *not,* at that moment, convey news of the resurrection. *(3) The women*, as instructed, leave the sepulchre to inform the disciples that the Lord had risen (Matt. 28: 2-8; Mark 16: 3-8; Luke 24: 2-11). *(4) Peter and John,* following Mary Magdalene's report, run to the sepulchre (Luke 24: 12; John 20: 3-10). *(5) Mary Magdalene* returns to the sepulchre, and becomes the first to **encounter** (but **not** the first to **know** He had risen) the risen Lord. "Jesus saith unto her, Mary, She turned herself and saith unto Him, Rabboni; which is to say, Master" (John 20: 11-17). Hence Mark 16: 9, "He appeared

Matthew

first to Mary Magdalene". ***(6) The other women***, *en route* to tell the other disciples, apparently not with Peter and John, perhaps scattered, are met by the Lord Jesus (Matt. 28: 9-10). ***(7) Mary Magdalene*** returns to the disciples with the news "that she had seen the Lord" (John 20: 18). But "they, when they had heard that he was alive, and had been seen of her, believed not" (Mark 16: 11).

"Go ye therefore"

Read Chapter 28: 16-20

The previous verses in this chapter can be nicely summarised in the words of John Phillips, "The women were about to confront the world with the most tremendous fact in history; the watchmen would soon confront the world with the most tremendous falsehood in history" (supplied by Justin Waldron). To which we now add that 'the disciples were about to confront the world with the most tremendous message in history': "Go ye therefore, and teach all nations, baptizing them in the name of the Father and of the Son, and of the Holy Ghost: teaching them to observe all things whatsoever I have commanded you: and, lo, I am with you always, even unto the end of the world" (vv.19-20), or according to Mark, "Go ye into all the world, and preach the gospel to every creature" (Mark 16: 15).

These verses contain what has been rightly called 'The Great Commission'. The passage may be divided as follows: ***(1)*** the place (vv.16-17); ***(2)*** the power (v.18); ***(3)*** the preaching (vv.19-20); ***(4)*** the period (v.20).

1) THE PLACE, vv.16-17

"Then the eleven disciples went away into Galilee, into a mountain where Jesus had appointed them. And when they saw him, they worshipped him: but some doubted". We must notice ***(a)*** the rendezvous (v.16); ***(b)*** the reservations (v.17).

a) The rendezvous, v.16

"Then the eleven disciples went away into ***Galilee***, into a ***mountain*** ('the mountain', JND) where Jesus had appointed them. As J.M.Flanigan observes, "There is a certain sadness in this expression, 'the eleven'. There had been twelve, but there had been a traitor among the twelve, a defector. Judas was the only one of the twelve who was not a Galilean. He was Judas Iscariot, Judas Ish-Kerioth, Judas the man of Kerioth, a village of Judea. The eleven knew Galilee well. It was their home country, as it was

His, their Master's. They now return to Galilee, in obedience to his word and that of the angel". A parallel passage is found in Mark 16: 15-18. Attention is drawn to the following:

i) ***The disciples were instructed to go to Galilee.*** Quite clearly, this was not to witness His ascension. When the ascension took place, the Lord "led them (including Matthew) out as far as to Bethany…And it came to pass, while he blessed them, he was parted from them, and carried up into heaven" (Luke 24: 50-51). The disciples then "returned…unto Jerusalem from the mount called Olivet" (Acts 1: 12). But although witnessing the Lord's ascension, Matthew does not mention it! Under the inspiration of the Holy Spirit, his Gospel ends in Galilee! The King had been rejected in Judaea and Jerusalem. See John 7: 1, "After these things Jesus walked in ***Galilee***: for he would not walk in Jewry ('Judaea', JND), because the Jews sought to kill him". And, ultimately, they did kill Him. They rejected their King. As Wm.Kelly observes, "in Matthew we are shown Jesus rejected by Jerusalem, yet found in Galilee, even after His resurrection". By commissioning His disciples in Galilee, the Lord Jesus set the scene for their coming service. In Paul's words, "through their fall (Israel's fall) salvation is come unto the Gentiles" (Rom. 11: 11). Galilee is called "Galilee of the Gentiles": "Now when Jesus had heard that John was cast into prison, he departed into ***Galilee*** and leaving Nazareth, he came and dwelt in Capernaum, which is upon the sea coast, in the borders of Zabulon and Nephthalim: that it might be fulfilled which was spoken by Esaias the prophet, saying, The land of Zabulon, and the land of Nephthalim, by the way of the sea, beyond Jordan, ***Galilee of the Gentiles***: the people which sat in darkness saw great light; and to them which sat in the region and shadow of death light is sprung up" (Matt. 4: 12-16). This leads to:

ii) ***The disciples were instructed to go "into a mountain ('the mountain',*** JND) ***where Jesus had appointed them".*** Most, if not all, commentators, understand the words, "where Jesus had appointed them", to mean the mountain to which the Lord had directed them, leading, for example, J.M.Flanigan to say, "The Lord meets them at the appointed place, on one of the hills of Galilee". However, it is worth considering that "the mountain where Jesus had appointed them" refers to the ***original*** appointment of the disciples: "And he goeth up into a ***mountain***, and calleth unto him whom he would: and they came unto him. And he ordained twelve, that they should be with him, and that he might send them forth to preach" (Mark 3: 13-14). See also Luke 6: 12-13.

If this is the case, then we can say that having been commissioned to preach by the Lord at the beginning of His ministry, the disciples had learned how to preach by watching and listening to their Master. They were therefore equipped to go further and preach, not now only to "the lost sheep of the house of Israel" (Matt. 10: 1-6), but to "all nations" (v.19).

We should add that they met the Lord on a mountain, reminding us that we hear Christ best when:

> Shut in with Thee, far, far above
> The restless world that wars below

Compare Exodus 24: 9, and note the contrast between Revelation 17: 3, where John is taken "in the spirit into the **wilderness**" to see the "woman sit upon a scarlet coloured beast", and Revelation 21: 10, where he is "carried away in the spirit to a great and high **mountain**" in order to see "that great city, the holy Jerusalem, descending out of heaven from God".

b) The reservations, v.17

"And when they saw him, they worshipped him: but some doubted". The principle of worship before service springs immediately to mind (see, for example, Ezekiel 1: 28 - 2: 1-2). But this leaves unexplained the fact that "some doubted". This is not altogether easy to understand when we remember that the disciples had already seen the Lord twice in Jerusalem (John 20: 19, 26). The word "doubted" (*distazo*, meaning 'to stand in two ways') implies uncertainty. Some commentators suggest that those who doubted were among the "five hundred brethren" (1 Cor. 15: 6), but this is rather speculative. There is nothing to indicate that they were present in Galilee. Perhaps the answer lies in the rendering, "And Jesus coming up spoke to them" (v.18, JND), in which case those who 'doubted' did so when the Lord Jesus first appeared in the distance. Compare John 21: 1-8. In this case, the disciples were about 100 yards away at the time, with "early morn already breaking" (John 21: 4, JND).

But there is something else here. The commission which follows was not addressed to people all having sublime faith! Those who worshipped and those who doubted, at least initially, all received the Lord's commission and promise. Where would any of us be if our service depended on unwavering faith and perfect understanding?

2) THE POWER, v.18

"And Jesus came and spake unto them, saying, All power (*exousia*, meaning authority) is given unto me in heaven and in earth". God has given to Christ the sole and undisputed right to direct His servants, just as "the Father hath committed all judgment unto the Son" (John 5: 22). *He* has absolute freedom of action. *We* do not. This is clear from the contrasting roles. The Lord said of Himself: "All power is given unto *me*" (v.18). The Lord said to His disciples: "Go *ye*" (v.19). He has the authority to direct His servants. His servants are under an obligation to obey. We must never forget:

- That the *church* has no authority of its own. The church does not formulate doctrine or direct the movements of its members. "Wives submit yourselves unto your own husbands, as unto the Lord. For the husband is the head of the wife, even as **Christ is the head of the church**...Therefore as **the church is subject unto Christ**, so let the wives be to their own husbands in every thing" (Eph. 5: 22-24). When Barnabas and Saul embarked on the first 'missionary journey', they were "sent forth by the Holy Ghost" (Acts 13: 4).

- That the *preacher* has no authority of his own. In the Old Testament, the prophets thundered "Thus saith *the LORD*". "The prophet that hath a dream, let him tell a dream; and he that hath my word, let him speak my word faithfully" (Jer. 23: 28). It is a question of "To the law and to the testimony: if they speak not according to *this word*, it is because there is no light in them"(Isaiah 8: 20). In the New Testament, Paul wrote: "And unto the married I command, yet not I, but *the Lord*" (1 Cor. 7: 10); "If any man think himself to be a prophet, or spiritual, let him acknowledge that the things that I write unto you are the **commandments of the Lord** (1 Cor. 14: 37). See also 2 Cor. 13: 10.

We cannot leave this without noticing that the Lord said, "All power (authority) is given unto me in *heaven* and in *earth*":

i) **All power is given unto Him "in heaven".** That is, at the centre and source of operations: in providing the gifts necessary for the purpose. "When he **ascended up on high**, he led captivity captive, and gave gifts unto men...And he gave some apostles; and some, prophets; and some, pastors and teachers; for the perfecting of the saints, for the work of the ministry, for the edifying of the body of Christ" (Eph. 4: 8-12). Paul himself recognised that in his own case, all power was given to the Lord "in heaven": "it pleased God, who separated me from my mother's womb, and called me by his grace, to reveal his Son in me, that I might preach him among the heathen" (Gal. 1: 15-16).

ii) All power is given unto Him "in earth". That is, in the field of operations: in directing the gifts. Having seen 'the vision of the man of Macedonia', Paul and his companions "endeavoured to go into Macedonia, assuredly gathering that **the Lord** had called us for to preach the gospel unto them" (Acts 16: 9-10). We are to "pray...therefore **the Lord** of the harvest, that he will send forth labourers into his harvest" (Matt. 9: 38).

3) THE PREACHING, vv.19-20
"Go ye therefore, and teach all nations, baptizing them in the name of the Father, and of the Son, and of the Holy Ghost: teaching them to observe all things whatsoever I have commanded you". In these verses the Lord Jesus speaks about making disciples and marking disciples, but before considering His teaching in this way we should notice the extent of the commission: "Go ye therefore, and teach **all nations**. This involved action: "**Go** ye therefore".

Earlier in the Lord's ministry He dispatched "the twelve" with instructions to confine their mission to "the lost sheep of the house of Israel". They were told, "Go not into the way of the Gentiles, and into any city of the Samaritans enter ye not" (Matt. 10: 1-6). "The twelve" went as the King's messengers, but as events were to show, "his own ('people') received him not" (John 1: 11). Their commission then differed considerably from the commission here: the King had been rejected by His people, and the message of divine blessing was to be extended to "all nations".

The disciples were to undertake their responsibilities as obedient servants. They were given a command, "Go ye", and as J.C.Ryle rightly says, "Let us never forget that this solemn injunction is still in full force. It is still the bounden duty of every disciple of Christ to do all he can in person, and by prayer, to make others acquainted with Jesus. Where is our faith if we neglect this duty? Where is our charity? It may well be questioned whether a man knows the value of the Gospel himself, if he does not desire to make it known to all the world". Amos recognised the Lord's authority in this way: "I was no prophet, neither was I a prophet's son...and the LORD took me as I followed the flock, and the LORD said unto me, Go, prophesy unto my people Israel" (Amos 7: 14-15).

In the words of the parable, the Lord still says to us all, "Son, go work to day in my vineyard" (Matt. 21: 28). Preachers have constructed challenging sermons on the basis of this verse. For example: *how* we are to work - in full consciousness of our relation with Him - "**Son**, go work to day in my vineyard"; *what* we are to do - "Son, *go work* to day in my vineyard"; *when* we are to work - "Son, go work *to day* in my vineyard"; *where* we are to work - "Son, go work to day in *my vineyard*". This brings us to making disciples and marking disciples:

a) Making disciples
"Go ye therefore, and teach all nations" or "make disciples of all the nations" (RV/JND). In the first place we should notice that the word of God is **applicable and workable universally**. It is above language, history and culture. It can be proclaimed to "all nations". It *is* to be proclaimed to all nations": "ye shall be witnesses unto me both in Jerusalem, and in all Judaea, and in Samaria, and unto the uttermost part of the earth" (Acts 1: 8). In Mark's words, "And they went forth, and preached every where, the Lord working with them, and confirming the word with signs following. Amen" (Mark 16: 20).

The instruction, "make disciples of all the nations" emphasises *long-term* results. The Lord does not say here 'Go ye therefore and preach' (as in Mark 16: 15), but "Go [therefore] and make disciples" (JND). The word 'disciple' means, literally, 'a learner' (*mathetes,* from *manthano*, to learn), and W.E.Vine points out that "A disciple was not only a pupil, but an adherent; hence they are often spoken of as imitators of their teacher; cp. John 8: 31; 15: 8".

The object is not to make converts, or to elicit decisions, but to "make disciples". This is something infinitely more thorough and comprehensive than 'making converts'. Disciples are people who recognise Christ's **authority**: "if thou shalt confess with thy mouth the Lord Jesus (*kurios*) or, "if thou shalt confess with thy mouth Jesus as Lord", JND, (Rom. 10: 9); Christ's **tutorship**: "Ye call me Master (*didiskalos*) and Lord; and ye say well: for so I am. If I then, your Lord and Master (*didiskalos*), have washed your feet; ye also ought to wash one another's feet" (John 13: 13-14); Christ's **ownership**: "meet for the master's (*despotes*) use" (2 Tim. 2: 21): the word *despotes* means 'one who has absolute ownership and uncontrolled power' (W.E.Vine).

As noted above, this involves preaching the Gospel: "Go ye into all the world, and preach the gospel to every creature" (Mark 16: 15). While, strictly speaking, it is not part of our current passage, it is worth emphasising that the Gospel is "the gospel of God" (Rom. 1: 1) and "the gospel of Christ" (Rom. 1: 16). As such it is "the gospel of the glory of the blessed God" (1 Tim. 1: 11, RV) and "the gospel of the glory of Christ" (2 Cor. 4: 4, RV). Like the Thessalonian believers, we should preach it with clarity: "From you **sounded out** the word of the Lord" (1 Thess. 1: 8). The words "sounded out" mean 'to sound forth as a trumpet or thunder' (W.E.Vine). The English word 'echo' lies in the Greek word (*execheo*). It is our duty to tell out **all** "the word of the Lord". It is our duty to tell out **nothing but** "the word of the Lord". See, for example, Acts 11: 19-20, "Now they that were scattered abroad upon the persecution that arose about Stephen travelled as far as Phenice, and Cyprus, and Antioch, **preaching** (meaning 'speaking') **the word** to none but unto the Jews only. And some of them were men of Cyprus and Cyrene, which when they were come to Antioch, spake unto the Grecians **preaching** (meaning 'heralding') **the Lord Jesus"**.

b) Marking disciples
Disciples were to be marked by undergoing baptism particularly, and by obedience to the word of God generally: "Go ye therefore, and teach all nations, **baptizing** them in the name of the Father, and of the Son, and of the Holy Ghost: **teaching** them to observe all things whatsoever I have commanded you".

i) **Baptising them**. The words "baptizing them in the name of the Father, and of the Son, and of the Holy Ghost" are not a baptismal formula, although "mentioning the name of the Holy Trinity at the time of baptism is a suitable way to indicate the relationship between God and the person receiving baptism" (Justin Waldron). Baptism marks the fact that on faith in Christ believers become indissolubly linked with God, that is, with "the Father, and...the Son, and...the Holy Ghost". This is conveyed by the use of the preposition *eis*, meaning 'into': "baptizing them into (*eis*) the name of the Father and of the Son and of the Holy Ghost" (RV). See also JND.

This emphasises that while believers are subject to harm and danger at the hands of men, their spiritual life is secure. The words "into (*eis*) the name (singular) of the Father and of the Son and of the Holy Ghost" (RV) underlines the impossibility of separation from God. The title "the Father" emphasises divine **love**; the title "the Son" emphasises divine **lordship and saviourhood**; the title "the Holy Ghost" emphasises divine **power**.

There is, of course, no conflict between the Lord's words here, and the later statements in the New Testament. In Acts 2: 38, Peter called on his Jewish audience to "Repent, and be baptized in (*epi* or *en*) the name of Jesus Christ for the remission of sins", and in Acts 10: 48, he baptized Gentile believers at Caesarea "in (*en*) the name of the Lord". That is, on His authority. See also Acts 8: 16, where Samaritan believers were "baptized in (*eis*) the name of the Lord Jesus". The preposition *eis* is used here to emphasise that the Samaritans, who were cut off from the Jews (John 4: 9), had been brought into the blessings of the Lord Jesus Christ, thereby acknowledging that "salvation is of the Jews" (John 4: 22). See also Acts 19: 5, where the former disciples of John were "baptized in (*eis*) the name of the Lord Jesus". Once they were identified with John, now they were identified with Christ.

ii) Teaching them. "Teaching them (compare v.15) to observe all things whatsoever I have commanded you". We could stop for a long time at the first two words "teaching them". Here is David Newell (*Believer's Magazine, August 2012*): "For God's people to get the full nourishment of His Word, all the Scriptures without exception must be on the menu. This requires system. Occasional, haphazard or *ad hoc* teaching will never provide a balanced diet of truth. The Lord Jesus made clear that we live by "every word that proceedeth out of the mouth of God" (Matt. 4: 4). Mark that: 'every word', not selected highlights or popular passages. If I am not feasting on every word I am not properly living". David Newell's article is worth reading in its entirety.

It should be noted that the Lord did not say 'teaching them...all things", but "teaching them ***to observe*** all things", reminding us that we are to be "doers of the word, and not hearers only" (James 1: 22). The word "observe" (*tereo*) means 'to watch over, preserve, keep, watch' (W.E.Vine). Interestingly enough, the same word is used of the guards at the tomb: "And for fear of him (the angel) the keepers (*tereo*) did shake and became as dead men" (v.4). Sadly, the Lord's people sometimes 'shake and become as dead men' when it comes to keeping the Lord's commandments. The Lord Jesus said, "If ye love me, keep (*tereo*) my commandments" John 14: 15. He continued, "He that hath my commandments, and keepeth (*tereo*) them, he it is that loveth me", and "If a man love me, he will keep (*tereo*) my words: and my Father will love him, and we will come unto him, and make our abode with him" (John 14: 21, 23).

Moreover, it should be noted that the Lord did not say 'teaching them to observe some things, but "teaching them to observe ***all*** things whatsoever

Matthew

I have commanded you". If **Bible teachers** are to emulate Paul in declaring "all the counsel of God" (Acts 20: 27), then, similarly, the **recipients** are to do nothing less than believe and practise "all the counsel of God". It should be added that both teachers and hearers are to do nothing *more* than keep the commandments of the Lord. The Saviour severely censured those who taught "for doctrines the commandments of men" (Matt. 15: 9). It is a matter of "whatsoever *I* have commanded you", not 'whatsoever *you* feel is suitable, desirable or logical. The Lord's word is binding upon us. It is obligatory. It is not a matter of our preference, which can only lead to a repetition of "every man did that which was right in his own eyes" (Judges 21: 25).

4) THE PERIOD, v.20
"And, lo, I am with you always ('all the days', JND), even unto the end of the world ('age', JND)" (Matt. 1: 23). Matthew's Gospel therefore ends as it begins. It commences with "they shall call his name Emmanuel, which being interpreted is, God with us", and ends similarly, "Lo, I am with you always", where the order of the Greek words is 'I with you am'. "He hath said, I will never leave thee, nor forsake thee" (Heb. 13: 5).

Preachers and teachers have not been slow to notice the four "alls" of the 'Great Commission": "all power (authority)…all nations…all things…always". Yes, "unto the end of the world ('age')" must include the end-time preaching (Matt. 24: 14), but it most certainly relates to *us* as well. In the following words, quoted by David Tinkler at the end of this final study in Matthew,

'Our first concern should be His last command'.